Uni

Ch

Subject

The Palgrave Handbook of Prison Ethnography

Palgrave Studies in Prisons and Penology

This is a unique and innovative series, the first of its kind dedicated entirely to prison scholarship. At a historical point in which the prison population has reached an all-time high, the series seeks to analyse the form, nature and consequences of incarceration and related forms of punishment. *Palgrave Studies in Prisons and Penology* provides an important forum for burgeoning prison research across the world.

Titles include:

Vincenzo Ruggiero and Mick Ryan
PUNISHMENT IN EUROPE
A Critical Anatomy of Penal Systems

Phil Scraton and Linda Moore
THE INCARCERATION OF WOMEN
Punishing Bodies, Breaking Spirits

Peter Scharff Smith
WHEN THE INNOCENT ARE PUNISHED
The Children of Imprisoned Parents

Thomas Ugelvik
POWER AND RESISTANCE IN PRISON
Doing Time, Doing Freedom

Marguerite Schinkel
BEING IMPRISONED
Punishment, Adaptation and Desistance

Mark Halsey and Simon Deegan
YOUNG OFFENDERS
Crime, Prison and Struggles for Desistance

Andrew M. Jefferson and Liv S. Gaborit
HUMAN RIGHTS IN PRISONS
Comparing Institutional Encounters in Kosovo, Sierra Leone and the Philippines

Deborah H. Drake, Rod Earle and Jennifer Sloan (*editors*)
THE PALGRAVE HANDBOOK OF PRISON ETHNOGRAPHY

Palgrave Studies in Prisons and Penology
Series Standing Order ISBN 978–1–137–27090–0 hardback
(*outside North America only*)

You can receive future titles in this series as they are published by placing a standing order. Please contact your bookseller or, in case of difficulty, write to us at the address below with your name and address, the title of the series and the ISBNs quoted above.

Customer Services Department, Macmillan Distribution Ltd, Houndmills, Basingstoke, Hampshire RG21 6XS, England

---

The Palgrave Handbook of Prison Ethnography

Edited by

Deborah H. Drake
Senior Lecturer in Criminology, The Open University, UK

Rod Earle
Lecturer in Youth Justice, The Open University, UK

Jennifer Sloan
Senior Lecturer in Criminology, Sheffield Hallam University, UK

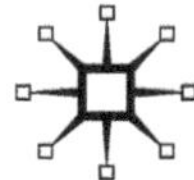

First published 2015 by
PALGRAVE MACMILLAN

Palgrave Macmillan in the UK is an imprint of Macmillan Publishers Limited, registered in England, company number 785998, of Houndmills, Basingstoke, Hampshire RG21 6XS.

Palgrave Macmillan in the US is a division of St Martin's Press LLC, 175 Fifth Avenue, New York, NY 10010.

Palgrave Macmillan is the global academic imprint of the above companies and has companies and representatives throughout the world.

Palgrave® and Macmillan® are registered trademarks in the United States, the United Kingdom, Europe and other countries.

ISBN 978–1–137–40387–2

This book is printed on paper suitable for recycling and made from fully managed and sustained forest sources. Logging, pulping and manufacturing processes are expected to conform to the environmental regulations of the country of origin.

A catalogue record for this book is available from the British Library.

A catalog record for this book is available from the Library of Congress.

Contents

Part II Through Prison Ethnography

Part III Of Prison Ethnography

Figures

Foreword

What has prison ethnography to offer in an age of mass incarceration?

Being invited to write a Foreword to this groundbreaking collection, following the equally impressive symposium on prison ethnography ('Resisting the Eclipse'), hosted by The Open University's International Centre for Comparative Criminological Research (ICCCR) just over a year earlier, is a great honour. But as I sit down to write a few words that will preface this testament to the importance of ethnographic studies of the prison, I have a slight nagging feeling that the mood of optimism and excitement that marked the conference in September 2013 may have diminished slightly. Many of us work in countries that are experiencing an era of highly politicised penal policy and, relatively rapidly, it seems that doing research in prisons has become a great deal more difficult. The necessary reliance on government agencies to authorise access to prisons, the sometimes tortuous process of liaising with gatekeepers and the intimidation that can be applied by organisations that do not like one's methods or findings have all made the ethnographic endeavour trickier than in previous times. From the perspective of someone working in the UK, it is tempting to rail against the current government and, in particular, at a Secretary of State for Justice who has taken the hardening of penal sensibilities to new levels, made swingeing financial cuts to prison budgets (resulting in many prisons operating with a skeleton staff) and back-pedalled on his predecessor's promise of a 'rehabilitation revolution'. In the current climate, many prison governors are understandably reluctant to open their doors to academic researchers. But, equally, these obstacles mean that prison ethnography has never been more necessary.

The impetus behind the symposium that precipitated this volume was Loïc Wacquant's *Ethnography* article 'The Curious Eclipse of Prison Ethnography in the Age of Mass Incarceration'. The presenters at the conference reminded participants that an eclipse is something hidden or overshadowed; not something that is not occurring. But if prison ethnography has been 'eclipsed', what accounts for its relative invisibility and what is overshadowing it? It has been suggested that one reason why prisons research may at times go on under the radar is that much of it is conducted by doctoral students, who are able to take advantage of the relative freedoms of the PhD, but often unable to generate the kind of attention that their work deserves (Crewe and Jewkes, 2012). This is changing (and in evidence I would point to the embryonic series that this volume is part of, *Palgrave Studies in Prisons and Penology*, which welcomes proposals from newly qualified PhD candidates), but the change is happening quite slowly, particularly for ethnographers writing in languages other than English.

There can be little doubt that in many countries ethnographic studies are overshadowed by a heavily quantitative approach to penology. But the bald statistics can blind us to the realities beneath. Organisation theorists have used the notion of 'dazzle' in relation to highly ornate and embellished buildings, arguing that excessive decoration can induce a kind of architectural and aesthetic apathy. In other words, their sheer brilliance induces a seemingly paradoxical anaesthetising effect, dulling or deadening the senses of those who occupy them or gaze upon them (Dale and Burrell, 2003). The idea of dazzle as deception actually comes not from architecture but from the 'camouflage' effect with which some battleships were painted in the two world wars. Dazzle painting (or 'razzle dazzle'), consisting of brightly coloured geometric shapes or bold black-and-white stripes, might seem an unlikely form of camouflage – one would imagine that a vividly painted, moving monument to cubist art, ploughing through the waves, might draw attention to itself. However, the technique was developed not to conceal the ship, but to disrupt the visual rangefinders used for naval artillery and make it difficult for the enemy to estimate the vessel's type, size, speed and heading. The dazzle eclipsed the target.

Prison statistics can similarly 'dazzle' and run risk of blinding or anaesthetising the observer. In an age of mass incarceration, it is not particularly surprising that the focus tends to be on the big numbers – of prisoners incarcerated, levels of mental illness and drug dependency, rates of suicide and self-harm, children left without a parent, recidivism, individuals dependent on the prison–industrial complex for their livelihood and so on. California, the US's largest state prison system, serves as an example. Since 2009 when its prisons housed more than 160,000 prisoners and employed over 69,000 personnel at an annual cost of $10.3 billion, California has been an enthusiastic adopter of Life Without Parole (LWOP), with well over half the life sentences imposed being LWOP (Dolovich, 2011). These almost incomprehensible numbers have placed the state's prison system under such severe strain that it has twice been subject to court orders requiring it to cut its prison population by tens of thousands. But between 2003 and 2008, 5,471 prisoners out of a total of 12,933 life sentences imposed received life with the *possibility* of parole, a statistic which might seem to cut against the notion of a widespread commitment to permanent penal exclusion. However, as Dolovich reminds us, the possibility of parole makes little practical difference; in most cases, it is a meaningless ritual in which the form is preserved but in practice is rarely enacted.

Ethnography can help us to understand such bureaucratic processes and the visceral effects they have on the flesh-and-blood people serving these horrendous sentences. Even allowing for the fact that life-sentenced prisoners might legitimately be regarded as dangerous beyond their recommended sentence, one might still expect parole boards to see an appreciable number of people, especially by the third or fourth time around, who could be released with minimal public safety risk. And yet, for the past decade, the Californian Parole Board has denied 98 per cent of the petitions it hears. From this, one might conclude that lifers in California are especially dangerous (which common sense would suggest is ridiculous), but we can't possibly hope to understand what is happening without engaging with the people at both ends of the decision-making process.

Engagement is also crucial because penal history can be painted in very broad brushstrokes, and it befalls ethnographers to find detail, texture and nuance within the big picture. (And can there be any more detailed, textured and nuanced evocation of prison life than the gendered power dynamics that imbue the making of a cup of coffee or the 'perfume of sweat', as described by two of the contributors to this book?) Of course, ethnographers are not the only people who can take on the task of revealing the prison. Critical criminologists have been amongst the most vociferous and passionate critics of prisons and have consistently challenged what they see as an increasingly punitive criminal justice agenda. But occupying the intellectual space between theory and politics, critical criminology sometimes appears curiously detached from the people most affected by the structural and systemic imbalances they are concerned with. Some of the most scathing critiques of prisons are written by individuals who appear never to have set foot inside a prison, or at least not for some decades. In some ways, this is understandable. Prison research is difficult, stressful and time-consuming, and many scholars leave the field early in their careers (often following completion of their PhD), never to return.

But critical perspectives have, to a large extent, shaped penology. They have done much to highlight atrocities, instigate reform and promote an abolitionist agenda, which sometimes precludes their authors from saying anything that is positive or progressive within penal systems: for example, about successful individual prison communities, about pioneering penal 'experiments' or about enlightened governors trying to change the system from within (all of which are represented within these pages). It is as if to illuminate pockets of good practice or individual agency, however small, would undermine their overarching message. Yes, prisons are, as Scott and Codd (2013: 170) remind us, 'places of sadness and terror, harm and injustice, secrecy and oppression'. But they can also be places of great humour and playfulness, friendship and camaraderie, educational enlightenment, successful therapeutic intervention and transformative achievement. All these emotional states and more are reflected in this volume. We may at times 'walk through graves', but we also witness the 'creation of miracles' when we infiltrate the prison.

This may be one of the reasons why, in comparison to many other fields of scholarly interest, prisons generate a high degree of curiosity, sometimes motivated by personal experience (not necessarily of confinement, but perhaps of perceived injustice or the power of the human spirit to survive in adversity). Criminology has largely resisted the notion that prisons are highly charged emotional environments and that qualitative inquiry has autoethnographic dimensions. Not in this book, though. Here we experience the prison from multiple perspectives – not just from particular demographic/status positions including gender, ethnicity, nationality, class, sexuality and sexual orientation – but from other standpoints: the prisoner, the ex-prisoner, the prison governor, the clinical psychologist, the policy advisor, the prison chaplain, the activist and many more besides. The stories they tell, or that are told on their behalf, remind us of the illuminating power of narrative.

One of the exciting things about *The Palgrave Handbook of Prison Ethnography*, then, is that, in myriad ways, it reveals why we do ethnographic research, what our conscious or unconscious motivations might be, how we feel about our research and our research participants and what the intended and unexpected outcomes of our ethnographic endeavours may be. The contributors tell their stories from the field without fear of exposure as human beings capable of compassion, empathy, excitement – and the rather more ambivalent or negative feelings, as described by some of the authors here. Far from producing 'soft' research, they succeed in retaining epistemological and theoretical rigour, whilst at the same time being highly reflexive about the research they are engaged in. Such interesting and honest accounts provide a benchmark for others trying to process their experiences about the ethnographic fieldwork they undertake and about the pains and gains of doing qualitative prison research (see Jewkes, 2012; Beyens et al., 2013; Jewkes and Wright, 2015; and the 2014 special issue of *Qualitative Inquiry* on 'Doing Prison Research Differently' for more detailed discussions).

In an era of mass incarceration, reflexive, human-centric ethnography is an important counter, not just to quantitative analysis, but to the 'official' audit culture that has led to prisons being judged on a plethora of government-instigated rules, directives and performance targets that render individual prisoners anonymous administrative targets. Recent decades have also witnessed the dominance of the empiricist, 'scientific' methods and findings of psychologists. The emergence of clinical programmes aimed at treating offenders' behaviour has resulted in prison psychologists being awarded an unprecedented level of power, including power over access to prisons by academic researchers. Government departments have further discouraged ethnographers with a variety of strategies questioning the methodology, objectivity and usefulness of sociologically imaginative studies of the internal life of prison. If this were not potentially obstructive enough, the prison administrators' demands for researchers to disclose information concerning inmate behaviour that breaks prison rules and can be adjudicated against, including illegal acts, and behaviour that is potentially harmful to the research participant, conflict with most university ethics committees' requirement that the researcher guarantees participant confidentiality. The demand that researchers within prisons will be expected to 'submit any questionnaires or interview schedules in advance for clearance' further obstructs ethnographers whose aims are to see what questions emerge whilst in the field. These obstacles to qualitative prison research are not insurmountable, but they are certainly challenging and, therefore, must be resisted if prisons and prisoners are not to be consigned to the deepest recess of knowledge and understanding.

Ethnographic research in custodial settings is, then, a challenging but rewarding endeavour. There may have been an 'eclipse' of prison ethnography, but this collection robustly counters any notion that we have witnessed its demise. Deborah Drake, Rod Earle and Jennifer Sloan – themselves all highly experienced prison ethnographers – have brought together an impressive collection of researchers from numerous countries doing important, insightful ethnographies across many diverse prison systems. Over a decade ago, John Pratt (2002) claimed that punishment had become anonymous, bureaucratic, rationalised and remote, returning us to a dark age of monstrous incivility and reducing individual lives to bureaucratic targets. The chapters that follow demonstrate that, despite the enormous challenges we face in our attempts to let a little light in on these dark ages of imprisonment, we are succeeding in deepening our understandings of the prison, in holding prison authorities to account and in giving voice to the individuals who, rich in experience and potential, are impoverished by the circumstances of their confinement. Prison ethnography seen through the lenses of performance, policy, participation, politics, power dynamics and personal biography are all represented in the pages of this book. *The Palgrave Handbook of Prison Ethnography* is a testament to the vibrancy, diversity and global reach of the field and suggests that, despite the pessimism with which I began, and the challenges to our work that are described throughout this collection, ethnography is succeeding in illuminating the shadows of the prison. We are making a difference. I hope that this book inspires many future researchers to do likewise.

Yvonne Jewkes
Professor of Criminology,
University of Leicester, UK

References

Beyens, K., Christiaens, J., Claes, B., De Ridder, S., Tournel, H. and Tubex, H. (eds) (2013) *The Pains of Criminological Research* (Brussels, Belgium: VUB Press).

Crewe, B. and Jewkes, Y. (2012) 'Introduction', *Punishment & Society* (Special Issue on 'The Pains of Imprisonment Revisited'), 13, 5, 507–8.

Dale, K. and Burrell, G. (2003) 'An-aesthetics and Architecture', in A. Carr and P. Hancock (eds) *Art and Aesthetics at Work* (Basingstoke: Palgrave Macmillan).

Dolovich, S. (2011) 'Creating the Permanent Prisoner', in C. Ogletree and A. Sarat (eds) *Life Without Parole: America's New Death Penalty* (New York: NYU Press).

Jewkes, Y. (2012) 'Autoethnography and Emotion as Intellectual Resources: Doing Prison Research Differently', *Qualitative Inquiry*, 18, 1, 63–75.

Jewkes, Y. and Wright, S. (in press) 'Researching the Prison', in Y. Jewkes, B. Crewe and J. Bennett (eds) *Handbook on Prisons*, Second edition (London: Routledge).

Jewkes, Y. (2014) 'Doing Prison Research Differently', *Qualitative Inquiry*, 20, 4, 387–488.

Scott, D. and Codd, H. (2012) *Controversial Issues in Prisons* (Maidenhead: Open University Press).

Wacquant, L. (2002) 'The Curious Eclipse of Prison Ethnography in the Age of Mass Incarceration', *Ethnography*, 3, 4, 371–97.

Acknowledgements

First and foremost, the editors would like to thank the contributors to this Handbook. Despite the breadth of this volume and the number of authors involved, we miraculously managed to hand the finished manuscript over to the publisher on time, which is often unheard of for a collection of this size. This is, in large measure, due to the professionalism, diligence and careful attention of our authors. It was a delight and a pleasure to work with you all.

The editors would also like to formally acknowledge the considerable intellectual contributions of our friends at the Global Prisons Research Network, especially Andrew Jefferson, Tomas Max Martin and Mahuya Bandyopadhyay. It was during a conversation amongst Andrew, Tomas, Mahuya, Deb Drake, Jen Sloan and Ben Crewe at the British Society of Criminology conference in Leicester in 2010 that the seed of an idea to hold an international prison ethnography symposium was hatched. It was subsequently agreed that the event would be hosted by the International Centre for Comparative Criminological Research (ICCCR) at The Open University in Milton Keynes, UK, and Rod Earle came aboard as another co-organiser. It is thus with thanks also to the ICCCR for their generous support and to Sarah Batt, specifically, for adding such professionalism and seemingly seamless organisation to the event. Many of those who attended that symposium are also present in this volume, but we wish to acknowledge those who, for one reason or another, were unable to contribute to it. Chris Garces and Sacha Darke – your contributions are sorely missed. If there is a second edition, you're both first on our list to cajole.

We also wish to extend our most heartfelt appreciation to Jules Willan, Harriet Barker and Dominic Walker at Palgrave Macmillan. Jules and Harriet – thanks for believing in the project at the outset, and Dom – thanks for seeing it through. We are also grateful to the *Palgrave Studies in Prisons and Penology* series editors, Ben Crewe, Yvonne Jewkes and Thomas Ugelvik, for lending their support to the collection (although, how could they not!).

We wish to extend our personal thanks to our loved ones who, invariably, helped to support and see each of us through this project (as well as our other respective projects, workloads and crazed ramblings on various prison-related issues of angst). So, from Deb – thanks, as ever, to my colleagues in the Department of Social Policy and Criminology at The Open University for their care, inspiration and support, particularly Steve Tombs, Louise Westmarland, Gerry Mooney and Ross Fergusson who provided seemingly endless advice, assistance and good humour. Thanks also, of course, to my co-editors Jen and Rod. You were both a pleasure to work with and although I am pleased that the project is complete, I will miss working on this with you. Finally, I want to thank my friends Tara Hackl, Joel Harvey and Daniel Wakelin for their steadfast support and my partner, Andrew Lindfield – for everything.

From Rod – thanks to all those who attended the *Resisting the Eclipse* symposium and got this ball rolling, particularly Deb and Jen for seeing it through. I couldn't hope to work with nicer people. Yvonne Jewkes was a supportive presence throughout, who both inspired and guided. I am grateful to colleagues in the Department of Health and Social Care at The Open University who continue to provide, and believe in, a sense of scholarly community in very trying times.

From Jen – there are so many people to thank for their support in this endeavour, not least those that I have worked directly with, including contributors, co-authors (Serena, you're fab!), publishers and, perhaps most importantly, my co-editors. Deb and Rod, you both have been wonderful in guiding a novice through the process and in giving me the confidence to take on such a role. Thank you for letting me be a part of this wonderful process. I would also like to thank my colleagues at the University of Sheffield and at Sheffield Hallam University who have seen me through the editorial process and put up with the worrier-that-is-Jenny! Finally, I thank my family for always being there – Mum, Dad, James, Oscar and Migsy. Without you, I don't know where I would be.

Finally, we extend our deepest gratitude to all those prisoners, prison staff and managers who have granted us the privilege of spending time with them and sharing their stories.

Contributors

Helen Arnold is Lecturer in Criminology in the Department of Psychology, Sociology and Social Work at the University Campus Suffolk, UK.

Lilian Ayete-Nyampong is Head of Research, Commission on Human Rights and Administrative Justice, Ghana.

Mahuya Bandyopadhyay is an Associate Professor in the School of Development Studies at the Tata Institute of Social Sciences in Mumbai, India.

Jamie Bennett is Governor of HMP Grendon/Springhill and holds a PhD in Criminology, University of Edinburgh, UK.

Kristel Beyens is Professor of Penology and Criminology at the Vrije Universiteit Brussel, Belgium.

Miranda Boone is Professor of Penitentiary Law and Penology at the University of Groningen and Senior Lecturer in Criminal Law and Criminology at the University of Utrecht, the Netherlands.

Lucy Carr is a PhD student in the Department of Law, University of Sheffield, UK.

Gilles Chantraine is a researcher and sociologist at the CNRS – CLERSÉ, France.

Ben Crewe is Deputy Director of Prisons Research Centre and Director of M.St. Penology Programme at the Institute of Criminology, University of Cambridge, UK.

William Davies is Senior Lecturer in Criminology in the School of Criminology Subject Group at Leeds Beckett University, UK.

Deborah H. Drake is Senior Lecturer in Criminology in the Department of Social Policy and Criminology at The Open University, UK.

Rod Earle is Lecturer in Youth Justice in the Faculty of Health and Social Care at The Open University, UK.

Elisabeth Fransson is an Associate Professor at the Correctional Service of Norway Staff Academy, Norway.

Martyn Hammersley is Professor of Educational and Social Research at the Department of Childhood, Youth and Sport at The Open University, UK.

Joel Harvey is Lecturer in Clinical Psychology at the Institute of Psychiatry, Psychology and Neuroscience, King's College London, UK.

Alice Ievins is a PhD student at the Institute of Criminology, University of Cambridge, UK.

Andrew M. Jefferson is Senior Researcher at DIGNITY: Danish Institute Against Torture, Denmark.

Yvonne Jewkes is Professor of Criminology at the Department of Criminology, University of Leicester, UK.

Berit Johnsen is Associate Professor at the Correctional Service of Norway Staff Academy.

Alison Liebling is Professor of Criminology and Criminal Justice and the Director of the Prisons Research Centre, Institute of Criminology at the University of Cambridge, UK.

Tomas Max Martin is Senior Advisor at the Danish Institute for Human Rights, Denmark.

Benita Moolman is a research specialist in the Human and Social Development Unit in Cape Town, South Africa.

Coretta Phillips is an Associate Professor at the Mannheim Centre for the Study of Criminology and Criminal Justice, Department of Social Policy at the London School of Economics, UK.

Laura Piacentini is Professor of Criminology at the Faculty of Humanities and Social Sciences, University of Strathclyde, UK.

Lorna A. Rhodes is Emeritus Professor, Department of Anthropology, University of Washington, USA.

Abigail Rowe is Lecturer in Criminology in the Department of Social Policy and Criminology at The Open University, UK.

Nicolas Sallée is Assistant Professor at the Department of Sociology, Université de Montréal, Canada.

David Scott is Senior Lecturer in Criminology at the School of Humanities and Social Sciences, Liverpool John Moores University, UK.

Jennifer Sloan is Senior Lecturer in Criminology at the Department of Law and Criminology, Sheffield Hallam University, UK.

Christina Straub is a PhD student in the Faculty of Education, Social Sciences and Law, University of Leeds, UK.

Thomas Ugelvik is an Associate Professor in the Department of Sociology, Political Science and Community Planning, UiT The Arctic University of Norway, Norway.

James B. Waldram is a medical anthropologist and Professor in the Department of Psychology, University of Saskatchewan, Canada.

Lindsay Whetter is a PhD student in the College of Life and Environmental Science at the University of Exeter, UK.

Serena Wright is a research assistant at the Prisons Research Centre, Institute of Criminology at the University of Cambridge, UK.

General Introduction: What Ethnography Tells Us about Prisons and What Prisons Tell Us about Ethnography

Deborah H. Drake, Rod Earle and Jennifer Sloan

The practice of ethnography as a research method has a long history that places special importance on understanding the perspectives of the people under study and of observing their activities in everyday life (Hammersley and Atkinson, 1983). It is a method used by researchers in a variety of disciplines, but it is perhaps most famously associated with social anthropology and the study of indigenous cultures (Malinowski, 1922; Evans-Pritchard, 1937; Turnbull, 1961). Ethnographers aim to produce rich and detailed accounts of people and the social processes they are embedded in. For these reasons, it is often employed by educational, health and social sciences researchers in a wide variety of institutional, community and other social settings.

This Handbook draws together a collection of papers that examine ethnography or ethnographic research practices undertaken inside prisons. In 2002, Professor Loïc Wacquant published 'The Curious Eclipse of Prison Ethnography in the Age of Mass Incarceration' in a special issue of the journal *Ethnography*. In that article, Wacquant expressed a visceral horror at what he encountered on entering a large US penal institution and his deep sense of foreboding about what such places mean. With US prison populations booming, he lamented the scarcity of ethnographic studies of American jails and prisons. He was troubled to note that, at a time when the detailed and sensitive examinations of prisons which ethnographic work can provide are most urgently needed, this kind of research seemed to be disappearing under the weight of more conventional and profitable 'correctional' research.

Some ten years later, in 2012, a group of prison researchers in the UK and Europe organised a symposium on prison ethnography. Supported by the International Centre for Comparative Criminological Research at The Open University and in collaboration with colleagues from the Global Prisons Research Network (GPRN), the symposium aimed to contrast the relative dearth of prison ethnography in the US with another story – one of a vibrant, critical and engaged body of prison research around the world. The symposium attracted over 100 delegates from 12 different countries, most with wide experience of long-term, in-depth research in prisons, and created a unique opportunity to share perspectives and dilemmas from the field. Those who came together at this event examined the many different challenges ethnographic researchers face in getting close to the experiences, feelings and understandings of prison life in North America, Africa, South America, India, the UK and other European countries. This collection not only presents versions of most of the papers that were discussed at the symposium, but it also draws in contributions from other prison researchers who were not present at the event but whose work informs the growing body of expertise on ethnographic methods, on prisons and on the research dilemmas associated with ethnographic work in a prison context.

In this introductory chapter, we present a consolidated overview of both what ethnography has given us in relation to our understandings of the prison and, in turn, what prison ethnographies have contributed to our understanding of the ethnographic enterprise. This Handbook offers contributions to existing literature on both of these fronts as well as an in-depth and critical examination of the continued and increasing use of imprisonment around the world.

Seeing with words: Prison through the lens of ethnography

Prison ethnography has some very distinctive difficulties as an approach to researching prison life. These difficulties become acute where the principal focus of interest is the lives of prisoners rather than the prison institution as a whole. Some might argue that in relation to prisoners' lives, ethnography is not 'real' ethnography, in the strict anthropological meaning of the process, where

> conclusions are based primarily on 'fieldwork', which involves entering the world of the people under study as a close observer or even as a participant over an extended period of time. By sharing in the daily life experiences of his or her subjects, the ethnographer becomes more attuned to the less visible conditions and situations that shape these lives.
>
> (Duneier et al., 2014: 2)

The majority of prison ethnographies which focus on prisoner cultures or 'societies' – including the majority within this Handbook – are done by people unlikely ever to be imprisoned, and who have never been sent to prison themselves, other than as a visiting researcher. Most of the authors in this collection are thus 'outsiders' who have not practically shared in the experiences of the core characters in the object of study – prisoners. They have not been deprived of their liberty and, in most cases, the researcher inevitably goes home and leaves the prison behind at the end of their working day. At very least, the outsider researcher always retains that option, thereby losing touch with the defining reality of the prisoners' experience – constraint on freedom and being locked up and under control. Immersion, in the traditional, direct ethnographic sense, is bound to be relatively shallow, particularly for those ethnographies that have aimed solely to focus on the prisoner society. That said, the tradition of prison ethnography reflected in this collection aims to capture a far wider range of perspectives than just that of the prisoner. Prison*er* ethnographies differ from prison *staff* ethnographies as well as from *prison-as-organisation* ethnographies.

By focusing on the nitty-gritty of the research method and the experiences of ethnographers in different prison contexts, this collection aims to draw out the nuanced differences between ethnographic techniques, approaches and practices. Moreover, as Hammersley points out in Chapter 1, negotiating the oscillations between the positions of an outsider and an insider (whether in a prison setting or amongst Melanesian Islanders) is part of the terrain the ethnographer must traverse, but it is central to the intrinsically complex journey. As Young points out, '[T]here is no singular insider or outsider position that researchers occupy during the course of fieldwork, but rather myriad positions and statuses that can be viewed by respondents either as insider or outsider depending on the social circumstances or conditions affecting the research endeavour' (Young, 2004: 192).

Within this collection, we view prison ethnography as an approach to conducting research in prisons. We define ethnography as a form of in-depth study that includes the systematic and impressionistic recording of human cultural and social life in situ. It includes observing and/or interacting with people as they go about their everyday lives, routines and practices. We contrast an ethnographic approach with purely interview-based research methodologies that tend to be episodic, short-lived and often take place outside of spaces the informant routinely occupies. In addition, we also recognise an ethnographic approach in commitments to the generation of 'thick' descriptive accounts of the research, though these may vary considerably in 'thickness', depth and texture.

Wolcott notes that the term 'ethnography' refers to both the process and the product – 'the presentation itself' (1990: 47) – and we embrace the interrelational continuity of this process. An ethnography does not emerge as a singular, fully formed product, but rather manifests in a variety of forms over the lifetime of the research. We welcome that this form of study is not an *-ology* but a *-graphy*,[1] tending towards the arts of depiction rather than the science of discovery. As Fassin (2014) remarks, there is much that connects the craft of ethnography with the world of literature, and the ethnographer with the novelist. The celebrated French novelist Marcel Proust's argument about 'not going too fast' and making time for detail can serve the ethnographer well.

Back (2007, 2012, 2013) contrasts the attentive, patient approach of ethnography with recent trends towards a journalistically informed, web-enabled, 'reality rush' of proliferating forms of social representation. Amid the torrents of journalistic exposé and reality TV, Back is concerned not only with voyeuristic intrusion into the lives of the poor and the marginalised, the vicarious glee with which those 'unfortunates' 'living at the bottom' are paraded across screens, but also with the claims of revelation, relevance and detail. It is as if the simple profusion of documentary data implies a genuine empirical provenance. Coinciding with this trend, there is, according to Back, a counter-movement – a second eclipse we might add – within academic sociology towards abstraction and theory, a disengagement in the face of such a volume of competing representations of the meaning of lives lived 'out there'. Tellingly, he notes a reticence or inhibition in some emerging sociological literature, such as PhD dissertations, to attempt 'thick' or 'rich' social description, to decline the invitations for a reflexive, ethnographically informed sociology (Bourdieu and Wacquant, 1992). In this collection, Sloan and Wright (see Chapter 7) and Waldram (see Chapter 11) engage directly with such problems, offering, respectively, their own experiences as hope and insight into a new generation of prison ethnographers and the complexities for prison ethnographers of capturing appropriate 'tone'.

Back (2007: 16) is scathing about a trend towards what might be called 'sound-bite' or 'sugar' sociology which confuses quotation for portraiture, sweetness for flavour. It is, he says, 'the task of sociological writing to bring to life the people we work with and listen to'. He quarrels with quotations used as if they were tables or graphs in a quantitative study, as free-standing, self-contained illustrations of some aspect of the text. He cites (2007: 17) the ethnographer Mitch Duneier's pithy remark:

> If you are going to get at the humanity of people, you can't just have a bunch of disembodied thoughts that come out of subject's mouths in interviews without ever developing characters and trying to show people as full human beings. In order to do that it is useful to have a character that lives in the text.

In this collection, one author, Lindsay Whetter (see Chapter 17), resorts to poetry (not her own) to work through and express the depth of feeling and the complexity of emotion she encountered through her work in prison. We welcome the exploration of lyricism as a genuine effort to better understand and to give more life and force to character, feeling and experience in prison texts (see Abbott, 2007; Wakeman, 2014).

Virginia Woolf is celebrated for breaking a prolonged silence in literature around women's lives and desires. Her experiments were not always accessible or accepted, but they almost always opened doors to new ways of knowing and knowing what was hidden. Similar ambition can only enhance prison ethnography, and Abigail Rowe's contribution (in Chapter 18) indicates some of the ethnographic possibilities of getting behind the 'psychic shields', the carapace-hard exteriors that prison excels in fashioning, and that so fascinated Woolf. Whether it is 'The Mark on the Wall' (Woolf, 1991) or 'a stain upon the silence' (Samuel Beckett quoted in Hillyard et al., 2004), the models and methods of literature should not be neglected by prison ethnographers.

Writing about what has been encountered in prison and making sense of it is one of the most demanding and elusive tasks of the ethnographic researcher (see Drake, Chapter 13, this volume). Taking a lesson from the priorities and methods of anthropology distinguishes prison ethnography from the positivistic predilections of more conventional criminological research in prisons. Ethnography is never about finding causes. It exists to demonstrate that there are so many ways of being human. As Lorna Rhodes demonstrates in Chapter 14, prison ethnography leads away from the dehumanising tendencies of criminology towards the more fully human concerns of an anthropology of prison.

Drawings from the past: Prison classics

The history of prison ethnography in England can trace its origins to the form of reflections committed to paper by prison visitors and reformists such as John Howard (1777) and Elizabeth Fry (1827). Howard toured the prisons and gaols of eighteenth-century England in search of models of good practice in the emerging penal estate. What he found appalled him so much that his lengthy report *The State of the Prisons in England and Wales* was published to expose the neglect, brutality and corruption that characterised the prison system. Elizabeth Fry's work consolidated the philanthropic and religious connection between establishing penitentiary prisons and campaigning for their improvement by reform. Her Quaker faith fed her activism, and her short, but influential, book *Observations of the Siting, Superintendence and Government of Female Prisoners* detailed the regimes of various early nineteenth-century prisons, graphically listing their many failings.

After a period of relative quiescence in the US, there was, in the mid-twentieth century, something of a resurgence in qualitative studies of prison life. It coincided with the blooming of American 'New Deal' sociology and the flourishing of what Sumner (1994) characterises as 'The New Disciplinary Matrix', gathering around sociology and psychiatry. Donald Clemmer's *The Prison Community* (1940) established the modern form. In his in-depth and richly detailed study of a relatively typical American state penitentiary, Clemmer eschewed the attractions of the notorious big city prisons, such as New York's Sing Sing, or the new generation of model prisons, such as Stateville, being built across the US at that time. He opted to write about where he worked, in Illinois. Clemmer's training as a sociologist as well as a criminologist resulted in him being appointed to the Classification Board and Mental Health Office of the Illinois State Prison System. He used his position to further his interest in prison culture and drew from prisoners' essays and autobiographical writings. He could refer to thousands of 'sympathetic conversations' with inmates gathered over his years of work in the prison, including a period spent as coach of a prison football team. Due to this depth of immersion and a variety of source materials, Clemmer's study is often credited as being the founding text of prison ethnography and consistently referenced for its originality and insight. Clemmer coined the term 'prisonisation' to capture the extent to which prisons generate and then inculcate their own distinctive cultures. As he notes, however distinctive they seem, and indeed are, prisons and the people within them are always part of society: '[I]n a sense, the prison culture reflects the American culture, for it is a culture within it' (1940: 298). He identified an 'inmate code' as a set of rules and sometimes specified rituals that men in prison adopted to establish a contrarian and self-sustaining identity from the prison regime. The idea of the inmate or a convict code has now acquired an almost mythical status, both in penal sociology and in prison vernaculars.

The convict code, prison culture and other aspects of the way prisoners collectively and personally respond to incarceration formed the basis of Gresham Sykes' (1958) now famous study *The Society of Captives*. Sykes, writing in the second wave of Chicago social interactionist sociology, provides another landmark text and indispensable reference point. Sykes paid early tribute to Clemmer's anthropological insights: 'It taught us to see the prison not simply as a grab bag of problems such as discipline, industry, sanitation and so on, but as a culture which could be fruitfully studied in its own right' (1958: 576).

Sykes entered a maximum-security men's prison in the US with the intention of investigating that culture. His account has become a landmark text, acquiring the dubious status of being 'part of the litany of penology' (Rock, 2008). In some senses, this is unfortunate because *The Society of Captives* is often taken to speak to a universal, almost timeless, prison experience. Reading it dispels this illusion quickly. With its vivid descriptions of armed guards and gun towers overseeing prison compounds, it is clearly driven by a sensitivity to totalitarian power that was inevitably sharper in context in which the study was conducted. In the mid-1950s, barely a decade after the defeat of fascism in Europe, the US remained in thrall to its power, the manner of its own victory and the lurking threat of the Soviet Union and the Cold War. 'The prison official is a bureaucrat' declares Sykes boldly in the introduction, 'but he is a bureaucrat with a gun.' Sykes indicates the shadows looming over him: 'the calculated atrocities of the concentration camps' and the 'ruthless exploitation' of the Soviet gulag. This helps to explain his overriding interest in 'total power' and the possibility that a maximum-security prison will furnish him with a 'prism through which we can see the spectrum of forces at work when social control nears its extreme' (1958: p. xxxiv).

His detailed study was the first to capture and conceptualise the deprivations of prison life. Sykes' 'pains of imprisonment' became a framework through which the distress experienced by prisoners as a result of their confinement could be better understood. The five pains identified by Sykes define the prisoner experience by the deprivation of liberty, goods and services, heterosexual relationships, autonomy and security. By identifying the deprivation of what are, fundamentally, essential human needs, Sykes made clear the inherent, intentional and profound inhumanity of the prison experience. Whilst the contribution of Sykes' work is frequently lauded in the prisons literature and continues to be widely cited, the lack of recognition of his work and findings in prison and criminal justice policymaking remains problematic.

Whilst the shadows of totalitarianism have now receded from the foreground, the reverse is true of issues of race and gender that Sykes' perceptive introduction also notes:

> Race relations take on new forms in the custodial institution where the ratio between Negroes and whites frequently approaches unity and both groups live under conditions of enforced equality. In prison, as in war, we find men without women and norms concerning the masculine role and the endurance of sexual frustration take on new guises.
>
> (1958: p. xxxii)

As several chapters in this collection attest to, the structuring and experiential features of race and gender have endured and evolved in scale, urgency and complexity in contemporary prison landscapes. Sykes' study is an invaluable reference point to the potential of ethnography to illuminate them.

After Sykes' contribution, and possibly even more widely known and highly regarded, Erving Goffman provides students of ethnography with another classic, *Asylums: Essays on the Social Situation of Mental Patients and Other Inmates*. *Asylums* is Goffman's account of three years, 1954–57, spent visiting The National Institute of Mental Health in Bethesda, Maryland, and working amongst the 7,000 inmates of St Elizabeth's Hospital in Washington, DC. It begins with his by-now famous definition of a total institution: 'a place of residence and work where a large number of like-situated individuals, cut off from wider society for an appreciable period of time, together lead an enclosed, formally administered round of life' (Goffman, 1961: xiii).

Prisons and mental hospitals make a paradigmatic form which is explored in the first essay, 'On the Characteristics of Total Institutions'. Significantly for our purposes here, in stressing the literary ambition of ethnographic writing,

Goffman is quick to deploy in his opening account of 'the inmate world' the words of the Irish poet and playwright, Brendan Behan. Goffman takes from Behan's autobiography, *Borstal Boy*, his description of the 'red and white and pity-coloured flashes' beaten out of him by the borstal wardens whilst inducting him to the institution's violent habits. Goffman's prose swings between the lyrical and the clinical, the historical and the biographical, to great effect. He quotes liberally from case notes and reflects at length on his own experiences in conducting semi-covert participant observation fieldwork in which he posed for nearly a year as an employee of the St Elizabeth's Hospital.

Asylums has been continuously in print since it was first published in 1961 and is widely hailed as a text that humanised, and rendered much more visible, a dehumanised and largely invisible group of people. If not formally a trilogy, these three books – *The Prison Community*, *The Society of Captives* and *Asylums* – established a form and an approach to ethnographic research in prison that has been sustained, albeit with difficulty and not without controversy, to the present day.

In a more contemporary context, Wacquant (2002) gives an excellent overview of the scene in the US, including the contributions of John Irwin's *The Felon* (1970) and James Jacobs' *Stateville* (1977), both of which are highly influential works that fit into the tradition of prison ethnography (along with others such as Toch, 1975, 1977), albeit not specifically identifying themselves as such at the time. As Hammersley argues in Chapter 1, the implied epistemic privilege that accompanies an ethnographic approach automatically, but sometimes spuriously, places certain expectations upon the work. As Wolcott notes, 'faulting a study because of an unwarranted claim to be ethnographic may overshadow the fact that, labelling error aside, the research is thorough, informative, and insightful' (1990: 45). Rather than tangling in arguments over ethnographic credentials and the exact methodological provenance of various prison studies, the approach we have taken, as editors, has been relatively open and eclectic. Whilst some anthropologists may be justified in defending the integrity of the method, our primary interest has been to embrace and reflect the diversity of ethnographic prison research to better challenge and champion its various potentials. Lorna Rhodes' contribution (Chapter 14) is an excellent example of this. Her work derives strongly from the disciplinary traditions of cultural anthropology and thus contributes powerfully to the range and breadth of otherwise more tightly focused prison ethnographies. Some of these adopt narrower and more conventional qualitative methodologies, deploy thinner description and display a more condensed analytical range. They are diverse.

Classifying a work as ethnographic can be problematic, and Wacquant's (2002) quarrel is more concerned with the precedence given to quantitative, instrumental and uncritical prison research operating in the service of an aggressively expanding 'prison-industrial complex'. He demonstrates how the growth of such correctional research has displaced the more open stance and critical opportunities of ethnography in the US. Although there was a period between the late 1970s and the 1990s when there appeared to be less prison ethnography occurring in the US, in line with Wacquant's identification of a dangerous 'eclipse' of prison ethnography (2002: 385), since the 1990s and outside of the US, ethnographic approaches to prison research have proliferated and thrived.

Ethnographic research has a long-standing tradition on the European side of the north Atlantic and perhaps is sustaining itself better. Thomas Mathiesen's sociological study of a Norwegian prison, described in his book *Defences of the Weak* (1965), was concerned with the extent to which the culture of prisoners in Norway mirrored or contradicted the culture of prisoners in American prisons (as described in the work of Clemmer, Sykes and others at that time). Mathiesen spent two years conducting fieldwork that aimed to capture the essence of Norwegian prisoner culture. His study offered a landmark contribution to the sociology of prison life because it demonstrated, in explicit terms, the importance of wider social and cultural norms on the shaping of prisoner societies. Mathiesen observed that, in Norwegian prisons, conflict between prison officers and prisoners took on a different form than that of American prisons. Conflict between staff and prisoners persisted in Norwegian prisons, but rather than manifesting through deviant prisoner countercultures, it took the form of more direct prisoner challenge of perceived inconsistencies or contradictions of 'the system' or, more precisely, the ways in which officers applied the rules and thus shaped the system. Mathiesen coined the term 'censoriousness' to describe this process, which he defined as a 'criticism of those in power for not following, in their behaviour, principles that are established as correct within the social system in question' (Mathiesen, 1965: 23). He further argued that the major functional element for censoriousness was that when officers were confronted with it, the lack of legitimacy on which their power was being wielded could be brought to their attention. These ideas have taken significant root in prison scholarship, perhaps most notably in the work of Sparks, Bottoms and Hay (1996) and their study of order in two maximum-security prisons in England and Wales,[2] which extended the idea of legitimacy as a key element of how prison order is won or lost. Likewise, the work of Alison Liebling and Helen Arnold (2004) on the 'moral performance' of prisons might also be viewed as having some genealogical connections to Mathiesen's earlier, groundbreaking work.

One of the first ethnographic prison studies in the UK, undertaken around the same time as Mathiesen's work in Norway, was carried out by Terence and Pauline Morris in London's Pentonville prison (1963). Their research provided a great deal of descriptive, ethnographic detail about Pentonville and drew comparisons as well as contradictions to the work of Clemmer and Sykes. Despite the relative importance of the work, as a strong critical and unrestrained description of prison life, the work was viewed by Pentonville prison staff and prison administrators as a polemical reading of the prison and was thus viewed as a somewhat controversial contribution to the prisons literature. It is sometimes suggested (anecdotally by prison service administrators) that the relative dearth of in-depth studies of UK prisons throughout the rest of the 1960s and into the 1970s was, in part, attributable to reactions against the publication of *Pentonville*. Meanwhile, back inside the prison estate, the 1970s and 1980s saw the state of prisons in the UK as sites of central concern to policymakers and critical researchers alike. For over 20 years, British prisons were troubled by prisoner riots and disturbances. During this period, a number of studies and writings about prison life aimed to draw attention to the chronic failure of prisons or to question the extent to which experiences of imprisonment were fulfilling the supposed or official purposes of prisons as a social institution (see, for example, Cohen and Taylor, 1972; Fitzgerald, 1977; King and Morgan, 1980; Fitzgerald and Sim, 1982; Boyle, 1984; Carlen et al., 1985; King and McDermott, 1989, 1990).

Of particular importance was the work of Phil Scraton, Joe Sim and Paula Skidmore, in *Prisons Under Protest* (1991), which examined the problem of prison protests through the study of Peterhead prison in Scotland. Using a detailed, case study approach that drew on first-hand enquiry-based research that was, by its very nature, ethnographic in scope, the book eloquently evidenced the way '[l]ife in most British prisons is an unrelenting imposition of authority' (1991: 62). Indeed, this work and many others produced throughout the 1970s, the 1980s and up to the mid-1990s, though not strictly ethnographic, nevertheless captured in rich, detailed and angry description, the crisis that troubled the British prison system throughout these years.

Since the mid-1990s, ethnographic studies of prison life have widened in diversity, geographic spread and focus. Of particular note are Platek's work in Poland (1990), Bosworth's study on women in prison (1999) and the works of Jewkes in England (2002), Piacentini in Russia (2004), Bandyopadhyay in India (2010), Crewe in England (2011), Phillips in England (2012), Drake's account of the High Security Estate in England (2012) and Darke in Brazil (2013), indicating some of the wealth of ethnographic research that has emerged since the endarkening tendency was identified in the US by Wacquant. This collection now attests to a sustained stream of ethnographic works that, at least for the time being, has assured a strong ethnographic tradition in prison research.

Seeing the ethnographer: Ethnography through the lens of prison

Since the 1940s, in a variety of disciplines where ethnography has been practised, there has been a much greater emphasis in the research literature on examining the role of the ethnographer in the ethnographic process, with ethnography often becoming paired with terms such as reflection and reflexivity (Davies, 2007). Amongst prison ethnographers, and particularly at the *Resisting the Eclipse* symposium, this has provoked fruitful discussion about its merits and methods. Reflexivity involves developing a consciousness of one's self in the process of research, and it is a familiar and almost unavoidable experience for ethnographers. Such reflection is inherent to the process because the researcher is 'the primary research instrument, as he/she has access to the field, establishes field relations and conducts and structures observations' (Claes et al., 2013: 59). Nonetheless, it is a widespread and controversial term in social science, qualifying its claim to objective knowledge because of the way the personal qualities of the researcher filter and shape the data collected and, therefore, the knowledge that emerges from it (Pels, 2000).

In some quarters, reflexivity has also developed a reputation for making academics even more self-absorbed than usual. Reflexivity, so it is argued, is a diverting hall of mirrors, best passed through quickly (Lynch, 2000). As Dick Hobbs (1993: 62) rather wearily asks: who wants to know about the valiant ethnographer 'who was nearly arrested, almost beaten up and didn't quite go crazy' as they bravely descended into the criminal underworld? Reflexivity, poorly practised, or uncritically indulged, simply turns the intrinsic voyeurism of the researcher back on themselves, a narcissistic self-absorption that confuses the object of study with the method (Skeggs, 2004). Perhaps Hobbs had in mind Geertz's (1988: 97) warnings about 'the unbearably earnest' fieldworker's confessional writing. The tendency, seemingly a trans-Atlantic one, for irritating neologisms such as 'mystory', 'Me-search' or 'I-witnessing' can be off-putting (Back, 2012). It is a difficult balance to strike between recognising that there is no 'view from nowhere' (Bourdieu, 2000: 2) and that you are not the story but the storyteller.

The Palgrave Handbook of Prison Ethnography

A turn towards greater reflexivity and a stronger emphasis on the positionality of the researcher runs the risk of moving focus away from prisoners and prison cultures. We do not want prisons or prisoners to be eclipsed in such a way. We favour Back's (2013) proposal for forms of imaginative writing 'that can capture a positioned observer's sense of things' rather than a barren 'correctness' in 'taking responsibility for your roots'. Whilst the importance of the findings of ethnographic research is of central importance to the wider socio-political project to which prison ethnography necessarily speaks to, the focus of this Handbook is on the method and experience of in-depth, ethnographic research. It does not, however, ignore the prison-as-place. Instead, it centralises the prison as a site of exploration, as an exemplar and as a lens by which to expose new insights on conducting in-depth qualitative research in a wide range of areas. At the same time, its focus on the prison across a variety of international contexts provides a unique opportunity to consider the social and political dimensions of the use and experience of imprisonment worldwide. This Handbook has four overall aims:

1. to expose what can be learned about contemporary prisons in different contexts through the use of ethnographic research methodologies;
2. to take stock of and examine the breadth of research dilemmas thrown up by the challenges of qualitative, and particularly ethnographic, enquiry in prisons;
3. to stimulate debate on enduring and emerging research dilemmas in a context of changing academic demands and differing political conditions and value systems; and
4. to provide an up-to-date, authoritative and illustrative account of diverse prison conditions around the world.

On the latter aim, the scope of this collection has been limited by the constraints placed on some of our invited authors by their academic institutions or their current projects in the field. Several were unable to contribute to this edited collection. However, our colleagues at the GPRN were instrumental in ensuring a wider geographical coverage than would have been possible otherwise. The collection includes contributions that speak of prison experience in more than ten countries.

Notwithstanding a high proportion of European jurisdictions amongst these, this Handbook successfully captures a richness of the ethnographic approach and offers essential illuminations of penal interiors that are otherwise and intentionally hidden from view. By collecting in one volume such a range of exceptional prison scholarship, this Handbook demonstrates how the increasing shift towards quantitative forms of enquiry in the social sciences, and in the field of criminal justice in particular, sacrifices enormous epistemological opportunities.

The Handbook is organised into four parts under the prepositions *About, Through, Of* and *For,* in order to situate the chapters that make up each part of the Handbook within a relational space to the practice of ethnography. Each part is introduced by one of the editors where the whole of the sum, which forms that part, is narrated and drawn together.

In 'About Prison Ethnography' (Part I), Rod Earle introduces a collection of chapters that present methodological, theoretical and pragmatic issues associated with using deep, immersive, qualitative approaches to understanding complex social and political problems. This part presents a range of diverse perspectives and positions on the challenges of 'doing' in-depth research and in so doing reveals much 'about prison ethnography'.

In 'Through Prison Ethnography' (Part II), Deborah Drake prefaces a series of contributions that consider what can be revealed 'through ethnography' and how an ethnographic approach can offer insights that are specific to a field of study as well as to wider social and political concerns. The collection of diverse international prison research experiences included in this part are considered as if through an adjustable lens, with the visual metaphor offering a way of developing critical analysis that 'zooms in' on the detail or 'zooms out' to capture the context (and thanks to Andrew Jefferson for suggesting this metaphor). The chapters demonstrate how the infinitely variable details of human existence can be analysed both in magnified detail and against a more panoramic theoretical perspective 'through ethnography'.

In 'Of Prison Ethnography' (Part III), Rod Earle returns to usher in a transition into a range of chapters which seek to unpack the extent to which ethnographers are 'of' the fields that they study. This part of the Handbook focuses on different aspects of the role of ethnographer and the way he or she negotiates the research setting. Many of the contributors in this part have worked or held different roles within prison environments prior to, during, or after studying the prison ethnographically. The chapters expose and illuminate the tensions associated with 'insider'/'outsider' statuses and the shifting boundaries and identities that combine to challenge the relationship between the ethnographer and his or her other roles in the research field.

The concluding part of the Handbook, 'For Prison Ethnography' (Part IV), is introduced by Jennifer Sloan and includes a range of chapters which make the case 'for' prison ethnography. Each of the chapters offers a distinctive, compelling and theoretically robust argument 'for prison ethnography' recognising that, ironically, the parochial, narrow vista of the prison environment can also be a site of meaning-making for wider social forces in an increasingly globalised and changing world. These final chapters in the Handbook not only take the case for prison ethnography well beyond the prison, but also remain anchored in the lessons to be learned there.

The chapters which form *The Palgrave Handbook of Prison Ethnography* provide a definitive source for students, practitioners, novice and seasoned researchers, both within and beyond criminological and prison studies. The collected works reflect upon, wrestle with and expose the means by which prison ethnographers aim to gain understanding, make sense of what they learn and then make it intelligible to wider audiences. Prison ethnographers, as Richard Quinney (2000) has argued about criminologists more generally, are given the opportunity to bear witness to experiences and practices that few other members of society have the opportunity to see. As a result, they hold a responsibility to communicate and to educate. This Handbook showcases a range of contributions by prison researchers who have resisted the eclipse of prison ethnography and remain committed to exploring and extending its potential.

Notes

1. We are grateful to Andrew Jefferson and Tomas Max Martin of the GPRN for this insight.
2. England and Wales have a common legal jurisdiction, with a unified prison service, which differs from other parts of the UK.

References

Abbot, A. (2007) 'Against Narrative: A Preface to Lyrical Sociology', *Sociological Theory*, 25, 1, 67–99.

Back, L. (2007) *The Art of Listening* (Oxford: Berg).

Back, L. (2012) 'Take Your Reader There' Department of Anthropology: Writing Across Boundaries Project [online resource] (Durham: Durham University), http://www.dur.ac.uk/writingacrossboundaries/writingonwriting/lesback/ [accessed 22/July/2013].

Back, L. (2013) 'Attentiveness as a Vocation: An Interview with Les Back', https://www.gold.ac.uk/media/Attentiveness%20as%20a%20Vocation%20-%20Back%20and%20Ruiz.pdf [accessed 7/November/2014].

Bandyopadhyay, M. (2010) *Everyday Life in a Prison: Confinement, Surveillance, Resistance* (India: Orient Blackswan Pvt Ltd.).

Bosworth, M. (1999) *Engendering Resistance: Agency and Power in Women's Prisons* (Dartmouth: Ashgate).

Boyle, J. (1984) *The Pain of Confinement* (London: Pan).

Bourdieu, P. (2000) *Pascalian Meditations* (Cambridge: Polity Press).

Bourdieu, P. and Wacquant, L. (1992) *An Invitation to Reflexive Sociology* (Cambridge: Polity Press).

Claes, B., Lippens, V., Kennes, P. and Tournel, H. (2013) 'Gender and Prison Ethnography: Some Fieldwork Implications', in K. Beyens, J. Christiaens, B. Claes, S. De Ridder, H. Tournel and H. Tubex (eds) *The Pains of Doing Criminological Research*, pp. 59–71 (Brussels: VUP Press).

Clemmer, D. (1940) *The Prison Community*, New edition (New York: Holt, Reinhart and Winston).

Carlen, P., Christina, D., Hicks, J., O'Dwyer, J. and Tchaikovsky, C. (1985) *Criminal Women* (Oxford: Blackwell, Polity Press).

Cohen, S. and Taylor, L. (1972) *Psychological Survival: The Experience of Long-Term Imprisonment* (Harmondsworth: Penguin).

Crewe, B. (2009) *The Prisoner Society: Power, Adaptation, and Social Life in an English Prison* (Oxford: Oxford University Press).

Davies, C. A. (2007) *Reflexive Ethnography: A Guide to Researching Selves and Others* (London: Routledge).

Darke, S. (2013) 'Inmate Governance in Brazilian Prisons', *Howard Journal of Criminal Justice*, 52, 3, 272–84.

Drake, D. H. (2012) *Prisons, Punishment and the Pursuit of Security* (Basingstoke: Palgrave Macmillan).

Duneier, M., Kasinitz, P. and Murphy, A. K. (eds) (2014) *The Urban Ethnography Reader* (Oxford: Oxford University Press).

Evans-Pritchard, E. E. (1937/1976) *Witchcraft Oracles, and Magic among the Azande* (New York: Oxford University Press).

Fassin, D. (2014) *Plenary Address, British Society of Criminology*, Liverpool University (personal recording).
Fitzgerald, M. (1977) *Prisoners in Revolt* (Harmondsworth: Penguin).
Fitzgerald, M. and Sim, J. (1982) *British Prisons* (Oxford: Blackwell).
Fry, E. G. (1827) *Observations on the Visiting, Superintendence, and Government of Female Prisoners* (Cornhill: John and Arthur Arch).
Geertz, C. (1988) *Works and Lives: The Anthropologist as Author* (Cambridge: Polity Press).
Goffman, E. (1961) *Asylums: Essays on the Social Situation of Mental Patients and Other Inmates* (Chicago: Aldine Publishing Company).
Hammersley, M. and Atkinson, P. (1983) *Ethnography: Principles and Practice* (London: Routledge).
Hillyard, P., Sim, J., Tombs, S. and Whyte, D. (2004) 'Leaving a "Stain upon the Silence": Contemporary Criminology and the Politics of Dissent', *British Journal of Criminology*, 44, 3, 369–90.
Hobbs, D. (1993) 'Peers, Careers and Academic Fears: Writing as Academic Fieldwork', in D. Hobbs and T. May (eds) *Interpreting the Field: Accounts of Ethnography*, pp. 45–66 (Oxford: Oxford University).
Howard, J. (1777) *The State of Prisons in England and Wales* (Warrington: Printed by William Eyres).
Irwin, J. (1970) *The Felon* (New Jersey: Prentice-Hall, Inc.).
Jacobs, J. B. (1977) *Stateville: The Penitentiary in Mass Society* (Chicago: University of Chicago Press).
Jewkes, Y. (2002) *Captive Audience: Media, Masculinity and Power in Prisons* (Cullompton: Willan Publishing)
King, R. D. and McDermott, K. (1989) 'British Prisons 1970–1987: The Ever-Deepening Crisis', *British Journal of Criminology*, 29, 2, 107–28.
King, R. D. and McDermott, K. (1990) ' "My Geranium Is Subversive": Some Notes on the Management of Trouble in Prisons', *British Journal of Sociology*, 41, 445–71.
King, R. D. and Morgan, R. (1980) *The Future of the Prison System* (Farnborough: Gower).
Liebling, A. and Arnold, H. (2004) *Prisons and Their Moral Performance* (Oxford: Oxford University Press).
Lynch, M. (2000) 'Against Reflexivity as an Academic Virtue and a Source of Privileged Knowledge', *Theory, Culture and Society*, 17, 3, 26–54.
Malinowski, B. (1922/1961) *Argonauts of the Western Pacific: An Account of Native Enterprise and Adventure in the Archipelagoes of Melanesian New Guinea* (London: Routledge and Kegan Paul).
Mathiesen, T. (1965) *The Defences of the Weak: A Sociological Study of a Norwegian Correctional Institution* (London: Tavistock Publications Limited).
Morris, T. and Morris, P. (1963) *Pentonville: A Sociological Study of an English Prison* (London: Routledge and Kegan Paul).
Pels, D. (2000) 'Reflexivity: One Step Up', *Theory, Culture and Society*, 17, 3, 1–25.
Phillips, C. (2012) *The Multicultural Prison: Ethnicity, Masculinity, and Social Relations among Prisoners* (Oxford: Oxford University Press).
Phillips, C. and Earle, R. (2010) 'Reading Difference Differently? Identity, Epistemology and Prison Ethnography', *British Journal of Criminology*, 50, 2, 360–78.
Piacentini, L. (2004) *Surviving Russian Prisons: Punishment, Economy and Politics in Transition* (Cullompton: Willan Publishing).
Platek, M. (1990) 'Prison Subculture in Poland', *International Journal of the Sociology of Law*, 18, 459–72.

Rock, P. (2008) Review of *The Society of Captives*, Second edition, 2007, *The Canadian Criminal Justice Association*, https://www.ccja-acjp.ca/en/cjcr200/cjcr279.html [accessed 6/November/2014].

Scraton, P., Sim, J. and Skidmore, P. (1991) *Prisons Under Protest* (Milton Keynes: Open University Press).

Skeggs, B. (2004) *Class, Self, Culture* (London: Routledge).

Sparks, R., Bottoms, A. E. and Hay, W. (1996) *Prisons and the Problem of Order* (Oxford: Oxford University Press).

Sumner, C. (1994) *The Sociology of Deviance: An Obituary* (Buckingham: Open University Press).

Sykes, G. M. (1958) *The Society of Captives: A Study of a Maximum Security Prison*, 2007 reprinted edition (Princeton: Princeton University Press).

Sykes, G. (1958) 'Review of "The Prison Community" ', *The Journal of Criminal Law, Criminology, and Police Science*, March–April, 49, 6, 576–7.

Toch, H. (1975) *Men in Crisis* (Chicago: Aldine Publishing Company).

Toch, H. (1977) *Living in Prison: The Ecology of Survival* (New York: The Free Press).

Turnbull, C. (1961) *The Forest People* (London: Cape).

Wacquant, L. (2002) 'The Curious Eclipse of Prison Ethnography in the Age of Mass Incarceration', *Ethnography*, 3, 4, 371–97.

Wakeman, S. (2014) 'Fieldwork, Biography and Emotion: Doing Criminological Autoethnography', *British Journal of Criminology*, 54, 5, 705–21.

Wolcott, H. F. (1990) 'Making a Study "More Ethnographic" ', *Journal of Contemporary Ethnography*, 19, 1, 44–72.

Woolf, V. (1991) *The Complete Shorter Fiction* (Susan Dick, ed) (London: Grafton).

Young, A. A. (2004) 'Experiences in Ethnographic Interviewing about Race', in M. Bulmer and J. Solomos (eds) *Researching Race and Racism*, pp. 187–202 (London: Routledge).

Part I
About Prison Ethnography

Introduction to Part I

Rod Earle

Part I of this Handbook introduces the complex field of prison ethnography. Collectively, the chapters examine their place in the wider ethnographic landscape and illuminate the particular challenges and triumphs of conducting ethnography in prison and how, and why, some ethnographers 'do' prison ethnography.

The first three chapters present distinctive and contrasting perspectives on prison ethnography. In Chapter 1, Martyn Hammersley writes 'from the outside', quickly indicating that he has no experience of prison ethnography. However, as many will recognise, and as his ubiquitous presence in the reference section of ethnographic texts attests to, Hammersley is very much 'an insider' when it comes to ethnography. He provides a succinct and lucid summary of many of the themes that animate this collection – the role of reflexivity in prison ethnography, the difficulties of rendering an authentic account of prison life and being sensitive to the power-soaked contexts of prison research. Writing with the benefit of long experience, Hammersley strikes a cautionary note, warning prison ethnographers not to 'over play their hand' in their enthusiasm for an 'ethnographic imperative'. The epistemic privilege this assumes can be a poison chalice, warns Hammersley, implicitly establishing a sterile hierarchy of methods that binds thought and action to the vertical at the expense of the horizontal. The three-dimensional research community Hammersley prefers may be a 'swamp', but we are all in it together, he insists, and 'there is no moral high ground'.

In Chapter 2, David Scott argues that the moral compass of prison ethnographers must be brought fully into view. Writing from direct experience of 16 different prisons, Scott declares them to be 'profoundly immoral places'. Laying his cards firmly on the table as a prison abolitionist, Scott fully reveals his hand. Having briefly outlined what is involved in contemporary abolitionism, he draws explicitly and evocatively from his research journals to provide the kinds of insights that propel ethnographic claims to epistemic privilege. His work with prison chaplains inevitably pulls him towards the moral core of penal practice. He describes prisons as 'dark places', 'graves for the living', as the title of his chapter puts it. Taking inspiration and direction from Stan Cohen's (2001) *States of Denial*, rich in first-hand ethnographic detail, Scott's chapter could not be more different from Hammersley's. The moral high ground is staked out and the hierarchy confronted. An abolitionist praxis that testifies against the denial and neutralisation of penal horror is proposed. Prison ethnographers, equipped as they are with privileged knowledge, must 'name the prison place for what it is – a place structured to deliver violence, pain and suffering'.

In Chapter 3, the 'moral performance' of prisons is a theme identified by Alison Liebling and her colleagues at the Cambridge Prisons Research Centre. 'Moral performance' offers a sophisticated metric for evaluating what prisons do (Liebling and Arnold, 2004), and few people in the UK have more combined experience of researching prisons than Alison Liebling, Helen Arnold and Christina Straub. This chapter finds firm, if not high, ground in Hammersley's swamp. The authors do this by revisiting Cohen and Taylor's famous study from 1972 in the context of their 2010–11 study of HMP Whitemoor. In doing so, they seek to reinvent the dialogue between prison researcher and researched prisoner. Vivid extracts from fieldwork notes illuminate the chapter, as they do in Scott's, but they are not just the researchers' notes. Prisoners contribute their perspectives and the work of the Cambridge Dialogue Group rises from the pages, meeting the force of Scott's argument with its own 'moral and emotional momentum'. According to the authors, long-term prisoners engaged in dialogue with long-term criminologists promise to become the new criminologists of the future. Two utopian visions, three chapters in!

The collapse of the twentieth century's largest utopian project, the Soviet Union, forms the backdrop to Laura Piacentini's contribution in Chapter 4 on researching Russian prisons. Transitions are her theme. Caught up in Russia's chaotic re-emergence from Soviet collectivity to national singularity, Piacentini cannot help but find her ethnography pulling her ever deeper into Russian penal culture and its people's orientations to the state and history. Prisons are the thread out of which Piacentini weaves a story that is both personal and ethnographically instructive. With the benefit of 20 years of experience in Russian prison research, she can retrospectively contextualise what it is about ethnography that has animated her career. She speaks of 'ethnographic mobilisation and immobilisation' to account for its differential presence in her work as she has moved towards the development of penal policy and practice in the new Russian state. As Russians reimagine their future, the penal structures of the past haunt their new institutions and visions. Piacentini wonders aloud how her research can be reconciled to the pains and urgency that accompany such a process. Just as Max Weber's experiences of the 1918 German Revolution pushed him to focus on 'self-clarification', 'inner consistency' and 'vocation', so Piacentini turns to 'integrity', in method and intent, as the answer to the questions that confront her. 'Honouring one's word' is the key to ethnographic authority she settles on, recognising ethnographers' responsibility to ethical practice; it also provides her with the means to survive the societal turbulence gripping contemporary Russia.

French penal practice may not have Russia's fragmenting history and uncertain future to contend with, but Gilles Chantraine and Nicolas Sallée report in Chapter 5 on the way technological innovation in youth custody settings in France both fit into and shape new patterns of control. The close engagement involved in ethnographic research allows them to identify how the introduction of an electronic logbook to record, compile and distribute staff observations of young people in prison generated revealing patterns of compliance, resistance and consternation. Their work highlights the role of the ethnographic in accessing a wider range of interpretive repertoires. Chantraine and Sallée identify the rhetoric of electronic communication as a transformative medium that extends well beyond the simple management of data. Through careful observation and sophisticated theoretical analysis, they note how the conventions of oral conversation between staff become locked into the new digital recordings and are thus radically transformed. In stark contrast to the organic dialogue championed by Liebling, Arnold and Straub, Chantraine and Sallée identify a new trend in communicative control. They call attention to the need for an even wider approach to prison ethnography, which can encompass 'an ethnography of writing'. Writing themselves against the eclipse of prison ethnography, they demand an inclusive prison ethnography that uses more imaginative ethnographic methods. Drawing from rich new French ethnographic practice (Fassin, 2013) and theoretical innovation across the new social studies of technologies (Latour, 2005), Chantraine and Sallée offer an exemplary case of how prison ethnography brings a novel visibility and intelligibility to the dark places described by Scott.

Getting close to the research subject is an intrinsic part of ethnography, but, in Chapter 6, Ben Crewe and Alice Ievins present a series of challenging examples as to how, in prisons, this can confront ethnographers with particular dilemmas. Taking as a starting point the account of an American journalist sued by a prisoner for misrepresentation and 'character assassination', they explore ideas about readership and writing. Compelling accounts of their work with prisoners and in prison draw the contours of moral quandaries they have negotiated, with varying degrees of satisfaction. They go on to ask searching questions about the capacity of researchers to extend empathy to men convicted of sexual offences and about their honesty in reporting feelings less readily 'owned' and disclosed than the more conventional ones. Here, the implications of a distinction drawn, tacitly or explicitly, between 'ordinary decent criminals' and an ultimate criminal 'other', are opened up. It is a conversation waiting to happen, a dialogue that prisoner ethnographers can begin.

The complex theoretical and methodological issues outlined by Hammersley in the opening chapter of this section benefit from his years of immersion in ethnography. The last chapter in Part I, Chapter 7, continues the theme of contrasting diverse perspectives by presenting a thoughtful, reflective account of two 'green' prison ethnographers. Jennifer Sloan and Serena Wright comment on their experience of ethnographic prison research as PhD research students, 'neophytes' to the world of prison and academic research. Taking inspiration from Jewkes (2012), they focus on the profound experiential impact of prison interiors. Treading a careful line between recognition of the emotional toll involved and the need to avoid the implication of any equivalence to the burdens shouldered by prisoners, Sloan and Wright add to a growing reflexive literature about prison ethnography itself. Many, more experienced prison researchers will recognise their dilemmas. Those new to the field, or considering their options, will benefit from their generosity and candour. Going further than simply sharing their own experiences, the authors present the results of a survey of more experienced prison researchers. This commitment to openness makes a substantial contribution to the kind of scholarly community that prison ethnographers need to thrive.

Max Weber (1968) thought of ecclesiastical institutions as merely burnt-out shells of a once-burning charisma. Prisons exert a kind of morbid charisma that is more continually bruising than 'once burning'. Nonetheless, it is a force less readily recognised than their simple authority and symbolic presence. As such, prisons exert a powerful magnetic pull on both the popular and the sociological imaginations. Collected in this first part of the Handbook are seven examinations of that attraction. They show prison ethnography as both diverse and disagreeing, a sign of its health and potential. Prisons exist in many more countries than it would be possible to include in this volume, but what drives prison ethnography forward is that it only takes 'one good case [to] illuminate the working of a social system' (Gluckman, 1961: 9). Going around and about prison ethnography, the following chapters demonstrate how this is accomplished.

References

Cohen, S. (2001) *States of Denial* (Cambridge: Polity Press).

Fassin, D. (2013) *Enforcing Order: An Ethnography of Urban Policing* (Polity: Cambridge).

Gluckman, M. (1961) 'Ethnographic Data in British Social Anthropology', *Sociological Review*, 9, 5–17.

Jewkes, Y. (2012) 'Autoethnography and Emotion as Intellectual Resources: "Doing Prison Research Differently" ', *Qualitative Inquiry*, 18, 1, 63–75.

Latour (2005) *Reassembling the Social: An Introduction to Actor-Network Theory* (Durham: Duke University Press).

Liebling, A., assisted by Arnold, H. (2004) *Prisons and Their Moral Performance: A Study of Values, Quality and Prison Life* (Oxford: Clarendon Press).

Weber, M. (1968) *On Charisma and Institution Building* (Chicago: University of Chicago Press).

1
Research 'Inside' Viewed from 'Outside': Reflections on Prison Ethnography

Martyn Hammersley

Introduction

My focus in this chapter is on the methodological implications of the inside/outside distinction for ethnographic research,[1] as illustrated by the critical case of prison ethnography (Jacobs, 1974; Liebling, 1999; Rhodes, 2001). Appropriately enough, in colloquial English, 'being inside' is a euphemism for 'being in prison', and this acknowledges, amongst other things, the sharp boundary around this type of setting, marking it off from 'the outside world' – a feature that is of considerable importance from the point of view of carrying out research and from other perspectives as well. As Rhodes (2004: 8) remarks: 'prisons create by their very nature sets of opposing and aligned positions.'

More generally, though, the distinction between inside and outside is central to much discussion of ethnography, since its advocates insist on the importance of finding out what goes on *inside* settings and of understanding the perspectives of *insiders*, asserting the capacity of ethnography to do this. Outside/inside also connects to the notion of reflexivity, which is often seen as a central feature of ethnography (Hammersley and Atkinson, 2007). Whilst many meanings have been given to the term 'reflexivity' in the literature (Lynch, 2000), the most common one involves the idea of stepping outside of an activity in which one is engaged (in this case research) in order to reflect back upon it. This type of reflexivity is an aspect of the task in which I am engaged here. As an outsider to prison ethnography (I have never done ethnography 'inside'), my reflexive credentials are no doubt open to question, but I can claim to be an insider to ethnography more generally. And the issues I will address – whilst prompted by reading and thinking about prison ethnography – apply beyond that specific field.

The features of ethnography I will be discussing have an ambiguous character. They can be positive, but they also harbour temptations, dangers and errors, which I will explore. In part, these are linked to a tendency to forget the metaphorical and functional character of the inside/outside distinction (see Lakoff and Johnson, 1980). I will discuss them under two headings: 'epistemological' and 'ethical/political'.

Epistemological issues regarding inside/outside

A starting point here is what might be called the *ethnographic imperative*; and this, I suggest, underpins concern over the 'eclipse' of prison ethnography (Wacquant, 2002a). This imperative asserts that in order to *truly* understand any social phenomenon, direct contact with it via participant observation is required. This was built into anthropological enquiry for much of the twentieth century. Also, symptomatic of the influence of this imperative is the way in which a famous quotation from Robert Park has been frequently repeated. This quotation, from the 1920s or early 1930s, reads:

> Go and sit in the lounges of the luxury hotels and on the doorsteps of the flophouses; sit on the Gold Coast settees and on the slum shakedowns; sit in the Orchestra Hall and in the Star and Garter Burlesk. In short, [...] go get the seats of your pants dirty in real research.
>
> (quoted in McKinney, 1966: 71)

In the context of prison research, King (2000: 297–98) provides an echo:

> This may sound obvious. But it has to be said. It simply is not possible to do research that will tell you much about prisons without getting out into the field. No amount of theorizing or reading in an office can substitute for the hands-on experience of spending your time in prison.

Integral to what I have called the ethnographic imperative is a claim to *epistemic privilege*: that ethnography, especially in the form of participant observation, provides superior understanding. For example, it is often argued that direct contact is required if the researcher is to be able to overcome her or his preconceptions and prejudices about the people and places being investigated. Or, it may be suggested that social institutions present misleading facades and that it is only by penetrating those facades that genuine knowledge can be produced: going inside to find out 'what really goes on', rather than accepting official accounts or more remote and mediated perspectives. The implication is that any other source of knowledge than ethnography (in the form of participant observation) is defective, or at least very much second class. Underpinning this is the idea that closeness, or involvement in a setting, provides access to data that cannot be obtained in any other way and offers genuine understanding of people and places. Thus, in the context of his study of Wellingborough prison,

Crewe (2009: 3) refers to ethnography as 'an approach that can pierce the skin of an institution, penetrate official descriptions and show the interconnections between apparently discrete elements of the prison social structure', and he claims that 'it makes possible a form of learning that is direct and experiential' (p. 477).

There is much to be said in favour of this general line of argument: getting close up to a phenomenon often provides information about it and understanding of it that is not easily available more remotely. And, not only may a view from afar lack detail, but it is certainly true that appearances can be misleading; that, indeed, some are *designed* to deceive. Furthermore, in the case of human social life, involvement in it – regular interaction with the people concerned over a lengthy period of time – will also frequently challenge prior assumptions and supply knowledge and understanding that would not otherwise be accessible.

At the same time, it is important to recognise that this argument does not provide an effective justification for ethnography. In particular, it cannot warrant what I referred to as the ethnographic imperative. There are at least two respects in which it generates problems.

Problems with insider knowledge

It is often argued that ethnography provides access to an insider perspective. This general idea is often traced back to Malinowski's (1922: 25) emphasis on the importance of grasping 'the native point of view'.[2] More recently, this argument has taken the form of claiming that ethnography provides epistemic advantage because it accesses experiences and views that generally go unrepresented in the public sphere, because the people concerned are marginalised: prisoners would be an obvious case in point, but by no means the only one. By enabling us to see and experience the world from the point of view of such groups, it is claimed, ethnography can provide more authentic or complete knowledge of society, as compared with other sources of social knowledge.

Some versions of this argument, for example those influenced by feminist standpoint epistemology (see Smith, 1974; Hartsock, 1983; Harding, 1992), attribute epistemic privilege to the marginalised in a universal way: that they are more likely to see and understand things as these really are, whereas others will be blinded by ideology. An alternative version simply stresses the uniqueness and virtually inexplicable character of other people's experiences and draws the implication that, given this, they must be treated as authorities on their own experience. Examples of both these lines of argument can be found in a variety of fields, for instance research on childhood (see, for example, Kellett, 2005) and disability studies (see Zarb, 1992).

There are two related problems associated with this claim that ethnography provides access to insider knowledge. First, there are questions about whether researchers can ever become insiders and what this would entail. For instance, aside from the barriers that often face researchers in gaining physical access to prisons (Cohen and Taylor, 1977; Rathbone, 2005; Bandyopadhyay, 2010), does the ethnographer ever actually become a member of 'prison society'? Some have argued that extreme measures are required for insidership to be attained. Thus, in the case of studying those belonging to a different religious faith from one's own, it has sometimes been suggested that religious conversion is essential (see Jules-Rosette 1978a, 1978b). Following a similar line of argument in studying prisons, must we, like Marquart (2003), become prison officers or even commit an offence that gets us confined as an inmate?[3] Jacobs (1974: 232) reports the complaint of an inmate: 'instead of doing your bull shit research from an armchair, why didn't you come in as an inmate so you could find out what it's all about, you phoney cock-sucker', whilst others asked in a more friendly way why he 'didn't become an inmate for a week or two in order to experience the totality of their world' (p. 237). At the very least it may be argued that researchers' personal and social characteristics need to approximate to those of the people they will be studying. Perhaps only ex-convicts can understand prisoners' lives properly (Ross and Richards 2003). But, of course, there are significant differences amongst prisoners, so that there may also be more specific requirements in particular cases. For example, in the case of studying Muslim prisoners, it may be proposed that researchers must share that faith (Quraishi, 2007).

Whilst there is undoubtedly some force in these arguments, any hope of achieving full identity between researcher and researched is, of course, futile. Each of us has many different social characteristics, and the combination of these makes us virtually unique. This is true both of researchers and of the people they study.[4] Moreover, whilst there can be barriers to understanding that result from the social characteristics and positionings of the researcher, it is often difficult to know which of these will be significant in any particular situation. Quraishi (2007) points out that, whilst he was a Muslim, there were still important respects in which he differed from the Muslim prisoners he was studying. Thus, intrinsic divisions within categories such as 'Muslim' and other characteristics such as home region or social class can prove significant. Furthermore, in any setting, we are usually investigating more than one group of people, and these may vary significantly in their characteristics, so that it is not possible for a researcher to be similar to all of the groups to be studied.

Whilst it is true that the distinctive characteristics of researchers may sometimes make it impossible or difficult for them to study particular sorts of people, it is easy to exaggerate the obstacles, and care must be taken not to prejudge what is possible. Indeed, in some instances particular kinds of difference may facilitate contact and understanding more than similarity. Given this, rather than the pursuit of similarity, what is important is reflexivity: awareness on the part of the ethnographer of how her or his personal and social characteristics, feelings or emotions, and behaviour may not only facilitate and illuminate but also restrict and distort the data and the analysis (Phillips and Earle, 2010; Jewkes, 2012; Drake and Harvey, 2014). This is required precisely because the ethnographer can never simply be an insider.

A second problem with the idea that ethnography provides access to insider knowledge is that, in terms of this argument, ethnography's epistemic privilege can be trumped by the claims to knowledge of 'real' insiders. In the case of prison ethnography, this would include not only inmates but also warders and others involved in the everyday life of prisons. Participants generally have far greater 'closeness' and longer-term involvement than ethnographers. This is an issue that comes to the surface particularly when an ethnographer puts forward an account that is at odds with the views of at least some of the people he or she is studying.

One response to this problem has been to reformulate the primary task of ethnography as 'giving voice' to insiders, especially those who are marginalised – enabling them to be heard by a wider audience. However, this is not unproblematic even in its own terms: there will often be insiders of diverse kinds, and they may have divergent perspectives, so which group is to be selected, and on what grounds? In the case of prisons, there are very significant differences not only between prisoners and warders, but also *amongst* prisoners. Is the task of the ethnographer simply to present these diverse views as all equally valid and of value? This is rarely done. But, in any case, in 'giving voice' the ethnographer is still playing a governing role, in the sense of filtering and formulating insider views, rather than simply preserving and voicing these in their own terms.

This criticism sometimes leads to the proposal that the task should be to enable insiders to carry out their own ethnographies, along the lines of participatory enquiry (Reason and Bradbury, 2001). But, again, the question arises as to which insiders are to be assisted in this way, and why. Furthermore, there are issues about in what sense the resulting enquiry represents a form of social science research. In particular, who is responsible for the nature, purpose and quality of the investigations carried out? Or, more fundamentally, who decides how these matters are to be decided and on what grounds?

For me, what these problems indicate is excessive emphasis on the value of insider knowledge. In summary terms, this emphasis is empiricist. Whilst ethnographic closeness or involvement may well increase the chances of gaining understanding in certain respects, or at least reduce the dangers of being misled in particular ways, it cannot *guarantee* understanding. Nor can we assume that other sources of knowledge can never provide understanding. More than this, there may be distinctive forms of error that are more likely when one is 'up close', 'involved' or 'inside'. Indeed, there has long been discussion of these in the ethnographic literature, under the heading of 'going native'.

Central to 'empiricism', as I am using the term here, is the idea that the world simply impresses its character upon us via direct experience. We must surely reject this, and recognise that understanding is an interactive process in which ethnographers necessarily bring something with them – knowledge of other situations, theoretical ideas and so on. Indeed, it has been argued that the source of ethnographic knowledge is not closeness or involvement, per se, but rather the dialectic between being an outsider and an insider (see, for instance, Hammersley and Atkinson, 2007). For this reason, in the terms provided by Freilich (1970), the task of an ethnographer is not to become an insider but rather to be a 'marginal native', or rather perhaps to make analytic use of the fact that at best one *will always be* a marginal native, never a complete insider (if that phrase even makes any sense). As Jacobs (1974: 238) remarks, in the context of his research on high-security prisons, the 'known observer can never really belong'.

This is, of course, a much more complex epistemological view than empiricism, and criticism of the latter in the context of ethnography has sometimes led to the adoption of a more radical position than I am suggesting here. For example, some claim that the accounts that ethnographers produce necessarily reflect their own identities, social locations and so on and the processes of production involved in the research, *rather than representing the character of independently existing phenomena*. Indeed, the very possibility of such independent phenomena sometimes seems to be denied, so that it is claimed that what are produced through ethnography (or other research strategies) are imaginary constructions that simply reflect our own positionalities, identities and so on. Thus, Denzin (1992: 124) claims that what I have been referring to as ethnographic empiricism assumes 'the camera theory of realism' and that this must be rejected in favour of a radical epistemological alternative:

> This [camera] theory presumes an external world that can be accurately recorded or photographed. It asserts that the closer you are to an event, the more accurately you can record its details [...]. But suppose that the camera theory of realism is wrong. Consider some troubling alternatives. The ethnographer's text creates the subject; subjects exist only insofar as they are brought into our written texts.

Here, I am prompted to quote the wise words of the eighteenth-century Scottish philosopher Thomas Reid (1785: 250):

> Let us remember how common the folly is, of going from one fault to the opposite extreme.
>
> (quoted in Haack, 2009:7)

There is no need to go from empiricism to radical constructionism of this kind, and there are good reasons for not doing so.[5]

Part of the problem here is a frequent tendency to assume that ethnography provides *pictures* of places, people and so on – an idea that is sometimes expressed in ways that do not explicitly appeal to the pictorial analogy. For instance, this is one interpretation of Crewe's (2009: 8) statement that 'the ambition is to provide a comprehensive sociological analysis of the prison'. Yet, in ethnography, as in any kind of research, we are never simply documenting what goes on 'inside', providing a picture or comprehensive account of it, we are always seeking to answer some particular set of questions about it. And the questions we address never exhaust the phenomena we are studying. Other questions can always be asked, and answering them will produce somewhat different accounts of the same phenomena, though hopefully not ones that are contradictory. Furthermore, to one degree or another, we are likely to bring in questions from 'outside'. And even if our questions are ones that arise 'inside', for example amongst inmates, we must take care neither to treat the inside, or insiders, as *unconnected to the outside* nor, as already noted, to assume that there is a single, homogeneous 'inside' or group of 'insiders'.

So, we can reconceptualise the idea that ethnography produces 'close ups' of social phenomena without effectively abandoning the idea that we can gain knowledge of phenomena that are independent of our understanding them. All ethnographies are necessarily perspectival, since they seek to answer particular sets of questions, but this does not lead to the conclusion that they 'create' the phenomena that they investigate, and that they cannot represent them more or less accurately. We should also note that the same epistemological argument can be applied to insider knowledge: this should not be treated as automatically valid, since it is always constructed on the basis of particular resources and for particular purposes. At the same time, it should not be dismissed for this reason as no more than ideological construction.

The problem of context

A rather different challenge to the notion of ethnographic privilege comes from the fact that, unless we are prepared to argue that social phenomena, including prisons, can be understood entirely in their own terms, we must locate them in some 'outside' – in a broader context that explains how they came into existence, why they take the form they do, what consequences they have and so on. In this respect, Wacquant's (2002b) critique of Duneier (1992, 1999; see also 2002) and other urban ethnographers is of interest, since part of his argument is that they failed to understand the lives of the impoverished black Americans they studied *largely because they did not take proper note of key structures and processes operating within US society* (see Hammersley, 2012). And in his own work on prisons, whilst emphasising the need to get inside them as an ethnographer, Wacquant also locates his analysis within a strongly framed theoretical perspective on the wider society (Wacquant, 2009).

It is certainly important to 'context' settings, but this carries problems for any claim to epistemic privilege on the part of ethnography. If we believe that ethnographic data must always be located in an understanding of the environment within which the phenomena studied exist, then this raises the question of how we are to gain knowledge of this context. After all, this cannot usually be done through participant observation, so that from the point of view of ethnographic empiricism this contextual information is necessarily weaker than that available about the setting itself. This might not be too much of a problem if we could treat 'context' as simply an add-on, but the interpretation of phenomena within an ethnographic setting is necessarily shaped by assumptions about how the setting fits into the outside, and the problem therefore becomes a much more serious one. Here, again, ethnographers' claims to epistemic privilege on grounds of close involvement, of 'getting inside', may be undermined.

Of course, there are some fundamental disputes about the nature of 'context' as this should operate within qualitative research. Some have argued that processes of social interaction context themselves – through the ways in which participants refer to various features of their world as relevant to their action in the course of it (see Lynch, 2000). This contrasts sharply with those approaches, such as that of Wacquant and some other 'critical' researchers, which insist on the importance of ethnography being clearly located within a broader theoretical perspective that makes sense of the whole to which the setting studied belongs.

Here, again, it seems to me that we must avoid 'faulty extremes'. It is true that when engaging in action people always have some sense of the context in which they are operating, and (to one degree or another) indicate this to fellow actors. It is also true that in studying people's behaviour we need to understand these perspectives. This is, of course, a standard premise of ethnography. However, it is a mistake to assume both that interactants always display this perceived context in full and that their understanding of their environment is sufficient for answering all the questions that a social scientist might reasonably ask about their behaviour. At the same time, to assume that there is some already-well-established comprehensive theory that can tell us how to understand the 'outside' of the phenomena we are investigating, and therefore how to understand them, flies in the face of what we know about the current state of social science today, which displays fundamental theoretical disagreements. Moreover, the very prospect of such a theory can be questioned precisely because any study addresses a particular set of questions, and these will determine, in large part, what counts as relevant context. Context is a functional category: there is not just one all-purpose, true context.

Social science provides a wealth of theoretical and empirical resources with which to formulate the context of any particular institution or practice for the purposes of enquiry, and we should make good use of these. However, our judgements about which resources are of value and how they should be interpreted and used must be shaped by our developing understanding of the particular phenomena we are studying and the questions we are seeking to answer. As in the case of insider knowledge, what is required is a two-way process.

I do not believe that this problem of context undermines the claims of ethnography to produce a distinctive and important kind of knowledge. But, as with the complexities of insider knowledge, it does undercut the ethnographic imperative and the strong assumption of epistemic privilege associated with it.

In summary, then, claims to ethnographic privilege must be moderated, in favour of recognising the dangers and disadvantages of 'closeness' as well as its advantages: that closeness and involvement are rarely sufficient to provide sound understanding. At the same time, we need to avoid going to faulty extremes in reacting to the problems associated with empiricism. As regards insider knowledge, neither redefining the goal as to amplify the voices of 'insiders' nor shifting to 'participatory enquiry' nor coming to view research as a process of imaginative invention is a sound solution to these problems. Similarly, we must recognise that whilst ethnography cannot be self-sufficient in producing knowledge of what goes on 'inside' a setting, we should not go to the other extreme: to a theoreticism which assumes that there is some already-available theory that can tell us the nature of the context and therefore of the phenomena we are studying. In fact, what counts as the appropriate wider context will depend upon the particular questions that we are addressing about those phenomena and will be determined in and through the research process.

Besides these epistemological issues associated with inside/outside, there are also some moral and political questions, and I turn to these next.

Ethical and political issues

A starting point for this second set of questions is the sense in which 'becoming an insider' involves a claim to entitlement, including perhaps the claim to 'speak on behalf of' insiders.

Speaking for others

In anthropology, and elsewhere, there are those who have challenged traditional kinds of ethnographic work on the grounds that it involved the fallacious and/or unethical claim to such a right (Hymes, 1974; Clifford and Marcus, 1986; Clifford, 1988; Said, 1989). Central to this critique, often, has been a play on the ambiguity of the word 'representation', suggesting that to represent – in the sense of documenting – the perspectives of some group of people and the settings in which they are located is, in effect, to speak on their behalf, this being interpreted as acting as their political representative.

Of course, ethnographers have sometimes acted as advocates for the people they study.[6] However, it is important to recognise that providing an account of the context in which people live or work, of their perspectives and values and of their activities is not equivalent to claiming to speak on their behalf. Doing that would involve an additional claim: to the effect that those people, if asked, would have provided the same account. And we have already seen why, in the case of ethnography, this is by no means to be expected. Aside from this, in our everyday discussions we often provide accounts of others' behaviour without claiming to speak on their behalf, indeed sometimes we specifically indicate that we are *not* doing this: 'I can't speak for her, but it seems to me that ...'. And there are good reasons why we should not conflate the two meanings of 'representation' – at the very least, political representation is not our primary task, if indeed it is part of our task at all. Others are often better placed, or better prepared, to take on this role. Finally, we should note that this conflation arises from the empiricism I criticised earlier: built into that epistemology is the idea that if only we can gain direct access to 'the inside', in other words to reality, it will speak to us, and we can relay its voice to others, so that we are speaking on its behalf. That this is not a defensible philosophical position is fairly obvious, I suggest.

Voyeurism

A second ethical or political criticism relating to the outside/inside distinction is the idea that ethnography amounts to a kind of voyeurism. This was the charge directed by Norman Denzin (1992) at William Foote Whyte's (1981) study of *Street Corner Society* and at the subsequent re-investigation of the same area of Boston by Marianne Boelen (1992). Here, as in the earlier quotation, Denzin's target is 'ethnographic realism':

> The charges that Boelen levels against Whyte are numerous. He was not an insider. He did not know Italian. He did not understand the importance of the family in Italian group life.
>
> (Denzin, 1992: 123)

However, Denzin continues:

> Whose Cornerville is it, anyway? The answer is obvious. Cornerville belongs to the people who live there. Whyte and Boelen entered this urban space and, like voyeurs, attempted to lay bare its underlying structures. Each found different structures because their angles of vision were different. But each of

their texts endorses the validity of the cultural voyeur's project. They refused to challenge and doubt their own right to look, write, and ask questions about the private and public lives that go on in Cornerville.

(pp. 130–31)

In these terms, prison ethnography would also be a form of voyeurism. And the feeling of being a voyeur has probably been experienced by most ethnographers at some times and in some places. Wacquant (2002a: 378) quotes his prison field notes at one point as follows: 'I can't tame the nauseating feeling of being a voyeur, an intruder into this plagued space.'

Whether ethnography is 'voyeurism' depends, of course, upon what is meant by that term. Its implication is observation of others, especially of their suffering or distress, *simply for personal satisfaction of some kind*, or perhaps *for the purposes of personal gain*, for instance in building a career. Bok (1984: 231) has argued that there is a temptation for researchers to misrecognise their own motives in a way that obscures their voyeurism. She suggests that the attraction of investigating private matters for many of them

is not rooted in their desire for knowledge alone, nor only in their hope that it might bring insight and possible benefits. They are also drawn to it by the allure of secrecy, of boundaries, and of the forbidden. Some take pleasure in dispelling the mystery, in showing it to be 'wholly superficial', in Durkheim's words. Others, on the contrary, want to get to the heart of the secret in order to partake of it, relish its intimacy. Trespassing on what is taboo attracts still others. The extraordinary amount of research into every minute aspect of sexuality or religious belief is simply not explicable on other, strictly scientific grounds.

It is certainly true that research could involve an unacceptable invasion of others' privacy. But it is not clear on what grounds Denzin could claim that Whyte or Boelen were guilty of this, and Bok's criticism of researchers in these terms is open to question: how does she know what their underlying motives were? Why is 'dispelling mystery' bad? Moreover, what counts as private is a matter of contextual interpretation, and often of contestation, since it is related to the ownership of places and information (Hammersley and Traianou, 2012).

By contrast with Bok, it seems likely that what is driving Denzin's charge of voyeurism is his apparent belief that observing people solely for the purpose of producing knowledge is unjustified, both because knowledge of the kind claimed is impossible (the 'camera theory of reality' is false) and because he believes that knowledge should always be produced to serve some political purpose or cause – all else is 'voyeurism'. I have already explained why the fact that ethnography is not a camera is no reason for denying that it can produce knowledge of phenomena that are independent of it. The second part of the argument is similarly defective. It is true that there is no justification for producing knowledge for its own sake, in the sense of aiming at *just any kind of knowledge*. For enquiry to be worthwhile it must be directed at answering questions that are of some genuine human interest or value. But this is very different from aiming at some other goal through the process of enquiry (Hammersley, 1995).

Espionage

If the charge of voyeurism makes us uncomfortable, the next criticism I will discuss is perhaps even worse. This is that ethnography serves to provide inside knowledge to the authorities that would not otherwise be available to them and assists their subjugation of the marginal and deviant. This was an accusation famously made by Martin Nicolaus, then a postgraduate student, at the Convention of the American Sociological Association in Boston in August 1968. He writes:

> Sociologists stand guard in the garrison and report to their masters on the movements of the occupied populace. The more adventurous [...] don the disguise of the people and go out to mix with the peasants in the 'field', returning with books and articles that break the protective secrecy in which a subjugated population wraps itself, and make it more accessible to manipulation and control. The sociologist [...] is precisely a kind of spy.

The more 'adventurous' sociologists criticised here are, of course, ethnographers. This criticism is also to be found in the piece by Denzin quoted earlier. He argues:

> Consequently, [Whyte and Boelen] keep in place the disciplinary eye of a positivistic social science. This science justifies its existence in terms of its 'positive' contributions to a surveillance society that requires greater and greater information about the private lives of its citizens. [...]
>
> (Denzin, 1992: 130–31)

And he concludes: 'it is appropriate to ask whether we any longer want this kind of social science.' We should note that the charge of 'spy' is not uncommon in the context of ethnography. Indeed, Jacobs (1974: 225) reports the suspicion that he was 'an agent for the F.B.I. or the Chicago Police Department's Gang Intelligence Unit, or an investigator for the Governor's staff', whilst Crewe (2009: 469) recounts being accused of spying by one of the prisoners he was seeking to study; and, of course, such suspicions are as likely to be harboured by prison officers as by prisoners.

This is a criticism that connects to the more general issue of how the findings of research may be used and abused by government authorities and others, one that certainly arises in the case of studying prisons. Crewe (2009: 2) has noted that classic studies of prisons in the US were 'highly influential in informing attempts by prison officials to design rehabilitative interventions and to maintain order'. There is clearly scope for different attitudes towards these interventions and towards the task of maintaining order in prison, and the idea that research serves domination may arise here. Sparks (2002) offers a more specific example, recounting how his own research may have played a role in prompting the closure of the special unit at Barlinnie. As these examples make clear, our research can sometimes have consequences, and we need to be aware of this. Yet, in my view, researchers seem to overestimate the potential impact of their work, whilst frequently complaining about its failure to have an impact. Here, there is a tendency, I suggest, to adopt an oversimplified conception of the interface between research, on the one hand, and policymaking or practice, on the other (Hammersley, 2002; 2013).

This concern with the political effects of research has prompted debates about 'whose side are we on' (Becker, 1967; Hammersley, 2000: ch. 3; Liebling, 2001). There is a fundamental issue to be addressed here. It is common for ethnographers and other social researchers to believe that there is a close affinity between the production and use of knowledge and progressive social change, or the achievement of more specific desirable practical outcomes. This is shared both by proposals for 'evidence-based' policymaking and practice and by much 'critical' social science (see Hammersley, 2013: Intro). However, this is an Enlightenment illusion. Whilst it is true that knowledge may often enable more effective pursuit of goals, it does not guarantee success and sometimes hampers it. Moreover, there is often scope for reasonable disagreement about which goals are and are not 'desirable', 'progressive' and so on. Nor is siding with some group the same as pursuing a political cause designed to serve their interests, a point that Leninism highlights (see also Gouldner, 1968; Hammersley, 2000: ch. 4).

Whilst I accept that there are genuine and difficult issues involved here, my attitude to these two criticisms – voyeurism and espionage – is that they are naïve. Doing social research of any kind, but perhaps especially ethnography, is almost inevitably occasionally ethically and politically uncomfortable, at the very least. I suspect that this is especially true when researching organisations that approximate to being 'total' (Goffman, 1961) like prisons, since these are set off from the rest of society in significant ways and also involve very sharp divisions between staff and inmates. The implication of Denzin's and Nicolaus's criticisms is that these problems could be avoided if the ethnographer were on the 'right' side or perhaps if the whole research enterprise were abandoned in favour of political activism. But whilst this might avoid these problems in the context of *research*, they would still arise in whatever other activity we chose as an alternative.

After all, encountering serious ethical and political concerns is hardly restricted to social researchers: it is a feature of many roles, including those of police and prison officers, social workers, journalists, politicians and extra-parliamentary political activists.[7] Moreover, the idea that such problems could be escaped through achieving solidarity or unity with the relevant group or community is an illusion, not least because we are rarely dealing with one homogeneous group alone. Real politics, along with the other kinds of work I have just mentioned, is frequently a dirty and difficult business, necessarily involving some manipulation, economising on the truth, and occasionally even outright lies. This is because much is at stake, by contrast with the relatively costless declaration of most political opinions within the academy, in the UK and other Western societies at least. So, the problem is not that there are two sides and that we are on the wrong one, which is the implication of Nicolaus's argument. It is that, if you like, there are always many insides and outsides, and that there is no way of negotiating around, or through, them that can be entirely comfortable, at least if one seeks to live without illusions.

For me, the value of producing knowledge about prison regimes, about the experience and effects of imprisonment and so on – and about other aspects of the social world as well – makes ethnography and other forms of social research undoubtedly worthwhile. But arguments to this effect will never entirely quell our doubts, or smooth over all worries and concerns. And they will certainly never silence critics, especially not in a culture where activities are increasingly judged entirely in terms of whether they have, or are assumed to have, good consequences, to 'make a difference' and/or according to whether they exemplify what are regarded as politically correct positions.

Of course, maintaining commitment to the production of knowledge – and belief in its value – is especially difficult in studying people who are suffering or are in distress, whether prison inmates or others. But whilst there are certainly occasions when one should abandon research in order to try to ease or remedy suffering, in my view this is only appropriate in very specific circumstances – notably where doing this could have a significant impact. Moreover, these circumstances are actually quite rare. Many criticisms of ethnographers for acting as voyeurs of suffering ascribe greater power for effective intervention to them than is realistic. Moreover, as with the journalist watching and reporting first-hand on the horrors of war, most of the time it is essential to stick to one's own task, indeed there is a duty to do so.

My position here is much the same as Stanley Fish's (2008) bullish defence of the study of literature against demands that it be directed towards political purposes. His position is encapsulated in the title of one of his books: *Save the World on Your Own Time* (see also Fish, 1995). Thus, he insists that academics 'do not try to do anyone else's job' and that they 'do not let anyone else do their job'. This echoes a similar sentiment expressed many years ago by Ned Polsky (1969: 140) in the context of doing research on criminals outside of prisons. He suggested that if someone wants to be a 'social worker', or for that matter a 'correction officer' (or, we might add, a political activist), that is 'their privilege', but that they should not do this in the name of social science.

Of course, many will disagree with my response to these ethical or political issues. Other types of response have been much more influential in recent years, from calls for partisanship to proposals for participatory enquiry designed to facilitate some of those on the margins making their voices heard. Whilst I would certainly not deny the potential value of these activities, for me they do not constitute research. Indeed, when done under its auspices, they amount to its betrayal.

Conclusion

I have tried to show how prison ethnography, and the inside/outside distinction, relates to some important methodological issues. There are sound epistemological arguments underpinning the rationale for ethnography, as a way of gaining knowledge from close-up participant observation, but they are sometimes pushed too far – into what I referred to as the ethnographic imperative and the claim to epistemic privilege associated with this. At the same time, reactions to the problems that this empiricism generates are sometimes equally problematic, such as attempts to redefine the task as amplifying the voices of the marginalised, as producing imaginative accounts that make no claims to objectivity or as requiring partisanship or participatory enquiry.

We must certainly abandon the ethnographic imperative and its claims for the intrinsic superiority of ethnography. There is no hierarchy of methods: different approaches tend to have varying advantages and disadvantages; none is superior on all counts. Indeed, there is usually interdependence, as with the way in which ethnography must depend upon other sorts of data for information about the contexts of the settings it investigates. At the same time, there are strong arguments in favour of ethnography as a method, in studying imprisonment and many other topics.

My underlying point is that we need to be very careful about the inside/outside distinction. It is misleading if interpreted in an abstract or fixed way. It should be obvious that there is no inside or outside per se. All perspectives and locations are situated, and the implication of this is that all reflexivity is itself from some particular angle: there is no view from nowhere that tells 'the whole story', whether conceived as outside or inside. This is not a matter of relativism – of a hall of mirrors, with each view necessarily being treated as justified in its own terms – or of a form of standpoint epistemology. It is true that there is no single view that can serve all functions, but there are better and worse approaches for answering particular questions. Perspectivism in this moderated form is the unavoidable reality.

In the case of ethical and political issues, too, there is no way of simply avoiding problems by adopting the 'right' stance. There is no moral high ground, 'inside' or 'outside' – we are all in the swamp. But, as researchers, our anchor must be a commitment to enquiry as an activity that, pursued with due modesty and moderation, is of value for the knowledge it produces.

Notes

1. Paper prepared on the basis of a talk given at the International Centre for Comparative Criminological Research annual conference, 'Resisting the Eclipse: International Symposium on Prison Ethnography', The Open University, September 2012.
2. His language here is sometimes taken to suggest the danger of Othering others. This should alert us to problems with the notion of 'insider' too.
3. Of course, events will unfortunately sometimes provide this experience for us; a famous example is Bettelheim's (1970) 'ethnographic study' of a German concentration camp in the 1940s.
4. Merton (1972) challenged insider arguments along these lines long ago.
5. For philosophical accounts offering, somewhat different, epistemological positions between these extremes, see, for example, Williams (2001) and Haack (2009).
6. For an illuminating discussion, see Hastrup and Elsass (1990).
7. For a good account of some of the problems in the context of journalism, not very different from those of ethnography, see Malcolm (1991).

Further reading

Liebling, A. (2001) 'Whose Side Are We On? Theory, Practice, and Allegiances in Prison Research', *British Journal of Criminology*, 41, 472–84.

Merton, R. (1972) 'Insiders and Outsiders: A Chapter in the Sociology of Knowledge', *American Journal of Sociology*, 78, 1, 9–47.

Hammersley, M. (1995) *The Politics of Social Research* (London: Sage).

References

Bandyopadhyay, M. (2010) *Everyday Life in a Prison* (Hyderabad: Orient BlackSwan).

Becker, H. S. (1967) 'Whose Side Are We On?' *Social Problems*, 14, 239–47.

Bettelheim, B. (1970) *The Informed Heart* (London: Paladin).

Boelen, W. (1992) 'Street Corner Society: Cornerville Revisited', *Journal of Contemporary Ethnography*, 21, 11–51.

Bok, S. (1984) *Secrets: Concealment and Revelation* (Oxford: Oxford University Press).

Clifford, J. (1988) *The Predicament of Culture* (Cambridge, MS: Harvard University Press).

Clifford, J. and Marcus, G. (eds) (1986) *Writing Culture: The Poetics and Politics of Ethnography* (Berkeley, CA: University of California Press).

Cohen, S. and Taylor, L. (1972) *Psychological Survival: Experience of Long-Term Imprisonment* (Harmondsworth: Penguin).

Crewe, B. (2009) *The Prisoner Society: Power, Adaptation and Social Life in an English Prison* (Oxford: Oxford University Press).

Denzin, N. (1992) 'Whose Cornerville Is It Anyway?' *Journal of Contemporary Ethnography*, 21, 120–32.

Drake, D. and Harvey, J. (2014) 'Performing the Role of Ethnographer: Processing and Managing the Emotional Dimensions of Prison Research', *International Journal of Social Research Methodology*, 17, 5, 489–501.

Duneier, M. (1999) *Sidewalk* (New York: Farrar, Straus and Giroux).

Duneier, M. (2002) 'What Kind of Combat Sport Is Sociology?' *American Journal of Sociology*, 107, 6, 1551–76.

Fish, S. (1995) *Professional Correctness* (New York: Oxford University Press).

Fish, S. (2008) *Save the World on Your Own Time* (New York: Oxford University Press).

Freilich, M. (1970) *Marginal Natives: Anthropologists at Work* (New York: Harper and Row).

Goffman, E. (1961) *Asylums* (Harmondsworth: Penguin).

Gouldner, A. (1968) 'The Sociologist as Partisan', *American Sociologist*, May, 103–16.

Haack, S. (2009) *Evidence and Inquiry* (Amherst, NY: Prometheus Books).

Hammersley, M. (1995) *The Politics of Social Research* (London: Sage).

Hammersley, M. (2000) *Taking Sides in Social Research: Essays on Partisanship and Bias* (London: Routledge).

Hammersley, M. (2002) *Educational Research, Policymaking and Practice* (London: Paul Chapman/Sage).

Hammersley, M. (2012) *What Is Qualitative Research?* (London: Bloomsbury).

Hammersley, M. (2013) *The Myth of Research-Based Policymaking and Practice* (London: Sage).

Hammersley, M. and Atkinson, P. (2007) *Ethnography: Principles in Practice*, Third edition (London: Routledge).

Hammersley, M. and Traianou, A. (2012) *Ethics in Qualitative Research; Contexts and Controversies* (London: Sage).

Harding, S. (1992) 'After the Neutrality Ideal: Science, Politics and "Strong Objectivity" ', *Social Research*, 59, 3, 568–87.

Hartsock, N. (1983) 'The Feminist Standpoint', in S. Harding and M. Hintikka (eds) *Discovering Reality* (Dordrecht: Reidel).

Hastrup, K. and Elsass, P. (1990) 'Anthropological Advocacy: A Contradiction in Terms?' *Current Anthropology*, 31, 3, 301–11.

Hill, M., Davis, J., Prout, A. and Tisdall, K. (2004) 'Moving the Participation Agenda Forward', *Children and Society*, 18, 2, 77–96.

Hymes, D. (ed.) (1974) *Reinventing Anthropology* (New York: Vintage).

Jacobs, J. (1974) 'Participant Observation in Prison', *Urban Life and Culture*, 3, 2, 221–40.

Jewkes, Y. (2012) 'Auto-ethnography and Emotion as Intellectual Resources: Doing Prison Research Differently', *Qualitative Inquiry*, 18, 1, 63–75.

Jules-Rosette, B. (1978a) 'The Veil of Objectivity: Prophecy, Divination, and Social Inquiry', *American Anthropologist*, 80, 3, 549–70.

Jules-Rosette, B. (1978b) 'Towards a Theory of ethnography', *Sociological Symposium*, 24, 81–98.

Kellett, M. (2005) 'Children as Active Researchers: A New Research Paradigm for the Twenty-First Century?' *ESRC National Centre for Research Methods*, NCRM/003. Available at http://eprints.ncrm.ac.uk/87/1/MethodsReviewPaperNCRM-003.pdf (accessed 25 September 2012).

King, R. D. (2000) 'Doing Research in Prisons', in R. D. King and E. Wincup (eds) *Doing Research on Crime and Justice* (Oxford: Oxford University Press).

Lakoff, G. and Johnson, M. (1980) *Metaphors We Live By* (Chicago: University of Chicago Press).

Liebling, A. (1999) 'Doing Research in Prison: Breaking the Silence?' *Theoretical Criminology*, 3, 2, 147–73.

Liebling, A. (2001) 'Whose Side Are We On? Theory, Practice, and Allegiances in Prison Research', *British Journal of Criminology*, 41, 472–84.

Lynch, M. (2000) 'Against Reflexivity as an Academic Virtue and Source of Privileged Knowledge', *Theory, Culture and Society*, 17, 3, 26–54.

Malcolm, J. (1991) *The Journalist and the Murderer* (London: Bloomsbury).

Malinowski, B. (1922) *Argonauts of the Western Pacific* (London: Routledge and Kegan Paul).

McKinney, J. C. (1966) *Constructive Typology and Social Theory* (New York: Appleton-Century-Crofts).

Marquart, J. (2003) 'Doing Research in Prison: The Strengths and Weaknesses of Full Participation as a Guard', in M. Pogrebin (ed) *Qualitative Approaches to Criminal Justice* (Thousand Oaks, CA: Sage).

Merton, R. (1972) 'Insiders and Outsiders: A Chapter in the Sociology of Knowledge', *American Journal of Sociology*, 78, 1, 9–47.

Nicolaus, M. (1968) 'Fat-Cat Sociology: Remarks at The American Sociological Association Convention, Boston'. Available at: http://www.colorado.edu/Sociology/gimenez/fatcat.html

Phillips, C. and Earle, R. (2010) 'Reading Difference Differently: Identity, Epistemology and Prison Ethnography', *British Journal of Criminology*, 50, 360–78.

Polsky, N. (1969) *Hustlers, Beats and Others* (Harmondsworth: Penguin).

Quraishi, M. (2007) 'Researching Muslim Prisoners', *International Journal of Social Research Methodology*, 11, 5, 453–67.

Rathbone, C. (2005) *A World Apart: Women, Prison and Life Behind Bars* (New York: Random House).

Reason, P. and Bradbury, H. (eds) (2001) *Handbook of Action Research: Participative Inquiry and Practice* (London: Sage).

Reid, T. (1785) *Essays on the Intellectual Powers of Man*, edited by J. Bennett, 2006. Available at http://www.earlymoderntexts.com/pdf/reidint1.pdf (accessed 12 October 2012)

Rhodes, L. (2001) 'Toward an Anthropology of Prisons', *Annual Review of Anthropology*, 30, 65–83.

Rhodes L. (2004) *Total Confinement: Madness and Reason in the Maximum Security Prison* (Berkeley, CA: University of California Press).

Ross, J. and Richards, S. (eds) (2003) *Convict Criminology* (Belmont, CA: Wadsworth/Thomson Learning).

Said, E. (1989) 'Representing the Colonized: Anthropologists' Intercolutors', *Critical Inquiry*, 15, 5–25.

Smith, D. (1974) 'Women's Perspective as a Radical Critique of Sociology', *Sociological Inquiry*, 44, 7–13.

Sparks, R. (2002) 'Out of the "Digger": The warrior's Honour and the Guilty Observer', *Ethnography*, 3, 4, 556–81.

Wacquant. L. (2002a) 'The Curious Eclipse of Prison Ethnography in the Age of Mass Incarceration', *Ethnography*, 3, 4, 371–97.

Wacquant, L. (2002b) 'Scrutinizing the Street: Poverty, Morality, and the Pitfalls of Urban Ethnography', *American Journal of Sociology*, 107, 6, 1468–532.

Wacquant, L. (2009) *Prisons of Poverty* (Minneapolis, MN: University of Minnesota Press).

Whyte, W. F. (1981) *Street Corner Society*, Third edition (Chicago: University of Chicago Press).

Williams, M. (2001) *Problems of Knowledge: A Critical Introduction to Epistemology* (Oxford: Oxford University Press).

Zarb, G. (1992) 'On the Road to Damascus: First Steps Towards Changing the Relations of Disability Research Production', *Disability, Handicap and Society*, 7, 2, 125–38.

2

Walking amongst the Graves of the Living: Reflections about Doing Prison Research from an Abolitionist Perspective

David Scott

Introduction

In my time as a researcher, I have walked amongst 'the graves of the living' (Minshull, 1618/1821) in 16 different prisons, predominantly in the North East or North West of England. My ethnographic research has primarily focused upon prison staff and the roles they *perform* in profoundly *immoral* spaces (Scott, 1996b, 2006, 2008, 2011, 2012, 2013a, 2014b, 2015). Whilst prison research aims to uncover lived realities and institutional policies and practices in a hidden world, not all accounts of prison life highlight the same issues and problems. There remain significant differences in terms of how the prison place is described and analysed. Whilst there are a number of reasons why this is the case, perhaps of greatest import is the fact that all [academic] writing is subjective, and prison narratives are influenced by the values and principles of a given author. The 'moral compass' of the prison ethnographer is crucial in the construction of penal theory and knowledge and their priorities; aims and objectives have enormous bearing upon their interpretation of the prison world. As this chapter title indicates, the following reflections on prisons, prisoners and prison workers are written from an *abolitionist perspective.*[1]

Abolitionism is a way of making sense of human experience and attributing meaning to social interactions as well as a normative framework critiquing repressive, dominating, dehumanising and authoritarian institutions. As a theory it prioritises the political values of freedom, liberty, equality, solidarity, non-hierarchical relationships and human emancipation and asks us to challenge, reduce or eliminate practices which infringe upon them. Abolitionists also promote the moral values of love, compassion, care, forgiveness, mutual aid and responsibility for others. They problematise acts that result in hurt, injury, pain and unnecessary suffering. In short, such thinkers focus upon what is morally unacceptable in human relationships and advocate non-repressive ways of responding to troubled and troublesome people (Scott, 2013b). For abolitionists, there can be no 'penal values' as the deliberate infliction of pain (the penal) is not something based upon intrinsic human good. Rather, pain infliction is an undesirable, detrimental, adverse and 'evil' deed reproducing ill feelings. Punishment and state institutions justified through pain delivery such as the prison are considered morally flawed. Abolitionist analysis is therefore sensitive to the inherent harms and structured constraints of confinement, illuminating the immorality of institutionalised pain infliction and is an approach, I think, which provides a valuable lens through which to examine daily penal practices.

Acknowledgement of human suffering is central to abolitionism. When we ask, 'who suffers the most in prison?' abolitionists recognise that only prisoners feel the full 'weight, depth and width' of dehumanising penal structures (Scott, 2015). Human suffering in prison, including that of prison staff, must be located within existing hierarchies of power. Analytically this operates on three levels: (i) the power relations pertaining inside a penal regime, (ii) the power to punish as operationalised and sanctioned through the penal authorities of the capitalist state and (iii) the role of prisons within wider constructions of power/powerlessness, inequality and structural division within society. I have argued elsewhere that prison staff are 'caretakers of punishment' (Scott, 2015) empowered in terms of the authority invested in the performance of their punishment role but at the same time low-status functionaries – caretakers – within a penal bureaucratic organisation. Staff, especially prison officers, suffer from the structured pains of confinement; not only do they do so to a much lesser extent than prisoners, but they also often fail to acknowledge the suffering of prisoners (Scott, 2006). In addition, prison work is no ordinary job: it is about maintaining an institution designed to deliver pain and create human suffering. As such, prisons are spaces of moral evaluation, and abolitionism places the moral legitimacy of penal institutions at the heart of its analysis (Scott, 2006; 2015).

Abolitionism not only is concerned with highlighting *what* happens to people inside the penal machine but also sensitises us to *who* is imprisoned and whether their voice is heard. Consequently, abolitionist analysis emphasises the lived experiences of those on the downside of power – the 'view from below' (Sim et al., 1987). Abolitionism legitimates rather than disqualifies accounts of prisoners but does not assume that prisoners are 'unproblematic bearers of truth' (Sim, 2003), acknowledging the right to democratically participate in a dialogue is not the same as suggesting that the prisoner experience should be privileged above all others in all circumstances. Abolitionists recognise that whilst scholars must provide a platform facilitating the emancipation of 'subjugated knowledge' (Foucault, 1980), they should also promote penological literacy by attempting to 'turn common-sense into good sense' (Sim, 2009). To do so, abolitionists focus on the inherent harms of imprisonment and situate the prison within its socio-economic and political contexts. For abolitionists, silence is not an option. If we have knowledge that can highlight the dangers inherent to the prison place, we must speak, whoever we are (Cohen, 2001; Mathiesen, 2004).

Abolitionist values, principles and sensibilities have influenced my research in terms of focus, the way I've observed prison life and the incidents and conversations I've considered most important to record and reflect upon in my writings. Abolitionism not only 'opened my eyes' by debunking some of the myths regarding prisons but also facilitated a more nuanced and sensitive appraisal of some of the most controversial aspects of its daily routine (Scott and Codd, 2010). Shortly before I undertook my first prison research in the mid-1990s, I read the second edition of *Psychological Survival* (Cohen and Taylor, 1973/81). This innovative phenomenological study recounted the experiences of long-term prisoners from E Wing in Durham Prison and revealed how its extreme environment undermined the meaning[s] of life. E wing was like 'living in a submarine', and the prison experience Stan Cohen and Laurie Taylor (1973/81) described was boring, depressing and lonely. Their unequivocal message was that the real problem prisoners faced was how to deal with the passing of wasted time. Such an approach to the prisoners' ability to cope, or not, with the 'saturation of time consciousness' (Medlicott, 2001; Scott and Codd, 2010) drew my attention not only to the inherent harms and pains of imprisonment but also to a focus on prison as a distinct moral space. My initial research focus was on how people who adhered to the moral teachings of Christianity – prison chaplains – could work within such an *immoral* institution, whilst my later work, on prison officers, explored how prison work can often entail a negotiation and neutralisation of moral principles and values. Both though highlight the difficult and unescapable moral dilemmas working within prisons engender.

I also read, and was strongly influenced by, the abolitionist perspective of Thomas Mathiesen, especially in his books *The Politics of Abolition* and *Prisons on Trial*, and that of Joe Sim in his books *British Prisons*, *Medical Power in Prisons* and *Prisons Under Protest* (Mathiesen, 1974, 1990; Fitzgerald and Sim, 1982; Sim, 1990; Scraton et al., 1991), before embarking as a prison ethnographer. Collectively, these texts not only are scholarly and thought provoking but also question the very nature, function and political legitimacy of penal incarceration. I found myself immediately and strongly drawn to the arguments of Mathiesen and Sim. Yet, it was only when I entered prison as an ethnographer that my moral and political commitments to abolitionism were confirmed. From the first time I entered the walls of a prison – HMP (Her Majesty's Prison) Frankland on 12 March 1996 – the experiences and knowledge gleaned through my research have led me to understand the prison as a profoundly abnormal, dehumanising and *immoral* place that does little good for those [socially disadvantaged people] contained within or indeed for those who ensure they remain so. For me, there has been a symbiotic relationship between abolitionist theory and the existential and emotional consequences of engaging in prison ethnography. In other words, the abolitionist values, principles and sensibilities underscoring my writings on prisons and punishment are derived, at least in part, from reflections upon prison realities I witnessed as a researcher.

A prison ethnographer's world view is illustrated in their research focus and publications, but it is also possible to identify their perspective through a careful analysis of their notes and diaries made during fieldwork. Central to this chapter is an overview, and self-interrogation, of my own field notes to illustrate the abolitionist perspective in my prison ethnographies. When I looked back at my prison journals[2] whilst preparing to write this chapter, rather than unlocking notebooks filled *only* with reflections on prison workers, I was struck by how often I wrote about prisoners and their general situation or observed their interaction with others. This was especially the case in my study *Heavenly Confinement?* (Scott, 1996b). Thus, though my research has focused on prison staff, this chapter draws extensively upon unpublished notes and comments about prisoners (Scott, 1996a).[3] These reflections are then embellished through reflections of observed incidents and contemplations about researching prison officers (Scott, 2002).

What is also clear from my field notes are the different feelings engendered when researching these two occupational groups. Whereas in my notes and observations on prison chaplains I can identify formative ideas about the importance of humanitarian interventions, with regard to prison officers, the picture is much more negative, emphasising the powerlessness of prisoners, moral indifference and denial. This is partly illustrated in the relative 'invisibility' of prisoners in my later prison notebooks (Scott, 2002). The narrative of this chapter consequently unfolds in chronological order. The next section primarily explores my reflections on, and interactions with, prisoners and staff when undertaking research on the role and perception of prison chaplains in six prisons in the North East of England in the mid-1990s. The chapter then moves on to consider my observation of prisoner–staff interactions when researching prison officers in HMP Preston.[4] The chapter concludes with a discussion exploring tensions and contradictions of doing prison research from an abolitionist perspective, revisiting the notion of context and 'speaking for others' and the implications of emancipating 'subjugated knowledges' for abolitionist praxis.

Acknowledging learning from the chaplains

As an undergraduate student in the early 1990s, I learnt about the central role prison chaplains had performed in reformed prisons such as HMP Millbank and HMP Pentonville. By all accounts, the chaplains' ministrations were the heartbeat of the penal machine for, alongside solitude and reflection, their religious instructions were to bring about the reformation of repentant lawbreakers (Scott, 1996b, 1997). Their moment of unassailable institutional power proved however to be relatively short lived. Historic evidence abounds of the abject failure and the subsequent abandonment of such penitentiary ideals by the 1860s (Scott, 2015). Though chaplain autobiographies continued to be written long after this point and the profession was given dedicated space in *Prisons Today* (Hobhouse and Brockway, 1922), as time has advanced detailed independent accounts of these 'superior officers of the prison' have become rare. Academic interest in the prison chaplain is negligible, evidenced, for example, in the *Prison Service Journal*-sponsored edited book *Understanding Prison Staff* (Bennett et al., 2008), which virtually fails to mention the chaplain at all.[5] Based on my historical prison studies, I became interested in the contrast between the chaplains' early prominence in the reformed prisons and their contemporary invisibility. I was also fascinated by what I considered to be a major contradiction between the values underscoring the [Christian] belief systems of prison chaplains – love, forgiveness, hope, compassion, kindness – and the daily realities of prison which seemed to be their negation. I wondered whether such a perceived tension between the chaplains working experiences and their professional values could result in an abolitionist critique of penal incarceration. This became the hypothesis of *Heavenly Confinement?* (Scott, 1996b).[6]

Many of the chaplains I interviewed had no developed theological perspective of imprisonment and merely justified the institution through secular philosophies of punishment. This being said, I did meet a few chaplains who were abolitionists – most notably the Anglican Chaplain of Durham Prison, affectionately known as 'Mick the Vic', who felt that the criticism highlighted in Thomas Mathiesen's *Prisons on Trial* were 'entirely right' and that prisons were fundamentally 'unchristian and ripe for abolition' (journal entry, 25 April 1996). Listening to those chaplains most critical of the prison, it was clear that they struggled with tension between reform and abolition. In my reflections in my journal, I wrote on a number of occasions about how I felt such 'chaplains walked a tightrope' (ibid.) for it seemed that those chaplains who most strongly felt prisons were immoral and counter-productive places were also those who held the strongest humanitarian commitment to do what they could on the ground to ease or mitigate the inherent degradations of imprisonment.

Despite being perceived by a significant number of prison officers and prisoners as simply talking 'mumbo jumbo' (journal entry, 2 May 1996), the prison chaplains I spoke with undoubtedly had a very sophisticated understanding of prison life. They felt they had to engage – it was, as some put it, 'their calling' (ibid.) – even though they knew that prisons did nothing but create further problems. This engagement with people working through the contradictory demands to both transform the penal system and at the same time help those in need right now is something which has significantly influenced my own understanding of what abolitionism entails (Scott, 2013b). I will return to this point again towards the end of this chapter, but for now I focus only on how the prison chaplain ethnography had a formative influence upon my understandings of imprisonment.

Prison chaplains 'officially' retain considerable power in the prison place. Though largely underplayed, the capacity to access all areas of the prison is still regularly performed. This gives chaplains a unique and envied freedom in a captive world. I accompanied the chaplains on their daily duties in six different prisons over a four-month period. In so doing, I witnessed virtually all aspects of prison life and had many opportunities to talk with prisoners and staff. This direct human engagement confirmed my belief that neither prisoners nor staff were 'radically different' from other people. Sensitised to the painful, degrading and dehumanising realities of penal incarceration by the abolitionist literature, the 'evening write ups' of my experiences in the prison were filled with accounts of prisoner experiences and interactions I had witnessed. This was significant not because of the locations – any penal tourist can see prison architecture – but because I saw prison life unvarnished and unannounced, whether it be the wings, reception, health care, segregation, visits, exercise, education classes, chapel services or food preparation in the kitchens. In a space of few months, I had witnessed nearly every possible dimension of prisons in their 'bare life' during the daytime[7] – literally un-stripped and naked.

In March 1996, I entered HMP Frankland in North East England, but most of my time was taken up with meetings with chaplains and negotiations for further visits in the coming weeks. Before I was to return to HMP Frankland, I was to shadow the Anglican Chaplain at Castington Young Offenders Institution (YOI) and undertake extensive observations and interviews at HMP Durham. I arrived early at Castington YOI on the morning of 27 March 1996 having already spoken extensively to the Anglican chaplain Fiona Eltringham in advance. I was to spend my first day at the jail shadowing her (journal entry, 27 March 1996). One of the first places that the chaplain attended was the segregation unit. Only one boy was being held in the 'seg' that day.

> As we walked through the door of the cell I was hit by the bareness of the room. The walls were cream and the window seemed quite high up in the wall of the room. It seemed clean and there was small blue mat on the floor but apart from that all it contained was the prisoner. He looked sad. He was maybe seventeen and was physically very small. I wonder[ed] what he could have done to end up in such a dreadful cell for 23 hours a day. More than

> anything the segregation cell reminded me of the small room in a swimming bath where you clean your feet when walking between the changing rooms and the main pool. It was not somewhere I would want to spend very much time.
>
> (ibid.)

One of the most significant events of that day revolved around the experiences of a young man called 'Thomas'. Below are two extensive extracts from my prison journal:

> My shadowing of the chaplain continued through the morning...I went with the chaplain to the visits room. The room was packed and prisoners were sitting talking with their visitors. The chaplain first went to talk to the prison officers who were supervising the visits. Standing at the front of the room – which looked like a gym hall – the staff explained that this had been a quiet visit. The visit was drawing to a close and Fiona [the Anglican chaplain] noticed that one boy was sitting by himself near the centre of the room. He seemed about eighteen. His hair slicked back and he was looking down on the desk [visits table] perhaps trying to make himself invisible. In a room full of talking he was sitting in silence alone. A visit is a really big thing in the prisoners experience – the anticipation of the visits in the days leading up to the event; the pride taken in telling other prisoners that they are going to be visited by a loved one; the time spent thinking about what is going to be talked about; the personal grooming directly before the visit. As soon as Fiona saw the boy she immediately went up and started talking to him. His name was 'Thomas'. He had been waiting for his girlfriend and best friend to come, but for some reason they had not turned up. Thomas not only had to deal with the disappointment of not having the visit, but also he now had to deal with the sadness of sitting alone among those who had visits and the humiliation that everyone would know that he had been stood up. Fiona asked 'are you ok Thomas?' Thomas explained that the officers would not take him off the visit until the end as they were short staffed and therefore none of the staff could be allowed to leave their supervisory roles. I think Fiona immediately recognised that he was pretty devastated and a really serious knockback for Thomas and so she said 'Are you coming to the chaplain's meeting tonight?' and Thomas said, 'Oh no, I can't go, I can't go, I didn't fill my forms in.' Fiona explained later that to come to the Chaplain's evening group you had to fill your forms in two days before for the class each week. Fiona then asked Thomas 'Would you like to come?' Thomas nodded and then the Chaplain and I made our leave, with Fiona saying 'Yes, see you this evening'. At that stage I hadn't realised the implications of this promise. For the next hour or so Fiona phoned and/or spoke with directly

> the prison bureaucrats so that Thomas could come to the evening session. She was eventually successful...
>
> (Journal entry, 27 March 1996)

This is not quite the end of the story of 'Thomas'. As per my journal entry for 27 March 1996, a little later I returned to the chaplain's evening class. Here, I was given the opportunity to speak with the prisoners, and I of course remembered Thomas from earlier in the day. I had devised a questionnaire for prisoners, which focussed on their 'perceptions of prison chaplains'. I had not really thought about the literacy levels of prisoners, especially young people in prison.

> I learnt some lessons this evening about using questionnaires with prisoners. Each questionnaire is really just a list of questions, tick boxes about what people think of the chaplains, and whether they would rather watch a TV programme like East Enders or go to an educational class with the chaplains. Perhaps unsurprisingly the results from the class at Castington indicate that telly wins every time. There are a number of open questions on the second page where prisoners can write more about their perceptions of chaplains. At least 12 of the young lads at the evening class filled in the questionnaires, including Thomas who I had met at the visit earlier today. He'd eventually been allowed to come and had duly turned up with the other lads. I didn't chat with him very much but he looked a lot happier than earlier in the day, even cracking a smile. I noticed how Fiona made a special effort that he felt included. All of the questionnaires were to be handed in at the end of the session. The questionnaires were all put on a table at the top of the room and most of the prisoners just put them down one on top of the other. Thomas came along with his questionnaire right at the end. He was the last lad to put his form down. I watched him and it was like when you are at school and you're a bit ashamed of the work you have done for he put his questionnaire right at the bottom of the pile. It was as if he didn't want anyone else to see it. Of course, the first thing I did as soon as he'd gone was I went to the bottom of the pile and read his questionnaire. At first I thought he'd not completed it, but at the bottom of page two there were four badly scrawled words – 'She is the best'. I've not really thought about prisoners not actually being very good at reading or writing. I feel like I've embarrassed some of the lads tonight, which is not a great start, given all the horrible things that happen in prisons.
>
> (Journal entry, 27 March 1996)

Prisons are *dark places* filled with loneliness, despair, mental anguish and suffering. Yet, there are always moments of hope – moments which stand out all the more in the memory because of the bleak normality. Irrespective of what this tells us about quantitative research with prisoners (and my own limitations as a researcher), Thomas's story is an illustration of how the human spirit can overcome obstinate and dehumanising bureaucratic realities and help mitigate another person's suffering. It is one I have never forgotten.

During the ethnography at HMP Durham, I was also keen to record my perceptions of prisoners. One experience that left a huge impression occurred on 22 April 1996. I was shadowing the Salvation Army chaplain Louis Kinsey when undertaking reception interviews. Though most reception interviews with the chaplains took place in a specially designated cell on the wing, the one that I wrote up most extensively took place in a prisoner's cell – indeed, it was primarily a description of the cell. Most of the reception interviews were quite brief – the chaplain asked the prisoners their name, address and offence. "They then briefly asked questions concerning their family and gave them advice like 'keep your head down and you'll be fine' " (journal entry, 22 April 1996).

> in one reception interview, the chaplain was greatly welcomed. The man had been in prison for nearly a week and was scared to leave his cell. He was older than most of the prisoners I had met thus far. He had greying hair and seemed to be in his fifties. He said the Chaplain was the first person he had spoken to in three days. The interview lasted much longer than normal. I felt uncomfortable writing in his cell, in fact I felt embarrassed being there at all – it felt like an invasion of his privacy. The prisoner did most of the talking and was very depressed. He had committed a sexual offence and had been abandoned by his family. The conversation between the chaplain and the prisoner was intense and I was trying not to look at him, so I discretely looked everywhere around the cell. It seemed cramped and decrepit. I felt that I could walk around the whole room in just a couple of paces. The light was not great and, of course, partly obscured by the bars in the window. The furniture was sparse – a table, a chair, a small wooden cupboard and single bed. There were dark orange stains on the bed legs [probably rust] and blankets on the bed were different shades of brown and little tattered. They looked like they had been there many years. The room stank of urine and the walls were just bear stones – they looked damp. The atmosphere in the cell was heavy as the chaplain and prisoner talked. The Chaplain has arranged to visit the prisoner again tomorrow to see if he could help him. I don't feel it would be right for me to return as an observer a second time.
>
> (ibid.)

On the afternoon of 22 April 1996, I visited Durham 'sHe wing' for the first time. It was 'a profoundly abnormal place' (journal entry, 22 April 1996), and it felt different from every other prison I had encountered till that time and indeed since. On my first visit to sHe wing, 'a woman prison officer was practicing her dance moves in one of the corners. It looked like she was dancing with a ghost' (ibid.). The claustrophobia, meaninglessness and pains of confinement were evident and etched on the faces of prisoners and indeed some staff. One of the first women prisoners I met there I initially thought had a skin complaint – it was only when I looked more closely and started talking to her that I realised that she had been self-harming and that her body was virtually covered with scars. She told me she was having difficulty finding new places on her body to cut. Still inexperienced in prison ethnography, I wrote how I found it hard at that time to understand why someone would want to cut and harm themselves.

When I was shadowing the chaplains, my presence was sometimes explained to prisoners and staff, though on numerous occasions it was not. This created opportunities and problems for the research. On the one hand, being there, especially with staff, was sometimes taken for granted and thus allowed a more open and honest dialogue to develop. On the other hand, because I was perceived as a 'trainee chaplain' or at least in some way connected to the Anglican Church, a number of those I spoke with, especially prisoners, initially thought that all I wanted was positive feedback and duly obliged. I became very aware of this problem at HMP Frankland when interviewing a prisoner called 'Lightning'. I noted in my journal how his account of the chaplains significantly altered when he realised I was doing independent research.

> At the afternoon chaplain's group I spoke to five prisoners... The most detailed discussion I had was with a prisoner who called himself 'Lightning'. At first he had nothing but positive things to say about the chaplains – he thought the chaplain's were 'great', 'fantastic', 'brilliant' and that he 'really liked them'. Lightning then asked me how long I had been training to be a chaplain. I explained that I was not a chaplain, but rather that I was doing a sociological study of prison chaplains and that I had no connection with the chaplaincy or indeed the prison service. This disclosure completely transformed our discussion. We continued to chat for maybe another ten minutes but now I was hearing a completely different tale. No longer were the chaplains 'friendly' and 'easy going'. Lightening in fact was a Rastafarian but until he started to say that he was interested in Christianity the chaplains wouldn't come and speak to him. Lightning said that the chaplains had ignored him and that he personally felt that he had been discriminated against on racial grounds... 'Who' the prisoners think I am is clearly linked to 'what' they will say to me.
>
> (Journal entry, 29 April 1996)

Earlier that morning, I had visited Frankland Healthcare centre whilst shadowing the chaplain and was confronted with yet another difficulty when undertaking research with prisoners.

> I spoke with Mo in Frankland Prison Healthcare Centre this afternoon. The Anglican Chaplain was visiting [...] a terminally ill prisoner who had only a short period of time to live and was desperate to be released before he died in prison.[8] Quite rightly the chaplain thought that my presence in the room with [...] would have been overly intrusive so whilst Stan [the chaplain] was busy I just hung around and spoke to three or four healthcare officers. After I explained I was investigating both the role and *perception* of the prison chaplains one of the officers (who I think was trying to be helpful) said 'Oh I've got exactly the man for you'. He shouted 'Mo, Mo come over here' and he got Mo to come across. Mo was a man in a wheelchair largely confined to Frankland healthcare centre, and said 'Mo you like the chaplains, come and say a few words to this man about what you think about them'. Whilst we were talking the officer stood just a little way from Mo and was definitely in hearing distance. The interview was awkward as I was pretty sure that Mo hadn't properly consented, so the discussion was relatively brief. This being said, Mo did give an amazingly positive appraisal of the prison chaplains – the chaplains were different, Stan was really friendly, the chapel was different to anywhere else in the prison ...[9] The problem is that in this 'coerced interview' it is hard to know if what Mo said was actually what he really believed.
>
> (Journal entry, 29 April 1996)

Bearing witness to denial

Doing an ethnographic study on prison chaplains proved to be a formative experience in terms of my understanding of prison life, doing prison research and abolitionism. Though a commitment to common humanity and human rights had been present in my research on prison chaplains by the time I came to undertake my second major prison ethnography on prison officers, this was much more explicitly articulated. Influenced by Stan Cohen, especially by his book *States of Denial*, my interest in prison officers was initially generated by an interest in their denial or acknowledgement of prisoner human rights (Scott, 2006, 2008, 2011). Prison officer research in the UK was still in its infancy, and as the ethnographic research gradually evolved, the focus drifted more and more towards understanding prison officer occupational culture (Scott, 2012, 2015). This was partly because the denials of common humanity and the invisibility of prisoner needs appeared so deeply embedded in the consciousness of the prison officers when I talked to them about 'prisoner rights' (Scott, 2006).

I had not up to this point considered human rights talk to be a particularly radical issue – it seemed obvious to me that prisons were painful experiences and that whatever a person had done it was impossible to become 'non-human' and therefore lose the right to be treated as a fellow human being. By now, my explicit interest in human rights further embedded a tension in my approach to prison abolitionism that I had first identified when researching the chaplains – the competing demands (or vociferous gods as Stan Cohen put it) between responding to human suffering in the present and promoting radical policies that can bring about a progressive transformation of the ways we deal with human problematic conduct (Scott, 2013b). Whilst I continue to advocate both forms of intervention – what I have recently referred to as an 'abolitionist real utopia' (Scott, 2013b) – the experience of doing research on prison officers in a 'fascist prison' (journal entry, 28 May 2002) certainly deepened my sensitivity to the need for a continuum between reform and abolition. Descriptions of the prisoner experience were not so prevalently recorded in my prison journal. Rather, the accounts recorded focused on the denial of common humanity (of both prisoners and staff) and the interactions between prisoners and staff. For now, the moral dimensions to the relationship between the prisoner and the prison officer had captured my imagination.

Between securing access and undertaking my research at HMP Preston, the prison governor had left. My first meeting to discuss how and when the research was going to take place was therefore held with the then acting governor. The governor was quite clear on the challenge that doing research on prisoner rights and subsequently prison officer occupation culture would entail. 'You're gonna come across loads of really fascist views', he said. He then did a Nazi salute to indicate to me the views of some of his staff (journal entry, 28 May 2002). Most of the research took place in the immediate aftermath of the Additional Days Awarded [*Ezeh and Connors v United Kingdom*] ruling of the European Court of Human Rights [ECtHR] in July 2002, which led to changes in governors' powers of adjudication. It was a unique and fascinating time as everyone had something to say about the ruling, albeit largely critical and hostile. I wanted to uncover if there 'was there a language of rights', and if there was, which 'rights' of prisoners were included and which 'rights' were excluded. It became very obvious within a matter of days that there 'probably wasn't going to be very many [officers] who had a language of rights'. And I kept on getting that response of, 'Why are you talking about these abstract human rights?' 'What are you talking about? You're on a different planet'. A rights language 'was completely alien to that kind of world' (journal entry, 10 August 2002).

There was hostility to the research and my presence in the prison at first and considerable concern that I was doing the research at all. I was often told that I should really be looking at officer human rights. One prison officer asked on the first day, 'Are you really interested in prisoner rights or is it just a job you have to do?' (journal entry, 30 July 2002). Initial hostility came from only a small but significant number of staff, epitomised in the attitude of one experienced prison officer called 'Charlie'. On the first day, I was warned by administrative staff that I might have problems with this officer.

I was introduced to this 'notorious' man in the first week. When he saw me, he came out with a tirade of abuse that would last a couple of minutes and go bellowing around the wing in a strong Scottish accent: 'Ooh I'm a child abuser and I have the human right to hurt and harm little kids... I have a right to beat up old grannies and take their pensions.... I have a right to rob banks... Fucken rights. They don't deserve any rights' (journal entry, 3 August 2002). I was determined to not be intimidated and resolved to speak with 'Charlie' at length – at the very least, I wanted to have a record of his abuse that I could then use as evidence in the research. I eventually arranged an interview.

> Charlie had said last week 'look you've gotta come in and talk one of the evenings' and so today we got chance to chat whilst he was doing the night-shift. When chatting to him, he told me how his wife had left him and how had all sorts of financial problems. It was a sad tale. He blamed the prison service, and especially those in the prison management, for his personal problems. He clearly didn't want to talk about the prisoners – they were an irrelevance to his daily existence – in his own words 'I'm sick of that talking about those bastards'. We then talked a little more about his life and that was as far we got. I think he is a cynical man who is very badly damaged.
>
> (Journal entry, 22 August 2002)[10]

A sense of moral indifference permeated the prison, which was not just restricted to the prison officer occupational grade. Prisoners were considered as manipulative and problematic people, who had to be contained. Drawing upon the notion of 'interpretive denial' (Cohen, 2001), I detailed the following incident:

> I was in the segregation unit this morning setting up an interview. The chaplain [a former nurse] and a member of the BoV[11] and three members of staff. The BoV man was telling me how much he liked and trusted the boys [officers], when we heard a number of large banging noises and a prisoner screaming. In the segregation unit office there was CCTV coverage of all the cells and we were all able to watch as the prisoner ran up to the cell door and bang it with his head. The prisoner repeated this process a few times and it was becoming clear that his head was now bleeding. The prisoner then had some kind of epileptic fit where he fell to the cell floor and began vomiting and shaking uncontrollably. The officers entered the cell, a few minutes later he calmed down and the doctor was called. What had looked to me like an obvious case of a prisoner in considerable suffering and pain was not considered this way by the expert panel in the segregation unit office. The problem prisoner was apparently just pretending. He 'recovered too quickly'

> according to the chaplain; he was 'just seeking attention and being childish' was the doctor's opinion. The incident had been successfully reinterpreted and the prisoner's suffering denied. The reality of the event was re-cast as another illustration of this prisoner's problematic behaviour.
>
> (Journal entry, 12 August 2002)[12]

My journal detailed a number of prisoner–staff interactions that once again indicated that prisoners were othered as lesser beings. One such entry concerned the hospital wing on HMP Preston. For many years it had been called 'F wing', but as staff used to call it Fraggle Wing, they changed it to H wing (journal entry, 4 August 2002). As one health-care officer told me, 'you can never change the name of a wing, at least not really. You'll never stop people calling it what they want. Though it is now H wing, people still say, "Oh are you going over to Fraggle Wing?" ' (ibid.). Whilst in the hospital wing, I observed a [probably uncharacteristic] violent confrontation between a prisoner and a maintenance worker.

> On the hospital wing this morning and the prisoners confined there are largely 'mentally ill' [people mental health problems]. I was hanging about the portacabin in the middle of the wing trying to informally talk to the officers. An officer from the works unit had come over to sort out some lights. He is a rather large overweight man. One of the prisoners was verbally abusive and said to him 'you're nothing but a big fat cunt'. He went up to him, grabbed the [rather small] prisoner by the throat and raising him from the ground said 'what did you say! I'm going to rip your fucken head open'. At this point [a senior prison officer] ran up to and said 'look he's mentally ill, let him go he's mentally ill!!' and [carefully] physically intervened to release the prisoner. An extreme situation to witness and it was over like a flash....
>
> (Journal entry, 5 August 2002)

As an abolitionist in such a hostile environment, my intention was to present a truthful with detailed account of what I observed. I did not find it easy to make 'allies' in this prison as I had done with my work on the chaplains. Looking back at my Preston prison journal, I have no heart-warming stories of humanitarian interventions by staff; I have only a small number of tragic accounts of conversations with prisoners with mental health problems and those prisoners who wanted to know more about their rights and thought I could help. The prisoners appeared 'crushed' and demoralised (journal entry, 17 August 2002). I had spoken at length with prisoners on the wings about prison officers, and their perceptions were largely negative in orientation. Prison officers in HMP Preston were 'cruel bastards' (journal entry, 17 August 2002), and prisoners recognised that the prison was 'a screws nick'. Whereas some prisoners felt safer because of this, others were intimidated.

I reflected how I personally was finding the research 'really tough' (journal entry, 24 August 2002) – the research experience in HMP Preston had been emotionally difficult – but barring my initial experiences at the start of the research, I had not found the prison officers personally antagonistic. Indeed, as the research progressed over a number of weeks, I found it easier to talk with many of the prison officers with whom I had regular contact. Yet, the sense of prison officer power in the prison was palpable. Overall, the prison officer had come to dominate and control the research in more ways than merely the core focus of the project. Within the 'fascist prison', my energies were focused on trying to understand how the 'officers ticked' (ibid.). As a consequence, prisoners became increasingly absent in my own personal reflections of the daily experiences of the research process, just like they appeared to be invisible in the eyes of many prison officers.

Contradictions, tensions and abolitionist praxis

In this chapter, I have attempted to explore in an honest fashion my development as a researcher, especially concerning the research I have undertaken on prisoners. I have given an unvarnished account, pointing to a number of mistakes and moral dilemmas I encountered. I hope some lessons may be evident such that they can be learnt by others. The use of questionnaires with prisoners must be carefully considered, and they may be highly inappropriate for young people in custody for [as I know now] many will have the literacy levels of seven-year-olds (Scott and Codd, 2010). My experiences have also made me very conscious of how the respondents' perception of the individual who is asking the questions has implications for the answers that they then provide. The power relations in a prison, and how they are enforced, should always be anticipated by the prison ethnographer. Power relations can also manifest themselves in other ways. For example, I have neither been asked to nor requested to 'hold the keys'. Not having keys can be important for two reasons. First, I question whether, as prison researchers, we should participate in the locking and unlocking of doors and gates, thus facilitating the operation of the penal machine. Second, and especially important when conducting research with prisoners, 'holding the keys' can be perceived as being part of the prison staff team. At times it may well be essential that researchers hold keys (access is denied otherwise or researcher is perceived as overly burdensome on staff time), but the implications of doing so must always be carefully considered

As an 'abolitionist on the inside', I have indicated not only how my abolitionist, principles, values and sensibilities influenced my research experiences but also how my experiences as a prison ethnographer have influenced my understanding of abolitionism. Witnessing first-hand the painful daily realities of penal incarceration can engender contradictory demands of bringing about the end of the penal machine as quickly as possible and of the necessity to do something about the worst excesses of prison life here and now. I am left with no doubt of the harmful nature of imprisonment and the fear it can generate. Abolitionists are likely to be sensitive to the nuances of penal realities and listen, observe and document the harms of imprisonment and in doing so may be more likely to problematise and denaturalise taken-for-granted aspects of prison life. Yet, I feel it would be unhelpful to draw the line too sharply between abolitionist research and other good prison ethnography. It may well prove very helpful to all those about to embark on prison ethnography to read *Psychological Survival, Prison on Trial* and *Medical Power in Prisons* as I did and perhaps for new researchers today to read also *Surviving the Prison Place, Punishment and Prisons* and *Controversial Issues in Prisons* (Medlicott, 2001; Sim, 2009; Scott and Codd, 2010) before they put their first step inside a prison. But the most essential aspects of good research – preparation, intellectual honesty, good listening skills and thoughtful research questions – should not be exclusive to abolitionists. If anything, it is the recognition of the moral failings of the prison and the reaction to, and what is done with, the knowledge of the inherent harms of penal incarceration that differentiate abolitionists. This I think reveals political commitments and moral values. It also means not falling into the trap of reinterpreting events to conform to the agenda of penal authorities but to use our 'sociological imagination' to understand how people act in the way that they do and how radical alternatives can be promulgated (Scott, 2013b, 2015).

Through my prison ethnographies, I have learnt a great deal about imprisonment and the importance of abolitionism. There is of course much we can still learn about the subjugated knowledge of prisoners. Ethnographies drawing upon the experiences of prisoners provide an important platform for the voice of the prisoner, but I think the prison ethnographer must also speak. Ethnographers must not remain silent or feel we cannot speak about own experiences of doing prison research, especially when critique of the repressive, authoritarian and dehumanising nature of penal confinement is located within wider abolitionist emancipatory politics. Indeed, bearing witness may have influence in shaping future policy. Ethnographers witness the mundane reality of wasting time, which I think is the greatest hardship of prison. There may well be moments of violence and physical confrontation in prisons – indeed, I was unfortunate enough to witness one such incident in the hospital wing of HMP Preston – but it is the repetitive daily humdrum of prison life that is the real problem.

For abolitionists it is essential to provide a theoretical and political context to the prison place and not to shy away from exposing the moral failings of imprisonment or its impacts upon prisoners and prison staff. When 'walking amongst the graves of the living', I have heard prisoners talk about their profound loneliness and how this exacerbated a sense of confusion and apathy. Many prison staff clearly find prison work very difficult. We should not be surprised about this. Prisons are toxic – they are places of pain, hurt and injury, and there can be no escape from this for those who work on the front line as 'caretakers of punishment' (Scott, 2015).

Such a critique of penal incarceration does not mean there are not moments of hope, friendship and compassion in prisons. What abolitionism recognises is that such moments shine so brightly because of the comparison with the dark backcloth of daily prison life. Whilst the story of 'Thomas', for example, gives us hope, it is not a story regarding human kindness *created* in the prison place. Rather, we should acknowledge how humanity has an extraordinary ability to overcome the hardest of obstacles in its way. Prison is such an obstacle that human beings sometimes overcome. Often, however, they do not. We should not be blinded by the light of rare penal successes but rather understand that because they contrast so sharply with the ugly realities of penal incarceration, they may quickly be snubbed out or overwhelmed by the everyday darkness of prison life.[13] We should ask what such moments of kindness, warmth and altruism tell us about the prison, and more pertinently, why are there not more triumphs of humanity. The point that I am making is that when investigating an institution structured by violence, we must always speak as we find – tell the truth – whether this is negative or positive. We all make metaphysical choices about what we *prioritise* in our writings. Denial or acknowledgement of human suffering, I think, most shapes the analytical imperatives and 'critical research values' of a penal abolitionist (Scott, 2014b).

Ultimately, the story of the prison and the people prisons hold is not a happy one. Prison ethnographers should use their knowledge to bring about radical and emancipatory change. For abolitionists this means abolitionist praxis – using their knowledge of the prison place to inform direct action, campaigns and lobbying against prisons and the wider confinement project (Scott, 2014b). Abolitionists have long been recognised as committed to social justice and recognition of common humanity. I think that it is essential that those who have knowledge of prisons come out and name the prison place for what it is – a place structured to deliver violence, pain and suffering. Though some may not wish to say it – or even for it to be said – the prison is inevitably a space characterised by *immoral performance*.

Notes

1. There are a number of different theoretical positions informing abolitionism, including Marxism, Anarchism, Christianity, Feminism, Virtue Ethics and Symbolic Interactionism. In this chapter, I talk about an 'abolitionist perspective' and focus on a number of values, principles and sensibilities shared by, or consistent with, these different traditions.

2. This is a rather grand name for a collection of unkempt fieldwork notebooks, in which I have written about my prison experiences. This chapter draws exclusively upon two such notebooks (Scott, 1996a, unpublished and unpaginated; Scott, 2002, unpublished and unpaginated).
3. For discussion of my research on prison staff and the implications for research values, see Scott (2014a, 2014b).
4. For further discussion of my prison research, see Scott (2006, 2015).
5. There are actually three page references to 'chaplains' in the index, though one of these refers to the word 'chaplain' listed in a table. There is no separate chapter on the prison chaplain.
6. The prison chaplain ethnography was conducted between 12 March and 17 June 1996 at six penal institutions in the North East of England: HMP Frankland, HMP Durham, HMP Acklington, HMP Askam Grange, Castington YOI and Deerbolt YOI. For discussions of my findings on the role and perception of the chaplain, see Scott (1996b, 1997, 2013a).
7. I did not witness the full prison experience, most notably what happened in prison at night.
8. I found out later that the prisoner died in Frankland prison a few weeks later.
9. There was a certain ambiguity in this last statement as the wheelchair-bound prisoner was unable to access many parts of HMP Frankland at that time – 1996.
10. I did not ever have another problem with 'Charlie' after the interview.
11. Board of Visitors, now called the Independent Monitoring Board (IMB).
12. See also observations from my journal, in Scott (2006), *Ghosts Beyond Our Realm*.
13. Thanks to Joe Sim for discussing this matter with me and to Rod Earle for clarification on wording.

Further reading

Cohen, S. and Taylor, L. (1977) 'Talking Prison Blues', in C. Bell and H. Newby (eds) (1977) *Doing Sociological Research* (London: Harper Collins).

Moore, L. and Scraton, P. (2013) 'Researching Prison: Women's Voices', in Moore, L. and Scraton, P. (2013) *The Incarceration of Women: Punishing Bodies, Breaking Spirits*, pp 54–71 (London: Palgrave).

Sim, J. (1990) *Medical Power in Prisons* (Buckingham: Open University Press).

References

Bennett, J., Crewe, B. and Wahidin, A. (eds) (2008) *Understanding Prison Staff* (Devon: Willan).

Cohen, S. (2001) *States of Denial* (Cambridge: Polity Press).

Cohen, S. and Taylor, L. (1973–81) *Psychological Survival* (Harmondsworth: Penguin).

Foucault, M. (1980) *Power/Knowledge: Selected Interviews and Other Writings 1972–1977* (London: Harvester Press).

Fitzgerald, M. and Sim, J. (1982) *British Prisons* (Oxford: Blackwells).

Hobhouse, S. and Brockway, F. (1922) *Prisons Today* (London: Longman).

Mathiesen, T. (1974/2014) *The Politics of Abolition* (Oxford: Martin Robertson).

Mathiesen, T. (1990) *Prisons on Trial* (London: Sage).

Mathiesen, T. (2004) *Silently Silenced* (Winchester: Waterside Press).

Medlicott, D. (2001) *Surviving the Prison Place* (Aldershot: Ashgate).

Minshull, G. (1618/1821) *Essayes and Characters of a Prison and Prisoners* (Edinburgh: W. And C. Tait).
Scott, D. (1996a) *Prison Journal*, Unpublished and unpaginated.
Scott, D. (1996b) *Heavenly Confinement? The Role and Perception of Christian Prison Chaplains in the North East of England's Prisons* (London: Lambert Academic Press).
Scott, D. (1997) *God's Messengers Behind Bars: The Role and Perception of the Prison Chaplain* (Ormskirk: Centre for Studies in Crime and Social Justice) [Report for HMPS Chaplaincy].
Scott, D. (2002) *Prison Journal*, Unpublished and unpaginated.
Scott, D. (2006) *Ghosts Beyond Our Realm: A Neo-abolitionist Analysis of Prisoner Human Rights and Prison Officer Occupational Culture*, Unpublished PhD Thesis (Preston: University of Central Lancashire/VDM).
Scott, D. (2008) 'Creating Ghosts in the Penal Machine: The Prison Officer Moral Universe and the Techniques of Denial', in J. Bennett, B Crewe and A. Wahidin (eds) *Understanding Prison Staff* (Devon: Willan).
Scott, D. (2011) ' "That's Not My Name": Prisoner Deference and Disciplinarian Prison Officers', *Criminal Justice Matters*, 84(1), 8–9.
Scott, D. (2012) 'Guarding the Ghosts of Time: Working Personalities and the Prison Officer-Prisoner Relationship', *Prison Service Journal*, 201, May, 18–23.
Scott, D. (2013a) 'God's Messengers Behind Bars: An Ethnographic Study of the Role and Perception of the Prison Chaplain in the North East of England', *Justice Reflections*, 33, June.
Scott, D. (2013b) 'Visualising an Abolitionist Real Utopia', in M. Malloch and B. Munro (eds) *Crime, Critique and Utopia* (Basingstoke: Palgrave).
Scott, D. (2014a) 'Prison Research: Appreciative or Critical Inquiry?' *Criminal Justice Matters*, March.
Scott, D. (2014b) 'Critical Research Values and the Sociological Imagination: Learning Lessons from Researching Prison Staff', in J. Frauley (ed) *C. Wright Mills and the Criminological Imagination* (Aldershot: Ashgate).
Scott, D. (2015) *The Caretakers of Punishment: Power, Legitimacy and the Prison Officer* (Basingstoke: Palgrave).
Scott, D. and Codd, H. (2010) *Controversial Issues in Prisons* (Buckingham: Open University Press).
Scraton, P., Sim, J. and Skidmore, P. (1991) *Prisons Under Protest* (Milton Keynes: Open University Press).
Sim, J. (1990) *Medical Power in Prisons* (Milton Keynes: Open University Press).
Sim, J. (2003) 'Whose Side We Are Not On', in S. Tombs and D. Whyte (eds) *Unmasking the Crimes of the Powerful* (New York: Peter Lange).
Sim, J. (2009) *Punishment and Prisons: Power and the Carceral State* (London: Sage).
Sim, J., Scraton, P. and Gordon, P. (1987) 'Introduction', in P. Scraton (ed) *Law, Order and the Authoritarian State* (Milton Keynes: Open University Press).

3

Prisons Research beyond the Conventional: Dialogue, 'Creating Miracles' and Staying Sane in a Maximum-Security Prison

Alison Liebling, Helen Arnold and Christina Straub

> There's no love in the concrete. It's almost... at times you feel like even the building despises people in here.
>
> (Prisoner, in Liebling et al., 2012)

This remark from a prisoner at HMP Whitemoor, England, expresses what we explore in this article: the extent to which relationships... constitute both 'the core of ethnographic fieldwork' (Agar, 1980: 53) and the quality of prison life.

Cohen and Taylor: Pioneers of prison Dialogue

In *Psychological Survival: The Experience of Long-Term Imprisonment*, Cohen and Taylor (1972) defied all rules of research access and created an opportunity to conduct one of the best, most authentic and insightful studies of long-term imprisonment available. They describe their work, carried out in HMP Durham between 1968 and 1971, as a 'collaborative' research project on 'how people survive in extreme and adverse situations'. Stan Cohen and Laurie Taylor – young sociology lecturers at the time – were invited to give weekly classes in social science to the long-term prisoners in E-Wing, a special security wing which they described as a 'submarine', with 20 prisoners and 40 staff. The wing had a turbulent history, having experienced disturbances, a barricade, hunger strike, staff resignations, violent incidents involving staff and a high-profile escape. These events formed a 'collective memory' which informed life on the wing for the quieter years of the research. The classroom in which the discussions took place had a symbolic significance since it had been converted from the chapel destroyed during a barricade. Staff were nervous about the classes and requested that Cohen and Taylor avoid topics 'connected to the men's lives' (Cohen and

Taylor, 1972: 29). They were identified by staff, based on their role, physical presentation and orientation, with the 'general forces of permissiveness'. Their attitude towards staff was rather derogatory ('we were foolish enough to visit the officer's social club'), and officers saw them as 'in league' with prisoners – they were criticised as engaging in a '*reciprocal granting of elite status*':

> We are university teachers, they are Category A prisoners. Outside on the landing sit the plebs.
>
> (ibid.: 33)[1]

The prisoners were high-status, high-profile individuals with strong public images and reputations (they included John McVicar and some of the train robbers). The classes were just over two-and-a-half hours long (they were held between 6 and 9 pm); tea was served; attendance was voluntary; the size of the class varied between 2 and 12 participants each week. It competed with television watching. The research project was initiated in 1968 during these classes:

> We had begun to move away from formal sociology towards unprogrammed discussions and it was during these that general criticisms of traditional prison studies was voiced.
>
> (ibid.: 32)

A Home Office-funded study was being carried out in the same prison at the time by a team of psychologists at Durham University (e.g. Banister et al., 1973). These authors were following up on indications that, since the abolition of the death penalty and consequently a rise in the number of prisoners serving long sentences, prisoners might reach a peak 'in their training' and then decline – or that they might form attitudes and characteristics that were detrimental to adjustment in society outside. This was a cross-sectional and longitudinal study of 200 men at four different stages of long sentences. It adopted a series of cognitive and other tests measuring spatial ability, visual reaction, manipulative dexterity and short-term memory. Prisoners were strongly critical of its methods, epistemology and ethics and had begun to boycott it. They raised their objections in a class with Cohen and Taylor and thus emerged a mutual research project, with the aim of adding something useful to policy debates about long-term imprisonment. Built around an explicit rejection of standard psychological personality tests and structured interviews, the research began 'without a problem', evolved its methods and 'blurred the distinction between the observer and the observed'. The authors employed four major research methods: unstructured group interviews (with observations and interpretations shown to prisoners); prisoners' writings: letters, stories, poems, essays; structured use of literature (books by Freud and novels and plays by Dostoyevsky, Serge, Camus and Genet); and sharing the writing drafts with prisoners. The researchers saw themselves as the least knowledgeable and the prisoners as knowledgeable agents. Trust was gradually built up on both sides.

Thus, they conducted a form of ethnography, or qualitative, interpretative research 'with' rather than 'on' prisoners. They bypassed the usual problems of access, funding and organisation, thereby avoiding the normal constraints of fixed budgets, time schedules and building relationships. Although Durham's governor was favourable, when a submission was made to the Home Office, they rejected the proposal on the grounds of its 'unscientific methods' (not a large-enough sample, no control group, no 'objective' tests and not measuring change over a long-enough period of time) and concerns about security and sensationalism. By this stage, most of the work had already been done.

Prisoners' reservations about traditional approaches to problems of psychological change were that the measures were not sophisticated or subtle enough to characterise their predicament. What Cohen and Taylor and their collaborators were interested in was 'mundane and untested matters' such as the passage of time, the making and breaking of friends, the fear of deterioration, the role of self-consciousness and the loss of identity. For long periods of time, Cohen and Taylor observed, they talked 'more intimately to these men than to any other people we know' (1972: 33). They noted that:

> the classes were more stimulating than those we took at the university; the men actually read the recommended books and had plenty of practical examples with which to refute our crasser generalisations.
>
> (1972: 68)

There was a gradual realisation that none of the available accounts of prison – by sociologists or psychologists – captured the predicament these men felt they were in and that the research was touching on the question of survival in extreme circumstances:

> Gradually we realized that we were not just trying to understand another group of prisoners. Instead, we were looking at the ways in which men in general might react to an extreme situation, a situation which disrupted their normal lives so as to make problematic such everyday matters as time, friendship, privacy, identity, self-consciousness, ageing and physical deterioration. Once we realised this we were able to turn to a range of other studies which looked at the more general questions of how men dealt with the stress produced by any massive disruption in their normal lives.
>
> (Cohen and Taylor, 1972: 41)

They reviewed the literatures on other dislocations and situations requiring endurance, for example on natural and war-related disasters, learning how sensitive accounts of the shattering and rebuilding of life could be applied to the experience of being a life sentence prisoner. These accounts enabled the 'mutual researchers' to see the long-term prisoners' predicament in a new way. They drew on material from concentration and labour camps, and prisons, whilst making several qualifications to the applicability of this material. The themes which survived application to prison were (i) extreme self-consciousness; (ii) the notion of resistance: that one should remain alive and unchanged; (iii) a preoccupation with having to take up a position: did one give in or fight back? and (iv) the question as to whether adversity 'makes' or 'breaks' the spirit. They looked at the prison literature to date and found it mostly concerned with social structures, institutionalisation, 'prisonisation' (a form of secondary socialisation), adjustment styles or types and the inmate culture. The literature came close to, but did not reach deeply enough, these questions of meaning and survival. The researchers wanted to emphasise human agency and creativity in the process of survival, rather than deterministically conceived modes of adaptation: how do individuals maintain a conceptual universe? How do they develop a plausible account of their situation and the environment in which they now live? How is life in this environment given meaning? How do they pass the time? How are friends made and lost? How do they adapt and how do they resist? How do they imagine, and then do, a 20-year sentence?

And so we come to our Dialogue Group at Whitemoor.

The context: Two studies of staff–prisoner relationships at Whitemoor

The research described below consists of a repeat and, in some respects, further development of an exploratory study originally carried out at HMP Whitemoor in 1998–99 by Alison Liebling and David Price (originally published as 'An Exploration of Staff-Prisoner Relationships at HMP Whitemoor') but in an entirely new context. The original study had been modestly funded by the Prison Service (at £15,000), had been unconstrained and had used mainly qualitative methods. It had included, for the first time in a research project, extensive use of Appreciative Inquiry (see Liebling et al., 1999). The idea of exploring the work of prison officers closely had emerged out of collaborative discussions between the research team and Prison Service personnel about an intriguing finding in a previous study – that officers deployed their discretion, or used their power, very differently on different wings (see Liebling, 2000). This study identified the characteristics of role model prison officers and described prison officer work at its best, as well as exploring the nature and quality of staff–prisoner relationships. The first study resulted in the publication of *The Prison Officer* (2001; and 2nd edition, Liebling et al., 2010).

The second project was more complex. The request for the research, and the negotiated agreement to follow, came from the chief scientific officer, and it was fully funded by the Home Office. Whereas the first study had been genuinely exploratory and unconstrained by specific policy concerns, in the second, the request for the research was external and direct. It was regarded as 'high risk research'. Ministers were 'genuinely worried' about the 'apparent risks of radicalisation' at Whitemoor, following a critical report on the quality of staff–prisoner relationships by Her Majesty's Chief Inspector of Prisons (HMCIP, 2008). Staff–prisoner relationships were 'distant', and a growing number of Muslim prisoners were expressing dissatisfaction with their treatment. A call for research had led to some unsatisfactory, 'naïve' and 'narrow' proposals, which were not going to answer the main questions of interest: 'have we got a problem at Whitemoor?', 'What sort of problem is it?' The brief was as follows: 'We need an exploratory piece of work, which considers "what is going on" at Whitemoor, in a properly social context'. So the idea of repeating the original exploratory study was offered, and accepted. We designed the study in a very similar way to the first, with some additional components (e.g. a detailed quality of life survey) based on conceptual and methodological developments made in subsequent research projects. One thing we were sure of was that we would welcome participation in a Dialogue Group as part of our 're-entry into the field'.

The Whitemoor Dialogue Group as a research method

In the original Whitemoor study carried out in 1998–99, the researchers had been made honorary members of the existing Dialogue Group, which consisted of prisoners, occasionally welcomed prison officers and other prison staff, and was led by one or more facilitators from outside the prison from the charitable organisation 'Prison Dialogue'. The existence of a group run by Prison Dialogue provided an excellent setting for the researchers to regularly meet with prisoners (sometimes with selected staff members present) and participate in an already-existing forum for open communication with members of the group. The team did not see their participation as a 'research method' at the time, but discovered this group was a place of deep conversation and relationship building.[2] Conversations were always energetic, fluent, powerful and often humorous. There were times when the themes were emotional for us as well as for prisoners (e.g. families, the importance of freedom, power and discipline, racism and intolerance, forgiveness and the experience of loss), but the topics were always compelling, even when more narrowly prison based (e.g. staff–prisoner relationships, breaches of trust, the impact of a violent incident on others or security categorisation and the impact of being Category A). We were expected to participate, reasonably enough, and so we did, whilst being careful never to 'set the agenda'. We were the focus of it once or twice – in a thorough interrogation about our research and when we were asked specific questions about how we lived or who we were. Prisoners told us during our various discussions in the group that we 'had got under the surface of the prison'. They also told us, 'we got under the surface of you'. Several of its members became key interviewees and advocates of our research elsewhere in the prison. We experienced unusually extensive conversation and contact with prisoners throughout the project and found ourselves being invited into its 'darker corners' by our prisoner participants. We were always warmly received, even when we returned to the prison several months or years after the research was completed. This assured us that, as a method, joining a Dialogue Group was both effective and appropriate.

Prison Dialogue Groups are 'more concerned with the humanizing of the society than the socializing of the individual' and achieve this 'through regular, open, on-the-level communication between a cross-section of those living and working in the prison'. They are underpinned by the notion that 'meanings are formed collectively as well as individually', and therefore they work by assisting participants 'to discover both the social and individual nature of their behaviour' and by 'establishing a community of enquiry' which 'addresses social fragmentation directly through open communication in a large group' (Garrett, 1991: 10–11). In short: 'Dialogue is an enquiry into what leads us to think, feel, speak and act as we do' (ibid.).

'The activity' of a Dialogue Group involves 15–20 people meeting weekly for a year or more; participation is voluntary; diversity is helpful; participants are seated facing one another in a single circle and have one conversation; there is no agenda or fixed topic of conversation, and there is no taught content; there is no objective; no subject is prohibited from conversation; everyone has the right to their own perspective and the responsibility of listening to other speakers seriously; it is not talk for talk's sake but facilitates talk in order to engage and exchange here and now; and attention is on the meaning of both the process and the content of conversation (Garrett, 1991: 11). During the early days of the Dialogue Group at Whitemoor, there were 'sometimes heated, and sometimes rounded, conversations for and against drugs, immigrants, abortion, violence as a means of implementing change, and pride and shame about being a criminal'. The group 'pondered on the media and reporting, royalty, former Yugoslavia, homosexuality and AIDS, abortion, contraception, religious experience, insanity, the Bulger murder, Zimbabwe, Nelson Mandela, money management, employment, friendship and love' (Garret, 1991: 16). At the end of one group we attended and to which an officer was invited, who participated fully, the officer thanked the participants for 'seeing him as the man behind the uniform'. In others, prisoners spoke with passion and insight about the effects of labelling and judgement and the question of 'where you draw the line':

> It is *when* you are being unfairly judged that you behave at your worst.
>
> (Dialogue Group participant, 5 May 1998)

Whilst the question of whether officers should be present generated considerable feeling, and sometimes resistance (depending on who they were), there was no question that when present, important connections were made and new perspectives understood. In this Dialogue situation, despite the pain and often pointlessness of prison, the participants seemed wise beyond their years, some coming to grasp the significance of 'life' on the face of their long sentences (perhaps more acutely than we did), expressing this movingly and personally:

> This will reduce my chances of having children... You have to reflect on the value of freedom... Sometimes people outside build their own prisons... This has moved me on from the material... I'd be happy outside now without a penny... Children just want Dad home, way above material things.
>
> (Dialogue Group participants, 4 August 1998)

From Dialogue to Cambridge Dialogue

The 'official' Dialogue Group ran from 1993 to 2001 (we joined it from January to December 1998) when a decision was taken to terminate the contract with the prison. When we returned to Whitemoor in 2009 to carry out the repeat study of staff–prisoner relationships, then, the group no longer existed. Given the important role the Dialogue Group had played during the first study and to remain true to its original spirit, the research team decided to set up its own Dialogue Group. We called it *Cambridge Dialogue.*

The team organised and facilitated a group for a period of ten weeks (from September to December, 2009). This was complex and involved some advertising, selection, approvals from the security department and negotiations with the establishment about 'the course' counting towards its purposeful activity figures. It was held in a carpeted workshop space that also functioned as the multi-faith room. It was large, and we made it comfortable, with prisoners' help (see below).

The exceptions to the principles outlined above were that Cambridge Dialogue Group consisted of fewer members than was recommended (there were up to 15, but usually around 11), and there was a planned theme or subject of conversation, nominated either by the research team or by the group in advance, which was informed by the sharing of a selected reading (chosen and distributed by the research team). We established a number of ground rules or guidelines for the group, which were agreed with the participants: (i) be polite and respectful of others in the group and their views; (ii) listen to the views of others and speak one at a time; let everyone have their say; (iii) we can't take up individual grievances or complaints; (iv) attendance is voluntary; if you feel after today that you don't want to come again, please let us know, but otherwise do try and come every week; (v) please try and do the reading we will give you for the following week to discuss, and make some notes if you wish; (vi) think about whether there is any particular topic you would like discussed at one of the groups; (vii) what is said in the group stays in the group, except for general analysis and final reporting purposes.

For Cambridge Dialogue, the 'formally' selected themes for discussion, chosen as a result of discussion during the first meeting, were the following: life on the streets and gun crime; psychological survival and coping in prison; trust; psychology and risk assessment; music; the prisoner society, doing prison research; legitimacy and order in prison; and faith and Islam. Despite these prison-specific themes, used as means to give an initial focus to the conversations, the talk that ensued encompassed in reality a wide range of topics, including in particular deprivation, social exclusion, schooling and education; differences in social class; voting, European Union legislation and The Lisbon Treaty; violence and the use of weapons, money and materialism, girls, women and relationships; hope; racism; and sexual harassment. At the end of the first exploratory meeting, at which these topics were proposed and discussed, prisoners shook hand with us, several saying 'nice one' as they left.

At the end of each Dialogue Group meeting, participants were given copies of the selected reading for the following week.[3] The topics and the readings were informed somewhat by the aims and nature of the research, but were also shaped by the wishes of prisoners. There was no conflict between these aims, as the Dialogue Group was a means of understanding life in the prison and getting to know a small group of prisoners well.

The Cambridge Dialogue Group differed from the official Dialogue Group in one other respect: it did not include prison staff. There was an officer presence in the room, for security reasons. In most cases, the officer(s) on supervisory duty in the workshop where the Dialogue Group was held remained unobtrusive and stayed a respectful distance from the conversation, mainly in the small staff office, which had a window onto the main room. For the first group, however, an officer sat himself within the circle of chairs (see below).

It took almost a month from our initial meetings with senior managers in the prison to set up and conduct the first group in mid-September 2009. As was generally the case with our fieldwork experience, and in contrast to the 'freedom' of the original study, there were more procedures to follow, more checking to be done and more concern about fulfiling performance targets. At the first meeting, we discussed our criteria for selection to the group: we wanted interested, able, articulate, intelligent prisoners who could read and who would contribute to group discussions; the prison wanted prisoners who were unemployed or otherwise not engaged in purposeful activity so as to boost their 'KPT out of cell activity hours'.[4] To gauge their interest, we asked our respective wings to suggest names of suitable prisoners who could be approached individually, and, to advertise the group, posters were placed on noticeboards in each of the three main wings inviting prisoners to participate in a regular Wednesday afternoon discussion course ('want a respectful and meaningful conversation about things that matter?'). The poster underwent several revisions in the light of discussion of 'content and workability' in order to meet the satisfaction of managers. It outlined the potential topics; explained that short readings would be distributed before each meeting 'to discuss and compare with your own experiences'; and specified that the course was 'aimed at those who are interested in conversation and study'. Those prisoners who were interested were asked to contact either their wing SO[5] or one of the research team. Places were limited to 20, and all those attending were to receive the sessional education pay rate.

The prisoners who expressed an interest in attending the Dialogue Group had to be risk assessed and receive security clearance, and after each meeting we were required to confirm their attendance with the Regime Office. For the first Cambridge Dialogue Group, 16 prisoners attended (6 from A Wing, 8 from B Wing, 2 from C Wing) from the list of 26 in total that we had given to Regimes (14 from A Wing, 10 from B Wing, 2 from C Wing). There had been some suggestion from security that two prisoners on the list may have had a longstanding 'issue', and we were aware that some prisoners may have declined to attend as a result of others in the group. The following fieldwork notes capture something of the problems we faced in the creating and conducting the Dialogue Group initially:

> When we entered the workshop the room had been prepared for us with chairs set up in a circle (Workshop 9 is also used for Induction and Muslim Prayers). There were cups, spoons, milk and coffee on a table to the side of the room. The room is large, clean and carpeted; a good facility although we had to move the chairs closer together due to the quite poor acoustics. We had brought in tea, coffee and biscuits, ignorant of the fact that it was Ramadan and therefore the Muslim prisoners were not able to eat or drink. The officer brought this issue to our attention and after consultation with prisoners we decided that we would provide the refreshments anyway. Everybody took a seat and the supervising prison officer sat within the circle; he said that he had been present in the former prisoner dialogue group and that it hadn't been a problem. The prisoners expressed their dislike for this officer (one of the group had been restrained by him during a family visit). Alison

> diplomatically put it to the group that it was negotiable whether we had an officer with us, and they said they weren't happy so we gently asked him if he would mind removing himself in order that we might build trust without officer presence for the first few weeks, in the first instance. He accepted this graciously. After the group we spoke with him again and Alison suggested that, as with a previous discussion group at Whitemoor, prisoners may start asking/wanting officers to listen to their views and be present for the discussions.
>
> We began by the three of us giving a short introduction about ourselves. Alison invited each prisoner to introduce himself and outline their interest in attending the group; the majority just gave their first/last name and their wing location. Several said they had come to the group for coffee and biscuits and [one prisoner] said it was because it was the only activity he was allowed to do and therefore the only opportunity he had to get out of his cell. There was some protest from members of the group about our original wish to record the discussion, so we agreed we wouldn't on this occasion. We never did.

After some settling-in troubles, relationships and conversation flourished. Prisoners said they looked forward to the meeting, and they greeted each other, and us, warmly, with news of the events of the week, banter about comings and goings or other incidents arising in the prison before settling into the group. The group consisted of 14 regular attendees from each of the three main wings in the prison. The average number of prisoners present was 11. Ten of the group were BME (71 per cent), and the remainder were white British.

The dialogue in the ten sessions that we held was, at times, lively, but it remained respectful, and the group were conscientious and well behaved. The tone of the discussion was generally serious, and there were many intelligent and insightful comments. There was humour; the main source of which was [a prisoner] who began nearly every comment with 'I'm IPP'.[6] He became known as 'Mr IPP'. There were many other examples of humour; for example, one prisoner asked if we had contaminated the biscuits we brought in with a special chemical that would make them talk! Light-hearted communication was mixed with more serious reflections. When one 'Exceptional Risk' prisoner was consistently late or was removed from the group by officers to undergo a strip search, the whole group felt for him, empathised with his situation and responded to his plight with both laughter at his regular disappearances and concerned comments about the structural meaning of this type of security measure. The afternoons were about shared experiences, not just conversation.

There was often a momentum to the conversations that reflected the need prisoners felt to have a voice; they wanted to talk constructively and to be treated, in some sense, as students. It was notable that the relationships the team developed with prisoners in these Dialogue Group sessions were more personal than in the original Dialogue sessions; the prisoners related directly to the team, without an organisation behind us, and this made for stronger interpersonal dynamics and a greater degree of authenticity. Prisoners felt that we were doing this 'for them', even though it was in part 'for us'.

Some topics worked better than others. For example, the conversations about psychological survival in prison and serving long sentences floundered at first. Prisoners could not consciously access or express any of the struggle for survival they experienced. The topic was almost unthinkable:

> I found myself rather disappointed (once the talk moved swiftly away from the reading) that there was not any protracted and honest discussion about ways of coping with long-term imprisonment; perhaps the pains and discomforts are buried just a little too deep to facilitate access and an inability or a lack of willingness to express their thoughts and feelings is in itself both an indication of pain and a means of coping with it.
>
> (Fieldwork Notes, 2009)

Prisoners said at first that they struggled to identify with the findings of Cohen and Taylor's study and saw little relevance of the chapter we gave them (on 'Survival in extreme situations') to their current situation. But the conversation soon developed into a more diverse analysis of the pains of prison life, such as the need to have a focus, learning to 'fight in the right way – via learning and courses', the feeling of powerlessness, the frustrations with rules about visitors' clothing on visits and the casual behaviour of prison officers. We found that, on the whole, this topic was better handled privately and at the interviewees' own pace.

The session on music similarly foundered. The problem – which we had not anticipated – was captured by one of the team in her fieldwork notes as follows:

> In our group today we were supposed to talk about music and what it means to us – we thought this would be light relief. The first 15 minutes were very awkward, until a white Muslim 'convert' told us he doesn't listen to music – it is forbidden. It 'leads to bad things'. The group were 'silenced'. Once this was acknowledged everyone opened up – we have now 'agreed' to have a discussion on the theme of 'faith'. The jugular. We might even give them Hamm's 'Muslims in prison' article as preparation. Right to the heart of things. But so risky and difficult.
>
> (Fieldwork Notes, 2009)

So sometimes topics were offered one week, and then events in the prison made them less easy to talk about. We were making inroads but finding opaque and multiple narratives. The change of heart about music followed a series of events over the weekend:

> Whitemoor was tough today. A 'good bad day' – loads of insight gained but all via bad events... a prisoner was stabbed and left for dead on Sunday, he survived and now there's a police investigation, apparently because he watched forbidden programmes on the TV at night. A Muslim. Attacked by 2 'extremists'.

There were other conflicting explanations for these events, emerging from the wings as we went about our research (see further Liebling et al., 2011; Liebling and Arnold, 2012). Direct discussions in groups about these serious incidents were, we understood, generally out of bounds.

The third session of the Cambridge Dialogue Group consisted of a discussion of trust (based on a reading from 'Prisons and Their Moral Performance', written by two of the research team). This theme worked well, particularly as its absence was illustrated throughout the meetings by the regular disappearance of one member for searching. Prisoners clearly identified and illustrated the 'lack of trust' in the environment. The physical environment of a prison epitomised the limitations of trust: 'distrust is built into the fabric and the architecture'. One regular participant had taken it upon himself to conduct his own research in advance of the meeting, asking staff and prisoners on his wing about trust. The outcome of his 'mini-survey' was that some prisoners trusted certain individuals, but some trusted nobody. He was proud to share his 'surprising' findings with the group: especially his discovery that 'staff don't even trust each other very much'. There were 'divisions' and 'loyalties'; male staff were 'sceptical' of young female staff and their apparent 'failure to impose appropriate boundaries'. Some female staff 'have told me things... there's a lot of harassment'. Despite the divisions, staff 'back each other up', making it hard for prisoners to trust individual staff members.

From this initial exposition the conversation flowed and was characterised by serious reflection and philosophical thinking – far from being a heavy and complex concept, trust was something prisoners knew and could talk about. The group discussed trust between officers, between officers and prisoners and amongst prisoners, as well as lack of trust in prison procedure and policy (e.g. distributive fairness, the use of the Incentives and Earned Privileges (IEP) policy as punishment, the adjudication process and the complaints system: 'I got a verbal warning for handing in the wrong menu slip!'). They acknowledged that whilst trust was often an individual matter, some groups of prisoners were trusted less than others: 'there is massive distrust of Muslim prisoners'. Black and mixed-race prisoners also felt less trusted: 'we are seen as a "gang" if we talk to each other'. Some prisoners gave examples of feeling trusted: 'I feel trusted in my job. They lock me in the yard by myself. That's putting trust in me'; or of others being trusted: 'some high risk prisoners are going to the gym every day (when they shouldn't) – that's gym staff putting trust in the kind of people they are'. So, staff were placing trust in certain prisoners, at specific times, and there was some consensus about where, and with whom, this was possible.

Prisoners did not trust staff who were 'a bit unsure of themselves; defensive'. The least trust in the prison was found between prisoners and psychologists ('we are their work subjects'). There was a 'complete lack of trust' in the criminal justice system as a whole. Trust was strongly linked to issues of staff professionalism, equality, discrimination, power and honesty. Where trust was lacking, there often existed stereotypical and unfounded assumptions as well as a reliance on formal warnings and sanctions.

A topic that worked particularly well was (street) life outside. Given that a considerable number of prisoners at Whitemoor had gang affiliations on the outside involving gun use, we asked the group to read Hallworth and Silverstone's 'That's Life Innit: A British Perspective on Guns, Crime and Social Order' (2009). The discussion was lively and fruitful with much talk about the role of the media glorifying gun use, using stereotypes and exaggerating both choice and glamour. Many of the group were highly critical towards the media, as it 'propelled consumerism', capitalism and 'envy'.

Much of the discussion centred on social exclusion by schools and the state, the influence of peers, family and role models, the psychology of the young (who 'feel invincible', that they 'still have time to change', that 'prison is cool and respected'), the snowball effect of crime ('once you're in this world'), including the risks of recall, and the disadvantages of 'not being middle class', therefore being ill-equipped to survive in contemporary society; experiencing barriers to aspirations; not possessing the 'right' values, 'weapons', clothes or support network/structure to succeed:

> You only see your growing up ideology is dysfunctional when you are inside. You end up living in the present. You think, 'when I make my first grand, I'll stop'. Then you get targeted: 'that's his brother'; families turn on whole families.
>
> (Prisoners, fieldwork notes)

Prison was like school – a cold, hard system, where there is 'no room to deal with individual needs'. Teachers could not relate to you. School provided 'the framework for your first social exclusion':

> Your parents don't know what to do, they are people from working class, school is a middle-class institution. You're automatically excluded because you didn't get the right middle-class mentality from your parents... Pupils

> and teachers don't understand each other because they are from different social classes. The teachers don't come from 'the ends', do they? They don't even know what you're talking about.
>
> (Prisoner, fieldwork notes)

This mutual exchange of childhood memories and past experiences (including ours) established trust between the group members and made us nostalgic and reflective. It helped us get to know the group and to learn something of their values and experiences. As many of the participants assumed that our lives were 'perfect' and privileged, we were able to correct this view – although they could each outdo us on adversity. The discussion had considerable momentum and included the hypocrisy of those in power ('MPs expenses', 'they invade Iraq', 'police lie and fit you up', 'it's all an old boy's network') and the awareness of the injustice of their harsh beginnings. Those who succeeded were 'nerds'; 'that's their middle class weapon, labelling us as rebels and criminals':

> Learning skills would have helped us – how to 'be a man'. We needed our kind of role models: boxers, runners, sports... it's how wild you are. I went with my friends. You only have to take one step. People brag about who they have shot.
>
> (Prisoners, fieldwork notes)

Despite the seriousness of the content, the mood was light throughout. There was much laughter about mistakes made in the past, reminding us all of our shared humanity. Their joint analysis of the role of class and inequality in society, and in their lives, was powerful and in stark contrast with the abstract, individualised risk model they found themselves caught up in, defined and constructed by.

Whilst the team were not there to teach or lecture, the Dialogue Group was a stimulating forum, and the prisoners took their role seriously, bringing with them their highlighted and annotated copies of the readings as well as additional letters to the team and particular books they had read, found interesting and wanted to recommend to us. Although 'from their point of view, such an academic ethos was a welcome relief from the usual relationships which they encountered within the prison' (Cohen and Taylor, 1972: 69), it was also much more than that.

Cohen and Taylor recognised that they 'began to talk rather than to lecture' when they 'ran out of material'. Their first conversations were 'rather wary exchanges' about culture and lifestyles; there was a trading of stories. They were candid about the extent and type of disclosure from themselves to the prisoners, in a role reversal of usual research practice. Unlike Cohen and Taylor, we did not come to rely on 'our subjects' to talk to intimately, although there were times when the team were asked personal questions such as whether we were married and whether we had been the victims of crime. They also made certain assumptions about the assumed stability of our lives and our apparent 'middle-classness'. In a dialogical and reciprocal spirit, we responded to these questions and assumptions in a way that revealed something of ourselves.

Dialogue as method and politics

As a research method the Cambridge Dialogue Group was a successful practice, which on reflection proved to be a vital process for building trust, establishing relationships and a presence in the prison, obtaining data and gaining access to prisoners throughout the prison, not least because 11 of the group were formally interviewed during the course of the research. That relationships had already been built with these prisoners prior to a more formal interview often meant that the recorded interviews took on a degree of sincerity and openness that might not otherwise have occurred. It enabled the team to glean a wider picture of their backgrounds and to uncover some of the central themes and meanings to prisoners of life in Whitemoor before talking with others. That we were warmly greeted on wings when we appeared helped us to establish conversation with others. The method permitted several values and practices to exist in an environment where they were typically constrained, feared, suppressed or denied: it promoted trust, respect, honesty, individuality and a sense of identity; it was humanising and thought provoking; it was full of emotions (laughter, pain, anger, frustration and disappointment): it provided a voice; it allowed for talk in an environment where talk was cautious and policed.

The discussions generated considerable insight, sensitised us to important and unexpected themes, in the prisoners' own vocabulary, and helped us to devise meaningful questions for the interview phase of our research. We were aware that feelings and attitudes are not always expressed in reasoned responses to direct questions. However, it was common for prisoners to return to issues arising in the Dialogue Group during interviews and to continue to illustrate them with detailed examples. The Dialogue Group shared some characteristics of focus groups (e.g. the participants were, to some extent, an established group or collection of subgroups; body language, teasing, humour and anecdotes were regarded as important; the group had a research purpose, and we took notes). It also shared some of the characteristics of therapeutic groups (it was supportive, exploratory and often raw, people were attributed or adopted 'roles' and it developed an 'internal life'). It was also distinctive from both of these types of group in important respects: it was educational, it had no therapeutic purpose, it was a shared forum or event and it was about more than the research project, communicating, we hope, respect and reciprocity.

As Cohen and Taylor wrote, 'we have not simply played the roles of detached seekers after information in this research project' (1972: 180). We intended to be appreciative and deeply engaged. This carried risks. In a prison concerned about 'conditioning', boundary maintenance, security breaches and the dangerousness of its population, 'getting close' had to be approached carefully. Being human, expressing sympathy or offering support, was regarded as a sign of naivety. We managed these matters as wisely as we could and talked to each other frequently to check our own instincts. In the end, when we had to stop, in order to turn to the more formal aspects of the research process (e.g. long one-to-one interviews), prisoners were 'gutted'. We were too. Running the group was taking a full day out of our working lives. The meetings had quickly become a valued routine, with meaning. We remained in touch with many of the participants and found some of them in a future research project, campaigning for a Dialogue Group. But that is another story.

From Dialogue to 'creating miracles'

Prisoners were appreciative of our efforts at Dialogue. At the same time, staff seemed to tolerate (if not quite approve) our modus operandi. The number of prisoners, who went on to agree to be interviewees in the project as it unfolded, suggested to us that our attempts at designing in creative, respectful 'deep- end' methods were successful. It was significant that throughout this process, we were also observing and interviewing staff, so they also had come to trust us and to feel that we appreciated their world view and the risks of operating in a high-security prison. The senior management team and some key staff continued to support our requests to 'make things happen', so that at about four months into the fieldwork, following protracted security procedures, we took ten of our one-year graduate students studying a prison sociology option into Whitemoor, to meet with our Dialogue Group members and share some reading. The prison's staff and senior managers were fully committed to making the event happen, once we had requested it, and so were extremely helpful over the complex arrangements both leading up to the visit and on the day. It was an important day, for all, as the students and the group shared experiences and perspectives and talked together about understanding prisons. The internationally diverse group of students were keen to acknowledge their struggles with reading and essay writing, which gave members of the group (several of whom were Open University candidates) hope and encouragement. That we were all free of the 'social control of talk' (Cohen and Taylor, 1977) was liberating and educationally important all around.

The 'miracle' (as prisoners referred to it afterwards) was creating these encounters – particularly getting the students so deeply 'in' (an ID check, a criminal records check, a search, 24 locked gates, a long walk along five corridors, downstairs into the workshops area and a wait) and the prisoners 'out' (of their cells, passed security checks and away from observing others for the afternoon) – so that they could talk together. It broke all the rules of distrust and made being human and curious together possible. The Dialogue Group laid the way for this event to take place.[7]

A second 'miracle' was the organisation of a table tennis tournament towards the end of the fieldwork stage of the research. One of the team had been asked by several prisoners to take part in a table tennis demonstration in the sports hall, as a result of her skilled playing on the wings in the observation periods of the fieldwork. Keen players in the prison had felt it would be a well-received event for prisoners from the main residential wings to attend a table tennis session in the sports hall where there would be an opportunity to see the game explained and played 'properly' and for prisoners to practise some of the technical shots. Various shots were demonstrated on one table by the researcher and a prisoner who had previously played to a high standard, whilst another prisoner provided an explanatory commentary. Prisoners were then invited to 'have a go' at some of the exercises themselves, and some competition was introduced whereby prisoners were tasked with, for example, seeing how many forehand shots they could play in three minutes, aiming for consistency and accuracy. Several tables were available for prisoners to practise. The event took place during a weekday afternoon in mid-June 2010 after several consultations between prisoners, the researcher and the Physical Education (PE) staff.

Such was the success of the event that prisoners wanted to resurrect the prisoner table tennis tournament, which had taken place in the prison on previous occasions but had lapsed. They were insistent that the researcher should endorse, encourage and support the event with her presence, which she gladly attended. The tournament was organised by prisoners and PE staff and took place on a Saturday at the end of July 2010. On arrival, the researcher found she too had been entered into the tournament, although she had been adamant that the tournament should be an event for the prisoners specifically. She was subject to friendly coercion and played a couple of early-round games. At the end of the tournament, prisoners were awarded prizes and photographs were taken of the participants, organising staff and the researcher.

The playing of table tennis (the organisation of a tournament, informal games on the wings and the table tennis demonstration), like others of the more participatory moments in the fieldwork (learning crafts, sitting in on classes, attending the gym), involved stepping outside of a role, shedding constraints and being authentic. It allowed the researchers to invest their role with their personalities, values and skills (much like good prison officers do). It meant that the researchers were not positioned by prisoners (and the PE staff) as 'just a researcher', and it meant that the prisoners were not positioned as 'just prisoners', but both were, for example, skilled players for that period of time. Both could reveal something more of themselves in a 'safe' and non-prison-specific setting. The playing of sport, with an outsider, allowed prisoners to transcend the boundaries of the prison walls and to alleviate the weight, depth and tightness of long-term imprisonment in a maximum-security setting. Much like the Dialogue Group discussions, there was a shared, novel, experience. The table tennis tournament could have been taking place in any sports hall, and the relationships and interactions that took place there could equally have happened outside of prison. In the case of the table tennis 'workshop' and tournament (and even in eventually gaining security clearance to bring in a personal table tennis bat), we had helped something happen that demonstrated our commitment not to' buy into' the rhetoric of 'public acceptability' and 'risk aversion' or 'risk management discourse': we were hopeful that where trust developed, between us and prisoners, us and staff and around the prison, unconventional events could occur despite 'security risks', but those risks could be managed. This had many positive outcomes.

In the end, the Dialogue Group became a form and mode of communication that set the tone for our research project. It enabled two-way conversation, some shaping of the research agenda and themes, and some sustained and meaningful talk by our participants about *their* world in our, or others', theoretical language. As Pawson has argued:

> Between them the researcher and the subject know a great deal about their subject matters, the trick is to get both knowledge domains – 'scholarship' and 'savvy' – working in the same direction.
>
> (Pawson, 1996: 303)

The Dialogue Group engaged prisoners in a way that has persisted and followed us into other prisons. It was difficult to organise and was time consuming, but it was worth every moment. It was organic and only loosely defined in our request for access. Trust got us the opportunity to do it, and our shared vision of the research process made it an important part of the project:

> Research is after all, an act of human engagement. To achieve criminological *Verstehen* – subjective understanding of situated meanings and emotions – researchers have to be *affectively* present *as well as* physically present in a social situation.
>
> (Liebling, 2001: 474)

There were times when the dialogue was challenging or so emotionally powerful that we found it hard to return to our outside lives. We naturally became engaged in the prisoners' lives and sometimes felt powerless to make anything better for them. We were listening to stories of trauma and chaos or, sometimes, of injustices. The trust built in this forum was in stark contrast to the realities faced by most of the participants in their current predicament:

> You can do good, change, work all this out, but you'll always be the biggest criminal in England in here.
>
> (Prisoner, Dialogue Group)

There was moral and emotional momentum in the group, and we were inevitably caught up in it. This both motivated us in our analysis and exhausted us. Staying sane (i.e. capable of doing the work on a long-term basis) required a wide range of strategies: team talk, reading and reflecting, writing, physical sports and time out. This was 'deep-end imprisonment', and we were immersed in it. As the fieldwork stage of our research came to an end, we were delighted to receive news by letter from several of the participants in our group. Some had moved on; others had moved on and returned. All gave us news of others in the group. We caught up with one or two in new places and watched their development with interest and sometimes with concern. We also retained a lasting interest in the prison and its evolution under new governors. The project became, in part because of the lives we encountered, 'unfinished business'.

The two Dialogue Groups described took place in somewhat similar settings, but in very different social contexts and political climates. Cohen and Taylor carried out their study during a 'wave of radicalism' in university and prison politics (Walton and Young, 1998), two projects with which they were aligned in their roles in the National Deviancy Conference and the New Criminology movement, as well as in their intellectual orientations, more generally (Taylor et al., 1973). They were critical criminologists, challenging the positivist tradition and the structure of power on which it rested. Their methodological and political commitments were well defined and complementary. Our Dialogue Group took place in the recent present, a time of narrower political vision in which the term 'radicalisation' has come to mean something quite different. But the same processes of social control in polarising, labelling and confirming its own stereotypes could be clearly observed.

Our criminology, originally grounded in and inspired by the sociology of deviance and the New Criminology, is more methodologically diverse, and it is politically constrained by the rules of funding and access. We are 'utopian realists', in Loader's term (1998), seeing links between our research and 'the public sphere', supporting a humanistic vision of the social world and believing in the 'basic unity and equality of human beings' (Harrison and Macfarlane, 2014: 108). Our view of power and the powerless is less idealistic and romantic than that of criminologists writing in the 1960s and 1970s, although our sympathy for, and often intellectual alignment with, members of our group was real. Through our Dialogue method, however, our participants expressed a reading of their predicament that was 'fully social'. Their political awareness was more dormant than in Cohen and Taylor's study, a characteristic of late-modern capitalism, but it was rising as prison sentences lengthened and penal policy hardened. Inequalities in life chances were obvious. Ethical and political themes emerged with power and energy. Long-term prisoners were the budding 'new criminologists'.

Our research task was 'to see the relevant individuals in their wholeness and particularity and to see what, morally speaking, is at stake', 'to grasp the "shape" of the situation' (Dancy, in Jollimore, 2013). Dialogue facilitated this and made us better interviewers and scholars. We found fundamental problems of social order, justice and humanity. This, in itself, is a normative and political act. As Richard Sparks has observed, long-term imprisonment 'points up rather sharply both the more brutal and the more humane poles of possibility' (Sparks, 2002: 578). The project we were invited to repeat had a 'civic' as well as intellectual importance (ibid.: 558), and Dialogue was a way to enter and explore the field respectfully and deeply. In the end, the research method shaped us and has had lasting effects on our vision of the kind of society we want to live in.

Notes

Universities of Cambridge, Suffolk and Leeds, respectively. Special thanks are due to our Dialogue Group participants and to successive governors and staff at Whitemoor prison for allowing and facilitating our research. Thanks are also due to Yvonne Jewkes for helpful feedback and editorial suggestions and to Rod Earle for stimulating comments on a first draft.

1. Whilst we are huge admirers of their work, our approach differs from theirs in several important respects. We fundamentally disagree with their approach to prison staff, which is demeaning and unscholarly, and we are not advocating the breaking of research rules but advocate a more flexible set of rules and assumptions about what constitutes good research.
2. Dialogue Groups were pioneered within Whitemoor as an 'innovative approach to groupwork ... based on meaning as the primary principle' (Garratt, 1991).
3. The readings included: Hallsworth and Silverston (2009) 'That's life innit: A British perspective on guns, crime and social order'; Hannah Moffatt (2005) 'Criminogenic needs and the transformative risk subject'; Sparks and Bottoms (2008) 'Legitimacy and Imprisonment Revisited: Some Notes on the problem of order ten years after; and Liebling, assisted by Arnold (2004) Prisons and Their Moral Performance, section on 'Trust', pp. 240–51.
4. Key Performance Target numbers.
5. Senior Officer.
6. Imprisonment for Public Protection: a version of 'two strikes and you are out'; an indeterminate sentence with a tariff.
7. The prisoners and the students still talk about this event, to us and to each other.

Further reading

Liebling, A. (2015) 'Description at the Edge? *I-It* and *I-Thou* Relations and Action in Research', *International Journal for Crime, Justice and Social Democracy. Vol. 4, No. 1 18–32.*

Liebling, A. (1999) 'Doing Prison Research: Breaking the Silence?' *Theoretical Criminology,* 3(2), 147–73.

Liebling, A. and Costa, J. (2016) 'Being Human as a Method and Research Finding in Social Science', in Coffman, D. (ed) *Festschrift for Jonathan Steinberg* (London: Palgrave Macmillan).

References

Agar, M. (1980) *The Professional Stranger: An Informal Introduction to Ethnography* (San Diego, CA: Academic Press).

Banister, P. A., Smith, F. V., Heskin, K. J. and Bolton, N. (1973) 'Psychological Correlates of Long-Term Imprisonment: I. Cognitive variables', *British Journal of Criminology*, 13, 312–23.

Cohen, S. and Taylor, L. (1972) *Psychological Survival: Experience of Long-Term Imprisonment* (London: Penguin Books).

Cohen, S. and Taylor, L. (1977) 'Talking about Prison Blues', in C. Bell and H. Newby (eds) *Doing Sociological Research* (London: George Allen and Unwin).

Dancy, J. and Jollimore, T. (2013) 'Godless but Good', *Aeon Magazine*, http://aeon.co/magazine/world-views/troy-jollimore-secular-ethics/

Garrett, P. (1991) 'Group Dialogue within Prison', in D. Bohm, D. Factor, P. Garrett, *Dialogues – A Proposal*, http://www.david-bohm.net/dialogue/dialogue_proposal.html

Hallsworth, S. and Silverston, D. (2009) 'That's Life Innit: A British Perspective on Guns, Crime and Social Order', *Criminology and Criminal Justice*, 9, 359–77.

Harrison, S. and Macfarlane, A. (2014) *Fieldwork with the Gurungs* (Cambridge: Harrison and Macfarlane).

HMCIP (2008) *Report on an Unannounced Full Follow-Up Inspection of HMP Whitemoor* (London: HM Inspectorate of Prisons).

Liebling, A. (2000) 'Prison Officers, Policing and the Use of Discretion', *Theoretical Criminology,* 4, 3, 333–57.

Liebling, A. (2001) 'Whose Side Are We On? Theory, Practice and Allegiances in Prisons Research', in E. Stanko and A. Liebling (eds) *Methodological Dilemmas of Research, British Journal of Criminology, Special Issue,* 41, 3, 472–84.

Liebling, A. and Price, D. (2001) *The Prison Officer* (Leyhill: Prison Service and Waterside Press).

Liebling, A., Price, D. and Elliot, C. (1999) 'Appreciative Inquiry and Relationships in Prison', *Punishment and Society: The International Journal of Penology,* 1, 1, 71–98.

Liebling, A., Price, D. and Shefer, G. (2010) *The Prison Officer,* Second edition (Cullompton, Devon: Willan Publishing).

Liebling, A.; assisted by Arnold, H. (2004) *Prisons and Their Moral Performance: A Study of Values, Quality and Prison Life* (Oxford: Clarendon Press).

Liebling, A. and Arnold, H. (2012) 'Social Relationships between Prisoners in a Maximum Security Prison: Violence, Faith, and the Declining Nature of Trust', *Journal of Criminal Justice*, 40, 5, 413–24.

Liebling, A., Arnold, H. and Straub, C. (2011) *Staff–Prisoner Relationships at HMP Whitemoor: Twelve Years On* (London: Home Office).

Liebling, A., Arnold, H. and Straub, C. (2012) *An Exploration of Staff-Prisoner Relationships at HMP Whitemoor: Twelve Years On* (London: National Offender Management Service).
Loader, I. (1998) 'Criminology and the Public Sphere: Arguments for Utopian Realism', in Walton, P. and Young, J. (eds) *The New Criminology Revisited*, pp. 190–212 (Basingstoke: Macmillan).
Moffatt, H. (2005) 'Criminogenic Needs and the Transformative Risk Subject', *Punishment and Society*, 7, 29–51.
Pawson, R. (1996) 'Theorizing the Interview', *British Journal of Sociology*, 47, 2, 295–314.
Sparks, R. (2002) 'Out of the "Digger": The Warrior's Honour and the Guilty Observer', *Ethnography*, 3, 4, 556–81.
Sparks, R. and Bottoms, A. E. (2007) 'Legitimacy and Imprisonment Revisited: Notes on the Problem of Order Ten Years after', in J. Byrne, F. Taxman and D. Hummer (eds) *The Culture of Prison Violence*, pp. 91–104 (Boston: Allyn and Bacon).
Taylor, I., Walton, P. and Young, J. (1973) *The New Criminology: For a Social Theory of Deviance* (International Library of Sociology, London: Routledge).
Walton, P. and Young, J. (eds) *The New Criminology Revisited* (Basingstoke: Macmillan).

4
'Get In, Get Out, Go Back?': Transitioning from Prison Ethnography to Prison Policy Research in Russia

Laura Piacentini

Introduction

Prisons are unpredictable worlds that exist in time and space. They are institutions people 'go to' acting as both a product and a generator of society's lost trust in acts of malevolence, crime and reoffending (Wacquant, 2002). Prisons have endured for centuries, and, consequently, the arrangement of people, activities and buildings are deeply implicated in a power–knowledge couplet (see Foucault, 1980) where phenomena, events and structures of history are registered and dispersed. Indeed, the prison is one of very few institutions where pain, suffering and power are depressed into the entire infrastructure and social fabric. In my ethnographic work, a combination of sheer curiosity that Russia remains an uncharted penal territory for Western scholars, coupled with a long-standing personal interest in the region that extended to mastering the language, made the site one of rich and potent allure. What I have learned about all prisons – from doing prison research in Russia – is that 'the place' (jurisdiction) and the 'the site' (the prison) are the repositories of a unique cultural relationship: the relationship between the prison and the state is a clear mirror reflection of the relationship between the person and the state. Thus, the prison reveals the state, which is why prisons are such unique sites of sociological enquiry.

In this chapter, I have two aims. First, I will reflect on almost 20 years of doing ethnography in Russian prisons. What I hope to achieve is a better understanding of the totality of the physical, emotional and intellectual challenges of researching a hidden penal system such as Russia's, one which looms large and vast across the European sphere and which weighs heavily in the histories of incarceration in high punishment societies. My own prison research journey is one in which the historical and cultural registers of incarceration can be understood as ruptured, contingent and in a state of cultural to-ing and froing. I now understand my long-term activity in prison research as characterised by moments of both *ethnographic mobilisation* and *ethnographic immobilisation* of the self in penal space.

When I reflect on ethnographic mobilisation, I was thrown into a jail environment so chaotic, remote, live, accessible, exciting and unusually welcoming (given its hiddenness from the scholarly world) that nothing less than total linguistic, cultural and residential immersion would have worked to complete my research. This is not to claim that mine's is an experience of personal incarceration, but my success in maintaining integrity in the field was measured by my psychosocial and cultural responsiveness to the *Rysski mentaliet* (Russian mind-set). The shock and awe of rapid mobilisation produced rich data from large-scale surveys, qualitative interviews, archival research, oral history analysis and participation in rituals such as collective mourning over incarceration ideals long since gone. Emotions – my emotions – played an integral role in the intellectual strategies and research design I employed. I discuss this further on but suffice to say, writing oneself into the lives of (penal) others and not hovering above the penal environment has elicited new insights into how people themselves navigate the vagaries of penal power and how they experience Russia's exceptionally complex penal history today. But whilst the Russian prison system has aged and attempted to become more modernised, it has also suddenly regressed. Its arrested development has been accompanied by an intensification in my own intellectual and, if I am frank, emotional commitment[1] to dig deeper inside this vast penal monolith to hopefully excavate for historical and cultural penal artefacts.

When I reflect on *ethnographic immobilisation*, I refer to overt and benign sexism, exploitation, humiliation, observing dire squalor, danger, risky self-placement and over-immersion in the field. But immobilisation of the self in my own prison ethnographic story also refers to my second aim in this chapter, which is to ask, as a postscript, how do we interrogate the effects of prison research on the self when the scholarship undertaken moves from field site to policy site? What is the place of emotions in policy critique, and where do emotions go? For it must also be said that prisons not only exist in space and time but also exist in policy and law. This begs the question as to whether in *penal policy scholarship* 'emotions' become invisible? Is there a need for emotional safety out of the prison field or is the place of emotion in policy critique the preserve of the penal reform movements?[2]

In the first part of this chapter, I offer my own considerations of why we need prison ethnography and its positionality as part of valid social science research design. In the second part, I reflect, and bring together, my thoughts on the ethnographic and ethical frameworks that I use in Russian jail research. In the third part, I change gear and ask how emotion is measured in policy analysis. That is, when we take the researcher's body out of the culture where prisons are and, therefore, take the body out of prison, what is left and can emotion have a place in critical policy analysis? In my conclusion, I introduce a discussion on the role of the researcher in policy critique and ask questions about the place for emotional narratives, when temporarily transitioning out of the prison field.

We need prison ethnography!

When referring to methodology, social scientists often debate the best methods for studying social phenomena and, quite often, disagree. The setting and the type of information sought remain the key drivers of the method to be utilised, with some arguing that the best methods are participant observation whilst others will rely on survey methods. Some settings provide particular constraints on researchers due to their configuration, the nature of the study, the subjects who are participating (and their place in society) and the overarching rules governing access to participants. Some forms of information sought are so complex, contentious and troubling that ethical matters can override the pragmatics of capturing everyday life in that particular social milieu. Nowhere is the setting and the type of information sought subject to such scrutiny and reflection than the prison, which since the mid-twentieth century, but particularly in the last 30 years, has produced a veritable avalanche of critical sociological insight, reaching wide audiences and creating new 'truths' about human behaviour, order, power, pain, discipline, hope and human relationships. John Irwin's path-breaking classic on prison ethnography shows a principled opposition to quantitative methods: 'any approach not based firmly on qualitative or phenomenological ground is not only a distortion of the phenomenon but is also very likely corruption' (Irwin, 1987: 42).

Irwin goes on to add that it is only through participant observation, guided by theoretical observation, that a researcher is able to reconcile the need for knowledge with the need for objectivity. In addressing these contrary ontological–epistemological tendencies, and the need for balance between being a 'complete participant' or an 'objective outsider', Davis (1973) makes the salient point:

> For in the end, the capacity to experience the word freshly from the outside and knowingly from the inside is part of the duality of intelligent social life itself. To replicate in our sociological research this duality through an ongoing *interior dialogue* which constantly counter poses the stark epiphanies of the one to the intimate knowingness of the other.
>
> (Davis, 1973: 342, emphasis added)

Clearly then, access to 'intimate knowledge' involves letting go of detached objectivity and seeing the group wholly from its members. To paraphrase Rabinow (1988), total immersion in the field changes what we see such that what had been a part has now become a whole, creating a completely new sense of the 'individual' in social settings. The classic prison sociology studies reveal a force of engagement with the field, its captives and custodians (and include Sykes, 1958; Clemmer, 1958; Goffman, 1958; and Cohen and Taylor, 1972) that we rely upon today because these studies address one of the central issues of our time: what are the social features of penal forms? Moreover, whilst many of these works do not describe their method as explicitly 'ethnographic' common to them all is the sociological significance of being there and a desire to 'know' and 'understand' over and above 'recording' what the research is really about. The focus on prisons' social effects has, until recently, overcrowded prison sociology to the detriment, some argue, of the effects of prison research on the emotions of the researcher despite this being a most fraught and intense environment (see Piacentini, 2004; Jewkes, 2014; Liebling, 2014). As Jewkes (2014) notes: 'there is an unspoken understanding that if we disclose the emotions that underpin and inform our work, our colleagues will question its "validity" and perhaps even our suitability to engage in criminological research' (Jewkes, 2014: 63).

Emotions, therefore, become the competing narrative between what is valid and reliable and what is, simply, 'over-emoting' or as an academic friend once said to me, 'go on, have a right good moan!' What the classic sociological studies of the prison from the 1960s onwards had not anticipated was the scale of imprisonment in the late twentieth century and, in particular, the immediate future of US imprisonment. Penal institutions the world over circulate continuously in both public consciousness and the sociological imagination, affecting what we think and feel about the idea of 'the carceral'. As one such member of the prison sociology community, I want to ask questions about the construction of this 'penal commonsense' and its worldwide spread. I want to know how penality coheres with crime, but I also want to know the place and purposes of how 'the state', 'culture' and 'community' are represented in penality's unfolding. This is because we are living through a period of deep cultural attachment to confinement in which ideas such as the 'new punitiveness' (Pratt et al., 2005), the 'new penology' (Feeley and Simon, 1992) and the 'culture of control' (Garland, 2001) place risk and danger at the centre of a new golden age of hyper-incarceration (see Wacquant, 2002).

Prison scholarship has never been healthier – or more international – because of the seemingly inexorable rise of prison populations in most Western nations but also due to the simple fact that the social response to crime and its control is so pervasive, so complex and so contested. It is in this sense that we should understand the incredible diversity of prison scholarship against a more sinister backdrop of penal excess. Thus, the embedded practice of carceralism has placed imprisonment centrally in public consciousness and everyday life. Of note, however, is that penal reform has had less of an impact on penal reductionism, which provokes the question as to how, when campaigns for penal reductionism are at their most visible and vocal, our cultural attachment to incarceration is intensifying. That aside, the setting of the prison is generating a profoundly self-reflexive research moment in sociology and criminology. It has been almost 20 years since I began researching the sociology of the prison and now make sense of the prison as a profoundly cultural world, a world in which when I enter I am forced to question the traditional modes of prison representation; I have come to understand the penal body politic as a complex and protean one. Yet, when I encounter prisons, anywhere, there is a residual taken for grantedness that goes along the lines of: this is a territory where the contained have become the subject of scientific scrutiny, to be studied in terms of causality. Or what Foucault (1980) refers to as the anatomical gaze where a modern conception of the diseased, the excluded, the-in-need-of-discipline is now constituted as a body subject to regulation and bio-power. Prison, therefore, is centrally about bodies held in regulatory space.

The diverse prison research landscape in front of us has led me and other prison sociologists to reach for new dynamic, epistemological possibilities in better understanding the embodied experience of prison. One development, introduced earlier, can be found in the idea of connecting to the research field through acknowledging the role that emotions, integrity and relational engagement play between researcher and participant. That is mapping the researcher's body on to the territory of prison research, which can produce meaningful and valid methodologies, enhance the data collection and produce substantive gains in the analysis and writing up. Rowe (2014), quoting Hammersely and Atkinson (2007), captures the essence of mapping the body on to the prison site well: 'the participant researcher is the research instrument par excellence' (Rowe 2014, 404, reprinted in Chapter 18, this volume). The ethnographic method – being there, getting close, deep immersion, navigating insider/outside boundaries, connecting to the hidden world and the participants of that world – has produced a polyphony of voices and emotional reactions to the socially complex and impaired world of incarceration.

In Forsythe's insightful study of ethnography in technology design research, she argues that ethnography looks and sounds straightforward, that anyone can do it, but as a method, ethnography *enables* deep perspective and an understanding of what events mean to actors themselves as opposed to what that they would mean if a fieldworker would have done them (Forsythe, 1999). Anthropologists have also expressed strong reservations at do-it-yourself ethnography because it might create superficial social research. Indeed, a trained prison fieldworker will always view ethnography as part of a design process, not a cognitive hall of mirrors. Ethnography helps me to avoid looking at the embodied experiences of incarceration from an (at times) disembodied perspective, or detached position. As others before me have stated, total disembodiment is simply impossible because doing prison ethnography can take the scholar to incredible depths of understandings that go some way in offering new sources of knowledge that do not rely upon a more desk-based approach (see Crewe, 2014a, 2014b). Jewkes (2014) goes further and argues: 'I believe that our personalities, histories and emotions penetrate our research in ways that can ultimately enrich our analysis, and give life, vividness and luminosity to our writing' (Jewkes, 2014: 387).

In addition, prisons do not represent 'normal life' but instead take the form of a purified shape whose outline is rejection, confinement and exclusion (Bauman, 2000). Of significance to the ethnographic craft, therefore, is the question of putting the visible self inside a social form of limitless contradiction, pain and intensity. The prison is where one simply cannot avoid affect on vision, mobility and hearing. Presented in these terms, the researcher's body cannot be ignored but becomes central to alerting us to new ways of understanding how the circuits of power flow, or are disrupted. Hence, if social research requires expertise in writing about emotions – which is not the same as writing emotionally – then ethnographic approaches can assist sociologists to challenge the realist traditions in research methodology and conventional assumptions about imprisoned bodies (see Clifford, 1983; Coffey, 2000). Turning attention to my own prison scholarship, in the following section, I describe the ethnographic experiences of prison research in Russia, and I provide new data from diary notes, findings and observations from the following published studies: Piacentini (2004, 2007) and Pallot and Piacentini (2012).

Transitioning in: Subject, project, me?

Earlier in the chapter, I referred to emotional commitment as part of a research design that includes ethnography. Emotional commitment has acted as my own personal benchmark of maintaining integrity and ethics in the field. Echoing Goffman, emotional reactions are entirely normal, indeed necessary, because they involve presenting the self to others (see Goffman, 1958; Jewkes, 2014). It is important to emphasise that emotional commitment is not a methodology in and of itself but instead part of a way of seeing and feeling events, populations and social milieu and placing private thoughts within a cultural and sociological context.

There is an unavoidable cultural repertoire associated with prisons in Russia because current carceral forms and norms contain remnants, or echoes, of wider cultural beliefs about 'being Russian' that provide for an intense common-sense coherence (see Smith, 2008). Kharkhordin (1999), mapping out the theoretical territory of what it means to be an individual in contemporary Russian society, makes the salient point that in the post-Soviet period 'collectivism', the professed hallmark of Marxist/Leninist life has given way to an outpouring of internal, previously privatised desires and emotions that are non-linear, fluid and messy. In the immediate post-Soviet period, there was a momentous cultural shift between an official discourse that banned the values of individual autonomy and expression, to one that reverses this and externalises values and practices. Nowadays, the present revival of authoritarian orthodoxy under President Putin represents a vision of the future legitimated through backward-looking nostalgia. Interestingly, there are echoes here of Stuart Hall's account of 'regressive modernisation' under Thatcher's authoritarian populism project in 1980s Great Britain. What is distinctive about Hall's theorisation (in relation to Russia) is how authoritarianism was harnessed to create a similar affect: populism which is intended to mobilise people through the 'fears, the anxieties, the lost identities of a people' (Hall, 1988: 167). As a result of over 20 years of amassing hundreds of prisoner and prison staff interviews, I have learned that the penal actor in Russia today has a rich emotional vocabulary that she or he wants to share and which expresses these intertwining ideologies of the self and the loss of the collective. Take this previously unpublished interview I carried out with a prison officer in 2003:

> Well I see myself as a prison officer, I see myself as a worker, a man who comes to work, does his job and then goes home.
>
> Interviewer response: I see. Do you think that these feelings are different from the late 1980s when you started out as a 'Soviet correctional officer'? Have your feelings changed at all?
>
> [ponders and looks downcast] Yes and no. I was so proud of my job. I was a Soviet prison officer! I think about this more now than I did then... I feel... I don't know how to say it... I feel like a different man... I am supposed to do X and Y now... human rights... [waves hand dismissively]... that was different from before... I feel.... I just feel... sadder now.

By putting aside what I knew intuitively would have been an impractical distance between respondent and interviewee, I respond to this despondent and sombre reflection with my own personal story of living in Odessa, Ukraine, in 1996. I am working towards emotional connectedness here and, therefore, integrity. My field diary response is as follows:

> I understand, I lived with a Russian couple of former engineers. The man was a bouncer now in a nightclub. He had lost his job in 1992 after 30 years as an army engineer. He was a big proud Russian man who drank too much and was depressed and alone most of the time. His wife had enough of the

> drinking and depression and just left! I was left alone with the bouncer for the rest of my time there but we started to bond and it became easier. He felt confused too.

In this interaction, a high-trust environment was created because it opened up a long series of conversations between several prison guards and me about 'being Russian'. I came to know 'the field', not just of prisons but of Russian culture, from an epistemological participative position. Most of the prison officers I have interviewed in Russia would spend the time together with me talking me through 'life in Russia'. Often I was told, 'Let's not talk about jails, let me tell you about me, my family, my life'.[3] This is similar to Liebling's (2014) observation that we 'forget we are in prison and feel a form of friendship building' (Liebling, 2014: 484), except that in my case it is *incumbent on me* to forget I was in prison. Looking back at these spells of fieldwork between 1997 and 2007, there was a lot of posturing and parading of masculinities, familial roles and paternalism leading to over-immersion in the field. Alternative research strategies were pointless. And my success at fieldwork was contingent on 'just being me', which initially was frustrating and disorienting because I was there to research imprisonment not engage in self-scrutiny (which is, of course, Jewkes' (2014) well-made point about how insights of self and insights of penal site meet and mesh). Smoothly run research encounters would have failed to materialise unless I was, and continue to be, willing to leave prison talk to one side. This is a further dimension to emotional commitment: suspending the academic self temporarily, with all the authority, labelling, suspicions and interrupted interactions this would be bring and engage in acts of 'speaking of feelings and minds in common'. In order to understand the larger, relational world I inhabited in Russian prisons, and to have a chance of moving the research towards critical prison sociology, a spirit of companionship was fostered. In my field diary on another evening, I have the following recorded:

> I found today's interviews a bit upsetting and confusing. I feel I have some idea about how the prison officers are struggling nowadays. I don't feel I spent much time today talking about imprisonment and I'm a bit panicked at this... not sure what data I have... but we did spend a long time just chatting about life in Russia. It was all quite sad really.

My subjective experience was later shared by two colleagues who participated in a major research study into the relationship between women's imprisonment and geographical distance in Russia. On a pilot trip in 2006 published in a study by Piacentini et al. (2009), myself and one other of our team were subjected to the *ethnographic immobilisation* referred to earlier. The limits of empathy and emotional commitment were tested after a cultural ritual. This event acted not as a catalyst in my quest for more knowledge (which the diary entry above shows was a matter of some concern), but was instead an undesirable by-product of deep cultural immersion and I felt neutralised and angry afterwards as the following diary extract shows:

> Conference event went ok and we've set up the main fieldwork sites for next year. Had to attend a banquet. Loads of booze, and an amazing table of food. Then the music came on. All the men and senior prison staff were pretty drunk, dancing with the Russian men and women who were singing national songs and dressed in traditional Slavic costume. At first it was ok and familiar and then we were invited up. We politely refused several times but were persuaded to the point of feeling like we had no choice and had to join in the dance.... We were both so embarrassed and nervous. I felt sick and angry because the Russians moved away and we looked pretty stupid just dancing.

At the time, a feeling of being a half person was overwhelming: one day one is showing emotions of warmth, engagement and connection, leading to positive data collection experiences, and the next day, feelings of anger, disgust and tension formed into negative judgements and a need for distance. As Katz (2004) has observed, moving from the emotion of connectedness to the emotion of disembodiment and detachment can create psychological chaos in researchers as they try to consider how a state of being bears upon the researcher's obligation to be reflexive about the position from which we choose to speak. The 'reality' was that many data collection experiences I have gathered – and will accumulate again in my next study – led me to pursue a particular path of epistemological enquiry, which is asking an empirical question about culture's bearing on penal developments.[4] Emotional identification with the field site revealed to me how the prison is a key arena of culture and ideology: 'penal practices' argues Garland 'are shaped by the symbolic grammar of cultural forms as well as by the more instrumental dynamics of social action, so that, in analysing punishment, we should look for patterns of cultural expression as well as logics of material interest or social control' (Garland, 1990: 199). Garland was examining Western penal development, and despite the paucity of scholarship on the cultural meaning of punishment in non-Western jurisdictions, Garland shows how *institutional language and values* come to be formed from outside-to-inside in non-Western penal cultures. According to Garland (1990) and Smith (2008), penality's role in the creation of culture is, therefore, to communicate meaning and is both its cause and its effect. Hence, Russia's cultural penal paradox is this: as the Soviet era is becoming more and more distant, remaining there, still, are signifiers of social/institutional life of prisons, from the architectural design of communal living, which carries forward Gulag prison design, to feminine-preserving beauty contests and the organised criminal gangs who practise a form of prisoner self-governance.

Integrity and emotional commitment

When transitioning into a prison site, the fieldworker makes multiple commitments to others on site. This has led to a very noticeable and recurring research dilemma of demonstrating integrity and accountability to a range of penal actors. My response to these dilemmas is to bring us back to what I think must be the central proposition for ethnographers and this is: 'what does an ethnographer hope to find in the ethnographic connection'? Jensen (2009), discussing integrity in business studies scholarship, writes:

> integrity [in our model] is a purely positive phenomenon. It has nothing to do with good vs. bad, right vs. wrong behaviour. Like the law of gravity the law of integrity just is, and if you violate the law of integrity . . . you get hurt just as if you try to violate the law of gravity with no safety device.
>
> (Jensen, 2009: 15)

In summarising my approach to prison ethnography, I would argue that the following four themes are useful as reflexive guidance questions for data collection, analysis and establishing boundaries:

- What I say – stating explicitly what I set out to achieve.
- What I know – doing research as I know it is meant to be done. Who do I hold myself out to be?
- What is expected of me – even when not explicitly expressed, what do others expect me 'to do'?
- What I stand for – fundamental to who I am and why I am there.

It is what is said by me and what is said by *my actions* that are the keys to my ethnographic approach, and at the centre of this is integrity. Integrity is the cornerstone of all research, yet it is not explored in great depth in ethnographic research and is taken to be as a given. Integrity is as much about virtue as it is about wholeness and completeness. It is about 'honouring your word', which is the same as saying, 'I will honour the standards for research that I set'. It cannot, therefore, be described as research instrument. In honouring standards set, appropriate parameters are laid down, and it is these parameters that make them effective tools for understanding the human behaviour that we study. Yet, integrity is also the consistency of actions, the clarity of thoughts and deeds and the truthfulness of values presented and developed. To have integrity, therefore, is to aim for wholeness and positivity and to produce workable frameworks that enhance performance in the research field. And so too is the case with accountability that without it the protocols we follow and the quality of the measures we put into place to ensure we protect our participants' confidentiality will fall apart. Without integrity, there is no accountability. The following two diary entries from 2007 reveal that despite the reality of feeling uncomfortable in the field, emotional identification with the external-to-prison context was vital to create effective integrity and robust research positionality:

> Set off to a beauty pageant alone from my prison digs through snow to the recreation hall. It was dark, cold and quiet. Overwhelming feelings of living in a jail, really cold, Russia, snow. Walked into find a sea of faces, dark prison clothes, shaved heads and silence. Couldn't stop thinking of prison memoirs. Loads of guards with rifles and then me and something like 300 male prisoners. Tried to smile at prisoners. They stared into space and when music came on and dancers appeared, the stony faces stayed and we all clapped at the same time. Had loads of questions but decided best to just clap along.
>
> (1997)

> Today was my third beauty pageant and talent show. All three of us went. Here we go again. Just a few guards this time and no prisoners. The young woman prisoner's ballet tutu fell to her feet. It was a moment of embarrassment for her and we just sat there... staring into space... she recovered well. We talked about it afterwards and we had different views but I just felt cynical even though we were told the women prisoners loved putting on the show.
>
> (2007)

These two excerpts reveal how the impact of how I am *for myself* and the impact on how I am *for others* were determined by the nature of what I stand for. Indeed, advancing of knowledge relies on trust and honesty that must be established well in advance of entering the field and always maintained whilst there. My story is therefore an *ethnography of discovery* conducted well in advance, even years before the site is entered. Yet, prison ethnography is more than a journey of discovery. It is also a process of theoretical validation. The get-close approach to prison ethnography demands often contradictory tasks where one has to develop a 'feel' for the prison through rapport building and management of multiple standpoints and interests. As Phillips and Earle (2010) note, knowledge produced from situated experiences not only creates nuanced knowledge of the realities of those under investigation but also represents social structures and multiplicities of experience that are intersectional and reflexive. By implicating oneself in the subject of choice, getting inside the field and then in the writing up, the researcher, as I have said elsewhere, is *writing themselves into the story*, and this can provoke a researcher into settling on a surer conceptual framework for the world they are observing (see Piacentini, 2007). A corollary of understanding prison fieldwork in this way is the disparate views that can be held between researchers coming from different disciplines into a shared field site (as was the case in the different interpretations of the beauty pageant of 2007).

Conclusion

Having integrity, honouring your word whilst articulating the conflicts of the social world and its consequences, is riddled with problems, especially where the political and social environment is as challenging and turbulent as it is in Russia. For prison ethnographers, the prison site is highly complex anyway, because it is subject to a particular form of *representation* (public/political/cultural/contingent/emotional), which means that the balance between integrity and accountability is more acutely felt as the choice of site is pointedly challenged (I refer here to the often-asked question, 'why prison research'?). A total and a totalising institution, the prison is both a closed space and a porous place where ideologies, practices and pains ebb and flow, where experiences are shared and stories with a beginning, a middle and an end unfold (sentences are completed, lights are turned off and on, timetables are set, doors are locked and opened, guards return home). Moreover, entries and exits are multiple and contingent. Prisoners also have to commute this emotional minefield. Preconceptions about penal punishment are disrupted as soon as you walk into a prison, because it is also a place where things are not said, truths are not admitted to, feelings are not shared and realties are not exposed.

Penetrating prison experiences creates immediate ethnographic burdens of seeing and then writing. It is this very essential nature of the penal sphere that demands of us openness to change and willingness to see everything. Going back to a point I made earlier about what the ethnographer hopes to find in the field, ethnography is both the story and the webs of meaning (Geertz, 1973) underlying 'the story'. Prison ethnographies, then, can never be fully fledged or completely whole unless we look at the totality of seeing that exists between people and the environment, all wrapped not very neatly around a highly regulated space. I also outlined how prison researchers often describe how their psychosocial defences are challenged. To be sure, what is demanded of me (from my participants) is a visible *ethnocultural* field enquiry. I have learned (accepted?), persuaded by my gatekeepers and my participants, that to silence the inquisitive voice and not interrogate 'life stories' would silence my participants' voices, would lead my participants to question my integrity and potentially shut down the research process. Thus, the cost, both personal and to research, is always potentially high when an ethnographer does not have integrity.

In summary, if integrity is the formal relation one has to oneself and standing for something, what are the effects of having integrity during prison research? I have in the past had an almost unimpaired access to opportunities to get as close as I could, and as close as I desired, to the field. This has now changed and my integrity, whilst creating hiddenness through acceptance and 'being one of them', nowadays, is subject to dispute not because I am not honouring myself but because the research environment is highly politicised. As a postscript then, I would like to raise a hitherto under-explored prison sociological question on the theme of *transitioning out*, temporarily, from field site to policy critique. The central question I ask below is: what is the place of emotions in policy critique? Where do emotions go?

Postscript: Transitioning out, ethnography or policy critique?

Forsythe (1999) describes ethnography as invisible work, adding that when a researcher is 'just chatting', this is no more than when a doctor is 'just talking to patients'. In other words, a competent prison researcher will take people's views and feelings as *data*, not as *results*. My intention to this point was to show how the analytical expertise deployed in prison ethnography is a form of 'cognitive walk-through', which can be understood as an experiential moment, a gathering of voices, a continual questioning of 'for whom and for what' and a heightened awareness of flows of meanings and ruptures in relationships. Whilst an approach of ethnocultural connectedness is essential in overcoming overgeneralisation and creating theoretical rigour, minimising overgeneralisation and heightening theoretical rigour are also tenets of good policy critique and cannot be said to be the preserve of field research. As mentioned in the introduction, prisons exist in space and time, but they also exist in policy and law, where a critique may reveal a heightening sense of how law and policy are mobilised into penal spaces. A heightened awareness of the text, of the discourse and of how penal spaces come to be composed of law and policy gives promise of a diagnosis of penal life that may not be too different in form from the ethnographer's perspective. As I embark on a new Russian prison project that takes me towards my 20th year of prison sociology on this subject, I face a challenge: in the short term, I will not be following the path of prison ethnography – that comes later – so where do I put my emotions when analysing Russian penal policy? Do emotions have a place in policy critique and is there a conflict of coverage between *being there* and *not being there*?

The most obvious place where emotional responses can arouse emotional reactions to imprisonment is the international penal reform movement. If putting more people in jail, and for longer, tests our conventional wisdom of what a prison sentence means, in penal reform discourse this conventional wisdom is emboldened with the narratives of rights violations, degrading treatment and penal atrocity. Penal reform as a movement, and as an ideology, provides the prison sociologist and citizen alike with a rich narrative of 'penal detail' and a place to put their emotional reactions to confinement. The multifaceted nature of penal reform strikes at the roots of penal legitimacy. That is, is the detention of citizens lawful, justified and humane? Penal reform critique is complex not least due to the question of how to enhance the legitimacy of critiquing systems of punishment and at the same time maintaining proximity to the audiences targeted. For our purposes here, this textual reading of penal pain has proved to be effective in mobilising emotional and psychological reactions. This is because of the highly valuable visual messages and textual stories that outline how imprisonment is a painful retribution that strikes a highly sensitive chord both in how the just measure of pain is turned into (sometimes inexplicable) sentencing policy (see Christie, 2000) and in how in prisons, in every context, are the so-called carriers of danger transferred into spaces from which they cannot escape (Bauman, 2000). Is it not, therefore, the case that the prison becomes a site of contested emotionality because we respond to stories of incarceration in a myriad of ways but all pointing unidirectionally towards the prisoner? For example, amongst numerous accounts of painful penal experiences, we often read of the regime that executes children, the death row inmate who was in terrible pain at the point of death, the woman who is stoned to death for 'adultery' or the suicide of vulnerable adult men for whom 'risk assessment' has failed. The above-mentioned examples take the reader and the viewer towards connecting to *prisoners*, to question the legal limits of *punishment* and to see and feel its ubiquitous presence. And yet, prisons' place within society and crime control has become so non-disrupted that we tolerate their normality whilst not tolerating the malevolence of the persons held within (the contained).

Reading penal reform campaigns can induce what Bauman calls 'emotional/attitudinal unity' (Bauman, 2000: 35), because the linguistic temperament of penal reform campaigns forces our eye to view penal experiences as truly atrocious, and we must respond. Thus, through exposing the illegitimacy of punishment forms, the legitimacy of penal reform processes is secured. One important matter that is excluded from the penal reform movement is the rendering of the prison itself as a socially constructed, normative world. A prison sentence is one that requires cultural, political and legal justification from the outside, a symbol not only of society's lost trust in legal obedience but also of society's justification for policies aimed at prisoners. It is the longing for order more broadly defined that ensures a prison's endurance, because, as both Foucault (1977) and Bauman (2000) note, the prison is an expression of society's quest for order, and in a well-ordered society, the norm of order tells people how to behave. It could therefore be argued that aside from penal reform campaigns the desire for a more general social order offers an excuse for 'whatever actions follow that sentiment' (Bauman, 2000: 23). In other words, the more we meet crimes with imprisonment, the more banal and emotionless imprisonment becomes. The question for sociologists of the prison then is whether we can merge the emotions of ethnography with the emotions of policy critique in settings where prisons are regularised, predictable and uniform institutions of norm regulation. There are many ways to conduct prison research, but if we take the researcher's body away from the site, we face the dangerous situation of training the critical eye only on prisoners and not on the site itself as 'the stage of human suffering' (Armstrong, forthcoming: 1). This is due to two factors. First, there appears to be a gap between critical expert knowledges and penal policy reductionism (despite expertise playing a bigger role in penal policy development). Second, as per Armstrong's (forthcoming) argument, there is the process of co-opting penal critique into penal management cultures that de-emotionalise the deleterious effects of incarceration. In effect what Armstrong is saying is that we have become expert in the 'dealing with prisoners' part but ineffective and nullified about the part dealing with the prison's wider social consequence. We have then become 'imprisoned by prison discourse' (Armstrong, forthcoming: 4), which is remarkable since prisons are politically cast and policy relevant (Katz, 2004).

And so there appears to be a growing gap between the high-quality prison ethnographic research outlined in this volume and away-from-prison critical, perhaps even emotional, responses to problematising the prison. This raises the important question: where is it safe to talk about emotions and think reflexively about confinement? As important as joining penal reform campaigns are in creating spaces for emotions to run freely, it is only part of a deeper change in conception, discourse and response to penal policy where we see emotions 'transitioning out' because in policy critique, the prison is understood through the bodies contained and not the through law and order rhetoric or populist punitiveness.

The thriving academic scholarship on prison ethnography speaks directly and powerfully to researcher accountability and non-estrangement. The rich variability of experiences reminds us also that doing prison research is akin to experiencing academic vertigo: not having integrity means being showing variously as inconsistent, unfocused, scattered, unreliable, undependable, unpredictable and generally unaccountable. A stark fact stands out: prison research pushes to the frontline Becker's oft-quoted statement: whose side are we on (Becker, 1967)? In constantly asking this question of ourselves, the moral and emotional density of meaning becomes less of a personal experience and more of one that is theoretically embedded. Moreover, it is also entirely sensible, indeed it is necessary, to ask 'whose side are we on' when conducting non-field site prison critique, not least because of the inevitability of incarceration. Whilst societal turbulence, the like of which I am currently witnessing in Russia, is impacting on how and when I return to the research site, I would suggest that the taken-for-grantedness of how the prison *institution* itself is a site of multiple, complex meanings that render the contained invisible must always be questioned. Thus, integrity is about *honouring* one's word, not *keeping* one's word. In this sense, integrity is 'privately optimal' (Erhard et al., 2009: 29), meaning, I can create meaningful, critical knowledge and have integrity even where the other is negative towards me and, moreover, when I am not 'there'.

Acknowledgements

This article draws upon some work from the study: *Women in the Russian Penal System: The Role of Distance in the Theory and Practice of Imprisonment in Late Soviet and Post-Soviet Russia* funded by the Economic and Social Research Council, RES-062-23-0026, 2006–10. It also introduces a new study funded by the Leverhulme Trust, commencing 2015 and titled *A Sociology of Rights Consciousness amongst Russian Prisoners*.

Notes

1. The term 'emotional commitment' refers here to personal motivation and how one feels and reacts to the penal degradations of living through cultural, political and psychosocial life in a post-Soviet world that many are still trying to come to terms with.
2. That is, we 'feel' the effects of incarceration when we are presented, through the lens of human rights campaigning or 'persons at risk' campaigns, the horrors of unfair trials, mistreatment of prisoners and human rights abuses in both sentencing and brutalising punishments, torture and arbitrary detention.
3. Similarly, see the work of Coretta Phillips and Rod Earle on ethnicity, identity and social relations in prisons published widely, but specifically, here, I refer to Earle (2013) where the author argues that entangled relations between white ethnicities in prison and penal strategies of control can lead to messy and disturbed identities around loss, melancholy and the historical and colonial histories of race, which create certain penal affects.
4. Empirical scholarship looking at culture's effects on penality has yet to be rigorously pursued.

Further reading

Alford, F. C. (2000) 'What Would Matter if Everything Foucault Said about Prison Were Wrong? *Discipline and Punish* After Twenty Years', *Theory and Society*, 29, 125–46.

Heinlein, S. (2013) *Among Murders: Life after Prison* (Berkeley: University of California Press).

Smith, C. (2009) *The Prison and the American Imagination* (New Haven: Yale University Press).

References

Armstrong, S. (forthcoming) *Prison as Stage and Actor.*

Becker, H. (1967) 'Whose Side Are We On?' *Social Problems*, 14, 3, 234–47.

Bauman, Z. (2000) 'The Social Uses of Law and Order', in D. Garland and R. Sparks, (eds) *Criminology and Social Theory* (Clarendon Studies in Criminology: Oxford University Press).

Christie, N. (2000) *Crime Control as Industry: Towards Gulags, Western Style*, Third edition (London: Routledge).

Clemmer, D. (1958 ed) *The Prison Community* (New York: Rinehart Publishing).

Clifford, J. (1983) 'On Ethnographic Authority', *Representations*, 2, Spring, 118–14.

Coffey, A. (2000) *The Ethnographic Self: Fieldwork and the Representation of Identity* (London: Sage).

Cohen, S. and Taylor, L. (1972) *Psychological Survival: The Experience of Long-Term Imprisonment* (Harmondsworth: Penguin).

Crewe, B. (2014a) 'Not looking Hard Enough: Masculinity, Emotion, and Prison Research', *Qualitative Inquiry*, 20, 4, 392–403.

Crewe, B. (2014b) 'The Emotional Geography of Prison Life', *Theoretical Criminology*, May, 18, 2, 56–74.

Davis, F. (1973) 'The Martian and the Convert Ontological Polarities in Social Research', *Urban Life and Culture*, 2, 333–43.

Earle, R. (2013) 'Inside White: Racism, Ethnicity and Social Relations in English Prisons', in C. Phillips and C. Webster (eds) *New Directions in Race, Ethnicity and Crime*, pp. 160–177 (Abingdon: Routledge).

Erhard, W., Jensen, M. and Zaffron, S. (2009) 'Integrity: A Positive Model That Incorporates the Normative Phenomena of Morality, Ethics and Legality', Harvard Business School NOM Research Paper No. 06-11.

Feeley, M. M., and Simon, J. (1992) 'The New Penology: Notes on the Emerging Strategy of Corrections and Its Implications', *Criminology*, 30, 449–74.

Forsythe, D. E. (1999) ' "It's Just a Matter of Common Sense" Ethnography as Invisible Work', *Computer Supported Cooperative Work*, 8, 127–45.

Foucault, M. (1977) *Discipline and Punish: The Birth of the Prison* (London: Penguin Books Ltd).

Foucault, M. (1980) *Power/Knowledge: Selected Interviews and Other Writings, 1972–1977* (London: Vintage).

Garland, D. (1990) *Punishment and Modern Society: A Study in Social Theory* (Oxford: Oxford University Press)

Garland, D. (2001) *The Culture of Control: Crime and Social Order in Contemporary Society* (Chicago: The University of Chicago Press).

Garland, D., Sparks, R. (2000) 'Criminology, Social Theory and the Challenge of Our Times', in D. Garland and R. Sparks (eds) *Criminology and Social Theory* (Clarendon Studies in Criminology: Oxford University Press).

Geertz, C. (1973) *The Interpretation of Culture* (New York: Basic Books.).

Goffman, E. (1958) *Asylums: Essays on the Social Situation of Mental Patients and Other Inmates* (Chicago: Aldine Publishing Company).

Hall, S. (1988). *The Hard Road to Renewal: Thatcherism and the Crisis of the Left* (London: Verso).

Hammersley, M. and Atkinson, P (2007) *Ethnography, Principles in Practice*, Third edition (New York: Routledge).

Irwin, J. (1987) 'Reflections on Ethnography', *Journal of Contemporary Ethnography*, 16, 41–8.

Jewkes, Y. (2014) 'An Introduction to "Doing Prison Research Differently" ', *Qualitative Inquiry*, 20, 4, 387–91.
Katz, J. (2004) 'On the Rhetoric and Politics of Ethnographic Methodology', *The Annals of the American Academy of Political and Social Science,* September, 595, 1, 280–308.
Kharkhordin, O. (1999) *The Collective and the Individual in Russia: A Study of Practices* (Berkeley: University of California Press).
Liebling, A. (2014) 'Postscript: Integrity and Emotion in Prison Research', *Qualitative Inquiry*, 20, 4, 481–86.
Pallot, J. and Piacentini. L. (2012) *Gender, Geography and Punishment: The Experience of Women in Carceral Russia* (Oxford: Oxford University Press).
Phillips, C. and Earle, R. (2010) 'Reading Difference Differently?: Identity, Epistemology and Prison Ethnography', *The British Journal of Criminology*, 50, 2, 360–78.
Piacentini, L. (2004) *Surviving Russian Prisons: Punishment, Politics and Economy in Transition* (Cullompton: Willan).
Piacentini, L. (2007) 'Handle with Care: New and Established Methodologies in Prison Research', in Y. Jewkes (ed) *The Handbook on Prisons* (Cullompton: Willan).
Piacentini, L., Pallot, J. and Moran, D. (2009) 'Welcome to "Malaya Rodina" (Little Homeland): Gender, Control and Penal Order in a Russian Prison', *The Journal of Socio-Legal Studies,* 18, 523–42.
Pratt, J., Brown, D., Brown, M., Hallsworth, S. and Morrison, W. (2005) *The New Punitiveness: Trends, Theories, Perspectives* (Cullompton: Willan).
Rabinow, P. (1988) 'Beyond Ethnography: Anthropology as Nominalism', *Cultural Anthropology*, 3, 4, November, 355–64.
Rowe, A. (2014) 'Situating the Self in Prison Research: Power, Identity, and Epistemology', *Qualitative Inquiry*, 20, 4, 404–16.
Smith, P. (2008) *Punishment and Culture* (Chicago: The University of Chicago Press).
Sykes, G. (1958) *The Society of Captives: A study of a Maximum Security Prison* (Princeton, NJ: Princeton University Press).
Wacquant, L. (2002) 'The Curious Eclipse of Prison Ethnography in the Age of Mass Incarceration', *Ethnography,* 3, 4, 371–98.

5

Ethnography of Writings in Prison: Professional Power Struggles Surrounding a Digital Notebook in a Prison for Minors

Gilles Chantraine and Nicolas Sallée

Introduction

The 'electronic logbook' (EL) is a penitentiary tool created in 2009 by three prison guards. This software application makes it possible to continually record and intensively circulate information on day-to-day events in prison, generating forms of knowledge on prisoners – key components of behavioural control.[1] The prison administration is currently trying to bring the EL into widespread use, arguing that since this system individualises the handling of detained persons, its implementation helps bring French prisons into conformity with the European Prison Rules (EPR). At the same time, the EL has been attacked by activists engaging in the 'legal guerrilla warfare' (Chantraine and Kaminski, 2007) that in part characterises contemporary militant activism in the prison sphere. Thus, taking advantage of a window of opportunity left open when the prison administration delayed having the tool approved by the Commission Nationale de l'Informatique et des Libertés (CNIL), International Prison Watch lodged an unsuccessful complaint with this body in late 2009, demanding that the system be abrogated, to stop what it viewed as the 'collection of sensitive personal data [...] operating outside of any legal framework'.[2]

As explained by Jean-Simon Merandat, head of the 'EPR' mission ordered by the prison administration directorate, the purpose of the EL is threefold: 'the observation and joint-handling of the prisoners; the general tracking of prisoners and prison life; the general observation of detention'. For this reason, the EL 'responds to three major objectives: to pool information with all actors in multiple disciplines supplying and sharing information in real time; to dematerialise procedures; to make information traceable through computerisation'.[3] If these are the formal objectives devolved upon the EL by the Prison Administration (PA), how is it used concretely?

The field study this article is based on was conducted in two prisons for minors (PMs) (Chantraine, 2011).[4] PMs, of which there are currently six, began opening in 2007. At the heart of their operation is the principle of professionals from multiple disciplines sharing responsibility for young prisoners. This requires unusually intensive day-to-day collaboration between prison guards, educators from the Youth Judicial Protection Service (or YJPS educators), teachers from the Ministry of Education and health-care personnel from outpatient consultation units (OCU), which are statutorily not subject to prison administration oversight, being tied to the Ministry of Health. In this context – at least in the prison administration's view – the EL is supposed to play a central role in realising the dream of partnership that the implementation of these new prisons promoted and promised.

Methodology

This contribution is based on ethnographic results stemming from long-term immersions in two distinct PMs. The exploratory phase of our research quickly led us to attribute particular importance to the work tools used by each professional group and especially to the modes of production and day-to-day uses of writings by professionals in the organisational context that shapes them. We consequently developed various complementary methodologies in order to understand the EL for what it is: both a special means of observing professional activity and its associated controversies and a component of this activity, which partially determines its structure and modalities. In this context, we first developed, in the interview guides, where to structure our interviews with professionals, a specific open section on various work tools, including the EL. Next, we negotiated with the directors at the two PMs being studied, and by guaranteeing the anonymity of personnel and prisoners, we obtained permission to print, with the help of the guard in charge of the 'detention management office,' all observations entered into the EL over a one-month period, in order to explore them systematically. We were also able to print – this time by clicking on entries concerning individual prisoners instead of clicking on 'detention' – all entries relating to the prisoners who participated in our semi-structured interviews (they too were anonymised to ensure confidentiality). Thus, we had access to all notes concerning these juveniles since their arrival. This second modality made it possible for us to see how some observations could serve as a 'representational foundation' that partially determines the future prison trajectory of the juvenile in question. Finally, we completed this collection of documents and interviews with two additional, original interviews with the guards in charge of the detention management office. Seated in front of the computer, they concretely discussed the application's complex operation: its advantages and drawbacks, its potential and the controversies it generates. Using these various methodological approaches, we hope to join Michèle Grosjean and Michèle Lacoste's effort to understand the written notes of professionals from several angles, 'by defining the interaction between their material aspects, representational characteristics, enunciative formats and uses within organisations' (Grosjean and Lacoste, 1999: 443).

In conducting our analysis, we will try to 'depart from an ethereal approach to utterance' (Fraenkel, 2007: 103) in order to examine writing – in the context of a 'pragmatic anthropology of the written' (ibid., 108) – as an integral part of a 'course of action'.[5] Similar to how Bruno Latour and Emilie Hermant, in their analysis of Paris signage, conceive of the labelling of streets (Latour and Hermant, 1998) as being part of a much broader apparatus for managing the city's writings, we consider the writing in the EL as just one of many elements in the practice of prisoner and prison surveillance and observation: human and technical surveillance of movement and circulation, prisoner and cell searches, listening in on telephone calls and so on. To this end, embracing the idea that there is an indissociability between, on the one hand, 'the deciphering of writings' and, on the other hand, 'ethnographic observation and in-depth knowledge of the environment in which they are written' (Laé, 2008: 25), it is appropriate to focus on what develops around the EL, in order to understand what is at play within it. We will also look at how notes in the EL written with a descriptive and informative aim fulfil a performative function, organising and structuring present and future actions.[6] We will then apply the notion of an analytical dissociation between the production and reception of acts of writing (Fraenkel, 2007: 104). Several studies show that writings in work contexts have a particularly small number of readers, the writing and its varied media delimiting a 'protected exclusive professional area' (Laé, 2008: 18).[7] However, the computer-based nature of the EL, which allows it to be read throughout the workplace and enables every actor in the PM to print information on paper, calls for a consideration of the extent of its distribution and of what role it plays through the appropriation of its contents in the day-to-day construction of prison trajectories. With the aim of implementing a sociology of professional practices that takes seriously the role of objects, equipment and the environment in the organisation of activities and knowledge (Conein, 1997), we will examine what the uses of the EL tell us about the work of various professionals in prisons and also look at how the EL causes professionals to act, thus shaping prisoner-handling methods whilst also crystallising the professional controversies that surround them. In conclusion, this analysis will highlight the need for ethnographers not only to renew their observation tools with a view to understanding the new complexity of the profession of prison guard but also to reconsider the connection of their empirical analyses to other, more theoretical and macro-sociological analyses, in order to consider contemporary methods of controlling and supervising stigmatised populations.

The writings: Mirroring professional identities

The EL is symbolic of the call, characteristic of the 'PM project,' for partnership and multidisciplinarity under the control of the prison administration. The way it is used or not used day-to-day sheds light on the professional controversies that are developing in relation to these new prisons. In fact, only prison guards use the EL regularly; other professionals tending to neglect it, despite the prison administration's ongoing efforts to encourage their partners to 'play along,' as shown in this statement by a guard in charge of the detention management office:

> What happens afterwards inside the PM isn't very traceable. Each administration individually makes its little contribution to handling the minor. But there isn't any real consistency or tracking. (...) In terms of what we're offering the minor, and whatever group you belong to – the YJPS, the Ministry of Education, or even the prison administration – what I've noticed is that each administration is working on it, but each is doing its own thing and the other administrations don't really know who's doing what (...). We have to succeed in sharing across all of the professional groups; traceability is part of that too.
>
> (Fernand, 38 years old, head guard, detention management office)

Despite these recurrent efforts and demands, most members of the YJPS and OCU make only minimal use of the EL to circulate general or operational information and usually avoid passing judgement on the prisoner's qualities or their attitudes. Others simply refuse to write anything at all in it. Often condemned as 'corporatist' and blamed by the PM hierarchy for hindering the prison modernisation process, the reactions of these professionals express specific visions of the young prisoners' health or education, historically shaped in the context of the development of different professional models.

Resisting the EL as a means of asserting and defending professional identities

EL utilisation and non-utilisation practices, the EL's contents and the way fragments of prison-life observation are recorded in it testify to (and are partially determined by) each professional group's respective history and the power balance between the various administrations within the PM. To clarify this argument, let us begin by looking at a health-care worker's description of his practices and the justifications it contains. Although some health-care personnel resign themselves to recording certain 'factual details' in the EL (e.g., to make it known that a sport certificate was granted to a prisoner), others, like this nurse, even fall below this minimal usage, defending a greater separation between their own administration and the prison administration:

> Do you use tools like the EL?
>
> – I go out of my way not to do so. We got a memorandum from a doctor (I think it was from the Lyon area), a GP in an OCU ambulatory facility who said 'It's very dangerous to write in the EL. This isn't our role. It's not for us to contribute to the EL. Written information concerning the monitoring of patients must not be divulged to the Prison Administration. Or in any case, if you give it to them, you do it at your own risk and peril. In legal terms.' So personally, I'm very careful with that. I go out of my way not to write. Because I tell myself that the EL is a penitentiary tool. To give you an example that reassures me about the idea of not doing it, in V., an adult prison where there are a lot more prisoners and a lot more nurses, no one writes in the EL. They don't even have access to the EL on their computers. The tools are kept very separate. We never touch this penitentiary software tool, and they never touch our computers. If I had to write in the EL in an adult prison, we'd be aware of it. (...) I'm saying that it's a penitentiary tool and that it's not up to me to go writing in penitentiary tools. I'd like to make a list on my computer of people who've been seen by the psychiatrist during the week, and then send it to them, but I don't want to write in a software application owned by the prison. I'm sorry but as a nurse that's not my role. We'll be discussing it with lawyers and jurists someday if it goes too far. Just like I don't think a guard or educator should be coming and writing something in the hospital software. We can't be told to collaborate with the prison and also work separately, and then at the same tell us not to differentiate ourselves when writing on the computers.
>
> (Paul, nurse)

In this nurse's statement, he expresses a combination of things: he mistrusts what he considers a 'penitentiary tool'; he uses other writing tools that allow him to avoid writing in the EL whilst still meeting the prison administration's communication requirements; and he is committed to legal prerogatives relating to 'medical confidentiality', which he presents not only as a legal constraint that in fact significantly restricts the range of data that can be recorded in the EL but also as one of a number of medical care conditions that are based on the establishment of a relationship of trust with the young prisoners.[8]

This nurse's refusal to use the EL has to be understood in light of two trends. The first trend concerns the health-care system's independence in relation to the prison administration, stemming from a reform in 1994. The second trend relates to challenges to this independence, both in the form of changes to penal legislation (Le Bianic and Malochet, 2011) and in the form of the 'PM project' itself, which presents transparency between partners as good organisational sense. It is in the context of this specific challenge that the nurse stresses the fact that health-care personnel in PMs should have the same relationship to the EL as their counterparts in any other prison, hence the reference to adult prisons, where resistance to the EL is just as virulent.

Amongst the administrations urged to collaborate with the prison administration, the YJPS also finds itself in an awkward position, for both historical and organisational reasons. From a historical point of view, in the first half of the twentieth century, the YJPS was built on the foundation of a rejection of the incarceration of juvenile delinquents, in the name of giving priority to their education; it also became an autonomous department of the Ministry of Justice in 1945, autonomising itself from the tutelage of the prison administration. When a decision contained in the Perben law of 9 September 2002 returned YJPS educators to work with incarcerated minors, many in the profession took this as an affront to its history and identity.[9]

From an organisational point of view, the YJPS occupies a unique position within PMs. Whereas the OCU and the Ministry of Education have their own premises within PMs (the 'health care centre' and the 'schooling centre'), making it easier for them to claim a substantial exteriority right inside the prison, educators are asked to work in close collaboration with prison personnel in the prison's housing units,[10] where meals and certain 'free periods' are led and controlled by an educator/guard pair (see Chantraine and Sallée, 2014). Consequently, for educators, establishing autonomy within the PM is something of an endless process, but it is still necessary in order to defend the specificity of their professional identity, as well as the singularity of a way of handling prisoners that cannot be based on the submission of educational practices to security needs serving the management of prison order.

In this context, the EL becomes a conflict object, the limitations on its uses appearing – in the eyes of some educators – to symbolise the independence they have preserved, which is an indispensable basis for individualised educational relationships unhindered by the prison administration's security prerogatives. The educators who oppose the use of the EL therefore emphasise their ethical need – one that stems more from a practical code of ethics than from a legally prescribed or codified element – to respect a 'duty of confidentiality' in order to respect 'the minors' private lives'. Highlighting the specific value attached to writing – which, amongst other things, 'freezes' statements by imprinting a recorded trace – one educator explained that she reserved the use of writing for the internal circulation of information within her administration (in logbooks separate from the EL) and only exchanged information with guards 'orally', 'on particular points that could have an affect on the collective handling of prisoners'. Although some educators use the EL anyway, this educator's position highlights the existence of a process of differentiation between the different professions' writing media and information circulation spaces.

The strategic use of the EL by educators

The ethical scepticism that educators have been developing towards the EL expresses itself in their collective mistrust, if not towards the whole guard corps, then at least towards certain guards. Although some educators – particularly certain contracted educators critical of the reinforcement of the 'YJPS identity' – believe their colleagues are making too much of a fuss about it, the majority of educators have these sorts of concerns about how guards could use the writings that educators record in the EL:

> The question is: who reads it, how is it analyzed, is it understood by the people who read it, is it taken into account by the people who read it? It's read by the prison staff, they [the guards] do of the descriptions, we do the analysis. I can't see myself writing ten lines when they write 3 . . . anyway we don't have the same writing practices . . . .
>
> (Christine, YJPS educator)

By contrasting – in a caricatural way – the guards' 'descriptive' writings and the educators' 'analytical' writings, this educator's criticism of the EL includes a comment on professional differentiation, no longer just in terms of writing media but also in terms of writing practices. Educators sometimes support this sort of comment with a critique of the quality of writings supplied by guards. Thus, one educator, making a joke in front of his guard colleague, explained to us, 'you don't need to know exactly who wrote the note to know if it was an educator or guard who added it. If there are mistakes then it's a guard [laughs].' An hour later, when we reminded him of this remark, he added that 'unfortunately, it's not just a joke . . . sometimes you look at the EL and you can't believe the stupid things written there'. This anecdote tells us something about the strategies educators use to distinguish themselves from guards. Making it possible to combine a consideration of EL use as a writing practice with a consideration of EL use as a reading practice, some educators make a distinction between what is written in the EL and 'truly important information':

> It's not that what's written there is useless, but frankly it's often unnecessary. No, personally, to get the really important information, I read the progress logbook,[11] or a ask the officer in the morning, when I run into him . . . .
>
> (Samia, YJPS educator)

In this statement, it is interesting to observe that the educator in question is not questioning the need to 'get information' from the prison side, but nevertheless considers a discussion with a guard more productive than reading the EL, precisely because the guard in question will have sorted and ranked the important information (compare this with the 'stupid things' mentioned above). In this respect, some educators even consider making ironic use of the EL 'by writing reams that add nothing' to highlight its 'often unnecessary' character. Other educators – a minority of them – consider it necessary to contribute to the EL to counterbalance what they see as the guards' often overly 'simplistic' view of prisoners. This requirement has been relayed by the director of the YJPS service in one of the two PMs, who urged educators to use the EL to 'assert our positions'. Conversely, against this 'clarification' strategy one educator contrasts another strategy of 'vagueness' and 'generality' that only an urgent situation could bring into question:

> I often record very general information because it concerns everyone, but on general matters. I don't go into details... it's very brief [...]. Or after an interview with a young person who'd just arrived, when he described an incident he'd just had with the guards, in which he was genuinely threatened; there was a suggestion that a possible attack might be repeated etc. And there was sincerity so I... I simply wanted to report it as a warning to be vigilant.
>
> (Guillaume, YJPS educator)

This is the strategy that is most successful amongst YJPS educators in the two PMs. Most educators agree to note in the EL only certain 'necessary' and 'sharable' information, particularly when it is a question of protecting a prisoner or member of the PM staff, the issues ranging from the risk of suicide to a suspected attack; we will return to this. This was particularly the case for one young person who was accused of rape and, not having succeeded in hiding the reason for his incarceration, had been targeted by other prisoners:

> 16/12/2009
>
> Subject: General atmosphere – (12:22pm)
>
> Validated 16/12/2009 at 17:00 by... (Head of the YJPS)
>
> Written by: YJPS educator
>
> Details: First contact with the boy. He seems a bit 'simpleminded'.
>
> I'm worried he'll be stigmatised in the living quarters. Pay careful attention!!!
>
> 08/01/2010
>
> Subject: Serious risk observed – (1:19pm)

> Validated 11/01/2010 at 12:01 by... (Head of the YJPS).
>
> Written by: YJPS educator
>
> Details: Following comments made by Baka (timekeeper), Lionel started crying after returning to his cell; the guard told me about this and I called the OCU [outpatient consultation unit] so the minor could see a psychologist. When I went to tell him, the minor was still in tears. I let him know it was possible to see Nadia [the OCU psychologist], and he agreed to go. Then I took a moment to chat in order to comfort him in the situation.

Two comments need to be made about these examples of observations, which are systematically read and validated by a superior. The first concerns the 'subject' of the note, which must be chosen from a predefined list.[12] Whereas guards make heavy use of the subject 'prisoner behaviour', educators rarely make this selection, preferring tabs whose more general headings are supposed to spare them from compartmentalising, potentially stigmatising connotations: 'general atmosphere', 'serious risk identified', 'information transmission file'. Symbolising the stability of their outsider's position within the EPM, professionals working for the Ministry of Education and the OCU use a narrower set of 'subjects'. Thus, teachers use the subject 'behaviour in the schooling centre', whereas members of the health-care centre use the subject 'OCU'.

The second comment concerns the fact that educators, due to their restricted used of the EL, need to separate 'sharable' information from other information that should be protected from general distribution throughout the prison. Educators therefore note this 'other' information in the two paper notebooks they mainly use, which the prison staff is prohibited to see. Guards readily scoff at the educators' writing practices. One guard joked about the educator he was paired with: 'the guy's on his tenth pen since the PM opened; I'm still on my first.'

Let us briefly detail the contents of these two notebooks. The first of them, the instructions and development notebook, is a 'unit book' that is filled out every day by the educator assigned to the housing unit in question. Unlike the EL, the notes are not about specific juveniles, but about the day's events in the prison – a central difference serving the objective of minimising the stigmatising effects of the recorded observations, which are placed in the more general context of the unfolding of the day. However, similar information is to be found in them, relating to the juveniles' behaviour and the general atmosphere in the housing units, in other words events that relate to the inside of the EPM. Very often the notebook is casually left on the educator's desk where it can be seen by everyone in spaces that, in every unit, are shared with guards. However, as soon as the information to be recorded concerns events outside the prison (information provided by the prisoner's family or outside educators, or information concerning the preparation of his release plan), this is noted in a second book, the 'juveniles' notebook', carefully placed in its socio-educational file, itself stored in a locked drawer. Thus, in their note-keeping methods, educators show that they specifically conceive the situation of young prisoners as extending beyond the prison walls. The observations they emphasise amongst themselves aim to place the juvenile's situation back in a broader context, relating it to his family and school situation and sometimes to his psychological state.

The EL's very contents therefore cannot be dissociated from these conditions underlying its use or lack of use by professionals, just as it cannot be dissociated from the alternative writing media used in prison. These contents are read, interpreted and deciphered by various professionals in the PM in light of the controversies surrounding the EL's validity, objectives, contributions, dangers and pernicious effects. However, as we will see below, in some situations the EL can be useful to all of the professionals – even its staunchest critics – as a harmonisation apparatus enabling some prison trajectories to be stabilised. This characteristic shows a diffuse infiltration by the essentially penitentiary categories contained in the EL.

Writings under control

One of the central questions that arises when studying the social construction of acts of writing concerns how public the writing will be. The form and content of a piece of writing, even if influenced by writing models internalised by the writer,[13] are partly determined by the expectation that it will be read and therefore by the nature, status and authority of its reader or readers. In this case, the readers are numerous since every professional in the PM can access EL content through one of the prison's computers by entering their username and password. This means that the EL's 'sphere of exchange', to use a term that Dominique Lahanier-Reuter borrowed from Mikhail Bakhtin, is that 'of a public institutional space' (Lahanier-Reuter, 2010: 61). This space is nevertheless institutionally segmented, and this is one of the EL's main characteristics. When an EL session is opened after a fieldworker logs in, no matter which administration they belong to, the names of the authors of notes do not appear. They will only see the author's grade and the administration he or she belongs to. However, when PM managers log in – again, regardless of which administration they belong to – then the authors' names appear on the notes.[14] As a result of this, the use of the EL is sometimes diverted from its primary function of producing and circulating information about the young prisoners, and it becomes a tool for controlling, even training, various field professionals. We will provide two examples of alternative uses.

The EL, a means of legal protection

As Michèle Grosjean and Michèle Lacoste (1999) have already pointed out in another context, the computerisation of written notes within organisations has reinforced and accentuated the role these play in protecting staff against legal action. In this respect, the EL becomes an essential legal protection apparatus when incidents occur in prison, particularly those relating to suicide prevention. The morally 'intolerable' (Fassin and Bourdelais, 2005) aspect of suicide in prison, especially by a minor, added to the legal responsibility assumed by the PA and the guards on duty the day of any potential 'drama'[15] make the suicide issue an inescapable theme in PMs. Not only do staff – essentially prison staff – believe, correctly or not, that their job is at stake, but they more broadly believe that the whole organisation's credibility is at stake, indeed its very survival. On the part of all members of the PM, regardless of the administration they belong to, this vigilance is not just about detecting the malaise of a juvenile who is unable to cope with prison, or spotting the tactics of a juvenile who is just 'putting it on'. It is also a matter of protecting themselves by making all prevention practices visible and traceable. It testifies to the importance of this prevention issue that it is the area in which one sees the least differences between the writing practices of educators and guards. The EL enables both sides to 'cover themselves' in the case of a suicide attempt, absolving themselves of responsibility, having 'done their job' by reporting a potential risk:

> The guard himself will report it, so it sometimes happens that we have concerns about a kid in his cell after sentencing; he's in tears and it's not doing well at all. So the night staff are immediately advised and he's placed under special surveillance. With the behavioral tracking [EL] it's the same, you can write something anytime. It's read regularly and can lead to special surveillance. (...) We would be responsible if we noticed something and didn't say anything. That's clear.
>
> (Fatima, 35 years old, YJPS educator in a housing unit)

For the same reasons, signalling a risk necessarily implies a reaction on the part of management, who cannot say they knew nothing, should a tragedy occur. Traces 'protect' whilst also triggering action, as we will examine later.

The EL: A means of checking and training prison staff

As a direct result of the conditions determining the distribution and accessibility of notes recorded in the EL (which, as we mentioned above, are differentiated according to the hierarchical grade of the professional who opens the session), the EL is used by prison management as an essential tool for regulating internal professional relations within the prison administration. In fact, writing in the EL is presented by prison management as an 'obligation'. This obligation not only takes on meaning in the process of certifying conformance to the EPR (laughing, an educator recalled that the EL was initially called the EPR by the PM's educators) but is also about the possibility of making the prison staff's work visible. This is what a prison director at one of the two PMs explained:

> When we evaluate interns or assess guards, we retrieve all their observations and look at them. And it's really necessary for understanding how it's used. So it's the number of observations, the quality of observation. I don't really care about spelling mistakes. What I'm really interested in is the relevance of the observation.
>
> (Séverine, PA director)

For field guards, the EL is therefore a means of archiving traces of their work and proof that they did it well. If it is true that, as an assistant director at one of the two PMs stated, 'if you don't know how to observe, you can't be a good guard; you'll always be missing something,' then one's observational abilities have to be made visible to management. Several times we observed guards trying to figure out 'what to write' in the EL, attempting to make the quality of their work and the relevance of their perspective on prisoners visible to management. On the other hand, this use of the EL can also be to a guard's detriment if the management believes his work was done badly. As this young guard explains, the prison management's desire for guards to regularly record notes ultimately 'turned against [him]':

> Actually, the management doesn't really know what goes on here, so the EL allows them to see what's happening. I recorded 13 observations in 3 months. Ok, I think the EL is a really useful thing, except that the management made some comments that I didn't really like. You see, the juvenile, Sofiane Z., was here for rape, and in my note I said that he has a problem with female authority, because he mouthed off at a female educator, and when they validated the comment they replied 'your role is to help the educator, not to analyze the situation'.... [silence]. So you can see there are some harmful effects.
>
> – Did you respond?
>
> – Nah, I kept a low profile but later I managed to make myself more visible, like when I stopped a big brawl in the gym, where I intervened. So at first, when I wrote notes, I did it without holding back, without filtering, whereas

> since then, I make relevant comments that don't go against the grain, just to say that I'm here, I'm doing things, that I'm doing my work well [smile] (...) We're asked to observe, not analyze. And yeah, we're told keep to our role as guards. So anyway, of course it's a bit frustrating, but it's true that I'm only category C staff... Anyway, because of all these things, I won't be spending the rest of my life in the PA.
>
> (Selim, PA guard)

Ultimately, this secondary application of the EL can be useful to prison management for instilling into field staff a certain way of viewing and categorising the young prisoners. Thus, the head of detention at one of the two PMs created a guide for optimal EL usage, listing a number of adjectives that guards could use to 'relevantly' characterise the behaviour of young prisoners:

> We also use it to see how staff use it... If someone says anything and everything, that's not useful, but if someone doesn't say anything, that's not useful either. They have to achieve a happy medium.
>
> – There are people who say anything and everything?
>
> – Yes because there are irrelevant observations. So what I did in the arrivals' wing was I put a... (...) I gave them examples of themes on behavior, habits, relationships, the mail, the visiting rooms, family situations, situation/development, relations with staff, with fellow prisoners, incidents, reactions, attitudes, activities, attentiveness in activities, in class, etc., appearance, hygiene, the canteens. And next to that, examples of terms. Like respectful, polite, obsequious, impolite... So they would know to speak, have ideas, write sentences and make relevant observations. I let them know that I didn't want to see 'nothing to note' (NTN). Because in the beginning, we had observations with 'NTN'. I don't give a damn about NTNs. So I've given them a bit of a framework. And based on that, they can develop observation themes. After, they just have to add the terms, which go in the next column. It's not an exhaustive list, there are certainly other terms.
>
> (Laurent, PA head of detention)

The list of suggested adjectives highlights some conceptual pairs based on an often-Manichean view of prisoners: respectful/disrespectful; polite/impolite; patient/impulsive; controls himself/lacks self-control and so on. Therefore, it would now be appropriate to look more closely at the contents of the EL, to try and understand the representations it conveys and appreciate how its uses – by writers and by readers – can orient prisoners' individual prison trajectories.

The role of the EL in the construction of prison trajectories

Reading the various notes in the EL allows us to identify the various ways young prisoners are categorised by prison staff. From a methodological point of view, at this stage the EL only acts a mirror of the dominant representations that influence the guards' activity. It would nonetheless be useful to go beyond this reading and understand how the EL – which consolidates these representations and circulates labels placed on prisoners – contributes to reinforcing individualised prison identities.

What the EL tells us about the young prisoners' representation in the prison

At the outset, in the EL one finds a differentiation in the nature of the recorded observations, according to the juvenile concerned and his progress along his prison trajectory. Reading the EL makes it possible to understand the prisoner representations and the operations of prisoner categorisation and classification that influence the action guards take day-to-day. Observations recorded during the juvenile's first week of incarceration concern his general state, the aim being to establish his 'profile'. Notes recorded during the rest of his time in prison mostly relate to isolated incidents that punctuate day-to-day life in the prison. With this 'knowledge' accumulated during the juvenile's first days in prison, it becomes possible to confirm, or more rarely invalidate, the judgement with which he is associated. Observation reveals that the recorded events tend mostly to be negative, creating a distorted view of reality that is disadvantageous to the juveniles. 'There's no point writing about what's going well,' said one educator.

Let us focus on analysing initial observations. These are made according to a prisoner categorisation system based on various conceptual pairs that overlap but can also conflict in certain situations.

The first pair opposes 'fragile' juveniles and 'comfortable' juveniles. Following from the importance of the suicide prevention objective and stemming from a representation of the PM, which must also supply a protective structure to some prisoners who would otherwise get 'walked on', one of the objectives is to identify possible weaknesses in the young prisoners. Guards therefore look for possible signs of 'incarceration shock':

> 12/03/2010
>
> Subject: Prisoner behavior – (11:48pm)
>
> Validated 12/03/2010 at 11:52pm by ... (1st guard)
>
> Written by: PA guard

Details: The prison registration process proceeded correctly. First-time prisoner does not seem to be experiencing incarceration shock. In the registration office he was quiet and polite [...]

In this context, judgements about prisoners have to achieve a fine balance. If it is quite clear that the juvenile is not too 'lost', it is also good that he 'shows his emotions'. The following two extracts from the EL, separated by an hour, concern a juvenile imprisoned for homicide who had previously never had any dealings with the law and was, upon his arrival, considered 'fragile, to be watched':

17/03/2009

Subject: Prisoner behavior – (6:27pm)

Validated 24/03/2009 at 14:37 by... (Lieutenant)

Written by: PA guard

Details: First contact with the juvenile. As soon as I opened the cell I noticed that he hadn't touched his dinner and that he'd slept with his personal possessions under the sheets. Very calm atmosphere at breakfast. The juvenile seems lost, talks very little and isn't eating. (...) At lunch, F. ate without making any attempt to converse with the adults. During the afternoon activity, his face opened up a little and you could see a smile between two table football balls. During dinner, there was a fun atmosphere thanks to the educator's eccentric conversation.

17/03/2009

Subject: Prisoner behaviour – (7:27pm)

Validated 24/03/2009 at 2:27pm by... (Lieutenant)

Written by: PA guard

Details: Something is bothering me about the juvenile's attitude. He seems to have a good understanding of the reason for his incarceration, but the coldness of his emotions or even the absence of emotion makes me wonder if maybe he still doesn't understand, or poorly understands, the act he has committed and its consequences....

To be followed up.

The second conceptual pair that structures the representation of the juvenile prisoners opposes 'first-time prisoners' and 'multi-recidivists'. Thus, some juveniles, even when they seem 'polite' and 'mature', must always be subject to special attention if they are too acclimatised to prison realities. Guards must be particularly vigilant upon the arrival of a juvenile whose prison record suggests his behaviour will be disruptive, especially in the case of a disciplinary transfer.

This is what is described in the following observation of a prisoner who arrived at the PM after 17 months of incarceration in a jail. The use of the expressions 'for the time being' and 'anyway' in the note tells us something about the prudence surrounding juveniles who are far too familiar with how the prison system operates:

> 25/03/2010
>
> Subject: Prisoner behavior – (7:36pm)
>
> Validated 26/03/2009 at 15:02 by ... (Lieutenant)
>
> Written by: ...
>
> Details: This prisoner arrived in the housing unit more tense than he was in the registration office.
>
> He was in conditions that were conducive to listening and discussion. For the time being, he has accepted all of our explanations about how the establishment operates. He was very pleasant and courteous towards the professionals, but should be watched anyway.

The third conceptual pair opposes 'nice' juveniles to 'pains in the neck', especially juveniles who 'ask a lot' from PM personnel. Although some prisoners are quickly categorised as 'having the right attitude' and are presented as 'positive leaders', whilst others will 'definitely present a problem' in the prison (as it was expressed by the head of detention upon the arrival of one juvenile), the judgement is sometimes difficult to consolidate. In these cases, the juveniles' prison history is often summoned, amongst other elements, to evoke a possible shift in representation. One juvenile was, in a guard's observation written at 10:27 am upon his arrival, characterised as 'comfortable', 'given that he has already been incarcerated in the PM', and it was predicted that he would 'likely not present any management problems'. But then, during an observation the same day at 6:15 pm, written by the same guard, it was suspected he might be a prisoner who was 'just waiting to play a nasty trick':

> 31/05/2009
>
> Subject: Prisoner behavior – (6:15pm)
>
> Validated 02/06/2009 at 2:37pm by ... (Head of detention)
>
> Written by: ...
>
> Details: A prisoner who wants to spend more time in his cell watching TV. I had to insist several times before he would go for a walk, knowing that he refused to go to his activity this morning.
>
> His behavior in the housing unit presents no problem and he does the tasks he's responsible for and obeys requests. He doesn't understand right away, you have to re-explain things, is he doing it on purpose or not????????

> He seems like he's just waiting to play a nasty trick, he tries to negotiate some things but in vain (juice in his cell, taking his walks in the recreation room...).
>
> One must be careful with him and not hesitate to take him in hand.

The EL, as an apparatus that translates day-to-day prison life, the fruit of the controversies and other exchanges between professionals highlighted earlier, also has the effect of consolidating prison identities that later influence how prisoners are observed and treated, thus shaping the course of their prison trajectory.

When the EL causes professionals to act

PMs operate based on a system of differentiated housing units: 'ordinary' units along with a 'reinforced' unit for problem prisoners and a 'liberal' unit for those who seem most 'deserving'. A central component in the construction of prison trajectories is the placement of prisoners in these different units. At least in principle, these placements are decided at 'single interdisciplinary commissions' (SIC), which are attended by prison guards, YJPS educators, Ministry of Education teachers and, more irregularly depending on the staff in attendance, health-care personnel (OCU). These meetings give these different partners the chance to present and defend their own representation of prisoners. They are also where EL usage becomes visible along with its label self-reinforcement effect. Prison personnel often come to the SIC with printouts of observations concerning the individual juveniles scheduled to be discussed. Although the observations can be debated through long discussions about the juveniles whose cases are being considered, the EL can also serve as a reminder of certain 'significant facts' that consolidate the juvenile's representation,[16] offering a stable cognitive framework that can orient subsequent discussions. In other words, oral discussion can clarify what has been written and enable actors to establish a context that will partially change the conditions of the writing's interpretation (Grosjean and Lacoste, 1999: 449–50), but in turn, writing, through the trace it leaves, restricts the redefinition of the 'case' discussed orally. Here, through the EL, what is written becomes the operator and driving force behind a process of stigmatisation.[17] This is shown by the following extract from an SIC that included a discussion about a juvenile whose case the OCU psychologist admitted was 'hard to understand'. One of the heads of the YJPS who supported the use of the EL, referring to its contents, got the SIC participants to agree on the 'profile' of the juvenile being discussed:

> Regarding Mahamadou, incarcerated for theft involving false imprisonment. According to the educator who introduced the juvenile, he 'recognises the

> seriousness of what he's done but coldly, without emotion ... it's bizarre.' She then says that based on initial observations of the juvenile in a group situation, he 'showed too little to be able to say right away whether he has the profile of a leader or follower.' After his schooling was discussed with the teacher who was there, the educator returned to this question of his 'profile,' which must be defined in order to determine which unit he should be assigned to. The head of YJPS, reading observations in the EL, suggested that 'he seems more like a leader than a follower.' The guard and the psychologist then agreed wholeheartedly.
>
> (Field journal)

It is nevertheless important not to generalise about the EL's operator role; it would then in every case become an actor in the process of constructing, consolidating and stigmatising prison identities. Sometimes it only conveys pre-existing representations. These remarks bring us to a consideration of the EL's uses, by placing them back in a broader action flow whose unique characteristics can shed light on this notebook's concrete role. In cases where the prisoner's 'profile' is relatively widely shared and consolidated, the EL only conveys a general feeling about the juvenile. Nonetheless, it can serve as the memory of this feeling, which, frozen and fixed by the writing, then provides a cognitive framework for orienting discussions. The very fact that many guards rely on EL observations to present the situation and discuss the juvenile's issues tells us something about the EL's role, which is consequently not limited to that of a passive conveyor but is extended to that of a distributor of categorisations carefully stored in its memory. In cases where the prisoners' profiles are less clear, less certain and even sharply disputed, the EL can become an actor in the controversy: 'on the EL, it is written that....' Consequently, not only do the EL's categories become party to the controversy, but the EL's legitimacy as an actor can be challenged.

This was particularly true in the case of a juvenile who the prison administration decided would receive a disciplinary transfer. The YJPS educators, who were very much against a decision they characterised as 'unjust', believed that the juvenile had been the victim of prison administration 'harassment'. At a meeting of the YJPS, one educator lost his temper:

> He's paying for being a big black person. How do you explain that one guy punches a guard in the face and gets 2 days in the disciplinary wing, and this guy gets 5 days! In fact right away, from the day he arrived, they told themselves 'we're going to transfer this guy'.

The educators then challenged the notes in the EL relating to this juvenile. According to them, these notes only relayed and reinforced an unjust, biased initial representation: 'it was long ago written in his behavioural record that he would be transferred.'

In every situation, it is important to ask oneself to what extent the EL plays the role of a conveyor of pre-existing representations, or that of an operator with the power to not only distribute but also produce prisoner categorisations, in which case it can then become a direct actor in the construction of prison trajectories. In other words, exploring the contents of texts written in the EL is not enough to understand this software's complexity and sociological significance. It is important to examine what takes place around it, to analyse not only the production of acts of writing but also their reception, interpretation and uses, as well as moments when the course of action overflows this strict content. In this sense, this anthropology of acts of writing offers a mise en abyme on the overall 'PM project'. Thus, we perceive the structural tension that pervades this project, caught between institutional calls for 'partnership' and 'interdisciplinarity' and each profession's struggle to preserve its own space and jurisdiction. We also perceive the need for the prison administration, in this project in which the prison's security prerogatives come into tension with its educational aims, to train its agents in 'good' observation. In this sense, on the one hand, controversies surrounding the need to use the EL – even surrounding its very existence – reveal the diversity of the different views of prisoners that coexist and clash every day in the PM; on the other hand, the concrete conditions of its appropriation shed light on the uniformisation of representations of prisoners, based on the intermingling of binary pairs. These results are reflected in how the EL is used to construct individual prison trajectories. The way that the EL is able to shape these trajectories, combined with the scepticism or even radical criticism that this use is subjected to, tells us something about the dominant role played by the prison administration and its system of categorisation in the construction of prison trajectories and about the occasional fragility of this dominance when it is scrutinised by professionals who can, in some situations, subject it to forms of verification or moderation.

Conclusion: What the ethnography of writings teaches us about prison and its socio-political rooting

A look at the principal ethnographic studies on the work of prison guards and their participation in behavioural control in detention reveals three axes that structure the core of their activity. The first axis is made up of the triptych 'supervising, separating, isolating' in which their supervision and 'movement' management activity – framed by each prison's particular architecture (Johnston, 2000; Mbanzoulou, 2011; Hancock and Jewkes, 2011; Simon et al., 2012) – organised within a fragmented penitentiary space (Demonchy, 2004; Milhaud,

2009), where each subspace (corridors, cells, health-care centre, etc.) has to pass a visibility test and is subject to particular security considerations (Chantraine et al., 2012). The second axis is made up of the triptych 'negotiating, discussing, punishing'. On this point, ethnographic research has amply described prison personnel strategies, which mainly consist in attempting to prevent incidents and reduce internal disorder by using various informal relational skills (Chauvenet et al., 1994; Chauvenet, 1996; Liebling, 2000; Liebling and Price, 2001; Crewe, 2009), in a constantly renewed effort to manage individuals, groups and 'atmospheres' in prison. These informal practices depend on the guards' ability to discuss and negotiate – an ability that could be likened to a perilous art of reassurance and psychological support in a stressful institutional context but is also like a subtle game of carrot (micro-reward) and stick (infra-disciplinary punishment). However, these practices assume diverse forms in different establishments and contexts around the country. They especially depend on the promotion and effectiveness (or ineffectiveness) of the defence of certain prisoners' rights, the formal regulation of the disciplinary regime, the promotion (or neglect) of 'communication' (McCleery, 1960) and, more generally, 'active security'[18] as a system-stabilising element and/or as a 'rehabilitation' tool.

The third axis is made up of the triptych 'observing, recording, tracing'. Analysis of this third axis, which has been the focus of this contribution, makes it possible not only to discover a new facet of the work of guards but also to gain a more subtle understanding of how practices of surveillance (first axis) and negotiation (second axis) – and, more generally, all of prison's behavioural control mechanisms – are being renewed as a result of the twofold injunction to partnership and traceability, as was pointed out by a British guard interviewed by Ben Crewe: 'All we've got is the power of the pen' (Crewe, 2011). This analytical enrichment will enable us to posit a first conviction: that ethnographers of prisons should not content themselves with resisting the potential 'eclipse of ethnography' (Wacquant, 2002), by 'going there to see' in order to describe the reality of prison from inside. They should also show sociological imagination (in Mills' sense, 1959): direct observation of interactions should of course remain the nodal point of their approach, but they must also give themselves the tools to explore other aspects of the activity of guards from an ethnographic angle. This would enable them to objectivise the way in which these aspects partly underpin and structure directly observable interactions.

But an ethnography of writings offers even more possibilities, if one accepts the idea (and this is our second conviction) that ethnographers of prisons should never forget to link their micro-sociological analyses to macro-sociological considerations. This means effecting 'a return to the motivations behind the first golden age of ethnographic sociological fieldwork in prison.' (Chantraine, 2013).[19]

In a theoretical contribution to a collective book on the topicality and fruitfulness of surveillance studies (Leman-Langlois, 2011), Fabien Jobard and Dominique Linhart suggest de-generalising the approach to surveillance, in order to grasp the diversity of the empirical realities that this concept encompasses. On the basis of two distinct ethnographies – the comparison of surveillance methods used at Orly airport (Paris) with those used in the underprivileged city of Dammarie-lès-Lys (a suburb of Paris) – they were able to construct two distinct surveillance ideal-types: 'liberal surveillance' and 'sovereign surveillance'. In the former ethnography, it is a matter of reconciling citizen rights with consumer comfort, whilst using specific indicators to try and identify potential terrorists. In the latter, it is no longer a matter of probing anonymous individuals, but perpetuating, personalising and individualising the observation of a population and individuals subjected and rooted to a territory, in the context of a relationship that is always marked by the immanent use of force.

In this respect, the observation of uses of the EL enables us to analyse PMs as 'pure' illustrations of sovereign surveillance ideal-types. If, from the perspective of the first axis of guard activity (supervising, separating, isolating), the prison administration has the ability to organise and control every movement through a subtle interweaving between remote surveillance (cameras) and close-up surveillance (in person) (Chantraine et al., 2012), the EL makes it possible to both de-spatialise observations and make them visible to everyone and also record and accumulate them; in short, they can be consigned to a past, present or future tense, making the EL something of an informational panoptic. This interpretation nevertheless has a weakness: that it underestimates the EL's possible uses. As we have seen, far from being reducible to an apparatus for supervising and observing prisoners, in practice it turns out to be also an apparatus for supervising and observing professionals, particularly guards. The judgements they express on prisoners are likely to be read and closely watched, even monitored, not only by their own superiors but also by the different professionals who work alongside them, or possibly by external third parties: sociologists and inspectors who work to improve living conditions in prison, or investigators who may intervene if a tragedy occurs in prison. This being the case, the sovereign surveillance of prisoners made possible by the EL starts looking like 'surveillance under surveillance' (Jobard and Linhart, 2011). If there is good reason to be concerned that these forms of surveillance under surveillance could lead to a sharp disconnect between real practices and those recorded in the EL, the potential impact of this surveillance on real social relations in prison should not be underestimated. In this respect, the routine use of the EL will likely increase the dynamism not only of the diffuse, consequential evaluation of prisoners, but also of the more general trend towards the judicialisation of social relations in prison (Rostaing, 2007). The effects of this increased judicialisation are themselves potentially open ended. Relative to the second axis of guard activity (negotiating, discussing, punishing), they might constitute a check – and a restraint – on infra-disciplinary arbitrariness in prison, but they could also lead to a decrease in social dialogue and informality in relations between guards and prisoners – a reduction could be increased by the systematic implementation of shields that protect and ultimately reduce responsibility.

Thus, the ethnography of writings in prison, when focused on the third axis of guard activity (observing, recording, tracing), enables us not only to enrich our understanding of the major changes taking place in the prison guards' profession and more generally in the prison administration as a whole but also, as long as it is allowed to be 'de-centred,' to provide us with tools to describe a contemporary – and sovereign – method of controlling the behaviour of stigmatised populations.

Notes

1. Originally called 'behavioral tracking', this software application was quickly renamed the 'electronic logbook', particularly because of the compartmentalist connotations of its first name, which left it open to criticism. Nevertheless, through interview extracts, we will see that some professionals are still using the term 'behavioural tracking'.
2. Sonya Faure, 'Captifs de la cellule informatique', *Libération*, 13 July 2010.
3. Jean-Simon Merandat, proceedings of the seminar 'La mise en œuvre des RPE', DAP, 10 April 2009.
4. Research conducted with the support of the GIP Law and Justice research mission.
5. This is also what Jean-François Laé stresses when he suggests that 'outside of the moment of action, [writings in work contexts] lose all consistency' [Laé, 2008, 14].
6. This 'pluri-functionality' characteristic of a number of work-related writings is highlighted by Béatrice Fraenkel in her analysis of how numerous organisations meet the objective of 'traceability' in writing (Fraenkel, 1993: 31).
7. Evoking so-called real work-related writings, which accompany work activity – those 'traces of knowledge that are unrecognized and unofficial, but are necessary if work is going to be carried out without continual incidents' – Josiane Boutet even stresses the frequent impossibility of distinguishing the author from the reader in them: 'these texts were not intended to be read by anyone but their author' (Boutet, 1993: 24).
8. More fundamentally, the protection of medical confidentiality, an issue that goes well beyond the EL, must be understood both as a means of protecting prisoners and as a means of defending the medical power against penitentiary power.
9. For an examination of contemporary changes in the profession of YJPS educator, see Sallée (2010).
10. These housing units constitute one of the original architectural features of the PMs. See Chantraine et al. (2012).
11. As we will see later, the progress notebook is one of the two notebooks most often used by educators. It concerns only one housing unit and aims to provide information about how day-to-day events in prison.

12. In this respect, the EL, like the 'care records' of hospital patients (Grosjean and Lacoste, 1999: 444), pre-formats and channels the writing of professionals: its contents are pre-organised and prioritised through categories. See also Acker (1997).
13. Anthropologist Aïssatou Mbodj-Pouye points out that 'the personal style of writing is not to be found far away from imposed styles of writing and injunctions to write, but rather in the way writers use the models imposed upon them' (2009: 870).
14. This game surrounding the identification of the authors of observations in the EL highlights the importance of the 'assignation function' fulfiled by writings in a work context, which strive for 'traceability' (Fraenkel, 1993: 35–6).
15. For an analysis of the evolution of the administration's responsibility in matters relating to suicide, see Cliquennois and Chantraine (2009).
16. This recalls the work of Donald A. Norman. For Norman (1991), writing constitutes a 'cognitive artifact', that is to say an artificial instrument designed to maintain, display or operate upon information in order to serve a representational function.
17. Erving Goffman (1975) has already pointed out the close connection between 'traces' and stigmata. In this case, the trace is no longer on the body (a lasting mark characteristic of an ailment) but rather in the software program. The trace is however no less visible.
18. Active security (formerly called 'dynamic security') aims to 'take account of the active role of social relations in the pacification of behavior' (Chauvenet et al., 2008, 152–53).
19. One thinks of Sykes, for example, who brilliantly showed how social relations in prison are the outcome of the clash between the various ends it is supposed to pursue (*Custody, Internal Order, Self-Maintenance, Punishment, Reform*). One also thinks of Goffman and his concept of the 'total institution', which, as a structural concept, questioned the social system as a whole.

Further reading

Bérard, J. and Chantraine, G. (2013) *Bastille Nation. French Penal Politics and the Punitive Turn* (Carleton: Red Quill Books Edition).

Chantraine, G. and Sallée, N. (2015) 'Educate and Punish. Educational Work, Security and Discipline in Prisons for Minors', *Revue française de sociologie*, 54, 3, English issue, 437–61.

Chantraine, G., Scheer, D. and Milhaud, O. (2012) 'Space and Surveillance in a Prison for Minors', *Politix*, 97, 1, English issue, 125–48.

Sallée, N. (2014) 'Juvenile Delinquents Educated Under Constraint: Responsabilisation, Discipline and the Return to a Republican Utopia in the French Youth Justice System', *Déviance et société*, 38, 1, French issue, 77–101.

References

Acker, F. (1997) 'Sortir de l'invisibilité – Le cas du travail infirmer', *Raisons Pratiques*, 8, 65–94.

Boutet, J. (1993) 'Quelques propriétés des écrits au travail', *Langage et Travail*, 6, 18–25.

Chantraine, G. (2004) 'Prison and Sociological Perspective', *Champ pénal/Penal field*, I, http://champpenal.revues.org/238.

Chantraine, G. (2013) 'Prisons Under the Lens of Ethnographic Criticism', *Criminal Justice Matters*, 91, 1, 30–1.

Chantraine, G. and Kaminski, D. (2007) 'La Politique des Droits en Prison', *Champ pénal/Penal field*, http://champpenal.revues.org/2581.

Chantraine, G., Scheer, D. and Milhaud, O. (2012) 'Espace et surveillances en établissement pénitentiaire pour mineurs', *Politix*, 1, 97, 125–48.

Chantraine, G. and Sallée, N. (2014) 'Educate and Punish: Educational Work, Security and Discipline in Prisons for Minors', *Revue française de sociologie*, 54, 3, 437–64.

Chantraine, G. (ed) avec Sallée, N., Scheer, D., Salle, G., Franssen, A. and Cliquennois, G. (2011) *Les prisons pour mineurs: Controverses sociales, pratiques professionnelles, expériences de réclusion, rapport pour la mission de recherche* (Droit et Justice: Clersé, 534).

Chauvenet, A. (1996) 'L'échange et la prison', in C. Faugeron, A. Chauvenet and A. Combessie (eds) *Approches de la prison*, pp. 45–70 (Bruxelles: De Boeck Université, Bruxellles).

Chauvenet, A., Orlic, F. and Benguigui, G. (1994) *Le Monde des surveillants de prison* (Paris: Presses Universitaires de France).

Chauvenet, A., Rostaing, C. and Orlic, F. (2008) *La violence carcérale en question* (Paris: PUF).

Cliquennois, G. and Chantraine, G. (2009) 'Empêcher le Suicide en Prison: Origines et Pratiques', *Sociétés Contemporaines*, 75, 3, 59–79.

Conein, B. (1997) 'L'action avec les objets: Un autre visage de l'action située?', in B. Conein and L. Thévenot (eds) *Cognition et information en société. Raisons pratiques n°8* (Paris: EHESS).

Crewe, B. (2009) *The Prisoner Society. Prison, Adaptation, and Social Life in an English Prison* (Oxford: Oxford University Press).

Crewe, B. (2011) 'Soft Power in Prison: Implications for Staff-Prisoner Relationships, Liberty and Legitimacy', *European Journal of Criminology*, 8, 6, 455–68.

Demonchy, C. (2004) 'L'architecture des prisons modèles françaises', in P. Artières and P. Lascoumes (eds) *Gouverner et enfermer: La prison, un modèle indépassable?* (Paris: Presses de Sciences Po).

Fassin, D. and Bourdelais, P. (ed) (2005) *Les constructions de l'intolérable. Etudes d'anthropologie et d'histoire sur les frontières de l'espace moral* (Paris: La Découverte).

Fraenkel, B. (1993) 'La traçabilité, une fonction caractéristique des écrits au travail', *Langage et Travail*, 6, 26–38.

Fraenkel, B. (2007) 'Actes d'écriture: Quand écrire c'est faire', *Langage et Société*, 3–4, 101–12.

Goffman, E. (1975/1963) *Les usages sociaux du handicap* (Paris: Minuit).

Grosjean, M. and Lacoste, M. (1999) 'L'oral et l'écrit dans les communications de travail ou les illusions du 'tout écrit', *Sociologie du travail*, 98, 4, 439–61.

Hancock, P. and Jewkes, Y. (2011) 'Architectures of Incarceration? The Spatial Pains of Imprisonment', *Punishment & Society*, 13, 5, 611–29.

Jobard, F. and Linhart, D. (2011) 'Surveillance libérale et surveillance souveraine', in S. Leman-Langlois (ed) *Sphères de surveillance*, pp. 103–36 (Montréal: Presses de l'Université de Montréal).

Johnston, N. J. (2000) *Forms of Constraint: A History of Prison Architecture* (Champaign: University of Illinois Press).

Laé, J. F. (2008) *Les nuits de la main courante: Ecritures au travail* (Paris: Stock).

Lahanier-Reuter, D. (2010) 'Livrets de bord et travail des enseignants du second degré', *Langage et Société*, 134, 55–78.

Latour, B. and Hermant, E. (1998) *Paris ville invisible* (Paris: Les empêcheurs de penser en rond/La Découverte).

Le Bianic, T. and Malochet, G. (2011) 'Soigner, évaluer, controller: Les dilemmes des soignants en milieu carcéral', in G. Benguigui, F. Guilbaud and Malochet, G. (eds) *Prisons sous tensions*, pp. 221–47 (Nîmes: Champ Social).

Leman-Langlois, S. (ed) *Sphères de surveillance* (Montréal: Presses de l'Université de Montréal).

Liebling, A. (2000) 'Prisons officers, Policing and the Use of Discretion', *Theoretical Criminology*, 4, 3, 333–57.

Liebling, A. and Price, D. (2001) *The Prison Officer* (Winchester: Waterside Press)

Mbanzoulou, P. (ed) (2011) *L'architecture carcérale* (Paris: L'Harmattan).

Mbodj-Pouye, A. (2009) 'Tenir un cahier dans la région cotonnière du Mali: Support d'écriture et rapport à soi', *Annales HSS*, 4, 855–85.

McCleery, R. (1960) 'Communications Patterns as Bases of Systems of Authority and Power', in R. A. Cloward (ed) *Theoretical Studies in Social Organization of the Prison*, pp. 49–77 (New York: Social Science Research Council).

Milhaud, O. (2009) *Séparer et punir. Les prisons françaises: mise à distance et punition par l'espace* (Bordeaux: Thèse de l'Université de Bordeaux).

Mills, C. W. (1959) *The Sociological Imagination* (London: Oxford University Press).

Norman, D. A. (1991) 'Cognitive Artifacts', in John M. Carroll (ed) *Designing Interaction*, pp. 17–38 (Cambridge: Cambridge University Press).

Rostaing, C. (2007) 'Processus de judiciarisation carcérale: Le droit en prison, une ressource pour les acteurs?' *Droit et Société*, 67, 577–95.

Sallée, N. (2010) 'Les éducateurs de la Protection judiciaire de la jeunesse à l'épreuve de l'évolution du traitement pénal des jeunes délinquants', *Champ pénal/Pénal field*, VII, http://champpenal.revues.org/7756.

Simon, J., Temple, N. and Tobe, R. (eds) (2012) *Architecture and Justice* (Ashgate: London).

Wacquant, L. (2002) 'The Curious Eclipse of Prison Ethnography in the Age of Mass Incarceration', *Ethnography*, 3, 371–97.

6

Closeness, Distance and Honesty in Prison Ethnography

Ben Crewe and Alice Ievins

Introduction

In their famously combative exchange in the *American Journal of Sociology* (*AJS*) in 2002, one of Loic Wacquant's many charges against Elijah Anderson, Mitchell Duneier and Katherine Newman is a putative lack of critical distance from their research participants. Wacquant's accusation is that all three authors detail rather than explain the behaviours and orientations of their research subjects and present (at least some of) them in a manner that is naively and needlessly favourable. The goal of ethnographic research, he argued, 'is not to exonerate the character of dishonoured social figures and dispossessed social groups', or to 'attract sympathy for their plight', as such, but to describe and dissect the 'the social mechanisms and meanings that govern their practices, ground their morality [...] and explain their strategies and trajectories' (Wacquant, 2002: 1470).

In his trenchant response, whilst refuting Wacquant's assertion that he presents his subjects as saints, or accepts their self-portrayals unquestioningly, Duneier asserts that one of his aims is to 'bring to light their basic humanity' (Duneier, 2002: 1575), an objective that represents one of the 'greatest strengths' of urban ethnography. Anderson's response, with its emphasis on accurately reporting the subjective experience, is similar: 'I try to write about the ghetto poor in a way that is *faithful to their understanding of themselves* [...] I regard this effort essential to the ethnographic enterprise and to the broader interests of an effectual social science' (Anderson, 2002: 1549; italics in original). Both writers, therefore, write 'from the ground up' (rather than 'from theory down'), as a means of 'moralising' their research subjects, making use of close and sympathetic description to illustrate the localised morality of their behaviour (Cole and Dumas, 2010). Here, then, is what Cole and Dumas (2010: 22) call the 'ethical-political dilemma at the heart of ethnography': in essence, whether one is more faithful to a theoretical or interpersonal commitment.

Wacquant's principal concern is the role of theory within ethnographic research, as well as his sense that some writers reproduce rather than theorise the 'folk explanations' of their research subjects (i.e. fail to interrogate how personal motives and beliefs are structured by broader mechanisms and conditions). Our aim in this chapter is not to engage with these issues specifically. Instead, our interest is in the politics of intimacy and honesty that this debate captures: how we, as prison researchers, seek not only to navigate the practical and philosophical problem of becoming intimate with our research participants, but also to honour their subjectivities, whilst at the same time providing a candid and objectively proper account of their practices and personhoods. In particular, and drawing primarily on Janet Malcolm's (1990) *The Journalist and the Murderer*, we highlight the tension between the need to establish closeness and distance at different phases of the research process and the associated difficulties of writing a truthful account whilst avoiding charges of duplicity. By then comparing the way in which scholars of mainstream prisoners and imprisoned sex offenders describe their experiences, the chapter also seeks to bring to the fore some of the inconsistencies in the ways that researchers approach and present these issues, as well as what appears to be an underlying process of moral reckoning and self-positioning on the part of the writer. It goes on to outline some personal experiences of trying to steer a course between intimacy and critique, through a particular form of accountability resulting from the maintenance of contact with research participants in the post-fieldwork period.

Intimacy and betrayal

Few academic reflections on the perils and paradoxes of writing about other human beings come close to Janet Malcolm's (1990) book *The Journalist and the Murderer*. Written ostensibly as an account of the lawsuit taken out by a convicted murderer, Jeffrey MacDonald, against an author, Joe McGinniss, the book is, in effect, an extended treatment of the complexities of the relationship between writer and subject. Having approached and persuaded McGinniss to author an account of his own murder trial, and invited him into his life (and that of his defence team) for a period of several months, MacDonald went on to sue McGinniss for 'a kind of soul murder' (p. 21), a fundamental breach of trust. McGinniss' crime, in the eyes of his subject, was not that, having become convinced of MacDonald's guilt, he had expressed this in print. Rather, it was that – in the interest of servicing his book – he had cultivated (or, at least, falsely maintained) a pretence of intimacy and friendship.

For McGinniss, the relationship was professional, that of author and subject, and much of Malcolm's book is spent debating the right of the journalist to engage in practices of bad faith and deception, given the discomfort they create for the writer, as well as for the subject, when they ultimately 'see the flash of the knife' (Malcolm, 1990: 145). Here, the opening passages of the book are worth quoting at length:

> Every journalist who is not too stupid or too full of himself to notice what is going on knows that what he does is morally indefensible. He is a kind of confidence man, preying on people's vanity, ignorance, or loneliness, gaining their trust and betraying them without remorse. Like the credulous widow who wakes up one day to find the charming young man and all her savings gone, so the consenting subject of a piece of nonfiction writing learns – when the article or book appears – *his* hard lesson. [...] The catastrophe suffered by the subject is no simple matter of an unflattering likeness of a misrepresentation of his views; what pains him, what rankles and sometimes drives him to extremes of vengefulness, is the deception that has been practiced on him. On reading the article or book in question, he has to face the fact that the journalist – who seemed so friendly and sympathetic, so keen to understand him fully, so remarkably attuned to his vision of things – never had the slightest intention of collaborating with him on his story but always intended to write a story of his own.
>
> (Malcolm, 1990: 3)

Later in the book, Malcolm elaborates on this fundamental distinction between the person who the research subject encounters (or assumes that they are encountering) and the person who eventually writes the text. Whilst the former is an 'all-accepting, all-forgiving mother', the latter is the 'strict, all-noticing, unforgiving father' (p. 32). Quoting Thomas Mann, she suggests that this reflects a split between the writer's personal and professional (or 'artistic') self:

> The look that one directs at things, both outward and inward, as an artist, is not the same as that with which one would regard the same as a man, but at once colder and more passionate. As a man, you might be well-disposed, patient, loving, positive, and have a wholly uncritical inclination to look upon everything as all right, but as artist your daemon constrains you to 'observe', to take note, lightning fast and with hurtful malice, of every detail that in the literary sense would be characteristic, distinctive, significant, opening insights, typifying the face, the social or the psychological mode, recording all as mercilessly as though you had no human relationship to the observed object whatever.
>
> (Mann, cited in Malcolm, 1990: 32–3)

Malcolm's position is to some degree a provocation,[1] and its rather cynical interpretation of the writer's behaviour may reflect the dynamics of journalism more than those of academic ethnography.[2]

Nonetheless, we suspect that few qualitative researchers will read Malcolm's text without recognising many of its key themes, or what Paul Rock (1979: 201) calls the 'predatory character' of fieldwork.

In fact, there are many ways in which the writer can betray the research subject. Malcolm's reflections cover a number of these possibilities, and at times, in her text, they are difficult to disentangle, but they merit some kind of classification and illustration. The first amounts to a kind of assassination, the portrayal of an individual in terms that they might find insulting or unkind, and which sit at odds with the interview experience. This mode of betrayal, in which the individual is personally defamed or *traduced*, is much more characteristic of journalism, where the unit of analysis is often the individual, and the subject of description is 'personality' or 'character', than sociological research, where the individual tends to be studied as a means of understanding social structures and processes.

A second way involves the re-telling of the personal narrative in a manner that deviates from the individual's self-understanding.[3] For the prison ethnographer, this mode of betrayal – the basis of the disagreement in the *AJS* – is much more likely, for something is always lost, or added, in the translation of the individual's story into sociological terminology. The individual prisoner is in effect *reduced* into a set of variables or a typological category, in a manner that risks violating the complexity of their inner experience, or their experiences, agency and attitudes are deemed false, and re-conceived as outcomes of social forces or abstract nouns ('neo-liberalism') that they do not necessarily recognise.

In the third way, the research participant is betrayed by a combination of their own naivety and the skill of the researcher, without any malice on the part of the latter. Malcolm is sceptical about this possibility (or rather, about the general possibility that the subject is unknowing). 'No subject is naive', she proposes, 'every subject of writing knows on some level what is in store for him, and remains in the relationship anyway, impelled by something stronger than his reason' (1990: 8). But it seems to us completely plausible that, within the comforting embrace of the interview – after the effort made by the interviewer to put the interviewee at ease – an interviewee says more than they later feel is prudent, or does not think through the reality of a distant publication. As Pierre Bourdieu (1996: 19) notes, good interviewing requires commitment to a form of 'active and methodical listening',[4] in which the interviewer displays 'total attention to the person questioned' (p. 19), and communicates to the interviewee that he or she 'is capable of *mentally putting herself in their place*' (p. 22, italics in original). Here, then, having opened up willingly in the interview room, the interviewee is *exposed* when the edited transcript is eventually made public, even when their contribution is anonymised. There is a distinction between 'whispering something beside a fire or across a counter and seeing it printed for the world to see' (Scheper Hughes, cited in Brettell, 1993).

To quote Bourdieu (1999: 1) again, when forms of intimacy that are generated in good faith are transformed into public discourse and academic capital, the researcher should feel some discomfort:

> How can we not feel anxious about making *private* words *public*, revealing confidential statements made in the context of a relationship based on trust that can only be established between two individuals? True, everyone we talked to agreed to let us use their statements as we saw fit. But no contract carries as many unspoken conditions as one based on trust.
>
> (Bourdieu, 1999: 1; italics in original)

Other forms of betrayal result not from any amendment of the research participant's truth, or from the exposure of private intimacies, but from putting into print public truths that may appear to cast judgment on professional competence. Since prison ethnographies are often focussed on a single research site, the governors and senior practitioners who lead them are liable to feel that their leadership is under scrutiny, even when this is not the aim of the study. Without the truthfulness of the account being compromised, it is important to give appropriate regard to the sensitivities of these particular research subjects, just as it is routinely given to other, less powerful, subjects.

Closeness and distance

Perhaps what is most interesting about Malcolm's reflections on the dynamics of writing and betrayal is her repeated allusion to their temporal and spatial dimension. McGinniss, she reports,

> made a point of distinguishing between the reporting and the writing phases of the journalistic enterprise, speaking of them as if the one had nothing to do with the other, and as if the reporting and the writing were done by two different people.
>
> (Malcolm, 1990: 59)

Whilst she notes that McGinniss was ultimately condemned in court by admitting this distinction, she does not disagree with its terms: 'An abyss lies between the journalist's experience of being out in the world talking to people and his experience of being alone in a room writing' (1990: 59–60). Later in the book, she makes a more striking statement: 'Only when a subject breaks off relations with the writer [...] is the journalist in a completely uncompromised position' (Malcolm, 1990: 142), unshackled from the relationship, and therefore able to write with greater candour or objectivity.

If Malcolm is correct in her argument that the writer is only free to write truthfully once the relationship with the subject is severed, then it should not be hard for prison researchers to be liberated from the supposed constraints of physical and psychological proximity. Prisons are bounded environments, whose rituals of entry and exit, and whose material borders, communicate unambiguously their sequestration from wider society. This is the case for researchers as well as prisoners. It is not difficult to create psychological distance from the site of fieldwork, should one wish to, all the more so because of the tonal difference between the austerity of the prison environment and the often cloistered world of the university. Meanwhile, most prisoners want to forget their period of confinement and return to their pre-prison lives as soon as they can. Most researchers will therefore be right if they assume that, unless they actively seek to maintain contact with their research participants, the likelihood that they will see them again is slim. Most researchers will also recognise Malcolm's (1990: 143) observation that, after a certain amount of time had passed after her own interviews with MacDonald – and despite their continuing correspondence – 'He had (once again) become a character in a text, and his existence as a real person grew dim for me.' In most large research projects, and no doubt some small ones, whilst some interviewees are imprinted in human form in the memory, most fade and are first reconstituted as transcripts and then dismembered into extracts.

But, for current purposes, Malcolm's argument is questionable for two reasons. First, it is too generous to the writer, and in particular to the journalist, for it assumes that the break in contact and the reconstitution of memory work only in the interest of truthfulness. Yet distance can enable carelessness. Freed from the feeling of responsibility to the research participant or environment, the writer may be more tempted to write hyperbolically, to caricature (in the interests of a typology), to 'neaten' excessively (in the service of an argument), to forget that people who hold power as well as those subjected to it operate under constraint and so on. As Wacquant suggests, distancing can also lead to sentimentalism, in which the writer forgets or disregards negative sentiments or awkward data, in order to make the subject of research more sympathetic. To take a well-known example, one wonders whether Cohen and Taylor (1972) stifled or came to forget any negative feelings about some of the individuals on HMP Durham's E-wing in service of an account which came close to celebrating their criminal lifestyles. Our attempts at the honest representation of our subjects can be diverted by many otherwise admirable objectives, including political ideology, theory and humanisation.

Second, Malcolm's formulation implies that any obligation that is felt to the research subject is a *threat* to objectivity. This reading of obligation is extremely limited. In what follows, we reflect on the merits of such feelings, arguing for a form of 'accountability' in which retaining a connection to one's research subjects makes the process and output of writing more rather than less accurate. To do so, we draw on three examples from the first author's research history in which participants have maintained an enduring presence in and beyond the research project. Here, for the ease of the reader, we shift to the voice of the first person.

Example one: Jason

I had met Jason – his real name, used here with his permission – when undertaking a survey exercise in HMP Wellingborough prior to the main period of fieldwork, and once fieldwork began, he had stood out as an engaging and intelligent prisoner who was interested in my study and keen to discuss a range of related and unrelated issues whenever I was on the lifer wing where he was accommodated. I could not quite tell whether Jason liked me, as he gave little away, but he was always willing to help me try to understand the prison's social and moral community, and was extremely articulate in doing so. When he left Wellingborough to go to an open prison, we remained in contact, and in the following year, when a colleague organised a conference on 'The effects of imprisonment' at my university, I invited Jason to attend, which he did as a form of day release. Jason had educated himself whilst in prison (he had served a sentence of over a decade, starting when he was 17), and on release he secured an undergraduate place at the London School of Economics. Our friendship developed – Jason invited me to parties in his student house, and I invited him to my flat for dinner – as did our more professional relationship. On one occasion, having sent him copies of a couple of draft publications, I interviewed Jason semi-formally about my findings, and he subsequently interviewed me about my experience of the research process.

Towards the end of his time as an undergraduate, Jason said that he was interested in coming to the Institute of Criminology, where I was based, as an MPhil student, and that he was keen, if possible, to eventually do doctoral research, potentially under my supervision. I had some misgivings, only because I was unsure how this might compromise the non-professional side of our relationship, but this seemed less important than his educational ambitions. Awarded an Economic and Social Research Council 1 + 3 bursary, Jason eventually became one of my PhD students. This involved some unusual and discomfiting situations. In my 2009 book, *The Prisoner Society*, I had described him within my typology as a *stoic*, and made a number of claims about him – and his 'type' – that he might want to contest. In MPhil classes, on the 'sociology of prison life' (co-taught with Professor Alison Liebling), we often discussed quotations, attributed to his pseudonymous persona, which I was using to illustrate analytic points about penal power and the prisoner experience. It was impossible not to feel somewhat awkward: about who, in the class, knew what[5]; about how I was representing him to others; and about who had the greater right to interpret his words.

Example two: Alfie

A second interviewee with I had stayed in touch was Alfie – this time, a pseudonym – a sardonic and intelligent prisoner, who had served a large number of sentences mainly as a result of crimes committed due to his addiction to heroin. Like Jason, Alfie had attended the philosophy classes on which I occasionally sat in, and described himself as having been transformed by his educational experiences in the prison. Alfie would often talk to me about his daughter: his attempts to resume contact with her and his anxieties about doing so. He did not like himself a great deal – certainly not his past actions, when 'on the out' – and was not optimistic about his chances of 'making it' on release, given his chronic and prodigious appetite for drugs. In the period after I finished my fieldwork, and before he was released, we corresponded twice, and although he claimed that he would write to me after 'a few weeks of his '"sojourn" into the real world' (Crewe, 2009: 489), I was doubtful that he would. As I wrote on the last page of *The Prisoner Society*, in the silence that followed, I assumed that he was either back on drugs, back in prison, or no longer alive.

Two years later, I received a brief email, from a woman who said that she was Alfie's daughter. He had died, she told me, and she had found my letters when clearing out his house. Could I send her some of the work in which I had written about him? Of course I could, I said; but, after some reflection, I realised that doing so was not entirely straightforward. Alfie had told me a great deal about the turmoil of his life and that of his wider family, and it was far from clear to me that he would have wanted anyone closely related to him to read about such things. He was dead, of course, but I could not predict how the revelation of family secrets, and of intimate feelings, might reverberate through the family he had left behind. Naturally, I had anonymised him in the book, and changed some identifying characteristics, but what was I now to do: maintain my commitment to anonymity, and send his daughter a copy of the book (a stupidly long book), without telling her who her father was within it (i.e. that he was 'Alfie'); or break it and potentially expose him, even when deceased? I chose the former, and did not hear from her again.

Example three: Prison Service practitioners

My study had been approved by the Prison Service. I wanted to disseminate its findings to senior practitioners within the service (amongst others), and the organisation had an official right, given the normal terms of access, to see copies of its outputs prior to publication. On submitting my first article arising from the research to a journal, 'The Prisoner Society in the Era of Hard Drugs', I sent a copy to the Director General of the Prison Service, Phil Wheatley. Although I had not expected a response, I was pleased to receive one. It thanked me for the draft article, made some complimentary (and non-defensive) comments about its content and argument and also raised some questions:

> What I thought wasn't brought out as clearly as I might have expected, was the explanation for the apparent contradiction in your description of Wellingborough between a relatively plentiful supply of hard drugs so that 'smack-heads' can maintain an almost street level of usage while, at the same time, others who are 'smack-heads' on the outside, find it relatively easy to give up while inside. Although I have nowhere near the detailed knowledge that you have of drug use in Wellingborough, my contacts with prisoners suggest that even regular users inside cannot sustain a street level habit because [...] security does succeed in restricting the supply somewhat and certainly, as you point out, puts up the price. It has also been suggested in other establishments, not only does the price go up but also the quality of the product on sale is not as pure as it would be on the street.
>
> (Wheatley, personal communication, March 2004)

The other practitioner to whom I sent the article was Jim Lewis, the man who had been the prison's governor (though not the governor who had originally granted access) during my fieldwork, as well as a student on the part-time Masters course on which I taught. I had been nervous about sending him the article: he had presided over a difficult period in the prison's history, and the article formed part of a wider description of a struggling establishment.

Like Phil Wheatley, Jim responded to the article in a way that was generous and insightful. Whilst Wheatley had identified a potential weakness in the argument, Lewis had identified a form of language that was careless:

> I really enjoyed the article and found much of what it said fascinating and would not want to suggest any changes to its substance. If it's not too late there is one comment that I would like to suggest. On page 8 you use the phrase that Wellingborough 'became flooded' with soft and hard drugs. I am not actually sure what that means, although it is a term that I hear used by some members of the security team. The rest of your article is very precise and 'became flooded' is such an emotive term that it seems a little incongruous. I don't think it is an accurate description and would prefer something like 'saw a significant increase'. You might say that this is a bit nit-picky.
>
> (Lewis, personal communication, March 2004)

Both respondents had raised legitimate and helpful points, which improved the final article.[6]

All of these examples help to illustrate the dynamics and benefits of a form of accountability that is often neglected in the literature on prison ethnography. Consulting with research participants, having a sense of them in our head, and maintaining a mental or material connection with them, need not, as Malcolm suggests, corrupt or compromise the process of writing accurately. The opposite should be true. Here, prison researchers might want to think, and be reflexively explicit, about the 'imagined' reader or readers in their heads – a term that is often discussed by novelists, but much less so, in our experience, by academics. Even where anthropologists have written on matters of readership and audience, the implication is often that research participants enter the process only at the point 'when they read what we write' (see Brettell, 1993). The temporal distinction between 'researching' and 'writing' therefore remains intact. The point that we wish to make is, first, that there is something to be gained from having in one's head a sense of the research participant (whether or not they become an actual reader), and, second, that the distinction between the phase of being in the field and being in the office (and our loyalties at these two moments in time) thereby collapses, at least in part.

Liking and disliking

In the dynamic described by Janet Malcolm, and in the debate in the *American Journal of Sociology*, the writer's attitude to the interviewee is initially and essentially sympathetic. The assumption is that the intimacy of the research process requires us to appear to like our interviewee or that it generates a genuine emotional affinity. Sometimes, though, even the most empathic interviewers are likely to encounter someone whom they dislike, who makes them feel unsafe or morally uneasy, or whose views repel them. The risk of this occurring seems particularly high amongst prison researchers, and many have written about such experiences. Phillips and Earle (2010) recount the difficulties of encountering attitudes towards race that they found highly unsettling in their study of ethnicity and masculinity in English prisons. In his highly candid account of his research in a Federal Penitentiary (in which he served as a corrections officer), Fleisher (1989: 110–11) explains his complete antipathy towards one inmate – 'From the instant I saw him in September 1986, I despised him.... The longer I sat next to him, the more I hated him' – and describes being disappointed in hearing that he had *not* been killed in a knife attack. Discussing her highly conflicted sentiments, and limit point of engagement, during her fieldwork in prisons in Ecuador, Fleetwood (2009: 42) quotes from fieldwork notes that describe: 'The tension between trying to balance up how I understand that guys that I like and have respect for and are good to me are murderers and have a capacity for cruelty and violence that I have no understanding of'. Such tales from the field are refreshing, for we should be suspicious of what Phillips and

Earle (2010: 374) call 'sociologically "airbrushed" accounts' of the research process. Authenticity is key to undertaking research, and an important component of authenticity is *disliking* some people (Bourgois, 1996: 254–5).

Fleetwood's representation of a kind of moral *ambivalence* is a more accurate reflection of our research experience than Malcolm's description of the 'fuzziness and murkiness, if not utter covertness, of purpose' at the heart of the journalist–subject relationship. Malcolm's claim is that 'If everybody put his cards on the table, the game would be over. The journalist must do his work in a kind of deliberately induced state of *moral anarchy* (Malcolm, 1990: 142–3, italics added). 'Ambivalence' captures the cognitive dissonance of liking and not liking someone simultaneously, for example, enjoying the company of someone who admits to having committed a grotesquely violent act, and who may describe it with little remorse. It suggests a suspension of judgment that is necessary in order to distinguish between the person and the offence, or an attitude that is genuinely conflicted. It also seems appropriate for describing the peculiar experience of not knowing whether we sympathise with someone or not because their index offence challenges our ability to separate out who they are from what they have done, whilst at the same time they may dispute the act that shapes this judgement.

Here, an example may be helpful. As part of a recent study of long-term imprisonment,[7] the first author of this chapter undertook an interview with a prisoner in open conditions, who had been incarcerated for over 30 years. In the interview, he explained that he had been convicted of murdering a child, but disputed his guilt, as he had done unwaveringly throughout his sentence. The use of a Google search prior to the interview – perhaps incautious – meant that first author/interviewer knew more about the offence details than the research participant disclosed. As the father of a young child, these details felt particularly morally troubling. It was harder than normal not to make a judgment about the person based on his offence. The interview was difficult: one of the very few occasions on which this interviewer has ever struggled to find a point of connection with the interviewee, who he found arrogant, angry and charmless. It was difficult to distinguish these sentiments about him as a person from an assessment of his guilt or innocence. But there was an alternative possibility that he was the victim of an obscene and devastating miscarriage of justice, one which would make almost anyone bitter and defensive.

There are questions here about whether or not liking or disliking someone matters, about whether their innocence or guilt is relevant to these processes, and about whether we should trust or discard our feelings about both of these issues. It is unsurprising that most empathic researchers find few interviewees dislikeable in person, and we agree with Drake (2012) that it is rare to feel that one is confronting someone who is monstrous, even when interviewing those who have committed extremely violent crimes. There are very few people with whom one cannot make a human connection, or find a shared moral framework. Conversely, we can dislike people not because they strike us as morally repugnant, but for reasons that are much more prosaic or difficult to justify, that is, because they are cocky, or boorish or dull. However, how this is telling or relevant is another matter: people are certainly more than their crimes, but so too are they more than the person we meet when we interview them. We do not seek to resolve these questions here. Rather, we want to highlight some of the ways in which prison researchers have described and addressed these issues, emphasising some characteristic differences between how they do so according to who their research subjects are, or what they have done.

Prison research and research sympathies

Echoing similar shifts in anthropology and other areas of social science, prison research seems to be undergoing a quiet revolution, in which the voices of the researched are increasingly being expressed in its writings. Many prison researchers pride themselves on giving voice to the voiceless, and, as Jewkes argues, criminologists often 'pursue particular research agendas precisely because they are drawn to marginalized, exploited, or dominated groups' (2012: 65). However, the voices and experiences of some prisoners have always been more valued than others. As Waldram argues, 'this new sensitivity [towards giving voice] did not transfer to all categories of the silenced. [...] Some, apparently, deserved to remain in the shadows; sexual offenders, for instance' (2007: 967). O'Donnell refers to this tendency for mainstream male prisoners to be more valorised than imprisoned sex offenders as a 'regrettable [...] bias' (2004: 253).[8] Sex offenders are an absent presence both within prison sociology and within prisons themselves, where they are often 'physically present' but 'shunned' (Holmberg, 2001: 86). In academic writing, where their exclusion and abuse is described, this is almost always from the perspective of mainstream prisoners (e.g. Åkerström, 1986), with very few attempts made to describe their own 'culture'.

More importantly, in the context of this chapter, whilst a considerable amount of research has been conducted with imprisoned sex offenders, its objectives generally seem to differ from research conducted with mainstream prisoners. Whereas the latter more often aims to understand the experience of imprisonment and thereby reform the prison (e.g. Liebling, 2014), the former is more often directed at reforming the offender, or preventing further offences, for example, by developing greater insight into treatment experiences and offence narratives (e.g. Blagden and Pemberton, 2010). In his article 'Everyone Has a Story: Listening to Imprisoned Sex Offenders', Waldram asks if we 'should [...] allow the stories of sexual offenders to be heard' (2007: 968) and justifies listening to sex offenders by noting that '[t]he only way to eliminate the problem and protect ourselves is to understand it as fully as possible' (p. 969). The implication is that sex offending is so dangerous, and sex offenders so abhorrent, that our rationale for researching them requires a consequentialist logic, organised around the *offence*. In contrast, researchers of mainstream prisoners are more often motivated by a desire to understand imprisonment, improve conditions and 'validate' (Bosworth et al., 2005: 259) the humanity of their research subjects.

These divergent aims are reflected in the different types of relationships researchers form with sex offenders and with mainstream prisoners. Because those conducting research with mainstream prisoners declare humanising motivations, typically, they make clear that they like and identify with mainstream prisoners, whilst questioning the ethics of researching (rather than advocating for) them (e.g. Bosworth et al., 2005; Liebling, 2014). Phillips and Earle, for example, acknowledge that the pain-imbued stories told by many prisoners can generate echoed pain in the researcher and lead to 'uncomfortable feelings of exploitation and disloyalty' (Phillips and Earle, 2010: 365, footnote 3). This model of relating to research participants can be understood as *sympathy-as-obligation*, in which the researcher feels discomfort for having taken advantage of prisoner-participants in narrowly defined research encounters. Jacobs, for example, describes feeling 'sincere concern for those inmates one knows personally as well as for inmates in general' and claims that 'it is scarcely possible to avoid being hounded by the feeling that one does not care enough' (1974: 237). He goes on to suggest that researchers should resolve this quandary and pay their 'moral debt' (ibid.) either through 'individual reciprocities (e.g. parole recommendations, help in finding employment)' (pp. 238–9) or by becoming involved in prisoner advocacy and prison reform.

Jacobs describes his ethical quandary in symbolic-interactionist terms as a 'gap between role and self' (p. 238). As a researcher, he was supposed to be impartial and to leave the research environment behind him once he left it every evening; as a human being, he felt sympathetic towards prisoners and compelled to offer them assistance. Other researchers working with mainstream prisoners have likewise explained that their personal characteristics, who they are as people, influences the work that they do. Phillips and Earle (2010), for example, advocate authorial reflexivity in order that researchers become aware of the ways in which 'we may distort, misrepresent or have subjects' experiences obscured from view because of *our* biographical experiences or subjectivities' (p. 374, italics in original); this should help to 'make more transparent the interpretive process' (ibid.). Like Jacobs, the emphasis is on researchers bringing their identities with them into the prison.

Those who discuss researching sex offenders, however, typically describe different relationships with prisoners, seeing them as something to be explained, excused or apologised for. This is a different ethical quandary – one which partly derives from a greater research focus on *offending* – and could be characterised as *sympathy-as-problem*. In this model, the researcher is focused on gathering information, and the development of a sympathetic research relationship generates *discomfort*. For example, both Scully (1990) and Hudson (2005) admit to feeling guilty for liking sex offenders. Scully suggests that her readers might be surprised that she empathised with some of the convicted sex offenders she interviewed. Such 'emotions may be more expected when the subjects are people with a sympathetic cause', she says, but 'convicted rapists too are human' (p. 18). Blagden and Pemberton report having 'to reconcile their own moral position as the building of rapport with research participants can sometimes lead to a genuine liking of that person' (2010: 272). As a corrective to the rapport that can be formed with violent and sexual offenders, Cowburn suggests that researchers should 'be mindful of the person who was hurt by the violence'; this is the only way of preventing the research from being 'a collusive engagement that ignores or denies the violence done to the victim(s)' (2013: 190), with whom the researcher's loyalty should ultimately reside.[9] Waldram comes closest to forming the kind of conventionally sympathetic research relationships that tends to be described in mainstream prisons research, but claims to have sought 'ethnographic empathy' (2012: 44), rather than sympathy.

Unlike Jacobs, whose sympathy with prisoners is seen as an *extension* of his non-researching self, Waldram's relationships with prisoners challenged his personal identity. He reports struggling to maintain 'disciplined empathy' because he 'was positioned not only as a researcher in hearing these tales but as a father and a husband and a member of the community' (2007: 966). Crewe (2014: 396) has suggested that these challenges are ultimately gendered, arguing that '[i]nterviews with sex offenders seem to bring into relief male scholars' self-conceptions in ways that research with mainstream male prisoners do not'. This is possibly because sex offenders 'often appear completely ordinary as men, [which] exposes the continuum on which both normative heterosexuality and criminally deviant masculine sexuality lie' (ibid.). This self-consciousness may be generated by similarity or betrayed solidarity rather than masculinity: Alisa Stevens, who conducted research with residents in prison-based 'therapeutic communities', found it hardest to differentiate between the offence and the offender 'with one of my female participants whose sexual victimization of women baffled and offended me, as a woman. I felt unjustifiably disappointed in her, as if she had betrayed "the sisterhood"' (2013: 46). Regardless, as well as discussing how they bring their identities with them into the field – as described above – those who conduct research with sex offenders instead describe their research experiences as *seeping out* of the prison and infecting their outside identities. Hudson, for example, describes 'a growing cynicism [...] with regard to other people's sexual and sensual actions' (2005: 8), which altered her relationship with her father. Similarly, hearing stories about sexual offences led Decoene (2013) to become self-conscious and uncomfortable with her own physical relationships with her children.

Here, then, we see a division between researchers' sense of identity in day-to-day life and the role they play as people researching sex offenders. What results is a form of alienation in which research encounters are not bound by the sorts of moral rules that researchers follow in normal life. In particular, many researchers are quite open about their pragmatic dishonesty during interviews. Cowburn (2007) and Scully (1990) listened to the sex offenders they interviewed passively and unchallengingly, critiquing them only when analysing their data and writing up; Scully presented 'a supportive, nonjudgmental, neutral facade – one that [she] did not always genuinely feel', but did not find it difficult to return to what she calls 'objectivity' (p. 18) after the interviews were over. Waldram felt ethical obligations to his research participants, but says that he was unwilling to spend too much time with prison and treatment staff as this might lead his research participants to assume 'that I was some sort of covert operative or else sympathetic to staff concerns and perspectives (I was, of course, but could not let on)' (2012: 43). The consequentialist motivation of these researchers – their commitment to preventing sexual offending – leads them to follow utilitarian ethics within the interview. Rather than being bound by virtues of honesty and integrity, they act instrumentally to obtain the information they desire. This is much closer to the 'deliberately induced state of moral anarchy' which Malcolm (1990: 143) depicts. They also appear less likely to share anthropologists' concerns about the ethics of returning research to the researched (e.g. Brettell, 1993), concerns which are increasingly reported by mainstream prison researchers (Cohen and Taylor, 1972; Bosworth et al., 2005; Farrant, 2014).

This author–subject hierarchy seems to result in part from concerns about 'offence-specific denial' which, Digard (2014: 429) argues, together with 'fear of manipulation [has] been generalised to invalidate sex offenders' voices more broadly'. These concerns about denial infiltrate the research encounter itself: many researchers express worries about reinforcing denial and cognitive distortions through 'passive collusion' with those they interview (Digard, 2010: 215; see also Scully, 1990; Cowburn, 2005b; Waldram, 2007). The language of cognitive distortion seeps even into discussions of the effects of the research on the *researcher*: Ó Ciardha (2014) has described the 'distortion' researchers sometimes develop when their empathy with sex offenders leads them to see victims 'as stumbling blocks to rehabilitation or as agents of risk'. When discussing an awkward encounter with one sex offender, Blagden and Pemberton describe it as 'vital [...] not to subscribe or fall victim to his attempts to justify his account' (2010: 273). The language here is striking. To believe a research subject is to fall victim to them, and the implication is that the researcher should start from a position of wariness and disbelief. Amongst researchers of mainstream prisoners, such terms are almost heretical.

Conclusion

In commenting on these distinctions between the ways that researchers of mainstream prisoners and sex offenders write about their research sympathies and loyalties, we do not wish to sound critical of scholars in either camp. Having undertaken research with sex offenders, both of us recognise the sentiments and misgivings that we have sought to describe (and can see why research that is focussed on serious sexual offending might generate such feelings all the more powerfully). But we are somewhat troubled by them and believe that they deserve further reflection, because they seem not only to reproduce wider discourses about particular kinds of offenders but also to challenge some of the claims that ethnographic prison researchers routinely make about their motivations. If – as Jewkes (2012) argues – we are drawn to marginalised people, we should be drawn to those prisoners who are especially marginal. If we claim to be driven by a desire to give voice to the voiceless, and to describe the experiences of the otherwise invisible, then what does it mean if the exercise of these drives is limited?

We would argue that a humanistic research orientation can be applied both to the process of ethnographic researching and to its writing. It should involve extending sympathy without prejudice, professionally (and not in the coldly instrumental manner that Malcolm implies). This will not prevent us as researchers from having more ambivalent sentiments, nor should we feel guilty when we do so. Indeed, ambivalence should be embraced, and may be an essential component of ethnographic research practice. It is possible and perhaps preferable to maintain a bifocal view of prisoners, in which we allow ourselves to like and dislike them. It is possible too to aim for a form of representation that is faithful to both human and theoretical complexity.

Notes

1. 'In that beginning of *The Journalist and the Murderer* I stated, in a very larger-than-life way, what the problem was. It was a piece of rhetoric' (Malcolm, cited in Wood, 2013).
2. However, we do not doubt that many journalists are much less cynical, and many academics much more, than is suggested here.
3. 'I ask Malcolm if she has done anything as an interviewer that she feels guilty about. There is a long pause, filled by birdsong and the sound of a breeze through the tall grass beyond the porch. "Well, I guess the general guilt is about stories. That you're telling a different story than the subject tells about himself or herself. There's just that yawning gap. That's the nature of the problem."' (Wood, 2013).
4. '...as far removed from pure laissez-faire of the non-directive interview as from the directiveness of the questionnaire survey' (p. 19).

5. Many people.
6. Both are quoted here with their permission.
7. Experiencing very long-term imprisonment from young adulthood, Ben Crewe, Susie Hulley and Serena Wright. ESRC grant ES/J007935/1.
8. The term 'mainstream prisoners' refers to those who have not been convicted of a sexual offence.
9. In this particular chapter, Cowburn discusses the ethics of researching all violent men, and not just those who have committed sexual offences. However, his findings are based on his earlier work with sex offenders (Cowburn, 2005a, 2005b, 2010).

Further readings

Any ethnographer will benefit from reading the argument between Wacquant and Duneier referred to in the chapter:

Duneier, M. (2002) 'What Kind of Combat Sport Is Sociology?' *American Journal of Sociology*, 107, 6 (May 2002), 1551–76.

Wacquant, L. (2002) 'Scrutinizing the Street: Poverty, Morality, and the Pitfalls of Urban Ethnography', *American Journal of Sociology*, 107, 6 (May 2002), 1468–1532.

Also recommended:

Malcolm, J. (1990/2012) *The Journalist and the Murderer* (London: Granta).

Waldram, J. B. (2012) *Hound Pound Narrative: Sexual Offender Habilitation and the Anthropology of Therapeutic Intervention* (Berkeley, CA: University of California Press).

References

Åkerström, M. (1986) 'Outcasts in Prison: The Cases of Informers and Sex Offenders', *Deviant Behavior*, 7, 1, 1–12.

Anderson, E. (2002) 'The Ideologically Driven Critique', *American Journal of Sociology*, 107, 6, 1533–50.

Blagden, N. and Pemberton, S. (2010) 'The Challenge in Conducting Qualitative Research with Convicted Sex Offenders', *The Howard Journal of Criminal Justice*, 49, 3, 269–81.

Bosworth, M., Campbell, D., Demby, B., et al. (2005) 'Doing Prison Research: Views from Inside', *Qualitative Inquiry*, 11, 2, 249–64.

Bourdieu, P. (1999) *The Weight of the World: Social Suffering in Contemporary Society* (Stanford, CA: Stanford University Press).

Bourdieu, P. (1996) 'Understanding', *Theory, Culture, Society*, 13, 17–37.

Bourgeois, P. (1996) 'Confronting Anthropology, Education, and Inner-City Apartheid'. *American Anthropologist*, 98, 2, 249–58.

Brettell, C. B. (ed) (1993) *When They Read What We Write* (Westport, CT: Bergin & Garvey).

Cohen, S. and Taylor, L. (1972) *Psychological Survival: The Experience of Long-Term Imprisonment* (Harmondsworth: Penguin Books).

Cole, S. and Dumas, M. (2010) Shadowboxing with the ghost of Bourdieu, Goldsmiths, University of London, https://www.gold.ac.uk/media/Cole-Dumasfinalpaper.pdf

Cowburn, M. (2005a) 'Confidentiality and Public Protection: Ethical Dilemmas in Qualitative Research with Adult Male Sex Offenders', *Journal of Sexual Aggression*, 11, 1, 49–63.

Cowburn, M. (2005b) 'Hegemony and Discourse: Reconstruing the Male Sex Offender and Sexual Coercion by Men', *Sexualities, Evolution and Gender*, 7, 3, 215–31.

Cowburn, M. (2007) 'Men Researching Men in Prison: The Challenges for Profeminist Research', *The Howard Journal of Criminal Justice*, 46, 3, 276–88.

Cowburn, M. (2010) 'Principles, Virtues and Care: Ethical Dilemmas in Research with Male Sex Offenders', *Psychology, Crime & Law*, 16, 1, 64–74.

Cowburn, M. (2013) 'Men Researching Violent Men: Epistemologies, Ethics and Emotions in Qualitative Research', in B. Pini and B. Pease (eds) *Men, Masculinities and Methodologies*, pp. 183–96 (Houndsmills: Palgrave-Macmillan).

Crewe, B. (2009) *The Prisoner Society: Power, Adaptation and Social Life in an English Prison* (Oxford: OUP).

Crewe, B. (2014) 'Not Looking Hard Enough: Masculinity, Emotion, and Prison Research', *Qualitative Inquiry*, 20, 4, 426–37.

Decoene, S. (2013) 'Criminological-Psychological Case-Work: Consequences of Visiting the Pits of Hell', in K. Beyens, J. Christiaens, B. Claes et al. (eds) *The Pains of Doing Criminological Research*, pp. 89–104 (Brussels: Vubpress).

Digard, L. (2010) *Sex Offenders and Their Probation Officers' Perceptions of Community Management in England and Wales.* Unpublished PhD thesis, University of Cambridge.

Digard, L. (2014) 'Encoding Risk: Probation Work and Sex Offenders' Narrative Identities', *Punishment & Society*, 16, 4, 428–47.

Drake, D. (2012) *Prisons, Punishment and the Pursuit of Security* (Basingstoke: Palgrave Macmillan).

Farrant, F. (2014) 'Unconcealment: What Happens When We Tell Stories', *Qualitative Inquiry*, 20, 4, 461–70.

Fleetwood, J. (2009) 'Emotional Work: Ethnographic Fieldwork in Prisons in Ecuador', *E-Sharp, Special Issue: Critical Issues in Researching in Hidden Communities*, 28–50.

Fleisher, M. (1989) *Warehousing Violence* (Newbury Park, CA: Sage).

Holmberg, C. (2001) 'The Culture of Transgression: Initiations into the Homosociality of a Midwestern State Prison', in D. Sabo, Terry A. Kupers and W. London (eds) *Prison Masculinities*, pp. 78, 92 (Philadelphia, PA: Temple University Press).

Hudson, K. (2005) *Offending Identities: Sex Offenders' Perspectives on Their Treatment and Management* (London: Willan Publishing).

Jacobs, J. B. (1974) 'Participant Observation in Prison', *Urban Life and Culture*, 3, 2, 221–40.

Jewkes, Y. (2012) 'Autoethnography and Emotion as Intellectual Resources: Doing Prison Research Differently', *Qualitative Inquiry*, 18, 1, 63–75.

Jewkes, Y. (2014) 'An Introduction to "Doing Prison Research Differently."' *Qualitative Inquiry*, 20, 4, 387–91.

Liebling, A. (2001) 'Whose Side Are We On? Theory, Practice and Allegiances in Prisons Research', *British Journal of Criminology*, 41, 3, 472–84.

Liebling, A. (2014) 'Postscript: Integrity and Emotion in Prisons Research', *Qualitative Inquiry*, 20, 4, 481–6.

Malcolm, J. (1990/2012) *The Journalist and the Murderer* (London: Granta).

Ó Ciardha, C. (2014) 'The Effects of Researching the Incomprehensible Nextgenforensic on WordPress.com'. Available from: http://nextgenforensic.wordpress.com/2014/March/16/the-effects-of-researching-the-incomprehensible/ (accessed 3 November 2014).

O'Donnell, I. (2004) 'Prison Rape in Context', *British Journal of Criminology*, 44, 2, 241–55.

Phillips, C. and Earle, R. (2010) 'Reading Difference Differently?: Identity, Epistemology and Prison Ethnography', *British Journal of Criminology*, 50, 2, 360–78.

Rock, P. (1979) *The Making of Symbolic Interactionism* (London: Routledge and Kegan Paul).
Roberts, S. (2011) 'Doing Research with Imprisoned Adult Male Child Sexual Abusers: Reflecting on the Challenges', *Child Abuse Review*, 20, 3, 187–96.
Scully, D. (1990) *Understanding Sexual Violence: A Study of Convicted Rapists* (Boston, MA: Unwin Hyman Inc.).
Stevens, A. (2013) *Offender Rehabilitation and Therapeutic Communities: Enabling Change the TC Way* (London: Routledge).
Waldram, J. B. (2007) 'Everybody Has a Story: Listening to Imprisoned Sexual Offenders', *Qualitative Health Research*, 17, 7, 963–70.
Waldram, J. B. (2012) *Hound Pound Narrative: Sexual Offender Habilitation and the Anthropology of Therapeutic Intervention* (Berkeley, CA: University of California Press).
Wood, G. (2013) 'Devil in the Detail: Janet Malcolm Interview', *The Telegraph*, 29 July 2013.

7
Going in Green: Reflections on the Challenges of 'Getting In, Getting On, and Getting Out' for Doctoral Prisons Researchers

Jennifer Sloan and Serena Wright

Introduction

Hardly any scholarly attention has been paid to the first-time prison researcher. What little commentary does exist (e.g. Smith and Wincup, 2000, 2002) is primarily focused on providing practical tips for novice researchers within criminal justice institutions which, whilst helpful, do little to prepare the inexperienced, 'greenhead' researcher for the lived emotions and experiences of the task of conducting prisons research. Even the most seasoned researchers are in no way immune to the 'pains' and 'turbulence' of prison-based fieldwork (cf. Liebling, 1999); however, for the *neophyte* prisons researcher, these pains can be magnified, particularly given the exhaustion, isolation and 'shock' of working in the field for the first time (Smith and Wincup, 2000). This 'shock' undoubtedly results from the lack of studies which exist to adequately equip and prepare novitiates to prisons research, an issue which is arguably part of the broader dearth of scholarly attention previously paid to the emotive aspects of work undertaken in this environment (see Liebling, 1999; Jewkes, 2012).

This chapter begins to redress this imbalance by engaging with the lived emotions and experiences of 'going in green' to prisons research. Both authors undertook prison research as part of the PhD process – Jennifer in an adult male, category C prison, looking qualitatively into masculinity and the adult male prison experience; and Serena in two closed female prisons, studying the life stories of repeatedly criminalised women. It details the authors' positive experiences of prisons research, as well as utilising some of the problems experienced as parables designed to help the first-time prisons researcher expect the unexpected. It offers instructional tips on gaining access, on conducting oneself in the prison environment during the research process, as well as on 'getting out' when the time comes to leave the field behind. Finally, the chapter also draws on the advice and guidance of experienced prisons researchers, to guide neophytes in 'getting in, getting on, and getting out' (key phases as suggested by Buchanan et al. (1988) in organisational research more broadly, and by Smith and Wincup (2000) in researching criminal justice organisations) of prison-based research.

Emotions, ethnography and the first-time prison researcher

A small body of research does exist to provide practical tips to the novice prison researcher. Smith and Wincup, whose piece stimulated the focus upon 'getting in', 'getting on' and 'getting out' that we follow here, speak of their doctoral research experiences, and the more practical aspects of the process in terms of identity negotiation, access, and politics in the research process. In another piece, they similarly brought the PhD experience to the fore (in prison and in bail hostels) regarding the ethical issues they experienced during their fieldwork. While their analysis is extremely useful with regard to the *practical* aspects of being a feminist criminological novitiate prisons researcher, rarely is space given over to considering the emotional, *visceral* experience of their respective projects; that is, their analysis lacks a view from 'both sides of the voyeur's keyhole', something which Denzin (1997: 47) has identified as being central to the ethnographic project. Smith and Wincup are not alone in this – a similar case in point is Townsend and Burgess's (2009) edited collection, which gives voice to various methodological issues rarely discussed yet also lacks the personal reflexivity inherent to ethnographic research.

King and Liebling (2008) made an important contribution to the discussion in terms of practical advice for those new to prisons research, suggesting 10 nostrums for embarking on studies within the carceral environment (King and Liebling, 2008: 442):

1. You have to be there.
2. You have to do your time.
3. You should not work alone unless you have to.
4. You have to know why you are there.
5. You must always remember that research has costs for staff and prisoners.
6. You must know when to open your mouth and when to keep it closed.
7. You must do whatever you have to do to observe but do not go native.
8. You should triangulate your data collection wherever possible.
9. You must strike a balance between publicity and anonymity.
10. You should try to leave the site as clean as possible.

Again, while King and Liebling acknowledge the potential for harm in Nostrum 3, overall their suggestions lack a degree of emotional engagement, eschewing the possibility that – expanding on Nostrum 5 – prisons research can also have 'costs' for those *undertaking it*.

While one can find reference to the emotional dimension of prisons research in a wide range of texts (cf. Crewe, 2014), it is perhaps only recently that the need to engage with the specific 'emotional demands' of ethnographic research in prison has come to the fore, particularly following the influential work of Jewkes (2012). In this, Jewkes charges prison scholars who decline to discuss the emotive landscape of their work with failing those who come after them (Jewkes, 2012: 64):

> [I]n failing to disclose their autoethnographic roles and their own emotional responses to what are frequently challenging and highly charged emotional environments, prison scholars are doing a disservice to those who follow them (e.g., doctoral students) who frequently approach the field with high levels of anxiety.

An important and rare exception to this rule can be found in Wacquant's (2002) appraisal of his first time in Los Angeles County Jail. Describing himself as 'literally gasping trying to keep my emotions under control' upon entering the prison, he presents his reaction to 'getting out' (Wacquant, 2002, cited in Crewe, 2014: 394):

> I am like *numb* coming out of this long afternoon inside [the prison], and I drive silently straight to the beach, to wallow in fresh air and wade in the waves, as if to 'cleanse' myself of all I've seen, heard, and sensed. I feel so bad, like scrambled eggs, that I chafe at writing up my notes until the following Tuesday... Every time my mind drifts back to it, it seems like a bad movie, a nightmare, the vision of an evil 'other world' that cannot actually exist.

While the difficult nature of prison research has been acknowledged in the past by a number of key researchers (e.g. see Liebling, 1999; Piacentini, 2007; Crewe, 2009; Drake and Harvey, 2013) – although perhaps not to this degree – none have spoken thoroughly about those issues which may be specific to, or more keenly felt by, those 'going in green' to prison research, nor engaging in practical talk to identify those lessons which have been learned in relation to going into the prison 'equipped' to deal with it.

Experiential context

The experiential context that informs these reflections comes from three studies that the authors undertook: two for doctoral research, and one directly to inform us regarding others' experiences of undertaking prison ethnography.

Study one: 'Men inside: Masculinity and the adult male prison experience'[1]

In this study, Jennifer undertook a period of ethnographic prison research in an adult male category C prison, spending a period of four months in the summer of 2009 in the prison, conducting 31 semi-structured interviews, wing observations, volunteering and doing small tasks in the offender management unit in order to remain immersed in the setting, and keeping reflexive research diaries. The research ultimately found that men in prison maintain their masculine identities in ways that conflict with how men are expected (and able) to be men outside prison, as well as finding that men maintain their masculinities in prison in varied (and sometimes unexpected) ways (Sloan, 2011; 2012a; 2012b). During the study, reflexive diaries were kept, initially as a means to record field notes, but also developing into a place where feelings and reflections on the process of doing research in prison could be maintained as a form of emotional purging at the end of a day. The research was done at a distance from any formal support networks in terms of academic supervisors and research community ties, so the researcher was somewhat academically isolated during the ethnographic period. Other than a single day spent visiting a prison, this was the first time that the researcher had been in a prison environment as a researcher so it was a new and different experience to interpret.

Study two: ' "Persistent" and "prolific" offending across the life-course as experienced by women: Chronic recidivism and frustrated desistance'[2]

The prison-based element of the second study, undertaken as part of Serena's doctoral research, centred on a series of in-depth life-history interviews with 12 women identifiable as 'persistent' (i.e. 6 or more convictions over the life course) and/or 'prolific offenders' (i.e. those officially identified as 'Prolific and Other Priority Offenders'). These interviews took place in the autumn of 2010 in two closed female prisons in England; one for remand and sentenced prisoners, and the other for sentenced prisoners only. While not established as 'an ethnography' in the purist sense, the study embodied many of the core values and practices of ethnographic work by being 'multiperspectival'. It was also a 'feminist' project and informed by feminist epistemologies (cf. Cook and Fonow, 1986; Davies, 2000). This involved an appreciation of the *viscerality* of 'understanding', and 'seeking to find a space and voice' for individuals, such as women in prison, who might not otherwise have a presence in the extant literature (Denzin, 1997: 45–6). The overall research findings drew attention to the centrality of addiction in the 'criminal careers' of female persistent and prolific [PAOP] offenders, and that these addictions often had their roots in women's acute trauma histories, and the subsequent adoption of substance use as a (maladaptive, and enduring) coping strategy. The biographical accounts provided by the women suggest that the language of 'persistence' may serve to obscure the lived realities of repeat criminalisation, which in their experience were better understood as recurrent episodes of attempted, or *frustrated*, desistance.

Similar to Jennifer's experience, research diaries were initially kept as a means of informing the later data interpretation and analysis, and to encourage a reflexive appraisal of oneself – in Denzin's words – 'from both sides of the voyeur's keyhole'; however these were similarly found to be exceptionally effective as a tool for 'self-debriefing' (or 'emotional purging', as Jennifer notes) following the day's interviewing. While having had previous experience of lone-working in a male category B prison, as a key-carrying member of the Independent Monitoring Board,[3] the environ of the *female* prison was a new experience, as was the nature of the prisoner–researcher interaction, and of returning alone to unfamiliar accommodation with only a digital recorder and a head full of the lives and experiences of the interviewees for company.

Study three: The 'Going in Green' survey[4]

The final study was conducted in response to being asked to write this chapter. We felt that it would be useful to get thoughts and reflections from researchers with more experience than ourselves, in order to help and provide suggestions to others in the position of starting out on the prison ethnography journey. This study took the form of a survey entitled *'Reflections on the challenges of 'getting in, getting on and getting out' for prisons researchers'*, which was sent out electronically to selected prison ethnographers, chosen as a result of their knowledge of, and experiences in, the field of prison ethnography. Participants could choose to have their names revealed or to remain anonymous. While we acknowledge that interviewing these individuals would have been a preferable method of data generation, resource restrictions necessitated a more flexible approach. In the survey, questions were asked about participants' first time in prison, the processes of getting in, getting on and getting out, and the perceived impact of their prison research. Of particular interest and relevance to this chapter were the suggestions and tips that participants would give to others starting out in prisons research – these will be discussed later.

Getting in

Negotiating access to any organisation – and particular criminal justice organisations – for the purposes of research is (Smith and Wincup, 2000: 335):

> a time-consuming and problematic process for outside researchers, not least because of the 'sensitivity' of much criminological research, but also because many areas of interest are surrounded by political controversy.

However, 'few writings' discuss these 'politics of negotiating access' (Smith and Wincup, 2000), nor 'the nuances of the micro-relations that prison researchers [in particular] must enter into in order to negotiate their access on a *daily basis*' (Drake and Harvey, 2013: 492). The difficulties in negotiating access to conduct research – particularly ethnographic research – within the closed 'total institution' (Goffman, 1961) of the prison should not be underestimated. As well as time-consuming, this process is bound up with both organisational and sectional interests, which – depending on which prison system you wish to 'get in' to – may act to render research plans all but impossible (e.g. for the US context see Wacquant, 2002).

As with most things in life, 'who you know' often serves one better than *what* you know in attempting to gain access to research in prison, making it a 'game of chance, not of skill' (Buchanan et al., 1988: 56). Jennifer was able to gain access to a prison that she had previously visited for reasons unconnected to her study. She had previously met the Governor of this particular establishment in the course of studying for her Master's degree where, in order to learn more about the prison setting prior to considering a PhD in the subject, she visited a prison in order to 'acclimatise' herself to the environment. This had the result that she was more of a known entity than simply 'cold-calling' for access. In an institution in which security is so important, being 'known' is important in instilling trust in gatekeepers. This in itself is of particular importance since the researcher is inherently 'dependent on the goodwill of organizational "gatekeepers"' (Buchanan et al., 1988: 56), who – in the case of prisons research – are numerous. The first gatekeeper to consider is the individual prison governor, as negotiating access with the second gatekeeper – the National Offender Management Service [NOMS] – may be dependent on evidence of an established relationship with the prison(s) identified as research sites (the NOMS application explicitly asks if prior approval has been gained from individual prisons).

Also, in addition to who you know, 'what you have *done*' may equally be of use, particularly where it indicates previous experience of time inside prisons. Serena's prior experience, for instance, as a member of the Independent Monitoring Board [IMB] at HMP Kingston may have acted as surety; a vote of confidence that she could not only work appropriately within the prison environment, but that – as a previous key-holder – she was perhaps less likely to represent a security risk than someone who had never held this relevant position of responsibility. Of course, 'what you have done' can also act to severely *impede* one's attempts at 'getting in' within this context; i.e. where the would-be prison researcher has served time on the other side of the door – where even decades later this can continue to be an issue, as is discussed elsewhere in this collection by William Davies (although see also Earle, 2014; Piche et al., 2014) regarding the positives that these experiences can bring. 'Who you are' can also be a problem – for example being young, and/or of student status which – even at doctoral level – can also serve to hinder one's progress in this respect (cf. Smith and Wincup, 2000; Gariglio, 2014).

At present (Summer 2014), the first step towards 'getting in' to the prison system of England and Wales is the aforementioned application to the National Offender Management Service, through the standardised NOMs application, or via the Integrated Research Application System [IRAS].[5] The Ministry of Justice website states that NOMS will support and 'encourage' research 'wherever it has the potential to increase the effectiveness of our services, either in the short or long term' (National Offender Management Service, *n.d.*). The arguably positivistic outcome-focused ethos implied here, in addition to the requirements placed on the need for the research to deliver demonstrable 'benefits' to NOMS through the planned research, could result in a scenario whereby avowedly-ethnographic researchers – committed to an open-ended and exploratory mode of inquiry, and who explicitly reject the validity and desirability of the tenets of positivism (cf. Denzin, 1997) – may neither want to meet, nor be *capable* of meeting, NOMS' demands for research which delivers such targeted and managerialist outcomes. As a result of this epistemological and methodological mismatch, it is likely that many would-be prison ethnographers – particularly those who lack insider support, and whose research motives are unlikely to meet the NOMS research criterion – may find themselves falling at the first hurdle, potentially leading to a decreasing likelihood that such studies will be carried out in the future.

Yet, this caution on allowing research within prisons has its advantages, not least for the individual prisoners who are protected (to a degree) from ending up as being used repeatedly as participants. On an ethical level, it must be recognised that prisoners have the potential to be extremely vulnerable people – captive, lacking in control over their lives, and in the power of others. Some degree of 'protection' is necessary in order to respect their privacy and position as autonomous human beings (albeit denied this recognition elsewhere), who may not want to be watched, questioned or commented upon. Also, novice researchers could be seen to be a bit like learner drivers – although often we have the skills and the knowledge, we are still in charge of a vehicle that has the potential to cause great harm, and should be observed and controlled with some caution.

Moreover, even when approval from NOMS is achieved, this does *not* guarantee that the research will take place, almost always for reasons beyond the researcher's control – for instance, of the four prisons for which Serena initially secured NOMS research approval, only three governors approved the research in their establishment. The fourth refused permission to research on the grounds that it necessitated – as oral/life history research often does – a recording device to be brought into the prison.

'Getting in' with a sound recording device – which, as indicated above, is an integral part of certain qualitative research methodologies – represented a potential stumbling block for both authors. After gaining NOMS approval for her study, Serena identified and directly approached the Heads of Security and the Governors or Deputy Governors at each establishment during pre-research visits, thereby signalling not only her familiarity with the organisational hierarchy, but also her capacity to establish relationships with the right decision makers and gatekeepers. This influenced the decision about whether to let her take recording equipment into the prison. Because the organisational hierarchy is so central to prison management, this familiarity with it is a useful skill to demonstrate. In negotiating access for the recording equipment, Serena explained how the recording device was crucial to the integrity of the research methods, and thus the integrity of the research findings (which – it had already been established – via gaining higher approval – were of interest/potential importance to NOMS).

In terms of practicalities, although Jennifer had secured written permission for her recording equipment from the Governor, there were different issues to be considered regarding the impact of the equipment on the interviewees. For example, one spoke of how it reminded him of the recording of his police interview,[6] something that had not even been considered in planning the research. The implications of using digital recording devices need to be considered carefully in advance. The use of recording technology conveys another layer of power over the participant through the recording of the spoken word, both in terms of the potential risk to confidentiality if the recorder is not kept secure, and also in a metaphysical way. Farrant struggled with issues of 'necromedia' (defined by O'Gorman as 'the incorporation of death and technology' (2003: 156)) stated that 'asking people who were generally strangers to tell me about their lives, and recording their words, felt like I was stealing part of them' (2014: 480; see also O'Gorman, 2003). The fact that the recording device held such sensitive data also means that there is a need to be aware of its whereabouts at all times, and the stories of the men contained within the device became valuable items which required protecting and nurturing, both literally in terms of keeping them safe in transit, and figuratively in terms of transcription and sense-making processes and doing them 'justice' in their interpretation. Researchers may be expected to commit to transcribing the interviews that evening, although in reality this may be impossible. In this case, committing to transferring each interview to a secure (i.e. password-protected and encrypted) location at the end of each night, wiping the recording device before entering the prison the following day, is important.

Getting on

Smith and Wincup (2000) discuss the process of 'getting on' in terms of gaining social access – how they gained acceptance on the inside and negotiated their identities as feminist researchers in sites of intense power relations. What tends to be left out of many accounts – particularly of PhD prison ethnographies – is the fact that being in prison can be scary. In the past, it has been said that one should not be afraid in prisons when doing research, and many feel that speaking of the fear that prison generates to show weakness (e.g. see May, 1993). Yet prisons, often austere and imposing structures, are *designed* to deter, and it seems somewhat naïve that a first-time researcher could enter such a cold institution and feel perfectly at home, a process that some prisoners themselves often try to resist to overcome the effects of institutionalisation. As Abusidualghoul et al. note in relation to the general context of conducting interviews (Abusidualghoul et al., 2009: 158):

> [N]o research methods handbook, no matter how popular, academically rigorous or acclaimed, prepares interviewers for the interview process. It has to be experienced [...] There is no training to help interviewers with the impending sense of excitement and fear.

In response to the lack of such texts about conducting prison research identified here, this section aims to give new prisons researchers a hint of the 'messiness' of our own experiences as some kind of preparation for the potential issues that may be encountered in relation to 'getting on' in prisons research.

A multitude of concerns related to 'identity', for example, may be experienced by the first-time researcher during their time in prison, largely due to the unique characteristics of this particular environment. In terms of presentation, it is easy to get this wrong, even with all the right intentions. Jennifer, while trying to maintain a professional identity, went in on her first day in a suit; unfortunately, she was subsequently (and frequently) misidentified as a member of the Senior Management Team [SMT].[7] When she attempted to change this portrayed identity, by dressing smartly (*sans* suit) on day two, she then acquired the label of psychologist – almost worse in a prisoner's eyes than being part of the SMT! (see Crewe, 2009; Maruna, 2011).

Based on her previous experience of prison identity politics during her time as part of the IMB, Serena was familiar with the need to avoid appearing as either part of the SMT or the psychology team, which involved dedicating far more time to clothing decisions than is ideal in this situation. Teaming a plain black top and cardigan with black jeans and Converse sneakers, with a smart scarf as a concession to looking less like a teenager, Serena was confident that this outfit would pose no threat to the women she intended to interview; certainly she was not mistaken as either part of the SMT or psychology team (although was still misidentified as a bereavement counsellor by two of the women). The unintended consequence of this however may have been to highlight Serena's lack of 'professional' identity, meaning that she was frequently mistaken by prison staff as an undergraduate student which may have shaped the degree of seriousness accorded to the researcher and, by association, the research itself.

Clearly then, acquiring the identity of 'researcher' is anything but simple, particularly where researchers often do not already have an established 'researcher' identity themselves (see also Rowe, this volume). Indeed, prison ethnographers may suffer from 'role strain' in the process of identity management within the prison, having to adopt numerous identities at different times, which may also have implications for the researcher as an individual in terms of 'a loss of a sense of self' (Drake and Harvey, 2013: 496). Moreover, such identities, once ascribed, were hard to escape, and made subsequent (and repeated) identity (re)negotiation even more strenuous and tiring – as noted above in relation to being mistaken for part of the SMT or a psychologist, it was not only a case of who to 'be' but also who not to 'be'. However, the good news is that the identity of the novice prisons researcher tends to be highly flexible – you have to try out new forms of 'you' to see which one works best, and while this can feel somewhat disingenuous, it must be remembered that even prisoners put on 'masks' in prison (see Jewkes, 2005b; Crewe, 2009).

As new researchers then, our experience demonstrates how one wishes to appear professional yet not 'of' the institution; knowledgeable, yet not arrogant or someone who knows it all; approachable, yet not standing out. As noted above, this can have implications for how one acts, talks, dresses and behaves; however, we have not yet addressed the ways in which these issues of identity politics clearly intersect with those of *gender*:

> Interesting that one of my questions is about being yourself in the prison – can I be me? I have to dress differently, smell different, wear different jewellery, have toned down hair, not for any written or spoken reason, but because I feel I should, so as to reduce my femininity in a place where it could potentially cause problems, and so that I don't stand out as an outsider (to prisoners I will by the fact that I am female, but to staff, I could just blend in – is that a good idea?). Attempting to be neutral – neither/both staff and outsider. All a matter of interpretation on the part of the observer, which I can do nothing about!
>
> (Sloan, Research Diary One)

The impact of gender in prison research has been noted in academic literature (Phillips and Earle, 2010; see also Sloan, 2011), yet this should not be assumed to be homogenously experienced by all female, and all male, researchers. The different ways in which gender *operates* (and in some instances, is wilfully used by researchers) for different researchers will, however, always have consequences – these can be both positive and negative. As a young female working in an adult male prison, for example, Jennifer found herself to be attempting to limit her own gendered displays, in an attempt to render herself as inconspicuous as possible, yet her femininity (and youth) was also useful in that some prisoners wanted to speak to a young woman, and others responded to her naivety with a greater degree of explanation, although, as the earlier extract from her diary reveals, this had some adverse implications, particularly in terms of staff being more protective of her/'looking after' her. This was problematic where it manifested in checking up on her during interviews, thereby interrupting the flow of some discussions with participants.

What we have aimed to show here is that, no matter how much you try to be 'the professional' in the research process, 'getting on'/doing research (in prisons, much like any other setting) is a messy process that does not always go to plan. As we found, the batteries for your recorder will run out during an interview (as happened to Jennifer); important paperwork will be left behind at your accommodation (Serena); the routines of the institution will *always* override your research priorities; and ultimately you will almost always (see Piche et al., 2014; Earle, 2014) be an 'outsider', no matter what identity you try to portray. It is perhaps somewhat ironic (cf. Earle, 2014) that the prisoners who participate in the research are experiencing a similar struggle in attempting to balance numerous identities (see also Schmid and Jones, 1991).

Getting out

Often considered only briefly with respect to leaving the field and the emotional isolation of the research experience, 'getting out' – and getting away mentally intact – is an important process that is rarely discussed in the research literature, particularly in relation to the potential for lasting effects prisons research, which can follow you out of the prison gates (this again represents an ironic similarity between the experiences of prisoners and those engaging them in research, although of course the long-term consequences implied here have far more profound implications for the future lives of former rather than the latter group). As Jewkes (2005a) found, individuals we meet in prison can have far-reaching impacts upon us and can affect us in deeper ways than we initially estimated. She refers to the story of one prisoner which has 'to some extent, haunted [her] over the intervening years' (p. 384; see also Jewkes, 2012). As one of the authors (Serena) can attest – one can be 'haunted' not just by the lives of the individuals met, but also more holistically, both by the sounds (e.g. women in the health-care unit screaming throughout the day) and the sights (e.g. fighting on the wing; the bloodied face of a woman who had self-harmed) of the prison environment. Such 'haunting' is not unknown in sociological research – indeed, Avery Gordon (2008: 22) notes (somewhat ironically when read in the context of prisons research):

> [G]hosts are never innocent: the unhallowed dead of the modern project drag in the pathos of their loss and the violence of the force that made them, their sheets and chains. To be haunted and to write from that location, to take on the condition of what you study, is not a methodology or a consciousness you can simply adopt or adapt as a set of rules or an identity; it produces its own insights and blindnesses.

One of the key elements in the 'getting out' process is keeping such ghosts, insights and potential 'blindnesses' in mind, and *listening* to those sounds and voices that we find so haunting, which can be a tricky task in a world that 'speaks rather than listens' (Back, 2007: 7). Such listening therefore has the capability to empower those who are ordinarily not listened to and rarely have the ability to be heard – in fact, the acknowledgement of such hauntings allows readers to 'situate and describe the voices of the people that have been transcribed onto the page' (Back, 2007: 17), and also to situate and understand the researcher a little bit more.

'Getting out' can be difficult when the individuals you interview – with whom you share conversation, a sense of rapport, and even a bond – and their current predicament are hard to push from one's mind. The accounts of sexual abuse and assault, of bereavement, of domestic violence, and of pain and despair are impossible to avoid amongst women and men in prison. They can also weigh heavily on the mind of any prisons researcher, particularly those researching in women's prisons, where one is statistically more likely to find such experiences, although both Serena and Jennifer (the latter in a male prison) found the disclosure of earlier trauma, abuse and forms of self-harm all too common, and the consequences all too visible. For the novice researcher, the weight of these experiences, and being so close to their consequences, even for a short time, can be difficult to bear.

For those who wish to return to the field (i.e. 'getting *back* in') – which may become increasingly necessary as NOMS place requirements on researchers to feed back their findings to the organisation/relevant establishments – there are also practical implications regarding going back. Prisoners, staff and other gatekeepers move. Prisons change hands, moving from the public sector to the private, for-profit, sector – or may be refurbished, rebuilt or, in some cases, closed. Priorities change. All this has to be borne in mind when deciding when and how to feed back to each prison. Jennifer chose to do this on a return visit, bringing copies of the full doctoral thesis, and abridged copies for each wing, as well as helping to draft a brief summary of the research findings to inform the prison. This requires quite a lot of thought, as the phrasing of findings needs to be carefully designed for a variety of audiences. Of course, as with any organisation, changes in management can alter the experience of operating within it, as Jennifer found – between leaving the prison and returning several years later, much had changed, as if it were a different prison. There were different gatekeepers and new and different degrees of access; all of this made for a strange and unsettling experience which individuals need to consider at the conclusion of their research. It is important to remember that the entire process of prison ethnography can take longer than many other types of research approach, and so such changes over time can be much more intrusive upon the sense-making process.

Of course, these examples only represent the authors' experiences; these are intended only as a means of communicating the *potential* for such experiences to occur, and to underscore the necessity to expect the unexpected. In this sense, what has been presented here should assimilated by potential prisons researchers as part of a *range* of potential experiences of prisons research. We hope this will not only serve to indicate to the future prisons researcher issues that might arise during their time 'inside', but might also to highlight the importance of appropriate support for *all* prisons researchers. As our survey indicated, the experienced prisons researcher may still expect to encounter issues relevant to the 'greenhead' researcher, even after several decades; however, *being prepared* and having recourse to *appropriate support* (whatever form that might take) is clearly crucial to becoming an effective and reflexive researcher in the carceral environment.

The 'Going in Green' survey 2014

In developing this chapter, the authors sought the views of known prison researchers through the use of a short online survey allowing for open comment against a series of queries. It included the question 'What three tips would you offer to new prisons researchers planning to do prisons research in 2014?' A range of prison experiences were shared, including work in both the male and female estate, in England and abroad, and in a variety of security categories. Some of the practical tips that respondents identified are shared here to help inform new prisons researchers and guide the next generation of prison ethnographers.

Tips for researching ethnographically in prison

1. Do it with another researcher, if possible.
2. Question and observe as much as you can with a critical eye.
3. Take time off from the fieldwork when you feel you need it.

The last point is of particular importance, and something that we also found to be crucial in our own research. When asked in the survey about advice for new prisons researchers, the same respondent went on to add:

> Everyone will have their own, unique experiences and remedies for them, so I wouldn't like to prescribe anything. I'd just say, whatever you feel as a result of prison research, don't ignore it – work through it. Your feelings may be telling you important things about the field or you may need to resolve whatever private emotional experiences you've had in order to ensure that you're robust enough to enter the field again and without a view that is too presumptuous or jaded.

Research fatigue is often acknowledged for populations subjected to multiple research studies, but it is also important to remember that a sustained period of emotionally demanding fieldwork can be tiring and draining to researchers. This is true for experienced researchers but all the more so for those who feel they have something to prove, as many new researchers do, and, as such, have yet to develop a wider repertoire of coping skills and strategies. The performance anxiety of academics may be more sharply experienced by the aspiring researcher. It combines with the harsh environment to challenge fragile confidence and uncertain capabilities. Both Jennifer and Serena noted this in their respective reflexive diaries during their research experience:

> I don't want to say about stress when inside – would be complaining and make me seem incompetent/incapable/not a good person to be doing the work.
>
> (Jennifer, Research Diary One)

> I am having trouble getting to sleep. And sitting here alone in this dingy pit, miles from home, isn't helping. The things I saw and heard today – well, I wasn't prepared for them. But what do I do with this? I still have to go into tomorrow, no matter what, and I need to be 'on it' – I won't get the chance to do these interviews again. Get the feeling that some of those officers I spoke with today just 'stamp on stress'; suppress it, ignore it. A trick I need to learn?
>
> (Serena, Reflexive Field Notes, November 2010)

Preparation is important prior to undertaking fieldwork. Although you can never fully predict what your prison research experience is going to be like, you can see how others have found it, and both authors agreed with the respondent who nominated the following three tips:

1. apply to NOMS early;
2. read prison biographies;
3. read ethnographic material.

This guidance was echoed by another, experienced senior prison researcher:

1. consult informally first;
2. build support for the topic;
3. be well informed.

These specific recommendations to new researchers, in relation to the initial access application to NOMS, were suggested by another:

1. Try to make your topic seem relevant and interesting to NOMS, that is, consistent with their strategic priorities.
2. Think about the resource implications for the prison you want to study. Be realistic about this.

Beyond these strategic recommendations, advice was also offered in relation to the wider ambience of the research context, implicitly acknowledging the significance of the emotional tone in which research is conducted: 'It gets better with experience' advised one respondent, suggesting that 'Being human, and supportive, whilst staying in "researcher role" works very well' in terms of protecting one's own emotional wellbeing during interviews.

Important tips were presented about the self-presentation issues we discussed earlier, the sense of the researcher as a person interacting with others in an ethical and engaging manner. This can often be assumed to be the case, but it is less invisible and more scrutinised by prisoners and prison staff than the researcher may care to know. So, as one participant noted:

1. Be open.
2. Look and listen very carefully.
3. Enjoy yourself.

This final point is of particular importance, and perhaps controversial – doing research in prison, and particularly conducting a prison ethnography where engagement and immersion are central to the research process, includes moments of joy, simple fun and more than a few games. As has been mentioned, the all too evident pain and suffering can follow you out of the prison, but the resilience, humour and energy found in so many aspects of prison life can be as intensely moving and even more inspiring. Acknowledging and expecting enjoyment and fun can do no harm.

At the same time, research in prison can have other effects on you as a person that you need to bear in mind three tips from another respondent with wide experience of prison cultures centred not only on preparing oneself, but on preparing a support network:

1. Be patient and persistent and prepare for the unexpected.
2. Discuss with an experienced prison scholar and conduct an honest self-appraisal of your own robustness and strength of character.
3. Make sure you have a back-up team of trusted people you can turn to if necessary for debriefing.

It is important not to keep the research to yourself and to talk to others who have gone through similar experiences. As discussed earlier, few people have prior experience of prison, and it is important to recognise the fact that, even though they can be profoundly fascinating places in which to conduct research, 'prison damages people' (Behan, 2002). Taking steps to look after yourself is crucial. Find something to do after your day in prison to relax and 'take you away from it'. For Jennifer, this outlet was swimming – it allowed her to have time to herself to think, and also played a role in 'washing away', as Wacquant (op. cit.) suggested, what the day in prison had laid on. Several survey respondents also noted the smells of prison, and this subject has parallels to some of the things prisoners do in prison and upon release, such as buying new clothes or having a bath (see Sloan, 2012a, 2012b). For Serena, spending as much time as possible in the company of 'trusted people' with whom she could relax, let off steam, and talk with at length (confidentiality permitting, of course) without fear of being judged was an important coping mechanism that sustained her through the fieldwork.

Joining a research network can be particularly useful (in the UK, for example, the British Society of Criminology (BSC) Post-Graduate Group, one of the BSC's specialist networks, or the Prison Ethnography Network), attending conferences, talking to other new researchers, and developing an understanding of the challenges of prisons research provide a way of relieving oneself of the burdens picked up in the research process. Crucially, acknowledging the fact that it can be both a negative and a positive experience helps to provide a more holistic way of making sense of the process. Prisons are not nice places, but they are very human places, fascinating sites of discovery where the worst and the best of life can often be seen in action. As one of the *Going in Green* survey respondents went on to say:

> Share with others; make sure you have trusted outlets for the sense of frustration you might feel; don't be tempted to stay in the field too long (even when the access has been so difficult to obtain). YOU are more important

than your study. Write down your doubts and feelings in a log – it helps to objectify them and provides material for a future article!

Conclusion

One of the interesting things about being a novice prison ethnographer lies in the similarity of experience with those more practised in the method. The stresses and strains seem to continue throughout the prison ethnographer's career, regardless of seniority, gender or time in the field. What does differ, however, is the confidence held in one's abilities in managing these experiences and making sense of them. The process of acknowledging such feelings and experiences and using them to inform the wider ethnographic project remains in its infancy in prison research. Finding one's feet in prison ethnography is hard, not least due to the expectations new prison researchers place upon themselves in the process – not wanting to appear naïve, unskilled or unworthy to be trusted with the responsibilities of prison ethnography. The need to respect the humanity of prisoners, and being sensitive to their predicaments and pains while advancing one's own career prospects, is fraught with complex ethical dilemmas. Experienced researchers may have either resolved these or developed ways of engaging with them more constructively and creatively (Chapter 3, this volume). For the greenhead researcher, they present formidable obstacles and disorienting dilemmas.

The advice given here is not intended to scare, but rather to *support* new researchers, in order that they may be better prepared to enter the field and know what to expect from an environment that is, in the main, hidden from public view. It would be irresponsible for a prison researcher who has had negative experiences not to make others aware of the risks, but at the same time, it is also important that we emphasise how extremely interesting, thought-provoking, life-changing and rewarding doing research in prisons can actually be.

What we have found in the process of reflecting upon our research experiences, and from drawing on the work of others (such as those within this collection), is that it is important to trust in yourself as a researcher. There is only so much advice that one can take from books regarding what is an extremely flexible, dynamic and unpredictable method of research – that is why the outcomes of prison ethnography are so highly valued. It takes bravery to discuss the emotional and difficult dimensions of research – few researchers wish to point out the things that they struggled with, did badly or perhaps could not cope with. Even those of us who do discuss such matters will undoubtedly hold some elements back – the ways in which our research changes us as individuals are inherently personal. We are not advocating 'navel-gazing' (cf. Cunliffe, 2004) or the prioritisation of reflexive accounts over those of the prisoners with whom we work, but we firmly believe that it is important to know that (i) reflexivity about such personal experiences is in itself informative data that can tell us about the prison as an institution (see also Drake and Harvey, 2013); (ii) such data feeds into professional self-development and, in turn, may contribute to enhancing the quality of one's research and thus the field of prisons research itself; and (iii) novice prisons researchers understand that they will be neither unusual nor alone in having such experiences as have been discussed in this chapter, and that the various hurdles of prisons research are conquerable.

Acknowledgements

We would like to express great thanks to all those associated with the three research projects undertaken that went towards this chapter, particularly those academics and prisoners who so kindly shared their experiences with us. Many thanks must also go to Rod Earle for his comments on our chapter.

Notes

Sheffield Hallam University and University of Cambridge, respectively.

1. This project was funded by the University of Sheffield and was granted ethical approval by the Ethics Committee at School of Law, the University of Sheffield.
2. This project was funded by the Economic and Social Research Council and was granted a favourable ethical opinion by the Ethics Committee at the University of Surrey.
3. In England and Wales, the Independent Monitoring Board is a group of volunteers that 'monitor the day-to-day life in their local prison or removal centre and ensure that proper standards of care and decency are maintained' (Ministry of Justice, 2014).
4. This survey was granted ethical approval by the Ethics Committee at the University of Sheffield in February 2014. It was not directly funded by any institution or funding body.
5. This is an online research application system, used by numerous bodies in the UK (including the Ministry of Justice, Cancer Research UK and the Welsh Assembly Government) to streamline applications to research within these organisations.
6. In England and Wales, under the Police and Criminal Evidence Act 1984, Code of Practice E, Section 1.5A, 'Recording of interviews shall be carried out openly to instil confidence in its reliability as an impartial and accurate record of the interview.'
7. That is, Governors and/or managers.

Further reading

Beyens, K., Christiaens, J., Claes, B., De Ridder, S., Tournel, H. and Tubex, H. (eds) (2013) *The Pains of Doing Criminological Research* (Brussels: VUB Press).

Drake, D. and Harvey, J. (2013) 'Performing the Role of Ethnographer: Processing and Managing the Emotional Dimensions of Prison Research', *International Journal of Social Research Methodology*, 17, 5, 489–501.

King, R. D. and Liebling, A. (2008) 'Doing Research in Prisons', in R. D. King and E. Wincup (eds) *Doing Research on Crime and Justice*, Second edition 431–51 (Oxford: Oxford University Press).

Townsend, K. and Burgess, J. (eds) (2009) *Method in the Madness: Research Stories You Won't Read in Textbooks* (Oxford: Chandos Publishing).

References

Abusidualghoul, V., Goodwin, J., James, N., Rainnie, A., Venter, K. and White, M. (2009) 'Sitting on a Wall in Northumberland Crying: Semi-Structured Interviews', in K. Townsend and J. Burgess (eds) *Method in the Madness: Research Stories You Won't Read in Textbooks* (Oxford: Chandos Publishing).

Back. L. (2007) *The Art of Listening* (London: Bloomsbury).

Behan, C. (2002) *Transformative Learning in a Total Institution.* Unpublished MA Dissertation (National University of Ireland, Maynooth).

Beyens, K., Christiaens, J., Claes, B., De Ridder, S., Tournel, H. and Tubex, H. (eds) (2013) *The Pains of Doing Criminological Research* (Brussels: VUB Press).

Buchanan, D., Boddy, D. and McCalman, J. (1988) 'Getting in, Getting on, Getting Out and Getting Back', in A. Bryman (ed) *Doing Research in Organisations* (London: Routledge).

Cook, J. A. and Fonow, M. M. (1986) 'Knowledge and Women's Interests: Issues of Epistemology and Methodology in Feminist Sociological Research', *Sociological Inquiry*, 56, 1, 2–29.

Crewe, B. (2009) *The Prisoner Society: Power, Adaptation, and Social Life in an English Prison* (Oxford: Oxford University Press).

Crewe, B. (2014) 'Not Looking Hard Enough Masculinity, Emotion, and Prison Research', *Qualitative Inquiry*, 20, 4, 392–403.

Cunliffe, A. L. (2004) 'On Becoming a Critically Reflexive Practitioner', *Journal of Management Education*, 28, 4, 407–26.

Davies, P. (2000) 'Doing Interviews with Female Offenders', in V. Jupp, P. Davies and P. Francis (eds) *Doing Criminological Research*, pp. 82–96 (London, UK: Sage Publications Ltd.)

Davies, Y. N. (2006) 'Intersectionality and Feminist Politics', *European Journal of Women's Studies*, 13, 3, 193–209.

Denzin, N. (1997) *Interpretive Ethnography: Ethnographic Practices for the 21st Century* (London: Sage).

Drake, D. and Harvey, J. (2013) 'Performing the Role of Ethnographer: Processing and Managing the Emotional Dimensions of Prison Research', *International Journal of Social Research Methodology*, 17, 5, 489–501.

Earle, R. (2014) 'Insider and Out: Making Sense of a Prison Experience and a Research Experience', *Qualitative Inquiry*, 20, 4, 404–13.

Farrant, F. (2014) 'Unconcealment: What Happens When We Tell Stories', *Qualitative Inquiry*, 20, 4, 477–86.

Ferrell, J. and Hamm, M. S. (1988) *Ethnography at the Edge: Crime: Deviance, and Field Research* (Boston: Northeastern University Press).

Fogg, A. (2014) 'Why Is Chris Grayling Blocking Research into Rape in Prison?' *The Guardian*, Tuesday 6th May 2014. Available at: http://www.theguardian.com/commentisfree/2014/may/06/chris-grayling-blocking-research-rape-prison-sexual-assault-jail [accessed 14th October 2014].

Gariglio, L. (2014) 'Gaining Access to Prison: Authority, Negotiations, and Flexibility in the Field', *Border Criminologies*, http://bordercriminologies.law.ox.ac.uk/gaining-access-to-prison [accessed 31st May 2014].

Goffman, E. (1961) *Asylums: Essays on the Social Situation of Mental Patients and Other Inmates* (Chicago: Aldine Publishing Company).

Gordon, A. F. (2008) *Ghostly Matters: Haunting and the Sociological Imagination* (Minneapolis: University of Minnesota Press).

King, R. D. (2000) 'Doing Research in Prisons', in R. D. King and E. Wincup (eds) *Doing Research on Crime and Justice*, First edition, pp. 285–312 (Oxford: Oxford University Press).

King, R. D. and Liebling, A. (2008) 'Doing Research in Prisons', in R. D. King and E. Wincup (eds) *Doing Research on Crime and Justice*, Second edition, pp. 431–51 (Oxford: Oxford University Press).

Liebling, A. (1999) 'Doing Research in Prison: Breaking the Silence', *Theoretical Criminology*, 3, 2, 147–73.

Jewkes, Y. (2012) 'Autoethnography and Emotion as Intellectual Resources: Doing Prison Research Differently', *Qualitative Inquiry*, 18, 1, 63–75.

Jewkes, Y. (2005a) 'Loss, Liminality and the Life Sentence: Managing Identity Through a Disrupted Lifecourse', in A. Liebling and S. Maruna (eds) *The Effects of Imprisonment* (Cullompton: Willan Publishing).

Jewkes, Y. (2005b) 'Men Behind Bars "Doing" Masculinity as an Adaptation to Imprisonment', *Men and Masculinities*, 8, 1, 44–63.

Maruna, S. (2011) 'Why Do They Hate Us? Making Peace Between Prisoners and Psychology', *International Journal of Offender Therapy and Comparative Criminology*, 55, 671–75.

May, T. (1993) 'Feelings Matter: Inverting the Hidden Equation', in D. Hobbs and T. May (eds) *Interpreting the Field: Accounts of Ethnography* (Oxford: Oxford University Press).

Ministry of Justice (2014) 'About the Independent Monitoring Board'. Available at https://www.justice.gov.uk/about/imb [accessed 14th October 2014].

National Offender Management Service (n.d.). 'Research at NOMS'. Available at https://www.gov.uk/government/organisations/national-offender-management-service/about/research [accessed 19th October 2014].

O'Gorman, M. (2003) 'What Is Necromedia?' *Intermédialités: International Journal of New Media*. Available at: http://cri.histart.umontreal.ca/cri/fr/intermedialites/p1/pdfs/p1_ogorman.pdfOliver [accessed 14th October 2014].

Oakley, A. (1981) 'Interviewing Women: A Contradiction in Terms', in H. Roberts (ed) *Doing Feminist Research* (London: Routledge and Kegan Paul).

Phillips, C. and Earle, R. (2010) 'Reading Difference Differently? Identity, Epistemology and Prison Ethnography', *British Journal of Criminology*, 50, 2, 360–78.

Piacentini, L. (2007) 'Researching Russian Prisons: A Consideration of New and Established Methodologies in Prison Research', in Y. Jewkes (ed) *Handbook on Prisons*, pp. 152–73 (Cullompton: Willan Publishing).

Piche, J., Gaucher, B. and Walby, K. (2014) 'Facilitating Prisoner Ethnography: An Alternative Approach to "Doing Prison Research Differently"', *Qualitative Inquiry*, 20, 4, 392–403.

Rowe, A. (2014) 'Situating the Self in Prison Research: Power, Identity, and Epistemology', *Qualitative Inquiry*, 20, 4, 464–76.

Schmid, T. J. and Jones, R. S. (1991) 'Suspended Identity: Identity Transformation in a Maximum Security Prison', *Symbolic Interaction*, 14, 4, 415–32.

Sloan, J. (2012a) '"You Can See Your Face in My Floor": Examining the Function of Cleanliness in an Adult Male Prison', *The Howard Journal of Criminal Justice*, 51, 4, 400–10.

Sloan, J. (2012b) 'Cleanliness, Spaces and Masculine Identity in an Adult Male Prison', *Prison Service Journal*, 201, 3–6.

Sloan, J. (2011) *Men Inside: Masculinity and the Adult Male Prison Experience*, Unpublished PhD Thesis, The University of Sheffield.

Smith, C. and Wincup, E. (2000) 'Breaking In: Researching Criminal Justice Institutions for Women', in R. D. King and E. Wincup (eds) *Doing Research on Crime and Justice*, First edition, pp. 331–49 (Oxford: Oxford University Press).

Smith, C. and Wincup, E. L. (2002) 'Reflections on Fieldwork in Criminal Justice Institutions', in T. Welland and L. Pugsley (eds) *Ethical Dilemmas in Qualitative Research*, pp. 108–20 (Cardiff: Cardiff Papers in Qualitative Research).

Townsend, K. and Burgess, J. (eds) (2009) *Method in the Madness: Research Stories You Won't Read in Textbooks* (Oxford: Chandos Publishing).

Wacquant, L. (2002) 'The Curious Eclipse of Prison Ethnography in the Age of Mass Incarceration', *Ethnography*, 3, 4, 371–97.

Part II
Through Prison Ethnography
Introduction to Part II

Deborah H. Drake

The chapters in Part II of this Handbook consider what can be revealed 'through ethnography' and, importantly, where some of the limits of ethnography are encountered. This part includes a diverse collection of contributions that demonstrate how the infinitely variable details of human existence can be revealed or may remain hidden during ethnographic encounters and analysis. Each of the contributions present various problems, solutions and unanswered dilemmas associated with ethnographic practices. They each shed some light on hidden or taboo subjects, whilst at the same time recognise that aspects of the field or the ethnographic endeavour itself remain in the shadows.

Chapter 8 opens this part of the Handbook with a compelling chapter by Andrew M. Jefferson, which looks 'beyond the West' to bring the inherent vulnerabilities of ethnography into particularly sharp relief. His chapter explores the performative and slippery nature of ethnographic research in non-Western prisons. Drawing on numerous examples from his wealth of research experience, Jefferson's reflections are sharp, riveting and candid as well as engagingly presented. This chapter authoritatively explores the interface between the ethnographer, the field and the resultant epistemological products of these encounters in order to reflect on and scrutinise prison practice, the role of the researcher and various aspects of the ethnographic method.

Capturing a similar tone to that of Jefferson but drawing on a starkly different approach to analysing their methods, Elisabeth Fransson and Berit Johnsen reflect on the gendered, social-material and relational dimensions of ethnographic prison research. In Chapter 9, they engage in a sophisticated and nuanced Deleuzian analysis of their respective affective journeys through two compelling and revealing vignettes that, in their telling, foreground and expose the complex, contradictory and dynamic processes that surround and infuse the production of knowledge when undertaking ethnographic prison research. Fransson and Johnsen's reflections consider the role of bodily experiences in relation to analytical, methodological and ethical questions. By so doing, their contribution is both thought-provoking and groundbreaking in its exposure and analysis of revealing and telling ethnographic moments.

Chapter 10 moves us on to explorations of the use of feminist ethnography as a methodological tool through which to examine the masculinities enacted in the prison context. Benita Moolman wrestles with gender relations and structures of power and authority as she describes her research with men convicted of sexual offences, serving their time in South African prisons. Her considerable contribution to this part argues for the merits of a narrative approach to a feminist ethnography, which encourages a strong investment in issues of representation of difference and of 'the other'. Moreover, Moolman makes a compelling argument for the importance of researcher reflection, particularly in relation to emotional experiences and personal reactions and to researcher praxis.

Picking up on both the idea of how to engage with ideas of 'the other' and the issue of representation, James B. Waldram focuses our attentions on the complexities of ethnographic writing, particularly for prison ethnographers who find themselves researching and writing about stigmatised populations. In Chapter 11, Waldram offers some general observations from many years of ethnographic research in Canadian prisons as well as a detailed exposure of the production and review processes within anthropology that he was subjected to when publishing his ethnographic work on men convicted of sexual offences. His chapter raises the uncomfortable problems that prison ethnographers can face when attempting to have their work published. However, Waldram's wealth of experience that he generously shares with us in this chapter, coupled with the strength of the argument he presents for perseverance, reassuringly persuades us that it is the responsibility of the prison ethnographer to represent our inmate participants as worthy human beings who have a story to tell.

The pains, struggles and tensions of the marginal positions occupied by prisoners and the way ethnographers 'see' their individual, personal and inevitably complex identities are brought into full and rich view in Earle and Phillips' contribution in Chapter 12. Their chapter considers the racialised dynamics of ethnographic research in two men's prisons in South East England. Earle and Phillips explicitly discuss and demonstrate how they accessed a reflexive ethnographic account of the identities of their research participants, in part, through the lens of their own diverse biographical identities. Through a range of enthralling examples, they illustrate not only the lived experiences and multiple features of contemporary racisms but also a convivial version of multicultural relational dynamics that can emerge through prison encounters.

Whilst the revelations of sustained ethnographic work can offer nuanced, fine-textured portraits that can startle and awe, my own contribution to this part of the Handbook considers those moments in ethnographic work when realities are only 'glimpsed at', but seem to suggest problematic or troubling secrets. Chapter 13 considers the deep, enduring tensions between care and custody, brutality and punishment that can accompany the prison officer role and, in turn, can also create structures and spaces that lend themselves to secrecy. A particular focus of the chapter is to consider the challenges for the ethnographer when only a sliver view of clandestine practices is obtained.

Part IV finishes on a crescendo of ethnographic reflection with a contribution from Lorna A. Rhodes. Her chapter further highlights the challenges faced by prison ethnographers in the specific conditions of the oppressive and secretive institutions they study. Rhodes' discussion authoritatively explores the ethnographic terrain of the prisons researcher ultimately arguing that the prison, as research site, cannot be grasped or comprehended entirely through standard ethnographic practices.

Part of the value of ethnography is being 'allowed' as a researcher to remain open to the meanings brought forth by the field and by your informants. As James Waldram (2009) has argued, although the rewards of prison ethnography are generous, the challenges are many. The intense, conflict-prone and relationally combative environment of the prison requires a fine-grained but robust filter through which observations and conversations can be passed and analysed. Moreover, once one has moved outside of the intersubjective relational encounter of the ethnographic field, it can be extremely difficult to translate one's observations; informants' subjective, emotional experiences; or the shared understandings that have been co-produced into a single, meaningful narrative. The processes through which ethnographic prison researchers achieve this and come to know what they come to know when they do ethnography is richly described in this part of the Handbook. The chapters in this part illustrate the messy, tangled and inherently idiosyncratic nature of the practice of ethnography that, in many ways, mirrors the messy, tangled and idiosyncratic nature of social life in general.

As an ethnographer, one's purpose is to absorb and to filter. The ethnographer 'takes into' himself or herself whatever is floating around in the atmosphere. He or she 'takes in' all that is seen. But also, and perhaps more importantly, s/he takes in what is unseen too. Through the chapters in this part, the stark revelations, conspicuous omissions and palpable residues of human existence are considered through myriad ethnographic encounters, analysed in magnified detail, but placed against more panoramic theoretical perspectives that demonstrate a flavour of what can be viewed, experienced and communicated 'through ethnography'.

Reference

Waldram, J. B. (2009) 'Challenges of Prison Ethnography', *Anthropology News*, 50, 4–5.

8 Performing Ethnography: Infiltrating Prison Spaces

Andrew M. Jefferson

Introduction

Based on a range of prison encounters in a variety of locations (Nigeria, Kosovo, the Philippines, Tunisia, etc.) but drawing primarily on material gathered during a seven-month fieldwork in Sierra Leone, this chapter explores the performative and slippery nature of ethnographic research in prisons. The main argument is that prison ethnography involves a high degree of embodied performance involving three fundamentally contingent and fragile relationships: to the field, to the self and to knowledge. These can be referred to as the inherent vulnerabilities of the ethnographic endeavour. Utilising (ethno)graphic examples the chapter discusses the interface between the ethnographer, the field and the imponderable knowledge that is generated as s/he attempts to scrutinise taken for granted aspects of prison practice.

The result is an inevitably personal account of what it can mean to infiltrate prison spaces. I take my point of departure in the assumption that modes of encountering research fields are as important to discuss as what we discover in them. The chapter addresses some of the possibilities and risks of prison ethnography and contributes to two of this Handbook's overall aims. It is about how the fieldworker generates knowledge *through ethnography*, and it illustrates the potential of field-based methods to reveal the underside of penal practices, meaning not the deliberately hidden but the taken for granted. The chapter considers how the ethnographic imagination is inevitably rooted in the situated, embodied, performative practice of the researcher as they encounter the field. Subjective? Yes – and proud of it.

Jewkes (2014a: 388–9) rightly claims that the prison is a unique institution, and Rowe (2014) similarly suggests that the prison positions the researcher more starkly than other institutions. My claim is simply that the prisons I have visited and studied around the world bring the inherent vulnerabilities of ethnography into particularly sharp relief. I draw on multiple field experiences over almost 15 years, mostly in non-Western contexts. My most classically ethnographic projects were in Nigeria and Sierra Leone where I spent initial periods of eight months and seven months, respectively. Despite the similarity in regard to length of time in the field, these projects were experienced quite differently. Although I approached Nigerian prison practice as an ethnographic novice, I was much less green when I arrived in Sierra Leone to study detention practices during and after the rebel war. The field notes drawn on below are mainly from the Sierra Leone experience.

Like many of the contributors to this volume, I am not an anthropologist and so cannot lay any kind of disciplinary claim to ethnography. But experience has taught me that an ethnographic orientation is best suited to pursue answers to the kind of empirical and theoretical questions that I find interesting as a social scientist (and as a scholar employed in an activist organisation). Choice of method depends not on disciplinary orientation but on the confluence of various contingent factors: research questions, feasibility, resources and even chance. Indeed, my initial introduction to prison ethnography was more by luck than design. This story demands telling.

Discovering ethnography

Over two decades ago, I was an intern in a UK social services department working with children in conflict with the law. I became friends with a colleague there who happened to be a former inmate of HM prison Grendon, a unique medium security prison in the UK based on therapeutic community principles. John himself was one of Grendon's successes. A year later, on his recommendation, I found myself as an intern in Grendon's psychology department, participating in therapy groups and community meetings and joining in evaluations of newly arrived inmates' suitability for the regime. At the same time, I shared a house with John and many a conversation about the inmates and staff whom he knew from a radically different perspective than I ever would. This was my introduction to the practice of understanding a site and its occupants in their own terms, almost from within. This was where an ethnographic orientation embedded itself in me, as the authoritative narratives of a former insider supplemented my outsider's youthful curiosity and impressionability.

Ethnography offers insights into the internal workings of prisons, but it is also possible to 'see through the prison' to gain understanding of wider social trends and structures. The prison as a site often seems to have punched beyond its weight in social science. Michel Foucault and Erving Goffman are perhaps the prime examples of utilising studies of enclosed spaces to make broader theoretical arguments about social and relational worlds, about knowledge and about power. The prison offers the social scientist a kind of intensified, rarefied context through which to theorise. At stake are notions of freedom, the classic relation between structure and agency, even what it means to be human. It would be ironic, then, if our accounts of prison research are reduced to the presentation of 'inhuman data' that is, if they are 'cold, calculated, (and) surgical' (Anon, 2005: 259). The ethnographic imagination offers an alternative way of seeing the prison, a way that grants us greater purchase (a better grip) on the phenomena at stake than more distant, cold, or hands-off methodological approaches. However, this is not without risks. Offering one's self as the fundamental research tool is challenging in any context. The prison presents particular challenges and threats (as well as unique opportunities[1]).

Some of the risks and opportunities presented by prison ethnography were at the forefront of our minds when Tomas Martin and I established the Global Prisons Research Network (GPRN[2]). From the beginning, we were preoccupied with overcoming the isolation of prison ethnographers working on prisons 'beyond the west'. And we were captivated by dilemmas about how to represent such places, and such a field. The GPRN was established to fill an empirical gap through field-based research and to rattle the cage of Anglo-American dominance of prison studies. We also wanted to support researchers working in emotionally demanding fields. We recognised that prison ethnographers are often highly invested in their projects, sometimes to the detriment of their own well-being.

There are of course textbooks that introduce ethnography to the novice, but it is not an approach that can easily be converted into a set of instructions or guidelines. It is intuitive, inter-subjective and thus largely learned 'on the run'. The following discussion is not a 'how to do prison ethnography' text. What I do hope to achieve, however, is to draw attention to the necessity of thinking more explicitly and more reflexively about the fieldworker's relationship to the field, to themselves and to knowledge. Forewarned may be forearmed. I turn first to consider the theme of the researcher's fragile relationship to the field.

Relating to the field

Infiltrating prison spaces is clearly about positioning. As Yvonne Jewkes has rightly noticed there are 'inevitable tensions that arise from positioning oneself, or being positioned by others' (Jewkes, 2014a: 389). This section is essentially about these tensions. First, I consider three forms of infiltrating the field that are more oriented to the way the ethnographer positions him/herself. Then I turn to some examples of the types of dilemmas that I encountered (that relate more to being positioned by others) and draw some general lessons from these.

When I reflect on my particular style of relating to the field, I can immediately identify three forms of infiltration: infiltration via cajoling; infiltration via accompaniment; and infiltration via gate-crashing.

Cajoling

Cajoling is part of the process of 'selling' a research idea to the prison authorities. Very rarely, in my experience, does access depend simply on providing a formal research protocol or project description and requesting approval. As a result, much care goes into establishing connections and credibility, gaining sympathy and branding the project in terms that will make sense to the authorities. This is often a delicate operation where certain aspects of the proposed project will be highlighted and others downplayed.[3] Just to give one example, in Nigeria, I adopted an incremental, tactical approach. First with the help of a local gatekeeper – a university professor – I was able to gain permission to spend time at the prison training schools. Then after four months I submitted a second application arguing that to really understand the role of recruit training I needed a better understanding of the places they were being trained to work in. This resulted in permission to access the prisons. Cajoling is about tactics, it is about knowing the audience; it demands patience, persistence and a sense of timing.

Accompaniment

To the ethnographer everything is potential material. I am fortunate to work at the intersection between research and intervention and increasingly I am presented with opportunities to access prisons around the world albeit relatively briefly. This can be in connection with the training of prison monitors or accompanying local non-governmental organisations (NGOs), who have a regular prison presence, during their activities. Often, the practice of accompanying others during their prison work can be a rich source of new knowledge. I recall one visit to the central prison in Sierra Leone, where the Officer in Charge – a man I had actually previously spent a weekend with in a rural village as the guest of another Senior Officer – reacted angrily to our NGO host's request to inspect the prison. His outburst revealed much about his fear of critique, his fear of losing his job, his livelihood and so on. And despite or because of the tension, it created an opportunity for me to test my cajoling skills. In this instance, I was able to draw on my previously established relationship with the Officer. He knew me, I argued. We had partied together in the village. He could trust me. Often such exchanges become quite ritualised and in a sense performative. He performed anxiety about what we might discover and expose. I performed our historic bond as a kind of guarantor of our trustworthiness. His relationship to me and his relationship to the NGO were being re-negotiated through the performance.

Gate-crashing

Another way of infiltrating is through gate-crashing. This is not such a relevant technique for getting into prisons or moving within prisons though I did once deliberately latch on to the delivery of morning tea to the VIP quarters of

Freetown's Central prison in order to get access to a very high-profile inmate accused of plotting to assassinate the vice-president. For a long while, I had wanted to speak with him but had not dared ask for formal permission in case it was refused. Tagging on to tea delivery proved a viable strategy in this case. Gate-crashing is more viable in criminal justice settings outside the prison, for example, at the courts as this account testifies:

> At court. A siren marked the arrival of the prison truck. I positioned myself close to where the arriving police set themselves, alongside one of the parked 4X4's, where I could see the back of the truck, the entrance to the holding cells and the escorting officers. The prisoners sullenly dismounted and entered the holding cells where, as per usual I could see them clamouring at the window of the bathroom. There were plenty of officers, some I knew some I didn't know. They are of course well within their rights to challenge me given my encroachment on their patch but the ones who do so are usually not very friendly about it. They look at me with hostility in their mouths and ask me what my problem is... [But] for the most part I get away with just assuming I will be accepted in close proximity to them. I don't ask permission... I sidle in... I am not exactly undercover or unobtrusive but neither do I interfere or cause them any problem.
>
> (Field note 200706)

Performative tactics and dilemmas

Perhaps 'infiltrating' is a strange term since none of the above tactics are particularly clandestine. They are rather particular examples of performance. They are fundamentally about the tactical presentation of self and the management of perception. Is it deceptive? Sometimes, sometimes not. Key to each of these examples is the issue of authenticity. As Abigail Rowe (2014) has argued, what is fundamentally at stake during prison ethnography is *who* we are and *what* we are. My point is we need to be aware of (and perhaps even wary of) what and who we *become* through our encounters with prisons. According to many published accounts, access to prisons for research is notoriously difficult. In West Africa, in actual fact, it is not as difficult as it sounds. But it can involve a sense of inauthenticity and a suspension of self. I was not always myself; I withheld; I compromised; I pretended; I was fundamentally ambiguous. These are aspects of the performance, the front, the cover (-up). The question is what does this mean for the much-lauded concept of integrity (Piacentini, 2013; Liebling, 2014); and what does it do to the ethnographer?

Rowe and others have made it quite clear that due to its inherently intersubjective and embodied nature, fieldwork in prison often thrusts roles upon us that we are less than comfortable with.

> This sense of being drawn more deeply into the action around me than I would have chosen frequently caught me by surprise generating feelings of discomfort and dissonance.
>
> (Rowe, 2014: 464; see also Liebling, 1999: 156)

In what follows, I present some of the uncomfortable ways in which I was both drawn in and sometimes kept at a distance.

My own work has featured a focus on groups typically understood as opposed to one another, for example perpetrators and victims or guards and inmates. I have as it were played both sides. My research in Sierra Leone came to focus on a group of former rebel fighters just released from six years in prison (Jefferson, 2010). I did this at the same time as I conducted observations in the country's prisons, interviewed staff and became 'friends' with the officer in charge of the prison. I recall one striking very mundane situation where the fact that I 'played both sides' became very obvious. I was driving in my battered red jeep – a big contrast to the big white land rovers of the United Nations and the Justice Sector Development Programme – together with a notorious former rebel leader (who now heads the current president's personal security detail) when in heavy traffic I suddenly cut in front of the (now retired) director of prisons, the man who formally speaking had granted me permission to study the prisons (after insistent pleading on my part). I remember feeling somehow compromised. Whose side was I on? Or whose side might I be perceived to be on? And what might the consequences be? As it was, there were none (that I know of).

On another occasion I drove prison staff *to* court and prisoners *away* from court! Did anyone really understand what I was doing or why I was there? Did it matter? Perhaps my role and position was as opaque as the carceral apparatus and the experiences of its occupants that I sought to understand?

A third example, from a different project, illustrates my shifting role through time. During a quite recent visit to Prison Headquarters in Freetown together with members of Prison Watch, a local reform NGO, I ran into the Officer who had signed the letter granting me access to the prisons back in 2006. 'You are becoming one of us' he said as he greeted me. Well, maybe, I thought. But maybe not. What he was noticing was my changed role. There I stood hand in hand with a critical NGO who were nonetheless working with the prison authorities. Somehow in his eyes that put me in a different position than the one he had imagined for me when I came to do independent research on detention issues so long before. Relationships are vulnerable to misinterpretation and often based on imagined perceptions over which we have no control. In Nigeria, there were at least five different roles ascribed to me. I was either a human rights activist, or a prison officer from the UK, or a spy, sometimes a researcher, or on one occasion simply 'the friend of the Officer in Charge'.

Similarly, Rowe identifies three different roles that were attributed to her in two women's prisons in Yorkshire: professional, naïve outsider and eccentric left-winger (Rowe, 2014: 470) and argues, as I have too (Jefferson and Huniche, 2009), that it is possible to exploit the inevitable fact of being ascribed multiple roles.

Increasing consciousness about the way the prison researcher is drawn in and ascribed roles and positions suggest increasing awareness of the importance of relationships for our conceptualisation of prison itself. I have come to consider the prison as first and foremost a *relational institution*. Rather than debating the function of the prison – is it for deterrence, or warehousing or rehabilitation? – and defining the prison in these terms I find it preferable to think about the way the prison experience is mediated through relationships and encounters. This involves paying attention to the way the prison researcher's experience is also mediated through relations (e.g. my pre-existent relationship with the angry officer mentioned earlier). Relationships with prison authorities and people in positions to grant or deny access have to be forged and continually nurtured. In Sierra Leone, I was often deliberately courteous and constantly anxious about causing offence. I always *felt* that my access was at risk and needed protecting, as indicated in the following note, though in retrospect it probably never was.

> I paid a courtesy call once more on the bakery where they were still busy preparing the dough. It seemed to take forever to get towards the gate lodge... I was briefly up to see the Officer in Charge [OiC] who was not there at first but then appeared from a back office. He has a winning smile in contrast to the junior officer who left his office without a greeting and whom, for a moment, I believed was the OiC ignoring me. Old fears and paranoia of screwing up my access.
>
> (Field note 110506)

Here, an example of perceived misrecognition awakened latent fears of having access curtailed. As well as seeking – often in vain – to manage others' perceptions of me, I also often tried to keep as low a profile as possible (despite being aware that this battle was lost before it began). Nevertheless, it led to a consciousness about where I situated myself not only socially but also spatially. The example is quite innocuous:

> Whilst he (an inmate) talked to me a queue (of inmates) gathered which later dissipated. I was rather conscious that I stood in full view of the office of the Officer in Charge and whilst he had said I might occasionally speak with prisoners this seemed a little blatant so I retreated into the arts workshop.
>
> (Field note 110506)

Basically I reduced my visibility; I hid.

The relationships that we are obliged to invest in are often a source of pressure and strain. Forced intimacy[4] involves the transgression of boundaries. Relational pressure can come from those we might naturally feel some sympathy with and those for whom we feel antipathy. It can also be a product of a failure to live up to the expectations or hopes of those with whom we interact (or our own). The following two excerpts reflect first a struggle I had exiting the field (frustration with self) and second the view of one prison officer on how I had failed to deliver.

> Taking leave. To Pademba road (prison) to confirm arrangement for this evening. The gateman pulled me to one side anxious for me to give him something, realising that I am soon leaving, claiming he would be on night duty next week. This is becoming a pattern, a difficult pattern to deal with. I have no pat response and seek avoidance and delay as the best strategy but it is distasteful; it is not a fine way to take my leave.
>
> (Field note 210706)

> The officer then rather directly asks me what I am going to give him in exchange for this information. I also told him I was unlikely to call him from Denmark because of the expense. I would have spared myself a verbal lambasting if I had lied. 'Am I American or British?' he asked. 'British'. 'Well, I prefer Americans'. Then he told a long story of a British woman called Ruth who learned their Limba language and lived in their village for years. But when she left she never gave anything back. She never took a small boy from the community, educated him and sent him back to develop that village. She was British. 'That is how the British are. I prefer Americans'. He insisted I record his words. 'The British' he said 'always try to gain from people'.
>
> (Field note 110706)

This was, more or less, my discomforting farewell to the prison, my exit from the field. Already from these accounts, it is clear that the vulnerability of the ethnographer's relation to the field is a deeply personal vulnerability. I turn now to consider a second major theme, the fragility of the relation to self that is a feature of the ethnographic encounter with the prison.

Relating to self

> For the (especially novice) researcher, the strain of continuous identity management; taut presentation of Self; and hypersensitivity to the ambient sounds, smells, and sights can be fatiguing and highly stressful.
>
> (Jewkes, 2014a: 389)

As is common, the issue of identity management and presentation of self 'dogged me throughout my fieldwork' to borrow the words of Abigail Rowe (Rowe, 2014: 471). The extensive examples shared below offer some further insight into the threats to identity and inherent vulnerabilities of the ethnographic approach to prisons.

Doing trust

One of the most fraught and strained features of ethnography is what I call 'doing trust'. When you are the tool, you are at risk. We do trust. It does not just develop. We put ourselves in situations that demonstrate we trust when there may be no grounds for trust. We bring trust into being.[5] The vulnerability of the prison ethnographer is part structural, part relational. There is the intimidation and irritation of fences, gates, security, patrolling dogs, surveillance, rules or their absence, queues of needy people deprived of justice, 'moral and institutional hierarchies' (Rowe, 2014: 465) we do not recognise or do not want to recognise, and so on. And then there is the intimidation that comes from other people. Most of my fieldwork in Sierra Leone was unproblematic but on occasion dynamics were deeply unsettling. The following excerpt captures some of the discomfort of a fraught relational encounter where alarm bells were ringing but appearances had to be maintained and offence not given.

> Strange day on trip to a village beyond the Waterloo checkpoint with XXX and his entourage comprising three former senior combatants. XXX is reticent to say the least and at the same time inclusive and resolute with his gestures but in a slightly intimidating, difficult to interpret kind of way. He slaps me on the back, holds me on the knee or leg and jabs his finger almost in my face as he speaks. He is emphatic. His whole being is as an exclamation mark at the end of a short sharp sentence... The intimidating atmosphere perhaps hung mostly around the fact that he wants to buy my vehicle for 2000 dollars less than I am advertising it for. I wondered whether the purpose of the trip was not to test drive and extort the car out of me. Probably only a secondary purpose; perhaps just a spontaneous one? I feel quite pressured. One of his entourage also argued on behalf of a cheap price for his 'boss' – 'think of our situation, think of our friendship'. All sorts of arguments were used for why I should sell it more cheaply including that XXX will need money to put fog-lamps and install air-con and get the windows tinted and the whole car re-sprayed. Hardly my concern and hardly negotiating chips.
>
> (Field note 050606)

Here we see how the aims of the research (understanding detention practices during and after the war) and the personal circumstances of the researcher (about to leave and needing to sell a vehicle) conspire, with the particular circumstances of having agreed to drive these former fighters to a village rendezvous, to leave me vulnerable, not because they were dangerous but simply because the field was open and unpredictable – as it must be. Interestingly, the member of the entourage who spoke up for his boss invoked central elements of the ethnographer–informant relationship to bolster his claims. When he says 'think of our situation', he is encouraging me to reflect on my own position of relative privilege vis-à-vis their own status as stigmatised former fighters. 'Put yourself in our shoes' he is saying, exactly what I am trying to do through my ethnography. And then he is even more appealing, 'think of our friendship', again tapping into a key trope of ethnography, the building of lasting relationships. Ironically this particular former soldier is someone whom I often seek out during return visits to Sierra Leone as I pass through the airport where he now shares responsibility for border security.

Sometimes I felt a sense of broader unease about conducting research within a post-conflict setting where I was unfamiliar with the way the state operated. At one point, a student colleague and I developed a rather healthy paranoia in the face of the arbitrary state apparatus we were slowly learning about. We asked ourselves to what extent our feelings of insecurity told us about the experience of our former combatant interlocutors. The broader framework, the penal politics and the nature of the implementing state can all be grounds for unease for the ethnographer whether this is in a place like Sierra Leone or a place like Denmark. The ethnographer's unfamiliarity with the field is the raison d'être for being there in the first place with all the risks and uncertainties that entails.

Bystander guilt and inaction

The above examples do not directly concern the prison though we should be aware that the perimeter fence should not limit prison ethnography. A quick review of my field notes from Sierra Leone suggests that the times I felt really vulnerable or afraid were mostly *outside* the confines of the prison. In the prison I felt not fear but guilt. I felt inconsequential and brutalised, not by the harshness of the atmosphere but by my choice to adopt a bystander/witness stance in the face of seemingly endless and tragic stories of *judicial limbo* (see Jefferson, 2011). I could not help. I chose not to help (mostly). The following excerpts capture some of the feelings of ambivalence this invoked and the strategies of avoidance that left me feeling somehow incomplete and dis-integrated.

> Prisoners are subtler (than prison staff who openly lamented about their sufferings). They approach me and engage me in conversation, tell me their

> stories try to extort my sympathy. I am beginning to develop immunity. I say first I am not a lawyer, second I am not ICRC, third I am not really mandated to even speak with them and am anxious I might get them as well as me into trouble. These are all strategies of avoidance, avoidance of obligation, avoidance of recognising and acting on obvious human need and obvious inhuman injustice.
>
> (Field note 110506)

Clearly, I was not immune as the following excerpt attests:

> During this visit I was deeply troubled at an emotional level by the depth of injustice and unmet need in the prison. The number of prisoners that approach me with similar stories of no bail granted, no appeal papers prepared on their behalf, ridiculous sentence lengths for minor crimes. The sense is that most of the inmates need not really be there at all, that their confinement is unnecessary. But that the randomness of justice delivery is deterrence; random acts of sovereign power reminding the population that anyone might be next. But it (what troubles me) is not so much the queue of injustice that the prisoners seem to represent as they approach me but the fact that I am consistently denying to help them in any way.
>
> (Field note 240506)

The following excerpt is taken from a description of my first meeting in prison with a group of Liberian refugees who had been in Sierra Leone for 18 years having fled from war in their own country. They had been arrested following a demonstration where some offices and vehicles were trashed at the United Nations High Commissioner for Refugees (UNHCR). It offers clues about how people, location and styles of relating all interact to exacerbate or mitigate vulnerability. I was in the remand section of the prison, checking the toilet facilities having withdrawn myself from the group a few minutes earlier:

> [T]he Liberians reappear. This time they are slightly more hostile . . . The *redband* (inmate leader appointed by authorities) seemed to act protectively towards me. I am uncertain whether the increasing agitation on the part of the Liberians was due to them having worked themselves up by their own accounts of injustice, my declarations that I had little power to affect the course of events regarding them or the change in location to a place where neither I nor they were visible from the admin block anymore. I had been happy about that as I moved with the *redband*, pleased to move beyond surveillance but now once more surrounded by disgruntled refugees expressing frustrations on behalf of family members waiting at court I felt slightly more vulnerable. Rain drops began to fall. No-one reacted. I wonder

> now how long I was there. It felt like an eternity barraged with information I could barely absorb, let alone process and respond appropriately to. I felt blurred, overwhelmed, struck by a profound inability to give what they wished for. They said they would demonstrate and protest if they were not soon taken to court. Indeed they actually said 'we will burn Freetown' but toned this down to a metaphorical burning in response to my frowns. 'Of course we won't burn anything but we will protest, make our grievances felt'.
>
> (Field note 200606)

This excerpt captures a number of the themes already mentioned pertaining to the vulnerability of the ethnographer: powerlessness, threat, the forging and maintenance of a relation, even a subtext of violence. Strangely perhaps, this encounter was to lead to a relatively long relationship and a relatively strong connection as I followed their court case, visited their homes and corresponded with their Chairman over a period of at least two years. But there was an extreme asymmetry to the relationship that is a feature of much prison ethnography. Whereas I learned much about the politics of victimhood, suffering as a quality of life, the vagaries of court cases, the slowness of justice and its punitive delivery, as well as the dynamics of disavowal featured in the UNHCR's interactions with this group, all I could give them was some temporary attention and recognition. I could not deliver on their dream of resettlement in a third country, though I felt keenly the weight and obstinacy of their hope (see Jefferson, 2014b, for further details).

Grief and suspicion

The experience of prison is sometimes described as social death. A Philippine inmate interviewed in connection with another research project talked about the prison as 'a cemetery of the living'. Sometimes the ethnographer is confronted with literal death. After attending the funeral of a very young child, the daughter of one of my informants in one of Freetown's poorest slum neighbourhoods, I wrote the following note which captures my grief, my frustration and my tentative distrust of the motives of the family. I had first seen Isatu, looking very sick, the day before and been asked whether I could provide money for a trip to the village to access local medicine.

> I weep inside myself for Isatu. Tears gather in the outer corners of my eyes but evaporate before they fall. Tears of humidity. Tears of futility. Tears in the landscape of grief. I feared for her. I distressed myself, not so much perhaps on her account if I am totally honest but on account of the impotence I felt trapped between competing discourses on health, illness and well-being. Not

> called to arbitrate or judge. Just to care, and to donate. A suspicion lingers that I may have just been called to fund the burial expenses. It seems an unfair suspicion. Did they know she would die? They have watched her suffer and deteriorate, kept her condition secret. They saw her pain. Now they grieve.
>
> (Field note 020606)

This quote is perhaps an appropriate place to flee the field and turn to the safer ground of the vulnerability of knowledge. At this point, the tone and tenor of the argument shifts. Inevitably, consideration of the vulnerability of knowledge is less personal and less reflexive than consideration of the vulnerability of the researcher's relation to self and to the field. However, perhaps this claim is, in fact, an illusion? Perhaps there is no safety in abstraction? Or perhaps the turn to knowledge is less abstract and more embodied and situated than we often imagine? It is, after all, the researcher's relation to knowledge that is at stake in the first instance and that knowledge is drawn, in part, from the researcher's own embedded experience in the field as we have already considered. If the ethnographer's relations to the field, to self and to knowledge are all contemporaneous and co-constitutive, as I believe they are, then we have no reason to consider knowledge to be 'safe' as I will suggest below (though it may feel safer than grief).

Relating to knowledge

> It is the relationship between what we know, what we do not know, what we cannot know and what we do not like to know that determines the cognitive frame for political practice.
>
> (Daase and Kessler 2007: 412)

In this section, I will argue that it is not only our selves and our relationships that are vulnerable but our knowledge too. The above quotation is taken from an article concerned with knowing and not-knowing. Somewhat playfully, but with deep seriousness the authors begin their article with a discussion of a poetically-rendered version of Donald Rumsfeld's (in)famous press conference remarks about *known knowns, known unknowns* and *unknown unknowns*. Daase and Kessler's analysis shows how the relationship between knowing and not-knowing is constitutive of social practice. This is no less the case for penal practice and no less the case for ethnographic attempts to understand penal practice. What – given the vulnerability of our relationship to the field and to self – can we know (or not know)?

Rowe has noted that debates over terminology (e.g. whether a particular prison study is *really* ethnographic) distract from more important discussions about epistemology (Rowe, 2014: 466) – about what we know or what can be known, or about what I am calling the vulnerability of knowledge. I am reminded of a common exchange when I try to hang out in reception offices or gate areas in prisons. After introductions the officers usually say something polite like 'fine we are happy to give you any information you need'. I was rarely able to convey to them effectively my lack of interest in their pre-packaged discourse, that is, their information. I was looking for raw, emergent material to slowly convert into data for analysis. Knowledge would come much later – hesitantly.

Ethnographic knowledge is always fragmented, partial and incomplete however long we spend in the field. Perhaps this is why it makes little sense to qualify the term 'prison ethnography' with epithets like 'quasi-' or 'semi-' as Lilian Ayete-Nyampong has argued (personal communication, 2014). All ethnography is either quasi or semi. There is no full picture, only fragments (see below). If this is the case then it calls for an extra degree of caution about the claims that we make for our ethnographically oriented knowledge.

Anthropologist Lotte Buch and I have been thinking for some years now about the importance of doubt, doubt as revealed in ethnographic human encounters and the doubt equally endemic to the process of translating ethnographically gathered material into uncertain, tentative knowledge (Buch and Jefferson, 2012). Drawing on the work of the American philosopher Stanley Cavell read, at least in part through the eyes and thought of Veena Das (2007, 2011), we have been wondering about a notion of imponderable knowledge. At a seminar on the topic held in Copenhagen in May 2012, we rhetorically posed the following question:

> Might ponderable knowledge be characterised as speculative, ivory tower, distant, contemplative even ascetic/hermetic (sealed). And imponderable knowledge as grounded, everyday, close, suggested, endlessly open, innovative and experimental, shimmering and hesitant. Not doubtful but expressive of doubt.

Not doubtful but expressive of doubt. Of course, we are not advocating that we not be believed, and that our writings are somehow unreliable or untruthful. But we are suggesting that the *doubt-filledness* of ethnography be acknowledged. Wittgenstein in *Philosophical Investigations* encourages his reader to:

> Ask yourself: How does a man learn to get an 'eye' for something? And how can this eye be used?

As already considered it is the entirety of the ethnographer enmeshed in his or her production of ethnographic material that is decisive for seeing and sensing and turning impressions, words, smells and flavours into knowledge. Ethnography seems to be precisely about learning to have that eye for something. In this light it becomes important to allow ethnographic projects to unfold slowly, to 'get to know', to invest in relationships, to not assume too much too fast. Such messy, muddy,[6] 'ordinary, chronic and cruddy' (Povinelli, 2011: 13) encounters demand, I think, modesty and hesitation both in the field and on exit as we wrestle with the doubt and uncertainty that our encounters throw up. Learning to have that eye for something is likely a career-long learning curve. As Jenny Sloan and Serena Wright document in this volume (Chapter 7), there is a long way from 'going in green' as a relative newcomer to becoming a relative old-timer. Which brings us towards a conclusion.

Conclusion: On marks, glimpses and ethnographic zoom

It is my hope that the glimpses of a vulnerable series of relationships shared in this chapter might stimulate more honest conversations about the intended and unintended consequences of field-based prison studies for the ethnographer and for knowledge. In this chapter, questions about *who* and *what* one is in the prison have been found to be fundamental questions that the prison poses. Recently, I drafted a brief blog-like piece for a newsletter where I reflected on some of the quandaries around the desire to know and not know the horrors of confinement. I called it 'lines of flight', an allusion both to Deleuze and Guattari and to my own ambivalent attitude when approaching a new prison. This brings the simultaneous desire to quench my appetite for knowledge and to flee or, to put it another way, I encounter a potent cocktail of anticipation and trepidation. I closed the 'meditation' with reference to the marks that the encounter leaves behind.

> For me, entering the prison, be it in West Africa or North Africa, Kosovo or the Philippines, involves stepping forward as much as stepping back. Each entry feels like two steps forward, one step back. A similar vacillation is involved on departure. The prison is not simply left behind. It becomes somehow inescapable. In the crucible of the prison something indefinable is left behind and an indelible, though hard to decipher, residue attaches itself. The prison leaves its mark, a mark that can be kept private or made public.
> (Jefferson, 2014b)

Researchers cannot help but be touched by the intensity of confinement, says Jewkes (2014a). There is an emerging consensus that prison ethnography is a vulnerable business and inevitably leaves marks. Rowe interrogates her own experience of women's prisons and finds echoes of prisoner pain. Her record of her own experience resonates with the experience of inmates (Rowe,

2014: 473). In the meditation mentioned above, I also wrote that 'all too often the prison transgresses my self-protective boundaries even as it transgresses the boundaries of its occupants' (Jefferson, 2014a). It seems clear that researcher emotions can resemble, echo or mirror the emotional impact of the prison on its occupants. Owning (up to) our (dis)comfort can be a clue to the (dis)comfort of the prison (see also Phillips and Earle, 2010; Yuen, 2011). Sometimes we fail to recognise ourselves in prison. This is when the threat to self is strongest. The questions 'Who am I? What am I becoming?' might be clues suggesting it is time to get out. Inmates, of course, do not have that luxury.

Does prison ethnography threaten identity? Yes. What do we become? That depends on how we handle the material and social differences and power inequalities we encounter. It depends on how we deal with the risk of becoming what we pretend to be, the risk of desensitisation and compassion fatigue and the encroachment of indifference. It depends on the degree to which we can resist the temptation to emotionally 'disconnect' (Reiter, 2014: 417).

Notwithstanding the cost, prison ethnographies do have the potential to elucidate much more than simply prison life especially if we experiment more with the zoom function of the ethnographic lens. Through ethnography the details of human existence, and social and political life can be calibrated both in magnified detail and against a more panoramic societal or theoretical perspective. Ethnography can allow the attentive scholar both to zoom in on local political and cultural versions of incarceration and to zoom out, bringing the nuances of confinement into focus and capturing global spectres of control. But however much we zoom in or out, we capture only glimpses (often 'blurry and pixelated' (Reiter, 2014: 417)) suggesting any idea of a comprehensive account of penal practices might be overambitious. Bandyopadhyay (Bandyopadhyay et al., 2013) problematises totalising tendencies, arguing that ethnography produces a view (based on fragments) that usefully disrupts 'myopic' readings of prison spaces. Taking fragments seriously fits with the idea that ethnography captures a snapshot, a cross-section of reality. Nevertheless, it is also true that ethnographers often forge long-lasting connections to particular sites and maintain long-term relations be these to key informants or specific locations. Thus, ethnography has the potential to zoom through time as well as space, though perhaps in a more limited way in prisons than other sites.

One final question: Is the idea of infiltrating prison spaces only apt for the West African context? There is a kind of informality and 'twilight' quality (Lund, 2006) to state institutions in West Africa that invites the kind of fieldwork style I have portrayed in this chapter. But I would hesitate to claim it is a special case. Most prisons would seem to invite to embodied performance, to the careful presentation of self and management of identity, to bluff and pretence, to the 'doing' of trust in a non-trust environment. To 'survive' in such climates and under such circumstances, we need to nurture our self-protective skills, and we need each other. Knowing the risks we may be able to ameliorate the costs. The organisers of the Prison Ethnography Conference that led to this volume took the first step. It is up to the old-timers and the novices together to continue the conversation so we can sustain each other as we continue to scrutinise sites of confinement in a bid to reveal their dynamics and their effects.

Notes

1. As Yvonne Jewkes puts it, prison research 'can have far-reaching and damaging effects but can also constitute an unexpected discovery of something else, something more' (Jewkes, 2014a: 388).
2. See www.gprnetwork.org.
3. I might, for example, highlight the value the project could have for the authorities. Sometimes by doing so I even realise the value the project might have for the authorities.
4. I am grateful to Steffen Jensen for this expression. He has used it to talk about the intense proximity of living in a poor urban neighbourhood in the Philippines. It also resonates with Gresham Sykes' *deprivations* (Sykes, 2007), reminding us of the parallels possible to make across different sites of confinement (Jefferson, 2012).
5. This is a deliberately alternative take on common, superficial, often blasé ideas of creating trust and building rapport (e.g. Patenaude, 2004).
6. See Decoene (2013) (in Beyens et al., 2014) who draws on Trotter's idea of 'cooking with mud' (Trotter, 2000), both cited by Jewkes (2014b).

Further reading

Maher, L. (2000) *Sexed Work Gender, Race, and Resistance in a Brooklyn Drug Market, Clarendon Studies in Criminology* (Oxford: Oxford University Press).

Martin, T. M., Jefferson, A. M. and Bandyopadhyay, M. (2014) 'Sensing Prison Climates: Governance, Survival, and Transition', *Focaal*, 2014, 3–17.

Jefferson, A. M. and Martin, T. M. (2014) 'Everyday Governance in African Prisons', *Prison Service Journal, Special Issue*, 212, 2–3.

References

Bandyopadhyay, M., Jefferson, A. M. and Ugelvik, T. (2013) 'Prison Spaces and Beyond: The Potential of Ethnographic Zoom', *Criminal Justice Matters*, 91, 28–9.

Beyens, K., Christiaens, J., Claes, B., de Ridder, S., Tournel, H. and Tubex, H. (2014) *The Pains of Doing Criminological Research*, First edition (Brussels: VUB University Press).

Bosworth, M., Campbell, D., Demby, B., Ferranti, S. M. and Santos, M. (2005) 'Doing Prison Research: Views From Inside', *Qualitative Inquiry*, 11, 249–64.

Buch, L. and Jefferson, A. M. (2012) 'Knowledge, Doubt & Obligation: Interrogating Imponderability', Unpublished manuscript, 2012.

Daase, C. and Kessler, O. (2007) 'Knowns and Unknowns in the "War on Terror": Uncertainty and the Political Construction of Danger', *Security Dialogue*, 38, 411–34.

Das, V. (2007) *Life and Words* (Berkeley: University of California Press).
Das, V. (2011) 'Time Is a Trickster and Other Fleeting Thoughts on Cavell, His Life, His Work', *MLN*, 126, 943–53.
Jefferson, A. M. (2010) 'Traversing Sites of Confinement Post-Prison Survival in Sierra Leone', *Theoretical Criminology*, 14, 387–406.
Jefferson, A. M. (2011) 'Glimpses of Judicial Limbo in West Africa', *Amicus Journal*, 26, 13–20.
Jefferson, A. M. (2012) 'Conceptualizing Confinement: Prisons and Poverty in Sierra Leone', *Criminology and Criminal Justice*, 14, 1, 44–60.
Jefferson, A. M. (2014) 'Lines of Flight – On the Desire to Know but Not Know Prisons', http://www.europeangroup.org/media/242#overlay-context=content/newsletters
Jefferson, A. M. (2014) 'Performances of Victimhood, Allegation and Disavowal in Sierra Leone', in S. Jensen and H. Ronsbo (eds) *Histories of Victimhood: The Ethnography of Political Violence*, pp. 218–38 (Philadelphia: University of Pennsylvania Press).
Jefferson, A. M. and Huniche, L. (2009) '(Re)Searching for Persons in Practice: Field-Based Methods for Critical Psychological Practice Research', *Qualitative Research in Psychology*, 6, 12–27.
Jewkes, Y. (2014) 'An Introduction to "Doing Prison Research Differently"', *Qualitative Inquiry*, 20, 387–91.
Jewkes, Y. (2014) 'Book Review: The Pains of Criminological Research', *Qualitative Inquiry*, 20 (4), 487–8.
Liebling, A. (1999), 'Doing Research in Prisons – Breaking the Silence', *Theoretical Criminology*, 3, 147–73.
Liebling, A. (2014) 'Postscript Integrity and Emotion in Prisons Research', *Qualitative Inquiry*, 20, 481–6.
Lund, C. (2006) 'Twilight Institutions: Public Authority and Local Politics in Africa', *Development and Change*, 37, 685–705.
Patenaude, A. L. (2004) 'No Promises, But I'm Willing to Listen and Tell What I Hear: Conducting Qualitative Research among Prison Inmates and Staff', *The Prison Journal*, 84, 69S–91S.
Phillips, C. and R. Earle (2010) 'Reading Difference Differently?: Identity, Epistemology and Prison Ethnography', *British Journal of Criminology*, 50, 360–78.
Piacentini, L. (2013) '"Integrity, Always Integrity"', *Criminal Justice Matters*, 91, 21–21.
Povinelli, E. (2011) *Economies of Abandonment: Social Belonging and Endurance in Late Liberalism* (Durham: Duke University Press).
Reiter, K. (2014) 'Making Windows in Walls Strategies for Prison Research', *Qualitative Inquiry*, 20, 417–28.
Rowe, A. (2014) 'Situating the Self in Prison Research Power, Identity, and Epistemology', *Qualitative Inquiry*, 20, 404–16.
Sykes, G. M. (2007) *The Society of Captives: A Study of a Maximum Security Prison, Princeton Classic Editions,* 1st Princeton classic edition (Princeton, NJ: Princeton University Press).
Trotter, D. (2000) *Cooking with Mud: The Idea of Mess in Nineteenth-Century Art and Fiction* (New York: Oxford University Press).
Yuen, F. (2011) 'Embracing Emotionality: Clothing My "Naked Truths"', *Critical Criminology*, 19, 75–88.

9
The Perfume of Sweat: Prison Research through Deleuzian Lenses

Elisabeth Fransson and Berit Johnsen

Introduction

This chapter draws on experiences of ethnographic research in closed male prisons in Norway. From the positions as researchers, our aim is to explore what our bodies can be in the field, what they can do to the field and what the field can do with them. By using the term 'can do', we want to draw the reader's attentions to affects produced in specific events through ethnographic fieldwork. Our analytical point of departure is to explore how our bodies enter into compositions with other bodies both human and non-human. Approaching the body as always more than itself, as an always relational and social-material event (Deleuze and Guattari, 1987), opens up questions related to what we can know together with prisoners. Inspired by Gilles Deleuze and Felix Guattaris' key concepts 'event', 'a body without organs' and 'the process of becoming', we explore the affective journey of our researcher bodies by sketching a couple of body assemblages[1] across two vignettes that we call 'a cup of coffee' and 'the perfume of sweat'.[2] Each of the two vignettes foregrounds the complex, contradictory and changing nature of becoming researchers and prisoners. Enlightening the process of becoming in the ethnographic prison research field, the chapter brings bodily experiences in touch with analytical, methodological and ethical questions important in newer prison ethnography.

How this became an issue

'I'm seldom as aware of my gender as when I am in male prisons.' This statement came up in a discussion between us sharing experiences on doing research – especially ethnographic research – in male prisons. Doing ethnographic fieldwork has opened a series of reflections we have been experiencing, through our time as researchers, in closed prisons in Norway. Being female researchers around our fifties with different research paths, different ways of doing fieldwork, different lengths of time within prison research, different bodies and also different ways of using the body in our research have given us the possibility of going into field experiences and revisiting field notes and affects related to these. In this chapter, we think and write with Deleuze, curious of what this philosophical approach can give us in our research.

Norwegian prison ethnography

Prison ethnography in Norway is strongly connected to fieldwork over time (Mathiesen, 2012), as well as to certain critical knowledge positions (Goffman, 1967; Foucault, 1995, 1991; Lipsky, 2010). Prison ethnography is subjected to strong control regarding access to the field, the collection of data and to discretion in presenting the data. These specific Norwegian contextual frames breed carefulness and a delicacy, and it is necessary to take into account their influence on how women researchers actually do prison ethnography. As researchers, trained in the Norwegian tradition of qualitative social research (Wadel, 1973; Gullestad, 1989; Kvale, 1989; Widerberg, 1994; Album, 1996; Løchen, 1996) and strongly influenced by our feminist scholars (Widerberg, 1996, 2001; Moi, 1998), the issue of gender and sexuality has always been an implicit part in our reflections of our work on prisons. As female researchers, we have to find strategies for how to overcome and find solutions of the problem of being a female ethnographic researcher in a male-dominated setting. In this chapter, we move further asking: 'What is the problem with this problem?' (Beauvoir, 2011). More than seeing our body as a problem, we want to explore what our bodies can be in the field, what our bodies can do in the field and what the field can do with our bodies. Could it be that we, going in depth in an affective methodology, can see something new? Using two vignettes, we explore our own experiences doing ethnographic work in prison. Before presenting the vignettes, we will introduce some of Deleuze's key concepts.

Prison walls, keys, uniforms and bicycles: The process of becoming female researchers

Event, body without organs and the process of becoming

Gilles Deleuze, together with Michel Foucault and Jacques Derrida, is regarded one of the most influential French philosophers of our time. Deleuze is known for his cooperation with the French psychoanalyst Fèlix Guattari. Their thinking of the body as always more than itself, as an always relational and a social–material event where the body makes things happen (Deleuze and Guattari, 1987), invites us into ethnographic prison research within the philosophy of post-humanism.

Event in a Deleuzian sense is the second when something HAPPENS! It could be something said that should not have been said, eyes in the wrong direction, a smell, a feeling of fear or knowing something that cannot be said. An event de-stabilises the order of things and opens up for vibrational, shadowy, virtual potentiality as a domain of becoming that cannot be grasped as an actualisation of the world external to it (Kapferer, 2010). We cannot know what is going to happen next. As researchers we prepare ourselves before going out in the field, we have a plan, but nevertheless we are often surprised. It does not go as anticipated. Our bodies meet other bodies; imprisoned bodies and prison officers' bodies, and we connect between keys, uniforms, smells, talk and walls. This mix or intertwined connection between human and non-human bodies makes us *a body without organs*.

Deleuze and Guattaris' (1987) concept 'a body without organs', often shortened to BwO, is a critique to a modernist conceptualisation of the body as a body with organs. A separated body defined by age, sex and gender. Individual bodies influenced by culture and other bodies, but nevertheless, separated from them. This does not mean that we are not bodies with organs. When we enter prisons, we notice anxiousness in our tensed muscles. We can sweat, feeling nervous and warm in meetings with prisoners. These feelings tell us something about the context and about us as prison researchers and they demonstrate how we approach the field with an open body (Solheim, 1998), absorbing what is in the prison setting. It is a kind of a 'bodily alertness', where some of our experience of the situation is to be found in what we notice in our individual body (Engelsrud, 2006; Leseth, 2008).

As an approach in research, the BwO focuses away from the individual human body and to the space in between bodies where humans and non-humans meet. It makes our bodies intertwine with non-bodily phenomena such as prison walls, tables, uniforms, keys, bicycles, sounds and smells. A body without organs approach makes us interconnect with the materiality around us and *become* something else (Deleuze and Guattari, 1987).

The process of becoming is, in a Deleuzian sense, not something that lies in nature and comes forward as something already in existence, like a child that becomes an adolescent, a girl that becomes a woman or as poverty leads to misery. Deleuze focuses instead on the process of becoming. What happens on the way, often illustrated as a line of flight, as raindrops falling on a window that separate and go off in different directions. The process of becoming creates room for surprises. Playing with this Deleuzian imagery opens up our capacities to see the man in the prisoner. It is not the young man who steals that is the prisoner; it is the becoming prisoner that produces a *universal* prisoner (Deleuze and Guattari, 1987: 277). By thinking philosophically and in a non-representative manner, Deleuze and Guattari argue that concepts should be developed by focusing events that can lead the thought to do thinking (Deleuze and Guattari, 1994 in Fuglesang et al., 2005). Let us turn to the first vignette.

'A cup of coffee'

I am on my way to my very first interview, in a small closed prison in the southwest part of Norway. Given the context of being a small prison, the prison governor invites me to his office and tells me that he has chosen Amin, 22 years old, imprisoned for gang violence for the first interview. He tells me that Amin is classified as a trusted prisoner and that he soon can ask for permission to be moved to an open prison. The governor is concerned that this is my first interview in prison and tells me that he has moved the place for the interview from the visitors' room downstairs, to the sitting room on the third floor where there are cameras and security buttons to press.

The governor follows me to the sitting room upstairs. This is an open space area adjacent to a kitchen. From the kitchen there are doors to three cells for the trusted prisoners. From their cell windows, they can watch the street life outside. Knives are affixed to the wall; clothes are hanging for drying. Photos of naked women are hanging inside the cell doors. The governor shows me the security camera and the alarm buttons – and those inside the cells. I feel a bit shaky, and I am sure that I would not remember the alarm buttons at all if I should need them. I also hope Amin does not hear the governor and his focus on my safety. When the governor calls him, Amin walks out of his open cell door. Of course, he has heard everything.

Amin is wearing a once white T-shirt, blue jogging trousers, socks and plastic sandals. He has his hands in his pockets, his shoulders are low, his eyes facing down to the floor. For me, the way he positions himself in the room and in relation to me, stand in contrast to his well trained and muscular young body. My mind flies away. I can imagine him in a fight. As we talk, Amin lifts his head, turns the chair more directly towards me and our eyes meet. At this point I feel comfortable. We talk about his position as a trusted prisoner, his wish for – but also fear of moving out. He tells me that his father has not visited him once. 'He is ashamed of me', he says. Amin also tells me about the medicine that keeps his body calm, and his longing for walking around in the street without anybody knowing him. The time flies and we are in the middle of important issues about being in a process of moving out of prison when a male prison officer comes in. He says that he wants to check the rooms. I notice that he wears blue gloves and I wonder why? He holds my eyes as if asking me if everything is okay? On his way out he tells me that the next prisoner is ready. It is like an electric shock going through my body. I feel so embarrassed over the way he says it. For a moment I don't know what to say and me and Amin just sit there.

Then Amin gets up and asks if I would like a cup of coffee? I feel relieved and thankful for the offer. Amin goes to the kitchen table and starts making

> the coffee. Again the prison officer comes in, more insistent this time and asks Amin to leave because the other prisoner is on the way. 'I cannot have two prisoners here at the same time', he says. 'I would just like to finish making her coffee', Amin answers. I feel a tense atmosphere. As if there was a silent struggle between the two of them. Amin is standing there with his back towards us making coffee. Again his shoulders are low, his eyes down. His voice is lower and the tone changed. I feel somehow responsible. In a desperate attempt to solve the situation I ask if I can use the bathroom. I thank Amin for the interview and the coffee and the prison officer says that he will follow me to the bathroom downstairs. When I come up again Amin has left, leaving fresh coffee for me and my next conversation partner.

Working with this event through Deleuzian lenses my perspective shifted. I started out analysing Amin's repressed subject-position. Working with the text while reading Deleuze I realised that Amin became silenced and that my voice came first, albeit in a very indirect way. Starting to work with the text as an event in a Deleuzian way, this logic changed. The connectedness I felt with Amin became more clear. I remembered how I, as we talked, felt that body-borders disappeared. That we connected and produced knowledge together about the process of becoming in prison and the processes of both fear and desire regarding moving out to an open prison. We became BwO to draw on another Deleuzian concept. It was not just me, the researcher, sitting there asking questions and Amin, that he as a prisoner, responded to. There in the room we connected until the prison officer arrived and our 'body-borders' were reintroduced.

In retrospect, I think it was my position, coming from outside, becoming connected with Amin and then again experiencing the border between us that made me feel embarrassed. The event, as I define it here, is when the prison officer comes in and ruins the BwO, reframed again when Amin repairs the damage and invites me for a cup of coffee. In this situation, Amin shows delicacy, takes a responsibility and shows me and the prison officer who he is, other than a prisoner. The reaction from the prison officer, in a matter of seconds, repositions Amin as a prisoner and demonstrates in this way the daily process of becoming a prisoner. The prison officer does not see or will not give importance to Amin's kind gesture; he does not allow Amin to be a non-prisoner – a normal and gentle young man.

The event also illustrates how the three of us through the uniform, the keys, the coffee and the mistrust in the room made us a new body without organs, but this time with a different atmosphere and different rules where both me and Amin follow the prison's power regime. It recreated the feeling I had when I arrived at the prison where the governor made me feel unsafe. A contrast to how I felt when I was alone with Amin.

By thinking with the concepts event, a body without organs and the process of becoming (Deleuze and Guattari, 1994) the ethical questions regarding my role as a researcher became clearer; whose side did I choose? Knowing that the staff had made arrangements for the next prisoner to come in, I followed their instructions, not making things difficult for them. But is this a good way to work as a researcher in prison? Should I instead have been standing up for me and Amin, saying that we needed more time? Should I have asked the correctional staff why he could not have two prisoners there at the same time? Should I have talked with the staff about the incident later on? Could I have talked with Amin about it? The interesting thing in this event is how I, as a researcher, was so willing to submit to the power and discipline of the prison officer. Looking at the event with a Deleuzian gaze opened up for new analytical, methodological and ethical issues that we will come back to in the last part of the chapter.

'The perfume of sweat'

> Berit: Do I influence you in the same way as a female officer when I exercise with you in the weight training room? Carl: A little bit. Yeees. But you are in a way, you are accepted in a little different way. Because you have a kind of defined task among us, you are in a way, you obviously come in among us with your own tasks in a way, so that's a bit different. But you are, though, a woman among us and, so you, that's a part of the same (laugh)... But for sure, when you take off your college-sweater then, then, it's (laugh) ten antennas that's just, that are tuned in at once. But it is, but it is just the way we are. Berit: But do you think it would have been the same if a female officer had done the same? Carl: A little different because there have been female officers that have trained with us too.... But it is not very different because, because for us are, are in a way things unattainable anyhow. So it is in a way purely, it is purely in a way just, just the autonomic[3] signals we react upon in a way. Berit: What kind of signals then? Carl: No, just that you take off your sweater, and that you, that we see your curves, and that you, that you sweat, that we can, that we can smell you and such things you know (clears his throat). It is different than we are used to, with just sweat from men and, and, these things we walk in all the time (clears his throat). And then it's men's fantasy, you know; when you see women not far away from you that, and if you're not used to seeing them then, then you think about, about things that have in a way a turn-on effect on you at once. Berit: Is that purely sexual? Carl: (Heave a sigh) Yes, yes I am sure you can say that it is, that it is something purely sexual. And that, but it is not like, it is not, it does not have to be something, something degrading for you in a way, or, or, or in relation to you. I mean it is just that it has a purely sexual effect. Not that you suddenly get attacked and raped in a way, but that your presence

> in a way touches the sexual sensors to, to, to those of us that are present in a way. Berit: Do I touch them more when I am training than when I am not training? Carl: Yes, for sure. Because you use yourself, you are more visible, and you (clears his throat), I am sure about that.

This text is a part of an interview with a prisoner in an ethnographic study of sport and masculinity in prison (Johnsen, 2001). I spent one year in a closed prison for men, exercising different sport and leisure activities together with them.

Today, about 15 years after the interview, I still remember very well the situation where we reached this point of the interview: In Carl's (a pseudonym) cell, we had been talking for 2–3 hours, Carl lying in his bed, me sitting in a chair, and a small table with the tape recorder on, between us. Little by little, we have been moving towards the issue of gender and sexuality. Then I became the subject of the conversation, and Carl's honest response changed the atmosphere between us. It became tense, eyes flickering around. Him restless in the bed struggling for words, but at the same time seemingly unaffected. Me, in the chair, uncomfortable in my body, warm and sweating. *Do I dare to continue? How far can I go?* Thoughts ran through my head. At the same time, we were moving into the core of the issue that I wanted to hear and learn more about! In a strange mixture of feeling excited, embarrassed and degraded (even though Carl told me not to), I carried on until Carl closed the event, after clearing his throat, by the phrase 'I'm sure about that'.

The event in this situation is both past and present. The 'present' event happens in the situation of the interview. Before the interview, there was a good dynamic between Carl and me. He was one of my key informants. He was curious about my study, and we often chitchatted 'in the field' even if I noticed him being a little hesitant each time we met, particularly at the start of a new conversation. It was like he was a little reluctant to come too close, but mostly when I somehow signaled that I wanted contact, often by eye contact and a smile, or when he saw that I was standing alone, he came over to me. I think he noticed my desire to have contact with him, and me noticing his desire to have contact with me (Deleuze and Guttari, 1987; Fox, 2011). In the field the two of us had established a BwO, involving a kind of friendship within the borders of him as a prisoner and me as a researcher. This constellation immediately found its forms in the interview situation; even the tape-recorder was incorporated in the BwO without problem. The unfolding of the creative potential embedded in the BwO (Deleuze and Guttari, 1987; Fox, 2011) enabled the BwO to reach a new dimension, by him sharing with me more private stories of his life. He showed me pictures of him in different situations, for example, on trips with friends, to illustrate his sportsmanship. In the interview, he became a man of different interests and an interesting person to listen to.

The event occurs when Carl reorganises the order between us. In his description of sexual arousal, I become something more than a researcher; I become a biological body of a woman. Carl becomes not merely a prisoner and a friend; he becomes the biological body of a man. This event involves an expansion of the BwO, which I did not desire. The established bodily borders, which carefully had expanded between us, exceeded their limits. Carl understood this, and by the use of the concepts 'purely sexual' and 'men's fantasy', he described the 'turn-on effect' as something outside his and the other prisoners' will. This was something happening because of sexual instincts.

At the same time, he understands how I feel. From his locked-up position as a prisoner, he sees me in the situation very clearly, and by pointing out the 'purely', 'not degrading' and 'not attainable' he gives me worth. This was something that I could not do anything about. Throughout the event Carl then carefully re-established the order of the bodily borders between us. The event did not frighten me, together with Carl in his cell I felt safe all the time. It made me rather reflect upon the past event and wonder: *What have I done by excising alongside these men in the gym?*

In the sweaty weight training room I was surrounded by bicycles, manuals and men, and a few times a female officer participating in the exercise. Being in this setting, I was very aware of how I dressed and how I behaved. Without being told so, I just knew that wearing tights and a tight fitting singlet, which would feel natural to wear in a gym outside the prison, was something that I just could not do. In big and baggy clothes, and *never* a white T-shirt that when wet of sweat would be transparent, I mostly sat on an exercise bike, my feet on the tread cranks moving round and round and the hands on the handlebars. With my body locked up in this position, I felt safe, and I felt accepted. On the prisoners' stage I felt I became a part of the BwO of humans – exercising sweating people, and non-humans – manuals, weights, barbells, benches, treadmills and bikes, together with caps tank tops and sweatpants.

Seemingly occupied with the exercise, I actually tried to hide my biological female body away. After a while on the bike, I got warm and sweaty. In order to keep up the exercise I had to take my college-sweater off, and there I was with the sweaty body and the wet non-white T-shirt stuck to my back. According to Carl, this was when the event happened. The antennas tune in on me, and the prisoners encase me with their gaze and their senses. In their eyes I became a woman, a biological body subjected for sexual desire. The prisoners were discrete, not showing me their attention in a direct manner. Actually, I did not notice the reaction of the prisoners, or rather – I think – I did not *want* to notice. Me, the wet non-white T-shirt, the baggy trousers and the bike carried on indefatigably determined to keep on and keep up the becoming a part of the BwO. The event was hidden for me, and I had forgotten to take into account the smell – *the perfume of sweat.*

Events leading the thought to do thinking

Discrete prisoners

Each of the two vignettes foregrounds the complex, contradictory and changing nature of becoming researchers and prisoners. Playing with Deleuze's concepts event, BwO and the process of becoming, we have brought effects in touch with methodological and analytical questions aimed at creating new knowledge in prison research.

Methodologically, the events have led us to lines of flights following affects such as voices, impressions, smells, fantasies and feelings as important parts of our research methods. The events de-stabilise the order of things, and in these happenings continuity is made visible. Analytically, we see how a BwO is connecting human and non-human things, to a space in-between, where something new is created (see Figure 9.1). Elisabeth connects and becomes a BwO with the table, Amin, the cup of coffee and the prison officer, the prison walls and the tense atmosphere. Berit becomes a BwO together with prisoners, bicycles, manuals and thick walls. Our bodies enter into compositions with the prisoners' bodies as well as non-human bodies, and make us remember the body is always more than just itself. It is always a relational and social–material event (Deleuze and Guattari, 1987). We are both in a process of becoming researchers and women.

The chapter enlightens how affects can be used productively as a source of awareness regarding the positioning of female researchers both within prisons

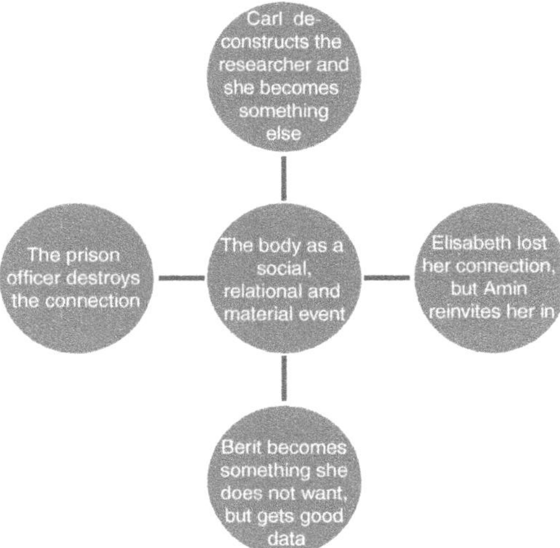

Figure 9.1 Sketch of the events

and within prison research. This question has a critical potential, regarding how we in our texts give voice to prisoners and people working in prisons (inspired by Alvesson and Sköldberg, 2009; Van Maanen, 2011). For us, this journey of thinking with Deleuze has been exciting and inspiring. It has given us the possibility to be explicitly concrete (Villani, 2006), and we have discovered new dimensions in our work. By analysing situations as events, our thoughts have been inspired to do thinking in ways that have been new for us. This has also given us the opportunity to take into account our thoughts that came into being in the event and to look upon them as valuable data in the analyses. We have come to appreciate the concept of BwO, in understanding how fruitful this approach is in the analyses of the possibilities of a researcher. While ethnographic methodological literature often refers to 'establishing rapport' (e.g. Bernard, 1995), the BwO takes the relational situation further, and it has made us reflect upon the creativity that occurs in the relational aspect. Through these reflections, it becomes clear that the integration of the relations to non-humans in the BwO is of crucial importance in doing ethnographic research in prison.

However, the most striking aspect to emerge from our 'play with Deleuze' is how the prisoners in the events presented have stepped forward in the text in new ways that contributed to other analyses. In writing the text, we have become aware of *the prisoners' discretion*. In both the events (also in the present and the past event in 'the perfume of sweat') it is the prisoners, with their discretion, who 'solve the situation' and re-establish the order. Amin makes Elisabeth a cup of coffee, rescuing some of their destroyed relation. Carl re-establishes body borders, and the prisoners in the weight-training room showed refinement and courtesy in not showing Berit their reactions to the sweat on her body. Both the events are characterised by an open ending, the outcome is not given. Even if we experienced the affections in the events as unpleasant, the prisoners with their discretion made us, in fact, become good researchers.

Closing remarks

Deleuze and Guattari are known for vital and expressive concepts that function as arrangements in their own right and in complex compositions that offset, warp, extend and double the conservative and disciplining doxa (Fuglesang et al., 2005: 254–5). The vignettes presented in this chapter foreground the complex and contradictory nature of body, body relations and body positions which we argue are important to map in prison locations where discourses of silence, classification and security dominate (Holford et al., 2013). Inspired by Deleuze, we will develop new regimes for our research, by simply being in the field with our bodies, using the Deleuzian conceptual tools towards a more sensible methodology. Starting to work with Deleuze and Guattari has changed our way of thinking about how we want to do ethnographic prison research. It has not made it easier, but it has certainly made it even more interesting.

Notes

1. Assemblages emerge from intermingling of bodies and effects that works in unpredictable ways (Deleuze and Guattari, 1987: 88; Fox, 2011: 361).
2. Inspired by Holford et al. (2013: 170).
3. In the interpretation of this sentence, 'autonomic' is understood as automatic.

Further reading

Deleuze, G. and Guattari, F. (1977) *Anti-Oediopus: Capitalism and Schizophrenia*, trans. R. Hurley, M. Seem and H. R. Lane (New York: Viking).

Deleuze, G. and Guattari, F. (1987) *A Thousand Plateaus. Capitalism and Schizophrenia* (Minneapolis, MN: University of Minnesota Press).

Deleuze, G. and Guattari, F. (1994) *What Is Philosophy? (Tomlinson and Galeta)* (New York: Colombo University Press).

Deleuze, G. (1994) *Difference and Repetition*, trans. P. Patton (New York: Columbia University Press).

References

Album, D. (1996) *Nære fremmede. Pasientkulturen i sykehus* (Oslo: Tano).

Alvesson, M. and Sköldberg, K. (2009) *Reflexive Methodology: New Vistas for Qualitative Research* (London: Sage).

de Beauvoir, S. (2011) *The Second Sex*, 1st Vintage Books edition (New York: Vintage Books).

Bernard, H. (1995) Research Methods in Anthropology, Second edition (London: Sage Publications).

Boundas, C. (ed) (2006) *Deleuze and Philosophy* (Edinburgh: Edinburgh University Press).

Deleuze, G. and Guattari, F. (1987) *A Thousand Plateaus. Capitalism and Schizophrenia* (Minneapolis: University of Minnesota Press).

Deleuze G. and Guattari, F. (1994) *What Is Philosophy?* (New York: Colombo University Press).

Engelsrud, G. (2006) *Hva er kropp?* (Oslo: Universitetsforlaget).

Foucault, M. (1991) 'Governmentality', in G. Burchell, C. Gordon and P. Miller (eds) *The Foucault Effect: Studies in Governmentality* (Chicago: The University of Chicago Press).

Foucault, M. (1995) *Discipline and Punish: The Birth of the Prison*, 2nd Vintage Books edition (New York: Vintage Books).

Fox, N. J. (2011) 'The Ill-Health Assemblage: Beyond the Body-with-Organs', *Health Sociology Review*, 20, 4, 359–71.

Fuglsang, M., Pedersen, M. and Sørensen, B. M. (2005) 'Skizoanalysens kartografiske optegnelser – om det sociales morfologi gos Gilles Deleuze og Felix Guattari', in A. Esmark, C. B. Lausten and N. Å. Andersen (eds) *Poststrukturalistiske Analysestrategier* (Frederiksberg: Roskilde Universitetsforlag).

Goffman, E. (1967) *Anstalt og menneske* (København: Paludans forlag).

Gullestad, M. (1989) *Kultur og hverdagsliv* (Oslo: Universitetsforlage).

Holford, R., Renold, E. and Huuki, T. (2013) 'What (Else) Can a Kiss Do? Theorizing the Power Plays in Young Children's Sexual Cultures', *Sexualities*, 16, 5–6, 710–29.

Johnsen, B. (2001) *Sport, Masculinities and Power Relations in Prison*, Unpublished PhD thesis (Oslo: The Norwegian University of Sport and Physical Exercise).

Kapferer, B. (2010) 'Introduction. In the Event – Toward an Anthropology of Generic Moments', *Social Analysis*, 54, 3, 1–27.

Kvale, S. (1989) *Issues of Validity in Qualitative Research* (Lund: Studentlitteratur).

Leseth, A. B. (2008) 'Hvordan kan vi forstå kropp?', in R. Säfvenbom and A. McD Sookermany (eds) *Kropp, bevegelse og energi* (Oslo: Universitetsforlaget).

Lipsky, M. (2010) *Street-Level Bureaucracy: Dilemmas of the Individual in Public Services* (New York: Russell Sage Foundation).

Løchen, Y. (1996) *Idealer og realiteter i et psykiatrisk sykehus* (Oslo: Universitetsforlaget).

Mathiesen, T. (2012) *The Defences of the Weak: A Sociological Study of a Norwegian Correctional Institution* (Abingdon: Routledge).

Moi, T. (1998) *Hva er en kvinne? Kjønn og kropp i feministisk teori* (Oslo: Gyldendal Forlag).

Russel, B. H. (2011) *Research Methods in Anthropology: Qualitative and Quantitative Approaches* (Lanham, MD: AltaMira Press).

Solheim, J. (1998). *Den iipne kropperz. Om kjtmnssymbolikk i modeme kultur* [The Open Body: Gender Symbolism in Modern Culture]. Oslo: Pax Forlag A/S.

Van Maanen, J. (2011) *Tales of the Field: On Writing Ethnography* (Chicago: The University of Chicago Press).

Villani, A. (2006) 'Why Am I a Deleuzian?', in C. V. Boundas (ed) *Deleuze and Philosophy* (Edinburgh: Edinburgh University Press).

Wadel, C. (1973) *Whose Fault Is That? The Struggle for Self-Esteem in the Face of Chronic Unemployment* (St. Johns: Memorial University of New Foundland).

Widerberg, K. (1994) *Kunnskapens kjønn. Minner, refleksjoner og teori* (Oslo: Pax Forlag).

Widerberg, K. (1996) 'Womens Experiences – Text or Relation? Looking at Research Practices from a Sociological and Feminist Perspective', *NORA: Nordic journal of womens studies*, 4, 128–36.

Widerberg, K. (2001) *Historien om et kvalitativt forskningsprosjekt* (Oslo: Universitetsforlaget).

Zourabichvili, F. (2012) *Deleuze: A Philosophy of the Event* (Edinburgh: Edinburgh University Press).

10
Ethnography: Exploring Methodological Nuances in Feminist Research with Men Incarcerated for Sexual Offences

Benita Moolman

Introduction

Prison and prisoner identities are often understood through discourses of carcerality and the Foucauldian analysis of prison as disciplinary space (Foucault, 1977). Carcerality is accompanied by social representations of prisoners as criminal, dangerous and pathological. The purpose of this chapter is not to contest this representation but rather to grapple with methodology as a process, as well as a vehicle through which research subjects are 'constituted' both through fieldwork and through the final text. Ethnography was chosen as a methodological tool to explore, examine and interrogate the meanings of identities as it was constituted through reference to inside and outside prison. In this chapter, I explore ethnography not as a method of data collection but rather as integral to the conceptual formulation of the 'written text' as a continuation of the methodological process of research. I explore 'the written' through an acknowledgement of the significance of narrative/storytelling as providing a means to tell 'more than one story'. I examine the meaning of fixed representation as opposed to it being fluid and dynamic, and then I explore the meaning and purpose of translation as a form of building bridges between the familiar and unfamiliar, signifying relationships between the researcher and the researched. I draw on research with men, incarcerated for sexual offending, carried out in three prisons in three different provinces in South Africa. Conducting research with human subjects is an intersubjective process, and so I end with some reflections on the use of my diary as a mediating tool to include my own shifting, multiple identities and lens to navigate the realm of 'who is valued as human?' in research with men labelled as 'sex offenders'. Ethnography is a useful methodological tool to situate the multiple identities in marginalised spaces and to illustrate the multiple dimensions of power in the research process. The purposes of this chapter are therefore twofold. Here I explore ethnography as a methodological approach to consider the nuances of researching and writing about people convicted of sexual offences, on the one hand, and to reflect on the relations (and perhaps limitations) of power in feminist ethnographies, on the other.

Place, prison and social identity

Historically, Goffman's (1961) concept of the 'the total institution' has been used to capture the idea of the prison as closed and static. As a 'total institution', prison is defined as a disciplinary space regulated through surveillance, management and control. This representation of prison is based on structural ideas of place as a closed system. Massey's (2005) concept of a 'sense of place' recognises the prison as a relational space that is produced through flows and relations of power, and more recent feminist geographers have acknowledged the prison as an embodied space (Moran, 2014). Baldwin (2012: 209), citing Massey (2005), emphasises that places are the products of the relationships negotiated with trajectories[1] by emplaced actors. Prisons are spaces in which prisoners negotiate their identities (bringing their pasts with them). Baer and Ravneberg (2008: 207) state, 'In highlighting the ways in which prison reminds us of non-prison surroundings, we depict prisons as everyday lived-in spaces and not as exceptional spaces for the other'. Social identities are made and remade through spaces and through the interactions in those spaces. Baer and Ravneberg (2008: 207) state, 'As a heterotopic space, prisons can seem set apart, as though there is always a clear distinction between prisons and other spaces but rather in some way prisons mimic broader frameworks of societal order and structures so they are not separate either.' The prisoners I interviewed had a very definite relationship with the 'outside' not only through a sense of who they were but also through continual contact with family and friends. However, there was also reference to prison as different to the outside, with its own rules and social practices. Prisons therefore have a little of both; they are places with their own histories and trajectories that are produced through practices and embodied performances by prisoners, wardens and the visitors who inhabit and visit this space (including researchers such as myself), but they are also constituted by their relation and location 'within' the outside, subjected to similar social norms and influenced by macro-social processes.

Social identities draw on the concept of subjectivities which is produced as multiple, shifting, fluid and, often, partial (Mama, 1995; Dolby and Cornbleth, 2001). This chapter is concerned with human life that defines social identities that include making connections between the 'inside' and 'outside'. These social identities are also transportable and transferable between prison and communities in South Africa. McKittrick (2011: 959), reflecting on work with female inmates, notes:

> Prison life, then, is extended to the streets, homes, courts, the department of justice, and across the state, as activists worked and work to share knowledge; it is inside and outside the prison walls that the labour of these women, their loved ones, and their children invokes relational and connective life-force in the face of gendered and racial apartheid and thus produce the conditions through which a radical black sense of place can be lived and imagined.

McKittrick draws on Massey's (2005) concept of a sense of place and includes the racialisation of place as critical in the reproduction of human life and space. Social differences of race, gender, sexuality, age, culture, religion, for instance, cannot be disregarded in the constitution of social identities and the experience of place. Social identities are powerfully relational and articulated through heteronormative practices of gender, race, class, sexuality and age as it interlinks with prison policies and legislation. Prison research on social identities highlights the prison as a hypermasculine space often entrenched in dominant practices of masculinity where violence and aggression are valued (Seymour, 2003; Bandyopadhyay, 2006). However, more recently researchers such as Bandyopadhyay (2006) and Rymhs (2012: 78) argue that the prison masculinities are 'more nuanced, complex and that there is space for improvisation', and that this practice of a particular form of manliness is not specific to the prison rather it demonstrates continuities with a wider social structure of masculinities. The purpose of this chapter is not to examine the continuum of practices of gender identity and specifically masculinities inside and outside of prison but rather to argue for ethnography as a methodological approach that provides a way of engaging this continuum.

Defining ethnography

Researching the lives of people convicted of sexual offences was always going to be a complicated and complex process and hence required a methodology that needed to grapple with the multiple tensions and contradictions of power. I say this because people who are convicted of sexual offences that fall within this category are regarded and often represented as dangerous, evil, hypersexual, savage and beyond redemption (Waldram, 2007). Of course, violence against women and children cannot be condoned or ignored, yet we need a more complex understanding of the multiple relations of power that constitute the lives of people involved in sexually violent crimes. When committing an act of sexual violence, a perpetrator often draws on practices of masculinities and the enactment of power. As a means of understanding the mobility of identities and the adoption of practices of masculinity that accompany acts of sexual violence, I had to find a methodological frame to give me enough proximity and distance with which to engage my 'research subjects' (I had to be both an insider and an outsider). Ethnography has historically been concerned with 'studying the other' and therefore provided a useful lens to think about the complexity of power that shapes the production of sexual violence and, hence, the lives of people involved in these kinds of crimes. Behar (2003: 271) argues, 'Ethnographic work is inherently paradoxical, being a process by which each of us confronts our respective inability to comprehend the experience of others even as we recognise the absolute necessity of continuing the effort to do so.' Ethnography, whilst attempting to understand the lives of others, can only provide partial understandings. As I listened to the interviews and during the transcription process, I realised that there was no definitive answer to who these men were or why they had committed acts of sexual violence. I had to find a way of sharing these complexities with a reader and work through the tensions of representation, translation and power differently. I realised that no ethnography could be, or could give, a definitive account of the 'life of the other', rather it is momentary, partial and represents an elusive search for truth. Therefore, no ethnographer can provide scientific truths, no matter how much there is a popular urgency and demand for definitive answers on 'why men commit sexually violent crimes'? Ethnographers have the authority to define and represent the research subject through the writing of the research project. I was interested in working differently with my own authority to define, represent and translate the lived experiences of the 'research subject'. I reflect on some approaches I used, such as narrative methodology, representation and translation in the research process, to develop a methodology that accounted for the complexity and mobility of social identities and relations of power.

Methods

This research was conducted with men convicted of sexual offences in three South African prisons. The prisoners ranged in ages from 14 to 76 and identified with a variety of cultural-linguistic groups, such as Xhosa, Zulu, Pedi, Tshwana, Sotho, and religions, such as Christian, Muslim and Hindu. Research assistants who spoke the languages of the participants assisted with data collection. The respondents were eager to participate and some of them have never spoken with an outsider or an internal support person (social worker, psychologist) since they were convicted of the crimes they committed. The interviews were conducted in the social work offices or spare room within the different prison units. The research was conducted with inmates from Medium A and Medium B and Maximum facilities. The prisoners at Medium A were close to their parole hearings and the inmates at the Maximum facility were labelled as 'serial offenders' who more often than not were serving sentences of life imprisonment.

I drew on an ethnography that consisted of the formal methods of focus groups and interviews but there were also many informal encounters just before or just after interviews, there were multiple conversations, across all three prisons with social workers, social work managers, wardens and so on. As an ethnographer I observed my physical surroundings, in and outside the physical prison building, I observed and participated in the everyday happenings of prisons, such as access and entry which had its' own routines. Lastly, this methodological approach included using my diary to record my own emotion throughout this research process but also as an intervention to engage with my research subjects in the writing of this research study. I end this section with my diary entries that started my fieldwork practice for my doctoral research study with men incarcerated for sexual offences.

> 4 September 2007 at 4pm
>
> I am about to enter my first interview with rapists and the more legally accepted term, sex offenders. Who will I be meeting? Will I like them? Will I reject them outright? No... my social work background has prepared me for this... my ability to relate to people irrespective of who they are and what they did. What am I doing entering their world?
>
> 4 September @ 8pm
>
> So, now 'They' are surprisingly normal. Even though I have said a rapist can be anybody, my reaction is still one of surprise. When one finally encounters 'the other'? Is this 'the other'? the 'other', what?
>
> The other, me
>
> The other, you
>
> The other, us
>
> Why have subordinated subjects always been considered the 'other'? Is my studying rapists an attempt at discovering an other, my other. They are not monsters. They are terribly human.

The recognition that 'sex offenders' are human was terribly disconcerting but also profoundly critical for the development of this research project. It was an uncomfortable reality to face 'sex offenders' (men who have committed serious acts of sexual and bodily violence) who are also so familiar in a sense. Familiar because they are men who grew up in neighbourhoods where I have lived and where my family and friends still live, they are men I could encounter in my work environment and the like, they are men who other than their sexually violent behaviours are very 'ordinary'. This first research encounter levelled the research playing field where my own sense of familiarity dissolved any preconceived notions of 'who' 'sex offenders' were, it simultaneously became the tool to develop an easy rapport and facilitated trust-building with my research subjects. My diary became a space of reflection as I studied the 'other' I was simultaneously reflecting my own understanding of power, difference and otherness.

My diary was a space for my own feminist politics and feelings and a place where my own voice as a woman could have a home. Furthermore, feminist research is grounded on contesting discourses that inscribe and re-inscribe difference as otherness, yet it has avoided confronting its' own biases in relation to discourses on the 'humanity' of people convicted of sexually violent acts. It was these tensions of difference, otherness and who is included in the definition of 'human' that persisted throughout the research process and throughout my diary reflections. Looking back at my diary entries, I notice the language and tone that is reflective of my preconceived notions and judgements about the men I was to study. I expected to meet men that I would be disgusted by, men that would be easy to dismiss and condemn. In my mind, the difference between 'them' and me was clear. It is this change in my own perceptions and process of introspection that I simultaneously explore in this paper. I now turn to explore ethnography as narrative/storytelling, as representation and as translation.

Ethnography as storytelling

Qualitative research has as its primary purpose uncovering the many layers of meaning attached to people's lives. I chose to tell the stories of my research subjects as narrated lives because it provided a means of understanding the complexity of lived experiences. Cole (2009: 72) states:

> Narrative can offer texts that are open to different readings – interpretations – while still being faithful to the teller. Critical discourse analysis may offer one way of enabling narratives to illuminate different inequities. Through critical exploration of the many different interconnected elements, it may offer insights into the 'cracks' of everyday lived experience, retaining complexity, blurring boundaries, and challenging dichotomies and powerful discourses.

Narrative methodology was a means of challenging linear understandings of the men who committed these acts of violence. I was concerned with not reducing these men into violent objects of study, nor as vulnerable prisoners at the 'mercy of the prison system'. They occupied these two positions yet they were also more than this which was evident in the time and care they took with representing themselves. The interviews reveal men who have had multiple life experiences, who come from differing community backgrounds and have, at times, moved between being victims and perpetrators of violence. Listening to them recount their stories, describing their childhoods and adolescences and their entries into manhood was filled with contradictions and blurred boundaries. Research subjects have an interest in presenting certain parts of them, I suppose we all do. Drivdal, Buire, Kinnes and Timm (2014: 3), citing Goffman (1959), state:

> By describing social interaction as a theatre where each individual is performing its own role according to an un-written script, Goffman built the ground work of a reflexive interpretation of social encounters as 'information games' in which certain information is played out, or hidden, to inform and influence expectations and reactions by others.

Waldram (2007) states that narrative in the prison context is contingent upon performance. He argues that to participate in treatment programs there are official discourses of truth that are framed through treatment programs based on Cognitive Behaviour Therapy (CBT). Waldram (2007: 152) states:

> To protect themselves, inmates characteristically attempt to persuade others of the details of their lives, their 'truth,' by employing selective biographical facts and strategic omissions, in combination with verisimilitude and even outright lies, all the while hoping to convince of the veracity of their accounts.

What they chose to share and how they chose to share information were determined through a number of factors. Whilst as a female researcher, they wanted to present their 'good side', yet as both a female and a social worker they also saw it as an opportunity for me to hear their side of the story, which meant the revelation of their sexually violent encounter(s) was often deemed by them to be necessary, albeit it was only one side of the story. For some of them, specifically those who were in treatment groups, sharing their stories was not new, for others this was a completely new experience.

The use of focus group interviews was also designed to examine the performance of masculinities with other men and thus the gendered relationships of this ethnography were not confined to only my relationship with them but also their relationship to each other and a different presentation of 'the self'. The presentation of the gendered self could be read in conventional ways, narrative methodologies exposed the diversity of experiences, and the interplay of emotion and rationalities in the constructions of masculinities. Viswesweran

(2003: 1) states that 'ethnography, like fiction no matter its pretence to present a self-contained narrative or cultural whole, remains incomplete and detached from the realms to which it points'. The performance of identities thus confirms the partiality and temporality of the research exchange. Presenting the full transcript as a narrative account in my subsequent writing up of the research (Moolman, 2011) provided a way to bring the voices of my interviewees into the text and a way for the reader to engage in their own interpretation of the meaning of the narrative of people who carry the label of 'sex offender'.

Ethnography as representation

Ethnography has been affected by the 'crisis of representation'. The perennial question that has challenged both feminism and anthropology is who has the power to represent who? Feminist methodologies have conventionally centred on the representation of women by women. Similarly to work by Newton (1998) who did research with academic, white men, this research challenged the taken-for-granted feminist assumptions by focusing on the study of men. I wondered 'how to represent' and make meaning of the lived realities of the men who were being interviewed. Yes there were clear indications of dominant performances and practices of heterosexual masculinity that pride themselves on sexual entitlement and violence, yet it was not the only story being told. As previously stated people convicted of sexual offences are represented as pathological, psychopaths or socio-paths, savages and monsters and predisposed to sexual deviance (Vogelman, 1990). Recent research, however, has more clearly identified risk factors associated with the perpetration of rape. Jewkes (2012: 30) states that 'there is strong evidence that five groups of amenable risk factors are important in rape perpetration: adverse childhood exposures; attachment and personality disorders; social learning and delinquency; gender inequitable masculinities; and substance abuse and firearms.' Some of these risk factors were apparent in the men's stories as they were described to me, but this simplistic reduction of their narratives would re-inscribe relations of power. These risk factors produce a static or fixed definition of a type or kind of man who rapes. Additionally, Waldram (2009) argues that the treatment models that are based on CBT re-inscribe fixed representations of men labelled as sex offenders. The danger of invoking these risk factors and psychological traits implicit in a CBT model promotes the idea that 'sex offenders' are a type of human being and thus obscures the many facets of the lived realities of the men who are convicted of committing these types of offences. I have argued elsewhere (Moolman, 2011) that men who commit sex offences sometimes mobilise different identities to establish power and authority over their victims and hence any fixed representation of identity ignores the mobilisation of power through the practice of multiple identities. Behar, describing her work with Esperanza, a woman who lived in Mexico and who was a street pedlar (2003: 270), states that, 'Before I could begin to understand Esperanza, I had to acknowledge that the figure of such a woman already exists in academic as well as mainstream reporting as a pre-theorised reality, an already-fixed representation'. Similarly, men convicted of sexual offences have a fixed representation in collective, social imaginaries. How do we, as researchers, interrogate these representations? Narrative writing provides insight into the complexity of the decision and choices people make. It highlights the contradictions and frailties of human life. In my diary entry I referred to my research subjects as 'normal' and 'human' because sitting and talking to them felt like talking to any group of men. There were moments of laughter and humour. I was left with thinking 'how do I tell this part of the story'? In the public imaginary, prison and prison inmates are so far removed from being 'human', what about my own 'imaginary'? How do I make sense of who I wanted them to be and who they were? Through my diaries, I was able to acknowledge the men labelled as sex offenders as human and began to understand the challenge of the recognition of 'the other' and when that moment happens, how does the space between the familiar and the unfamiliar become translatable?

Ethnography as translation

Ruth Behar's book, *Translated woman*, challenges us as ethnographers to think about the process of writing and the way we locate the subjects we write about. Studying 'the other' is also about becoming familiar with a cultural and social world that is unfamiliar. How do we relate to the unfamiliar? Becoming familiar with the unfamiliar is a process of building bridges that is pregnant with interpretation embedded in relations of power. Behar (2003: 229) states, 'It has to be about the way transfers from our different borders and class locations have been renegotiated, for the "process of cultural translation" is inevitably enmeshed in conditions of power – professional, national, international.' Whilst (we in the prison focus groups) were all South African, there were cultural, gender, racial and age differences. Cultural translation goes beyond social differences of culture, gender, and age and is about human life being mutually understood and valued but very differently. How do you translate a set of values that are completely different from your own? So how do I translate the stories as close to their own interpretation as possible yet remain committed to my own feminist politics and values?

By identifying my own research principles and drawing on postcolonial feminisms, I believed that using a narrative approach would allow spaces for interpretation, as well as choices for the reader to decide 'what parts of the story were the truth', if any. In the literature on psychological assessment and interventions with 'sex offenders', they are often described as being 'manipulative'

(Beech et al., 2003). Treatment programmes of men who have committed sexual offences identify 'cognitive distortions' and 'distorted perceptions' as repetitive and, at times, psychopathological and socio-pathological behaviours depending on the levels of risk for reoffending (Olver and Wong, 2013). Yet, 'sexual offenders' are also human beings, and they are also men with their own histories and explanations for the way their lives have unfolded and for the choices they have made. For example, my research subjects were also racialised subjects who had lived through and during apartheid. Most had lived their lives in poor communities, where their families had struggled economically. Whilst the violence they perpetrated cannot be excused or justified, their narratives also revealed the other sides and dimensions of their lives. In my subsequent writings about my research (Moolman, 2011), I have chosen to intersperse the narratives of my research participants with my own diary reflections, either at the beginning or at the end of each transcript. In this way I found my own voice mediating some of their voices, in conversation with them yet also set apart from their voices. I knew that I viewed the violence very differently from some of them (even though there were those who, during the interview, had acknowledged their own levels of violence and brutality). Prior to undertaking this research, I had worked at Rape Crisis Cape Town and had heard the 'other side' of the stories and I knew the extreme levels of violence against women in South Africa. My research and my feminist politics were not separate engagements, rather they are entangled within this research process. How do we move towards a common humanity when at first we are seemingly worlds apart? The next section is an account of some of my reflections on this entangled space of feminist ethnography.

Reflecting on 'being a feminist ethnographer'

Jewkes (2012: 68) states, 'Knowledge, then, is not something objective and removed from our own bodies, experiences, and emotions but is created through our experiences of the world as a sensuous and affective activity.' Researching men convicted of sexual offences from a feminist position creates dilemmas around both praxis and politics. My relationship to this research has never been neutral, yet I am committed to ethical research that acknowledges the dignity of the researched (even and maybe particularly when the researched is 'othered' on so many levels). As a woman I had a vested interest in understanding why and how they had committed their crimes as well as finding ways of holding them accountable for their crimes. Besides my emotional investment in the research, I was also interested in working differently with power as an academic and intellectual. Whilst I did not necessarily agree or believe everything that my research subjects shared with me, what was apparent was that these were powerful stories that could not be reduced to explainable quotes.

To parse their narratives into de-contextualised quotations would have diluted the meanings of the lives and the stories of these men. It simultaneously could not explain the fluidity of power that accompanied the research process, and it would not have explained the comfortable and easy conversation and relationship I had developed with my research subjects who were, at once, the normal men I engaged with in conversation as well as people who had once committed violent acts of extreme sexual aggression.

Hedge (2009: 279) asks, 'How do we represent lives and sensibilities from a space of otherness and render them intimate and with the dignity they deserve?' This methodological approach has its own contradictions and challenges for me, as a feminist researcher. How would I make sense of the graphic explanations of violence against women that I would encounter? Would I judge the men in that moment? How will that impact trust-building and rapport process in the encounter between the researcher and the researched? How would I respond to the levels of denial and rationalisation that can be typical of people convicted of sexual crimes? These questions forced me to think through and find a place for my own emotion, hence the necessity of 'keeping a diary' during this research process. In my writing, I have tried to incorporate the use of 'my diaries' to provide a degree of reflexivity on my own attachment and political position to the subject and 'subjects' of this research. My own struggles and tensions were particularly evident when I listened to the descriptions and explanations for the perpetration of sexual violence within the family, where the victims/survivors of intra-familial rape are particularly silenced through the narrative of the perpetrator. It renders knowledge production intimate, and the political as decidedly personal. An excerpt from my diaries details my emotional response and me trying to make sense of 'research', researcher and researched.

> 16 June 2009
>
> ...doing feminist research with women is so clear, empathise, empathise, empathise...but doing feminist research with men, it is harder to define what is appropriate and what is not, particularly interviewing sex offenders when the boundaries of victim and oppressor shift multiple times within the interview period...yes, this man was also raped as a boy...he did not tell anybody since nobody would believe him...where does this information sit...within the dynamic of empathy and manipulation...of sex offenders....What is good or the right feminist research practice is harder to know...driving away I was wondering if I made THE blunder of my research study by not probing for more detail...yet I have justified this by saying I can go back and interview him...which I might do...but this in some ways is not the point...the complexity of what this encounter

> has highlighted is an indication of the complexity of this research... when theories alone are not enough when interviewing people... where is the feminist theory to tell me what to do in moments like this... is it stick to the line of questioning no matter what?... radical feminist theory... or will the postmodern or postcolonial stuff be more applicable... black men's subjectivity sure is complicated and even more so... studying it from a postcolonial perspective... and a black women's perspective...

Whilst the diaries created a space for my own emotion, it simultaneously gave me a voice beyond official 'researcher'. I became the woman 'who had a say' about the violence that was spoken about. Fox (2008: 345) states, 'Narrative occurs in context, and is spoken or written through the lens of both the narrator and the researcher.' As a researcher I had a multiple presence in the interviews and the focus groups; at times I was woman, I was heterosexual, I was coloured yet I was also a social worker, a mere witness of 'their side of the story' and at other times a gender activist knowledgeable on rape and sexual violence. As a woman I was asked to play the role of explaining women's reasons for their behaviour, I somehow represented the voice of women as their girlfriends, sisters and so forth; as a gender activist I explained and defined the meanings of rape and sexual violence and some of the legislation on rape and sexual violence; as a witness I had to listen to their own stories of trauma and victimisation. I also had to listen to their stories of perpetration. During the interviews, my own emotion had to be suspended to create a non-judgemental and trusting space for the 'sex offender' as research subject. Whilst during this time my diary was helpful to record some of the emotion, it was only really during the data analysis and writing up of the stories that I had the personal space to name and feel emotions such as anger, sadness, disappointment and hurt for the intensity and brutality of the violence being described to me. Keeping a diary assisted with mediating my emotions, reflecting my own voice and for maintaining the complicated relations of power. My research subjects remained men with inherent privileges of masculinities both in and outside of prison. In the field of the prison, there was no clear pathway for a feminist researcher, I had to shift across multiple positions and find ways to be comfortable in an uncomfortable place. Behar (2003: 297) states that '[t]he feminist ethnographer is a dual citizen who shuttles between the country of the academy and the country of the feminism'. The politics of feminism requires that sexual violence must be confronted, challenged and eradicated. To do this, we have to understand the men who perpetrate these crimes. Yet, studying these men exposes the limitations of feminist research. Viswesweran (2003) reflects on the 'betrayals' of feminist theories yet encourages an ongoing commitment to conduct feminist ethnographies that confront complex power relations. Feminist research has to stretch beyond historical-gendered boundaries and strive to be inclusive of multiple forms of difference yet remain committed to a politics of gender and sexuality.

Conclusion

Ethnography with men labelled as 'sex offenders' provided a reflective space to rethink social identities, social difference and power relations in the research process. Traditionally, social identities get re-inscribed and 'solidified' in different phases of the research process. I argue that employing ethnography as a methodological tool that encompassed the data collection and writing up process provided opportunities to undo taken-for-granted social identities and for identities to be dislodged from fixed representations. This process was not uncomplicated, particularly when working with a highly politicised topic of sexual violence. The different layers and phases of ethnography revealed the different contours to 'producing knowledge on identities and difference' and examining relations of power and authority in knowledge production. Methodologies that shed light on the shifting power relations of the research process are central in understanding our own authority as researchers. Methodologies that are cognisant of politics and process are fundamental in producing discourses of difference that are disruptive of borders and otherness. The use of the diary to trace, track and engage my own emotion and politics of the research provided insights into my own understanding of what it means to be human, as well as of the imagined borders and limits of feminist ethnographies.

Ethnography was a lens to manoeuvre fixed notions of researcher and researched; human and non-human; violence and non-violence; woman and man; inside and outside; logic and emotion and, lastly, physical and social. Ethnography was a lens through which to constitute identities as transportable across and between notions of 'inside' and 'outside' and so who these men were on the outside (of prison) remain who they are on the inside of prison, they still exist in their capacities as fathers, grandfathers, uncles, neighbours and/or husbands. Ethnography as a methodological tool provided a means to recognise the permeability of boundaries and to recognise that 'difference' can be translatable and if we are open to the shifts between inside and outside as researchers we will be able to utilise the collective production of knowledge. This research with men labelled 'sex offenders' has provided (for me) a space to reflect on and appreciate the tapestry of human life.

Note

1. Baldwin (2012: 208–209) 'Trajectories are ideas, practices, and material processes that can affect people in the conduct of their daily lives, in their quest to live well; they are relationships and processes that affect others and may be authored by individuals, groups, and by non-humans'.

Further reading

Behar, R. (2003) *Translated Woman: Crossing the Border with Esperanza's Story*, Tenth anniversary edition (Boston: Beacon Press).
Massey, D. (2005) *For Space* (Thousand Oaks: Sage).
Steinberg, J. (2004) *The Number: One Man's Search for Identity in the Cape Underworld and Prison Gangs* (Cape Town: Jonathan Ball Publishers).

References

Baer, L. D. and Ravneberg, B. (2008) 'The Outside and Inside in Norwegian and English Prisons', *Geografiska Annaler: Series B, Human Geography*, 90, 2, 205–16.
Behar, R. (1999) 'Ethnography: Cherishing Our Second Fiddle Genre', *Journal of Contemporary Ethnography*, 28, 472–84.
Behar, R. (2003) *Translated Woman: Crossing the Border with Esperanza's Story*, Tenth Anniversary edition (Boston: Beacon Press).
Bandyopadhyay, M. (2006) 'Competing Masculinities in a Prison', *Men and Masculinities*, 9, 186–203.
Baldwin, J. (2012) 'Putting Massey's Relational Sense of Place to Practice: Labour and the Constitution of Jolly Beach, Antigua, West Indies', *Geografiska Annaler: Series B, Human Geography*, 94, 3, 207–21.
Beech, A. R., Fisher, D. D., Thornton, D. (2003) 'Risk Assessment of Sex Offenders', *Professional Psychology: Research and Practice*, 34, 4, 339–52.
Cole, B. (2009) 'Gender, Narratives and Intersectionality: Can Personal Experience Approaches to Research Contribute to "Undoing Gender"?' *International Review of Education*, 55, 561–78.
Dolby, N. and Cornbleth, C. (2001) 'Introduction: Social Identities in Transnational Times', *Discourse: Studies in the Cultural Politics of Education*, 22, 3, 293–6.
Drivdal, L., Buire, C., Kinnes, I. and Timm, S. (2014) Urban agency and the presentation of self: insight from comparative ethnographies in Cape Town. Unpublished paper.
Foucault, M. (1977) *Discipline and Punish: The Birth of the Prison* (London: Vintage Books).
Fox, C. (2008) 'Postcolonial Dilemmas in Narrative Research', *Compare*, 38, 3, 335–47.
Goffman, E. (1959) *The Presentation of Self in Everyday Life* (New York: Doubleday Anchor Books).
Goffman, E. (1961) *Asylums: Essays on the Social Situation of Mental Patients and Other Inmates* (Garden City: Anchor Books).
Hedge, R. S. (2009) 'Fragments and Interruptions: Sensory Regimes of Violence and the Limits of Feminist Ethnography', *Qualitative Inquiry*, 15, 276–96.
Jewkes, R. (2012) *Rape Perpetration: A Review* (Pretoria: Sexual Violence Research Initiative).
Jewkes, Y. (2012) 'Autoethnography and Emotion as Intellectual Resources: Doing Prison Ethnography Differently', *Qualitative Inquiry*, 18, 1, 63–75.
Mama, A. (1995) *Beyond the Masks: Race, Gender and Subjectivity* (London: Routledge).
Massey, D. (2005) *For Space* (Thousand Oaks: Sage).
McKittrick, K. (2011) 'On Plantations, Prisons, and a Black Sense of Place', *Social & Cultural Geography*, 12, 8, 947–63.
Moolman, B. (2011) *Permeable Boundaries. The Construction of 'sex offender' Masculinities in South Africa*, Unpublished Dissertation (University of California, Davis).
Moolman, B. (2014) 'Rethinking "Men in Transition" in South Africa: Considering the Intersectionality of Race, Class, Sexuality with Fender', *African Identities*, DOI:10.1080/14725843.2013.775843.

Moran, D. (2014) 'Leaving Behind the Total Institution? Teeth, Transcarceral Spaces and Re-Inscription of the Formerly Carcerated Body', *Gender, Place & Culture: A Journal of Feminist Geography*, 21, 1, 35–51.

Newton, J. (1998) 'White Guys', *Feminist Studies*, 24, 3, 572–99.

Olver, M. and Wong, S. (2013) 'Treatment Programs for High Risk Sexual Offenders: Program and Offender Characteristics, Attrition, Treatment Change and Recidivism', *Aggression and Violent Behaviour*, 18, 5, 579–91.

Pettinger, L. (2005) 'Representing Shop Work: A Dual Ethnography', *Qualitative Research*, 5, 3, 347–64.

Rymhs, D. (2012) 'In This Inverted Garden: Masculinities in Canadian Prison Writing', *Journal of Gender Studies*, 21, 1, 77–89.

Seymour, K. (2003) 'Imprisoning Masculinity', *Sexuality and Culture*, 7, 4, 27–55.

Viswesweran, K. (2003) *Fictions of Feminist Ethnography* (Minneapolis: University of Minnesota Press).

Vogelman, L. (1990) *The Sexual Face of Violence: Rapists on Rape* (Appalachia: Ohio University Press).

Waldram, J. B. (2007) 'Narrative and the Construction of 'Truth' in a Prison-Based Treatment Program for Sexual Offenders', *Ethnography*, 8, 2, 145–69.

Waldram, J. B. (2009) ' "It's just You and Satan, Hanging Out at a Pre-School": Notions of Evil and the Rehabilitation of Sexual Offenders', *Anthropology and Humanism*, 34, 2, 219–34.

11
Writing Bad: Prison Ethnography and the Problem of 'Tone'

James B. Waldram

Introduction

My contribution to this volume focuses not so much on doing ethnographic research in prisons, but rather on writing and presenting ethnographic research that has, as its subject, individuals who have committed criminal acts – often of a horrendous nature – or who are, in a word, 'bad' (Waldram, 2009). Whilst there are many methodology textbooks that detail how to engage in data collection ethnographically, few pay more than lip service to how to write it up, and none that I am aware of deal with what can be referred to as the 'tone' of the representation of research participants. Murchison's (2010: 208) fine methods text is a case in point, as he comes about as close as anyone to the issue when he advises, 'The tone you strike in your presentation can help by communicating a sense of shared empathy or even common cause with informants, but that sort of tone is not always possible or advisable.' There are few guidelines anywhere that explain when an empathetic tone is ill-advised, and more importantly, why. This represents a major gap in our understanding of the impact of ethnography as it speaks directly to issues of voice and audience and, more broadly, to the dominant, even hegemonic, grand narratives that affect how we write and read ethnographic products. It poses questions of when an empathetic rendering is not appropriate in ethnography, and why, and in what ways does bowing to dominant narratives affect our ability to understand and communicate our participants' lives to a broader audience?

Prisons – total institutions housing those convicted of criminal offences – provide excellent ground to examine how such moralised grand narratives about good, bad and evil play out in our ability to research and write ethnography. In this chapter, I present both some general observations from many years of ethnographic research in Canadian prisons and a case study of sorts involving the production and review process of my ethnography, *Hound Pound Narrative: Sexual Offender Habilitation and the Anthropology of Therapeutic*

Intervention (2012). I place my experiences talking and wiring about prison inmates within the broader context of recent trends within my discipline of anthropology, a discipline quite avowedly in love with victims and angst-ridden over its right to speak authoritatively about the experiences of those whose lives we study. In doing so, it is my goal to provide a correction to this trend by reminding ethnographers of their responsibility to represent the experiences and perspectives of their participants equally, regardless if they are victims or perpetrators, good, bad or evil.

'Why would you study *them*?'

I began my ethnographic study of Canadian prison inmates in the early 1990s, at a time when relatively little ethnography was being done in these institutions (Wacquant, 2002). Over more than a decade, I would say that I have interviewed some 300 inmates and participated in dozens of prison activities, recreational and therapeutic. When I began my prison research it seemed there were no other anthropologists doing similar work; eventually, at least in a North American context, I was joined by Lorna Rhodes (2004). But it was an academically lonely time, and the early lack of interest in (and, in some cases, hostility towards) my presentations and manuscripts betrayed what I would learn was a fairly strong sentiment within my discipline against prison research or, more accurately, against prison inmates. In a nutshell, the reaction I garnered was incredulity: 'Why would you study *them*?'

My first research project emerged from a very simple question put to me casually by a prison staff member who popped into my university office one day. He had been consulting on a data analysis matter with some statistics professors further down the hall and found himself in the adjacent Native Studies Department office block as he passed by towards the exit door. 'Do you think culture matters in the treatment of Aboriginal offenders?', he asked. 'Why yes, yes it does' was my brief response. We talked and he invited me to come out to the forensic psychiatric prison – a federal-level institution treating individuals sentenced to more than two years and who were generally seen as difficult cases – where he worked, where I met several research psychologists and psychiatrists who likewise were wondering if their treatment programmes were appropriate or effective for the substantial Aboriginal population, typically found in Canadian prisons. From these conversations emerged my first study, an effort to uncover and articulate how and in what contexts Aboriginality – the lived experience of being an Aboriginal Canadian – was meaningful. I spent many hours in interviews with Aboriginal inmates and Elders, and through the latter I became involved in the Aboriginal healing and spirituality programmes that were developing. It was at this point that several of the Elders who worked in the prisons requested that I study their healing programmes, to help explain what they do and how they do it, and how it is an effective form of treatment that complements that of mainstream forensic programming. This research continued for several years and led to a variety of publications that assisted the Elders in their efforts to both legitimise and properly fund their healing programmes in penitentiaries (e.g. Waldram, 1993, 1994, 1997, 1998).

As this work was winding down, an Elder asked me if I would undertake another study, focused specifically on the programme he had developed for Aboriginal men imprisoned for sexual offences. Together, we generated a research proposal for a collaborative project, but this was turned down by correction officials who found our refusal to hand over completed interview transcripts to be problematic. However, a few years later, and following a change in some correctional research staff, I resurrected the idea. The Aboriginal-specific programme had been terminated after a very short life, but the opportunity to research the main treatment programme for perpetrators of sexual crimes was open, where there was typically a 50–50 mix of Aboriginal and non-Aboriginal inmates. After much discussion and negotiation, the correctional research staff accepted my ethnographic approach as an opportunity to gain otherwise inaccessible insights into inmate experiences of treatment. Whilst there was a great deal of psychological research involving the 'sexual offender' programmes, these typically employed a pre-/post-test methodology, assessing inmates before and after treatment. What happened in treatment, how the inmates experienced it on a daily basis over the eight months of their residential programme, was a complete unknown. Indeed, no one had ever really thought much about it.

The unit where I worked employed a therapeutic community approach (Lockwood et al., 1997; Deleon et al., 2000; Shuker and Sullivan, 2010), and every four months or so a new cohort of inmates was assembled at the forensic prison hospital to start the programme together. There were always two cohorts in residence, one typically half way through as the other was beginning. They shared common areas, and their cells or 'houses' were intermixed. Their unit, like the others, was isolated and locked down for much of the day, but there were times and circumstances in which inmates could mingle with the general population of the institution. For the most part, though, this was a closed, small community of roughly 34 men forced to interact, organise, socialise and help each other in their daily lives and therapeutic programmes. Staff members of various types were on site 24 hours a day, but most of the therapeutic programming occurred during business hours, five days a week. Inmates were locked into their cells at 10 p.m. and not released until 6 the next morning, overseen the entire time by correction officers.

Over the course of 18 months of fieldwork, I engaged with four inmate cohorts. I was given largely unfettered access to the inmates outside of lockdown times. I could attend all group therapy sessions, the mainstay of the programme and participate in leisure activities and the daily life of the unit, seven days a week. I was not allowed to observe confidential, one-on-one therapy sessions, nor was I allowed to interview staff (more on this later). The initial reluctance of inmates to my presence soon gave way to acceptance such that my occasional absences from the unit were remarked upon, and I became a sounding board for many as a 'normal' outsider representative of the community as inmates drafted and worked through various homework and group presentations. The fact that I was learning the programme alongside them, and clearly had little relationship with staff, served to reinforce my status as an outsider who was there to learn about their experiences in as unbiased a manner as possible. For an inmate population, this is crucial, and there is no way that I would have gained the access I did if they believed that I was also working with the staff and getting their perspectives too.

Overall, I have spent more than a decade hanging out in prisons and getting to know inmates who have committed, in some instances, some very egregious crimes. My participants have included medium- and maximum-security classified men, in seven different federal penitentiaries and provincial correctional centres, with crimes ranging from drug offences, break and enters, robbery and assault, to sexual assault and murder. The sexual crimes run the gamut from those against children to those against adult males and females, from 'date rape' cases where the victim and perpetrator are known to each other to the stereotypical 'predator' stalking victims. Most men had lengthy criminal records involving various sexual and other offences.

From the very beginning of my work, I have been confronted by individuals suggesting that legitimate work with inmates is not possible because 'they all lie', that I will just be their dupe or worse, their apologist, or that they have no 'right' to have research done (Waldram, 2007). My work with men imprisoned for sexual crimes in particular has aroused great suspicion, with suggestions that I must be a pervert or an offender myself. Even worse, by the very fact of doing research with these offenders I have been accused of 're-victimising' those who were the targets of the crimes by giving a voice to the perpetrators. Those convicted of sexual crimes, it seems, should be neither seen nor heard.

Over the years, I have also had some very interesting reviews of manuscripts that I submitted for publication, reviews which frequently as not suggested that the reviewers saw those convicted of sexual crimes and other serious criminals as essentially evil, immune to rehabilitation and not worthy of being 'celebrated' (as one reviewer wrote) through a research article (Waldram, 2009). In two instances, editors confided to me that they were having trouble finding someone to review manuscripts precisely because of the subject matter. It was not relevant that leading experts have remarked that, rather than 'hideous monsters', those who have committed sexual crimes are more accurately thought of as 'everyman', largely indistinguishable from others

(Marshall, 1996). Indeed, perhaps this is what repulses – or frightens – people even more, that those who commit terrible crimes may otherwise appear as normal, like our neighbours, and not the drooling, hiding-in-the bushes cretins, as many want to imagine. I am reminded of Alexander Hinton's (2005: 2) description of an infamous genocidal murderer who arrived for an interview, looking like 'a poor farmer in his late thirties, who greeted me with the broad smile and polite manner that one so often encounters in Cambodia'. Those convicted of crimes, and especially sexual crimes, perhaps remind many of the frailties and foibles of the human condition. They have stories, families and are loved too. But it is far easier and more satisfying to essentialise them, to think of them as monsters!

'Tone' and *Hound Pound Narrative*

I think at its most fundamental the problem with tone represents a disinclination to allow the prison inmates – or any 'bad' people for that matter – to speak for themselves, or for me as ethnographer to provide an interpretation of their experiences that moves the reader closer to capturing that element of inmate subjectivity. An empathetic stance is not welcome in this kind of ethnography because the bad things that they have done preclude any right to be understood as complex human beings with psyches and emotions and perspectives. It is a totalising stigma.

Let me provide some examples of this from *Hound Pound Narrative*. As we all know, a scholarly book manuscript undergoes peer review at the behest of the publisher, and authors are expected to respond to any criticisms that emerge from this process. The categorical rejection of criticism is not viewed favourably by publishers. Authors are expected to take the criticism seriously, even when it is apparent that the reviewer is hostile, biased or incompetent. In this sense, reviewers have enormous power to shape the final manuscript if it is accepted by the press. One reviewer of the *Hound Pound Narrative* manuscript in particular noted that 'throughout the work there is a problem of tone'. What I offer here is a brief engagement with the reviewer's critique of tone and how I responded.

Example 1

In my analysis of the role of mandated autobiographic disclosure in the sexual offender programme, I employed the work of narrative scholars Ochs and Capps (1996: 34) to frame it in parallel to narrative forms of religious confession. In my draft I wrote:

> The disclosure of their crimes, as the dominant point of the Autobiography, represents a form of 'forced confession', reflecting 'the principle that human

> beings must divulge their sinful acts and thoughts to avoid damnation' (Ochs and Capps, 1996: 34). The similarity between this form of disclosure in therapy and confession in religious contexts is striking (Rose, 1992), and even though the program lacks such overt religious referents, the centrality of moral instruction represents a parallel: beginning with the Autobiography, the inmate must confess or be removed from the program and returned to the 'damnation' of the penitentiary.

'This kind of language is not helpful to the author's cause', responded the reviewer. 'Of course the inmates are removed from the programme if they do not comply with treatment... There is, of course, an implicit critique here that this is somehow unjust... These individuals have the opportunity for treatment... and they elect to participate. The point of the treatment is to change them. I do not understand why it is therefore unjust to expect them to follow the rules of the program to remain there.' My argument, which was central to the ethnography, was that it was the inmates who felt this was unjust, who viewed life back in the penitentiary as a form of 'damnation' and who 'volunteered' for the programme because they were informed quite clearly that parole, or movement to a lower-security facility, would be contingent upon successful completion. The moral principle at work in the treatment programme – that confession is an absolute necessity and refusal is a punishable offense – is clearly based on broader moral scripts. In the final draft, I did hang tight on this point and did not change anything. This was not the case in many other areas.

Example 2

In the draft, in a section called 'Broken Narratives or Breaking Narratives', I wrote: As Gergen and Kaye (1992: 174) have so eloquently put it, 'there is no justification outside the narrow community of like-minded therapists for battering the client's complex and richly detailed life into a single, pre-formulated narrative, a narrative that may be of little relevance or promise for the client's subsequent life conditions.' The reviewer responded that 'the terminology of 'battering' and 'breaking' the narrative seems not only overdrawn here but potentially offensive given the violent nature of the crimes these men are convicted of committing. The author ends up implying that the treatment team are as violent as inmates... setting up this kind of parallelism is really troubling.' In the final version, I muted the tone by removing the term 'eloquently' from the sentence introducing the quote and by adding this clarifying sentence immediately following: 'While I can appreciate the problematic issues inherent in utilising metaphors of violence and victimhood to speak about the experience of sexual offenders, the use of the descriptor "battering" does resonate with what I observed in the group sessions' (p. 234).

Example 3

In the draft, I wrote:

> Initially enticed by the illusion of agency, the request and opportunity to tell one's story – and especially to an audience partially composed of presumably sympathetic allies – most inmates are ultimately subdued by the weight of a therapeutic narrative crashing down on them, an authoritative voice fuelled by a massive dossier of previously acquired information about the inmate and supported by a cognitive behavioural science research paradigm designed to help them see how their personal narrative is problematic.

With respect to the phrase, 'most inmates are ultimately subdued by the weight of a therapeutic narrative crashing down on them', the reviewer commented that 'the choice of language seems overdone here'. I responded in the revised version by completely rewriting the offending part of the sentence to read, 'most inmates ultimately and to varying degrees come to terms with the therapeutic paradigm, some for instrumental and others for therapeutic reasons (and some for both.) This authoritative paradigm is backed by a massive dossier of previously acquired information about the inmate and supported by a cognitive behavioral [*sic*] science treatment model that is designed to help him see how his personal narrative is problematic' (Waldram, 2012: 7).

Example 4

The inmates are required to sign 'treatment contracts', which as I demonstrate in the book are rather coercive, the one-way documents that carry many penalties for breaches. Despite the appearance of the possibility of negotiation, '[t]he contract leaves no question as to who is in charge' – I wrote in the draft and retained in the book (Waldram, 2012: 94). This is a statement of fact. But the reviewer suggested that I was 'presenting this as if it is somehow "obviously" problematic'. In the draft I wrote, 'The spectre of individuals being removed, occasionally by force, looms large over the daily life of the unit. The consequences for violating the contract can be extreme.' The consequences to which I refer include not only being sent back to the penitentiary, which means in most cases no chance for parole, but being only partially 'rehabilitated' at the time. And there were instances where a contract violator resisted expulsion and had to be forcibly removed from his house by the heavily armoured cell extraction team. The reviewer suggested that '[t]he implication here is that this is unreasonable [and later in the review, 'unjust'], and this is a common tone throughout the book'. I think the reviewer's biases showed clearly here, and I stood by my view that the 'tone' was not one that engages with reasonableness of the actions, but rather the implications of them as understood and explained to me by the inmates. This underscores how, in writing the research, attempting to understand and manage the biases that readers will bring to the material is important, even if it is a losing effort. Nonetheless, in order to 'tone' down the meaning of this passage, in the final draft I substituted 'significant' for 'extreme' in the second sentence.

Example 5

A core element of the cognitive behavioural therapy used with these inmates is that they suffer from 'cognitive distortions' or 'thinking errors'. In my work I argue, through narrative theory, that whether one is a criminal or not rationalising, justifying and denying one's actions is normative and research suggests it is difficult to separate sexual offenders from others on the basis of cognitive distortions. My argument, in effect, is that the intense focus on identifying cognitive distortions is misplaced. The reviewer stated rather bluntly that this is 'a dangerous argument', reminding me that '[i]t is quite another [thing] to have a cognitive distortion or thinking error that a six-year-old wants you to have sex with her'. Hyperbole aside, the reviewer missed the argument that I was making, and one which I clarified in the revised text: it is not a question of the existence or content of so-called cognitive distortions that is the issue, but rather the extent to which one does or does not act on them, an area that attracts much less attention. But to be accused of making a 'dangerous' argument hyperbolically conflates my critique of the treatment process with a risk to public safety. In response, I added to the revised text: 'This is not to discount the significance and impact of their crimes, but rather to emphasise that to view these inmates solely or even primarily in the context of their criminal acts serves to oversimplify human existentiality and hence poses a risk to public safety, the opposite of the intended goal of prison treatment' (p. 225).

Example 6

The reviewer questioned my phrasing when I wrote that the therapists 'pass judgment on [inmates'] lives'. 'This', he or she suggested, 'is an example of problematic terminology with important implications. Do they? Or are they trying to shape their stories?... Unless the author can give us examples of the treatment staff talking about how the inmates are degenerates, or corrupt, or awful people, or whatever, he cannot make this claim.' My original passage was bracketed by a critique of cognitive behavioural therapy and cited leading authorities who explained how the narratives of those in treatment are typically 'destroyed or incorporated – but in any case replaced – by the professional's account' (Gergen and Kaye, 1992: 169). Of course, everything that I witnessed, and argued in the book, suggested quite clearly that stories were being judged in accordance with both official crime narratives contained in police and court records and in terms of compatibility with the cognitive behavioural model. Inmates were often told in very clear terms that their narratives were not adequate in either one or both contexts, and in some cases were forced to repeat until they were. I do not think referring to this process as 'passing judgement' was inappropriate here, and the inmates certainly viewed it this way. Nonetheless, in the book I changed the last phrase here: 'The inmates in my study are even provided with reviews of scientific research on sexual offending to bolster the authority of the treatment paradigm and its practitioners *to pass judgement on their lives*' to 'evaluate and assess the inmates' lives as a whole as well as their treatment progress' (Waldram, 2012: 15).

Example 7

There was concern that I described the efforts to learn the treatment programme by saying that the inmates were '*forced* to learn a whole new language' [emphasis in original to the reviewer]. Again, the requirement to learn how to speak in terms of cognitive behavioural therapy and the therapeutic community is a fact, and men are assessed on their ability to learn the language. The issue for the reviewer was my use of the term 'forced'. The reviewer explained, 'Certainly the author is entitled to his opinion, but this kind of word choice throughout the text presents the material in such a way that description comes to stand in for argument.' I used 'forced', noted the reviewer, 'instead of, for example, "invited", "mentored in", "taught", "offered" ', as if these other verbs – for those convicted of sexual crimes at least – are simply descriptive and not argumentative. In response, I changed the word 'forced' to 'required'.

Example 8

The reviewer also stressed what he deemed to be a 'potentially fatal flaw' in the manuscript, that I did not interview treatment staff members or correction officers. This was particularly problematic in the sense that 'many of the inferences and conclusions offered bank on an assumed perspective of the treatment staff that the author simply cannot substantiate'. I did accept the recommendation that at the very least I should place a discussion of this much earlier in the manuscript. But my concern here is that this obsession with staff perspectives attempted to undercut the validity of the ethnography by suggesting that it was biased in favour of the inmates. My explanation as to why I focused solely on the inmates fell on deaf ears. First, I was not allowed to formally interview them as a condition of the research. In this prison at least, only the inmates are subjects of research. However, I was able to talk with staff members off the record, observe them in group therapy sessions and casual interactions with inmates and read all of their reports, which I explained in the manuscript and which I believe did indeed give me solid insight into their perspectives even if I could not directly refer to those insights. Second, in my efforts to be as experience-near as possible and 'go down with the hounds', I was better positioned ethnographically to understand the inmates' experiences by not having too much contact with the staff. It was my call to read their reports only after the inmates had completed their programme, so that I could engage in as unbiased manner as possible with their experiences, observations and insights. And this approach did allow me to get much closer to the research participants than have many other ethnographers, where typically access to inmates is rigidly controlled. In the end, I could only conclude that the reviewer, in essentially declaring my bias in favour of my participants (quite normal in ethnographic research), was himself exposing a common bias in favour of the treatment staff, that is, that inmates lie, cheat and manipulate, and therefore I should not trust anything they tell me, whereas the staff have the 'truth'. In a sense, the book as submitted in manuscript form, and then again in its final form, sought to argue against such a perspective, and the reviewer reinforced in my mind why this was essential.

Example 9

After describing one case where a man was denied a family visit because he had offended against his stepson, I attempted to capture his despair. I quoted him from group therapy and added a verb that turned out to be particularly problematic: ' "I don't want to erase them from my life", he *laments*' [emphasis added here]. The reviewer responded that 'the author presents this as yet another institutional power play that is suggested as extreme or unjust'. Actually, I offered no such judgement, rather simply attempting to capture the facts and the emotions of the case. In the book, I deleted the verb 'laments' and simply quoted him. Apparently, sexual offenders cannot lament!

Certainly, it is entirely possible that this reviewer was attempting to save me from myself, to help me craft my ethnography that would reduce the likelihood that I would be targeted as a sympathiser of or apologist for these men. In isolation, I might agree, and there were also many valuable suggestions for revision. But as I have discussed so far, this reaction to the 'tone' in which I describe my research participants is actually quite common. Whilst I did indeed defer to some of the reviewer's concerns by changing certain passages (all authors appreciate the need to accept at least some of the reviewer's suggestions!), and the review made me very aware of the need to scrutinise my language carefully to be certain that I was comfortable with how the men were being portrayed. It also encouraged me to address the issue of 'tone' much more directly in the revised and resubmitted version of the manuscript. I began by again referencing Hinton's (2005: 4) work with Cambodian military mass killers, who writes that we should strive 'to resist simple, reductive explanations' of the behaviour of those we find repugnant or evil, or who we deny their potential for change. Instead, we are encouraged 'to see them as complex, multidimensional human beings who often have family and people who love and care for them and who want the same things in life as the rest of us – individuals who, like us, live within a moralised social world in which they, by and large, not only see themselves in moral terms but are quite prepared to question the morality of others' (Waldram, 2012: ix). I would direct the reader to the preface of the book for the detailed accounting of my position. But it is important to stress here, following Goffman (1961) who insisted that a 'partisan' view is necessary to understanding inmates of total institutions, that accurately understanding and relating the experiences of our participants, no matter who they are, is at the core of the ethnographic enterprise. As I explained in the preface:

> No matter how disagreeable my participants are, it serves no constructive purpose to 'tone' down an inmate's outrage at being removed from the treatment program and sent back to his home prison, for instance, no matter the reason or legitimacy of the action by prison officials. He *is* angry and upset, and I see it as my job to communicate that to the best of my ability. When an inmate 'laments' that he cannot have any family contact while in treatment, I must try to convey his emotional state, even though the treatment staff have very legitimate reasons for their actions. My research is not about their reasons, it is about the inmate's experiences. (p. xiii)

In response to a very fair critique that the victims of sexual crimes were largely invisible in my ethnography, I added in several places comments about the irony of treatment, where the victims are talked about, fantasised about and even portrayed by their victimisers whilst being, quite necessarily, invisible in the research. I was never in a position to meet or interview any of the victims of these crimes; indeed, to do so would have surely biased my ability to 'go down with the hounds' in an effort to capture as much as possible, in an experience-near manner, their thoughts and feelings as men convicted of sexual crimes in a prison treatment programme. I recognised, as most good researchers do, that going into any research situation entails identifying and managing one's own biases, and in previous prison research (not related to sexual crimes per se) I had been quite shocked at hearing some of the stories. So at the risk of again creating a bit of a critical backlash, in order to understand the experiences of these inmates I needed to manage my own views of their crimes and render invisible their victims, who would be understood only through the lens of their perpetrators. But this approach raised an important question: Can we only research and write about 'bad' people if we provide equal time to those who they hurt?

The morality of disciplines

The experiences that I have had talking and writing about men convicted of sexual crimes underscores that there is a moral dimension to disciplines, a kind of moralised grand narrative or paradigm that tends to dominate at specific historic moments and that serves to shape what can and cannot be said about a specific topic, and how it can be said. It even defines what constitutes a researchable topic in itself. This is compatible with Foucault's (1970) notion of the 'episteme', and underscores that anthropology, and its signature method and mode of presentation, ethnography, are characterised by a dominant and powerful moral ethos. There are accepted ways of talking about people, and accepted analytical frameworks, that are often only truly evident when there are breaches of the moral etiquette. Such breaches constitute a 'moral breakdown', as Zigon (2007) defines it, the moment when we are shaken out of our unreflective moral state to consider the appropriateness of a topic or representation. I believe that my sexual offender research presents one such example of this.

There are two components to a view of the moral ethos of ethnography that have coalesced in recent years. The first is the 'crisis of representation' in ethnographic writing, and the second is the rise and, I would suggest, hegemony of the anthropology of suffering paradigm. Together, these have served to shape the moral epistemic contours of contemporary ethnography in anthropology.

The 'crisis of representation' in ethnography is 'the uncertainty about adequate means of describing social reality' (Marcus and Fischer, 1986: 8). James Clifford identified the 'symptoms of pervasive postcolonial crisis of ethnographic authority' embedded in foundational questions such as 'who has the authority to speak for a group's identity or authenticity' (1988: 8). The inspiration for this reflexive turn came from the realisation that those typically under the lens of anthropological ethnography, the 'non-western other', were now able to read works written about them, respond and critique. Emerging from this movement was the gradual concern for how ethnographers portray their participants; we all became cautious that our descriptions did not invoke images of primitiveness, the 'darker side of life' (Edgerton, 1992: 5), so much so that we turned away from interpretations that could paint participants' societies in a negative light. We dropped the 'barbarian' and embraced the 'arcadian' notion of non-Western or traditional societies as fully functioning, healthy and harmonious (Lucas and Barrett, 1995). In turn, this propensity towards the positive came to reflect ethnography more broadly as anthropology came to identify strongly with, first, the victims of colonialism, and then victims of postcolonial poverty, inequality, violence and suffering.

To say that 'the varieties of human suffering have spurred the anthropological imagination' (Chuengsatiansup, 2001: 31) may be an understatement. Aimed 'at unveiling the social origins and structural sources of human misery' (p. 31), anthropological ethnography has fully embraced victims. The social suffering paradigm has emerged as a dominant one in cultural, psychological and medical anthropology, focusing on the consequences of the exertion of power on people (Kleinman et al., 1997). Taken to the extreme, such enquiry becomes 'militant', justifying the usually tabooed technique of disguising our identities to undertake what is, in effect, undercover research to expose those who seek to perpetrate the suffering (Scheper-Hughes, 1995, 2004). Such a black-and-white rendering of the world does little to help us fully understand the daily lives of those who suffer – and who, of course, do not suffer all the time! – and it also does a disservice to our ability to understand those who stand accused of creating the conditions of suffering. A focus on the 'people who get rubbished' (Scheper-Hughes, 1997) is not counterbalanced by meaningful investigations into those who do the rubbishing. And this is an ethnographic problem.

Together, the crisis of representation and the social suffering paradigm have created a hostile climate for research on those who perpetrate violence and, especially in my case, for how we represent them in our ethnography. One might think that these two intellectual movements are actually contradictory, that the crisis of representation would encourage us to understand and represent our perpetrator participants as faithfully as we do victims. Joel Robbins (2013) suggests that the ethnographic 'other', the non-Westerner that was the concern of the representationalists, has in fact been replaced by the 'suffering subject'. I would suggest that there is more of a synergy, that the ghost of the 'other' is very much evident in the power of the suffering paradigm. The 'empathic connection and moral witnessing' (Robbins, 2013: 453) that characterises the suffering paradigm is highly selective. Contrary to Robbins (2013: 454) and those whose work informs his own (e.g. Daniel, 1996; Fassin and Rechtman, 2009), the 'universality of suffering' is not so universal, at least in ethnographic terms. Only the victims of suffering have the right of fair ethnographic representation. When the 'subaltern' speaks (Spivak, 1988), we are to listen, accept and not challenge. When the murderer or rapist speaks, we are to question, condemn and reject. It does not matter if the perpetrator were once the victim, as is often the case with men who commit sexual crimes. Perpetrator status supersedes victim status. Here, Robbins (2013: 456) and I agree when he writes that social suffering ethnography 'is secure in its knowledge of good and evil'. But it is precisely the apparent fact that the purveyors of the suffering paradigm believe in the existence of evil as some kind of essentialist, universal and *real* phenomenon that is at the heart of the problem. Cultural anthropologists are dropping their cultural constructionist ball when it matters most! How can we understand suffering if we do not seek to understand the perpetrators of that suffering? And how can we understand the perpetrators if we in turn slot them into a singular category, that of the evil, and hence meritorious of only our disdain and worse?

Conclusion

Arthur Kleinman (1999: 418) has accentuated how, through ethnography, we are 'called into the stories and lives of others by the moral process of engaged listening, the commitment to witnessing, and the call to take account of what is at stake for people'. How is it, then, that with *some* people this moral process has less 'take' due to their own questionable moral status within our community?

Ethnographers are privileged by the intimate access they gain to the lives of their participants, and to bend to status quo pressures allowing for only certain kinds of representations not only does a great injustice to those participants and the tradition of ethnography, but is fundamentally unethical. Prison ethnography must be an ethical pursuit, and this requires that ethnographers write their results in a manner that faithfully reflects the humanity that even those imprisoned for crimes possess. The tone that we use must be compatible with our experience-near comprehension of inmate experiences, and we must resist those who would retreat into essentialist understandings of the world, to offer 'simple, reductive explanations' (Hinton, 2005: 4) of complex lives and acts. We will not always be successful in our resistance, as my experiences with *Hound Pound Narrative* show, but we have no right undertaking prison ethnography if we are unable or unwilling to see our inmate participants as worthy human beings who see themselves as morally grounded and who have a story to tell us. If we cannot write bad, how can we write at all?

Further reading

Waldram, J. B. (2007) 'Everybody Has a Story: Listening to Imprisoned Sexual Offenders', *Qualitative Health Research*, 17, 7, 963–70.

Waldram, J. B. (2009) ' "It's Just You and Satan, Hanging Out at a Pre-School:" Notions of Evil and the Rehabilitation of Sexual Offenders', *Anthropology and Humanism*, 34, 2, 219–34.

Waldram, J. B. (2009) 'Challenges of Prison Ethnography', *Anthropology News*, January, 50, 1, 4–5.

Waldram, J. B. (2012) *Hound Pound Narrative: Sexual Offender Habilitation and the Anthropology of Therapeutic Intervention* (Berkeley: University of California Press).

References

Chuengsatiansup, K. (2001) 'Marginality, Suffering, and Community: The Politics of Collective Experience and Empowerment in Thailand', in V. Das, A. Kleinman, M. Lock, M. Ramphele and P. Reynolds (eds) *Remaking a World: Violence, Social Suffering, and Recovery*, pp. 31–75 (Berkeley: University of California Press).

Clifford, J. (1988) *The Predicament of Culture: Twentieth-Century Ethnography, Literature, and Art* (Cambridge, MA: Harvard University Press).

Daniel, E. V. (1996) 'Crushed Glass, or, Is There a Counterpoint to Culture?', in E. V. Daniel and J. M. Peck (eds) *Culture/Contexture: Explorations in Anthropology and Literary Studies*, pp. 357–75 (Berkeley: University of California Press).

DeLeon, G., Melnick, G., Thomas, G., Kressel, D. and Wexler H. (2000) 'Motivation for Treatment in a Prison-Based Therapeutic Community', *American Journal of Drug and Alcohol Abuse*, 26, 1, 33–46.

Edgerton, R. B. (1992) *Sick Societies: Challenging the Myth of Primitive Harmony* (New York: Free Press).

Fassin, D. and Rechtman, R. (2009) *The Empire of Trauma: An Inquiry Into the Condition of Victimhood* (Princeton: Princeton University Press).

Foucault, M. (1970) *The Order of Things: An Archaeology of the Human Sciences* (London: Tavistock).

Gergen, K. J. and Kaye, J. (1992) 'Beyond Narrative in the Negotiation of Therapeutic Meaning', in S. McNamee and K. J. Gergen (eds) *Therapy as Social Construction*, pp. 166–85 (London: Sage).

Goffman, E. (1961) *Asylums: Essays on the Social Situation of Mental Patients and Other Inmates* (New York: Anchor Books).

Hinton, A. L. (2005) *Why Did They Kill? Cambodia in the Shadow of Genocide* (Berkeley: University of California Press).

Kleinman, A. (1999) 'Experience and Its Moral Codes: Culture, Human Conditions, and Disorder', in G.B. Peterson (ed) *The Tanner Lectures on Human Values*, pp. 20: 357–420 (Salt Lake City: University of Utah Press).

Kleinman, A., Das, V. and Lock, M. (eds) (1997) *Social Suffering* (Berkeley: University of California Press).

Lockwood, D., Inciardi, J. Butzin, C. and Hooper R. (1997) 'Therapeutic Community Continuum in Corrections', in G. De Leon (ed) *Community as Method: Therapeutic Communities for Special Populations and Special Settings*, pp. 87–96 (Westport, CT: Praeger).

Lucas, R. H. and Barrett, R. J. (1995) 'Interpreting Culture and Psychopathology: Primitivist Themes in Cross-Cultural Debate', *Culture, Medicine and Psychiatry*, 19, 287–326.

Marcus, G. E. and Fischer, M. J. (1986) *Anthropology as Cultural Critique: An Experimental Moment in the Human Sciences* (Chicago: University of Chicago Press).

Marshall, W. L. (1996) 'The Sexual Offender: Monster, Victim, or Everyman?' *Sexual Abuse: A. Journal of Research and Treatment*, 8, 317–35.

Murchison, J. M. (2010) *Ethnography Essentials: Designing, Conducting, and Presenting Your Research* (San Francisco: Jossey-Bass).

Ochs, E. and Capps, L. (1996) 'Narrating the Self', *Annual Review of Anthropology*, 25, 19–43.

Rhodes, L. A. (2004) *Total Confinement: Madness and Reason in the Maximum Security Prison* (Berkeley: University of California Press).

Robbins, J. (2013) 'Beyond the Suffering Subject: Toward and Anthropology of the Good', *Journal of the Royal Anthropological Institute*, 19, 447–62.

Rose, N. (1992) 'Engineering the Human Soul: Analysing Psychological Experience', *Science in Context*, 5, 2, 351–69.

Scheper-Hughes, N. (1995) 'The Primacy of the Ethical: Propositions for a Militant Anthropology', *Current Anthropology*, 36, 3, 409–40.

Scheper-Hughes, N. (1997) 'People Who Get Rubbished', *New Internationalist*, 295. Retrieved 6 February, 2006, from www.newint.org/issue 295.

Scheper-Hughes, N. (2004) 'Parts Unknown: Undercover Ethnography of the Organs-Trafficking Underworld', *Ethnography* 5, 1, 29–73.

Shuker, R. and Sullivan, E. (eds) (2010) *Grendon and the Emergence of Forensic Therapeutic Communities: Developments in Research and Practice* (Chichester, UK: Wiley-Blackwell).

Spivak, G. C. (1988) 'Can the Subaltern Speak?', in C. Nelson and L. Grossberg (eds) *Marxism and the Interpretation of Culture*, pp. 271–313 (Urbana, IL: University of Illinois Press).

Wacquant, L. (2002) 'The Curious Eclipse of Prison Ethnography in the Age of Mass Incarceration', *Ethnography* 3, 4, 371–97.

Waldram, J. B. (1993) 'Aboriginal Spirituality: Symbolic Healing in Canadian Prisons', *Culture, Medicine & Psychiatry*, 17, 345–62.

Waldram, J. B. (1994) 'Aboriginal Spirituality in Corrections: A Canadian Case Study in Religion and Therapy', *American Indian Quarterly*, 18, 2, 197–214.

Waldram, J. B. (1997) *The Way of the Pipe: Aboriginal Spirituality and Symbolic Healing in Canadian Prisons* (Peterborough: Broadway Press).

Waldram, J. B. (1998) 'Anthropology in Prison: Negotiating Consent and Accountability with a Captured Population', *Human Organisation*, 57, 2, 238–44.

Waldram, J. B. (2007) 'Everybody Has a Story: Listening to Imprisoned Sexual Offenders', *Qualitative Health Research*, 17, 7, 963–70.

Waldram, J. B. (2009) ' "It's Just You and Satan, Hanging Out at a Pre-School:" Notions of Evil and the Rehabilitation of Sexual Offenders', *Anthropology and Humanism*, 34, 2, 219–34.

Waldram, J. B. (2012) *Hound Pound Narrative: Sexual Offender Habilitation and the Anthropology of Therapeutic Intervention* (Berkeley: University of California Press).

Zigon, J. (2007) 'Moral Breakdown and the Ethical Demand: A Theoretical Framework for an Anthropology of Moralities', *Anthropological Theory*, 7, 2, 131–50.

12
Prison Ethnography at the Threshold of Race, Reflexivity and Difference

Rod Earle and Coretta Phillips

Introduction – Prison identities

Our objective in this chapter is to offer some insights from a broadly ethnographic study of two men's prisons in South East England conducted between 2006 and 2008. The study sought to explore the dynamics of difference and their impact on social relations in the late modern prison. We wanted to examine the relative importance of Sykes' (1958) model of a universal prisoner collective, united by common experiences of brutalisation and degradation (the 'indigenous model'), and Irwin and Cressey (1962) and Jacobs (1975, 1977) model, which, in contrast, saw identities external to the prison, including those of race and religion, informing social relations inside ('importation model').

The racialised dynamics of incarceration have been an increasingly prominent feature of Western criminal justice systems (Tonry, 1994; Wacquant, 1999; Wacquant, 2001; Wacquant, 2006), most prominently in the US, but no less significantly in England and Wales (Phillips and Bowling, 2002; Phillips, 2012). The dangers posed in the UK by racism in prison achieved wider exposure after the murder in his cell, in 2000, of the teenager Zahid Mubarek by his white cellmate in Feltham Young Offender Institution (YOI) (CRE, 2003b, 2003a). This and other revelations about ingrained racial discrimination in the criminal justice system and racial prejudice amongst its staff combined with new legislation that placed formal responsibilities on public bodies to promote 'good relations' (thus, *between* prisoners) and equal treatment (by prison officers *of* prisoners) between people 'of different racial groups' (NOMS, 2008).

However, despite recognition of the urgent need to address widespread racism in British society, its complex, shifting dynamics and locally specific manifestations can be challenging to conventional empirical inquiry. Our ethnographic and reflexive approach offered the opportunity to scrutinise some of these dimensions, to recognise their nuanced specificity and to acknowledge our own identities and biographical histories as mediums through which we could understand the late modern multicultural prison.

Two prisons out of a possible 146, between them containing less than 1,000 men amongst a total prison population of approximately 80,000, are not necessarily typical of the UK's carceral archipelago, but they were most definitely revealing. Our study involved spending three to four days a week in conversation, interaction and observation of prisoners for eight months in each prison. Semi-structured interviews with 60 prisoners in Rochester and 50 interviews in Maidstone were conducted, with slightly over one-half coming from informal contacts we made during the observational and interactional work and the remainder drawn randomly from the prison roll, stratified by ethnicity, nationality and faith.

Two prisons, the metropole and the garden of England

The two prisons lie just beyond the boundaries of the largest and most cosmopolitan city in Europe, the capital city of the UK and the erstwhile centre of the world's largest Empire: London. Home to over 8 million people, it is a vibrant, shouting advertisement for all the perils and pitfalls and wonders and windfalls of globalisation. It is the archetype metropole. Both prisons are in the county of Kent, commonly referred to by the tourist industry as 'the garden of England'. For the many men from London and its surrounding counties who serve their sentences in HMYOI Rochester or HMP Maidstone, the distinction between urban metropole and rural idyll and between minority ethnic multiculture and white mono-culture is a sharp one. For prisoners, it is a distinction experienced not through the contrasting landscapes of the physical environment, as it might be by the casual visitor, the tourist or ourselves as researchers, but in the characteristics of the prisoners themselves. Their habitus and collected dispositions are thrown together into the barren architecture of prison space where they must live together in cells and on prison landings. Up close, razor wire, metal mesh, concrete walls and iron bars look more or less the same in the city or the country, even if the sounds and the light around and above a prison's open spaces may vary. Inside each prison, we discovered it was the meeting of men's different locales, diverse histories and cultural biographies that mattered. With their different languages, manners, voices, accents, actions, looks and silences, with their various skin colours, complexions and hairstyles, the men gave us stories to tell about the multicultural prison. The juxtaposition of their being 'of London' or 'of Kent' (and/or somewhere else) but not in London or really in Kent, but in prison, was the ethnographic core of the study.

HMYOI Rochester is a prison for about 400 young men aged 17–21. It lies on the site of the original Borstal institution. Established in 1908 at the high point of British imperial ambition to ensure British masculinity remained robustly 'fit-for purpose', Borstals were correctional 'camps' for wayward young men

(Earle, 2011b). The Kent village of Borstal lies just above the port of Rochester on the eastern reaches of the Thames estuary. It is an area made famous by its most celebrated resident, the Victorian novelist Charles Dickens, and now made retrospectively available to the world at large courtesy of a theme park, Dickens World (http://www.dickensworld.co.uk/). Rochester and the other north Kent estuary port of Chatham were once the gateway to London and central to its imperial trading. Now declining and marginal, they are overshadowed by Dover and Ramsgate ferry ports and the tunnel route farther south connecting England to mainland Europe. The prison itself comprises a number of older brick-built, barrack-style accommodation blocks that betray their early twentieth-century origin. The wider prison compound includes more modern prison facilities and is ringed with high metal mesh fences that complement the perimeter wall of the old Borstal camp. The disused outdoor swimming pool just beyond the prison officer's car park is now a gloomy relic, a reminder of the benign intentions of its patrician Edwardian founders.

By contrast HMP Maidstone sits adjacent to the remodelled centre of the market town, a stone's throw from its pedestrianised commercial hub. The river Medway runs through the town, connecting it to Rochester farther downstream. It provides the town with its status as the agricultural axis point of the county of Kent, centre of the garden of England. Inside thick and imposing white limestone walls, erected almost 300 years ago in 1740, nearly 500 men are housed in five old and more modern prison blocks. It is one of the oldest penal institutions in the UK. In the middle of the eighteenth century, the prison reformer John Howard noted its overcrowding and poor ventilation (see also HMP Maidstone, 2009). At the time of our research, at the beginning of the twenty-first century, the prison inspectorate issued a damning report, listing much the same, with the contemporary embellishment of a thriving trade in drugs (HMCIP, 2007). Towards the end of our fieldwork, one wing was closed due to an outbreak of listeria.

Entering and being in the field: Enough about us . . .?

In recent prison scholarship, there has been a fruitful discussion about the value of 'tell it like it is' accounts (Hollway and Jefferson, 2000) or what Rowe (2014: 410) refers to as 'univocal realist ethnography' and analyses which privilege the role of emotions and reflexivity in the interpretation of the field and the construction of knowledge about the prison (Bosworth, 1999; Liebling, 1999; Crewe, 2009; Carlen, 2010; Phillips and Earle, 2010; Drake and Harvey, 2013; Jewkes, 2014). Given our research questions and being primed to issues of identity, race and multiculture, in hindsight we paid rather scant attention to questions of researcher positionality before entering the field. Our first day of fieldwork, which included 'hanging out' with prisoners at Rochester, alerted us to this omission and the implications of the polarities of our research team, with regard to race, gender, age and social class (for more on this, see Phillips and Earle, 2010). An early field note at Rochester recorded by Coretta, a black/mixed-race female researcher, about time conversing with a mixed-race prisoner on B wing during association, was illuminating:

> John tells me that a gov has told him about a nursery rhyme which refers to niggers and God not having time to make them white. He tells me that white prisoners tell them [minority ethnic prisoners] about how racist govs are, and they [white prisoners] don't like it either. He tells me that 'it's because they're [prison officers] from Kent. They're not from London, they don't know Miss that it's all unity and love in our [urban London] communities!
>
> (Field note (CP): 26 July 2006)

Later on the same field note and the corresponding one by the co-author, Rod, a white man of middle-class origin, signalled a substantive partiality in the engagement of prisoners around issues of racism from prison officers, a finding often observed in other studies (CRE, 2003a; Cheliotis and Liebling, 2006; NOMS, 2008; Phillips, 2012) but one which emerged differently for the two of us:

> Almost every prisoner that I meet wants to tell me about how bad the govs are here, and particularly the minority ethnic prisoners come to tell me about their [prison officers'] racism. Are they doing the same to Rod?
>
> (Field note (CP): 26 July, 2006)

> Coretta says all the black guys are telling her stories of the racism they face in the prison from the screws. It seems very striking, that they all have the same story, and want to tell her. She asks if I am getting the same and I have to say that I'm not. My interactions seem to be rather more mundane, low key, chit chat. I am worried about this as it seems a critical point of the project, and says something about the significance of identity – mine as a white researcher, and Coretta's as someone with whom such stories are meant to register.
>
> (Field note (RE): 26 July 2006)

The beauty of ethnography is that what we learn through one approach, in this case observation and interaction, may be contradicted or qualified by another approach, such as formal interviews. And indeed, this was the case; our interviews revealed an array of perspectives that ranged from the infrequent but determined accusations of blatant racism by a few prisoners to more tentative suggestions about the potentially racialised sources of differential treatment and even flat denials of the incidence of prison officer racism (for more on this, see Phillips, 2012). Notwithstanding, there was no getting away from the fact that Coretta's racial identity provided somewhat of a privileged access to minority ethnic (and some white) prisoners in a way which was denied to Rod, as a white man, and this feature continued in Maidstone prison too. Practically, this meant that more of the informal contacts who were from minority ethnic groups and who also became interviewees were interviewed by Coretta rather than by Rod.

This, of course, set up the potential problem of insiderism and outsiderism, which Merton (1972) long ago believed would lead to the 'balkanisation of social science'. In its starkest forms, black researchers alone are assumed to be able to access knowledge from black research participants/subjects. It holds out the promise of tapping a racialised authenticity otherwise obscured by divided and segregated societies in which race is subjectively lived (Phillips and Bowling, 2003). These idealised insider identities presume to offer black researchers a monopoly on access to a universal black experience, a singular black identity. Sobering then, are the observations of black American scholar, Winddance Twine (2000), entering the field to study race and racism in multicultural Brazil. Twine was disoriented by the force of remarks by black Brazilians, who appeared to wholeheartedly endorse the cultural valorisation of whiteness. She reports how unsettling it was to find her professional identity as a scholar repeatedly thrown into doubt by suggestions that she was the maid, the illegitimate sister of her white partner or even his whore. Mistakenly, she had assumed a shared, diasporic, black affinity with black Brazilians of African descent, as collective victims of white supremacy, which would provide her with privileged access to their experience that would be denied to a white researcher. As it turned out, Twine was a long way from having the inside track on their black subjectivity and experience.

We have learned from our experiences as a two-person research team, with self-evidently contrasting identities along the axes of race, gender and class, there can be no convenient, prescriptive conventions to guide the empirical study of race, multiculture and racism. Certain privileges of 'insiderism' may be part of the mix in any research encounter or interaction, but crude binary conceptions are less helpful than intersectional ones (for more on this, see Duneier, 2004; Phillips and Earle, 2010; Earle, 2010; 2011a; 2015). Ironically, however, the binary features of our research team, unusual in terms of Coretta's academic seniority, mixed-race ethnicity and working-class background, provided significant epistemological opportunities. What concerns us are the ways these are largely overshadowed, and thus obscured, by a fatalistic accommodation with their scarcity. The social, structural and institutional barriers that reproduce an almost exclusively white, middle-class academic community result in a research community ill-equipped to transcend the binaries it critiques.

Time and again, we found our respective identities, in terms of ethnicity and gender, throwing up 'angles' around which we would negotiate our research. In what follows, we present another discussion of how we encountered these differences and considered their epistemological implications. Focusing on our interactions with four men, we examine how their identities and social relations were shaped by 'race' and ethnicity.

Abbott – A man out of time

At the start of the fieldwork in Rochester, steered by prison officers who perceived our primary research interest to be about *racism*, we were alerted to the presence of a young white man recently transferred to the prison from another in the south west of England. Abbott, we were told by prison officers, was a self-declared supporter of a far-right, neo-fascist political party, the National Front. He had a swastika tattoo on his hand. More than one prison officer suggested that Abbott would be an 'obvious choice' for interview. He seemed to be regarded with an ambiguous mixture of contempt, pity and curiosity. It was not that he was seen as a celebrity, nor even as particularly notorious; he was simply and literally marked out as a known quantity, 'a racist', because of his tattoo and open political identification with the iconic symbol of British racism – the National Front. Abbott was seen, we were told by officers, as someone out of place, in more ways than one. His transfer eastwards to HMYOI Rochester arose from his being involved in fights and disciplinary issues at other institutions, and the isolating effect of his transfers was progressively more punitive the farther he was moved from his west country home. Through a combination of his own preferences and officers' assessment of his predicament, he was kept isolated from most other prisoners most of the time, for his own safety. This was consistent with data we subsequently gathered on the policing of overt racism by minority ethnic prisoners and the likelihood of violent retaliation against its presence.

Was he an obvious choice for interview, as the prison officers suggested? Even as we struggled to keep an open mind about Abbott, to allow him to be as much an 'unknown quantity' as any other respondent, we could not avoid the prescriptions offered to us, or deny how our own ethnicities and biographies were inevitably implicated in the choice. We discussed our approach. Was it an unexpected opportunity to exploit to the full? How could we avoid colluding with the implication of being presented with 'a specimen'; a real, live and captive, racist case study just waiting for us to interview? How problematic, how revealing was this presentation of Abbott? As ever, in the research field, such decisions are a tangled knot of pragmatism, principle, opportunity and external constraint. We had just entered the field and were already struggling to develop a coherent interview strategy that would have to surface complex and subdued questions of ethnicity (what is it like to be white?), subjective experiences of gender (what does masculinity mean to you?) within the constraints of an austere prison regime. We resolved that it was worth Rod approaching Abbott to explain our project and ask if he would agree to be interviewed. It seemed unlikely that he would have agreed to have been interviewed by Coretta, and even if he had, we were concerned that it may not be safe to do so.[1]

Rod interviewed Abbott along the lines of the semi-structured interview schedule we had laboured over for hours. As with the other nine pilot interviews, we discovered how difficult it was to establish a discussion around different identities, ethnicities and masculinities, how little time we had and yet how tiring and challenging our young respondents found it to engage in a two-way conversation for much more than an hour. Abbott's interview was entirely typical in that and in many other respects. After an hour and a quarter, his interest in, and energy for, the conversation was flagging and the interview concluded. What he talked about in the sections that focused on ethnicity distilled much that we were later to find in several of our interviews with white prisoners: avoidance of ethnic others; retreat into white enclaves and a preference for mono-cultural sociality; resentment towards policies designed to address discrimination and promote equalities; open and explicit hostility to Muslims as the symbol of a collective threat (Phillips, 2012).

When it came to discussing ethnicity, Abbott's account included justificatory references to his political affiliations: 'I think my political beliefs are a lot different for a start... ' and acknowledgement that he 'is going to sound very controversial'. To Rod, the white male interviewer, he was happy to describe his avoidance in prison of people from minority ethnic groups as being simply consistent with his behaviour outside prison and the political beliefs 'drummed into my head since I was a little boy'. It seems unlikely he would have been so candid with Coretta. What was unusual about Abbott was not so much his difference from other white men in the prison but the explicit political register of the sentiments and views he expressed. These appeared anchored in loyalty to his family and their white rural working-class community in South West England. His explicit rejection of a white British identity as being a national identity already compromised by ethnic diversity is symptomatic of the political contortions and confusions that have gripped racist and nationalist politics in the UK since the mid-1970s. Asked to identify which ethnic group he belonged to or how he would describe himself in terms of ethnicity, Abbott responded with the following:

> White British, white English, I would say, although that sounds a bit strange, but what is British? You know what I mean? That sounds a bit nasty, but that's just the way I've been brought up. I see myself as white English. The reason why I say that is because you don't know what British is. There's just so many ethnic minorities, not even minorities now, majorities should I say.

> They're everywhere and they never say, the African minorities, never say they're English, they say they're British, so I'd like to be separated from that. I don't wish to be too close to that. I know it's a bit controversial, but that's what I believe. I think where I come from we don't wish to even associate with any ethnic minorities, you know what I mean, we fear them... That's how I've always felt, I've been brought up like that. I've had that drummed into my head since I was a little boy. I'm not being silly now but you can probably see it yourself, there's a lot of white people trying to act black and trying to be involved in them lot, and I don't wish to get involved in that because I don't like it, I think it's wrong. I'm not saying that people shouldn't mix, they should, but not when you're trying to act like them and trying... we should have our own culture and like Muslims, they've got their own culture, we should have our own culture as well. And I think it's going downhill compared to the 50s and 60s, do you know what I mean, it's all going downhill.

In this commentary compiled from one of the first interviews we conducted in the study, Abbott quickly indicates themes we subsequently found amongst other interviews with white respondents and that were consistent with our fieldwork interactions. Abbott, as an 18-year-old, was born in the late 1980s, so his evocation of decline, of 'going downhill since the 50s and 60s', echoes the political rhetoric of Britain's nationalist politics as much as it does his own experience. The irony is that although Abbott was presented to us as a display specimen, and exceptional, his views were very similar to that of many other white men in the prisons. This bogus exceptionalism has been a consistent feature of studies of perpetrators of racist violence (Sibbitt, 1997; Ray et al., 2004; Gadd and Dixon, 2011). The difference was that Abbott had a political vocabulary and grammar for his views and an alibi in a family aligned with the open racism and nationalism of the National Front.

In the contemporary political landscape of the UK, the National Front is an organisation long since collapsed into eccentric factions or displaced by reconstituted and politically more nimble alternatives, such as the British National Party or, more recently, the English Defence League and UKIP.[2] As such, the National Front, far from mirroring the success of its similarly named French counterpart, exists more as an exotic relic, surviving on the lunatic, rural fringe of English society – a sort of rare breed farm for almost extinct political mavericks. Though Abbott's politics appeared out of place and out of time in HMYOI Rochester, his presence was offered to us as a kind of stable compass point, indicating a recognisable, and thus manageable, polarity of race. This willingness to present him as a known quantity is suggestive of anxiety over the unknown qualities of contemporary racism, the loosening of its moorings from the classical bearings of old-school 'racism'.

Warwick – A man out of place

In other aspects of the fieldwork, the shifting uncertainties of ethnic identification that coexist uneasily with the legacies of colonial history confronted Coretta with a series of dilemmas. Coretta's 'lox' (dreadlocked hair) assumed symbolic significance in the prison. This was based on their association with an emblematic form of black oppositional identity derived from Jamaican Rastafarianism (Kuumba and Ajanaku, 1998), but they were also simply an aesthetic marker of black femininity. Coretta had no intention to present herself as an authentic black liberationist or Rastafarian, and her 'lox' were principally a resistant stance against chemical 'relaxing' (hair straightening) as the main method for 'managing' Afro hair. Yet, in the first week of fieldwork at Maidstone prison, we met Warwick, a first-time prisoner and a Rastafarian from the Caribbean. It was immediately obvious that he was struggling to understand prison life – how he got there, how he could get in contact with his family in the Caribbean, whether he could survive on his vegan diet as the nearest approximation to Rastafarian 'ital' food, whether an appeal might help to get him out and whether he might be vulnerable to deportation. His soft-spoken bewilderment and fear was palpable and a reminder of how the prison disorients in just the way Goffman (1961) described in *Asylums*. Any first-time prisoner might be similarly felled by such alien circumstances, regardless of their 'imported' racial identities, but Warwick's pain and trauma was definitely less suppressed, less modified and more anguished than most. It was upsetting to see someone so obviously 'out of their depth' and in need of help. Over the following weeks, it was noticeable that as we regularly bumped into Warwick around the prison, his attention was almost always directed at Coretta rather than at Rod. Such instances of 'persistent following' of researchers by prisoners will be familiar to anyone who has done research in prisons. Sometimes believing, erroneously, that researchers offer a new opportunity to have their case heard or to act on their behalf as advocates means such interactions are not uncommon. What seemed important to understand, given the study's intentions to explore prisoners' identities, was not why Warwick sought our assistance as researchers but why he insistently chose one member of the research team and not the other. It is possible that this was gendered and that Warwick saw an approachability and willingness to listen in Coretta's femininity that he did not in Rod's masculinity, but as one of Rod's field notes (4 July, 2007) recorded, Warwick, on one occasion, appeared 'delighted' to see her, gently breathing the word 'Rastafari!' as he passed Rod en route to seek her attention, and this seemed to indicate that ethnic identification played a significant part in this particular research relationship.

Coretta – Mixed race, connected and out of place

Coretta's lox also seemed to have symbolic resonance in encounters with prison staff. During the fieldwork at Maidstone prison, Coretta established a friendly relationship with Lawrence, a British black Caribbean prisoner. 'You and me connect', he said, and whilst this connection was undoubtedly forged on the basis of more than simply race (such as age, parenthood and an allegiance to London), a later exchange suggested once again that our racial identities were part of the mix:

> Lawrence tells me he will be happy to talk (he's not scared what he says to us) at a later date – he warns me that the officers are not happy about my presence – that they do not want prisoners talking to me, whatever they say to the contrary. The female gov has already come in to check what is going on – making it clear to prisoners perhaps that they should be careful what they say to me? He says this is particularly so as I am a dread.[3]
>
> (Field note (CP): 8 July, 2007)

On another occasion, Rod noted the look of mute incomprehension, even fear (dread), on the face of a white, female administrator as we both entered an open plan office and engaged with her colleague, who had offered to provide some data to us. Rod noticed the woman staring past him at Coretta and remarked later to Coretta that the sustained duration of her stare, and its perplexed focus, seemed to convey a concern about Coretta's presence in the prison, her 'blackness' an unwelcome intrusion into the almost exclusively white populated office space of the prison. This snub was personally stinging, but tellingly significant for appreciating the complexities of race in the late modern prison.

We are grateful to Rhodes (2012) for drawing our attention to Barthes' (1981) concepts of the *punctum* and the *studium*, in a photograph which are helpful analytical insights for an ethnographer (see also Chapter 14, this volume). The punctum is that part of a picture which pierces the surface of a scene to puncture our consciousness or subconsciousness, a small but telling detail that, on being noticed, reconfigures the sense made of the whole. In this case, it reminded one of us of our difference from the majority. For Coretta, the punctum – the 'accident which pricks me (but also bruises me, is poignant to me)', to quote Barthes (1981: 49) – was a forceful and uncomfortable reminder of the small distance between vibrant multicultural conviviality and brutish everyday racism. Likewise, when Asad, a British Bangladeshi prisoner at Rochester, recalled putting his name down to play pool on an officer's list, but then saw white prisoners' names being placed before him, he wondered whether this was an act of discrimination. It was a small detail in the general flux and flow of the association period, but an unsettling one that he could not dismiss.

The suspicion of hidden injuries (Sennett and Cobb, 1972), inflicted with casual indifference, was reinforced by Anthony, a white British prisoner at Maidstone, who reported to Coretta overhearing white officers referring to 'fucking bastard blacks'. The routine power of prison officers to withhold access to goods and services in the prison is a disempowering commonplace of prison life, an experience inherent to life in prison and noted by many prison ethnographers (Liebling, 1999; Liebling, 2001; see also Crewe, 2009; Rowe, 2014). When this power is couched in a way that communicates their racialising sense of your own inherent worthlessness, their investments in your own subordinated racial status and their conviction that you can do nothing to change even though you are not a prisoner, it is even more painful. It is a shared injury and a form of inside knowledge. As Rowe (2014) observes, for ethnographers in prison such troubling and disruptive moments can be enlightening, and that it is by attending to such moments, being committed to the details of everyday interactions and providing dense descriptions of them, that we afford ourselves the opportunity of finding punctums and revealing hidden fields of meaning beyond the culturally familiar (the 'studium' of the whole picture). In these details, these punctums, Coretta felt the overwhelming weight of disenfranchisement which comes with the arbitrary *and* racialised exercise of power by white prison officers. As Jewkes (2014: 387) has noted, 'our personalities, histories, and emotions penetrate our research in ways that can ultimately enrich our analysis and give life, vividness, and luminosity to our writing.'

Neal – Heading south and spinning

If Abbott pointed 'due north' on an imaginary racial compass, another of our white respondents in the pilot interviews revealed himself to be operating 'due south'. Neal had expressed interest in our research and his willingness to be interviewed. He was a tall, thin young white man, who talked energetically about his growing up in the outer reaches of west London. He had secured a place in the prison's rehabilitation wing, a wing reserved for prisoners demonstrating commitment to the constructive use of their sentence and thus rewarded with more resources and privileges and subject to a looser regime.

The opening sections of the pilot interview schedule were designed to gather some fairly routine biographical data about where the men lived and how they had arrived at the prison. It included a question on any languages spoken, and Neal responded that he spoke Hindi and Punjabi. He lived in an area of London well known for being home to a diverse range of migrant communities, including those from Ireland, North and East Africa, the Eastern Mediterranean,

India and South East Asia. Neal went on to explain: 'I'm half Asian and half white... My dad's Asian and my mum's white', and that though they were now separated, he had grown up in a bilingual household and learned his father's first languages. As a result of this dual heritage, he had adopted the nickname 'Switch' and declared himself to be 'the only white Asian who knows more about the Asian culture than Asians themselves'. Asked what ethnic group he belonged to, he replied without hesitation, 'I'd say I was white British, I was Asian, I was white, a white Asian, British, an Asian, British Asian, whatever you want to call it that, you know what I mean'. He went on, 'I'm white. I look white. All my friends are Asian. They don't see me as a white person. They see me as an Asian person because they know my heritage... If I want to talk about someone, or if I'm on a bus and someone sits in front of me and I'm with my friend I'll talk to them in our language. Otherwise I speak in English, you know what I mean. So people will see and respect me for who I am not what I look like.'

The contrast with Abbott's refuge-seeking apologia and Neal's assertive cosmopolitanism could not be more apparent. Whilst one appears diminished and excluded amongst the already excluded, the other claims cosmopolitan inclusion. One appears to feel abandoned and quarantined, the other embraced and engaged. Using Gilroy's (2004) work as a compass, we came to recognise these polarities as melancholia and conviviality. In the latter, Gilroy suggests that amongst some of Britain's urban young people, race has become an irrelevance, remote from lived experience and rejected in principle. Others, however, remain haunted by race, bound into its denials of common humanity, anchored to its nostalgic hierarchies and invested in its privileges. This backward-facing melancholic dread is the counterweight to a convivial multiculture surfacing in unruly patterns across Britain (Gilroy, 2004). Neal and Abbott were of course much more complex and contradictory than these two brief vignettes suggest, and our subsequent fieldwork in HMYOI Rochester and HMP Maidstone revealed more of the consistencies, tensions, contradictions, morbidity and vitality that prisons capture and conceal under the dull rhetoric of punishment.

Emerging in immersion – The different sides of Jonathan

The principal value of sustained immersion in the field is that it necessarily involves using a variety of tools of observation, participation, conversation and interview – the hanging around and drifting combines with more targeted activity. In more conventional, short-term, qualitative research, these techniques may be deployed but rarely will the benefit of their interplay become as apparent as it does when conducting an ethnography. In the following discussion of Jonathan's contribution to the research, the various modes of interaction allowed us more insights than any single or episodic form of research would have provided.

Just as it would be wrong to characterise vertical relationships in Rochester and Maidstone between prison officers and prisoners as being singularly organised and mediated through racialisation and racism, the same simplistic assumption of a white oppressor–black victim binary had to be jettisoned when exploring prisoners' horizontal relationships with each other. Returning to the compass analogy, Jonathan was neither due north nor due south. He provided us with a variety of contributions to the research, which indicated the mercurial qualities of identities.

At HMYOI Rochester, a performance poetry workshop with prisoners was convened by the energetic and imaginative work of their 'writer-in-residence'. It involved inviting prisoners to add their own lyrics to musical backing tracks and then performing them to a small audience of peers. At the final workshop, the set was closed by a performance from Jonathan, a white British prisoner, who was later interviewed from the study's 'random sample'. A field note of the observation of the workshop drew from earlier casual conversations with Jonathan on the wings recorded in field diaries.

> He starts with a swift talking and rhyming rap – a story, funny and anecdotal, with lots of puns. His ultra-fast-chat stylings drew from his itinerant immersion in a criminal lifeworld that extended from the ports of Kent to the suburbs of London and beyond. When finished, he is pulled back to the mike and he launches into an almost unintelligible garage rap. The delivery is so quick fire it assumes a staccato rhythm of its own, with only the occasional word recognisable. Jonathan won the contest by popular acclaim.
>
> (RE Field note, 13 January, 2007)

This brief insight into the vernacular currents of youth and popular culture that drift easily into the young men's prison evokes the cultural hybridity that sociologists of race have long insisted are a characteristic feature of the changed times of late modernity (Brah, 1996; Sharma et al., 1996). The cross-fertilisation and fusion of sometimes disparate cultural styles and practices represent new, emerging, plural and hybrid identities, which displace notions of fixed, closed and homogenous racial identities tied to biological origins. Jonathan, whilst white, and hailing from traditionally ethnically mono-cultural Kent, gained the respect of the predominantly black group of prisoners in the workshop by easily emulating the vocal and linguistic vitality of black music forms. This emulation transcended the conventions of dismissive racialising mimicry by inflecting it with his experience of deep immersion in the circuits of criminal marginality, the shadowy but vital fringe economy of port life. Not unlike white rap artist, Eminem (Armstrong, 2004), Jonathan was comfortably at ease discussing the postures and posing that accompany men's fascination with guns (and marginality). Drawing with demonstrable ease on the cachet of black cultural forms which were dominant in the prison provided a means for him to boost his status and credibility inside (Phillips, 2012).

In interview with Rod, the white researcher, Jonathan had a different story to tell, one in which racial boundaries of belonging and exclusion could all too easily be reimposed (Frosh et al., 2002; Nayak, 2003; Hughey, 2011). The first part of his interview reflected on his bullying by black prisoners as a juvenile prisoner, which led him to deny his Kent upbringing – with their taunts of 'White Boy', 'you country bwoy, country bumpkin, osty boy'. Instead, he pretended to have come from Brixton, the symbolic location of black residential dominance, particularly socially and culturally. However, by the time we met Jonathan in Rochester prison, he had moved onward and upward, now standing as a 'big lad', unashamed of his Kentish roots and confident in the liquidity of his cultural capital.

Given below are two composite extracts from Jonathan's interview which reveal a cultural hierarchy inside prison and outside where black men rather than white men are considered powerful, superior and dominant. This inversion of colonial hierarchy brings confusion, uneasiness and strained relations inside, especially for white prisoners. Even those, like Jonathan, who shift with relative ease between the two, and are adept in and can adopt black cultural practices when it suits them, find themselves unsettled:

> black people seem to think that every white person is a mug... Because I get quite embarrassed by quite a few of the white lads being like that, coming down here just to get mugged off. Just because... it's not a racial part of it, it's just a matter of black lads look more intimidating like and they'd got dreadlocks, gold teeth, a little bit of an attitude and the way they talk. And you get a white lad and he says, 'Hello mate, are you alright?', and you get a black lad saying 'Wha Gwaan[4]! Pussy[5]!', whatever, what's it. Right, what's more intimidating? So as soon as you realise the lingo, yeah, and you understand it, I talk like that in front of them, I switch, you know, I don't even mean to do it...

> [Asked about his friendship groups]... I'd be with the white guys, straight up. I'm not racist or nothing like that it's just black guys will obviously respect black guys more and white guys always respect white guys more. It's nothing to do with racist or anything like that. But I believe black people are more racist than white people, and that's what I've watched. And religion-wise yeah, Muslims yeah, they are highly racist. 'You're a Cafar', that means a non-believer, yeah. So if you're a Cafar I will not talk to you. So that's highly racism in my book yeah... I had an argument like the other day yeah,

> but it was behind closed doors like, a couple of cells up. And the kid said I looked like Elvis, we were having a laugh and a joke through the pipes and that, 'you look like fucking Elvis'. I said, 'you're funny mate' [unclear–00:23:13], you know having a laugh with him. I said, 'you look like Side Show Bob[6]' mate, you know, coming back to him, then 'fuck you I don't joke with white boys', you know what I mean. I said, 'why are you bringing the racial issue like?' And I can talk like that you know, because I like arguments, I enjoy it you know, I've got a good opinion on it yeah. And I said, 'fuck it mate you're like Aladdin[7] mate,' you know, not racial, and he said, 'why you being racist?'... and then my [person] next door was stirring him up, he says 'oh you've got a magic carpet and you've got a monkey as a best friend' and all this. I said 'no mate, I didn't say that mate'. He said, 'you're racist, you're racist like, fucking you Cafar', and all this like. I was like, 'No mate'.

In the above-mentioned extract, the racial compass is spinning and being spun with malicious intent. The reported conversation travels quickly from the benign to the racialised, the personal to the collective, as other prisoners start to involve themselves in its rising tempo. The episode reveals the continually negotiated context of race in late modern culture, the stress and strain of doing so and its disorienting ambiguity (Phillips, 2008). In this reported exchange, there are mocking references to features of the Disney cartoon, Aladdin, a magic carpet and a monkey. These film references are themselves imbued with racial stereotype, with Disney studios notorious for reproducing narrow, stereotypical characterisations of Arabic people and culture. The film is populated with characters who are more than literally two-dimensional. Amongst the 'barbarian' types, the treacherous thieves and belly dancers rise the heroes, lighter skinned and overtly Americanised. The principal villain, Jafar, is darkest skinned of all. Here, a children's cartoon becomes loaded ammunition, improvised, explosive and disruptive. Jonathan's identification of Muslims as the 'most racist' signals how they have assumed the position of black people in the 1970s and 1980s as a popular target for racialisation (see Earle and Phillips, 2012).

As in every research enterprise, leaving the field means leaving things behind, discovering missing pieces and gaps you would like to fill. Even though ethnography takes, and makes, more from the field than most research processes, the gaps and missing pieces in this account are frustrating. We don't know of whom Jonathan is speaking. We don't know why his interlocutor is stung by the allusion to Sideshow Bob, though presumably the hair is a clue, a large Afro style. The rapid escalation and the turn to conflicted ambiguities of racialisation are sharp. Jonathan's reaction is defensive and quickly invests in the new hate figure of the Muslim. It is a far cry from the harmonious switching described by Neal but also a long way from Abbot's embattled muteness and nostalgic retreatism.

Con-viviality, new ethnicities and confliction

One of the remarkable features of prison life is its peculiar combination of torpor and vitality, mixing, clustering and segregation. We have adapted Gilroy's (2004; 2005) ideas about conviviality to accommodate this prison concocted 'con-viviality' of which Jonathan's performance poetry is a prime example, but underlying this are more unstable, brittle relationships between prisoners of different ethnic origins. The diversity of the multicultural prison is a contested one, shifting and unpredictable in its balance between racialised hostility, white retreatism and ethnic presence. Indeed, Hall (1987) puzzled over this paradoxical dynamism in 1987 as he began formulating the 'new ethnicities' paradigm. How is it, he asked, 'that young black people in London today are marginalised, fragmented, unenfranchised, disadvantaged and dispersed. And yet, they look as if they own the territory'. That we should encounter something so similar in HMYOI Rochester, and, to a slightly lesser extent, HMP Maidstone is indicative of the enduring power and continuing appeal of Hall's work.

In fact, we are writing this chapter shortly after the death of Stuart Hall, *the* pre-eminent black scholar of our times. Hall's (1991–2000) groundbreaking work on 'new ethnicities' has been a powerful influence on our thinking. His analysis and propositions around new ethnicities exist in considerable tension with the once-dominant forms of national identification that characterised colonial modernity. These were the privileged birthright of the white bourgeoisie (and in the trickle down, the white working class, too). Unquestioned and invisible until relatively recently, these white identities are not easily or happily exchanged for the contingencies and uncertainties of ethnicity. Naidoo (2000) notes that being the racial 'other' and embracing an ethnicity that jostled 'the difference between nationality, ethnicity, language and political affiliation' was a difference 'learned as children' by his generation. The familiarity of determining a sense of self or presenting one on demand from shifting repertoires is, suggests Naidoo (2000: 79), relatively banal for him, but for his white 'English counterparts [who] took it for granted that their cultural identities held no such conflicts', it is a hard lesson, a lesson too far or a lesson they refuse to learn. Naidoo suggests that for his white English friends, difference is resented because ethnicity is something others do or have. Thus, for Anglo-white people in the fragmenting realities of the UK, national identity no longer offers them a tacit but stable reference point for their sense of self. Reluctant to locate themselves in the ambiguities of ethnicity, the white English feel homeless, an experience that echoes harshly back at them in the arid landscapes of a prison. This is the post-imperial melancholia that is vividly portrayed in Gilroy's book *After Empire*. In our prison study then, Abbott is poorly equipped to manage his encounter with this new world of new ethnicities. In a multicultural world, Abbott has no compass to guide him but drifts with the melancholic phantasms of his parent's identification with the National Front. Other white men in the prison, such as Neal with more experience of living with 'no nation but the imagination' (Walcott, 1986), find it easy enough to position themselves in a sliding scale between Asian, British and English. Some like Jonathan are confident of their bearings, but uncertain of the horizon, sensing 'that immense process of historical relativisation which is beginning to make the British, at least, feel just marginally marginal' (Hall, 1987: 45) but unsure of where it leaves him.

Hall (1978) is best known amongst a criminological readership for *Policing The Crisis*. Interestingly, Campbell (2013) points out how frequently it is overlooked that the defining incident of *Policing The Crisis*, the 'mugging' in the Handsworth district of Birmingham, involved 'three boys of mixed ethnic background' and that the victim was an older white Irishman. One of the boys sentenced to over ten years in prison for the 'mugging' was himself a young Irish migrant, and each of the three 'muggers' had 'diasporic backgrounds: Irish, Caribbean and Turkish' (Farred, 2010: 264). As the text established itself as a landmark in the analysis of crime, order and social control, the complex ethnic dynamics so central to the new ethnicities framework have been traduced to the familiar dyad of black and white: 'a robbery initiated in Handsworth by three black youths on an elderly white victim' (Hallsworth, 2005: 85). Campbell's article challenges the specific erasure of the Irish in Britain from such accounts and connects it to particular formations of Anglo-whiteness that narrow the empirical gaze. Significantly, for our purposes here, Campbell (2013) also draws attention to the potential impacts of research personnel and the ethnic composition of academic research communities. They impact on what becomes known and how it becomes known (see also Phillips and Bowling, 2003; Phillips and Earle, 2010; Earle, 2015). Tellingly, in the follow-up publication to *Policing the Crisis, The Empire Strikes Back* (CCCS, 1982), Gilroy acknowledges the influence of the ethnic mix of the research centre in setting research agendas and shaping research methodologies. For Gilroy, the unevenness of their text in relation to the experiences of Britain's South Asian communities was directly attributable to the fact that 'only one of us has roots in the Indian subcontinent whereas four of us are of Afro-Caribbean origin' (see also Modood, 1994). Hall's work and the implications of a new ethnicities paradigm involve recognising that everyone 'speaks' from certain places and histories, not just 'minorities'. This is particularly challenging if you are of the majority, more accustomed to speaking from nowhere and in generalities, which is frequently the case if you are a man, middle-class and/or Anglo-white. In subsequent critical reflections on how some experiences 'count' whilst others remain peripheral, Gilroy (cited in West, 1992: 701) elaborates on the theme, 'It's probably got to do with who owns and manages and controls the spaces in which such discussions appear, and the particular definition of race politics they want to trade in.' The idea of trading in 'race politics' challenges us to think about which voices count in the academy and in our host discipline.

For every African Caribbean male undergraduate at a Russell Group University, there are three African Caribbean men aged 18–24 in prison. In this age group, 7 per cent of the prison population is made up of African Caribbean men, but they constitute only 0.1 per cent of the undergraduate population of Russell Group universities (Sviensson, 2012). This makes it quite unlikely that researchers going into prisons are going to find themselves contending with the kind of dilemmas of ethnic (mis)recognition and (mis)identification that we have found to be such a stimulating aspect of our ethnography, because the researchers are likely to be white. Writing through these experiences as a two-person research team composed of contrasting identities has provided a particular kind of reflexive ethnography, perhaps more open to difference by being different, but hopefully not unique.

Closure

The racialised dynamics of late modern, multicultural prisons are bound to be diverse and cannot be ignored. One of the beauties of ethnography is its insistence on the specificity of its craft. The ethnography outlined here, and in other writings, does not tell the whole story of English prisons. We have been in two prisons in South East England. The men in these prisons encounter race, racism and ethnicity and give them shape in varying degrees of intelligibility. There are struggles taking place over their respective meanings, inside the prison, in wider society and in our own lives. Ethnography's anthropological origins mean that it is rarely seeking causes, especially not those that so energetically animate criminology and penology. Its defining and distinctive mission is to render more intelligible the many ways of being human in the world. It involves listening to people, seeing what they do, attempting to feel what they feel and hear what they say. It thereby creates an implicit politics of affinity. Prison ethnography, thus practised, embraces radical alterity, an openness to otherness (Hage, 2010; 2012). Our prison ethnography sheds some light on those struggles and offers resources that they might be rendered more adequate to the full breadth of human potential.

Notes

1. This is not meant to suggest Abbot necessarily posed a physical threat, but as we have discussed elsewhere (Phillips and Earle, 2010), Abbott epitomised the white racist

bogeyman, reminiscent of figures and experiences of racism from Coretta's past. The National Front's reputation for racist violence, and open valorisation of its political efficacy, was also a consideration, and a potentially unnerving feature of the prospective interview.
2. United Kingdom Independence Party.
3. Jamaican-derived patois and slang for the overt expression of 'blackness', from the aforementioned 'dreadlocks' of Rastafarianism.
4. Jamaican patois for 'What's going on?'
5. Derogatory reference to female genitalia.
6. From *The Simpsons*, US cartoon series, a criminal character, 'white', and known for his large head of eccentrically curly hair.
7. An explicitly ethnic reference to the person's non-white identity.

Further reading

Gilroy, P. (2012) *After Empire: Melancholia or Convivial Culture?* (London: Routledge).
Overing, J. and Passes, A. (eds) (2000) *The Anthropology of Love and Anger: The Aesthetics of Conviviality in Native Amazonia* (London: Routledge).
Phillips, C. (2012) *The Multicultural Prison – Ethnicity, Masculinity, and Social Relations among Prisoners* (Oxford: Oxford University Press).

References

Armstrong, E. G. (2004) 'Eminem's Construction of Authenticity', *Popular Music and Society*, 27, 335–55.
Barthes, R. (1981) *Camera Lucida: Reflections on Photography. Translated by Richard Howard, Hill and Wang* (New York, NY).
Bosworth, M. (1999) *Engendering Resistance: Agency and Power in Women's Prisons* (Aldershot: Dartmouth Publishing Company Limited).
Brah, A. (1996) *Cartographies of Diaspora* (London: Routledge).
Campbell, S. (2013) 'Policing the Irish: Whiteness, "Race" and British Cultural Studies', *European Journal of Cultural Studies*, 16, 135–54.
Carlen, P. (2010) 'Book Review of the Prisoner Society: Power, Adaptation and Social Life in an English Prison', *British Journal of Criminology*, 50, 977–80.
CCCS (1982) *The Empire Strikes Back: Race and Racism in 70s Britain* (London: Hutchinson in association with the Centre for Contemporary Cultural Studies).
Cheliotis, L. K. and Liebling, A. (2006) 'Race Matters in British Prisons: Towards a Research Agenda', *British Journal of Criminology*, 46, 286–317.
Crewe, B. (2009) *The Prisoner Society: Power, Adaptation and Social Life in an English Prison* (Oxford: Oxford University Press).
Drake, D. (2012) *Prisons, Punishment and the Pursuit of Security* (Basingstoke: Palgrave).
Drake, D. H. and Harvey, J. (2013) 'Performing the Role of Ethnographer: Processing and Managing the Emotional Dimensions of Prison Research', *International Journal of Social Research Methodology*, 17, 5, 489–501.
Duneier, M. (2004) 'Three Rules I Go by in My Ethnographic Research on Race and Racism', in M. Bulmer and J. Solomos (eds) *Researching Race and Racism* (Basingstoke: Palgrave).
Earle R. (2011a) 'Ethnicity, Multiculture and Racism in a Young Offenders' Institution', *The Prison Service Journal*, 197, 32–38.

Earle, R. (2011b) 'Boys' Zone Stories: Perspectives from a Young Men's Prison', *Criminology and Criminal Justice*, 11, 2, 129–43.

Earle R. (2014) 'Inside White-Racism, Social Relations and Ethnicity in an English Prison', in C. Phillips and C. Webster (eds) *New Directions in Race, Ethnicity and Crime* (London: Routledge).

Earle, R. (2015) 'Race, Ethnicity, Multiculture and Prison Life', in Crewe, B. and Jewkes, Y. (eds) *Handbook on Prisons*, Second edition (London: Routledge).

Equality, C. f. R. (2003a) *A Formal Investigation by the Commission for Racial Equality into Hm Prison Service of England and Wales – Part 2: Racial Equality in Prisons* (London: Commission for Racial Equality).

Equality, C. f. R. (2003b) *A Formal Investigation by the Commission for Racial Equality into Hm Prison Service of England and Wales – Part 1: The Murder of Zahid Mubarek* (London: Commission for Racial Equality).

Farred, G. (2010) 'Out of Context: Thinking Cultural Studies Diasporically', in T. Olaniyan and H. Sweet (eds) *The African Diaspora and the Disciplines* (Bloomington, IN: Indiana University Press).

Frosh, S., Phoenix, A. and Pattman, R. (2002) *Young Masculinities* (Basingstoke: Palgrave).

Gadd, D. and Dixon, B. (2011) *Losing the Race: Thinking Psychosocially About Racially Motivated Crime* (London: Karnac).

Gilroy, P. (2004) *After Empire: Melancholia or Convivial Culture?* (London: Routledge).

Gilroy, P. (2005) 'Multiculture, Double Consciousness and the "War on Terror" ', *Patterns of Prejudice*, 39, 431–43.

Goffman, E. (1961) *Asylums: Essays on the Social Situation of Mental Patients and Other Inmates* (New York: Anchor Books).

Hage, G. (2010) 'Negotiating the Passion for the Political', *Thesis*, 11, 100, 37–40.

Hage, G. (2012) 'Critical Anthropological Thought and the Radical Political Imaginary Today', *Critique of Anthropology*, 32, 3, 285–308.

Hall, S., Critcher, C., Jefferson, T., Clarke, J. and Roberts, B. (1978) *Policing the Crisis: Mugging, the State and Law and Order* (London: Macmillan).

Hall, S. (1987) 'Minimal Selves', in H. Bhabha (ed) *Identity: The Real Me* (London: Institute of Contemporary Arts).

Hall, S. (1991/2000) 'Old and New Identities, Old and New Ethnicities', in L. Back and J. Solomos (eds) *Theories of Race and Racism*, pp. 144–153 (London: Routledge).

Hallsworth, S. (2005) *Street Crime* (Cullompton: Willan Publishing).

HMCIP (2007) *Report of an Announced Inspection of Hmp Maidstone 19–23 February 2007* (London: HMCIP).

HMP Maidstone (2009) *Within the Walls: A History of Maidstone Prison, 1819–2009: [Brochure to Accompany an Exhibition at Maidstone Museum and Bentlif Art Gallery, May 28th–26th July 2009]* (Maidstone: Maidstone Prison).

Hollway, W. and Jefferson, T. (2000) *Doing Qualitative Research Differently: Free Association, Narrative and the Interview Method* (London: Sage).

Hughey, M. W. (2011) 'Backstage Discourse and the Reproduction of White Masculinities', *The Sociological Quarterly*, 52, 132–53.

Irwin, J. and Cressey, D. R. (1962) 'Thieves, Convicts and the Inmate Culture', *Social Problems*, 10, 142–55.

Jacobs, J. B. (1975) 'Stratification and Conflict among Prison Inmates', *Journal of Criminal Law & Criminology*, 66, 476–82.

Jacobs, J. B. (1977) *Stateville: The Penitentiary in Mass Society* (Chicago: The University of Chicago Press).

Jewkes, Y. (2014) 'An Introduction to "Doing Prison Research Differently" ', *Qualitative Inquiry,* 20, 387–91.

Kuumba, M. B. and Ajanaku, F. (1998) 'Dreadlocks: The Hair Aesthetics of Cultural Resistance and Collective Identity Formation', *Mobilization: An International Quarterly,* 3, 227–43.

Liebling, A. (1999) 'Doing Research in Prison: Breaking the Silence?' *Theoretical Criminology,* 3, 147–73.

Liebling, A. (2001) 'Whose Side Are We On? Theory, Practice and Allegiances in Prisons Research', *British Journal of Criminology,* 41, 472–84.

Liebling, A., Arnold, H. and Straub, C. (2012) *An Exploration of Staff-Prisoner Relationships at Hmp Whitemoor: Twelve Years On* (London: NOMS).

Merton, R. K. (1972) 'Insiders and Outsiders: A Chapter in the Sociology of Knowledge', *American Journal of Sociology,* 78, 9–47.

Modood, T. (1994) 'Political Blackness and British Asians', *Sociology,* 28, 859–76.

Naidoo, R. (2000) 'No Place Like Home', in J. Rutherford (ed) *The Art of Life – on Living, Love and Death* (London: Lawrence & Wishart Ltd.).

Nayak, A. (2003) *Race, Place and Globalization: Youth Cultures in a Changing World* (Oxford: Berg).

NOMS (2008) *Race Review 2008: Implementing Race Equality in Prisons – Five Years On* (London: NOMS).

Phillips, C. and Bowling, B. (2002) 'Ethnicities, Racism, Crime, and Criminal Justice', in M. Maguire, R. Morgan and R. Reiner (eds) *The Oxford Handbook of Criminology* (Oxford: Oxford University Press).

Phillips, C. and Bowling, B. (2003) 'Racism, Race and Ethnicity: Developing Minority Perspectives in Criminology', *British Journal of Criminology,* 43, 269–90.

Phillips, C. and Earle, R. (2010) 'Reading Difference Differently: Identity, Epistemology, and Prison Ethnography', *British Journal of Criminology,* 50, 360–78.

Phillips, C. (2012) *The Multicultural Prison: Ethnicity, Masculinity, and Social Relations among Prisoners* (Oxford: Oxford University Press).

Ray, L., Smith, D. A. and Wastell, L. (2004) 'Shame, Rage and Racist Violence', *British Journal of Criminology,* 44, 350–68.

Rhodes, L. (2012) 'Ethnographic Imagination in the Field of the Prison', *Paper Presented at the 'Resisting the Eclipse Symposium'* (Milton Keynes: The Open University).

Rowe, A. (2014) 'Situating the Self in Prison Research: Power, Identity, and Epistemology', *Qualitative Inquiry,* 20, 404–16.

Sharma, S., Hutnyk, J. and Sharma, A. (eds) (1996) *Dis-Orienting Rhythms: The Politics of the New Asian Dance Music* (London: Zed Books).

Sibbitt, R. (1997) *The Perpetrators of Racial Harassment and Racial Violence* (London: Home Office).

Sparks, R., Bottoms, A. and Hay, W. (1996) *Prisons and the Problem of Order* (Oxford: Oxford University Press).

Sviensson, K. P. (2012) 'Introduction', in K. P. Sveinsson (ed) *Criminal Justice v Racial Justice: Minority Ethnic Overrepresentation in the Criminal Justice System* (London: Runnymede Trust).

Sykes, G. M. (1958) *The Society of Captives: A Study of a Maximum Security Prison* (Princeton: Princeton University Press).

Tonry, M. (1994) 'Racial Disproportion in Us Prisons', *British Journal of Criminology,* 34, 97–115.

Twine, F. W. (2000) 'Racial Ideologies and Racial Methodologies', in F. W. Twine and J. W. Warren (eds) *Racing Research, Researching Race: Methodological Dilemmas in Critical Race Studies* (New York: New York University Press).

Wacquant, L. (1999) '"Suitable Enemies": Foreigners and Immigrants in the Prisons of Europe', *Punishment & Society,* 1, 215–22.

Wacquant, L. (2001) 'Deadly Symbiosis: When Ghetto and Prison Meet and Merge', in D. Garland (ed) *Mass Imprisonment: Social Causes and Consequences,* pp. 82–120 (London: Sage).

Wacquant, L. (2006) 'Penalisation, Depoliticisation, Racialization: On the Over-Incarceration of Immigrants in the European Union', in S. Armstrong and L. McAra (eds) *Perspectives on Punishment: The Contours of Control* (Oxford: Oxford University Press).

Walcott, D. (1986) *Collected Poems 1948–1984* (New York: Farrar, Straus and Giroux).

West, C. (1992) 'The Postmodern Crisis of the Black Intellectuals', in L Grossberg, C Nelson and P. A. Treichler (eds) *Cultural Studies* (London: Routledge).

13
Finding Secrets and Secret Findings: Confronting the Limits of the Ethnographer's Gaze

Deborah H. Drake

Introduction

Ethnography, inevitably, can only provide a partial account of the culture, society or field under study. James Clifford (1986: 7) wrote, 'Even the best ethnographic texts... are systems, or economies, of truth. Power and history work through them, in ways their authors cannot fully control.' Here, Clifford was referring to the *construction* of ethnographic writing and the fact that ethnographers inevitably must translate the reality of informants into a finished, narrative account. It is the ethnographer who ultimately chooses what to include or exclude in their authored expression of the cultures, lives and meanings that were observed and described to them in the field. Far from threatening the empirical value of the ethnographic endeavour, its partial nature can mirror 'the partiality of cultural and historical truths, the ways they are systematic and exclusive' (p. 6). Hammersley and Atkinson (1995: 255) argue, 'The relationship between the ethnographic text and its subject-matter may not be entirely straightforward. But it is not totally arbitrary... There are social actors and social life outside the text, and there are referential relationships between them.'

The limitations and partiality of ethnography are aspects of the craft that must be acknowledged by the ethnographer throughout the whole of the research process. Both the collection and the *interpretation of the meaning* of particular narratives within the society or culture being studied are fundamental to the practice of ethnography, and it is these narratives that form the substance of evocative and nuanced ethnographic representation. However, during an ethnographic endeavour, some stories from the field only seem to emerge in fragments or as partial accounts from a single informant. Some of these narratives are verifiable and 'factual' – for example, when an informant describes an incident or event they shared with someone else. The framing and meaning of the event will, of course, be imbued with the subjective experience of the storyteller(s), but the basic facts of the narrative can be corroborated through other sources. There are other stories or cultural practices, however, that an ethnographer might begin to uncover that will be difficult to verify, such as when an informant discloses or hints at a guarded secret. Moreover, an ethnographer may piece together fragments of a story from the field that informants want to actively keep hidden. During ethnographic work, the researcher sometimes has a sense of or hears the whisper of a taboo subject or an underground cultural practice that informants will not confirm and which has not been directly observed by the ethnographer himself or herself. Secret, taboo or more 'deviant' aspects of a given society, culture or organisation are always the most difficult to research and capture. Whilst the study of underground practices or activities may not be the focus of a particular ethnographic study when the ethnographer becomes aware that something clandestine may be going on, it can be troubling because it may suggest that she has not achieved full acceptance, has failed to gain a sense of mastery over the field (Drake and Harvey, 2014) or something meaningful is being missed.

In this chapter, I consider the moments during ethnographic practice when realities or meanings are 'glimpsed at', but are not fully revealed to the researcher. To do so, I draw on ethnographic research experiences during two projects conducted in English men's maximum-security prisons (see Drake, 2012, 2014). I consider some of the moments during these projects when organisational secrets seemed to emerge but which could not be fully verified. In the closed, secretive and often paranoid environment of the prison, some aspects of the field can remain obscured to the outsider researcher, no matter how much time he or she spends with informants or observing in the field. The chapter considers the potential relationship between the conditionality of prison officer collegial culture and the emergence of 'dark' practices. It is argued that the deep, enduring tensions between care and custody, brutality and punishment that can accompany the prison officer role can also create structures and spaces in which hidden practices can be both exercised and kept hidden. A particular focus of the chapter is to consider the challenges for the ethnographer when only a sliver view of clandestine practices is obtained.

Secrecy in groups and organisations

Simmel (1950: 463) provided the first sociological theorisations of secrecy and argued that it was a 'universal sociological form' – meaning that the potentially negative contents of a secret are, in some respects and in many situations, irrelevant. It is the significance of secrecy in the maintenance of social structure that Simmel was concerned with. Goffman (1959: 142), likewise, discussed the importance of 'inside' secrets, 'whose possession marks an individual as being a member of a group and helps the group feel separate and different from those individuals who are not "in the know" '. He further stated: 'Inside secrets give objective intellectual content to subjectively felt social distance.' Thus, as Simmel (1950) also noted, even though the content of a secret may be incidental, it is the exclusion from possession of it that gives a secret its cultural and psychological power. Secrets bind individuals together whilst simultaneously excluding 'outsiders'.

The interpersonal and social significance of secrets is an area under-considered in the research literature. However, recent sociological research on secrecy in organisations has been conducted by Chris Grey (2014), who considered the power and strength of secrecy in relation to one of the most secretive operations in living memory – the workings of Bletchley Park during World War II. Grey's analyses of Bletchley Park are based on declassified papers, interviews with veterans and published, publicly available first-hand accounts of Bletchley. This historical and sociological work on Bletchley Park offers insights on aspects of social, cultural and organisational secret keeping that have previously and perhaps inevitably been limited due to the inherent difficulty associated with researching organisational secrets and secret organisations.

Grey (2014) examines the culture of secrecy which operated at Bletchley. He outlines the instructions staff were given on matters of secrecy, the security checks they were subjected to, the conventions of 'not telling' and 'not asking' that developed and the 'rigid compartmentalisation of work and restriction of information... that was central to [Bletchley Park]' (p. 112). Grey notes the apparently durable seal of this secrecy culture and its longevity beyond the closure of Bletchley and draws out the elements that seemed to secure the strong secrecy culture that was established there.

In further work on processes of secrecy, Costas and Grey (2014) examine the theoretical and social dynamics of secrecy, as opposed to the informational aspects of secrets. By so doing, they make clear the power that secrets or, more precisely, 'secret keeping' can wield within organisations. They take a neutral approach to examining secrecy in organisations, choosing analytical examples that are not compromised by moral considerations of the secrets themselves or by salacious examples which may be drawn from secret organisations. By examining secrecy as a social process (as opposed to examining the informational elements of secrets themselves), Costas and Grey are able to hone in on the interpersonal dynamics that surround secrecy in organisations. Thus, they illustrate that the mere act of secret keeping wields power and results in organisational consequences that are entirely independent of the information that is being kept secret. They argue:

> Secrecy is constituted through social interactions and, specifically, needs to be understood in terms of its conditions and consequences for identity and

> control. By depicting social process in terms of conditions and consequences we suggest that what is at stake is not a linear cause-and effect relationship but an ongoing, iterative dynamic relationship.
>
> (Costas and Grey, 2014: 2)

Two particular social 'stakes' are identified by Costas and Grey in relation to secrecy: identity, and the capacity of secrecy to establish in-groups and out-groups, and control, and the way power can be maintained by secret keeping. With respect to identity, they suggest that a social understanding of secrecy recognises that 'secrecy is not just about the legitimate or illegitimate concealment of valuable information, but is also about the social aspects of organizational life, such as the cementing of group identity' (p. 8). Being trusted to keep a secret has the capacity to make people feel special and important, and thus it also has an impact on individual identity. With respect to control, the work of Grey (2014) and Costas and Grey (2014) make it clear that secrecy is often highly associated with the exercise of social power. Placing limitations on the sharing of information can be a means by which interests and boundaries are protected. The keeping of secrets can create the impression of special knowledges in order to bolster power. Thus, the work of both Grey (2014) and Costas and Grey (2014) make it clear that practices of secrecy can impact heavily on both group and personal identities and that acts of secret keeping enable, exert and require control.

The issue of secrecy has been discussed in the ethnographic literature by a few researchers in relation to family secrets (Poulos, 2008), religious communities of Indonesia (George, 1993) and Africa (Diamitani, 2011) and the archive on the secret police in Romania (Verdery, 2013). In addition, there have also been a number of studies in sociology and criminology which have discussed the ethical dilemmas of encountering corrupt practices in the field, particularly in relation to policing (Norris, 1993; Reiner, 2000; Marks, 2004; Rowe, 2007). Whilst some of these accounts discuss the difficulty a researcher faces in gaining access to private information or how to ethically respond to the discovery of hidden practices, there are few that focus explicitly on encounters with secrecy (but see also Chapter 14 in this volume, where Rhodes discusses some related ideas). Goffman (1959: 141) discussed the desire of both individuals and groups to engage in 'information control' wherein a given audience is not provided with 'destructive information about the situation that is being defined for them'. Goffman states: 'a team must be able to keep its secrets and have its secrets kept.'

Noticing forms of secret keeping amongst a group is not necessarily unexpected during an ethnography. However, encountering secret keeping that seems to cloak negative or possibly corrupt information or practices presents ethical and practical challenges for the ethnographer (as the policing literature attests, see Norris, 1993; Marks, 2004). Whilst there are different types of secrets that a group or organisation might hold, this chapter is primarily concerned with what Goffman identifies as 'dark secrets'. These are secret facts about an organisation, group or subgroup that are incompatible with the image that the group wants to convey. Goffman argues that such dark secrets are 'double secrets', stating that 'one is the crucial fact this is hidden and another is the fact that crucial facts have not been openly admitted'. For the ethnographer encountering the suggestion of a 'dark secret', the 'crucial fact' of the secret may or may not be meaningful or worthy of exposure and condemnation, but finding a hidden sphere of the field presents a frustrating dilemma for the ethnographer.

Secrecy in high-security prisons

The illustrative examples I will outline in this chapter are drawn from two related research projects (see Drake, 2012, 2014). The initial project was an ethnographic study of prison life in two English maximum-security prisons (Full Sutton and Whitemoor) in 2005. The subsequent study, which took place from 2007 to 2009, was an extension of the first and included the other three English long-term, maximum-security prisons (Frankland, Wakefield and Long Lartin). This second study, however, was conducted in collaboration with prison officers, who I had trained in ethnographic methods. The purpose of this second study was, in part, concerned with understanding the meaning and experience of imprisonment for prisoners. But it was also concerned with providing prison officers with an opportunity to gain a more nuanced understanding of prisoner experiences through ethnography (see Part III of this volume for examinations of the relationship between ethnography and practice). The scope, methods and dilemmas of this project are discussed more fully elsewhere (see Drake, 2014). This chapter is my first written attempt to consider material that is gleaned from the field during both of these research projects and which relates to hidden or 'underground' elements of prison life and prison officer culture. Before doing so, however, I first set the scene by considering the 'security environment' which permeates maximum-security prisons in England and the role that secrecy sometimes plays in these prisons.

> From the moment you reach the outer gate you feel the intensity of the environment. Staff wait in long queues as everyone arrives for their shift at the same time. Officers speak of feeling concerned about reaching their wing on time, but no one *really* wants to enter the prison early to avoid being late. At the gate, staff pass through full body metal detectors, are physically wanded down,[1] and on occasion are randomly searched by hand. After being searched, officers re-fasten watches, belts, staves, key pouches and chains,

> and groups of staff are slowly fed into the prison through the airlock.[2] After queuing again to retrieve keys and radios everyone must then face long walks through a countless series of doors and gates to get to their home departments or wings. The oppressive environment hangs in the air as groups of staff trudge through hollow and austere concrete corridors.
>
> (Excerpt from field notes)

As the above field note excerpt indicates, the volume of security measures in maximum-security prisons in England can be felt simply upon entering these establishments. There is a seemingly endless array of procedures, systems, codes and contingency plans all concerned with maintaining security. There is a tangible tension in the atmosphere that is the result of a focused emphasis on security, rooted in institutional memory and manifest in an underlying sense of anxiety – amongst the staff – of the potential of what might happen in the event of a serious incident, escape or the outbreak of disorder. Across the five long-term, maximum-security prisons, the staff operate under a constant background of 'potential disaster'. In these prisons, the anticipation of what might hypothetically 'go wrong' has seemingly become inextricably intertwined with organisational as well as living memory of real incidents that actually had occurred (e.g. serious assaults, riots or escapes) in the past and the consequences that subsequently resulted (see Drake, 2006; 2012). Recollections and frequently told narratives originating in lived institutional experience of terrifying incidents with riotous prisoners, serious staff assaults or the fall-out from previous high-profile escapes hold real purchase in staff cultures and in the minds of individual members of staff. The accumulated history of disorder in long-term maximum-security prisons in England is important to understanding the cultural structures that have come to shape what I have described elsewhere as the 'habitus' of maximum security (Drake, 2011), wherein almost every aspect of maximum-security prison life has come to be viewed through the filter of security.

Security maintenance, as practised through intelligence gathering, surveillance, searching procedures or other physical security measures, orients so much of the daily working lives of prison staff that it can create a kind of 'security thinking' that seems to spread, as if contagious, to almost every aspect of prison work. Although it might be expected that the concept of security would be inextricably associated with practices of secrecy, this was not necessarily the case in all aspects of the day-to-day practices of high-security prison staff, particularly when it related to information about the general population of prisoners. For example, intelligence information about prisoners was fairly freely shared amongst members of staff and with their managers (and in the presence of this prison ethnographer). Presumably the relative powerlessness of prisoners and the operational goal of maintaining security and (as a result, control) meant that certain kinds of 'intelligence' information were willingly and unproblematically shared with anyone who was inside the prison but who was not a prisoner. However, practices of secrecy were apparent in other aspects of high-security prison work.

There were some formally sanctioned secrecy practices in high-security prisons which were a matter of routine. For example, the management of high-profile prisoners who were also categorised as 'high risk' often involved the need for secrecy around their movements or other arrangements to do with their secure custody. In addition, at the time of the research, high-security prisons had groups of staff called Dedicated Search Teams (DST), which, in some respects, fulfilled a policing role within each prison. These teams, as a matter of routine, could turn their sights on both individual prisoners and individual members of staff or wider staff or prisoner groups (e.g. through unannounced searching of staff or prisoner areas or through clandestine intelligence gathering operations) in the interests of maintaining security.

Formally sanctioned secrecy practices coupled with the heavy security focus in maximum-security prisons could serve to create an atmosphere of tension, paranoia and distrust not just amongst staff and prisoners but also amongst individual members of staff and different staff groups. This was especially true if the security regime turned in on itself, which could occur exceptionally when a member of staff was suspected of inappropriate behaviour with prisoners or other prohibited actions undertaken during the course of their duties. Secrecy then became a paramount concern to the few members of staff who were investigating the matter, and thus the control of information became crucial, as the secrecy of the operation played a key role in the gathering of evidence. However, operations such as these planted seeds of distrust that could divide some staff groups quite significantly. For example, in two of the maximum-security prisons in which I conducted research, the DST were viewed with hostility by a number of staff due to the surveillance and intelligence-gathering activities they sometimes conducted on staff. The DST seemed to have a reputation not dissimilar to an 'internal affairs' department that is concerned with identifying corruption or other illegitimate or inappropriate practices. Thus, some members of staff would actively (though clandestinely) attempt to undermine or besmirch the reputation of the DST – either as a group or individually.

In addition to the formal and official uses of secrecy in high-security prisons, informal secret keeping was also apparent within and between staff groups. Moreover, the tension of the maximum-security prison environment seemed to create a potent atmosphere for the proliferation of practices of secrecy, which, in turn, played a role in creating and maintaining in-group and out-group affiliations between staff groups. The strength of certain elements of the staff cultures that operated in high-security prisons meant that individual members of staff or staff groups who undertook duties or exhibited attitudes that contradicted firmly held beliefs within the wider prison officer culture could be viewed with deep mistrust by other members of staff (see also Crawley and Crawley, 2008; Sim, 2008). For example, staff who delivered rehabilitative or 'offending behaviour' programmes or those who ministered to prisoners' health-care needs were sometimes viewed with suspicion by pockets of the wider staff group. These members of staff could be seen as 'insider-outsiders' and, as a result, were sometimes labelled by other groups of staff as 'untrustworthy' or 'not one of "us"'. Staff who were thus labelled would not enjoy the same levels of camaraderie in the workplace as some of their colleagues, and due to their perceived 'sympathy' with prisoners, they were excluded from informally defined staff cliques who, for example, actively concerned themselves with the punishment of prisoners – either in conversation or in the way they carried out their duties. At the extreme end of these invisible dividing lines within the staff culture, 'out-group' staff could be ostracised and subjected to harassment or bullying. Bullying between members of staff took place in private, and these practices were, unsurprisingly, shrouded in secrecy. Likewise, the members of staff who were preoccupied with the punishment of prisoners were more closed off and seemingly secretive towards anyone who was deemed an 'outsider' (either as a member of staff or as an ethnographer), and their ranks could close very quickly if questions about their practices were raised.

The bullying of certain members of staff and the suggestion of cultural practices that seemed to be explicitly oriented towards the punishment of prisoners blurs into secrecy of another kind – the intentional obscuring of inappropriate or prohibited practices. These categories of practices can be the most difficult for the ethnographer to observe because they require the admission of and exposure to carefully guarded secrets. Uncovering deviant practices in prisons is a complex, multilayered and high-stakes task. Such practices may range along a scale that, at one end, includes more transgressive acts, which are not illegal, but are in contradiction to policy or staff culture and, at the other, include activities which are, in fact, legally prohibited. In either case, these activities are the 'double secrets' that Goffman (1959) identified (referred to above) and which staff groups will closely guard and deny when questioned about them.

Encountering 'dark' secrets in the field

The parts of a cultural landscape that may be blanketed or kept secret by members of a group should be respected by the ethnographer when privacy surrounding a particular issue appears to be collectively agreed and/or culturally important because the exposure of such secrets is not always necessary in gaining a deep and nuanced understanding of the field or culture being studied. However, there are other situations when an ethnographer might begin to uncover hidden stories that are seemingly distressing or deeply meaningful for certain individuals or a group of informants. Under these conditions, uncovering concealed strands within the matrix of cultural practice can facilitate prisms and depths of understanding that would otherwise be one dimensional and shallow. At the same time, however, conducting ethnographic research in closed institutions or other hard-to-access settings is a rare privilege that may be accompanied by a responsibility to call attention to practices which would raise public alarm. Despite the potential vital importance of uncovering hidden practices or narratives, doing ethnography is complexified when the ethnographer happens upon only a hint that there are cultural practices that are clandestine and cannot gather 'hard evidence' of either their presence or their absence.

The hidden area of prisons, which I want to focus on first, seemed to lie beneath the more apparent and sometimes blatant conditionality of prison officer culture, briefly discussed in the last section of this chapter (also see Crawley and Crawley, 2008). The existence of clique-like subgroups amongst prison officers could create an unmistakable atmosphere that gave the impression that there were fine layers of cultural practices that needed to be carefully observed and peeled back:

> It is startlingly evident that an individual prison establishment is a collection of many different cultures and micro-climates. Each residential area or wing seems to have its own atmospheric texture and each can feel uniquely different, as though you are moving between entirely different prisons each time you enter a different residential unit. This change of atmosphere seems attributable as much to the 'society of staff' as it is 'the society of captives', although wing design, layout and facilities seem to play important roles too. Moreover, the 'society of staff' allocated to a residential location in a prison changes according to shifts, with different teams working together on different shift patterns. Staff teams are often organised through 'divisions' or 'divs' that include a core team who all tend to work the same shift pattern on a given wing. A wing might, therefore, have two 'divisions' of staff, where, for example, 'Red Div' is allocated to one shift pattern and 'Black Div' is allocated to another (though this specific language differs from prison to prison). Thus, there are sometimes micro-climates within microclimates wherein the atmosphere of a wing might change fairly significantly, depending on which 'Div' is working.
>
> (excerpt from field notes)

The atmospheric changes, described above, can be clearly observed and felt not only by an 'outsider' – for example, the ethnographer – or by prisoners, but also by other prison officers who may be randomly allocated to a particular wing in order to make up the numbers (due to staff shortages or sickness, for example). Whilst, on one hand, prison officers will often verbally describe their collegial relationships as cohesive and supportive, they will, on the other hand, sometimes ignore or ostracise certain members of the staff group. Crawley (2004: 185–98) has discussed group rivalry in and between prisons. Prison staff will often fiercely defend the establishment in which they work in the presence of prison officers from other prisons. However, at a local level, wing-to-wing rivalries between groups of staff are common.

> I am on [X] Wing all day today. It is hard going. I am currently in the centre office [where officers are often located] and I feel tension, as though I am unwelcome. A governor grade has just come in. The tension does not improve. She asks one of the officers if all is well on the wing. She receives a perfunctory: 'all present and correct.' She acknowledges me and asks if I am getting what I need. I say: 'I'm just getting a feel for things.' She seems to want to leave and does so. After she has left, the member of staff she was speaking to phones a colleague to let them know she is on her way. The conversation is curt and factual, I suspect because I am there and he should not be 'warning' his colleague that a governor is on her way...
>
> ...
>
> It is now evening and a member of staff has come for the evening shift who is not normally allocated to this wing. He is not made to feel welcome either. He seems reluctant to speak openly to me here, although we have spoken before and he has been quite friendly. He suggests we perhaps speak somewhere else, another time. He doesn't look comfortable here. I go off to spend association time with the prisoners.
>
> [Excerpt from field notes]

The wing described above had a reputation for being a 'bad wing' by staff due, they argued, to the 'nature' of the prisoner population allocated there. Prisoners on this wing were described by staff as being exceptionally dangerous and hard to manage. However, the prisoners described the staff as being inflexible, unhelpful and, at times, brutal. The member of staff referred to in my field notes who worked the evening shift, but did not normally work on that wing, subsequently discussed with me how ostracised he felt whenever he had to work there. He was a newer member of staff and felt he had not yet earned the respect of his colleagues, especially those on that particular wing. This, he felt, was specifically related to the way he spoke to prisoners, which was with courtesy and respect. His experiences spoke to the fact that some 'in-group, out-group' delineations were drawn by staff on the basis of conflicting approaches and attitudes to prison officer work. Where these divisions existed, hostilities and divisions between colleagues could develop and were apparent.

> Yes I think it can be clique-y and I think it depends where you work. Some areas are more clique-y than others, some wings are more clique-y than others. The thing that annoys me the most about this job is that the more you try to better yourself or diversify the more you become ostracised. So I think that is the most really, really annoying thing about this job.
>
> (Prison Officer)

The division of opinion amongst prison officers on the different ways of performing the role of prison officer is well reported in the research literature (Crawley and Crawley, 2008; Scott, 2008; Sim, 2008; Liebling et al., 2010; Tait, 2011). During my own ethnographic work in prisons, the most obvious divisions often arose in relation to what was viewed by the dominant staff groups as the 'right way' of speaking to prisoners:

> I would say it is more with the interacting with prisoners, where you see it the most. We got trained, that you need to go out there and talk to prisoners, etc. – to build up dynamic security, but you don't see that as much. There are officers who just... very rarely do you see them talking to prisoners or maybe they do talk to them, but they talk to them differently to what I do and it's a bit of an 'us' and 'them' sometimes. If you are breaking that, it's not looked upon well... I have heard it mentioned around the jail, guys who have worked on other wings who talk to prisoners and people say: 'what are you doing? We don't do that here or you don't address them as Mr.' There is an officer who trained with me and calls every prisoner Mr and his name is being bandied around and he's been told not to do it.
>
> (Prison Officer)

Disclosures of this nature, coupled with observations of staff divisiveness and the 'insider-outsider' positioning between some prison officers, provided a glimpse into aspects of the conditionality of prison officer collegial relationships that seemed only to scratch the surface.

During both research studies, the staff who more openly spoke about the potentially conditional nature of prison officer culture were those who delivered offending behaviour programmes (though they were not the only members of staff who seemed to experience ostracism, at times). These staff were often viewed by the main body of discipline staff as 'care bears' or conversely as 'con shy'.

> ...the wing I was on wasn't too bad, it was more off-wing, other people looking at that wing and saying: 'oh you work with nonces[3] and stuff' because they were sex offenders... There is still a bit of that there, but it is not as out in the open, it is not as blatant, it is not as obvious.
>
> (Prison Officer)

It was, perhaps, easier for those who worked on programme delivery to discuss the difficulties they had with some of their colleagues because they had support from fellow programmes staff and, also, because they tended not to have to work closely with wing-based colleagues. There were, however, residential members of staff too who alluded to difficult relationships with colleagues and the suspicion that there could be a darker side of prison officer culture. However, I was not able to draw out explicit disclosures on these issues, only furtive and nervous suggestions.

During some of the informal conversations, I had with staff I got the impression that there was an element of fear that could surround collegial relationships. If an officer wanted to 'fit in' and be protected by his or her colleagues, he or she had to carry out their role in a specific way, even if that went against his or her own conscience. This was perceived by some staff as a high-stakes dilemma because not 'fitting in' was viewed as being potentially dangerous. Good collegial relationships were felt to be crucial because, firstly, the staff generally felt they needed to rely on colleagues if the need for 'back up' arose in a confrontation with prisoners. But, secondly, it was also suggested to me that a member of staff who was viewed as an 'outcast' could be 'set up' and deliberately placed in a dangerous situation wherein prisoners would be given false information about the 'outcast' member of staff who might then experience some form of retaliation from prisoners. Whilst this sort of scenario was not observed or explicitly reported to me during the field work in any of the prisons, it was a fear that some members of staff seemed to feel extremely concerned about.

Quotations like the two that follow only obliquely reference the possibility of a potentially darker side of prison officer collegial relationships, but they do signal the sharp divisions within the staff group that can manifest in ostracism and bullying.

> ...you know you get trained to do stuff... but when we get on the wing you have got to conform because you don't want to be seen as an outsider.
>
> (Prison Officer)

> You are fighting two battles, in a sense, aren't you? The prisoners might not like you, and then if the other officers don't like you, it's isolating.
>
> (Prison Officer)

Encountering a desire amongst the staff to conceal aspects of collegial relationships from an outsider does not necessarily mean that they were concealing anything untoward. As Simmel (2005) noted, secrecy in and of itself is not inherently good or bad. For example, George (1993: 236) has argued that insiders might want to maintain secrecy from an outsider ethnographer in order to 'protect their sense of being and their control of meaning'. However, the clear existence of small groups of staff 'cliques' and the evident fear and concern of some staff about being labelled an 'outsider' seemed to suggest that prison officer work could be deliberately and actively made more difficult if you were deemed to be an 'outcast' by your colleagues. Moreover, the presence of some apparently very tight and closed staff groups, coupled with some troubling disclosures from prisoners, seemed to suggest that some of the secret keeping I encountered were due to the concealment of 'dark secrets' and crucial facts.

Getting inside insider secrets

Prison work can be a high-stakes enterprise in prisons of every security category. However, in maximum-security prisons in England, a 30-year history of riot, disorder and staff–prisoner conflict had left a seemingly indelible mark on the institutional memories and on the discipline staff groups in each of these prisons, albeit in uneven ways and through differing means (Drake, 2006, 2009, 2012). The strength and perceived threat of the recurrence of these histories continued to shape staff cultural practices in myriad ways. As suggested above (and see Drake, 2011, 2012), the strength of the 'security regime' in high-security prisons is difficult to subvert because the ideology of security permeates, influences and regulates practitioner discretion in ways that are self-reinforcing. However, despite the pervasiveness of 'security' and its seemingly ubiquitous influence over the thoughts and actions of prison staff, the suggestion of underground practices amongst prison officers indicated that the 'security regime' may not reach into the deepest corners of prison officer culture.

In more than one of the five maximum-security prisons in which I carried out research, I was told troubling stories by prisoners about staff impropriety. These stories ranged from exploitation of the vulnerabilities of prisoners to outright brutality against them to descriptions of financial corruption (e.g. trafficking drugs in prison or extorting goods and services on the outside from prisoners' friends or families). Fully verifying the authenticity of these stories for the purposes of officially reporting them was not possible. However, over the course of the two projects, there were unexpected instances when I became privy to 'insider knowledges' either by being in the right place at the right time to overhear a partial conversation or via a few members of staff who were willing to corroborate some of the stories that prisoners had told me. In any event, a second-hand story corroborated by another second-hand source remains an unverified rumour. Accounts of impropriety that are unverifiable are not unique amongst academic work on closed institutions or criminal justice professionals such as the police (see, for example, Norris, 1993; Carlton, 2007), and they present particular dilemmas for the researcher, especially in relation to both the responsibility of privileged access and maintaining academic rigour. Whilst

I therefore do not deem it appropriate to describe the unverified allegations that were made during my research, it is of interest to at least examine them in categorical form.

The alleged deviant practices of the staff were suggested by prisoners to range along a scale of transgressive practices. These activities were reported to be carried out by small groups of staff – operating at extreme ends or the fringes of the 'security regime'. Allegedly, these were officers who would engage in *sub rosa* activities that might be categorised as various forms of corruption. For example, financial gain or acquisitive corruption, 'punishment' of prisoners or brutal corruption or, more curiously, care for prisoners or what might be called palliative 'corruption' (Blundo and de Sardan, 2006).

This final category of alleged underground staff activity – which might be called palliative 'corruption' – is of a different order and character to the other two and requires separate consideration. In some respects, it might provide potential evidence of the authenticity of the other deviant practices, because, as an inversion of harmful corruption, it speaks to the capacity for normative brutality and callousness within maximum-security prison staff culture. That is, if 'care' for prisoners – as manifest in acts of human kindness or tactile comforting (e.g. an arm around a shoulder or a comfort-giving hug) – could be viewed within staff and prisoner cultures as a form of corrupt practice, then it makes the possibility of normative brutality against prisoners more plausible. Palliative 'corruption' was a secret practice that was relatively more easily uncovered during the research, but it was still difficult to view or discuss. Additionally, it may also have (in certain circumstances) slipped into actually prohibited activities when clandestine relationships were formed between a member of staff and a prisoner and, thus, it could shift from a rather benign (and benevolent) secret to a secret that concealed a strictly prohibited action.

Against the historical-contextual background of long-term maximum-security prisons, the hegemonic masculinity inherent in the prison environment, as discussed by Sim (2008), could result in extreme and perverse permutations of cultural practices. The concept of practical norms, as discussed and deployed by de Sardan (2008) in his examination of African public services, provides helpful insights in understanding corrupt or informal practices (thanks to Tomas Max Martin for bringing this concept to my attention; see Chapter 22 of this volume). De Sardan's work considers the problem of everyday corruption and examines it as a social activity that is regulated by tacit, informal rules or norms that differ from official or legal rules. Practical norms, in de Sardan's terms, include practices that do not follow official, formal policies but which are nevertheless regulated by tacitly agreed schemas. During the period in which I carried out my ethnographic work in maximum-security prisons, and as suggested in the earlier sections of this chapter, there were two cultural dimensions which I would argue were pivotal factors in determining and shaping the tacit understandings the staff had about performing the role of prison officer. Of particular significance during the research were, firstly, a distrust and suspicion of members of staff who attempted to 'care' for prisoners or those who delivered offending behaviour programmes (as discussed above). Secondly, due to the fact that maximum-security prisons hold 'some of the most difficult and dangerous prisoners in the country' (HMCIP, 2002: 9), the delivery of 'punishment' was seen to be a key part of the prison officer's role by some officers. Whilst these two manifestations of prison staff culture are commonly reported in prisons across the UK and elsewhere, the high-stakes nature of the high-security prison environment meant that the 'suspicion of care for prisoners' and the 'need to deliver punishment' could be, arguably, more easily activated within cultural subgroups of these prisons to serve nefarious intentions. That is, the boundaries of informal practical norms could, arguably, be more easily pushed to extreme limits, given the harsh status quo of the maximum-security prison environment.

Sim (2004; 2008) has noted that violence perpetrated by the state in the exercise of criminal justice is a neglected field. He argues that where it is discussed within criminology, it is considered 'the result of an individual, unmanageable state servant deviating from cultural and institutional norms that are otherwise benevolent and supportive' (2004: 115). Likewise, the same arguments are often presented by state officials when specific questions of corruption arise. Despite the limited capacity I had as an ethnographer to fully reveal the 'dark secrets' of prison officer cultural practices in high-security prisons, the partial view that I was able to obtain suggested that corrupt or informal practices were not committed by lone, renegade state servants but by small clusters of tight-knit groups of staff. Moreover, these practices seemed to be supported, organised and 'regulated' (to some extent) by staff cultures that had been shaped by a convergence of traumatic institutional memories and the infiltration of 'security thinking'. Whilst engaging in any of the forms of alleged corruption, mentioned above, staff had to have operated outside the majority of colleagues. It is evident that more research is needed in this area, but gaining access to hidden practices of this particular nature is a tricky business.

Crucially, if the threads of observation and narrative accounts that I drew together on brutal and acquisitive corrupt practices are accurate, then it was not so much that staff were significantly deviating from cultural or formal institutional norms, it was more that they were performing extreme versions of them. That is, within the cold, brutal, masculinised, punishing and repressive environment of maximum-security prisons, allegations made by prisoners of brutality and of exploitative acquisitive corruption (particularly) could plausibly be viewed as small subgroups of staff simply taking a commonplace series of punishing and painful practices to their logical and ruthless conclusion. It was, in fact, more difficult to imagine the conditions under which the allegations of surreptitious care were taking place, as these activities were more of a deviation from accepted and official practical norms.

Concluding summary

When researching in prisons for long periods of time, it is often the case that a researcher will hear second-hand (and some first-hand) accounts of underground activities carried out by either prisoners or staff. For the ethnographer who hears these stories, it is not always necessary to determine their validity. If the stories hold meaning amongst the staff or prisoner groups, their authenticity may be inconsequential because what matters is their influence over the cultural landscape from the perspectives of those who repeat and believe in the stories. Moreover, if unverified 'horror' stories (which may, in actuality, be myths) about certain prisons can hold weight and purchase within the prisoner society, this can also be equally true amongst the staff group, who may operate as if the stories are authentic. The power of such stories can infuse the ethereal environment of a prison with an ominous vapour that is absorbed by both staff and prisoners alike and which manifests in various ways as both groups interact with one another.

Whether verifiable or not, stories of staff corruption permeated some of the staff and prisoner cultures in the high-security prisons I studied in tangible ways. Becoming aware of stories of corruption either through explicit disclosure by prisoners or through sliver views and informal corroborations during the ethnographic encounter led to my own further analytical reflection, filtering and meaning-making. In particular, when stories of alleged prison officer corruption were analysed together with the observed conditionality of prison officer collegial relationships, they brought into fuller view concealed strands of a matrix of cultural practice. The role of prison officer appeared to be heavily impacted by the power of collegial conditionality. Formal and informal secret keeping as well as the shadows cast over prison practice by the possibility of hidden secrets seemed to converge in sets of beliefs held by some staff that there were real dangers associated with being relegated to an 'out'-group. By examining the conditionality of prison officer culture, the potential ways in which extreme versions of institutional norms could break off into deviant and corrupt subcultural forms were brought into fuller view. As a result, it became possible to better understand the processes by which staff and organisational cultures might not only stimulate but also effectively demand or require mass indifference, negligence or outright brutality.

The ethnographic lens, however partial and limited, offers the potential to glimpse at a field of vision that may be impossible to obtain in any other way. However, as this chapter illustrates, there are some aspects of the field that may remain frustratingly out of reach and concealed in the shadows. This chapter opened with a brief discussion on the partial nature of ethnographic work and the difficulty of verifying the basic facts of a narrative uncovered in the field when, for example, an informant discloses or hints at a carefully guarded secret. Not gaining full access to all of the secrets hidden within an organisation during the course of an ethnographic study is not an incomplete ethnography. Leaving some quadrants of the ethnographic field undisturbed is not a sign of failure. Discovering practices of secret keeping during ethnographic work can still be meaningfully analysed and understood by an ethnographer without actually gaining full disclosure of the secrets being kept. As Grey (2014) and Costa and Grey (2014) argue, often the secret itself is entirely irrelevant, it is the practice of secret keeping that holds the most stakes and meaning for organisational members. However, under other circumstances, both the secret keeping and the secret being kept are of crucial significance to understanding certain cultural practices and the potential importance of exposing them.

Acknowledgements

Many thanks to Rod Earle, Steve Tombs and Reece Walters for reading and commenting on earlier versions of this chapter.

Notes

1. Being 'wanded down' means having a hand-held metal detecting wand passed over you.
2. An airlock consists of two airtight doors, in series and with a chamber between, which do not open simultaneously.
3. 'Nonce' is an acronym for 'Not of Normal Criminal Element' and is widely colloquially (and pejoratively) used in British prisons to refer to people convicted of sexual offences.

Further reading

Ferrell, J. and Hamm, M. S. (eds) (1998) *Ethnography at the Edge: Crime, Deviance, and Field Research* (Boston: Northeastern University Press).

George, K. M. (1993) 'Dark Trembling: Ethnographic Notes on Secrecy and Concealment in Highland Sulawesi', *Anthropological Quarterly*, 66, 4, 230–39.

Sim, J. (2003) 'Whose Side Are We Not On: Researching Medical Power in Prisons', in S. Tombs and D. Whyte (eds) *Unmasking the Crimes of the Powerful: Scrutinizing States and Corporations* (New York: Peter Lang).

Verdery, K. (2013) *Secrets and Truth: Ethnography in the Archive of Romania's Secret Police* (New York: Central European University Press).

References

Blundo, G. and de Sardan, J. P. O. (2006) *Everyday Corruption and the State: Citizens and Public Officials in Africa* (London: Zed Books Ltd.).

Carlton, B. A. (2007) *Imprisoning Resistance: Life and Death in an Australian Supermax* (Sydney: Institute of Criminology Press).

Clifford, J. (1986) 'Partial Truths', in J. Clifford and G. E. Marcus (eds) *Writing Culture: The Poetics and Politics of Ethnography*, pp. 1–26 (Berkeley, Los Angeles, London: University of California Press).

Costas, J. and Grey, C. (2014) 'Bringing Secrecy into the Open: Towards a Theorization of the Social Processes of Organizational Secrecy', *Organization Studies*, published online first DOI: 10.1177/0170840613515470.

Crawley, E. (2004) *Doing Prison Work: The Public and Private Lives of Prison Officers* (Cullompton: Willan).

Crawley, E. and Crawley, P. (2008) 'Understanding Prison Officers: Culture, Cohesion and Conflict', in J. Bennett, B. Crewe and A. Wahidin (eds) *Understanding Prison Staff*, pp. 134–52, (Cullompton: Willan).

de Sardan, J. P. O. (2008) 'Researching the Practical Norms of Real Governance in Africa', Discussion Paper No. 5, Dec, London: Overseas Development Institute.

Diamitani, B. T. (2011) 'The Insider and the Ethnography of Secrecy: Challenges of Collecting Data on the Fearful Komo of the Tagwa-Senufo', *African Archaeological Review*, 28: 55–70.

Drake, D. (2006) *A Comparison of Quality of Life, Order and Legitimacy in Two Maximum-Security Prisons*, Unpublished PhD Thesis, University of Cambridge.

Drake, D. (2009) *Prisoner Experiences and Quality of Life in Dispersal Prisons*. Research Report Submitted to the Directorate of High Security, NOMS.

Drake, D. (2011) 'The "Dangerous Other" in Maximum-Security Prisons', *Criminology and Criminal Justice*, 11, 4, 367–82.

Drake, D. H. (2012) *Prisons, Punishment and the Pursuit of Security* (Basingstoke: Palgrave Macmillan).

Drake, D. H. (2014) 'Researching Prisoner Experiences with Prison Officers: An Action Research Inspired Approach', *Action Research*, March, 12, 1, 94–109.

Drake, D. & Harvey, J. (2014) 'Performing the Role of Ethnographer: Processing and Managing the Emotional Dimensions of Prison Research', *International Journal of Social Research Methodology*, 17, 5, 489–501.

George, K. M. (1993) 'Dark Trembling: Ethnographic Notes on Secrecy and Concealment in Highland Sulawesi', *Anthropological Quarterly*, 66, 4, 230–39.

Goffman, E. (1959) *The Presentation of Self in Everyday Life* (London: Penguin Books).

Grey, C. (2014) 'An Organizational Culture of Secrecy: The Case of Bletchley Park', *Management and Organizational History*, 9, 1, 107–22.

Hammersley, M. and Atkinson, P. (1995) *Ethnography: Principles in Practice*, Second edition (London: Tavistock).

HM Chief Inspector of Prisons (2002) *Report of an Unannounced Follow-Up Inspection of HM Prison Whitemoor 15–17 July* (London: HMSO).

Liebling, A., Price, D. and Shefer, G. (2010) *The Prison Officer*, Second edition (London: Routledge).

Marks, M. (2004) 'Researching Police Transformation: The Ethnographic Imperative', *British Journal of Criminology*, 44, 866–88.

Norris, C. (1993) 'Some Ethical Considerations on Field-Work with the Police', in D. Hobbes and T. May (eds) *Interpreting the Field: Accounts of Ethnography*, pp. 122–43 (Oxford: Clarendon Press).

Poulos, C. N. (2008) *Accidental Ethnography: An Inquiry into Family Secrecy* (Walnut Creek, CA: Left Coast Press).

Reiner, R. (2000) 'Police Research', in R. D. King and E. Wincup (eds) *Doing Research on Crime and Justice*, pp. 205–35 (Oxford: Oxford University Press).

Rowe, M. (2007) 'Tripping Over Molehills: Ethics and the Ethnography of Police Work', *International Journal of Social Research Methodology*, 10, 1, 37–48.

Scott, D. (2008) 'Creating Ghosts in the Penal Machine: Prison Officer Occupational Morality and the Techniques of Denial', in J. Bennett, B. Crewe and A. Wahidin (eds) *Understanding Prison Staff*, pp. 168–86 (Cullompton: Willan).

Sim, J. (2004) 'The Victimised State and the Mystification of Social Harm', in P. Hillyard, C. Pantazis, S. Tombs and D. Gordon (eds) *Beyond Criminology*, pp. 113–32 (London: Pluto).

Sim, J. (2008) 'An Inconvenient Criminological Truth: Pain, Punishment and Prison Officers', in J. Bennett, B. Crewe and A. Wahidin (eds) *Understanding Prison Staff*, pp. 187–209 (Cullompton: Willan).

Simmel, G. (1950) 'The Secret and the Secret Society', in K. Wolff (ed) *The Sociology of Georg Simmel* (Glencoe, IL: Free Press).

Tait, S. (2011) 'A Typology of Prison Officer Approaches to Care', *European Journal of Criminology*, 8, 6, 450–54.

Verdery, K. (2013) *Secrets and Truth: Ethnography in the Archive of Romania's Secret Police* (New York: Central European University Press).

14
Ethnographic Imagination in the Field of the Prison

Lorna A. Rhodes

Introduction

In this chapter, I propose that something about ethnographic practice itself can help us expand our understanding of what is possible for the ethnography of prisons. As other chapters in this volume attest, ethnographers of prisons face challenges specific to oppressive and secretive institutions (see particularly chapters 2 and 13). The extent and intensity of these challenges vary widely, but in many cases we encounter an inversion of the guiding premise of our craft, as the fundamentally relational quality of the ethnographic method encounters restriction, surveillance and suspicion. My aim here is to explore the territory that emerges from these pressures, such that the field site, or specific events within that site, cannot be grasped or comprehended entirely through standard ethnographic practices. By seeing ethnography as a specific perception of our surroundings – an apprehension of figure and ground – I suggest one way we might approach our collective imagination as prison ethnographers in creative and perhaps unexpected ways.

I begin with a brief description of a particular detail that entered my imagination during a day of observation in Washington State prisons, a detail that eventually helped me cut through the bureaucratic underbrush obscuring my topic.[1] I then turn to two discussions of photography: Roland Barthes' *Camera Lucida: Reflections on Photography* (1981) in which he explores a metaphor of figure and ground as a way to see beyond the photographic image and a passage in Avery Gordon's *Ghostly Matters: Haunting and the Sociological Imagination* (1997) that extends Barthes' argument to encompass a larger field of social suffering. Drawing on Barthes' and Gordon's discussion of the *punctum* and *studium*, my third section briefly explores examples from other prison ethnographers that suggest how suggestive, incomplete moments of fieldwork can open out onto unseen territory. Finally, I explore the notion of this territory, described by Barthes and Gordon as the 'blind field', and suggest ways in which it can be applied to prison ethnography.

I want to note at the outset that this chapter is not about method as such. I am making the important assumption that basic ethnographic practices – responsible behaviour, careful observation, sustained and detailed note taking – are firmly in place as the foundation for ethnographic work, in prison as in any other research site. I also do not mean to separate the conduct of field research as such from analysis, writing or reading; rather, this chapter suggests one of many ways to see them as dynamically related, iteratively and inseparably entangled throughout the ethnographic process.

A haunting detail

In my book *Total Confinement: Madness and Reason in the Maximum Security Prison*, I describe the process of 'receiving' at a prison in Washington State. Arriving by bus from county jails,[2] prisoners shackled together 'on the chain' are led into a large, specially organised area where they are released from restraints, given prison-issue clothing in return for the orange jumpsuits worn in transit and moved en mass through a series of steps. During a day when I observed this process, I watched the procedures at each step – paying particular attention to the process of screening for mental illness – and talked with prisoners and staff members. At that point I had been conducting ethnographic research in the Washington State prisons for some time and 'the mentally ill in prison' constituted my specific point of entry. How were mentally ill prisoners recognised, classified, disbursed and treated? What could they expect from prison? Towards the end of my visit, I watched the officer working at the photo ID station, where prisoners' previous IDs (from jail) were removed, their pictures were taken and they were issued new badges. I lingered near some prisoners, who had, at that point, finished all the steps. And there I noticed something.

> Next to the photo ID station I find a big box full of discarded identification badges. Dozens of pictures of prisoners fill this box, men staring warily out of the laminated plastic. Some have closed, defiant faces, others are studiedly neutral; some are sad and exhausted, their eyes full of fear, and I see in one man the over-wide eyes of the fetal alcohol affected.
>
> (Rhodes, 2004: 102)

When I left the prison that day, my mind full of impressions, the one that rose to the surface – and that kept coming back to me, lingering in my imagination – was that box of photos. The photos were haunting and upsetting. Later, as I worked on assimilating my experience, that one unforgettable detail opened out onto something I had not seen clearly until then. Mentally ill prisoners are not a neatly separate category, entering and moving through the prison as a 'population'; rather, psychiatric impairment is inextricably tied to the ways in which these institutions manage the relationship between the individual and the group. In this context, as I later wrote, 'treatment is more than an enclosure of specialised attention' (2004: 130).

We are trained to think that ethnographic writing emerges systematically from a massive pile of notes – and it goes without saying that my immersion in my research allowed me to see what I saw. But an emphasis on methods as such can obscure the fact that the 'field' is not a level plane to which we give an even, flat attention. Rather, even as we are engaged in observing as much as possible (thus, I tried to attend to all the steps of receiving), our attention can be *caught*, illuminated by the unexpected and serendipitous. This experience, common to ethnography more generally, emerges with particular force in the prison environment. The problem often glossed as 'access' (Waquant, 2002) is more than a matter of whether one gets through the gate, is given a set of keys or manages to talk at random with prisoners. My initial understanding of receiving, for example, was shaped by what Pat Carlen calls 'imaginary penality', 'institutional practices [conducted] "as if" all objectives are possible' (2008: 1). Because my entry into the system was mediated by these practices – by administrative interactions focused on policy – I did not initially see the 'mentally ill offender' or 'MIO' as a construct dependent on the tension between group and individual that pervades prison management. A different ethnographer working in a different system might encounter or arrive with some other source of influence. Many researchers are limited to a single prison or to only one area or programme within a prison or find that only prisoners, or only staff, are available for interviews. And, of course, navigation of the built environment of the prison – for instance, in some institutions, the requirement for constant escort – necessarily shapes the experience of research. One challenge of prison ethnography, then, is to avoid missing those shaping elements that remain beyond our conscious awareness as we go about the obvious tasks of fieldwork.

Punctuation points

In *Camera Lucida*, his long illustrated essay about photography, Roland Barthes notes that many photographs have something in the image that catches us, a telling, haunting detail that he calls the *punctum*. He writes:

> This element rises from the scene, shoots out of it like an arrow, and pierces me ... the word [*punctum*] ... also refers to the notion of punctuation ... photographs speckled with sensitive points – the telling detail, the punctuation mark
>
> (1981: 26–7)

One of Barthes' illustrations is a photograph by George W. Wilson, taken in 1863, of Queen Victoria on her horse. The queen, in a sort of cape with a ruffle around her face, sits side-saddle with her huge skirt covering most of the horse's side. A man in a kilt stands holding the horse's head.

> This is the *punctum*; for even if I do not know just what the social status of this Scotsman may be... I can see his function clearly: to supervise the horse's behavior: what if the horse suddenly began to rear? What would happen to the queen's skirt, *i.e., to her majesty?* The *punctum* fantastically 'brings out' the Victorian nature (what else can one call it?) of the photograph....
>
> (Barthes, 2008: 57, also quoted in Gordon, 1997: 107)

The queen's attendant (or perhaps, more accurately, one who attends to the horse) is the 'off-centre detail' (Barthes, 1981: 43) that sparks out of the photograph and captures Barthes in a way that the queen – the expected element – cannot. In my experience of the box full of discarded ID photos, it was the faces of the prisoners that shot out of the scene; they were the off-centre detail that animated the orderly succession of screening practices I had set myself to observe. If my day in receiving was the photograph, they were the *punctum*.

In her book *Ghostly Matters: Haunting and the Sociological Imagination*, sociologist Avery Gordon turns briefly to Barthes' discussion of the *punctum* as a way to talk about those who disappeared between 1976 and 1983 (*los desaparacidos*) under Argentina's military junta. Gordon writes about how photographs of the dead, with their capacity to 'bruise' and 'animate' the viewer (Barthes, 1981: 27, 20), became the medium through which the Mothers of the Plaza de Mayo (*Los Madres)* communicated the nature of their loss, the experience of both knowing and not knowing that their children were dead. Held up in public by the Mothers, the photographs acted as *punctums*, which 'make meaning meaningful, convey the existence of something... eloquently... [have] power to attract, to draw me in, sometimes beside myself' (Gordon, 1997: 106). The *punctum* breaks through the everyday surface papering over events – in Argentina, the silence of the military junta, the pretence that life could go on as usual – and unmistakably *catches* our awareness.

Many photographs have no sensitive point, no punctuation. In this case, what we see is a flat field – Barthes called it the *studium* – offering a kind of general interest (p. 26).[3] The *studium* 'yields those details which constitute the very raw material of ethnological knowledge' (p. 28) and evokes what Gordon describes as 'participation in the cultural, historical, and politically transparent information of the photograph' (p. 106). Describing the *studium* as 'a kind of education' (p. 28), Barthes offers as an example a 1959 photograph by William Klein entitled 'Mayday, Moscow'. We see a group of people standing in a crowd; for Barthes, nothing in particular catches the eye. 'The photographer teaches me how the Russians dress... I *note* a boy's big cloth cap, another's necktie... [photography] supplies me with a collection of partial objects...' (p. 30). The act of noting demanded by the *studium* is not the same as the apprehension – or perhaps more accurately the experience of being apprehended by – the *punctum*.

In Barthes' analysis, the *punctum* points to something hidden that he calls the 'blind field'. As Gordon explains, the blind field 'is never named as such in the photograph... It is precisely what is pressing in from the other side of the fullness of the image displayed within the frame; the *punctum* only ever evokes it and the necessity of finding it...' (p. 107). A photograph from which a *punctum* emerges is not transparent, not a conveyor purely of information, but a suggestion of what is not seen. 'However lightning-like it may be,' Barthes says, 'the *punctum* has, more or less potentially, a power of expansion' (p. 45). Both Barthes and Gordon see the *punctum* as fundamentally relational; because it sparks from the photograph, from the scene, it connects the viewer with what the photograph *doesn't* explicitly depict. What Gordon calls the 'other side' enters into the viewer – in fact, it cannot be avoided. Once you've imagined the queen falling off her horse, you cannot *not* imagine it. Interestingly, Barthes notes, 'In order to perceive the *punctum*, no analysis would be of any use to me (but perhaps memory sometimes would...)' (p. 43). This suggests that the photographer and the viewer, as well as, by analogy, the ethnographer, experience the moment apart from any analytic relation to the subject, but in the context of relations and images built up over time in memory. Perhaps for me, for example, the photographs in the box were more noticeable – more capable of being noticed – because I had been struck, on other prison visits, by a poignant disjunction between the greying hair of older inmates and the younger selves displayed on their IDs.

Reading punctuation

Before turning to three telling details found in recent ethnographic accounts of prison, I should address the obvious question: *for whom* are these the punctuation marks? We can't know what an ethnographer actually experiences, either at the time of observation or when writing, going over notes or simply remembering. The *punctum* is thus, necessarily, a subjective experience – not only at the moment of its emergence but also as it finds its way onto the page, guiding the reader's experience of the text.[4] Nevertheless, because of the way contemporary ethnography is written, I think it is safe to assume that many striking images and incidents, often highlighted as chapter headings, italicised passages, title or epigram quotes or quotations from notes, were experienced by the ethnographer as precisely those telling details and sensitive points that become, in turn, memorable to the reader.[5] The following examples are *punctums* for me – I read each one as a striking detail that opens out onto the liveliness and depth of the ethnographic account in which it appears.

In an article entitled 'The Embrace of Human Rights in an Ugandan Prison', Tomas Max Martin aims to show that human rights reform is appropriated in complex ways by prison staff. The article begins with this excerpt, italicised in the original, from his field notes:

> Henry and another guard attack a young prisoner, who has apparently provoked them by asking a question. They slap him repeatedly and Henry kicks the prisoner in the back as he covers his face with his hands and cries: 'Oh forgive me, forgive me!' The other guard takes one of the belts that the prisoners have just been ordered to drop on the ground and lashes the young prisoner on the back and the head.
>
> A superior officer, who has been hanging around outside, yells to them:
>
> 'You make sure that you are not violating their human rights. Don't you know that the system has changed?'
>
> 'Eh, this is human wrongs!' the guard with the belt replies and hits again. The superior officer approaches, laughing. The guard makes a few feigned lashes with the belt and then stops and continues to search the other prisoners.
>
> (Martin, 2014: 69)

In this passage, the emergence of 'human rights talk' as a joke in the middle of an episode of abuse points to a blind field. The joke invites the reader to ask: What is going on? How, and for whom, is this being funny? By what route has this vocabulary entered this particular scene? As Martin subsequently shows, no oversimple dichotomy serves to describe the actions of Ugandan prison staff, who are pressed by international agencies to adopt 'human rights'. 'Staff submit to human rights, but through this submission, they take ownership of human rights, diffuse them and put them to use' (p. 79).

My second example is from James Waldram's *Hound Pound Narrative*, an account of the use of Cognitive Behavioural Therapy for sex offenders in a Canadian Prison. In the programme Waldram describes each prisoner works individually to prepare an autobiographical account and then presents it to therapists and other prisoners in a small group session. Waldram describes how one prisoner, Sam, becomes anxious under pressure as therapists and fellow prisoners question his story. At one point, a therapist intervenes: 'It's *your* life story', she says, 'Try to do it in a neat, chronological way' (2012: 3). 'It's *Your* Life Story' becomes a chapter heading (pp. 106–24), as Waldram shows that hidden behind the stated intentions and therapeutic façade of CBT as practised on this unit is a studied effort to mould prisoners' narratives into a predetermined pattern. The blind field here is all that the men are not allowed to say, for, as Waldram follows them through this process, he realises that 'autobiography' actually conceals those aspects of prisoners' lives, such as early abuse, that might help them understand their own behaviour. 'It's *your* life story' is so telling precisely because, in fact, it wasn't really Sam's story at all.

The *punctum* in my third example has a more complex referent. Mahuya Bandyopadhyay (2010) opens her account of *Everyday Life in a Prison* by describing her awkward early days of fieldwork in an Indian prison. She was made to wait in the prison's main office, where one day she found that a frail old man was lying in a corner waiting to be taken to the hospital.

> The office carried on without heeding him. I too went largely unnoticed. An officer's attention was suddenly drawn to me and the old man, almost simultaneously. Addressing no one in particular he ordered: 'Take *this thing* away from here. This is an office.'
>
> (2010: 3)

The blind field opened out by this brief interaction is not, as one might expect, an account of callous staff, though callous staff appear. Rather, Bandyopadhyay asks the reader to reverse conventional expectation and understand 'that first encounter [as a] backdrop against which prisoners' worlds can be positioned' (p. 4). Her account examines the 'constructive processes' engendered by prisoners' resistance to this backdrop – thus opening out unexpectedly onto the relationship between the interior of the prison and the neighbourhoods from which the prisoners come (2010: 4). The *punctum* – the man spoken to as a 'thing' – points to a blind field that is as invisible to her initially as it is to us as we read the first page of her book.

Barthes describes the *punctum* only in terms of the visual medium of photography. Following his lead, I offered as an initial example a visual image featuring photographs in some ways parallel to those Gordon describes, of those who have been disappeared, though less brutally, by the state. But to extend the idea of the *punctum* to ethnography, more generally, we must include the verbal punctuation mark: an ethnographic *punctum* often emerges from what is spoken. We can't know from the accounts of Martin, Waldram and Bandyopadhyay whether these telling details – the joke, the command, the dismissal – caught them at the time of hearing or shot out from the page later, in writing. The result, though, is that they write so that we as readers experience these brief events as *animating*[6] for us and for the story as a whole. As we read them, we can see that they have been carefully recorded (on paper or in memory), treasured as touchstones of analysis and finally incorporated into the written account for the reader to experience as well.

Barthes objects to the possibility that a telling detail may be placed on purpose to catch the viewer's eye. For him, deliberate punctuation is manipulation – such details, no longer spontaneous, do not pierce us.

> Hence the detail which interests me is not, or at least is not strictly, intentional, and probably must not be so; it occurs in the field of the photographed thing like a supplement that is at once inevitable and delightful... above all, imitating Orpheus, [the photographer] must not turn back to look at what he is leading – what he is giving to me!
>
> (1981: 47)

Here, the parallel with ethnography cannot be sustained. For the ethnographer, the initial experience of a *punctum* is indeed a 'supplement' – the unexpected, startling emergence of an event, sometimes only grasped in retrospect. As Gordon puts it, 'the enchanting detail cannot be predicted in advance or calculated for methodological rigor' (1997: 108). But in the long process of moving from fieldwork to the published page, the ethnographer enters into a conscious relationship to the *punctum*, which becomes good both to think with and to write about. As Gordon notes, a *punctum* – 'the little but heavily freighted thing' – is always social, 'if highly particularised' (p. 108), and it is this conjunction of the social and the particular – the social in its particularity – that eventually becomes the fabric of ethnographic writing.

Blind fields

The prison and its surrounding security state are inherently *opaque*. They cannot be understood simply on the terms in which they present themselves to us. The ethnographer hopes to penetrate this opacity, ideally moving from an initial ignorance (common to all ethnographic projects) to greater familiarity. But the multiple limitations of prison ethnography, differing in extent and degree, seem to be built into the institutional site itself. For example, Sacha Darke, writing about a jail ('lockup') in Brazil to which he was granted exceptional access, notes that some inmates were transferred to remand prisons (2014: 56). These constitute an 'elsewhere', a blind field – inaccessible to Darke, perhaps less open than the facility he studied and no doubt essential to the operation of the larger system of which that site was a part. Was that other prison available for ethnographic work? If, as seems likely, it was not, then how might he – or any ethnographer in the face of similar opacities – grasp, or at least indicate, the 'other side', that which lies outside the frame of the 'picture' the ethnographer is able to record? In these situations, the *punctum* enables 'the moving field beyond the four corners of the image [to] emerge for us' (Gordon, 1997: 107). That blind field is what we cannot, in fact, observe directly but must, instead, approach more obliquely.

Gordon develops the contrast between *punctum* and *studium* in the context of the photographs carried by the Mothers of the Plaza de Mayo.

> For the Mothers, the photographs were a spirit guide to the desaparecidos and to disappearance as an organised system of repression. The photographs – 'tokens of absence' [quoting Sontag 1977, p. 16] and potent evidence of what is harrowingly present – [were] part of a movement to punctuate the silence, to break the stadium-like quality of disappearance...The Mothers transformed the docile portrait...into a public *punctum.*
>
> (1997: 109)

Certainly, the ethnographer of prisons does not face this kind of personal loss and danger. What is similar, however, is the necessity to 'punctuate the silence' – to break through into the blind fields that lie behind institutional routines and publicly available information. The Mothers found a powerful way to reference the violence behind the silence surrounding the disappeared. Violence also pervades the examples I have offered so far of physical violence, erasure of identity and humanity, and manipulation of narrative. But violence may differ widely in how it appears to the ethnographer and in terms of which aspect of the prison is silent at any particular moment. Thus, for example, Bandyopadhyay brings forward an overt episode of violence not as a prelude to further violence but rather to highlight a covert landscape of resistance.

I encountered a similar element of reversal – an unexpected background to the foreground constraint and threat – in the course of research on solitary confinement. One day I was visiting a staff member at the home of his parents when he and his mother recounted this story:

> The staff member had been placed in charge of transporting to a distant state a prisoner who was notorious for a history of violence and had been in unremitting solitary confinement for many years.[7] In standard procedure for interstate transport, the prisoner was strapped into a stun belt, cuffed, and loaded onto a special plane with a two-man escort. Few prison routines are more rigorously security driven. But the night before the flight, the staff member – who knew the prisoner well – asked his mother to make a batch of chocolate chip cookies; these he took for the prisoner to eat as they flew toward their destination, another maximum-security facility. Both he (and later the prisoner) pointed out that this might be the prisoner's only chance, for the remainder of his life, to eat food from outside the walls.

I observed none of this directly, but the details of the story are vivid in my mind: the staff member holding the activation button for the stun belt in one hand and the bag of cookies in other, the two of them pursuing, in spite of everything, their long years of conversation. Here, violence is right on the surface, above all in the overt threat of the belt.[8] But behind that surface is a blind field of forbidden contact, covert mutual respect and staff joined by collegial silence.

The story of the cookies suggests four ways in which we might expand on the possibilities opened up by the blind field. First, and most obviously, the *punctum* points to what we cannot see at the time but might be able to explore in the future. Imagine, as a thought experiment, that I could have gone along on the next transport plane. The story of the interstate transport, with its strange *punctum*, would have told me not to assume that the security procedures, which the transport officers would likely be eager to highlight, were the whole story. Alerted to other possibilities, I might have asked questions about a more unexpected and invisible aspect, the peculiar secrecy made possible by these flights. In this sense, the recognition of a *punctum* accords with much advice to ethnographers about attending to and recording details in order to follow up on them more fully over time. In an article entitled 'The Hidden Side of the Moon', Annette Liebling suggests that ethnographers be alert to 'the veiling of data'. 'Veiling' can result, as she discusses, from the human limitations of the researcher – blind spots and inadequacies that prevent us from widening our field of attention (2007: 145).[9] But beyond these limitations, prison ethnographers face the 'veiling' of sites, complexes, stories and histories; sometimes we are, in fact, trying to study the hidden side of the moon. Liebling offers a phrase (borrowed from Gendlin): 'lifting out' (2007: 145; Gendlin, 1978). Our work, she says, is to lift out, to take on 'elements that are sensed as problematic' and make sense of them in their context – with that context including as much as possible what is hidden (p. 145).

A second possibility, though, is that direct 'lifting out' may not be an option. My thought experiment is a dead end, because I would not have been allowed onto a transport plane, and other opportunities to follow up on the story turned out to be limited. In situations like this, a different approach to the *punctum* is in order, for we must acknowledge that some aspects of our research field are, quite simply, beyond our grasp. Yet, they are not absent. This is Gordon's point: the *punctum* points to that place where something ghostly, a shaping absence, can be apprehended but not overtly or methodically 'lifted out'. The Mothers of the Plaza de Mayo demonstrated through the *punctum* of the photograph that their children were gone, yet in that very demonstration evoked their ghostly presence. Those cookies were enjoyed at a moment of extreme securitisation, yet evaded the pervasive managerialism underlying the transport operation.

A third aspect of the blind field is suggested by the story of the cookies, for the institutional landscape itself can have a *studium*-like quality for its participants – flat, repetitive and driven by rituals of security. This background, with its emphasis on learned routine, is one source of correctional officers' complaints about the tedium of their daily work. But the same sparks that strike the ethnographer can also strike others in an institutional setting. The story of the cookies was memorable not only for me, but for others as well – for the prisoner and his escort, of course, but also for other staff members below a certain level in the operational hierarchy. Such stories circulate precisely because they point beyond themselves, off-centre, accidental and enchanting; they may serve to attune the institutional imagination to hidden possibilities (which could be positive or negative). It is not just the prison complex itself that constitutes a public secret (Taussig, 1999; Daniels, 2007); public secrets circulate within prisons as well. The presence of an audience in the person of the ethnographer may constitute an opportunity for participants in a familiar scene to signal precisely those charged moments when underlying meanings and structures make themselves visible.

Finally, the blind field can help us distinguish overdrawn, fetishised depictions of the prison from those details that tell us something we don't already know. In his discussion of the *studium*, Barthes notes that some journalistic photographs 'shout' – but they lack the poignancy of those whose *punctums* draw him beyond himself (1981: 41). Similarly, much popular representation of prisons is illustrated with familiar (though often shocking) tropes of violence and punishment. These correspond in some respects to the *studium*, which Barthes writes can be 'receive[d] as political testimony' (1981: 26). There are important exceptions, and one certainly doesn't need to be trained in ethnography to trace out the complexity that unfolds between figure and ground, but ethnography is especially suited to an exploration of blind fields that lie beyond or behind the most immediately striking details. Ethnographic practice supports the momentary suspension of judgement and tolerance for ambiguity out of which sparks of punctuation not only emerge but also lend meaning and energy to the various fields they reference. Thus, the telling detail is not the one we already know we are going to see, but that made visible by preparation and time – the beginning of a story that expands, troubles and, in the process, resists the pervasive fetishisation of the prison.

Conclusion

In this chapter, I have suggested that the visual metaphor proposed by Roland Barthes, in which a 'punctuation point' expands the field of certain photographs, can be extended to ethnography and, more specifically, to the ethnography of prisons. Without diminishing other necessary aspects of research, awareness of the difference between what he called the *punctum* and the *studium* offers a kind of permission: we can attend to – even cherish – those elements of ethnographic experience that truly 'grab' our attention. This form of attention then becomes a guide to navigation, the starting place for what is sometimes called the ethnographic imagination. As we incorporate it into our writing, we signal to our readers the existence of an 'other side', what is hidden makes its presence known. Thus, our attention, which has been affected, changed and, in her words, 'haunted' by our experience becomes our readers' attention as well – and we hope, eventually, that our reader too will be haunted by these moments.

Notes

An earlier version of this chapter was presented at The Open University Conference 'Resisting the Eclipse', held under the auspices of The International Centre for Comparative Criminological Research (ICCCR), Milton Keynes, 18 and 19 September 2013. I am grateful to the organisers for inviting me, to Deborah Drake and Rod Earle for their encouragement and advice and to the conference participants for their attention and comments.

1. The examples and perspective presented in this chapter are drawn from ethnographic research conducted between 1993 and 2002 in Washington State Department of Corrections supermax (control) and psychiatric facilities (see Rhodes, 2004). The restrictions and difficulty surrounding research in US prisons account for some of the emphasis in this chapter on issues of opacity; however, as the 'Eclipse' conference made clear, ethnographic research on prisons worldwide, as well as in the US, is increasing in scope and importance.
2. In the US, most prisoners at the state level begin their contact with the criminal justice system with a stay in a county jail; those who receive sentences longer than a year are sent to state prisons.
3. Barthes writes that his difficulty finding a French word for this quality led him to the Latin *studium*, which means 'a kind of general, enthusiastic commitment... but without special acuity'. The Latin *punctum* means a 'prick, [a] mark made by a pointed instrument' (p. 26).
4. Michael Fried writes that 'commentators on *Camera Lucida*, when glossing the *punctum*, have stressed the importance of the individual viewer's sheerly personal response' (Fried, 2005: 543).
5. This highlighting of striking details seems to be characteristic of contemporary ethnography. Earlier writing, modelling itself on natural science, was more likely to relegate such details to introductions and footnotes.
6. 'The photograph is in no way animated... but it animates me' (Barthes, 1981: 20; Gordon, 1997: 109).
7. Interstate transport is a system for moving or exchanging prisoners and can occur for a variety of reasons; in cases like this one, transport is arranged for a prisoner who has become, for a variety of possible reasons, too difficult to maintain where he is.
8. See Rhodes (2004: 90–5) for a discussion of the use of stun belts as restraints.
9. In an argument that complements Barthes' analysis of the *punctum*, Liebling suggests that 'seeing' – in the sense of understanding deeply – goes beyond visual observation and description (2007: 144).

Further reading

I strongly recommend reading the whole of Avery Gordon's *Ghostly Matters: Haunting and the Sociological Imagination*; the discussion of Barthes takes up only a few pages of this rich and inspiring work. For a useful look at note taking and its integration with every aspect of ethnographic research, see *Writing Ethnographic Fieldnotes* by Robert M. Emerson, Rachel I. Fretz and Linda L. Shaw (University of Chicago Press, 2011).

References

Bandyopadhyay, M. (2010) *Everyday Life in a Prison: Confinement, Surveillance, Resistance* (New Delhi: Orient Blackswan).

Barthes, R. (1981) *Camera Lucida: Reflections on Photography* (trans. Howard, R.) (London: Fontanna).

Carlen, P. (ed) (2008) 'Imaginary Penalities and Risk-Crazed Governance', *Imaginary Penalities* (Cullompton, Devon: Willan Publishing).

Chartraine, G. and Sharon, D. (2007) 'Public Secrets', *Vectors: Journal of Culture and Technology in a Dynamic Vernacular,* 2, 2, http://vectors.usc.edu/issues/4/publicsecrets/ Accessed 8 January 2014.

Darke, S. (2014) 'Managing Without Guards in a Brazilian Lockup', *Focaal – Journal of Global and Historical Anthropology*, 68, 55–67.

Fried, M. (2005) 'Barthes's Punctum', *Critical Inquiry*, 31, 3, 539–74.

Gendlin, E. T. (1978–79) 'Befindlichkeit: Heidegger and the Philosophy of Psychology', *Review of Existential Psychology and Psychiatry*, 16, 1–3, 43–71.

Gordon, A. (1997) *Ghostly Matters: Haunting and the Sociological Imagination* (Minneapolis: University of Minnesota Press).

Harcourt, B. (2005) 'Carceral Imaginations', *Carceral Notebooks*, 1, 3–19.

Liebling, A. (2007) 'The Hidden Side of the Moon, or, "Lifting Out" in Ethnographies', in A. McLean and A. Liebling (eds) *The Shadow Side of Fieldwork: Exploring the Blurred Borders between Ethnography and Life* (Oxford: Blackwell).

Martin, T. M. (2014) 'Reasonable Caning and the Embrace of Human Rights in Ugandan Prisons', *Focaal – Journal of Global and Historical Anthropology*, 68, 68–82.

Rhodes, L. A. (2004) *Total Confinement: Madness and Reason in the Maximum Security Prison* (Berkeley: University of California Press).

Sontag, S. (1977) *On Photography* (New York: Dell).

Michael, T. (1999) *Defacement: Public Secrecy and the Labor of the Negative* (Stanford: Stanford University Press).

Waldram, J. B. (2012) *Hound Pound Narrative: Sexual Offender Habilitation and the Anthropology of Therapeutic Intervention* (Berkeley: University of California Press).

Waquant, L. (2002) 'The Curious Eclipse of Prison Ethnography', *Ethnography,* 3, 4, 371–97.

Part III

Of Prison Ethnography

Introduction to Part III

Rod Earle

> You must learn to use your life experience in your intellectual work: continually to examine and interpret it. In this sense craftsmanship is the center of yourself and you are personally involved in every intellectual product upon which you work.
>
> (Mills, 1959: 196)

This part of the Handbook includes chapters by authors examining the relationship between themselves as ethnographers and their prison fieldwork. The six chapters focus on different aspects of the role of the ethnographer and the way she or he negotiates the research setting. Most of the contributors in this section previously worked in the prison environment, and their chapters expose and illuminate the tensions associated with their different 'insider'/'outsider' statuses. Each author explores the shifting boundaries they encountered in the challenges and benefits of this occupational proximity. For all but one of these researchers, prison settings were not unfamiliar landscapes populated by strangers; they were on home territory. They appear to follow C. Wright Mills's advice on crafting a sociological imagination as they 'examine and interpret' how their life experiences and their intellectual work are so intimately linked.

Ethnographic immersion in prison life posed unusual dilemmas for Jamie Bennett (Chapter 15), because, as a prison governor, he was far from being an unknown entrant to the field; he was already an established player on it. For Bennett, the problem was not so much how to get in to the prison, but how to get out of the role of prison manager. Recognised by prison staff and other managers, he encountered various degrees of deference and professional circumspection. Bennett found he could sometimes exploit the conventions of dress codes to get around such obstacles. Dressing down, and casual, allowed him to traverse and negotiate shifting boundaries of insider and outsider, signalling to him the power of those conventions and his sometimes unconscious investments in them.

Several of the six authors refer to becoming self-conscious of the way their modes of dress and self-presentation had to be adapted to their new ethnographic role. The title of Chapter 16, by Lilian Ayete-Nyampong, refers to this process as 'changing hats', a deceptively simple analogy for a complex exchange. Bennett's chapter title alludes to the exposure ethnographers both feel and need as they enter the field and the power implicit in his role as a governor. In the allegorical tale of the emperor's new clothes, the nakedness of the emperor is obvious to all, but is remarked upon only by the innocent child. Bennett's account bravely reveals the vulnerability involved in switching roles and the struggles involved in 'looking the part'. For Ayete-Nyampong similar dilemmas surfaced as her professional 'hat' opened doors and smoothed her access to research sites. However, as she describes, dipping below the surface and gaining the trust of children could be another matter, requiring another hat.

For Lindsay Whetter, in Chapter 17, the struggle was more metaphysical and tangled in the transcendental qualities of her commitments to the community she was researching, a faith-based community inside an English men's prison. Whetter provides a thoughtful and compelling account of the 'wonderful yet harrowing' journeys between her immersion in the community as a volunteer and her modes of inquiry as a researcher. Ideas about gender, femininity and masculinity are threaded through Whetter's reflections on the unavoidably messy management of her sense of self. Her account is distinguished by a candour that is sometimes avoided in the more conventional academic literature on prisons. She reports on how the anguish and loneliness of prison life resonated uncomfortably in the singularity of her research role. Her chapter adds to a growing literature on the 'affective toll' of researching prison. Poetry has a place in this literature, and Whetter dares to find room for it in her chapter.

Unlike most of the authors in this part of the Handbook, Abigail Rowe had little prior experience of prison life before becoming a prison researcher. Her account in Chapter 18 of feeling intensely 'outside' narrates, in telling detail and insight, the journey inward and onward through a variety of fieldwork encounters. By attending carefully to the texture and tone of her own experience, Rowe reveals how the troubling disquiet she felt provided unexpected opportunities for analysis and understanding. Rowe connects the routine disclosures and concealments of ethnographic fieldwork with the dynamics of sexual identity and 'coming out'. With exceptional acuity, Rowe finds her way inside the women's prison to places few others have reached, leaving a trail that others will surely follow.

The increasingly prominent position of research evidence in prison management is a feature of Chapter 19, by Lucy Carr. Carr's journey is a bumpy ride from one kind of research to another. Having been appointed to provide HMPS with data and research findings from an English women's prison, Carr reports on her transition to other agendas and methods as a PhD student whilst remaining in the same institution. As with Ayete-Nyampong's experiences in a young men's prison in Ghana, Carr finds that the two hats do not switch easily or always fit comfortably. Like Bennett, she both resists and resents being taken as a 'known quantity' and struggles with those who recognise her but not her new role, her new self. Carr also has to contend with those who do not know her or her role, but cannot fathom her ease of movement and apparent familiarity with her surroundings. Is she 'a spy', governor's stooge or an 'undercover copper'? Whilst these may be familiar dilemmas to any prison researcher, for the ethnographer seeking intimacy and inclusion, they can be profoundly compromising. For Carr, some of the affinities of gender, of being a woman in a woman's prison, facilitated her acceptance, but in ways that were rarely straightforward or simple. Her relative youth, for instance, and being seen as naïve, or 'green' as Sloan and Wright referred to in Chapter 7, could be worked to her advantage. She found that having shed her professional armour as an official HMPS researcher and demonstrated her intentions to seek closer understanding of women's predicaments in prison, she was regarded by some women as deserving of their protective care. Carr's account provides a fascinating accompaniment to Bennett's tale of the 'Governors new clothes', mediated, in part and in places, by women's experiences of solidarity, sociality and mothering.

For Joel Harvey, in Chapter 20, an ethnographic role in prisons is contrasted and compared with the role of clinical psychologist working in secure settings, and, through his text, these roles are retrospectively illuminating. Having conducted a sustained ethnographic study of an English young offenders' institution, Harvey finds that his research methods of immersion and engagement find an echo in his subsequent therapeutic practice. Negotiating the boundaries of being an insider and outsider in the course of his ethnographic research equipped Harvey with skills he found to be all too relevant to his position as a psychologist on an 'in-reach' team working for a National Health Service Trust. The formal professional status of being a psychologist with a defined role is contrasted to the more liminal condition of the ethnographer, constantly shifting from one position to another. From his prior ethnographic experiences, Harvey found resources and insights that equipped him in his therapeutic practice. The social closeness he sought as an ethnographer had no direct equivalent in his clinical practice, but furnished him with experiential knowledge of prisoner's lives that he found invaluable in a therapeutic context. He proposes a hybrid, a synthesis, in the form of 'an ethnographic practitioner' that might bring the richness and depth of ethnographic knowledge to bear on the training and practice of the clinician.

The intrinsic humanistic features of ethnography are noted by Hage (2012), and the potential, but unintended, therapeutic impact of social interviews is recognised by Illouz (2007). Illouz, for example, notes that the famous Hawthorn Effect arose at least in part out of the unseen affective impact of the (mostly female) factory workers being interviewed by attentive researchers who appeared to value their opinion, whereas the (mostly male) management appeared indifferent to them. The art of listening (Back, 2007) soothes as well as reveals.

Much of what is discussed in this part of the Handbook has antecedents in critical social science and the wider ethnographic literature (see Liebling, 2001). The dilemmas and paradoxes of the insider and the outsider are the stock-in-trade of the ethnographer. The role of the ethnographic researcher, their personal characteristics and peculiarities and their social position and orientations have all become more fully recognised as epistemologically significant. Who you are, what you do and how you do it increasingly matter in contemporary ethnographic research in prison. The craftwork advocated by Mills involves weaving this personal biography into social, situated history.

What is new and collected here are six detailed and candid accounts of this process. Although largely focused on English research experiences in men's and women's prisons, the account from Ghana of similar dilemmas, negotiations and epistemological implications indicates that such experiences might not be exclusive to the metropolitan, Anglophone, North. Recognising the international diversity of prison experience depends on a diversity of ethnographic accounts. Particularly welcome, therefore, is Ayete-Nyampong's insightful account of ethnographic work in Ghana's correctional youth custody projects. It implicitly reveals the reach of English penal practice and the excluding legacies of colonialism. Borstal and Bentham are conjoined and co-opted in a complex web of history that takes a village in Kent and an Enlightenment philosopher to a coastal city and teenage boys in modern West Africa. What lies between and beyond are questions of prison ethnography yet to come.

References

Back, L. (2007) *The Art of Listening* (Oxford: Berg).

Hage, G. (2012) 'Critical Anthropological Thought and the Radical Political Imaginary Today', *Critique of Anthropology*, 32, 3, 285–308.

Illouz, E (2007) *Cold Intimacies: The Making of Emotional Capitalism* (Cambridge: Polity Press).

Liebling, A. (2001) 'Whose Side Are We On? Theory, Practice and Allegiances in Prisons Research', *British Journal of Criminology*, 41, 3, 472–84.

Mills, C. W. (1959) *The Sociological Imagination* (New York: Oxford University Press).

15
Insider Ethnography or the Tale of the Prison Governor's New Clothes

Jamie Bennett

Introduction

Whilst many ethnographic and anthropological studies report the work of outsiders exploring remote and alien cultures, in this chapter I will discuss a different approach: that of 'insider' ethnography. This is concerned with ethnography 'characterised by significant levels of initial proximity between researcher and researched' (Hodkinson, 2005: 132). Drawing upon my own research on prison managers, funded by HM Prison Service and conducted whilst I myself was a prison manager, I will discuss the origins and design of my ethnographic work. It is a reflexive account of conducting fieldwork that considers how the dual identities of insider and researcher were entangled in ways that are significant not only methodologically but also in revealing dynamics of power (Sparks et al., 1996), in this case between researcher, researched and the host organisation, who was also my funder and employer.

My ethnographic research considered the working lives of prison managers in the context of late modernity (Bennett, 2012). I was particularly concerned with the impact of neo-liberal globalisation, as reflected specifically in managerialism, a broad set of organisational practices and values that have reshaped public sector management including the importation of commercial practices such as performance measurements and monitoring, market competition and economies of scale. The work was interested in how this intersected with localised cultures, including prison occupational cultures and individual agency. I concluded that the working lives of prison managers was dominated by '*prison* managerialism', a term which endeavoured to encapsulate the duality of internal culture and globalised trends, capturing the way they intersected and interacted sometimes in harmony and sometimes in conflict. The everyday practice of prison managers was characterised by the navigation and negotiation between these forces.

The origins of this project lay in my own professional and personal experiences. In 1996, with the intention of extending my interest in social justice into a career, I joined the Prison Service on a fast-track management programme, becoming a governor grade in 1999. During my time managing prisons, I have wrestled with complex and unresolved moral dilemmas. How far can I progress issues of social justice within prisons and how far does that have a broader impact on society? Does the structure of society mean that imprisonment merely entrenches, legitimates and enforces power and inequality? What is my role as a public 'expert' on criminal justice issues – to advocate on behalf of an optimistic approach to prisons or to problematise it and argue for its abolition? The origin of this research was therefore personal but also brought into focus wider sociological issues, including the relationship between agency and structure and that between global and local forces. I sought, through ethnographic research, an opportunity to explore and understand in a more systematic way my own working world and indeed myself. From the outset, the research and my role as a working prison manager were inextricably linked.

Choosing research methods

In order to explore the working lives of prison managers, I decided that an ethnographic approach was required, one that was 'grounded in a commitment to the first-hand experience and exploration of a particular social or cultural setting on the basis of (though not exclusively by) participant observation' (Atkinson et al., 2001: 4). There were some specific features of both the subject that had been identified and the setting in which it was taking place that made this approach relevant.

In relation to the subject, ethnography has been identified as being particularly relevant to exploratory or 'pathbreaking' research (Fielding, 2001), and this project fitted that in as much as it involved a relatively unexplored area with a broad agenda. The nature of the research was to address the lived experiences of work, including how rules and routines were understood and enacted. Ethnography of work has been able to explore this whilst also linking this with broader sociological questions such as the relationship between agency and structure (Smith, 2001), organisational and occupational culture (Frow and Morris, 2000; Parker, 2000) and issues of power and inequality (Smith, 2001).

Ethnography also has an established track record in British prisons (e.g. Sparks et al., 1996; Liebling assisted by Arnold, 2004; Crewe, 2009; Drake, 2012; Phillips, 2012), specifically in researching prison staff (Liebling and Price, 2001; Crawley, 2004). This work has revealed the complex social interactions that shape the prison world, shed light upon what are often obscured and hidden aspects of the institution and has connected this with wider sociological perspectives (Wacquant, 2002).

The central approach taken in ethnography is the use of participant observation (Fielding, 2001). However, approaches to observation vary along a spectrum from participant to non-participant and even within one study, such as this one, the role and identity of the researcher will be unstable and vary according to circumstances at different moments. A range of other strategies are also deployed in ethnographic research such as formal and informal interviewing, systematic counting and examining documents. Such a wide range of strategies are now being used that it has been suggested that there is 'a carnivalesque profusion of methods, perspectives and theoretical justifications for ethnographic work' (Atkinson et al., 2001: 3). In this particular study, there were three sources of data generated: 62 days of observations of managers in their day-to-day roles, 60 semi-structured interviews with them and documentary evidence collected in the sites.

The fieldwork for this study was conducted in two medium-security prisons in England over a 12-month period. The two prisons were relatively modern, both being constructed and opened in the mid-1980s. Their organisational life took place against the background of the growth in the use of imprisonment, which dramatically accelerated from the early 1990s. Their institutional history was entangled with this, and both prisons had subsequently been expanded with the addition of extra prisoner accommodation and facilities. At the time the research was conducted, both held over 600 prisoners and both were undergoing further expansion.

Much of my research was located in spaces away from the maelstrom of the prisoner society and staff–prisoner interactions on wings, workshops and exercise yards. Significant time was spent in offices and meeting rooms in 'admin' areas. Even those interactions with prisoners generally took place with individuals in office-based interviews, disciplinary adjudications or in the conduct of routinised processes such as on reception and discharge. More unstructured interactions in social spaces did take place, often at times where there was a high concentration of prisoners such as the serving of meals, coming in or going out from exercise or during movements to and from work. Rather than management being located in a 'backstage' world, there appeared to be a number of distinct but intersecting social milieus – including that of staff, prisoners and managers. The spaces inhabited by managers in some respects replicated those of the typical bureaucratic organisation – bland beige offices and meeting rooms with functional furniture, motivational posters and displays of corporate information, the multiplicity of computers, telephones and filing cabinets. However, to suggest that they were identical would be to ignore the bars on the windows, the locks on the doors, the key chains and security cards and the uniforms worn by some staff. The milieu of the prison manager reflected the dual pressures of both a homogenised organisational regime and the distinctive local aspects of the prison world.

Entering the field

Gaining access to prisons can be 'a time consuming and problematic process' (Smith and Wincup, 2000: 335), and certainly there have been many examples of researchers being denied access or having their ambitions curtailed in the process of negotiating access. However, as an insider negotiating access was less time consuming and was not problematic in the same way. In practical terms, gaining entry to the prisons was straightforward. Personal contact was made with the senior managers in the two prisons, the research explained, and they immediately consented.

The complexity of conducting insider ethnography has often been discussed in epistemological terms. Whilst historically insider ethnography was viewed negatively within the field (see Eriksen, 2001), it has become increasingly accepted (Jackson, 1987). In contemporary ethnography, a more nuanced view of insider ethnography has emerged (Hodkinson, 2005). This recognises that there are risks the insider needs to be conscious of, including failing to explore and reveal 'taken for granted' aspects of a culture and failing to adopt a sufficiently critical perspective. However, there are also potential benefits including being able to screen for credibility, being able to deploy knowledge to identify salient issues for research and being able to establish rapport. The role of insider researcher requires a degree of reflexivity and discipline in order to realise the potential benefits, whilst avoiding the potential pitfalls. Such theoretical exploration of the role of insider research does, however, risk imposing an artificial neatness on the process itself and the complex ways in which the researcher and the researched interact and understand one another.

On my first day conducting fieldwork, I quickly gained a sense of how my identity as both a researcher and a prison manager would shape people's perspectives in diverse ways. I attended the daily management meeting at nine o'clock, which involved a range of managers from around the prison and discussed operational incidents, the absentee staff and other policy and performance issues. I briefly introduced myself and the purpose of my research. During the meeting, a manager made a series of risqué jokes, firstly about his relationship with his wife and then about his dog which had been 'shagging sheep'. At first there was little laughter, and one person said that they did not want to join in because of 'our guest', referring to me. To this the manager responded by saying, 'Don't worry, he's not bothered about that.' This seemed to encapsulate how for some I was a harmless colleague used to the masculine banter of prison life, whilst for others I was a potentially dangerous outsider of whom they should be wary. After the meeting, I met with a manager who had an extensive academic background and found myself being seen from a different perspective, focusing in detail on my researcher position. Later in the day, I toured the prison and was introduced to a variety of staff, who, when

I said I was researching managers, would often respond with mocking, though good-natured, laughter and comments such as 'if you can find them'. When my role as a prison manager was disclosed, this was often met with excessive deference in a similarly mocking, but good-natured, tone. These responses again drew upon my dual identities and revealed some of the barriers I would face on being seen as an 'outsider' by some groups, not only as a result of being a researcher but also due to being a prison manager. Whilst such interactions revealed to me the complex and diverse ways in which I would be perceived and people would interact with me, I also spent the day feeling uncomfortable in my new role, not entirely understanding what it was to be an insider researcher. The routines and practices of prison life were familiar to me, and I struggled to have a clear sense of my new role and the perspective that I should adopt. My field notes were heavily descriptive, lacking in detail and largely ignoring my own feelings and personal reflections. My experience was that becoming an insider researcher was a messy, inelegant, even crude process which only came incrementally through practice over time and sometimes involving uncomfortable reflection. I would also not wish to suggest that my experience of being an insider researcher was ever accomplished in the sense that it was complete; instead, it always felt inchoate and incomplete, a constant process of navigation and negotiation, with myself as well as those around me. However, this was a process which was potentially rich with meaning and one which not only could enable the process of observing and understanding the field from a new perspective but was also a conduit through which the tensions and conflicts of the field could be expressed and sited. It is to this process which I now turn.

Conducting the fieldwork: Problems and challenges

Whilst some other research studies by prison management insiders have simply stated their personal experience and affiliations and treated it as a declaration of interests (e.g. Bryans, 2007), I will attempt to provide a more reflexive account of the research process. This section broadly covers three issues: identities, power and confidentiality and interventions.

Identities

Identity is the idea that individuals have a concept of the self, a sense of who they are and their place in the world, what has been described as the 'sustaining of coherent, yet continuously revised, biographical narratives' (Giddens, 1991: 5). In the process of carrying out this research, there were shifts in my own sense of identity, but there were also responses from subjects regarding who they thought I was and how they understood my identity. These two aspects will be discussed below.

My own sense of identity was intimately bound up in the research methodology and my role as an insider researcher. For an ethnographer studying a field they are familiar with, the challenge is identified as achieving sufficient critical distance, a process of 'getting *out*, of distancing themselves from their far-too-familiar surroundings' (Lofgren, 1987). In that way, a position is sought which is intimate enough to gain access, empathise and understand but at the same time sufficiently detached in order to reflect and analyse what has been described as walking a tight rope between 'empathy and repulsion, home and strangeness, seeing and not seeing' (Sarsby, 1984). It is this position between distance and intimacy that has been described as the essence of ethnographic fieldwork; 'it is out of this experience of being simultaneously an insider and an outsider that creative insight is generated' (Fielding, 2001: 151).

There were some ways in which I tried to create distance through the research design itself. In particular, I selected prisons that I was not familiar with and therefore they and the people who worked there were largely unknown to me. By having sites that are separate from my direct personal experience, this helped me to see things anew and to feel some unfamiliarity in a familiar environment (Strathern, 1987). The planning of the research and background reading gave some shape and structure to the observations, shifting me from my work identity or at least providing me with a reflexive appreciation of it and helping me to view the environment from a sociological rather than a managerial perspective. The use of field notes, the constant carrying of a notebook and frequently writing observations and entries also anchored me into the purpose for which I was there. In these ways, I was trying to manufacture and sustain a sense of disciplined subjectivity (Wolcott, 2005).

There was also a more intimate, intense and personal experience that I went through in order to achieve a sense of detachment. I can now 'reflect on the self that [I] had to become in order to pass in the setting, and how that temporary, setting-specific self differs from the person that [I] normally [am]' (Fielding, 2001: 151). The most visible and outward manifestation of the changes in my identity were in my personal appearance. Before entering the first research site I had to decide what I was going to wear. This was a more challenging and complex issue than simple vanity. This struck at the heart of my identity and the change that I was undertaking. Clothes are not merely for discretion or warmth but are also related to identity: 'Essentially people use clothes to make two basic statements: first, this is the sort of person I am; and secondly, this is what I am doing' (Ross, 2008: 6–7). In prisons, clothing has a particular meaning and is used in order to communicate distinctions of status. There is a long history of prisoner clothing being used as a reflection of changing penal philosophies from the uniformity of arrowed and striped clothing to the liberalism of prisoners wearing their own clothes and on to new punitive practices using high-visibility clothes (Ash, 2010). For staff also, the use of prison uniform and military style insignias of rank are used in order to convey a sense of order, status and discipline, with governor grades distinguished by the fact that they wear suits rather than uniform, sometimes even being referred to as 'suits' and promotion into their ranks being described as 'getting your suit'. My decision about what clothes to wear therefore took on a particularly potent texture and felt that it went to the essence of both who I had been and who I was attempting to become.

I decided to wear casual, reasonably smart clothing but avoid suits and ties. This decision was intended to convey a difference from my previous identity as a prison manager and to mark myself out as someone who was not in the prison as an employee. This change in status and role did not go unnoticed by others. One officer directly asked me what it was like going from a 'high-powered job' to coming in speaking to staff wearing a T-shirt and jeans (I was wearing a polo shirt and chinos, but the question was still a good one). Other staff, including senior managers, did occasionally comment on my casual attire, usually in a light-hearted way, but also in sufficient numbers to indicate how important this was in defining my change in role and perceived status.

I also found myself going through changes that indicated a personal journey I was undertaking. I became increasingly comfortable in casual clothing and increasingly uncomfortable in a suit, so that those occasions outside of the research when I had to wear a tie, I found it strangulating and almost impossible to wear. I grew my hair longer and even sported a beard at one stage. The way that research can have an impact on the researcher and is manifested in personal appearance was graphically illustrated on the cover of Malcolm Young's *An Inside Job* (1991), where two photographs of the author contrasted the clean-cut police officer with the hippyish researcher. These changes are not superficial, but reflect a deeper questioning taking place as a result of the temporary role in the field. Young observed that there is an intense, intimate and personal experience, a 'radical reflexivity' (ibid. p. 25), which is needed to create the distance required:

> It requires a conscious act of experiencing a reflection of yourself and of how you have become what you are. It can be quite painful, for the insider is studying his own social navel, with the potential always present that he will recognize this to be only one of a number of arbitrary possibilities and perhaps also find that many practices are built on the flimsiest of moral precepts.
>
> (ibid. p. 9)

Rather than drawing me in to 'going native', the research led me to question my profession and my own role, reflect on the morality of practices I engaged in, choices I made and accommodations I accepted. These are not always comfortable considerations. I particularly questioned the role of prison in society and its role in maintaining and reinforcing power and inequality (e.g. see Bennett, 2008). This also led me to question my role as a prison manager, as well as those of other prison managers, whether I and they reinforce, resist or ameliorate these conditions. This questioning is difficult but is also creative and rewarding as part of the process of exploring the field from a space that is both intimate but also sufficiently detached in order to facilitate meaningful observation. When I had entered prisons as a professional, I rather idealistically felt that this was an opportunity to engage with issues of social justice, but by the end of the research, my perspective had shifted and instead I saw myself engaged in a messy set of compromises and challenges regarding values and beliefs, getting my hands dirty in a social field of struggle.

Whilst these changes in my own identity mark the journey I was undertaking, no researcher acts in isolation. Those who are the subject of the research also have a sense or perception of my identity. This is often intertwined with organisational culture and structures as it is related to any personal identity I projected. There are seven predominant ways in which I felt that I was perceived by those in the field.

The first is as a *colleague*. As has been described earlier, the fact that I was an insider meant that access was easier and also meant that I understood the language, acronyms and technicalities of processes in prisons. This is useful in enabling staff to speak to me with some degree of confidence that their perceptions would be understood and empathised with. I did not face any resistance as an 'outsider' or have to undertake any rites of passage in order to be accepted. In fact, that acceptance was often instant; for example, one senior officer went as far to describe me in a team briefing as 'one of us'. This sense of shared experiences and belonging did create some challenges in focusing on the research issues. Some outside researchers can adopt a position of naivety which would allow them to explore what were taken for granted assumptions and practices. I had to manufacture this sense by explaining to people that although I was familiar with the technicalities or mechanics of prison management, my role as a researcher meant that I was looking at it from a different perspective. Generously, everyone was willing to do this, although it did illustrate that the first perception that many people had of me was as a fellow member of prison staff rather than a researcher.

The second identity is that of *superior* in an organisational hierarchy. As those I was interacting with knew my background and previous roles, some were conscious that I held a formal rank and status within the organisation. For example, occasionally I would be called 'Sir' or 'Governor', and one interviewee asked, 'is it okay to call you "Jamie" since you're an ex-Dep?'[1] Such forms of address and the seeking of permission to drop formalities convey a sense of the importance of status and hierarchy within the organisation. However, such interactions also perform a function for those who are using them, acting as signals that they should be cautious about what they say and do.

A third, and related, identity is that of *expert*. I was sometimes asked by individuals or in meetings to comment on policies, practices or provide feedback. I studiously avoided doing this, always explaining that I was there in a particular role of researcher. This was never pushed by the questioners and was accepted on the face of it. However, this did disclose a degree to which participants were aware that I was not a naive observer but instead carried a professional history and knowledge.

The fourth identity is that of *mentee*. Some managers, notably some who were older, more experienced and particularly those who were more senior than me in the organisational hierarchy, adopted a mentoring role towards me. They were willing to spend additional time with me, ensuring that I had support and access, willing to share their thoughts and experiences and also offer unsolicited advice on my future career. This benevolent interest was helpful and appreciated but was also an assertion of hierarchy, control and a tacit reinforcement of my insider position.

These first four identities are linked in as much as they all relate to hierarchical position, rank or status within the organisation. They reveal that whilst I was not in a formal position, I was perceived by many to carry residual status and identity as a prison manager.

The fifth identity is *auditor*. Some managers asked how the outcomes of my research would be used within the organisation. Although I explained that this was not the purpose or nature of the work, some managers found this difficult to comprehend. For example, many people asked about or referred to the 'report' I was writing, a term that implied that it has some official purpose. Another example is where one governor grade approached me anxiously saying that he had been told I was completing 'a cost-benefit comparison' between the two prisons. Although I had previously explained the nature of the research and reiterated this, there remained a residual anxiety from that individual, reflecting a concern about the purpose and uses to which the research may be put by the organisation. Some managers also responded to the research by putting on a performance as if they were being tested and were anxious to pass. These individuals would often use management phrases and clichés in order to respond to questions and would constantly seek to give positive examples of what they had done, claim credit for innovations and provide 'spin'. Given that I had spent some considerable time in the field by the time I carried out the interviews, these distortions were relatively easy to detect and were themselves telling about the individuals and sometimes about wider prison management. Nevertheless, they also reveal one of the ways in which I and my research were understood and approached by the participants.

The sixth identity is as an *enigma*. For some people, I was difficult to understand and to pigeon hole, and they appeared bemused as to what I was doing and why I was doing it. This was revealed in some of the comments that were made about my personal appearance as described above. Indeed, one senior manager, during the phase that I had longer hair and a beard, described me in a joking way as 'Che Guevara'. Whilst this may just have been a reference to my appearance, it may also have indicated that beyond curiosity, there may have been suspicion or discomfort about my motives or that I deviated from and subverted cultural expectations by undertaking this research role.

The final way in which I was understood was as a *researcher*. However, this was not discrete from my organisational identity and in many ways was a manufactured identity. There were some managers who had themselves undertaken research and were able to discuss meaningfully the research process and my role. They particularly understood what I was doing, how I was doing it and some of the complexities. As the research progressed, other managers also seemed to accept that I was there in a particular role and started to become protective of that. For example, when I was asked in meetings to comment on issues, other managers would step in on my behalf explaining that I was there as a researcher. Whilst this may have also been about protecting their own status and position, the fact that this appeared to happen more as time went on indicated that this at least in part reflected that they accepted my role as researcher. However, for some there was an inherent problem with being a manager and a researcher. On more than one occasion, I was asked penetrating questions about my motives and any personal or career advantage that I may accrue from conducting the research. One manager took a different angle and asked candidly whether it was possible for me to be unbiased, given my background, and describing how they felt judged by my observing them. My identity as a researcher appeared manufactured, incomplete and inextricably bound up with my organisational position, although it did form part of how I was understood and viewed by others.

Power

Power in its most general terms refers to the production of causal effects (Scott, 2001). This is not only a subject of this research, but is an ethical and practical problem in its conduct. As an 'insider', I am someone who potentially holds power, but I am also the subject of power and potentially the medium for it. There is therefore a particular issue about the potential effects of the research for myself and for others.

I will start by discussing the ways in which I may have been the subject of power. This has been described as the 'special problem' of prison research where access and funding are restricted, and therefore there are risks regarding the control and shaping of research (Sparks et al., 1996: 339). There are both formal and informal ways in which organisations can attempt to shape and control research outcomes (Whyte, 2000; King, 2000). However, the argument that organisations will overtly control research can be overplayed, and it should be recognised that the process of gaining access and conducting research is negotiated, meaning that the researcher themselves exercise significant power (Hammersley, 1995; King, 2000). In my specific case, the research was funded initially by the Leadership and Development team of the Prison Service as an individually negotiated personal development opportunity. The head of that particular team was keen to promote innovative development opportunities and was willing to make funds available to support this. Although that individual asked me to include in the research some analysis of data that had already been generated on prison managers using Myers-Briggs personality assessments, this was quickly forgotten as that individual moved on from their role, and it has not been part of the research project. Each year I have had to resubmit an application for funding which has asked for little more than an update on progress. As has already been described, access to the prisons was straightforward without any attempt to alter or shape the research agenda. There was not therefore the intimate scrutiny and collaboration in establishing the research agenda that have been discussed elsewhere (Sparks et al., 1996; Smith and Wincup, 2000).

During the conduct of the research, there were not any overt attempts to control or shape what was happening. There were rare comments made, including an offer to keep a senior manager 'informed' about a prison being researched, occasional requests to ignore or overlook comments that may have been seen as inappropriate or unprofessional ('don't write that down', 'you're not making a note of that?') and a prodding desire that the outcome of the research would be 'favourable' to a particular prison. However, these comments were never made with a sense of any meaningful pressure and were never taken seriously by me or followed up by those who made them. Later, questions about the research by those people were satisfied (or deterred) by general feedback about which stage the research was at or sociological concepts that may be relevant, no information was directly asked for or disclosed that would have breached confidentiality. Similar comments frequently crop up in methodological accounts and should not be considered indicative of any serious attempt to corrupt or distort the research findings, but were instead a reflection of the natural uncertainty and nervousness of research subjects who surrendered considerable power to a researcher.

However, overt power is not the only way in which control can be exercised, and there are often soft forms of power that achieve the same outcomes. There are more subtle ways in which the values of funders and researchers can become inexorably interlinked through their relationship (Cheek, 2000), and this can be a particular issue where, like me, they are an employee (Sparks et al., 1996). I have acquired a certain amount of organisational trust and have accepted the obligations and responsibilities that come with that, including that publications are subject to official approval in order to ensure that they are not overtly political or breach the Civil Service Code. However, within those constraints I have also cultivated an alternative identity as a commentator on prison issues, being editor of the *Prison Service Journal* since 2004, a member of the editorial board of the *Howard Journal of Criminal Justice, Criminal Justice Matters,* the author of a number of articles and the editor of three books. Some of these articles have been critical of prisons generally or Prison Service policy in particular. In these ways, I have a developed and practised critical appreciation of the work that I do and the field in which I operate. Whilst the final thesis is not polemic, it does include observations that are critical of or are at odds with official accounts.

As an insider, my experience as the subject of power was different from that of external researchers. In the design, funding, approval and fieldwork stage, there was an absence of formal control, and I was able to proceed with minimal scrutiny. Indeed, the most striking feature has been the absence of control rather than the exercise of it.

I will now turn to the ways in which I may have been the facilitator of power. My intention was to carry out research on prison managers, who are people who themselves hold significant power over others. In his work, Bryans (2007: 6) described prison governors as a powerful 'criminal justice elite'. Pahl (1980) has argued that sociology has largely ignored the powerful in favour of the powerless and addressing this deficit could have significant value:

> If the everyday worlds with which we are most familiar are mainly those of the underdogs or, at best, the middle dogs, we are forced to fall back on the accounts of non-sociologists for an understanding of the top dogs... If one argues that our understanding of the powerless has been greatly improved through sociological analysis, surely our understanding of the powerful could also be improved.
>
> (p. 130–1)

However, are prison managers really a powerful elite? Gouldner (1973) also argued in favour of undertaking sociology of the powerful but argued that prison managers, school head teachers and hospital administrators were not the powerful but were also underdogs. He described that these 'local caretaking officials' were generally depicted in sociology as ignorant and poor managers. He went on to say that these depictions carried

> a political payload. For it is this discrediting of local officials that legitimates the claims of the higher administrative classes... and gives them an entering wedge on the local level.
>
> (ibid., p. 50)

A study of prison managers therefore has to be conscious of the risks of being used in unintended ways and for reasons that are not approved or supported by the researcher (for a poignant example, see Sparks, 2002). As a result, this study attempted to avoid appearing as a formal evaluation of effectiveness and instead was an attempt to provide a sociological exploration. By the very nature of the subject of agency and structure, prison managers were explored not only as the holders of power but also as the subjects of it. It was therefore not attempting to place prison managers in the position of being elite or the sole holders of power. It is as much about their powerlessness as much as it is about their power.

Finally, I will address the ways in which I was the holder of power and others were the subjects of it. I have already touched upon some of these, but they are worth reiterating. The first was that any researcher holds some power in as much as people exposed themselves and their work to the scrutiny of someone who would analyse and write about it without them having control. This was a significant act of trust by the participants and an accumulation of power and responsibility by the researcher. As has been previously mentioned, my role as an insider may have carried with it expectations about comradeship and may have facilitated access, it was therefore important for me to structure expectations by being clear about the nature of the research, the areas being considered and to provide commitments about confidentiality. The second aspect of my power related back to my role as a serving prison manager. This was brought sharply into focus on the one occasion when a member of staff declined to be interviewed. I had intended to go back to the manager in charge of the prison on that particular day and arrange an alternative interview, as they assisted me by making staff available. The interviewee expressed concern about this and stated that they may be challenged or criticised for refusing to take part, not by me but by the manager I would be speaking to. As a result, I decided not to arrange an alternative interview and went home for the day. Although on this occasion the risk was managed and avoided, it nevertheless highlighted that I was perceived by some as having power through the support of senior people within the establishment. Although I did not sense that others were concerned about this, it was an issue that I became increasingly conscious of as a result.

As an insider, the complexities, challenges and risks of research display both similarities and differences compared with external researchers. In some ways, the process of the research was eased and the logistics were more straightforward. There were the same risks of control and misuse of findings. However, there were more subtle challenges both in the ways that organisational power flowed in shaping the researcher and the response of the participants. As an insider researcher, it is essential that one is alert to this and open to ways in which this can be manifested and managed.

Confidentiality and intervention

Many researchers report ethical dilemmas presented where they have to ask themselves whether they should maintain the mask of the neutral and passive researcher or whether they should intervene (for particularly vivid examples, see Crewe, 2009). This was a dilemma that I faced on several occasions throughout the research; again, my insider status made these challenges at least feel different to those situations presented in other research.

As was mentioned previously, the only time in which there appeared to be a request to breach confidentiality was when a senior manager asked me to keep him 'informed' of the research. This appeared to be an implied invitation to do more than simply discuss the sociological findings but instead to pass judgement and nuggets of information about the organisation and individuals. As I have said previously, this was not followed up and subsequent conversations and feedback were in the most general terms regarding the progress of the research, and I was not directly asked to breach any confidentiality.

There were a number of occasions during the research where people made comments that I felt were distasteful and sometimes racist or sexist. One in particular had a strong impact. On that occasion, a manager shared an anecdote about a conversation he had with a more senior, female colleague at a previous prison, during which he had described overweight women as 'pigs in knickers'. This left me feeling sickened at the degrading language and attitude displayed. Many researchers have reported having 'well-bitten tongues' from remaining silent when comments are made (Crewe, 2009). However, this left me sharing Crewe's feelings of shame at the 'collusive silences' (ibid.: 475) that were maintained. In my circumstances, I was particularly concerned as my organisational status may have conferred a greater degree of tacit approval to what was said, but I had to balance that with the potential benefits of gaining a rounded picture of the world I was examining.

During the research, people appeared to become increasingly relaxed, testing me with disclosures about their views about managers, and once established that I would listen and hold confidences, they opened up to disclosures about a range of issues. As ever, it was the disclosures of breaches of formal rules that provide a barometer of the honesty and openness of participants. Some revealed experiences of witnessing the abuse of prisoners in the distant past, many disclosed practices such as manipulating performance information and others disclosed more individual but deeply held personal beliefs about issues such as religion or politics. As with the comments described above, the balance seemed to lie in maintaining openness rather than shutting this down and breaching confidentiality.

On one occasion, I felt that the balance lay differently. In this situation, I was shadowing a manager, who had to carry out a series of checks in the reception area of the prison. A prisoner had arrived, who claimed to have been assaulted by prison staff at the prison he had just left. Initially, it was not clear that there was going to be any follow up on this. I decided that the risk was serious and immediate and therefore wanted to be assured that the prisoner was receiving medical attention and that the matter was properly recorded. In the event, the manager I was shadowing did ensure that these things happened without the need for me to intervene. I am sure that the questions I was asking betrayed more than a research interest at the time and that my concern was clear. Although I was satisfied that my conduct was necessary in the circumstances, it illustrates that I always acted as a researcher on a contingent and inchoate basis.

One issue that is often raised in research is about loyalties and taking sides, again a particular issue in prisons where the divisions between groups are sometimes marked, such as between prisoners and staff or between managers and the managed. In one of the sites, I was present during a one-day strike by the Prison Officers' Association. Some managers were members of the union and therefore joined the strike (most senior and principal officers) whilst others were not and therefore operated the prison during the day. I decided that I would cross the picket line and enter the prison. I did not feel compromised by this; as a result, both of the fact that I was researching managers and was therefore interested in how they would deal with the situation and also that as a governor grade I would not be expected by those on the picket line to join a strike and instead would be expected to go in. My dual identity acted as a protection on this occasion. During the day I was able to talk to managers on both sides and afterwards I was able to discuss the strike openly with those who took part without any adverse reaction. Whilst in the prison, I also made it clear that should the need arise I would be willing to assist with the operation of the prison. This assessment was based on the immediacy of the risk that can accompany a strike situation. With just a small number of people on duty during strike action, the safety of staff and prisoners can be compromised. However, in the event I was only asked to cover a unit during a meal break, but again this reveals how my responsibilities as an employee remained extant, even if temporarily subdued.

These dilemmas about when to stand back, when to intervene, when to keep confidentiality and when to break it are always presented in the field. However, there were occasions when my dual role had an influence, in shaping the nature and context of these dilemmas.

Leaving the field

In each prison, there was a pre-arranged fixed period for my stay (six months) and a set programme of work that I intended to carry out. It was therefore a straightforward logistical task to end the research. I offered to return in due course to present some of the findings but it would be four years before that happened.

Leaving the field was not, however, simply a technical task but was instead part of a personal journey or 'rite de passage' (Young, 1991: 63) which had seen me change in many ways. As I prepared to leave the second research site, my casual clothing started to become smarter, my hair shorter and ties felt less constricting. Within two months of completing the fieldwork, I had taken up a post as governor of a prison. Although I outwardly returned to my previous occupation, I did not feel like the same person who had gone into the research. I felt more questioning, less attached to the organisation for its own sake, more conscious of the social web that imprisonment formed part of and more conscious of the strengths and limitations of managerial practices. This made me a different prison manager, although I make no claims to be a more effective one, but that, after all, was never the purpose.

On taking up my new post, I became immediate colleagues with the governors of the two prisons I had conducted the research in. We had to re-establish our relationships in new roles and were able to move on. However, the need for me to maintain confidentiality was apparent, and they both respected that my research would develop at its own pace and in its own way. Apart from the occasional polite question about when it would be completed, neither has ever wanted to know more about it nor asked to intervene in any way.

Having undertaken this research, it also meant that I would now be marked not only in how I saw the world, but also how I would be perceived. Although there may not be the open and intense hostility towards inside researchers as there has been in the past (Young, 1991 see also Mascarenhas-Keyes, 1987), there is a degree of antagonism that could arise from being so publicly identified as a prison manager with an interest in research, intellectual inquiry or academic study. This is an antagonism that was, in itself, revealing about the culture of prison management. There is a cultural tension within prison management in which some prison managers define the world of prison management as being made up of two mutually exclusive groups, the first was described using terms such a 'academic' or 'process-orientated' or 'strategy', in contrast to the second group that were described using terms such as 'practical', 'people-orientated' and 'operational'. Whilst such distinctions were false and incomplete, the language and tensions are important in understanding culture (Parker, 2000), but were also part of my own personal story.

On leaving the field, I completed a phase in the research, but I also entered into a new phase of my personal and professional life. In this phase, I certainly did not claim to have the answers but I did have a better understanding of the questions, issues, complexities, tensions and problems of the world in which I worked and researched.

Note

1. That is, Deputy Governor.

Further reading

Hodkinson, P. (2005) 'Insider Research in the study of Youth Cultures', *Journal of Youth Studies*, 8, 2, 131–49.

Jackson, A. (ed) (1987) *Anthropology at Home* (London: Tavistock Publications).

Young, M. (1991) *An Inside Job: Policing and Police Culture in Britain* (Oxford: Clarendon Press).

References

Ash, J. (2010) *Dress Behind Bars: Prison Clothing as Criminality* (London: IB Tauris).

Atkinson, P., Coffey, A., Delamont, S., Lofland, J. and Lofland, L. (2001) 'Editorial Introduction', in P. Atkinson, A. Coffey, S. Delamont, J. Lofland and L. Lofland (eds) *Handbook of Ethnography* (London: Sage).

Bennett, J. (2012) *The Working Lives of Prison Managers: Exploring Agency and Structure in the Late Modern Prison*, Unpublished PhD thesis, University of Edinburgh, Edinburgh.

Bennett, J. (2008) *The Social Costs of Dangerousness: Prisons and the Dangerous Classes* (London: Centre for Crime and Justice Studies). Available at http://www.crimeandjustice.org.uk/opus540/Dangerousness_finalweb.pdf [accessed August 2011].

Bryans, S. (2007) *Prison Governors: Managing Prisons in a Time of Change* (Cullompton: Willan).

Cheek, J. (2000) 'An Untold Story? Doing Funded Qualitative Research', in N. Denzin and Y. Lincoln (eds) *Handbook of Qualitative Research,* Second edition (London: Sage).

Crawley, E. (2004) *Doing Prison Work: The Public & Private Lives of Prison Officers* (Cullompton: Willan).

Crewe, B. (2009) *The Prisoner Society: Power, Adaptation and Social life in an English Prison* (Oxford: Clarendon Press).

Drake, D. H. (2012) *Prisons, Punishment and the Pursuit of Security* (Basingstoke: Palgrave Macmillan).

Eriksen, T. (2001) *Small Places, Large Issues: An Introduction to Social and Cultural Anthropology,* Second edition (London: Pluto Books).

Fielding, N. (2001) 'Ethnography', in N. Gilbert (ed) *Researching Social Life,* Second edition (London: Sage).

Frow, J. and Morris, M. (2000) 'Cultural Studies', in N. Denzin and Y. Lincoln (eds) *Handbook of Qualitative Research*, Second edition (London: Sage).

Giddens, A. (1991) *Modernity and Self-Identity: Self and Society in the Late Modern Age* (Cambridge: Polity Press).

Gouldner, A. (1973) *For Sociology: Renewal and Critique in Sociology Today* (Harmondsworth: Penguin).

Hammersley, M. (1995) *The Politics of Social Research* (London: Sage).

Hodkinson, P. (2005) '"Insider Research', in the Study of Youth Cultures"', *Journal of Youth Studies,* 8, 2, 131–49.

Jackson, A. (1987) 'Reflections on Ethnography at Home and the ASA', in Jackson, A. (ed) *Anthropology at Home* (London: Tavistock Publications).

King, R. (2000) 'Doing Research in Prisons', in R. King and E. Wincup (eds) *Doing Research on Crime and Justice* (Oxford: Oxford University Press).
Liebling, A. assisted by Arnold, H. (2004) *Prisons & Their Moral Performance: A Study of Values, Quality and Prison Life* (Oxford: Clarendon Press).
Liebling, A. and Price, D. (2001) *The Prison Officer* (Leyhill: Prison Service Journal).
Lofgren, O. (1987) 'Deconstructing Swedishness: Culture and Class in Modern Sweden', in A. Jackson (ed) *Anthropology at Home* (London: Tavistock Publications).
Mascarenhas-Keyes, S. (1987) 'The Native Anthropologist: Constraints and Strategies in Research', in A. Jackson (ed) *Anthropology at Home* (London: Tavistock Publications).
Pahl, R. (1980) 'Playing the Rationality Game: The Sociologist as Hired Expert', in C. Bell and H. Newby (eds) *Doing Sociological Research* (London: George Allen and Unwin).
Parker, M. (2000) *Organizational Culture and Identity* (London: Sage).
Phillips, C. (2012) *The Multicultural Prison: Ethnicity, Masculinity and Social Relations among Prisoners* (Oxford: Oxford University Press).
Ross, R. (2008) *Clothing: A Global History* (Cambridge: Polity Press).
Sarsby, J. (1984) 'Special Problems of Fieldwork in Familiar Settings', in R. Allen (ed) *Ethnographic Research: A Guide to General Conduct* (London: Academic Press).
Scott, J. (2001) *Power* (Cambridge: Polity Press).
Smith, V. (2001) 'Ethnographies of Work and the Work of Ethnographers', in P. Atkinson, A. Coffey, S. Delamont, J. Lofland and L. Lofland (eds) *Handbook of Ethnography* (London: Sage).
Smith, C. and Wincup, E. (2000) 'Breaking in: Researching Criminal Justice Institutions for Women', in R. King and E. Wincup (eds) *Doing Research on Crime and Justice* (Oxford: Oxford University Press).
Sparks, R., Bottoms, A. and Hay, W. (1996) *Prisons and the Problem of Order* (Oxford: Clarendon Press).
Sparks, R. (2002) 'Out of the "Digger": The Warrior's Code and the Guilty Observer', *Ethnography,* 3, 4, 556–81.
Strathern, M. (1987) 'The Limits of Auto-Anthropology', in A. Jackson (ed) *Anthropology at Home* (London: Tavistock Publications).
Wacquant, L. (2002) 'The Curious Eclipse of Prison Ethnography in the Age of Mass Incarceration', *Ethnography* 3, 4, 371–97.
Whyte, D. (2000) 'Researching the Powerful: Towards a Political Economy of Method', in R. King and E. Wincup (eds) *Doing Research on Crime and Justice* (Oxford: Oxford University Press).
Wolcott, H. (2005) *The Art of Fieldwork,* Second edition (Walnut Creek, CA: AltaMira Press).
Young, M. (1991) *An Inside Job: Policing and Police Culture in Britain* (Oxford: Clarendon Press).

16
Changing Hats: Transiting between Practitioner and Researcher Roles

Lilian Ayete-Nyampong

Introduction

Ethnographic fieldwork in a site of human confinement over a prolonged period can be challenging and requires a cautious but determined approach. It necessitates being part of the daily lives and routines of two opposing worlds: staff and officers. This challenge is further exacerbated by the diverse roles ascribed to the researcher or those which the researcher assumes.

This chapter brings to the fore some practicalities that confront the ethnographic researcher, who also at the same time retains a practitioner status. It draws from two years of ethnographic research in Ghana from 2009 to 2011 in two confinement sites for children in conflict with the law. This chapter addresses the question: 'what ethical dilemmas does changing hats from practitioner to researcher, and vice versa, present for prison ethnography?' By referring to correctional centres as prisons, I establish the relevance of discussions which draw on my ethnographic research to prison ethnography in Africa. These discussions problematise a research reality that stems from a serendipitous fieldwork experience characterised by the duality of roles and complex entanglements. They also explore the epistemological shifts and power dynamics associated with the respective roles of practitioner and researcher. By recognising my human rights or practitioner status, which facilitated access to these institutions, I acknowledge that the ensuing double role was fraught with challenges which I grappled with throughout the entire research process. In a bid to access information, my researcher role required greater sensitivity and responsiveness to the feelings and sentiments of research informants rather than the mere reliance on a legislative mandate to access these institutions for monitoring purposes. Nevertheless, I was also mindful of the pro-active agency of research informants, who could deliberately conceal information, conduct their own 'impression management' and engage selective gatekeeping.

Reflexivity was central to the research process as my intentions were not only obscure to the various actors in detention but even to me as researcher. Efforts to maintain a delicate balance between my practitioner and researcher selves, the overt and the covert as well as the home (familiar) and the field (strange) did not come easy. This chapter concludes that whereas sticking to blueprints and ethical guidelines may be useful, ethical challenges are often unpredictable, evolving with time and thereby require constant negotiation; they rely on everyday practical remedies and considerations.

Correctional institutions as prisons

Correctional centres or prisons do not lend themselves to a singular definite meaning. Whereas architectural delineations, such as Jeremy Bentham's panopticon, provide some defining features, confinement sites that lack most of these traditional architectural features can be even more repressive due to their sophisticated monitoring mechanisms that deprive the prisoner of his or her liberty as well as dignity.[1]

Two correctional centres provide resources for this chapter: the Senior Correctional Centre (SCC), the only institution for young male offenders in Ghana, and the Junior Correctional Centre (JCC), the only institution for juvenile female offenders. In accordance with Ghana's Juvenile Justice Act 653 of 2003, a juvenile offender is a child under 18 years of age, who has been convicted of an offence, whereas a young offender is one who is 18 years or above (but less than 21 years), who has been convicted of an offence. Juvenile and young offenders are held in junior and senior correctional institutions, respectively. The latter additionally hold juvenile offenders below 15 years who have committed serious offences. The Juvenile Justice Act does not set a lower-level limit for a juvenile offender; this gap is however filled by Section 4 of the Criminal Code (Amendment Act 554 of 1998), which sets the legal age of criminal accountability at 12 years.[2] The Juvenile Justice Act, Section 47 (3), sets the upper limit for children in conflict with the law at 21. By this age, young offenders in committal will have completed their term in the state's senior correctional centre.[3] The legal definition of juvenile and young offenders in detention covers persons between the ages of 12 and 21 in accordance with the relevant laws in Ghana. Similarly, the legal definition of a juvenile delinquent in most African countries is usually restricted to persons under 21 years, though the exact lower- and upper-age limits differ from country to country (Igbinovia, 1985).

The SCC and the JCC were established as separate and distinct institutions by the Juvenile Justice Act in 2003. Prior to the passage of the act, a place for holding juvenile and young offenders were referred to as 'an Industrial school' and 'a Borstal institution', respectively, reflecting the practice of the former British colonial government in the pre-independence Gold Coast state. This change in name, as well as the low-fencing walls that surround these centres, seeks to emphasise the correctional policy of these institutions. In everyday talk, however, these institutions appear more like conventional prisons. Staff and youngsters still refer to the former names of these institutions, which suggest these centres are, effectively, prisons. Low walls and absence of fencing, which is meant to emphasise correction rather than imprisonment, tend to induce the opposite of its intention amongst the young offenders I researched. According to the youngsters, the lack of fencing gave them a feeling of being imprisoned (Ayete-Nyampong, 2013). Also, youngsters expressed surprise, during my focus group discussions, that the institution was not a prison but a correctional establishment. In fact, eight of ten youngsters, prior to committal, had heard that the Borstal, as they were referred to, was 'a prison for bad boys'. Similarly, senior officers of the SCC also sometimes perceive the correctional institution as a prison. They lament that the institution is still being run by prison officers, who have virtually no training in handling children and youngsters. An assistant officer in charge commented: 'This institution was governed by rules formulated by the Ghana Prisons Service and yet these inmates are children. Almost all of us are transferred from adult prisons and so we do not have any particular training to equip us to work with them.' (Ayete-Nyampong, 2013: 67; 2014). Thus, whereas correctional centres established under the new law in Ghana undertake various educational and religious activities in a bid to promote appropriate behavioural changes, the label 'correctional centre' makes little sense to detainees, or even to their staff. In practice, such institutions are still perceived as prisons.

On the basis of such actor perspectives, I conceptualise correctional centres as prisons, thereby locating my research and discussions in this chapter within the context of prison ethnography. An actor-oriented approach is a counterpoint of structural analysis in development sociology (Long, 2001), which recognises that various actors, such as detainees and detaining staff, have differential responses to similar structural causalities of crime and everyday confinement (Ayete-Nyampong, 2013). This approach acknowledges the efforts of social actors as invaluably contributive to any change concerning them. A social actor in this respect is neither merely a synonym for an individual nor is it a fixed social category such as social class or gender, but it is a social construct (Long, 2001). Thus, correctional institutions, prison officers and young offenders are examples of social actors to whom agency can be attributed.

Relevance of the current study: The case for prison ethnography in Africa

In the field of youth justice, the majority of studies in Africa are survey based, with the exception of few studies which employ interviews and direct testimonies from young people. Such survey-based studies aim at formal penal and criminal justice reform and are not well equipped to reveal the context of everyday prison practices. Qualitative studies on juvenile justice in Africa are relatively few in number. South Africa is credited with a high proportion of these studies with a particular and necessary focus on HIV/AIDS in prisons and correctional centres (Gaum et al., 2006); diversion programmes (Cupido et al., 2005); sexual violence, youth gangs and child soldiers (Steinberg, 2004; Petersen et al., 2005).

Ethnographic field studies in Africa's prisons and correctional institutions are scarce. The research by De Kock (2005) on youth in conflict with the law examined life stories of young people awaiting trial in Gauteng, South Africa, but it does not include young offenders in detention. Jefferson (2007), in an eight-month ethnographic field study on prison officers' training and practice in Nigeria, examined penal philosophy and practice of the Nigerian Prisons Service (see also Chapter 8, for Jefferson's contribution to this volume).[4] Lindegaard (2009) did some work on male youngsters in Cape Town. Similarly, Sauls (2009) researched violence and the daily management of children in a place of safety in Cape Town. Some ethnographic research has also been conducted in Uganda, focusing on the justice sector and policy transfer in the global south (Martin, 2012; and see Chapter 22, this volume).

My research and discussions complement scholarly work in Africa, which is mostly preoccupied with 'free youth' in contexts of war, conflict, violence and politics (Honwana and De Boeck, 2005; Christiansen, 2006; Christiansen et al., 2006; Peters, 2006; Abebe and Kjorholt, 2009; Omoniyi et al., 2009). Discussions in this chapter are innovative, given their focus on confined youth. My research approach also abandons dominant domestic and international discourses that have pigeonholed African prisons and correctional centres as characterised by poor material conditions in need of change and reforms (Sarkin, 2008).[5] These perspectives, though useful, have over the years been over-rehearsed, and the repetitive calls for reform and change have not yielded much result.[6] Yet, change is incomplete when it is devoid of context or without regard to insider perspectives.

Researcher status and attendant epistemological shift as well as power dynamics

My research status involved negotiating a shift from my practitioner training in human rights monitoring that drew from epistemological approaches that sought an absolute truth by means of generalisations and statistical representations. This shift in approach sought to address patterns and variations of experience amongst young people in custody. It sometimes required the need to observe the same or different situations continuously for long periods so as to grasp the full import of their diversity. Sustained immersion in the field provides rich empirical data from which theoretical and interpretative frameworks emerged. For instance, I observed that escapes in correctional centres could not be reduced to preventing inmates from absconding and punishing those who escape. Such reduction glosses over the complexities of confinement practice (Sparks, 1996) as depicted through the narration of three cases on escapes (Ayete-Nyampong, 2013: 110–32). These three cases portray the dynamism and paradoxes that surround escape attempts in daily detention life. These escape incidents demonstrate varying acts of everyday negotiations with other youngsters as well as officers in attempts to defy institutional rules. Such escape occurrences are also replete with paradoxes of violent acts and institutional efforts to control such acts. Prior to escapes, youngsters are usually violent and defiant; they are likely to be isolated or confined under harsh conditions. However, instead of promoting compliance with institutional rules, such conditions, rather, tend to make youngsters more violent and defiant. Confinement life is therefore organised around the anticipation of violence and by so doing invites violence. Correctional centres are therefore not only repositories of violence by virtue of housing inmates who possess a history of structural violence. Everyday happenings of confinement life generate and produce violence.

Crucial to my new approach therefore is an ontological and a methodological viewpoint that does not assume a unitary or fixed reality; for instance, the fact that escapes are characterised by both structural and everyday forms of violence as well as constitute an integral part of everyday entangled relationships of confinement life.

Stemming from this open-ended and immersive methodological stance, I could not employ a definite set of questions, as was the case during previous visits to detention institutions associated with my practitioner status in monitoring their compliance with international human rights. On the contrary, I avoided from the start the idea of developing a fixed set of questions. At first, I was primarily interested in the meanings that the young people there associate with human rights and framed my research question accordingly as: 'What sense do juvenile offenders make of human rights in their day-to-day life in detention?'

I commenced the preliminary research work with my 'almost framed' central research question as a starter and a loose guide. Then I saw the need to slightly alter my research question again, upon realising that young people in custody seldom had anything to say about human rights. Also, youngsters' and officers' diverse constructions of correctional centres as prisons could not be ignored. Shifting from a human rights practitioner status and seeking to make meaning of youngsters' perspectives as well as experiences made me realise that the way I conceived human rights did not seem to be part of their language or experience. It appeared evermore necessary to put aside normative conceptualisations of human rights and to go with another research question: *How do juvenile and young offenders make their everyday life meaningful in correctional centres in Accra?*

My researcher approach therefore differed significantly from my practitioner approach where structured questions around prearranged agendas were prepared ahead of visits to detention institutions. My research was not based on hypothesis testing but required that the research process and my research role be guided by emergent empirical data. Whilst this inductive approach is often characterised by serendipity and was exciting, given the surprises associated with it, it was also marked by insecurity and powerlessness experienced by both the researcher and the researched. Distinct boundaries were not set, and one could not clearly predict the next step nor strategise ahead in terms of what methods to employ. The power that I enjoyed as a human rights practitioner from the presentation of questionnaires, as well as subsequent discussions that ensued about compliance or non-compliance with various human rights standards, seemed lost in the new process. I also experienced the loss of power associated with the formal presentation of a team of human rights monitors in a formal dress code representing a state institution. I was sometimes plunged into a sort of identity crisis. This was because the institutions and detaining authorities, in spite of the acquaintance I had developed with them stemming from my monitor role, sometimes questioned my new role. The daily quiet and unannounced research visits could not be compared with the official annual visits associated with my practitioner status. Whilst such situations of identity crisis provided the opportunity to further clarify my new researcher role, it constituted a potential source of insecurity. In one instance, I was denied access to one group of youngsters by an officer in charge (OIC), although I had already gained permission from the OIC, as well as from a higher oversight authority. I was given access only after I had reproduced my introductory letter.

My approach also reflected a state of powerlessness on the part of the institutions I was visiting. Detention authorities sometimes counted on the Commission on Human Rights and Administrative Justice CHRAJ (my employer) as a voice in presenting their grievances of poor conditions of work (by means of reports and the media coverage that such visits attracted). Such reports and media coverage sometimes prompted discussion with the institutions and provided them the opportunity to share with the public not only their grievances but also their achievements. Such opportunities seemed lost with my current researcher status which could offer them little in return, even though the institutions had provided me with more sustained access relative to the one- or two-day annual visits as a human rights monitor.

The institutions derived some benefit nevertheless as they sought my views on certain crucial issues as diverse as those around adoption, the incarceration of a pregnant female and various matters pertaining to escape occurrences, as well as my views on punishment. Even so, this was difficult and sometimes delicate for me as my views were sought as a human rights practitioner and not a researcher. I needed to make a clear distinction in the dual roles that I assumed, but it was not easy or straightforward. Whilst my role as a researcher was undoubtedly clear to myself, some situations and predicaments made such roles appear fuzzy even to me. Not only did I have to consciously remind myself of the perspective from which I shared my views, but I also needed to remind myself that my viewpoints elicited various interpretations according to the 'hats' that the institutions saw me wearing. Whilst such varied interpretations by themselves constitute useful data, I discuss later how I also consciously employed impression management so as to create certain effects associated with my researcher role.

The feelings of uncertainty and powerlessness, as well as insecurity that characterised my new researcher status, however, motivated certain innovative methods. During the initial stages of fieldwork, some detainees and staff would hardly speak to me, even with the increased acquaintance that came with extended participant observation, not much changed. I got round this difficulty by using what I termed 'conversational interviews', interviews that formed an integral part of my participant observations. Consequently, people were more willing to chat and respond to questions whilst we engaged together in various activities such as dress-making lessons and farmwork. Such conversational interviews proved to be useful means of gathering data, which I employed throughout the research process.

The Intricacies of Access – Going beyond mandates and legislation

In discussions that follow, I consider my human rights practitioner status which facilitated access to these institutions but which also raised further ethical challenges.

One key consideration for institutions and individuals that visit detention centres is whether or not there is a clear mandate stemming from a legislative instrument that gives power to access these places. The CHRAJ is specifically mandated by Section 42 of the Juvenile Justice Act (653 of 2003) of Ghana to visit and inspect any correctional centre for juvenile and young offenders in the country. On the basis of the CHRAJ's mandate, I could access these institutions. In addition, I had also struck up an acquaintance with the detaining authorities due to many years of conducting monitoring visits to these institutions. I therefore gained entry to my research sites on the basis of this mandate and level of acquaintance. Nevertheless, whilst I entered the institutions with my CHRAJ's employer's hat on, I also had another hat on – the researcher's – and this was the intricate bit, to get the various actors to appreciate my other hat: my research role. The initial stages of my fieldwork concentrated on explaining the demands and dictates of this other hat. I tried to clarify that though

I remained an employee of the CHRAJ, my academic research and daily visits were independent of the CHRAJ and that the methods associated with the former were markedly different from the latter.

Another difficulty was the fact that, despite the mandate or power to visit, coupled with the acquaintance and rapport I had established over the years, I was struck by a number of newly pertinent questions after I had negotiated entry and was preparing to commence my fieldwork:

- Does Section 42 of the Juvenile Justice Act (653 of 2003) mandate me to enter the private worlds of offenders?
- To what extent does a piece of legislative instrument mandate me to intrude into someone else's personal and subjective world?
- What ethical justification do I have to demand responses from children just because my entry was negotiated with an OIC (synonymous with parents or adults giving consent on behalf of children)?
- Have the children themselves given me access to their world?
- Does agreed access to one child, 'Abena', entail access to another child, 'Kwabena'?

Thus, although I could access the various buildings and structures on the basis of a legislative mandate, I still needed to negotiate consensual social access to the youngsters. Though I had been permitted to arrange interviews with youngsters, I considered the paramount need to respect their right to provide information only willingly and not to impose my power as a researcher on them.

Throughout the process of fieldwork, negotiation of social access to youngsters and other actors within the detention environment was a continuous process and not a one-off attainment. This was not due to a feeling of strangeness on my part or that I had not gained a sense of familiarity with the young people, though that seemed to be the case at the initial stages, and due to uncertainties sometimes associated with my researcher role. Respecting children's right to consent entails being sensitive to their non-verbal expressions such as body language as well their facial expressions. Sometimes children may consent to participating in an interview and yet their facial expressions are not in conformity with such consent. Such contradictions gave me a feeling of uneasiness to go ahead without a brief explanation or assurance of confidentiality. The question of whether it was right not to proceed with an interview also depended on the subject under discussion. Sometimes youngsters might convey their discomfort in the form of a pause, a break in the flow of their talk, or start talking faster, or even begin shedding tears, all of which were useful indications to suspend or pause an interview. Thus, continuous negotiations were necessary for youngsters, who during the initial stages of my fieldwork expressed such discomfort mostly as a result of fears of possible victimisation by their officers. The passage of time coupled with the continuous interaction as well as increased acquaintance and familiarity allayed such fears and feelings of discomfort to a large extent. I observed that confinement settings characterised by close monitoring could never entirely be devoid of such suspicions and fears; my task was to endeavour to reduce such fears to the barest minimum.

The question as to whether or not a formal mandate was enough also extended to the usage of research instruments. I was sensitive not to disclose the identity of youngsters even though permission was granted to use a voice recorder and a digital camera (these instruments are usually not allowed even during CHRAJ visits). I noticed that my use of the instruments was intimidating for youngsters. I could read the anxiety in their faces during the initial periods that I used the camera, even though I did so with their consent. The strategy of allowing youngsters to take pictures of themselves was not successful either. The act of youngsters handling cameras and taking pictures was somehow considered a privilege not compactible within a disciplinary confinement setting. I however managed to take few pictures at the latter stages of my fieldwork.

I was also unsuccessful with the use of the voice recorder as the youngsters' gazes were kept more often on the voice recorder, and their attention, as well as the flow of conversations, was hampered. My compromise was a small note pad[7], which I cautiously used as I noticed that even the note had sometimes affected the flow of conversations. Overall, I needed to strike a bargain between what was ethically acceptable in a particular context and whether or not to seek information according to my terms at the expense of the feelings of the children.

In sum, although I had obtained formal access to the institutions as a human rights officer, my inductive approach stemming from my researcher status re-orientated my motives to be more considerate of the best interests of the children, allowing them to determine more of my research instruments, such as pen and paper rather than recorder. I was equally mindful of the need for equity between the researcher and the various actors in the research. Ethics, in this regard, went beyond a legal mandate to enter custodial premises as adherence to a set of principles and rules of conduct, or a 'go ahead' nod from an ethical committee, to being genuinely sensitive to the wishes, feelings, sentiments, perceptions and experiences of children (Graham, 2008) and other actors. Access in this respect was 'far more than the granting or withholding of permission for research to be conducted' (Hammersley and Atkinson, 2007: 43).

Agentic research informants

Being sensitive to the feelings and sentiments of research informants is as important as being mindful of how such people can also deliberately conceal information. I observed this on the part of both officers and youngsters. Gaining access to informants in correctional centres or prisons is as important as negotiating access to physical settings (Hammersley and Atkinson, 2007). Due to the regimentality and repetitiveness of detention life, one might tend to assume that things continue to go the same predictable way day in, day out; and yet detention life is active, dynamic and dotted with frequent changes. Following a short break from the research, I assumed that I could return to continue with my regular routines. I was mistaken; the terms had changed without me realising. I had visited after the break as I had not seen the officers and youngsters for some time and took for granted that I could dash to the classroom to speak briefly with them. However, I noticed hesitation on the facial expression of one of my gatekeepers, a senior officer. I ignored the indication and went ahead to the classroom. As I did so, the senior officer called me back, his reason being that he had planned to hold a meeting with the teachers and, so, I could only talk to them later. During later conversations with him, I realised that he was now the second in command and had begun to restrict some of the freedoms I enjoyed probably because he had to satisfy other interests.

Youngsters also deliberately choose what information to release or not to release. During what I term 'interrogative encounters' (Ayete-Nyampong, 2013: 151) with their officers, I observed how they manage to steer conversations in directions that favour their own interests. I have witnessed instances when professionals visited and interviewed youngsters and the latter did not say a word; during other times, youngsters decided what information to release. In conversations with other professionals such as human rights officers, clinical psychologists, social workers and NGO workers, youngsters may make an attempt to conceal certain information. On one occasion, I was with some girls in the hall where they usually held one-to-one meetings with a clinical psychologist in a nearby office. The girls looked happy and were chatty, particularly two of whom had just returned from meeting the psychologist. The two commented (Ayete-Nyampong, 2013: 153):

> This white lady is very troublesome, she continued to ask us what bothers us even when we continually say to her that we did not have any problems and that we were just fine.
>
> (There were giggles from the others)

Even with the increased level of acquaintance that came with extended participant observation, not much changed. During the period of fieldwork, female youngsters, except a few, would hardly speak to me on a one-on-one basis.[8] I noticed that whereas researchers and other professionals are very eager for information from youngsters, the latter are just as eager to withhold information unless they realise this is in their interest.

Another strategy that youngsters employ in order to conceal vital information is to adopt and sometimes modify the expressions of officers or other professionals. A youngster who was popularly known by both staff and inmates as 'pastor' because of his active involvement in church activities, as well as his compliance with the rules of the institution, was caught a number of times smoking 'weed', to the surprise of the officers. Some youngsters adopted strategies of open compliance with their officers so as to conceal less acquiescent behaviour from such officers or other staff. The word 'change' or 'reform' pervades most spheres of the correctional centre and is common on the lips of staff and other professionals who visit. Youngsters such as 'Kofi'[9] subscribe to such similar usages during conversational interviews (Ayete-Nyampong, 2013: 153):

> On the whole I think I have really changed. I am glad I came here, if I had not, maybe something more terrible could have happened to me. When I watch what people suffer as a consequence of bad behavior, it scares me and I do not want to be part of that. Sometimes when I watch TV and see people being killed for committing crimes I get really scared.

Whilst 'Kofi' may have actually changed, like the 'youngster pastor', inmates sometimes try to act the perfect inmate. As Goffman observed in a term he describes as 'conversion', such inmates take over completely the official or staff view of themselves so as to better act out the role of the perfect inmate (Goffman, 1968).

The balance of being able to remain sensitive to matters of access as well as the various power influences exerted by the research informants comes with a continued presence and a growing acquaintance in the field. Regardless of the degree of acquaintance, I observed that research informants have their own agency and agendas and will seek to influence researchers and their results (Emerson et al., 1995; Monahan and Fisher, 2010). Whilst such influence by itself constitutes relevant data and should not be simplistically dismissed as relevant or irrelevant, true or false, I also sought reliance on a variety of gatekeepers as well as my own impression management to facilitate and strengthen my access to numerous sources of information and insight.

Researcher agency

One important skill associated with my new researcher role was to identify certain people who police the formal physical and social boundaries in detention institutions. Gatekeeping played a vital role in promoting access to youngsters and officers.

My initial point of contact was one officer who usually conducted visitors and human rights monitors around the centre as this afforded him more social interaction than his repetitive office work. He was keen on introducing me to other officers and conducting me round, probably ascribing to me a practitioner role and mistaking me for a human rights monitor. However, he became less interested when he realised that I was less keen on tours and sat more often with youngsters and other staff in the yard.

I encountered another officer who supervised educational activities of the centre. He seemed pleasant and showed me around the centre's educational facilities, yet was circumspect as to the information he released to me. His responses and information were more idealised than what actually pertained (Rubin and Rubin, 1995). I noticed that most information he provided contradicted what I observed; whilst he would say, for instance, that the centre had an abundance of text books and teachers, I realised that the opposite prevailed when I visited classrooms. He continued to facilitate my access to youngsters and to staff, but I no longer relied on him for information when I noticed his tendency to project a particularly positive image of the institution. I however maintained the friendship with him as he facilitated access to both youngsters and officers.

Another senior officer was equally helpful in terms of providing access to youngsters and officers. Unlike the previous officer, the information he provided tallied mostly with my observations. However, upon his promotion to management status, this officer assumed a more formal stance in terms of his associations with me as his interests tended to be steered towards that of management and those in authority.

Being partly aware of blurred boundaries associated with my entangled roles, as well as the ambiguity of how I was perceived by staff and youngsters, I made special efforts to convey an impression that distinguished me from staff and partly from my former practitioner status.

Each of the correctional centres prompted different responses from me in terms of impression management. I dressed in traditional blouse (*kaba*) and cloth, a traditional outfit which matches a 'mum's' role anytime I visited the SCC. This attire distinguished me from prison officers, who were all dressed in formal uniform. When I began to hold focus group discussions and engage in one-to-one interviews with youngsters, most would call out to me from their dorms addressing me as 'mum'. However, at the JCC, I dressed casually in 'jeans' and 'a buttoned shirt', as officers, who were mostly social workers, were themselves dressed in their traditional Ghanaian attire and not in uniform. I consciously reminded myself not to convey a 'monitor' or 'inspector' status, which is usually associated with officers of the CHRAJ who visited prisons or correctional centres, as this could create a power gap and inhibit a free flow of conversations. Conversely though, where necessary, I drew on my human rights practitioner status to facilitate access to some informants, such as those for higher-level interactions, which required a formal appearance.

Apart from managing the impression that I conveyed, personal characteristics such as my gender and being able to speak local languages contributed to easing or inhibiting access to information. Senior officers – most of whom were male – were delighted to share views with a female colleague or researcher. At the same time, I blended quite well with the female officers, engaging in womanly talk. Other factors, such as being able to speak two local languages, Akan and Ewe, were also an advantage. But being familiar with the local conversational dynamics, such as posing questions to oneself and providing responses as a means of maintaining the flow of conversations, was even more important. In spite of these efforts, some officers simply ignored me, whilst some youngsters were hesitant to speak.

Researcher as practitioner

During the initial stages at one of the centres, I rarely witnessed officers beating young inmates with the cane. Having accessed the institutions on the mandate of my human rights employer and being viewed in that regard, initial situations were probably presented to me with that in mind. Officers and detaining authorities were well aware of the position of human rights institutions regarding the use of the cane or any form of corporal punishment. Later in the course of my fieldwork, I noticed that officers used the cane and seemed completely oblivious of my presence. Somehow, it was an indication that I had blended and that my practitioner status had been forgotten.

This seemed to augur well for me as a researcher, suggesting that I was gradually gaining insider trust, and I was even assigned a staff rank by some officers. On the other hand, I wondered whether my familiarity had grown to the extent that I was losing my practitioner self entirely. Maybe I had been so immersed that I had lost my objectivity and human rights sense of judgement such that I could no longer recognise an abuse. Or was it that my research priorities and the quest for information had taken precedence over my professional ethics. I tried to think about how I would have reacted if I had witnessed such incidents when I visited as a human rights monitor.

In the first place, even though corporal punishment contravenes the provision of the United Nations Convention on the Rights of the Child (CRC), corporal punishment has not been outlawed under Ghana's educational policies despite several calls by the CHRAJ and other human rights organisations to do so. The majority of educational institutions in Ghana therefore use corporal punishment but under certain conditions. Regardless of whether it had been outlawed or not, I would have, in my practitioner role as a human rights officer, drawn the attention of the authorities to the provisions of the CRC and would have included it in my monitoring report. Not so this time round as I considered, on the basis of the actor perspective stance as well as the inductive approach I had adopted, that it was necessary to first consult the various actors about their views.

Different views were expressed. Some youngsters said such caning toughened them and gave them more recognition amongst peers; as a result they commanded more respect and were able to stand up to harsher treatment. They regarded it as training that offered them progression from one level of toughness to the other. Some youngsters were of the view that such caning was less painful than certain cruel treatment meted out to them by their fellow juveniles or senior inmates. My later interactions with the youngsters also reveal that the majority of them had experienced physical abuse and similar treatment during their pre-custodial period whilst living with their families. Other youngsters considered corporal punishment as a form of discipline that shaped them for acceptable behaviour in conformity to the rule. Whatever the views, I observed that none of the youngsters seemed immune entirely to pain.

According to the officers, corporal punishment served as a deterrent and also a means of ensuring compliance with the rules. I observed during interactions with staff and youngsters that detention institutions must be seen to be exerting some form of social control for the purpose of public safety and security even if the desired ends are not achieved (Ayete-Nyampong, 2013). Such acts of punishment in themselves guarantee employability and job security, and officers must be seen to be doing what they have been employed to do – enforce compliance.

My observations and interviews thus provided a different outlook to my approach to corporal punishment. My human rights position had not been entirely compromised, because I realised that actors' views were vital in informing remedies and action concerning them. If prison officers had known of the evidence that caning did not yield the desired results for some children but that it rather tutored them to do 'worse things', they may have considered other alternatives. In a similar vein, if human rights officers and related professionals had taken full cognisance of everyday life in detention and respected actors' own constructions and children's perspectives (Graham, 2008) of their experiences in correctional institutions, they would have considered more useful approaches rather than to simply impose the provisions of a convention or legislation on reluctant, unpersuaded actors.

Oscillating between the overt and the covert

I assumed an overt status as I explained my researcher role to detaining authorities and respondent groups as distinct from my practitioner role which required little explanation. Yet, I also adopted an implicitly covert role because I could not fully declare my research objectives, due to the lack of a defined research plan and questions stemming from my ethno-inductive approach. This approach sometimes kept prison authorities in a state of suspense because they were acquainted with my practitioner status and accepted it as adequate for access to the institutions.

Authorities in secure institutions, many a time, demand a clearly demarcated scope of one's research and do not want to be in doubt as to the demands it will place on them or their staff, or the whole institution. The authorities wondered why, this time round, I could not share a definite research plan and questions with them. For instance, in the course of my fieldwork, one of the OICs asked, 'what, indeed, I was up to?' and demanded that I clarified certain processes again. I tried to appreciate the difficulty of the OIC, who was not being able to reconcile to the role of a practitioner who attends one- or two-day annual visits, as compared to one who has virtually become part of the correctional community. Also, one of the OICs demanded during the middle stages of my fieldwork that I reproduce my letter of introduction before being granted access to a related institution.

The sense of insecurity and unpredictability was therefore experienced by both the researcher and the researched. A gap between the intentions of the ethnographer and the authorities is created right at the outset of the research process, a gap which, though it creates discomfort for both researcher and researched, should not be hastily closed but openly discussed. Keeping these authorities regularly informed and updated was one effective way by which I addressed this gap. Hammersley and Atkinson (2007) discuss a similar gap between the practicalities of ethnographic research and the expectations of relevant academic gatekeeping authorities, such as ethical committees. According to Hammersley and Atkinson, the deliberations of authorities including ethical committees can frustrate the work of the ethnographer, as committees are premised on a psychological, biomedical or survey research model and tend to object to ethnographic research which may dwell on single case, particularistic, and non-generalisable situations.

The strange and the familiar

The confusion and the insecurity that came with the lack of definite boundaries that characterised my practitioner and ethnographic role even extended to my private sphere. The home and the field seemed two distinct places, and 'I was moving between the strange and the familiar on a regular basis' (Hume and Mulcock, 2004: xv).[10] I had to switch frequently from a homely and familiar site to a closed site characterised by strangeness – vulgar language, defiance, verbal and physical confrontation, traumatic experiences, narratives about murder, defilement, assault, unpleasant smells and other characteristic features of prison settings. This required continuous adjustments as I sought to maintain the terms of my social, emotional and psychological well-being.

These places were however part of one continuous space, quite different from the distinctness that existed between my practitioner and personal space. Monitor visits were once-a-year events, whereas my research role demanded my continued presence for the period of two years. On one occasion, following a conversation with one of the boys prior to his discharge from the centre, I realised that no relative was available to collect him and he hardly had enough money to take him to his destination, besides lacking some basic necessities. I therefore drove him home, gave him some food and some other items before taking him to the lorry station. Some of the youngsters from the rural areas may not have been to the city for the entire period of their detention and so they would not know their way around. However, on reaching home, my family bombarded me with a barrage of security-related questions; they felt my action was unusual and risky, particularly given that over the years as a human rights practitioner such an interaction between my home life and my work life had never occurred. In my ethnographer role, however, I had undoubtedly struck up an acquaintance and familiarity with the 'stranger'. Relationships in the field can be profound as well as intense, and I found myself struggling to understand my family's legitimate concerns of security and safety. The distinction between the strange and the familiar, for me, had become blurred, and whilst this had its advantages for me as a researcher, there were also ramifications when those blurred boundaries were seen as sharp and clear by others.

Conclusion

The foregoing discussions depict the serendipity associated with ethnographic research into everyday confinement life, as well as the intricacies of transiting between diverse roles. The awkward experiences and interdependencies between the practitioner and researcher, covert and overt, as well as the strange and the familiar are practical realities that have characterised my fieldwork experience. The practitioner and researcher roles are not in themselves problematic; the challenge lay in their entanglements and negotiation, as well as interdependencies provoked by the uncertainties, unpredictability and powerlessness that are intrinsic to an ethno-inductive approach. The recognition that the various actors, as well as the researcher, could come under various influences that could impact on their actions and choices is an important one. Rigidly sticking to the demands of my practitioner role or insider grounding, adhering to some set rules or blueprints, would have deprived me of the required capacity for reflexive analysis. Such reflexive analysis involves being able to see with both sets of eyes,[11] that of a practitioner as well as a researcher. Yet, it also demands being able to make some distinction between diverse positions and not to amalgamate such positions, however entangled they seem. I tried to manage these positions by stepping back from my acquaintance and familiarity afforded me by my practitioner grounding and yet not stepping back entirely away from the scene. In sum, when practical remedies are sought, rather than reliance on blueprints in response to everyday situations in a confinement setting, serendipities as much as uncertainties and awkwardness can yield useful insights.

Notes

1. Similar discussions were held at a conference in Bordeaux in 2013 that featured various presentations on varied detention institutions.
2. The Criminal Code (Amendment Act 554 of 1998) raises the age of criminal responsibility from age 7 to age 12.
3. The legal protection that the Juvenile Justice Act offers juvenile and young offenders between ages 12 and 21 is of little relevance to young female offenders who are older than 18 years. Whereas young offenders older than 18 can be admitted to the SCC, this is not so with girls as there exists no SCC for them. The implication is that girls could be finding themselves in prison at earlier ages than boys (or disappearing elsewhere), which possibly explains the very low committal rates at the JCC.
4. Dr. Andrew Jefferson has also done some ethnographic work in Liberia and Sierra Leone. There are other few upcoming doctoral studies identified, such as a proposed research looking at 'street children's' experiences of juvenile justice practices in Kenya by a doctoral student.
5. Sarkin, J. (2008). *Human rights in African Prisons* (Capetown, South Africa: HCRC press).
   In fact Sarkin (2008) notes that worst conditions in prisons are prevalent in other parts of the world.
6. A special rapporteur on Torture, who assessed the situation of torture, inhuman and cruel treatment in Ghana's detentions institution, commented in his preliminary observations on 14 November 2013, that conditions in Ghana's prisons and police cells are still poor and amount to human rights violations. See http://antitorture.org/ghana-country-visit/ [accessed 19 February 2014].
7. I tried to listen attentively, write brief notes and note clues and catchy words that made me remember details of the conversation later, before the day ended.
8. On the contrary, with increased acquaintance, I held successful one-on-one conversations with young male offenders.
9. All names of youngsters used in this paper are pseudonyms.
10. This reference by Hume and Mulcock to the home differs from my usage. Mulcock refers to the home as the city where she had grown up and therefore familiar, yet there were certain spirituality and health scenes that were unfamiliar and strange to her.
11. I draw on discussions on 'Awkward Spaces, Productive Places', by Hume and Mulcock, who share similar views that the ethnographer must be able to see with both the eyes of an outsider and an insider and be able to maintain an intellectual distance for a critical analysis.

Further reading

Ayete-Nyampong, L. (2014) 'Entangled Governance Practices and the Illusion of Producing Compliant Inmates in Correctional Centres for Juvenile and Young Offenders in Ghana', *Prison Service Journal: Everyday Prison Governance in Arica,* 214, 27–32.

Hammersley, M. and Atkinson, P. (2007) *Ethnography. Principles in Practice,* Third edition (London: Routledge).
Hume, L. and Mulcock, J. (2004) 'Introduction: Awkward Spaces, Productive Places', in H. Lynne and J. Mulcock (eds) *Anthropologists in the Field, Cases in Participant Observation* (New York: Columbia University Press).

References

Abebe, T. and Kjorholt, A. T. (2009) 'Social Actors and Victims of Exploitation: Working Children in the Cash Economy of Ethiopia South', *Childhood,* 16, 2, 175–94.
Ayete-Nyampong, L. (2013) *Entangled Realities and Underlife of a Total Institution,* PhD thesis, Wageningen University, Wageningen.
Ayete-Nyampong, L. (2014) 'Entangled Governance Practices and the Illusion of Producing Compliant Inmates in Correctional Centres for Juvenile and Young Offenders in Ghana', *Prison Service Journal,* 214, 27–32.
Christiansen, C. (2006) *Youth, Religiosity and the AIDS Pandemic. Faith Friends and Family Virtues in Uganda,* Unpublished Paper presented at the Youth and the Global South Conference, Dakar.
Christiansen, C., Utas, M. and Vigh, H. E. (eds) (2006) *Introduction: Navigating Youth, Generating Adulthood: Social Becoming in an African Context* (Uppsala: Nordiska Afrikainstitutet).
Cupido, M., Kritzinger, A. and Van Aswegen, F. (2005) 'The Implementation of a Diversion Programme for Juvenile Offenders: Problem Areas and "Pitfalls" ', *Social Work,* 41, 3, 251–64.
De Kock, D. (2005) 'Youth in Conflict with the Law and Socio-Economic Experiences in Their Childhood: A Relationship', *Journal of Child and Youth Care Work,* 20, 56–71.
Emerson, R., Fretz, R. and Shaw, L. (1995) *Writing Ethnographic Fieldnotes* (Chicago: The University of Chicago Press).
Gaum, G., Hoffman, S. and Venter, J. H. (2006) 'Factors that Influence Adult Recidivism: An exploratory Study in Pollsmoor Prison', *South African Journal of Psychology,* 36, 2, 407–24.
Goffman, E. (1968) *Asylums: Essays on the Social Situation of Mental Patients and Other Inmates* (Hammondsworth: Penguin).
Graham, A. (2008) 'On Researching Children's Experiences: Methodological and Ethical Issues Paper', Unpublished presented at the *Children and Young People as Social Actors' Research Cluster Symposium.*
Hammersley, M. and Atkinson, P. (2007) *Ethnography. Principles in Practice,* Third edition (London: Routledge).
Honwana, A. and De Boeck, F. (2005) *Makers and Breakers. Children and Youth in Postcolonial Africa* (Dakar: Codesria).
Hume, L. and Mulcock, J. (2004) 'Introduction: Awkward Spaces, Productive Places', in H. Lynne and J. Mulcock (eds) *Anthropologists in the Field, Cases in Participant Observation* (New York: Columbia University Press).
Igbinovia, P. E. (1985) 'Perspectives on Juvenile Delinquency in Africa', *Journal of Juvenile Law,* 9, 1, 12–35.
Jefferson, A. M. (2007) 'Prison Officer Training and Practice in Nigeria: Contention, Contradiction and Re-imagining Reform Strategies', *Punishment and Society,* 9, 3, 253–69.

Lindegaard, R. (2009) *Coconuts, Gangsters and Rainbow Fighters. How Male Youngsters Navigate Situations of Violence in Cape Town, South Africa* (Amsterdam: PhD University of Amsterdam).

Long, N. (2001) *Development Sociology: Actor Perspectives* (London: Routledge).

Martin, T. (2012) *'Human Rights in Ugandan Prisons'*, Unpublished paper presented at *An International Symposium on Prison Ethnography* (Milton Keynes: The Open University).

Monahan, T. and Fisher, J. (2010) 'Benefits of "Observer Effects": Lessons from the Field', *Qualitative Research,* 10, 3, 357–76.

Omoniyi, T., Scheld, S. and Oni, D. (2009) 'Negotiating Youth Identity in a Transnational Context In Nigeria', *Social Dynamics,* 35, 1–18.

Peters, K. (2006) *Footpaths for Reintegration; Armed Conflict, Youth and the Rural Crisis in Sierra Leone* (Wageningen: Unitversiteit van Wageningen).

Petersen, I., Bhana, A. and McKay, M. (2005) 'Sexual Violence and Youth in South Africa: The Need for Community-Based Prevention Interventions', *Child Abuse and Neglect,* 29, 11, 1233–48.

Rubin, H. J. and Rubin, I. S. (1995) *Qualitative Interviewing. The Art of Hearing Data: Choosing Interviewees and Hearing What They Say* (Thousand Oaks: Sage).

Sarkin, J. (2008) *Human rights in African Prisons* (Capetown, South Africa: HCRC Press).

Sauls, H. (2009) Delinquency or Resilience? How Interpretations of Violence Translate Into the Daily Management of Children in a Place of Safety in Cape Town, Unpublished paper presented at the *Medical Anthropology at Intersections: Celebrating 50 Years of Interdisciplinarity* (New Haven, CT: Yale University).

Sparks, R. (1996) *Prisons, Punishment and Penality* (London: Sage).

Steinberg, J. (2004) *One Man's Search for Identity in the Cape Underworld and Prison Gangs* (Johannesburg: Jonathan Ball).

17
'To Thine Own Self Be True'[1]: Having Faith in the Prison Researcher

Lindsay Whetter

Introduction

> If you love your neighbour as yourself, then you won't rape his daughter, sell drugs to his children, you won't kill your neighbour.
>
> (Geoff Hebbern, HMP The Verne Chaplain)[2]

This chapter is based on findings from an ethnographic exploration of Kainos, the first faith-based prison unit to be established in the Western world. Kainos was opened in April 1997[3] in The Verne prison.[4] Kainos is unique in that it combines a hybrid therapeutic community with cognitive behavioural therapy in open dormitory living conditions. The foundations and ethos of Kainos are Christian, based on concepts of 'loving thy neighbour'[5] and restorative justice. The course programme is secular and the community is open to prisoners of all faiths and none. As I began my research (having previously been a volunteer on the Kainos Community wing), my role was seen, by both prisoners and staff, as sometimes interchangeable between that of a volunteer, a researcher and even a member of staff. For the most part, this 'messy' identity perception added to my research experience. I will critically discuss how the blurring of these role boundaries can become messy, but enriching. I explore the dilemmas of balancing professional research detachment with compassion, especially when immersed in the community on a daily basis for such a long period of time, and how easy it was to become weighted down by the hopes and fears of the prisoners in such an all-consuming environment. I discuss the challenges of being a lone prison ethnographer and the need for self-reflexivity, not just for methodological rigour but also as a coping strategy as a researcher (and a person of faith) in the deep, and sometimes dark places of prison. There is currently a lack of literature on self-reflexivity of the faith-motivated prison researcher. By sharing my experiences in an informed and transparent way, I hope to offer a unique understanding of this, thus far, rarely discussed, perhaps 'hidden' researcher positionality.

A suitable method

The advice of C. Wright Mills (1959: 211) is that '[y]ou do not really have to study a topic you are working on... once you are into it, it is everywhere'. Prison is a 'site of intractable conflict' (Sparks, 2002: 556), which makes prison ethnography unique and challenging. It is a multi-layered, multifaceted process and requires a unique research stance. There are the processes of negotiating access to participants, building trust in a sometimes frenetic and volatile environment and conducting your research study to the best of your ability within the confines of a very restricted regime of rules and regulations, power and control. In addition, there is the process of a sincere attempt to participate, observe and become 'part of' the environment in order for the more organic, free-flowing process of ethnography to happen. Prison ethnography is a wonderful yet harrowing dichotomy between constraint and creativity; it can be disturbing, yet there can be glimmers of hope and laughter too.

Some prison researchers attempt to act as a conduit for the voiceless, marginalised 'others', as a way to 'give voice' to the underdog, to help see the world from the viewpoint of the oppressed rather than the oppressor (Becker, 1967; also see Hammersley, Chapter 1, this volume). Ethnography is also a resistance against a preoccupation with prison statistics and the audit culture that tends to dehumanise prisoners. In an attempt to re-humanise prisoners, one has to engage in real-life human interactions. In an environment where prisoners' voices are rarely heard, I wanted to give prisoners the opportunity to participate in an interactive ethnography where they could be an active part of the research process. Rather than simply participating as observee and interviewee, prisoners actively engaged in the creative process of this research by keeping their own research journals, writing poetry, participating in informal discussions as well as taking part in interviews.

The 'insider' perspective has often been excluded in academic criminology by neglecting the 'real-life' experiences of the prisoners. Dissatisfied with the absence of the voices of prisoners in research, convict criminology 'approaches existing practices, research and political commentary... with a critical lens that is not only informed by personal experiences, but [is] underpinned by these experiences' (Aresti, 2013: 19). Attaining knowledge should be experiential; you cannot gain true insight into what is 'hidden' simply by reading about it: 'No amount of theorizing or reading in an office can substitute for the hands-on experience of spending your time in prison' (King, 2000: 297–8). It is important to balance the 'deep' ethnographic accounts of the intricacies of day-to-day prison life in the broader context, looking out into society as a whole. Of equal importance, however, is to look inwards at the researcher. Ethnography permits researchers to expose some of their own identity and motivations. As Liebling explains, when studying the prison 'it is impossible to be neutral' (2001: 472), and as researchers we have a responsibility to be transparent about who we are and what our motivations are:

> The fieldworker cannot and should not be a fly on the wall. No field researcher can be a completely neutral, detached observer, outside and independent of the observed phenomena.
>
> (Pollner and Emerson, 1988: 1)

The remainder of this chapter is split into five themes. In the next section, I introduce the concept of 'situating the "self" in ethnography'. This is followed by a more detailed look at 'the faith position'. I then discuss the complexities of my 'messy identity' and the challenges faced by 'the lone researcher'. The final section 'learning to breathe under water' takes a deeper look at balancing professionalism with compassion in the challenging world of prisons research.

Situating the 'self' in ethnography

> We see the world not as it is, but as we are.[6]

Placing oneself in the field is a tricky business. Before entering the prison, having been security cleared and trained in matters of safety, security, conditioning, manipulation and hostage situations, you have to think carefully about 'who' is entering the field and about how much of your own personal identity will be and can be (security permitting) revealed. As Denzin points out, researchers are integral to the society being studied and as such both the researcher and the researched are very much intertwined in the research process; subsequently, 'the others' presence is directly connected to the writer's self-presence in the text' (1994: 503). In being careful to avoid self-indulgent narcissism, a semi-autoethnographical approach seemed to be a way of adding richness and context to my study. My interpretations and perceptions of the world are coloured by my past experiences of the criminal justice voluntary sector (CJVS), my personality, gendered experiences, my beliefs, my academic knowledge and myriad other life and personal experiences that make me the individual I am. My work is informed by my 'insider' perspective, not of incarceration but of the CJVS and of the faith-motivated volunteer perspective. I seek to fuse the prisoner's 'insider' perspective with my own 'messy' 'insider–outsider' perspective:

> The most time consuming element of 'true' ethnography (rather than mere observation) is the need to embed yourself into a community until you see

> something as an insider, and therefore are able to tell what's important and what's not; the search for a 'native perspective'.
>
> (Richards, 2012: 6)

Perhaps the most obvious aspect of identity worthy of reflexivity is gender. I am a female in an adult male prison. Prisoners are not permitted conjugal visits, and many are therefore experiencing a degree of sexual frustration.[7] I always dressed in a 'prison appropriate' way and consciously wore 'non-feminine' clothes; my 'prison uniform' subsequently comprised dark baggy trousers, brown gender-neutral boots and an array of muted-coloured baggy shirts. I did not wear perfume or make-up. There were other careful considerations about my appearance too. I did not want to look 'too smart' for fear of being perceived as a member of staff, a solicitor or a psychologist, but I wanted to look respectable and to 'blend in' as much as possible. I decided on 'respectably casual' – I emphasised the 'student' part of my identity rather than the 'professional' one so as not to appear as having any kind of authority or to be seen as part of the system. I chose not to have my own set of keys for the same reasons.

In the male-dominated environment of the prison, I found I was generally treated in a respectful way by everyone who lived and worked in the prison, albeit sometimes in a paternalistic way.[8] As Luke,[9] one of the prisoners pointed out, 'right now all women look positive because it's something we're deprived of – you're not gonna get anything bad said by anyone in prison'. I found that there were times when I seemed to be categorised into certain gender-specific and age-specific roles. Sometimes I felt that I was fulfilling a role that the men were deprived of, becoming surrogate or pseudo 'sister' or 'daughter'. Spending so much time 'hanging out' with the residents, I was sometimes perceived as a 'mate': 'you're one of us – you should get a Kainos certificate too' (Tommy, prisoner).

There is little research literature about the experiences of women working in men's prisons. Kumara et al. (2012), however, conducted research on women's experiences of working in a men's therapeutic community prison and found that women can find themselves playing different gender-specific roles and that these roles were also influenced by personality. The study reported that women found their work distressing and challenging at times (Kumara et al., 2012); I discuss the effects of bearing witness later in the chapter. Being without many of the usual symbols of my femininity and 'full' identity whilst in prison gave me a little insight into the stripping of identity prisoners must experience.

Spending time in prison enables you to notice the little things that can speak volumes about a particular issue. Prisoners wear an assortment of, often ill-fitting grey, green and blue prison-issue clothes; 'Prisons are full of grown men who are like old men shuffling round in clothes that look like pyjamas.'[10]

One day I noticed that they were all wearing the same grey prison socks, and then I noticed that there were acts of individuality that were being expressed, through their appearance. I noted in my field diary:

> Prisoners do small things to make a big statement about their identity. Rick wears dreadlocks and often wears a homemade hat with his pagan symbol or a feather in his hair. Tommy has cut off the bottoms of his tracksuit bottoms to make long shorts. Rob wears a bandanna. Tony wears a Rastafarian coloured hat and has dreadlocks.

Once a person enters prison and puts on prison clothes, their old identity is immediately lost and replaced by a new one, the prisoner identity. It is a matter of considerable debate amongst researchers as to whether or not adaptation to prison life is 'indigenous' (Sykes, 1958), influenced by the environment itself or 'imported' (Irwin and Cressey, 1962), or influenced by the prisoner's characteristics and pre-prison life experiences. In my observations, I noticed interactive effects of both models. Talking to one of the prisoners about the issue of identity, he made an interesting point:

> Because we [the prisoners] wear the same clothes, in prison, there is no class – everyone is equal – outside you can tell what class someone is by their clothes – if you wear Gucci you're middle class, if you wear a hoodie you're working class – in prison we are all the same.

Seeing a prisoner in his own clothes, in a different context is a striking reminder of this identity loss. I recall being shocked when I met one of the prisoners outside the gate on the day of his release[11]:

> At first I didn't recognise James and thought he was a gym instructor. He looked so different outside of the prison and out of his prison clothes; the only way I can describe it is that he looks like a 'real person' now. In the 24 hours of him changing status from a prisoner to a 'free' man James didn't look like a prisoner anymore – just by seeing him in his own clothes I could see his uniqueness and individuality.
>
> (Field diary)

What I saw in James that day was more than a simple change of clothes: perhaps what I saw was not just a change in the fabric of his clothes, but a change in the fabric of his soul. The 'massive assault' (Berger, 1963) on his identity as the result of incarceration had finally ceased and free from the constraints of the prison society and free from his 'false prison self'; perhaps he felt safe to be his 'true self'.

As a result of wearing my 'prison uniform', I felt a part of my identity was suppressed. Because I felt 'asexual' in prison, when I was not in prison I found myself adopting an exaggerated sense of 'femininity' – I wore skirts and heels more often and delighted in wearing make-up and perfume – I felt the need to celebrate my femininity more. There were other aspects of my 'self' that were suppressed in the prison too; as both volunteer and researcher I felt the need to be aware at all times of how I conducted myself. Conscious of constant surveillance I was ever mindful of my actions with regard to ethics, professionalism and security, and due to the vulnerability[12] of the prisoners I constantly analysed my own words, actions and motivations, ever mindful of balancing my roles as volunteer and researcher with professionalism, integrity and my values as a person of faith.

The faith position

> When I began to talk to the men on D wing, I thought to myself – there but for the grace of God go I. It was a very humbling experience.
>
> (Research journal)

> This is more than a PhD to you isn't it. Are you a Christian?
>
> (Michael, prisoner)

Quite simply, everyone has a faith position, be it 'spiritual', religious, agnostic, atheist or humanist; it is impossible not to have a faith position.[13] For the researcher it is part of his or her identity which extends to gender, race, ethnicity and a multitude of other cultural, societal and personal identity nuances, which make each one of us unique. As a researcher, one's faith position needs to be put into context with the rest of one's biography and this biography can be an important part of the ethnographic process. It is imperative to acknowledge and be open about one's positionality as researcher's perceptions and beliefs can change throughout the ethnographic process. A good researcher will question and probe his or her own beliefs whilst holding on to the integrity of why he or she is doing the research, and be firm in his or her values and motivations.

There are a number of reasons why people from a Christian faith position may want to work with prisoners and aim to establish communities within a prison: concern for prisoners; human decency; justice and just punishment; relationships and spiritual transformation (Burnside et al., 2005; see also Scott, 1996; 1997, as well as Chapter 2, this volume). Visiting people in prison resonates deeply with some Christians as some believe that when they go into prison they meet with Jesus: 'I was in prison and you visited me' (Matthew 25: 36).[14] Part of Christian doctrine contends that through the actions of God in Jesus, true change only occurs through redemption, restitution and forgiveness.

Christians are not a homogenous group, however. Researching Christianity is complicated as there are many different denominations and new churches emerging, often with very different hermeneutic stances which influence the ways in which they perceive the world and interact with others. On one end of the scale there are fundamental Christians and on the other end there are very liberal Christians, and there is everything in between. As a result there are huge differences in motivations and performances of beliefs amongst Christians working in the prison system. There is a common misconception that all Christians want to proselytise (Goode, 2006) and public criticism of faith-based organisations tends to focus on the assumption that the faith-motivated volunteer seeks to convert, sometimes through manipulative and controlling means (Elisha, 2008). There are myriad differences and nuances in Christian belief and praxis but there are commonalities too, especially regarding an avowed theo-ethics of love and charity.

There are different narratives to any faith-motivated individual or group in prison and in a political climate of fear about the rise of Islam and wider insecurities, amongst which Christian and other faith radicalisation in prison is a modern reality, there are real concerns about the potential damage of a faith-motivated agenda in prisons: vulnerable people can sometimes become caught up in a world view that they lack the freedom and criticality to evaluate. Within prisons, the authorities worry that radical agendas are utilised by some prisoners to manipulate systems to their advantage. This, in turn, can create a division in the prison population between believers and non-believers, and discriminates against the latter; animating homophobia, and other forms of prejudice.[15] Although the terminology of 'radicalisation' has been lodged principally as an accusation against Islamist agendas in prison (see Liebling et al., Arnold, 2011; Earle and Phillips, 2013), there has been some research that suggests prisons can serve as incubators for radicalisation and fundamentalism of all faith groups (Neumann, 2010). The Institute for Social Policy and Understanding (2013) report found that in the US prison radicalisation is not exclusive to Islam but also extends to fascist or neo-Nazi organizations and extremist Christian groups. In The Pew Report (2012), US prison chaplains reported fundamentalist groups present amongst Islamists, Pagans, Protestants, Other non-Christians, Native American Spirituality and Jews amongst others.

Fundamentalist, extreme faith views can have lasting detrimental effects on vulnerable people but there are other narratives; religious belief is not a fixed category and to question, to doubt, to be uncertain is an essential part of some faiths. Anglicans, for example, are encouraged to question, to think, to analyse. Speaking in Exeter Cathedral in 2012 Canon Carl Turner described Christianity in terms of resonant frequency and how this can be dangerous; he gave an example of how soldiers marching across a bridge caused a frequency so powerful that the bridge collapsed and because of this they now march out of step when they cross a bridge; he spoke of how dangerous resonant space and frequency can be in the Christian context because some churches want everyone to be the same and to think the same – he spoke about his gay and lesbian friends and said that Christians are *not* as one and we *should* be out of step with one another and embrace difference; the type of evangelism that preaches uniformity is shallow because it preaches that God fixes everything and, within Anglicanism, that is not true; God experiences things with us but does not fix things.

My personal theology is very much like my ethnography – it is organic, immersive, ever unfolding. For me, faith is a verb; it is about Christianity in action, serving the common good. Indeed, during this research process I questioned my beliefs about humanity, justice, forgiveness, and where God is in people's suffering. To be 'called' by God to work with prisoners is an extraordinary and inexplicable thing to do. I believe something greater is working through me when I find myself praying with vulnerable prisoners,[16] some of whom have committed acts that horrify me. For me, it is a gift to be able to see their vulnerabilities, their humanness, their brokenness.[17]

My own understanding and interpretation of Christianity is not about being morally pure; much of the vocal and prominent atheist thinking against Christianity draws its energy from moral protest (Woodhead, 2004) and yet Christianity is quite the opposite: 'As it is written: There is no one righteous, not even one' (Bible NIV. Romans 3: 10). Christianity, then, from my perspective, is about knowing we are all fully human and being fully human means we all carry with us human failings, fallibilities, 'sin', 'character defects'. What is important is to acknowledge and accept this humanness.

We are not necessarily so different from those who find themselves in prison and perhaps it is in the similarities that human relationships can be built, the foundations of which can lead to the process of narrative change imperative in the desistance process (Maruna, 2001).[18] There are Christians, myself included, who are secure enough in their beliefs that they are willing to look outside their faith and adopt and embrace other belief systems to work towards the common good, and who are concerned with Christian service rather than conversion. All faith perspectives have truths and commonalities. It is in the similarities between various perspectives that understanding, collaboration and 'the quest for the good' can be achieved. Speaking about changes within prison chaplaincy in 2014, the then Chaplain General William Noblett explains that chaplaincy and Christian ministry 'is evolutionary . . . The journey involves an openness to the ideas and theology of different faith traditions, and the theory and praxis of prison ministry place it at the forefront of inter-faith dialogue' (Noblett, 2014: 57). There are parallels in belief, praxis and values between faith and secularity, theology and psychology. Perhaps the only barrier is language:

a person of faith will speak of 'unconditional love', someone with a different belief may speak of 'unconditional positive regard'; a psychologist will talk of 'self-actualisation',[19] a theologian 'transcendence'. Much can be borrowed and learnt from one another if we focus on the similarities, not the differences.

A messy identity

Ethnography involves observation of a particular kind. It is done with rigorous and sound research methodology, which includes a degree of self-reflexivity, especially for the researcher who may already be embedded in his or her research environment. Having been a Kainos volunteer for two years prior to undertaking my study, I was faced with how to make the transition from volunteer to researcher: How do I maintain the focus, reliability and validity of my research whilst maintaining my integrity as a volunteer and a person of faith? As a volunteer I was already very much an integral part of my research environment and thus had already become the 'accidental observer', ever curious to know what happened on the wing on a day-to-day basis when we (the volunteers) were not there. Self-confessed 'accidental observer' Kantrowitz (1996) studied an Illinois prison whilst working as a prison guard. It was his 'intimate acquaintance with the people and the places' (cited in Philo, 2001: 485) that allowed him to describe and explore the intricacies of the daily routines and activities in order to understand the true nature of control as 'the answer is to be found precisely in the detail, not in the grand scheme' (Philo, 2001: 485).

On a practical level there were some immediate benefits to my 'insider' status. Gaining access to prisons to carry out research is a complicated and lengthy process. I had already been security cleared and trained and as I had already built up a trusting relationship with Kainos and prison staff, I was subsequently granted permission by the Director and the CEO of Kainos and The Verne's forensic psychologist in training had expressed her support of my research after an initial meeting.[20] The issue of trust is imperative in prisons research and is tied in very closely with ethics and integrity. There was an already established element of trust between myself and those who resided and worked on D wing.

Volunteers have a unique relationship with prisoners due to their perceived status as 'altruistic', 'there of their own free will' and 'not part of the system'. Although there is little in the way of literature on prisoners' experiences of volunteers and the relationships between volunteers and prisoners (Armstrong, 2012: 145), mutual trust coupled with sharing of vulnerabilities was a relationship dimension that made the volunteering experience differ from that of the prisoner-staff relationship:

> It's so weird the highlight of my week is going into the prison. I feel able to offer a listening ear. I'm not trying to convert them. It's Christianity in action – it's by your work that you are known.
>
> (Yvonne, volunteer)

> They [volunteers] treat me like I'm a person not a prisoner. Maybe it is not by your words or your actions but just the fact that you're here.
>
> (Luke, prisoner)

Volunteering in prison enables relationships to be established, making connections as individual human beings rather than focusing on the offence committed. Kainos volunteers are explicit about this: 'we are not interested in why someone is here; we want to get to know him as a person' (Dianne, volunteer). As I began my research, I felt I had already established a relationship with the men that was separate from the prison system and as one of 'walking alongside' rather than to judge or to convert. Due to the various roles I had in my research setting, over time I was able to notice small changes in various men, the sum of which amount to enormous change that cannot be 'measured' in positivistic or statistical terms:

> Johnny was serving tea tonight – he is being transferred to another prison in a few days. As I walked up to him he said 'I'm gonna miss you miss. I don't wanna go – they might tie me up and beat me up and put me under the bed.' He was being jovial but there was a real apprehension in his voice too. He has grown so much since I have known him. When I first met him he was shy and walked with his head down. During his time on the wing, with each new responsibility he has been trusted with, he had grown in confidence and in stature. He no longer looks at the floor when he walks past, he looks you directly in the eye and he always speaks and asks how you are.

There were other glimmers of hope to be found in this community. As I spent time 'hanging out' in the community, I could see relationships forming and there were acts of kindness and laughter to be found in the community.[21] Due to the longevity of my time on D wing, it was possible to experience a total cultural immersion which enabled me to experience some of what life is like for those who live and work in this prison community. Having made a decision not to have my own keys, I had to enter and exit the prison with staff which meant being 'imprisoned' on the wing for 9–12 hours at a time. I found spending long hours on D wing physically exhausting as there was little natural light or fresh air and the heating was on constantly. I gained some understanding and empathy towards prisoners who 'sleep their way through time' and also of some of the frustrations of life passing you by; 'life stands still while you're in prison' (Ben, prisoner). I found it increasingly frustrating not having my mobile phone or laptop with me and not being able to access the Internet. I felt completely cut off, like my life was on hold for the hours I was in prison. I never did 'miss' anything important whilst in prison, unlike prisoners who are powerless over their circumstances outside prison. Their lives literally are 'on hold' and they do miss out on opportunities and experiences: 'prison doesn't scare me, what I'm missing out on does' (Luke, prisoner).

Ferrell and Hamm (1998) describe the criminology of emotional attentiveness as the way in which ethnographers tell the research story through establishing feelings of trust, affection, identification and allegiance; the most rigorous analysis is achieved through affective fieldwork. In such work, the less distance there is between researcher and participant, the better and more methodologically sound the research is. However, this often produces conflicting emotions on the part of the researcher. In terms of identity, researchers have described feeling odd or feeling without position or purpose (Sparks et al., 1996). There were times when I felt uncomfortable being present during certain conversations and there were times when I felt my presence was a burden, but for the most part I was generally accepted as being a part of the community, whatever my role: 'you're part of the furniture miss' (Johnny, prisoner). I genuinely felt privileged and honoured to have been welcomed into the community by the prisoners, staff and the officers, especially when my role changed from volunteer to researcher. I am sure, at times, they must have felt uncomfortable with me and my notepad.

My 'messy identity' enriched my experience in the field as it gave me insight into the many dimensions of life on D wing. Both prisoners and officers sometimes perceived my role in different lights: as a volunteer, a researcher and even member of staff and sometimes I was asked to do things that staff should do – sometimes it was ethical and other times I had to question whether or not it was ethical. There were times when I was even confused as to what my role was. One extract from my research journal reads:

> I feel I have lost my way as a researcher because I have been so drawn into the depths of prison life. I have been so absorbed by the environment, the men's lives and wanting to walk alongside them – this has become more important than doing my research. Prison is an all-consuming environment – it is of the world but separate – part of society but shut off from it.

This 'messy' identity enriched my experience as I became more immersed in the community. At times I was fulfilling different roles simultaneously as researcher, volunteer and 'staff'. For example, because I knew the workings of the programme and the routine of the wing I was able to answer questions from new residents; I have taken minutes in meetings and generally 'helped out' on the wing. There were times when prisoners just wanted to offload and I was confident in my role to act as confidant as long as no ethical or security issues were raised. There were times when prisoners told me things they said they had never told anyone. To this day I respect and honour those conversations and they will not be a part of my future writings. The most beneficial element of having multiple identities in prison was that I realised that the most important factor is not 'what' role you have but 'who' you are. 'Prisoners know when you're genuine, that's why they relate to the volunteers; prisoners are very astute' (Lucy, Kainos staff). It is in your treatment of those around you that enables relationships and trust to be built, without which an ethnographically grounded understanding cannot fully materialise.

In many ways there are similarities between researchers and volunteers. As a volunteer you are a 'guest' in the prison and have to adhere strictly to prison service rules and Kainos codes of conduct. Volunteers and researchers, like prisoners, must obey prison officers' orders at all times. A volunteer has no authority and, like the researcher, must 'hide' judgements on occasion. 'The prison researcher is faced with a balancing act of giving an intellectual account of "what is happening" whilst suspending "what ought to be"' (Liebling, 2001: 49). A prison researcher has to assert a number of different positions in terms of identity and conduct; 'one has to build social rapport while suspending (or hiding) moral judgements; cope with an intricate ethnography whilst establishing position and purpose in an unfamiliar "deep" place; and navigate the complex power relationships between prisoners and staff' (Piacentini, 2007: 155).

The insider–outsider debate raises some interesting issues. It can be argued that 'insider' positionality can engender a myopic view of social reality, whereas the 'outsider' can objectively enquire of social groups' significant practices or experiences because they are unfamiliar' (Phillips and Earle, 2010: 1). However, these claims are refuted by many, who argue instead that both social groups borrow from each other and both have a distinct set of biases, liabilities and assets (Phillips and Earle, 2010). I too ascertain that although the 'insider' risks maintaining a myopic view, rigorous and thorough research practices can become the lens through which the researcher can adopt a wider, clearer view of social reality, whilst holding onto the original image. With carefully considered research methods, intellectual autonomy and transparency, it is possible to maintain integrity and professionalism. I found that, whilst in the field, the solution was to remain true to both identities as volunteer and researcher and to approach my identity as a whole rather than to try to separate them out; they are interwoven and part of the fabric of my identity. I sought to blend them in a way that maintained my personal integrity and that of my research. The key to any good ethnography is transparency. As a Kainos volunteer and person of faith I am an 'insider' and as a researcher and as a non-incarcerated person I am also an 'outsider' but this identity is much messier in practice and adds to the richness of ethnographic exploration. Ethnographic practice traces the movement to and fro, back and forth, inside and out.

The lone researcher

For the lone researcher, the need for self-reflexivity and good field notes is vital. The key to writing a good prison field diary is to write as much as possible about as much as possible. In practical terms, for me this meant using a notepad and pen whilst in prison and typing up my notes when I left prison each evening; this in itself is an important method of reflexivity and analysis. Field diaries act as a way of thinking through the research process, helping the researcher to reflect on their interactions with people, places and things. The process of 'writing it all out' helps to trace the development of (mis)understandings (Cook and Crang, 2007) and is also a means of embracing the creative process of ethnography. The researcher's own responses and reactions are an important part of how the research will develop. The prison is a constantly moving space, where time can freeze and the unsaid can speak volumes, and where much of what is being observed is 'hidden'. The acknowledgement of a researcher's emotions is a vital part of prison ethnography; to write *about* emotions, not to write *emotionally* (Piacentini, 2013).[22] Writing reflective accounts of disturbing events, a general 'feeling' on the wing can help to make sense of what is actually happening; close proximity allows you to pick up on important things that might be missed as a casual observer:

> I felt rather paranoid in the classroom today – there is something going on I don't know about – everything looks 'normal' but there is an undercurrent, I can feel it, it's almost sinister – the men are quieter than usual. I spoke to Jack during the break and he said 'there's a funny atmosphere on the wing at the moment because of what's going on in one of the dorms. Rob is causing problems'.
>
> (Field diary)

The importance of emotions in prison ethnography was discussed by Lorna Rhodes at the International Prison Ethnography Symposium in 2012; she said that there should be no avoidance of the emotional aspect of what prison researchers do and that these narratives can lead to re-evaluation and re-clarification of an issue (see also Rhodes' Chapter 14, this volume). For her, thinking, speaking, observing and writing are all one thing and it is this total immersion into the field that enables the researcher to tell the story of what is really happening. Jewkes (2012) refers to the significance of auto-ethnography and emotion in prison research, suggesting that prison ethnographers do prison ethnography a disservice by not acknowledging emotion; acknowledging emotion is an essential part of the researcher's responsibility to manage his or her identity (Jewkes, 2012).

Prisoners suffer from deprivation of liberty, lack of privacy, separation from family and loved ones and are thereby vulnerable adults. It is almost inevitable that the researcher who embarks on an ethnography among such people, most of whom have suffered various other traumas, will themeselves end up with vicarious trauma or compassion fatigue to some degree. Drake and Harvey (2014) discuss the complexities of disentangling the underlying causes of this 'affective toll' which can manifest as physiological health symptoms, especially for the lone researcher who may have no forum to openly discuss his or her emotional state. There is little research thus far on the effects on the researcher of carrying out research with prisoners; there is, however, abundant literature on the effects of working with traumatised people on mental health professionals, whose spirituality and sense of hope and meaning have been disturbed due to vicarious trauma (McCann and Pearlman, 1990).

In addition to my field diary, I also kept a personal research journal where I recorded my thoughts and feelings. Certain ideas and theories have been formulated out of its writings, reinforcing my sense that the act of writing is part of the ethnographic process; 'How can I tell what I think till I see what I say' as novelist and critic E. M. Forster puts it (1927).[23] During the fieldwork phase, my journal became hugely important as a cathartic tool to make sense of each day by writing about my experiences and emotions. It was for my eyes only and it was a safe space for me to offload in an unrestricted way my concerns, upsets, angers, frustrations; it was an outpouring of ideas, thoughts and feelings. Some of my best conceptual ideas have been born out of these pages. Reflexivity as part of a therapeutic process of self-comprehension also helps one make sense of situations; often, the point of maximum insight in the field occurs at the point of most disturbance, which is when you need time to write and reflect until you know what it is about; it is about trusting and knowing your instincts.

Learning to breathe under water

Balancing professionalism with compassion and ethics with security issues were challenges I faced on a daily basis. Disassociating from the research environment can be difficult and keeping an emotional distance is not always easy, especially when you are bearing witness. Reflexivity can, therefore, be partly used as a therapeutic tool, because researching prisons can be a lonely process. Balancing research detachment with compassion, especially when immersed in the prison community on a daily basis for such a long period of time, was dilemmas I frequently encountered. It was easy to become weighted down by the hopes and fears of the prisoners in this all-consuming environment. A number of months into my fieldwork, I wrote:

> My head never stops – it's like a washing machine. D wing is so draining – there is no air or natural light. I am doing so many hours in prison, I am so tired. I am only beginning to acknowledge that it is emotional work dealing with broken people. I am so worried and upset about Charlie today – I feel so sad when I look at him – what a tragic waste of a young life. I feel so powerless. How can I change the prison system? I feel overwhelmed about the pain and suffering. I am exhausted.

Shortly after I wrote this, I spoke to a prison chaplain who assured me that it is perfectly natural to 'crash' when you work in prison and that you will then find your own way of dealing with it. He suggested I read 'Sharing the Darkness: The Spirituality of Caring' by Sheila Cassidy.[24] A poem in the book gave me great strength as I felt it was symbolic of what I had been experiencing in prison. The poem deploys a metaphor of a house built by the sea that is eventually overwhelmed by it. It ends with the observation:

> *That when the sea comes calling you stop being good neighbours*
> *Well acquainted, friendly from a distance neighbours.*
> *And you give your house for a coral castle*
> *And you learn to breathe underwater.*[25]

I understood the 'sea' in this poem as the presence of God and His strength to carry you through what might seem an impossible task; at times I felt like I was drowning in the horrors of prisoner's stories. Cassidy explains that the sea is both God and the slow encroachment of the world's agony upon one's conscience; the two are actually as one (1988: 9). Having read Cassidy's book I was able to put my creative energy into breathing in goodness, not drowning in the darkness of prison and to focus on why I was there – to carry out research and to walk alongside. In a strange dichotomy, the intensity of emotions felt in prison is coupled with a gradual desensitisation of the dark realities found within the prison walls. I found myself challenging my own thought processes; it had become 'normal' to talk about horrific acts of abuse, cruelty and violence; one minute we'd be talking about last night's dinner, the next we'd be talking about the events leading up to someone's murder. I was aware of becoming desensitised and did not want this to happen. I never want not to be shocked at abuse, neglect, violence and cruelty. However, part of becoming desensitised and becoming comfortable with openly discussing the darkness of humanity is to see prisoners as God intends us to see them – as fully human, frail and fallible. To see through another's eyes is to see your own failings and that is frightening for most because society prefers to believe that 'they are not like us'. When you go into prison you face yourself, and that can be a powerful experience. Having a faith gives me a lens and a framework with which to make sense of the environment, the prisoners, myself and creation. I recorded a defining moment in my field diary when I was talking to one of the prisoners in the classroom one day:

> It feels strange that I don't feel strange talking to men who have done terrible things – I was in the classroom with Tim this morning – I was sitting at a table and he was standing behind me and over me showing me his book. As I watched his hand move across the page I thought this hand has killed someone and I don't feel afraid of you and I don't think you are a monster.

Detaching with compassion and without losing sight of why I was there was sometimes a difficult thing to do. There were times when I had to keep firm boundaries in my mind and remember what my role was, as this field note records:

> I interviewed Ben today and he told me so much about some of what happened to him in prison. I actually stopped at one point as I needed to process what I was being told and said to him 'that's a lot to take in' and I just had to sit there and pause for a minute. All I could say was 'that's horrific'. I just wanted to say something inspiring and helpful but I couldn't so I breathed and carried on. Driving home I felt traumatised as I have been reminded of the dark reality of prisons.

I was literally left speechless during this interview, and I wanted to do or say something helpful or useful but I was powerless. It was not my place and I had to remember this boundary. I was not a therapist or a member of staff. I did feel like a failure for not being able to offer anything. Speaking to a prominent member of prison chaplaincy some months later, he told me 'when you are listening to something horrific sometimes there are no words and just being there, listening is what matters'.

Conclusion

Conducting prison ethnography is challenging and at times joyful. It requires resilience, integrity, professionalism, patience and compassion. Positioning your 'self' in your research setting coupled with sound, rigorous methodology and reflexivity produces insightful, experiential knowledge and 'thick descriptions' of the 'hidden' world of the prison. The depth and longevity of this interactive, semi-autoethnographic study demonstrates the importance and value of prison ethnography in order to understand the diversity of prison on a more human level. The blurring of my role boundaries and 'messy' identity perception added an invaluable dimension to my understanding of and analysis of the intricacies of relationships within the prison community and this added a richness to my experience of a total cultural immersion. Balancing professional research detachment with compassion and becoming weighted down by the hopes and fears of the prisoners in such an all-consuming environment are realities researchers have to face and overcome. Working within a framework of integrity, compassion and accountability, one can make scholarly, value-based judgements and remain true to one's values as a person and a researcher. Being a lone prison ethnographer comes with its own unique challenges, and the need for self-reflexivity, not just for methodological rigour but also as a coping strategy in the deep and sometimes dark places of prison, is imperative.

As a prison ethnographer, I am a privileged member of society. To be given the opportunity to engage in an organic, creative process within a tightly controlled, regimented environment is both challenging and humbling. Very few members of the public enter into the prison world; so it is my responsibility as a researcher to educate and to engage with the public in shaping understandings of the horrors, and also of the shimmers of light, to be found in prison. As a researcher and person of faith, I have a lens to help make sense of my environment and a theological framework with which to critique the modern prison system:

> While no Biblical blueprint exists for how Christians are to engage the prison issue, the biblical witness offers us a moral compass. The direction is clear. The details are left to us to work out.
>
> (Parham, 2011)

For me, it is about Christianity in action in the form of discipleship and service: walking alongside, listening, being present, embracing a positive response to the problem of imprisonment, in the knowledge that God's justice is a renewing and restoring one. As another prison researcher asserts, 'my scholarship must have stakes in the greater good' (Shabazz, 2010). I still pray for the men in my study, and my writing continues as a creative act of prayer for all people in prison. By sharing my experiences of the faith-motivated researcher in an informed and transparent way, I hope I have offered a unique understanding of this, perhaps 'hidden' researcher positionality. I find guidance and solace in the remarks of Revd John Davies (2005) that such work 'is to do with embracing the discomfiting realities of the world without drowning in the terrors they hold for us. We can't ignore these realities. They are the atmosphere we live and breathe in, they are the flow between the places we inhabit... if we breathe in the Spirit we inhale healing here.'

Notes

1. *Hamlet* (Act I, Scene iii).
2. Geoff Hebbern made this comment in 1996 when he was a principal officer and not a chaplain; it was in response to being asked by a rather hostile person from the prison service to explain why he thought the project would work.
3. Originally as Kainos-APAC Trust.
4. HMP The Verne has now closed as an adult male, category C prison for prisoners and now houses detainees.
5. Bible (NIV: Mark 12:31).
6. This quote has been attributed to a number of people: Anais Nin, Talmud, Anonymous.
7. Kainos volunteer handbook.
8. This is my experience of a single prison wing and women's experiences in other wings and other male prisons can vary.
9. All prisoners' and volunteer's names are pseudonyms.
10. Frances Crook, speaking at The Howard League Student Conference, 2013.
11. Residents who are living on Kainos at the end of their sentence are taken for breakfast in the local town by staff and volunteers on the day they are released.
12. Prisoners are vulnerable adults due to their very status as suffering from deprivation of liberty, lack of privacy, separation from family and loved ones and so forth.
13. I am indebted to my supervisor, Associate Professor Nick Gill, for this point.
14. Bible (NIV).
15. I am indebted to Dr. Christopher Southgate for these insights.
16. As chaplaincy volunteer (Exeter Cathedral Prison Prayer Support Team) for HMP/RC Exeter.
17. This is not to condone or excuse their acts, it is to see them wholly, fully as human.
18. See Maruna et al. (2006b) for narrative change in relation to religious conversion.
19. Maslow's 'Hierarchy of Needs' (1943).
20. My proposal then had to be approved by NOMS (National Offender Management System) through IRAS (Integrated Research Application System).
21. I write in more depth, in my PhD thesis, about the hope and humanity found in this community.
22. Speaking at *The International Prison Ethnography Symposium*, 2012.
23. From E. M. Forster's (1927) *Aspects of the Novel*.
24. Sheila Cassidy was imprisoned and tortured in Chile in 1975 for drawing attention to human rights abuses.
25. Originally from an unpublished work by Sr Carol Bialock, RSCJ.

Further reading

Cassidy, S. (1988) *Sharing the Darkness: The Spirituality of Caring* (London: Darton, Longman and Todd Ltd.).

Jewkes, Y. (2012) 'Autoethnography and Emotion as Intellectual Resources: Doing Prison Research Differently', *Qualitative Enquiry*, 18, 63.

Noblett, W. (2009) *Inside Faith: Praying for People in Prison* (London: Darton, Longman and Todd).

References

Aresti, A. (2013) 'A Convict Perspective', *Prison Service Journal*, Perrie Lectures, January, 211, 19–24.

Armstrong, R. (2012) *Searching for Mercy Street: Examining the Re-Entry of Ex-prisoners Released From a Faith Based Prison Unit,* Unpublished PhD Thesis, University of Cambridge.

Becker, H. S. (1967) 'Whose Side Are We On?' *Social Problems,* 14, 3, 239–47.

Berger, P. L. (1963) *Invitation to Sociology. A Humanistic Perspective* (Garden City, New York: Doubleday/Anchor Books).

Burnside, J., Loucks, N., Adler, J. R. and Rose, G. (2005) *My Brother's Keeper. Faith-Based Units in Prisons* (Cullompton: Willan Publishing).

Cassidy, S. (1988) *Sharing the Darkness: The Spirituality of Caring* (London: Darton, Longman and Todd Ltd.).

Cilluffo, F. (2006) *Statement to the Committee on Homeland Security and Governmental Affairs on Prison Radicalization: Are Terrorist Cells Forming in US Blocks?* Hearing, 19 September 2006.

Crang, M. and Cook, I. (2007) *Doing Ethnographies* (London: Sage).

Davies, J. (2005) www.johndavies.org [accessed May 2014].

Denzin, N. K. (1994) 'The Art and Politics of Interpretation', in N. K. Denzin and Y. S. Lincoln (eds) *Handbook of Qualitative Research* (Thousand Oaks, CA: Sage).

Drake, D. and Harvey, J. (2014) 'Performing the Role of Ethnographer: Processing and Managing the Emotional Dimensions of Prison Research', *International Journal of Social Research Methodology*, 17, 5, 489–501.

Earle, R. and Phillips, C. (2013) 'Muslim Is the New Black – New Ethnicities and New Essentialisms in the Prison', *Race and Justice*, 3, 2, 114–29.

Elisha, O. (2008) 'You Can't Talk to an Empty Stomach: Faith-Based Activism, Holistic Evangelism, and the Publicity of Evangelical Engagement', in R. Hackett (ed) *Proselytisation Revisited: Rights Talk, Free Markets and Culture Wars* (London: Equinox Publishing).

Ferrell, M. and Hamm, M. S. (1998) *Ethnography at the Edge: Crime, Deviance, and Field Research* (Boston: Northeastern University Press).

Goode, J. (2006) 'Faith-Based Organisations in Philadelphia: Neoliberal Ideology and the Decline of Political Activism', *Urban Anthropology*, 35, 2–3, 203–36.

Irwin, J. and Cressey, D. (1962) 'Thieves, Convicts and the Inmate Culture', *Social Problems*, 10, 145–55.

Institute for Social Policy and Understanding (2013) Facts and Fictions about Islam in Prison, January 2013.

Jewkes, Y. (2012) 'Autoethnography and Emotion as Intellectual Resources: Doing Prison Research Differently', *Qualitative Enquiry,* 18, 1, 63–75.

Kantrowitz, N. (1996) *Close Control* (Albany, NY: Harrow and Heston).

King, R. D. (2000) 'Doing Research on Prisons', in R.D. King and E. Wincup (eds) *Doing Research on Crime and Criminal Justice* (Oxford: Oxford University Press).

Kumara, N., Caulfield, L. and Newberry, M. (2012) 'The Experiences of Women Working in a Male Therapeutic Community Prison', *Prison Service Journal*, May, 201, 7–11.

Liebling, A. (2001) 'Whose Side Are We On? Theory, Practice and Allegiances in Prisons Research', *British Journal of Criminology*, 41, 472–84.

Leibling, A., Arnold, H. and Straub, C. (2011) *An Exploration of Staff-Prisoner Relationships at HMP Whitemoor: 12 years on* (Cambridge: CICPRC).

Maruna, S. (2001) *Making Good: How Ex-Convicts Reform and Rebuild Their Lives* (Washington, DC: American Psychological Association).

Maruna, S., Wilson, L. and Curran, K. (2006b) 'Why God Is Often Found behind Bars: Prison Conversions and the Crises of Self-Narrative', *Research In Human Development*, 3, 2–3, 161–84.

McCann, I. L. and Pearlman, L. A. (1990) 'Vicarious Traumatization: A Framework for the Psychological Effects of Working with Victims', *Journal of Traumatic Stress*, 3, 1, 131–49.

Mills, C. W. (1959) *The Sociological Imagination* (New York: Oxford University Press).

Neumann, P. R. (2010) *Prisons and Terrorism: Radicalisation and De-radicalisation in 15 Countries* (London: International Centre for the Study of Radicalisation and Political Violence (ICSR)).

Noblett, W. (2009) *Inside Faith: Praying for People in Prison* (London: Darton, Longman and Todd).

Noblett, W. (2014) 'Interview with the Venerable William Noblett CBE', *Prison Service Journal,* January, 211.

Parham, R. (2011) www.ethicsdaily.com [accessed October 2011].

Pew Research Centre (2012) *Religion in Prisons: A 50-State Survey of Prison Chaplains* (Washington: Pew Research Centre).

Phillips, C. and Earle, R. (2010) 'Reading Difference Differently? Identity, Epistemology and Prison Ethnography', *British Journal of Criminology,* 50, 2, 360–78.

Philo, C. (2001) 'Accumulating Populations: Bodies, Institutions and Space', *International Journal of Population Geography*, 7, 473–90.

Piacentini, L. (2007) 'Researching Russian Prisons: A Consideration of New and Established Methodologies in Prison Research', in Y. Jewkes (ed) *Handbook on Prisons* (Cullompton: Willan Publishing).

Piacentini, L. (2013) 'Integrity, always Integrity', *Criminal Justice Matters*, 91, 1.

Pollner, M. and Emerson, R. M. (1988) 'The Dynamics of Inclusion and Distance in Fieldwork Relations', in R. M. Emerson (ed) *Contemporary Field Research: A Collection of Readings* (Prospect Heights: Waveland Press).

Richards, C. (2012) 'Auto-Ethnography: How Respondent Researchers Helped Bring Ethnography in from the Cold', *International Journal of Market Research*, 54, 1, 28–34. [Available online: https://www.mrs.org.uk/pdf/Richards%20-%20IJMR%2054.1%202012.pdf].

Scott, D. (1996) *Heavenly Confinement? The Role and Perception of Christian Prison Chaplains in the North East of England's Prisons* (London: Lambert Academic Press).

Scott, D. (1997) *God's Messengers Behind Bars: The Role and Perception of the Prison Chaplain* (Ormskirk: Centre for Studies in Crime and Social Justice) [Report for HMPS Chaplaincy].

Shabazz, R. (2010) www.uvm.edu/~geograph/?Page=RashadShabazz.php [accessed March 2010].

Sparks, R. (2002) 'Out of the "Digger": The Warrior's Honour and the Guilty Observer', *Ethnography,* (special issue) 3, 4, 556–81.

Sparks, R., Bottoms, A. E. and Hayward, W. (1996) *Prisons and the Problem of Order* (Oxford: Clarendon Press).
Sykes, G. M. (1958) *The Society of Captives. A Study of a Maximum Security Prison* (Princeton: Princeton University Press).
Woodhead, L. (2004) *Christianity: A Very Short Introduction* (Oxford: Oxford University Press).

18
Situating the Self in Prison Research: Power, Identity and Epistemology

Abigail Rowe

Introduction

From the middle of the twentieth century onwards, ethnographic methods have had a central influence on sociological research in prisons (Clemmer, 1940; Sykes, 1958; Ward and Kassebaum, 1965; Giallombardo, 1966). It is a tradition that continues to make a significant contribution to the sociological understanding of imprisonment in jurisdictions across the globe, in spite of concerns that, in an age of mass incarceration, ethnographic research has become relatively marginalised since its mid-century 'golden age' (Wacquant, 2002). The contribution that participant observation has made to the understanding of imprisonment and prison institutions is clear. However, as Jewkes (2012) has observed, ethnographies of prison life have tended to avoid acknowledging the emotionality and autoethnographic dimensions of the participant observation on which they rest. Criminology, she suggests, has not been receptive to accounts of the emotional subtext of field research. Although a reflexive tradition is well established and vigorous in many fields of contemporary ethnographic research (see, inter alia, Van Maanen, 1995; Emerson et al., 2001; Atkinson et al., 2003; Davies, 2008), in written ethnographies of prison life, the researcher often all but disappears, confined to methodological footnotes and appendices and seldom visible or acknowledged in the analysis proper. This evasion of self and emotion in written accounts of prison research defies the ineluctably embodied and – despite its realist and positivist origins – subjective character of ethnographic methods.

This chapter seeks to extend Jewkes' argument that admitting to emotion is key to understanding the research process by exploring the substantive gains in understanding, which can emerge from acknowledging the (inter)subjective and embodied dimensions of fieldwork in prisons. In the analysis presented

First published in *Qualitative Inquiry*, 2014, 20, 404–16.

here, I take up Hammersley and Atkinson's (2007) suggestion that the participant researcher is 'the research instrument par excellence' to explore the epistemological possibilities of making the self of the researcher visible (see also Spry, 2001; Anderson, 2006). The discussion draws on data and reflections from my own research in two English women's prisons and focuses on moments of disruption, emotion and 'trouble' generated by my presence in the field. They revealed my different modes of participation in the social world of the prison and, in turn, illuminated some of its characteristics. I was aware of my presence disturbing established patterns of interaction as I slipped in and out of visibility as a stranger there, giving brief insights into otherwise unobserved relations, and the meanings and values of people and practices within the prison. I felt myself drawn uncomfortably into institutional and moral hierarchies that I wanted to resist, illustrating sharply their pervasive power. I found my own established self-meanings unsettled by the need to manage a research identity in the field. In particular, managing my position as a gay woman researching in a setting in which sexuality was a salient and contentious theme felt at times like a form of emotional participation, perhaps invisible to others, but a powerful source of understanding for me. These were embodied encounters, emotionally marked by my own or others' responses.

Taking a properly reflexive approach to participant observation is not then simply a question of making one's various positions and allegiances accountable to the reader to buttress researcher objectivity (see Primeau, 2003; Anderson, 2006; Davies, 2008). Neither is the attentiveness to subjectivity and emotionality which is implied by an autoethnographic approach necessarily the solipsistic exercise that Jewkes (2012) suggests criminologists often believe it to be. Rather, as Ruth Behar (1997) has written,

> [t]he exposure of the self who is also a spectator has to take us somewhere we couldn't otherwise get to. It has to be essential to the argument, not a decorative flourish, not exposure for its own sake (p. 14).

This discussion, then, seeks to do more than produce a 'confessional tale' (Van Maanen, 2011 [1988]) of the experience of fieldwork. Rather, it attempts to integrate the researcher-self more fully into what Atkinson et al. (2003: 59) term 'the ethnography proper' and examine what can be learned from reflecting on the ethnographer's presence in the prison that we could not otherwise have access to.

The study

This chapter is based on eight months of fieldwork during 2007–08, which was conducted in two women's prisons in the north of England within a broader study of prisoners' coping and social support practices. The research combined participant observation, semi-structured research interviews with prisoners and uniformed staff, and a structured survey administered to prisoners.[1] Following a brief pilot study, fieldwork was conducted at one 'open' and one 'closed' prison for women – (Her Majesty's Prisons) HMP Askham Grange and HMP New Hall.[2] The pilot phase was carried out at HMP Drake Hall in Staffordshire, then a semi-open prison for sentenced women prisoners.[3]

HMP Askham Grange is an open prison occupying a former manor house set in modest grounds in the centre of a village just outside York. At the time of the research, the prison held approximately 100 prisoners aged 18 and over in a staged resettlement regime. Prisoners (or 'residents' – the preferred term of prison managers and one of a number in common usage) worked towards voluntary and paid employment or study in the local community. The prison's administrative offices, education department, and most of the accommodation were in the main house, with a small, relatively self-contained modern annex of single rooms for women in paid employment outside. The prison's separate mother-and-baby unit could hold 10 women with children aged up to 18 months, although it was under-occupied for most of the research period. Its nursery was open to children of prison staff and from the local community.

HMP New Hall is a closed prison approximately 35 miles away from Askham Grange, also in Yorkshire. The prisons' geographical proximity meant that there was some movement of both staff and prisoners between the two, and that – in theory at least – some services, such as Psychology, could be shared.[4] At the time of the research, New Hall had a population of approximately 400 remand and sentenced prisoners in closed and, on one wing, semi-open conditions. A separate unit held 'juvenile' prisoners, aged 15–18 years. The prison's diverse mixture of cellular and dormitory accommodation reflected its piecemeal development from its earlier role as a boys' detention centre. Separate buildings housed a unit of small wings, larger galleried wings and a small prefabricated unit that served as the semi-open accommodation. Dedicated wings held new arrivals, women detoxing from opiates, and mothers with babies aged up to 9 months, although for most of the research period the latter was either out-of-use or was used as an additional accommodation to ease overcrowding elsewhere. The 'healthcare' wing housed prisoners with the most acute mental health problems, and a small number of women lived on the segregation unit, either for their own protection or because their behaviour could not be managed elsewhere. The women worked in light assembly or textiles workshops, attended education classes or contributed to the running of the prison by working as cleaners, orderlies[5] or in the kitchens.

Discussion

The central participant-observation approach of ethnographic methods makes available a range of positions from complete participant to complete observer

(Gold, 1958), the relative merits of which have long been described and debated by ethnographers. In penal and secure settings, the nature of the institutional environment pushes most researchers towards the 'observer' end of Gold's spectrum, bringing with it well-rehearsed anxieties about the inevitable disruption the researcher's presence in the field will cause to the situated activity, the relations and practices, that she wants to observe (for surveys of these debates, see Hammersley and Atkinson, 2007). With Hammersley and Atkinson's (2007) conception of the ethnographer as research 'instrument' in mind, this chapter considers disruption, and the emotion that attends it, as a source of ethnographic insight, rather than necessarily a problem to be circumvented. Rhodes (2012, and see Chapter 14, this volume) borrows Barthes's (1981) notion of the 'punctum' – the detail in a photograph that 'pricks' and 'bruises' – to highlight those moments in ethnographic fieldwork that break through the surface of the everyday and penetrate the consciousness of the researcher to generate new or deeper insight (see also Earle, 2013). Here, I reflect on just such emotional 'punctuation points' (Rhodes, 2012); moments in my fieldwork when I was either aware of disturbing settled patterns of activity around me or experienced the process of fieldwork as unsettling to my *self* in ways that seemed to reveal something about the social life of the prison.

In the PhD thesis that presented the first iteration of this study's findings (Rowe, 2009), autoethnographic reflections were largely tidied away into a more-or-less neatly bounded methods chapter. This discussion has its origins in the process I began then of reflecting on and trying to account for my methods. For many prison researchers whose methods include participant observation of some kind, claiming the term 'ethnography' raises some fraught questions about the extent to which we really can participate in or gain access to prison life, and in exactly what ways our research should or should not be regarded as ethnographic (Rhodes, 2001). Few experience what it means to sleep in a locked cell, for example, or to dispense the authority of the penal system. In this vein, Mathiesen (1965) remarks of the limitations to his study of male prisoners in preventive custody in Norway that, 'I could quite obviously never become *one of them*' (p. 236, italics added). A number of researchers have sought qualified descriptors of their methods in recognition of this. Owen (1998) and Crewe (2006), for example, acknowledge the limits to outsider participation in prison settings in their respective (and I think useful) use of the terms 'quasi-' and 'semi-'ethnographic methods to describe their approaches. In being handed about between disciplines, definitions of ethnography have become elastic and contested. Whilst for some ethnography remains nothing less than total immersion in the host community, for others it can encompass almost any qualitative method concerned with culture and meaning-making (Chambers, 2000; Hammersley and Atkinson, 2007). At times, sociologists and anthropologists researching prison life have perhaps focused on such questions of taxonomy at the expense of arguably more fundamental epistemological questions about how the field can be known, and on what basis our claims are made. Even so, it was entering into this near-ritual consideration of what kind of ethnography I thought this was, that led me to examine in detail the senses in which I thought I had been a *participant* in the social world of the prison.

As I've suggested, the structures of a prison make it difficult for an outsider to assume anything other than a marginal position. I was also both temperamentally most comfortable in the role of reserved participant and committed to gaining insights into the perspectives of both prisoners and staff, which seemed to demand a relatively high degree of 'mobility' between groups, so limiting the depth of my identification with either (see Hammersley and Atkinson, 2007). Despite my reserve, however, it seemed to me that there were two senses in which I couldn't avoid participating in the social world of the prison: First, in its hierarchies and second, in its pervasive identity politics. I felt continually positioned along these two axes, and was conscious of needing to manage and, at times, resist this. This sense of being drawn more deeply into the action around me than I would have chosen frequently caught me by surprise, generating feelings of discomfort and dissonance. The terms of my presence in the prison, and the modes of my participation there, thus proved unstable and beyond my ability to determine. Reflecting on the experience once the uncomfortable moment had passed, however, it was clear to me that this subjective, embodied, emotional engagement was itself a powerful means through which I was able to gain a deeper understanding of the prison's relations and practices. As Alison Liebling (1999: 164) has commented, 'our emotions do not need to be reconciled with our so-called data. They constitute data.' Furthermore, making emotion and the self visible in research accounts may offer a partial solution to the problems that these questions of managing identity and power present to conducting and writing prison ethnography.

Troubling the field: Identity, hierarchy and the 'properties' of social actors

Negotiating access is an iterative process in much qualitative research. In the controlled and surveilled environment of the prison, this may be exaggerated yet further. For most prison researchers, accounting to participants for oneself in the prison is continual: moving around secure areas; negotiating the habitual guardedness of many prisoners and officers; navigating an institution in which, although one often encounters strangers, all can be rapidly and precisely placed (Drake and Harvey, 2013). My own experience of fieldwork in penal establishments was shaped, I think, by my being, on the whole, a fairly inconspicuous presence in a women's prison. As a white woman below 30, I was squarely within the demographic of most of the prisoner population at the establishments in my study. Potential points of difference – my southern accent, my odd purpose there, my identification as gay – either emerged later or remained unarticulated. Dressed in civilian clothes, I could have been a member of a number of groups as neither prisoners, civilian workers, nor senior staff wore uniforms, although as a student and an observer I probably looked both less smart and less purposeful than many prison workers. Always uncomfortable with markers of status, I wore the ID badge that marked me as an 'official' visitor and the keys I was issued at New Hall to allow me to move around independently, as inconspicuously as I could. The recording equipment I used for interviews was small enough to be carried unnoticed in a pocket. Although I clung to a notebook like a security blanket, at a glance, and especially in a crowd, I was probably not easy to 'read', and I seemed to be difficult for staff and prisoners to place without asking. On the occasions when I became aware that there was confusion about who I was, I was generally taken for a prisoner. Or perhaps it was those that I noticed, because it was that mistake that caused most ripples.

I quickly became aware both that people were *trying* to place me, and that in prison, the *kind* of person I was had a heightened significance. It seemed to illustrate the pressures and anxieties of institutional living, and some of the imperatives of penal institutions in particular: I remember being asked early on 'what I was' by a prisoner who'd thought I might be, as she said, 'one of us' because I was 'little' and 'looked young', but who was trying to identify someone to help her see a dentist before she was released; another who wanted to make a private phone call in a wing office where I was sitting asking the officer who was taking her through into the back office where the phone was, 'What about that girl?' meaning me, taking me for an inmate and clearly vigilant about the risks of discussing personal matters in front of an unknown prisoner; a uniformed officer asking me when I walked into a staff room at Askham Grange, 'Are you a governor, or a prisoner?' – half joking but nonetheless clearly seeking to establish the terms on which we would engage with one another. Like both the staff and the prisoners around me, then, I was identified, positioned, and managed accordingly.

In this hierarchical and relatively low-trust environment, efforts were visibly being made to manage impressions (Goffman, 1959) by controlling the flow of personal information and selecting the appropriate mode of address for whomever one was speaking to. Conditions of need, material scarcity, and patchy service provision charged interactions with instrumentality as individuals sought to secure services and support. Being embedded (embodied) in these encounters gave a very immediate insight into the caution and pragmatism with which people inside prisons conduct their everyday lives; *experiencing* them directly meant that I *had* to engage with their significance to be able to respond. In contrast, my presence as an outsider sometimes seemed initially not to register at all, only to be redoubled in its impact when it slipped back into view. The ensuing confusion or emotion was the 'punctuation point' that drew my attention, underscoring the recognition that a mistake had been made, and emphasising its significance. The disruption, caused by two incidents at New Hall in which I initially escaped notice as an observer, recorded afterward in my field diary, were, as Rhodes (2012) would lead us to expect, fruitful to my understanding:

Tuesday, 23 October 2007

> [I spent part of the afternoon observing an IT lesson.] There was a boisterous girl in the corner, Kirsty[6] ... I sat and chatted to a woman I recognised from G Wing as she did her work ... [The lesson wound down] well before the end of the session. A young female officer came in to search the women before they left. Sitting apparently aimlessly at one of the computers, she took me for an inmate ('Come on, Miss!,'[7] chivvyingly). My thoughts were elsewhere and it took me a moment to work out what she meant ('Oh! Oh no, I'm not a prisoner ... '). When she left, Kirsty commented [of the officer], with some enjoyment, 'She went well red!'

Several elements of this incident are noteworthy: what looked to me like the officer's embarrassment at making an error in front of inmates; her apparent sense that she had insulted me; and the prisoners' pleasure at her discomfort, all spoke to the often-strained quality of relations between staff and prisoners at this establishment. Where the categorisation of bodies is a bureaucratic and moral imperative, a failure of this kind troubles the settled order that the prison regime seeks to achieve. Here, the officer's efforts to 'make' an authoritative role for herself (Goffman, 1959; Rowe, 2009) faltered, itself a small victory for the prisoner. That this mattered was marked by the emotion it generated in both.

Confusion of this kind continued, to a degree, even as I became an established presence at New Hall:

Monday, 7 January 2008

> [I was standing on the upstairs landing on E wing at lunchtime, talking to Helen and Jan] ... Miss Lewis approached, locking in. Jan commented that it was time for them to go back in, and something about my having been caught 'Speaking to the enemy.' As I headed back downstairs, Miss Caldwell, seeing me out of the corner of her eye, began to say, 'Where are you going?!,' then saw it was me and apologised, embarrassed.[8]

The moments in which I was absorbed into the action of the prison – at least in the awareness of some of those around me – were no doubt fleeting. As I have already suggested, they felt like slippages between invisibility and visibility as an outsider to the institution, and where they were marked like this by embarrassment or confusion, they were revealing of social norms. They exposed – if only momentarily – the tone of the *un*observed officer addressing an inmate. The intensity of the officers' discomfort in these moments seemed to reveal a consciousness of the gap between the way in which I had been addressed as an imagined prisoner, and the more respectful tone usually afforded to a visitor. Perhaps this might be called something like quasi-participation: being subsumed briefly by the action completely and then slipping back into visibility as an observer. This was one of the ways in which my participant position seemed unstable, as if shifting from total participant to total observer, at least in the awareness of others. Owen (1998) similarly notes how being mistaken by staff for a prisoner during her fieldwork in a Californian women's prison gave emotional insights into the experience of confinement. In my own research, the degree of discomfort caused by such miscategorisations varied between establishments. In the more relaxed atmosphere of Askham Grange, endearments such as 'love' and 'duck' were usual terms of address both within and between the staff and prisoner groups. There was less often a significant difference in the tone in which staff and prisoners were addressed, so mistakes were less marked and less charged with obvious meaning.

In these moments, slight disturbances caused by my presence felt instructive. Goffman (1971) remarks that the purpose of ethnography is to 'derive the properties of individuals from observable situated activity'. On several occasions, the confusion I generated seemed to expose the 'properties' of particular social actors and the significance of the practices I observed more clearly than if everything had continued smoothly and uninterrupted. The fieldwork incident that illustrated this most vividly to me took place during an early observation in the busy Reception at New Hall:

Tuesday, 13 November 2007

> [One of the Reception officers] Jo Moore ... seemed to adopt me – I don't know why. Having begun the day as 'Abigail,' by the end of the shift I was 'Little Abi.' It was Jo who made sure I was offered drinks, and – because I ended up staying so late – that I got a meal. She progressively put me to work – initially just asking me to pass her this or that, and then ultimately helping her fill in prop [property] cards.... Reception is made up of three sections: an entrance area with some holding rooms and a counter; a middle room with a counter and the SO's[9] office off it; a back area where the shower, kitchen and an 'inner' holding area are. I was standing in front of the counter in this middle room when Jo asked if I wanted a drink and asked Margaret the orderly if she'd 'Get Miss a black coffee.' She duly brought me a coffee,

> and a little while later, standing in the doorway between the two outer rooms while Jo and a couple of other officers went through some property, I lifted the cup to take my first sip. Jo was facing me, caught sight my light blue plastic cup and looked absolutely aghast: 'Where d'you get that?!' I (nonplussed) said that Margaret had brought it to me. Jo – seemingly quite horrified – said that it was a prisoners' cup: 'Don't drink from it.' I said I really didn't mind, but she shook her head, wrinkling her nose, and took it from me back out to the kitchen. A minute or two later, Margaret brought me a replacement coffee, laughing in embarrassed apology that she'd thought I was a prisoner. I told her that it was fine – I didn't mind what I drank from – there'd been no need to change the cup, and it had been perfectly natural to take me for a prisoner, standing where I had been...

I felt drawn into the prison's power relations in a number of ways here. Participating in the officer's work seemed to add a note of ambiguity to my position; and, as always, I forgot in my gratitude at being offered a drink by an officer that accepting it would probably mean that a prisoner would immediately be instructed to bring it. I never got used to, or felt comfortable with, this. I experienced ongoing, irresolvable tensions between the imperatives to respond positively to the officer's social overtures, meeting the physical demands of my own thirst, hunger and caffeine withdrawal during a long day at the prison, and trying to hold myself apart from the institutional power by which prisoners were processed and subordinated.

This internal discomfort was all displaced, however, by the crisis of confusion and panic about the cup I had been given. The fallout from this simple misunderstanding drew my attention to the different crockery used by staff and prisoners, and its previously unconsidered significance. I'd seen that the officers used their own ceramic mugs, which were kept on a separate shelf in the kitchen area, but without this incident would probably not have thought much more about it than I would about the cups in a school staff room, or that office workers choose to bring in from home. Here, I was taken aback at the visceral disgust manifested in the immediacy and strength of the officer's reaction, the ideas of stigma and contamination that it revealed, and the suspension of the norms of politeness that would in another setting have made it unacceptable to express revulsion or insist that the mistake be corrected. It seemed to me that the cluster of ideas and beliefs exposed in this moment were not ideas that the officer would have (could have?) articulated in a research interview. In any case, I wouldn't have known how to formulate a question that 'tapped' it, and even if these associations were conscious ones, I suspect she would have been reluctant to express them. These were not insights that would have been available by any means other than *being there* as an embodied social presence, a *person*[10] with particular 'properties' of my own, albeit uncertain ones. The disruption that accompanied the process of ascribing 'appropriate' meanings to me was instructive. Again, the emotion generated when mistakes were made – disgust, embarrassment – gave an uncensored commentary on their significance that was unlikely to have been accessible in any other way.

In a smoothly realised routine encounter, the tacit rules organising a setting's relations and practices remain submerged and may go unnoticed by the outsider-observer, because there's little to direct attention to things that have an unanticipated meaning; before the officer reacted as she did, it hadn't occurred to me that the mug I'd been given had symbolic significance. Lacking an 'indigenous role' and ignorant of social norms, the outsider-observer is not easily placed and may disrupt established relations in ways that 'trouble' the smooth-running of social transactions (notwithstanding, of course, that the actors inside prisons may not be invested in things running smoothly; many prisoners actively resist in all kinds of ways, and officers themselves adopt variant roles (Ben-David and Silfen, 1992; Farkas, 2000; Tait, 2011)). This seems to me to be one of the ways in which the practice of ethnography can 'make the familiar strange', both to the observer and, perhaps, to participants in the field, itself 'punctuating' the situated activity under observation and making it legible.

The prison officer in this incident had – in her attempts to be welcoming by occupying me – drawn me slightly beyond my preferred position of detachment by involving me in her work. However, my corner of Reception felt sufficiently 'backstage' that any compromise to my appearance of independence felt tolerable, and the trade-off against my desire to acknowledge the officer's kind intent, and avoid alienating her as a potential interview participant felt worth it. It did feel odd to contribute to official prison documents, however, and I was struck – as so often in the course of my fieldwork – by how rapidly decisions about how to present and conduct myself had to be made, and how uncertain the consequences of those decisions were. I often wanted time I didn't have to consider how I felt and what I should do, and the case for reserve felt impossible to make 'in the swim' of the action to hard-pressed prison staff who wanted an extra pair of hands to carry out what to them were straightforward, everyday tasks, but which to me – with my unease at practices of power and punishment and desire for separateness – felt fraught with confusion and compromise.

During my fieldwork, there were a number of other occasions on which members of prison staff – seeing me, I think, as being there in some kind of 'professional' capacity (although who knew quite what, or why?) – also asked me to help out with little tasks. Although undoubtedly due in part to the pressure staff were under (women's prisons are relatively lightly staffed, and New Hall at this time was experiencing high levels of both staff absence and prisoner receptions), some of these instances may have arisen from attempts to manage the discomfort of feeling observed, or even to 'colonise' and domesticate a potentially threatening stranger. Some of these experiences felt more deeply compromising to my efforts to hold onto and make visible my distance from the institution. One such incident took place during a day's observation on the semi-open wing at New Hall:

Friday, 2 November 2007

> The day's post arrived just before the women returned from work for dinner. The post was sorted into ordinary post, which had been opened already, and legal post, which was separate so the women could open it themselves in front of staff. As they got in, the women came to the office to ask for their post. They came in throughout their lunch hour, and while the officer oversaw the lunch queue she asked me if I'd mind handing out letters if anyone asked (this arose because the servery is just outside the office door, and space is so short that there wasn't really anywhere other than the office for me to be while everyone queued for food because it was a bit of a crush). Although I've come across and chatted to a number of the women on the wing, I've certainly not met anything like a critical mass of them to make me feel as though I'm generally known by prisoners, or that it's clear that I don't work for the prison, so this was a little uncomfortable. One of the women I'd seen coming through Reception the other day came and asked for a letter from the pile of unopened post, in addition to an ordinary letter. I told her that I didn't think I was allowed to give it to her because it needed to be opened in front of an officer (and that I was not one). She kept insisting (slightly aggressively) that the letter was there and yes she could have it. It felt as though it took a lot to persuade her that I couldn't give her the letter, and she kept agitating for it. I felt incredibly uncomfortable, and very annoyed that I'd been put in this ambiguous position...

This experience left me reeling. It was the stuff of a very ordinary, low-level confrontation between a prisoner and a member of staff. Exercising this kind of discretionary power in face-to-face encounters is continual in prison officer work (Mathiesen, 1965; Willet, 1983; Liebling, 2000; Liebling and Price, 2001) and as soon as I was placed in this role – even without any of the authority that made it meaningful – I felt myself positioned within this potentially conflictual dynamic. The reasonableness of my explanation that I *had* no authority didn't matter to the woman who wanted her letter. It was of no importance to her whether or not I had any investment in the rules that said she couldn't have it, any more than it had occurred to the officer that this task might make me uncomfortable, or be incompatible with my own purpose there.

Here again, were tensions between the need – common to all ethnographers – to maintain civility to my 'hosts' in the field in recognition of my imposition on them and in return for the access I was granted, and to remain visibly distinct from it. But who were my hosts? The officer here had allowed me to spend the morning sitting in the wing office. She did not have to and could have asked me to leave. My presence was at least as great an imposition on prisoners, however, who could not choose to refuse me admittance, except to their own rooms. The discomfort and anxiety I felt on this occasion pointed to the singular transactions of power that structured my encounters with the officer and the prisoner. In this moment, the dilemmas arising from my conflicted position felt intractable. It may be, however, that writing these dissonances back into my analysis of the incident not only puts the self to epistemological use by making the emotional responses that so clearly delineated the power transactions here but also offers a way of managing some of that conflict. Denzin describes what he terms 'messy' ethnographic texts (Denzin, 1997. See also Denzin and Lincoln, 2000; Lincoln and Denzin, 2005) as reflexive, multi-voiced, exposing the writer and refusing the authority promised by 'the myth of silent authorship' (Charmaz and Mitchell, 1996). Making the self visible as situated and subjective makes a different kind of position available from that of the univocal realist ethnography still typical in prison research. This circumvents the need to adopt a stable set of allegiances, and so perhaps offers a way of mitigating my sense that I must either be complicit in the disposal of forms of power that I could not fully endorse or was rejecting the hospitality of my hosts (see also Liebling, 2001).

As I have already suggested, and as Goffman (1971) implies it should, thinking autoethnographically about my own encounters in the field reveals some of my own 'properties' in that context. Because my outsider status and apparent rolelessness made me an obscure presence for many, there were times when others seemed to 'fill in the blanks' with meanings that perhaps shed more light on the social world of the prison than they did on me. I felt myself positioned variously as *professional, naïve outsider, eccentric left-winger*. The glimpses I caught of the ways in which others appeared to imagine me were often seemingly generated by others with little prompting from me, and clear reflections of the preoccupations, assumptions, and self-conceptions of actors in the field. As in previous examples, the position I occupied was not stable, and was as much ascribed to me as chosen by me. One example of being positioned by a basic-grade prison officer as 'the professional' who could adjudicate on appropriate practice was rich with layered meanings about punishment, penal practice, and status of prison officers. I was spending the day on the largest wing in the prison, which held the long-term prisoners. During a discussion about the types of prisoner held on the wing, the conversation turned to the Governing Governor's recent decision to grant permission to two women in a relationship to share a cell, which overturned what had until then been official policy. There were several of us in the office, but one long-serving but basic-grade officer steered the conversation:

Wednesday, 7 November 2007

> ...She clearly disapproved. I asked if couples sharing cells presented specific managerial/operational problems (such as – though I didn't suggest anything to her – coping with the fallout of intense relationships: frequent moves when relationships began/broke down; staff having to distinguish between serious/non-serious and healthy/unhealthy relationships...). She said, 'Well why should we?! It's like giving them their own self-contained flat!' Her reaction was clearly completely visceral (mildly interesting in light of the fact that I think she might be gay, in which case I suppose this instinct would be about punishment...). 'You're the professional – what do you think?' Were there murmurs here from her colleagues to tone down what they read as antagonistic? I think there was certainly an edge of that, at which she protested, 'No! I'm interested!' I think my response was that in this, she was the professional, not me...

I had perhaps irritated the officer by asking for an explanation of what was probably to her self-evident, but there was an audible sharpness to the word 'professional', amplified by what I thought was the demurring of the others present and my own obvious attempt to deflect it. It was not, after all, an identity that I had sought to claim for myself. Her use of the term seemed loaded with the sense of injury shared by many of her colleagues at that time: overruled and subordinated to prisoners' interests by new-broomish managers; their experience and procedural knowledge unvalued and irrelevant; hurried into change they did not necessarily approve of (see Liebling and Price, 2001; Crawley, 2004). It was challenging and defensive, tinged with suspicion, even scorn, of the views of those who – like me, like the Governor – viewed and understood the prison from the comfortable distance of our ivory towers rather than her own more grounded vantage point on the landings.

My presence as an observer, then, seemed to 'trouble' the field in a number of enlightening ways. The ways in which I felt my presence disturbs the setting were often deeply revealing of attitudes, practices, and social relations. They underscored the significance of the embodied character of ethnographic research, its 'relational, emotional, personal' nature (Atkinson et al., 2003: 56). As Jewkes (2012), Liebling (1999), and others indicate, however, and as suggested at the outset of this discussion, the relationship between field and researcher is a recursive one. I found as I attempted to navigate the structures and social relations of the prison and negotiate a tenable position for myself, that there was an insistence to the social dynamics in each of the prisons that was difficult to resist, a persistent pull to position me along those indices of identity and hierarchy on which the compelling logic of the prison demands that everyone be placed. As so often in fieldwork, 'making' and holding my chosen role as a reserved participant was a continuing negotiation, and often felt deeply compromised by the nature of the setting in ways that unsettled me.

Troubling me: Sexual identity, silence and the contours of power

Ethnographic fieldwork is not simply a personal process, but a dynamic one; 'the actual lived experience of fieldwork confronts, disrupts, and troubles the self' (Atkinson et al., 2003: 54). Atkinson et al. (2003) primarily consider how the experience of fieldwork impacts on the ethnographer's experience and understanding of self-identity. The confrontation, disruption, and troubling of the self that they describe, however, also offer a source of insight into understanding the experiences and practices of actors in the field. In this way too, then, the self is the ethnographic 'research instrument' (Hammersley and Atkinson, 2007).

Themes of identity and power run together hand-in-hand – always, but especially in prisons, where no-one ever *just happens to be*, and in which who one *is* of profound material and moral significance. Many ethnographers describe navigating dilemmas of self-presentation in the field as a process of finding a position that balances their own comfort and that of the group under observation. The researcher-self must be *made* in order to achieve a position as an 'acceptable marginal member' (Hammersley and Atkinson, 2007). In prisons, this means managing the impressions of both staff and prisoners (Liebling, 2001; Drake and Harvey, 2013). I was most conscious of doing this work in micro-level improvisations in the kinds of encounters I have discussed above: attempts to distance myself from the regime in the eyes of prisoners without seeming to cast negative judgment on the business of staff; seeking a line between appearing trusting and credulous; trying to ensure that I was as responsive and reliable I could be, but without sacrificing boundaries. I was certainly conscious of making mistakes. It was precisely when things went wrong, however, that I became conscious of these as power-laden transactions. Changes to arrangements for interviews with prisoners, for example, were hampered by the obstacles to direct communication and vulnerable to being overwritten by institutionally shaded scripts of disingenuousness and disrespect. Likewise, my anxieties at being aligned with the symbols of regime power: cups and keys and refreshments offered by staff but brought by prisoners. Attempts to 'make' my researcher identity and to position and re-position myself within complex encounters in the field often felt reactive and largely instinctive.

Some decisions about my self-presentation, however, were perhaps more strategic: how to present the project to make it understandable and seem worthwhile (with inevitable changes of emphasis in versioning this for different staff groups, managers, and prisoners); how to dress to convey an impression of being credible and 'together', but approachable and – preferably – distinct from prison staff; what personal information I would disclose or withhold. As an (usually) 'out' gay woman researching in women's prisons, questions and anxieties about self-presentation coalesced around ideas of (not) coming out. This was a uniquely persistent dilemma in the research, partly, perhaps because, transposed to the prison, my settled patterns of identity management were unsettled somewhat. The anxiety it generated was indeed a 'confrontation of the self', to revisit Atkinson et al.'s phrase. It dogged me throughout my fieldwork. Although this anxiety felt in some ways like a burden and an obstacle, I came to understand it as itself a kind of emotional participation in prison life and capable of illuminating something of what it is like to manage an identity in a closed and often hostile institution.

In another research project, my sexual orientation might have felt completely irrelevant. In women's prisons, however, sexuality is significant. Since the early twentieth century and up to the present day, sexual and romantic relationships between women prisoners have been a preoccupying theme for researchers (inter alia, Otis, 1913; Ward and Kassebaum, 1965; Giallombardo, 1966; Howe, 1994; Freedman, 1996; Severance, 2008; Einat and Chen, 2012), and gay and bisexual-identified women represent a significant minority of prison officers. The lesbian, gay, bisexual, and transgender (LGBT) staff group is active and visible. During my preliminary visit to Askham Grange, for example, I noted a large, framed rainbow flag carrying its logo displayed in one of the prison's central corridors. I thus began my fieldwork knowing that same-sex sexuality was likely to be in some way significant in the research sites, and participants confirmed early on in the research that in many English women's prisons it is not uncommon for even straight-identified women to enter into erotic and romantic relationships with one another. Added to my desire for personal reserve, the significance of sexuality in this field left me uncertain as to whether or not coming out myself would be either expedient or comfortable.

Although 'coming out' is commonly treated as a one-off rite-of-passage event in queer lives (see Orne, 2011), it is of course a recurrent experience, rehearsed and revisited as one encounters new people and places. Orne describes what he terms 'strategic outness' as a 'continual contextual management of sexual identity'. Day-to-day, 'outness' – for me – is almost always preferable. Conducting fieldwork, deciding whether to disclose this concealable characteristic became folded into and complicated by those other questions about managing an identity in the prison.

Not generally being 'read' as gay, coming out for me usually entails some kind of active disclosure. When others assume heterosexuality, *not* making that act of disclosure can quickly come to feel like an act of concealment.

An observation very early in my fieldwork at Askham Grange made me feel I needed to understand more about the significance of sexuality there before deciding to come out. I was spending a slow Friday afternoon in the prison's Reception and the two officers posted there – Beth Clarke and Miss Harvey in the field note below – had called over the tannoy to an officer working elsewhere in the prison, their friend Em, to come and join them for a cup of tea. Two others, Miss Campbell, who was 'young-in-service' but herself somewhere in her 40s, and a woman I didn't know had also dropped in for a chat on their way past. Also there was the Reception Orderly, who was a similar age and whose relationship with the officers seemed relaxed, but distinctly subordinate:

Friday, 18 May 2007

> Beth Clarke, Miss Harvey and Em are all gay ... and this definitely affected the atmosphere in the room, which seemed to a degree sexualised – when discussing Em's recent weight loss, Beth and Miss Harvey agreed she'd lost enough, Beth saying, 'You've gone too far for me now – I've gone off you' and there was quite a lot of mock-flirting; Beth told Em and Miss Harvey about a young blonde woman in an officer's shirt but no epaulettes she'd noticed in the car park slightly earlier and wondered who she was, which became a conversation about who the 'fit blonde' was. I suppose the majority of the well-established officers in the room were gay, i.e. a majority of the high-status people in the room, which seemed to facilitate a kind of homonormativity in the conversation, so that the couple of straight officers, notably Miss Campbell, were kind of falling in with that norm, and laughing along with the conversation; it struck me as being the obverse of the more common situation of being the only gay woman in an office laughing along with the girls/trying to keep your head down when the conversation turns to firemen and hoping no-one addresses you directly on the subject ...

I was fascinated by this scene and the dynamics between the women in the room that it suggested. The confidence shown by Beth, Em, and Miss Harvey not just in referring to their shared lesbian identities in a mixed group of colleagues, but doing so in undoubtedly sexual terms was striking. Furthermore, their conversation held the floor, so that it was the others of us in the room who were positioned as marginal. As I noted in my field diary, I felt as though I recognised in Miss Campbell's demeanour an inverted version of a social awkwardness, an embarrassed marginality, and desire to avoid attention, that I was familiar with from the experience of being amongst groups of straight women talking about men. It confirmed absolutely her heterosexuality, and struck me as something I'd not seen in quite this way in any other workplace I'd known. It resonated with my expectation that sexuality might prove a salient – and perhaps sensitive – theme, and increased my uncertainty about what I would disclose.

The conversation raised questions about the prison that made me cautious about outing myself. If the small, but mixed, staff of uniformed officers contained a visible clique of assertive and assertively gay women, how might that affect relationships? Was there any backlash from their male and heterosexual female colleagues? What did prisoners think? The experience I brought with me to the field of managing my own sexual identity and outness sensitised me to the scene I had witnessed, the possible meanings it might hold, the probable emotions and relations in which it was rooted. These were things I knew intimately and felt I recognised immediately. The officers' own openness about expressing their sexual identities did not, of course, indicate that the meanings they carried within the institution were positive, or even neutral: might not a close, confident minority, coloured in the eyes of others by wider social stigma, attract some more ambivalent responses from colleagues and prisoners? In an organisational culture characterised by at least surface friendliness (and a fair measure of backstage bitching) would I be able to explore any such ambivalences if I were out myself? The officers' excitable response to the appearance of the unknown woman made me worry that disclosure might – with the ready bonding that often arises between members of all kinds of minority groups – lead to a level of assimilation by this group of women (if, of course, this *was* a group in a meaningful sense). As Moore and Jenkins (2012) point out, disclosure is irreversible, and I worried that an association with a particular group (and a potentially divisive one?) might threaten my 'mobility' within the field. Prisons are also characterised by high levels of gossip, and most agreed that this was especially true at Askham (as indeed this scene suggested), where staff were less guarded than in closed conditions, and there were few restrictions on prisoners' ability to socialise with one another. It seemed unlikely, then, that I would be able to differentiate the way I presented myself very effectively between individuals. I probably needed to regard coming out to one person as a public declaration, and should avoid disclosing to anyone what I was not willing to be universally known. This element of self-presentation, only half-considered before the fieldwork began, touched some deep and even painful places. I began to *feel* a little of the process of identity management that membership of a total institution must entail. I'm not sure I would have noticed it had I not had to *do* it in a way that felt so deeply exposing and personally risky.

Despite the familiarity of these anxieties, however, the contours of this dilemma were unique in my experience, running along lines that were specific to the prison setting and giving insights into its topography. As I moved from open to closed prison conditions, I became aware of the sense of sexual vulnerability shared by many prisoners, who commented on the experience of seeing a male officer's eyes at the cell door when they were undressing, and the inconsistency whereby a man could not strip search them, but a lesbian could. This became connected with my consciousness of eroticised cultural fantasies of women's prisons and the stereotype of the voyeuristic, predatory dyke (Freedman, 1996; Herman, 2003; Ciasullo, 2008; Rowe, 2012), with which I had a horror of being associated in the eyes of participants who knew better than I did that prisons are about *pain*. The details of my uncertainty about coming out, then, were partly responses to the institution, conditioned by my consciousness of the steeply asymmetrical power relations of the prison, and my desire to remain outside them as far as I could. Also unsettling was the incongruity of finding myself suddenly reticent about my sexual identity in a setting where – of all places – it shouldn't raise an eyebrow (should it?), where I saw obviously gay women every day, and where (at New Hall especially) it was not uncommon to hear even straight-identified women chatting openly about their current and ex-girlfriends, and where gossip about flirtations and break-ups between inmates was frequently shared by staff and prisoners alike.

My reflections brought insights into the pressure that the prison exerted on the process of identity management that I think all experience (see also Greer, 2002). My position as an outsider was also crucially significant to the complex social and institutional power relations associated with these issues that I began to perceive. Both my understanding of the profound disempowerment that made prisoners a potential object of a voyeuristic gaze and my awareness of the stigmatised societal meanings that still attach to lesbianism were in play in my anxiety. I was at once, then, worried by my marginality, vulnerability, and my relative power. My settled practices and self-meanings were disturbed by the context of the prison, and the research, but this disturbance was a means through which I could understand it.

The position I came to occupy never felt like an easy or stable one, neither politically nor personally satisfactory. The decision to not/come out became a rolling deferment until time ran out. By not disclosing, I gained some data I might otherwise not have done: confidences from straight-identified women about their shock and unease when they first came across lesbian activity amongst prison inmates; discussions about how the prison should manage prisoners' intimate relationships. Other lines of enquiry were somewhat circumscribed, however. Unwilling to ask questions that I wasn't sure I would answer myself, I did not instigate personal discussions about prisoners' experiences of sex and relationships in prison, although they were volunteered by some and appeared as footnotes in the narratives of others. I would not lie, but I nevertheless remember the rush of panic I felt when, during an evening event in the Chapel at New Hall, two women playfully involving me in their bored banter seemed suddenly to stray into my buffer zone of silence:

Wednesday, 31 October 2007

> Frances and Stella were messing about and kind of drew me in. Stella said to me (something to the effect) that, 'Frances fancies you...' I (a bit embarrassed) made some remark about knowing Frances to be a respectable married woman and a grandmother, so I knew that she didn't. Frances (who must be in her forties), a little distance away, was protesting to Stella (also to me, indirectly) that she didn't but that Stella did and she was a lesbian. *Stella*: 'I'm not! I'm not! I gotta man in prison!' They'd been having a bit of a tussle a couple of feet away and directing some of their interaction to me. Now Stella came back up to me and said directly to me, with animation and standing quite close, 'There is a thing called gay, and a thing called jail bent – and I'm jail bent.' Then a brief pause (like beginning a new paragraph), and then, 'Are you young?' I misheard her, thinking she'd said, 'Are *you* one?' (like, a lesbian). I felt flooded by embarrassment... It took me a moment or two of (I'm sure) flushed stuttering to work out what she *had* said, and find I didn't quite know how to answer that, either: 'Er, don't know. I'm twenty-eight...?' The verdict was positive – she nodded approvingly that anything in the twenties was okay...

Before Stella asked her misheard question, my interest had been absorbed by her complex attitudes and identifications: Comfortably calling herself 'jail bent' (and flirting a little while earlier, with apparent intent, with the girl sitting in the row behind her), but lesbianism itself still eliciting giggles and vehement denials. In that moment I was caught off balance, again wishing I had more time to steer a more careful course. The wave of relief I felt at realising I did not have to answer a question that would either out me decisively or prompt a denial that was dissonant with my deeper identifications and commitments was accompanied by some amusement at the nakedly Freudian nature of my mishearing, which highlighted to me the evasions I had been relying on. My strong and physical reaction to this incident demonstrated that more was at stake emotionally than I had been aware of. It was the punctuation point that illuminated this tangle of meanings around prison sexualities.

The kind of collision between inside and outside behaviours and identities that I experienced in attempting to negotiate a 'prison persona' was described time and again in my interviews with prisoners; painful disjunctures and tensions between self-conceptions, expedient self-presentation and the perceptions and positionings of others. In experiencing my *self* as disrupted, just as when my presence seemed to *cause* disruption, my embodied and emotional involvement in the field allowed me to come to particular understandings of the social world of the prison that might not otherwise have been available to me. It is this opening up of otherwise unavailable meanings that Behar (1997) suggests must be achieved by making the ethnographic self visible if it is to earn its place in the text. It both illuminated specific norms and practices and offered insights into the emotional tenor of prison life: the challenge of identity management in a closed, low-trust, inward-facing institution; the pressure of managing dissonances within and between 'imported' and 'situational' selves. For me, this affective involvement in these ubiquitous negotiations felt like an additional, if unspoken, form of participation in prison life, which carried an epistemic impetus of its own.

Conclusion

In its minimal form, reflexivity in the realist ethnographic tradition serves as a way to manage and neutralise the 'problem' of researcher subjectivity. As Davies (2008) reminds us, however, it is that very subjective, intersubjective, presence of the researcher that generates the data on which all ethnographic analysis rests, whether this is acknowledged or not. This discussion has argued that the disturbances that arise from the ways in which the researcher and the field act on one another can give rise to substantive insights. Atkinson et al. (2003) suggest that – whilst the researcher-self has always been at the heart of ethnographic methods – the significant innovation of post-realist ethnography is to make that self visible in the text. Whilst this visibility has often remained marginalised in confessional 'tales of the field', more recent studies have sought to integrate the two, making the self an analytic tool. Following this, I have suggested that admitting to our embodied and subjective presence in the field becomes both a source of substantive understanding and a solution to the discomfort and compromises that even marginal participation in a complex field like a prison inevitably entails. In renouncing the fallacious and epistemologically untenable position of 'silent authorship' (Charmaz and Mitchell, 1996) and showing the self, it becomes possible for the researcher to occupy a more dynamic, conflicted role because it ceases to be necessary to hold a single position and set of allegiances.

Considering the multiple ways in which I thought I had been a participant in the world of the prison led me to reflect on how difficult I had found it to remain outside the prison's hierarchical structures and its persistent demands around identity: *what* are you? *who* are you? Power flowed in both immediate and diffuse ways around and through those negotiations. These were questions of instrumental significance – who could do what *for* or *to* whom; a multi-layered moral ordering of 'spoiled identities' and 'normals' (Goffman, 1963); collisions and strain between outside and inside selves and statuses. The *experience* of being drawn into and having to navigate those relations –

both internally and in encounters with others – became a way of accessing, understanding, and organising glimpses into the prison world, its powerful logics, practices, and emotional pressures.

There are, of course, clear dangers in making the researcher-self visible in social research. As Davies (2008: 10) warns, excessive reflexivity is as unhelpful as the extremes of realist and positivist ethnography, risking 'sterile and precious self-consciousness' or an absolute blurring of the distinction between subject and object. Furthermore, there are sound reasons for safeguarding a sense of the 'real' in ethnography (Anderson, 2006; Davies, 2008; Van Maanen, 2011 [1988]), which must be especially true in a politically charged field like criminal justice. Nevertheless, all ethnography relies on the perception of the researcher, who comes to know the field bodily, intuitively and emotionally, as well as intellectually and through the accounts of others. Through attentiveness to all these ways of knowing, we can engage more fully with the social worlds we study, and come to insights that might not otherwise be available.

Acknowledgements

The author declared the following financial support for the research, authorship and/or publication of this chapter: The research was funded by a grant from the UK's Economic and Social Research Council (ESRC), Ref. PTA-030-2005-00058.

Notes

1. For a fuller account of the research sites and methods, see Rowe (2009).
2. Because of the size of the women's penal estate in England and Wales, it is impossible to anonymise the prisons effectively without removing almost all descriptive detail.
3. Because of their relatively small number, women's prisons are categorised as simply 'open' or 'closed', rather than by the more differentiated levels of security used in the men's prison estate. An open prison equates to the lowest category of security in the male estate. There are no internal locks, except on staff offices, and the site is not secure. At Askham Grange, the building was locked only at night. 'Semi-open' conditions allow prisoners to move freely within a prison or a wing within a secure perimeter. Since the research, Drake Hall has been 're-roled' as a men's prison, and this classification no longer exists for any whole prison, although, as at New Hall, otherwise closed prisons may include some semi-open accommodation.
4. The two prisons were administered separately at the time of the research, but have since been brought together under the management of a single Governing Governor.
5. 'Trusted' prisoners employed to support officers by carrying out work essential to the running of the prison.
6. All names are pseudonyms. The same pseudonyms are used in all written accounts of the research.
7. 'Miss' was the typical title for both female staff and prisoners. A member of staff would generally address a prisoner s/he didn't know as 'Miss' but call a woman s/he knew by her preferred forename.

8. At New Hall in particular, which had a reputation as slightly old-fashioned, modes of address operated rather like those in a school. Staff usually addressed each other in front of prisoners (and often even in 'backstage' areas) as Miss or Mr So-and-So, so that this is how I often thought of officers. My interchangeable use of forenames and titles for staff reflects this. Except on the couple of occasions when I was telephoned by the Gate at New Hall to admonish me for forgetting to inform them when I was onsite out of hours, when I was 'Miss Rowe', I was always called 'Abi' or 'Abigail'.
9. Senior Officer: middle-ranking uniformed officers.
10. I follow Cahill's (1998: 135) usage of the term 'individual' to denote an 'organic bodily being', 'person' to refer to what Harré (in Cahill) calls the 'socially defined, publicly embodied being', and 'self' to mean the being's 'reflexive awareness of personal agency and identity'.

Further reading

Cunha, M. (2014) 'The Ethnography of Prisons and Penal Confinement', *Annual Review of Anthropology*, 43, 217–33.

Greer, K. (2002) 'Walking an Emotional Tightrope: Managing Emotions in a Women's Prison', *Symbolic Interaction*, 25, 117–39.

Owen, B. (1998) *In the Mix: Struggle and Survival in a Women's Prison* (Albany: State University of New York Press).

References

Anderson, L. (2006) 'Analytic Autoethnography', *Journal of Contemporary Ethnography*, 35, 373–95.

Atkinson, P., Coffey, A. and Delamont, S. (2003) *Key Themes in Qualitative Research: Continuities and Change* (Walnut Creek, CA: AltaMira).

Barthes, R. (1981) *Camera Lucida: Reflections on Photography* (New York, NY: Hill & Wang).

Behar, R. (1997) *The Vulnerable Observer: Anthropology that Breaks your Heart* (Boston, MA: Beacon).

Ben-David, S. and Silfen, P. (1992) 'Staff-to-Inmate Relations in a Total Institution: A Models of Five Modes of Association', *International Journal of Offender Therapy and Comparative Criminology*, 36, 209–21.

Cahill, S. E. (1998) 'Toward a Sociology of the Person', *Sociological Theory*, 61, 131–48.

Chambers, E. (2000) 'Applied Ethnography', in N. K. Denzin and Y. S. Lincoln (eds) *Handbook of Qualitative Research*, Second edition (Thousand Oaks: Sage).

Charmaz, K. and Mitchell, R. G. (1996) 'The Myth of Silent Authorship: Self, Substance and Style in Ethnographic Writing', *Symbolic Interaction*, 19, 285–302.

Ciasullo, A. (2008) 'Containing "Deviant" Desire: Lesbianism, Heterosexuality and the Women-in-prison Narrative', *Journal of Popular Culture*, 41, 195–223.

Clemmer, D. (1940) *The Prison Community* (New York: Holt, Rinehart and Winston).

Crawley, E. (2004) *Doing Prison Work: The public and Private Lives of Prison Officers* (Cullompton: Willan Publishing).

Crewe, B. (2006) 'Prison Drug Dealing and the Ethnographic Lens', *The Howard Journal*, 45, 347–68.

Davies, C. A. (2008) *Reflexive Ethnography: A Guide to Researching Selves and Others*, Second edition (Abingdon: Routledge).

Denzin, N. K. (1997) *Interpretive Ethnography: Ethnographic Practices for the 21st Century* (Thousand Oaks: Sage).
Denzin, N. K. and Lincoln, Y. S. (2000) 'Epilogue', in N. K. Denzin and Y. S. Lincoln (eds) *Handbook of Qualitative Research,* Second edition (Thousand Oaks: Sage).
Drake, D. and Harvey, J. (2013) 'Performing the Role of Ethnographer: Processing and Managing the Emotional Dimensions of Prison Research', *International Journal of Social Research Methodology,* 17, 5, 489–501.
Earle, R. (2013) 'What Do Ethnographers Do in Prison? Reflexivity, Trialties and Error in Prison Ethnography', *Criminal Justice Matters,* 91, 18–19.
Einat, T. and Chen, G. (2012) 'Female Inmates' Perspectives Toward Consensual Same-sex Relationships in an Israeli Prison', *International Journal of Comparative and Applied Criminal Justice,* 36, 25–44.
Emerson, R. M., Fretz, R. I. and Shaw, L. L. (2001) 'Participant Observation and Fieldnotes', in P. Atkinson, A. Coffey, S. Delamont, J. Lofland and L. Lofland (eds) *Handbook of Ethnography* (London: Sage).
Farkas, M. (2000) 'A Typology of Correctional Officers', *International Journal of Offender Therapy and Comparative Criminology,* 44, 431–49.
Freedman, E. (1996) 'Race, Class and the Construction of the Aggressive Female Homosexual, 1915–1965', *Feminist Studies,* 22, 397–423.
Giallombardo, R. (1966) *Society of Women: A Study of a Women's Prison* (New York: John Wiley & Sons).
Goffman, E. (1959) *The Presentation of Self in Everyday Life* (London: Penguin).
Goffman, E. (1963) *Stigma: Notes on the Management of Spoiled Identity* (Harmondsworth: Penguin).
Goffman, E. (1971) *Relations in Public* (New York: Basic Books).
Gold, R. L. (1958) 'Roles in Sociological Fieldwork', *Social Forces,* 36, 217–23.
Greer, K. (2002) 'Walking an Emotional Tightrope: Managing Emotions in a Women's Prison', *Symbolic Interaction,* 25, 117–39.
Hammersley, M. and Atkinson, P. (2007) *Ethnography: Principles in Practice,* Third edition (London: Routledge).
Herman, D. (2003) 'Bad Girls Changed My Life: Homonormativity in a Women's Prison Drama', *Critical Studies in Media Communication,* 20, 141–59.
Howe, A. (1994) *Punish and Critique: Towards a Feminist Analysis of Penalty* (London: Routledge).
Jewkes, Y. (2012) 'Autoethnography and Emotion as Intellectual Resources: "Doing Prison Research Differently" ', *Qualitative Inquiry,* 18, 63–75.
Liebling, A. (1999) 'Doing Research in Prison: Breaking the Silence?' *Theoretical Criminology,* 3, 147–73.
Liebling, A. (2000) 'Prison Officers, Policing and the Use of Discretion', *Theoretical Criminology,* 4, 333–57.
Liebling, A. (2001) 'Whose Side Are We On? Theory, Practice and Allegiances in Prison Research', *British Journal of Criminology,* 41, 472–84.
Liebling, A. and Price, D. (2001) *The Prison Officer* (Leyhill: Prison Service and Waterside Press).
Lincoln, Y. S. and Denzin, N. K. (2005) 'Introduction', in N. K. Denzin and Y. S. Lincoln (eds) *The Sage Handbook of Qualitative Research,* Third edition (Thousand Oaks: Sage).
Mathiesen, T. (1965) *The Defences of the Weak* (London: Tavistock Publications).
Moore, J. and Jenkins, P. (2012) 'Coming out in Therapy? Perceived Risks and Benefits of Self-disclosure of Sexual Orientation by Gay and Lesbian Therapists to Straight Clients', *Counselling and Psychotherapy Research,* 12, 308–15.

Orne, J. (2011) '"You Will Always Have to 'Out' Yourself": Reconsidering Coming out through Strategic Outness', *Sexualities*, 14, 681–703.

Otis, M. (1913) 'A Perversion Not Commonly Noted', *Journal of Abnormal Psychology*, 8, 113–16.

Owen, B. (1998) *In the Mix: Struggle and Survival in a Women's Prison* (Albany: State University of New York Press).

Primeau, L. A. (2003) 'Reflections on Self in Qualitative Research: Stories of Family', *American Journal of Occupational Therapy*, 57, 9–16.

Rhodes, L. (2001) 'Toward an Anthropology of Prisons', *Annual Review of Anthropology*, 30, 65–83.

Rhodes, L. (2012, September 18) *'Ethnographic Imagination in the Field' of the Prison Paper Presented at the Resisting the Eclipse Symposium* (Milton Keynes: The Open University).

Rowe, A. (2009) *Negotiating Disempowerment: Coping and Social Support in Women's Prisons*, Unpublished PhD thesis, The Open University, Milton Keynes.

Rowe, A. (2012) 'Sexuality, Criminality and the Women's Prison: Pat Arrowsmith's "Somewhere Like This"', *Prison Service Journal*, 199, 32–34.

Severance, T. (2008) 'The Prison Lesbian Revisited', *Journal of Gay & Lesbian Social Services*, 17, 39–57.

Spry, T. (2001) 'Performing Autoethnography: An Embodied Methodological Praxis', *Qualitative Inquiry*, 7, 706–32.

Sykes, G. M. (1958) *Society of Captives: A Study of a Maximum Security Prison* (Princeton: Princeton University Press).

Tait, S. (2011) 'A Typology of Prison Officer Approaches to Care', *European Journal of Criminology*, 8, 440–54.

Van Maanen, J. (ed) (1995) *Representation in Ethnography* (Thousand Oaks: Sage).

Van Maanen, J. (2011 [1988]) *Tales of the Field: On Writing Ethnography*, Second edition (Chicago: University of Chicago Press).

Wacquant, L. (2002) 'The Curious Eclipse of Prison Ethnography in the Age of Mass Incarceration', *Ethnography*, 3, 371–98.

Ward, D. A. and Kassebaum, G. G. (1965) *Women's Prison: Sex and Social Structure* (New Brunswick: Aldine Transaction).

Willet, T. C. (1983) 'Prison Guards in Private', *Canadian Journal of Criminology*, 25, 1–17.

19
Re-entry to Prison: Transition from HMP Researcher to 'Independent' Researcher

Lucy Carr

Introduction

Ethnographic work within a prison setting is challenging for any researcher. Seeking to document the world of those around them, prison-based ethnographers do not merely note what can be interpreted through observation of their surroundings, but endeavour to establish field relations encompassing trust and rapport with those working and living within the prison walls in order to gain a deeper insight into the lives and experiences of those imprisoned. Prison ethnographers face the challenges of appearing unthreatening so as to form a connection with the research subjects by seeming impartial and without institutional power. Entering a prison site attempting to establish such an identity might be problematic for any ethnographer, but for a previous prison service employee, the prospect of acceptance from prisoners may seem especially challenging.

In this chapter, I provide an account of my 're-entry' into a women's prison as an independent researcher undertaking doctoral research,[1] who had recently been employed by Her Majesty's Prison Service (HMPS) as a researcher at the same prison. In this account, I explore the particular issues associated with the adoption of a new (researcher) identity, as well as the ways in which my personal characteristics and biography impacted and shaped interactions during the research process. Here, I expose the details through personal reflections of my research experience, incorporating how my personal biography, identity and emotions became 'entangled' with and inevitably shaped the data gathered during the process, starting with access to the research site and the cooperation I gained within it, independence and matters of personal safety and how I managed these dynamics.

I reveal the methods I employed in my aim to appear 'unofficial' and approachable to prisoners, giving explanation for the considerations and conscious decisions I made in the management of my identity, such as dress and the possession of prison keys. Here, I also reflect on my identity within the social relations of fieldwork by considering how biographical aspects such as my gender, age and personal character generated unforeseen reactions from the prisoner society, and how these personal aspects impacted upon the power dynamics in the relationships I formed within the prison. I describe the tensions and challenges I encountered in retaining neutrality during my time in the prison and discuss the emotional dimension of my research experience.

Background

My interest in women prisoners and their experiences began whilst working for the prison service as a researcher and data analyst (2008–11). I was fascinated by the different lives these women experienced and saddened when many of them seemed unable to survive in the world outside the prison, realising they would likely return. At the time, I was based at HMP New Hall, a closed establishment located in Wakefield, within the North East of England, which accommodates adult female prisoners of all categories, and was conducting research which explored the clinical and psychosocial interventions available to drug users in custody, many of whom were categorised as short-term repeat 'offenders'. Repeat offending statistics associated with the short-term prisoner population had become a subject of significant interest to New Hall prison since the publication of the 'Reoffending of Adults in England and Wales' report (Ministry of Justice, 2010) that demonstrated an increasingly high percentage of women reoffending upon release. HMP New Hall was reported to have the highest one-year re-conviction rate for short-term prisoners discharged from all (female and male) English and Welsh prisons, at 76.6 per cent (MoJ, 2010) making New Hall an ideal location in which to explore the experiences of women repeatedly imprisoned for short periods of time.

Conducting research within my employed position had become increasingly difficult due to internal funding restrictions, making it almost impossible to complete work effectively or to meet ever-tightening deadlines. The desire to continue research with the necessary research training, supervision, funding and, most of all, time to do qualitative work that allowed for prisoner involvement formed my determination to undertake doctoral research at the University of Sheffield. When approaching the prison with this proposal, the prison officials were in full support. Upon leaving my employed position at New Hall prison, my staff access remained open to allow me to return to the establishment to carry out fieldwork for the PhD. Although, at first sight, this may seem relatively straightforward given the difficulties usually reported by researchers seeking access to prison, in reality this arrangement generated its own set of difficulties which I endeavour to illustrate in this chapter.

The PhD research involved a prison-based ethnography being carried out as an aid to understanding how the women lived and experienced short-term imprisonment. It allowed me to build a rapport with the women (and staff) that were later recruited as interview participants. The fieldwork took place over a period of 18 months (between January 2013 and June 2014), including visits at different times in the day, on weekends and at night. I spent an intense period dedicating three to four long days a week in the prison over six weeks, before slowly reducing my appearances. The ethnography allowed me to observe the women in the prison setting and gain an understanding of the sorts of issues they experienced during imprisonment and upon release, which I later explored further through in-depth interviews in which prisoners would be asked about their life histories, experiences of offending, imprisonment and previous resettlement attempts. In order to investigate the contribution of the prison, interviews also took place with the people who work with the women in custody, including prison employees of various positions and grades, police and probation officers and workers from third sector agencies.

My ethnographic experience was very much participatory. I immersed myself with the women by taking part in daily activities in the prison. This included acquiring a 'job' in the prisoner workshops: for the most part a sewing factory, but also for a short period in an assembly workshop where I spent my days packaging toilet rolls. In the assembly workshops I worked hard, contributing fairly to the workload and would take my breaks at the customary times alongside the other prisoners as if the work were officially imposed on me as it were for them. I would often eat with the prisoners and spent association time on the prison wings alongside the women doing things I would not ordinarily do, such as sitting watching television soaps, doing the ironing, playing pool and sitting with women looking at clothes in mail order catalogues, and I tried to join in discussions on subjects I often knew very little about. Some occasions saw me attend the chapel and sports and fitness classes in the prisoner's gymnasium, again things I would not typically do in my normal daily life. Not only was I in unfamiliar surroundings, I was engaging in activities and affairs that would have been alien to me even outside the prison walls, which added to my uneasiness. Had I been a confident volleyball player, been able to hold a snooker cue properly, had some knowledge of Coronation Street's storyline and so forth, I might not have felt so far out of my depth. A hand-written diary was kept to encourage reflection on my research experience.

Access, arrangements and cooperation

Much of the literature on gaining 'access to prisons' and 'gatekeeping' discusses the many difficulties and barriers would-be researchers must face. King and Liebling (2007) explore the lengthy processes and challenges in acquiring access to prisons for research purposes. They explain that the would-be researcher is expected to produce a viable research proposal presenting something additional to the 'official' research agenda that could have some benefits for the institution(s), but is not too disruptive and that there is the funding, or at least the prospect of funding. On top of that, the would-be researcher needs to evidence they have the right credentials for conducting such research in the establishment. Difficulties do not stop at gaining initial, physical access, but is reportedly an ongoing struggle, as Malloch (2000: 16) states, 'Throughout the research project, gaining access continues to be an ongoing process often strengthened by the gatekeepers' expectations of what they might gain through co-operation.' For my part, physical access to the prison proved less problematic than gaining access and cooperation from staff within the establishment. I had to acquire the trust, cooperation and assistance from staff within the prison using tact, diplomacy and interpersonal skills.

Access to New Hall for the purpose of doing my own research had been granted on the basis that I would use my existing knowledge of the establishment to manage the logistics of the project independently, occupying very little of prison staff time. Because of this prior understanding, I was not handled in the way other visiting researchers to the prison would have been. For example, I was not allocated a 'contact' staff member who helped orchestrate and supervise my work within the prison and I used my staff identification and access to prison keys in order to move around the prison independently. It was taken for granted that I would follow correct protocol for accessing what I needed using my existing familiarity with the establishment and the prisoners, causing little distraction to other prison workers. The downside was that nobody was obligated to accommodate my needs, and my research, although recognisably beneficial to the prison, was no longer part of the prison inspectorate requirements and consequently not a key priority to the prison. Carlen and Worrall (2004: 185) highlight the dilemmas of working to suit the prison, noting that prison staff can often be 'wary of researchers, especially of any who fail to show their full appreciation of prison staff priorities and institutional concerns'. I felt I was expected to appreciate the establishment priorities even more so, due to having previously been a part of the prison community.

No longer working directly for the prison meant becoming overlooked and I soon realised how unimportant I was. In some respects this proved advantageous; it gave me the freedom to conduct the research as designed, not subject to influence and close scrutiny from the prison officials. The negative aspect of this arrangement meant that assistance was not easily obtained when it was required. Lack of supervision within the prison also raised some concerns with regard to my personal safety. The prison relied on me using my own discretion and previous experience on matters of personal safety. The location of all prisoners is closely monitored, therefore, officers knew when I was occupying an individual and the location, but concerns as to whether I was with support or unaided were never questioned. I did not carry a radio, nor did I have access to a panic alarm of any sort; I relied on my common sense and caution when conducting the research.

Identity

Liebling (1992: 118) describes the identity dilemmas that quickly gather around the prison researcher:

> [D]on't get involved, don't take sides, express opinion, breach confidences or react to very much at all; don't be mistaken for a probation officer, social worker, psychologist, volunteer or governor grade – or 'someone from the parole board' – or identify with any of the last; don't be dependent on the staff, but never overlook them; don't get in the way, but don't neglect to explain yourself, sometimes apologetically, to each individual when they ask: 'Who did you say you were exactly?'

There was much confusion as to my identity for those employees who did not know me, due to my level of access and familiarity with the prison and many of its staff members. It was noticeable I was not a conventional 'visitor' to the establishment. I was often cast in a number of different roles, most commonly mistaken for a psychologist or external agency worker. In most instances, I was able to disclaim my employee status and describe my role as a research student. However, at times, being identified as a student seemed to work against me and I occasionally encountered some anxious attitudes from staff members who showed concern over my unsupervised access to all areas of the prison, including staff-access-only IT systems, prisoner files and records and the prisoners themselves. The apprehensions exhibited by staff were perhaps professional concerns over access to the protected material (and the prisoners themselves) since I presented no evidence of having approved clearance for retrieving such data and staff perhaps feared being held liable for allowing my apparent misconduct to take place under their watch. More often it seemed like sheer interest, curiosity and confusion from staff as to whom I was and what I was doing which prompted their interrogations. However, this occurrence was rare and, as previously mentioned, I was generally overlooked. My apparent inexperience also resulted in prison staff rendering the full description of terms and abbreviations used in the prison community and describing issues and functions to me in the simplest terms. Although some might consider this condescending, it was intended in a helpful and accommodating manner rather than an intention to belittle or patronise me. On these occasions, I would react by showing appreciation for their instruction and support rather than describing my pre-existing knowledge of such information.

Yet, certain biographical elements contributed to the processes of developing relationships and of overcoming the institutional fear of outsiders. I sensed staff appreciated the fact that I had not come from a purely academic background but had some experience of working on the wings and could empathise with the difficulties of 'the job'. Like Liebling (1992), I consider that having an understanding of the concerns pertinent to staff (job security, privatisation threats, limitations of role and so forth) minimised hesitation about conversing with me.

Prison employees who knew me in my previous capacity were often unaware of my new 'independent' researcher and student status. It was commonly assumed that I had been absent from New Hall to undertake research in another prison (not an unusual scenario in my previous role). Staff would often introduce me to other staff members as 'a HMPS researcher' and fail to mention my student status. Staff would occasionally call upon me to carry out duties pertinent to my previous employed role and I would have to inform them I no longer held such responsibilities and was there only to conduct my own research, which left me conscious I may be perceived as uncharitable and self-seeking. Despite my best efforts, but perhaps inevitably and necessarily, my identity remained blurred throughout the course of the fieldwork.

Prisoners also expressed great confusion over my identity. Again, my familiarity with the establishment and its staff seemed dubious for someone claiming to be an 'outsider'. A number of the women recognised me, or knew me, from my previous position causing further suspicion. They would question my employment status and dispute my claims to being a student. For example, one prisoner asserted 'you're not a student, I remember you, you were doing those questionnaires at Askham [Grange prison]'. The woman announced that three years earlier I had interviewed her as part of an investigation I had carried out under the direction of the governor at HMP Askham Grange which assessed the quality of various aspects of the prisoner's lives in custody. The women lightheartedly made jokes concerning my identity and motives after recognising me as an ex-prison employee. The women alleged I was an 'informant' of some kind, covertly gathering intelligence and 'snitching' or feeding back to authorities. Unfortunately, the nicknames I was assigned by this particular group of women, the 'undercover copper', 'Governor's spy' and so forth, stuck with me for a number of weeks. These playful, teasing remarks actually enhanced the relationship with the women.

I would typically overcome any suspicions by explicitly clarifying, quite honestly, that I left my employed position in order to conduct research objectively as an 'independent' which allowed me to explore the women's experiences and include their viewpoints and perceptions. This usually relieved the women's concerns and allowed me to build a rapport. By sharing this personal biographical account, it felt I had offered something of my life which meant the women sharing detailed accounts of their lives in discussions or interviews were somewhat reciprocal. This not only allowed me to develop a relatively trusting relationship with the women, in an environment where trust is valuable, but also opened additional doors as some of the discussants and interviewees were recruited on a rolling basis. During the fieldwork, the women would essentially vouch for my credibility to other inmates, often affirming 'she's alright, you can talk in front of her'. The encounter described in the following diary extract demonstrates such dilemmas:

> When [Zoe] returned from her video link [session with her wife] she became emotional. I tried to comfort her and made her a cup of tea from my tea pack (a form of sharing which is forbidden amongst the prisoners)... [Zoe talked at length] about her relationship with her wife and disclosed how she was abusing the use of [prescribed medication] she had traded... to help with the pains of separation. At this point [Anne] interjected and [scolded Zoe] for talking so openly to me, stating in front of me 'watch what you say to her' and pointed at me!... [Zoe] was quick to jump to my defence saying 'she won't say shit.' Not knowing how to respond, I sat in silence while they argued my allegiance in front of me!... [Anne] has been more wary of me than the others from the start; I've noticed she is the only one who doesn't take her turn for a smoke in the toilets (a forbidden act) until she thinks I'm not looking. When I see them signal for her turn [to smoke], I purposely go to talk with [Amanda] at the folding table so that I have my back to the toilet door... and I saw [Anne] [signal] towards me [as if to warn of my presence] when [Charlie] was describing her techniques for hiding the lighter in her bra. [Charlie] just shrugged it off though.

Managing my identity: Disposing of suits and uniforms

There were a number of ways in which I tried to manage my identity by considering factors such as self-presentation. My aim was to appear non-threatening and without institutional power to the prisoners in order to encourage the building of trust and rapport.

Although dress might seem a trivial matter, I was conscious of how it fundamentally represents power within the establishment and I was keen to exhibit my transformation from staff member to independent researcher by abandoning my recognised formal wear. It was noted during the fieldwork that women would occasionally refer to discipline staff as 'the uniforms', and, similarly, Governors, Senior Management Team members and high-ranking visiting officials, for example, were dubbed 'the suits' (see also Bennett, Chapter 15, this volume).

Female prisoners at New Hall are permitted to wear their own clothes if deemed appropriate. Many women arrive at New Hall with only the clothes they are wearing; many have lived homeless, dependant on drugs and working as prostitutes; where clothes are deemed inappropriate (e.g. excessively damaged, insanitary or exposing), a set of alternative attire is provided from a depository of unwanted prisoner clothes. In many cases, a workplace uniform is prerequisite, such as kitchen whites, gardening overalls and so forth; but generally the women opt for casual or comfortable wear – typically tracksuits, hooded sweatshirts and trainers. Although my aim was to appear approachable and accessible to prisoners, at the same time, I was aware that I would be expected to present a professional image. I did not wear a suit, nor did I wear a tracksuit and trainers; however, I did try and dissociate myself from the institution by wearing clothes that made me look unofficial. The downside to this was the attention it attracted from prison staff; it highlighted me as the unsupervised visiting student I essentially was. On occasions where I visited the gymnasium wearing casual sports clothing, I noticed a difference in the way I was received by prisoners as I was often mistaken for a prisoner.

In my previous capacity, prisoners would routinely address me as 'Miss', as would staff in the presence of inmates. During the fieldwork, I continually insisted on the abandonment of formal terms of address and insisted on being called Lucy. Prisoners acknowledged this request and used my given name comfortably, whilst staff, particularly discipline officers, continued to address me as 'Miss'. Prison officers at New Hall often use formal terms of address for one another but call prisoners by their first names; therefore, it was considered that staff may have felt uncomfortable with using my given name since it would have been almost marking me a prisoner (see also Rowe, Chapter 18, this volume). Nonetheless, I did note that other visitors were customarily called by their first names by staff, and therefore by addressing me formally officers were essentially categorising me as one of them. It was also considered that the use of formal address could have been simply due to their forgetting my name.

What I initially feared would be the most destructive factor to my attempts to appear 'unofficial' to prisoners was the matter of prison keys since they are emblematic of institutional power within prisons. A number of authors have discussed the issue of researchers holding keys within prison (Liebling, 1992; Genders and Player, 1995; Sparks, Bottoms and Hay, 1996; King, 2000; Mills, 2004; King and Liebling, 2008), and opinions on the matter are somewhat divided. King (2000: 305), for example, argues that researchers should not hold keys to the prison as 'the possession of keys is so symbolic of the difference between freedom and captivity that it would place the researcher too close to staff' and thus decreases trust. I did not at any time feel that my keys negatively impacted my efforts to appear approachable and accessible. Mills (2004) also debates the need for researchers holding keys, in reference to issues of personal safety, particularly as a female researcher. However, Mills (2004) was conducting research in a male establishment investigating rape perpetrators, which certainly raises issues of personal safety less pertinent to my own experience.

Possessing keys was the inescapable compromise I made for having unsupervised access to all areas of the establishment. My access arrangements required me to carry keys in order to limit the burden on prison staff by diminishing the need for an escort. Although they may have contributed to some of the women's confusion over my identity, despite my initial concerns, I did ultimately view them as valuable. Without the possession of keys, I would have been fully reliant on staff escorts and I would not have enjoyed some of the experiences and developed the relationships with prisoners I was able to with a uniformed escort in constant close proximity to me. Keys granted me freedom to move around the prison between wings, workshops, classrooms and offices during the course of the day, allowing me to manage my time more effectively. The women appreciated my capability to offer privacy; keys allowed me to take the women to a space where they could talk without interruptions and the presence of discipline officers.

Social identity

There are many aspects of my identity I am not able to control or manage which arguably impact my role as a researcher; for instance, my age, sex, ethnic origin, regional background and accent, vocation and so forth. According to Warren (1988: 13):

> The fieldworker's reception by the host society is a reflection of the cultural contextualisation of the fieldworker's characteristics, which include marital status, age, physical appearance, presence and number of children, and ethnic, racial class, or national differences as well as gender.

Bosworth et al. (2005) argue that qualitative researchers should reflect on their identity within the social relations of fieldwork. Nonetheless, there is little discussion around what impact social identity factors have, if any, on the research's role. This omission in the literature is highlighted by Gelsthorpe (1990: 95) who argues these factors are 'often underplayed, if not ignored' in the research literature as they 'do not ask how far personal biography and experience influence the research role, what the significance of age is on field relations, what it is like to be a woman/man doing research in a male/female setting' and so on, despite its significance.

With regard to race, I am a white British researcher in a predominantly white setting (with more than 85 per cent of New Hall population's racial category being white, and correspondingly, 15 per cent of my informants represented ethnic minority groups). There were no apparent issues of ethnicity differences impacting the relationships with participants. I did not observe or encounter any incidents of racism, and there was no mention of it being a feature in their lives; however, this outcome may have differed had I represented a different ethnic group.[2] However, in the course of conducting the research I noted a number of significant dynamics, particularly my gender, age and personal biography.

The HM Inspectorate of Prisons (2013) recognises that 'the management of prisons, and individual prisoners, can often be dominated by men ... The ratio of male to female staff is too high in some prisons.' Employees at New Hall appeared relatively gender balanced with a seemingly equal number of women and men in positions of management, administrative and discipline roles.

A female prison researcher is not a new phenomenon; much research has been carried out over the years in both male and female establishments by female researchers (e.g. Morris and Morris, 1963; Scully, 1991; Liebling, 1992, 2001; Genders and Player, 1995; Gelsthorpe, 2000; Campbell, 2002). In relation to the prisoners at New Hall, I consider being female an influential factor to the positive engagement and trusting relationships I built with the women which helped with the recruitment of interviewees. Conversely, Martin (2000) argues, 'It is the skills, not the gender, of the researcher that establishes his/her credibility and this is the crucial factor in determining the willingness of prisoners to participate in a research project.' I would argue that many of the women would be more open to discussion on certain issues, perhaps, motherhood, prostitution, sexual assault, with another woman. Many of the women reported being in, or having previously been in, intimidating, violent and/or sexually abusive relationships with men. HM Inspectorate of Prisons reported in its most recent inspection report of New Hall prison (2013) that 38 per cent of women had experienced sexual abuse or rape, 38 per cent had experienced emotional abuse, 21 per cent of women had worked in the sex industry and 41 per cent had experienced physical abuse, most of which was at the hands of a male perpetrator. Therefore, although it cannot be verified, I would contend being female proved advantageous in speaking with vulnerable women on such sensitive topics. I encountered this resonance from some of the women's comments implicating identification with me as a woman. For example, one woman when discussing feeling overpowered as a woman and dominated by her male partners, she alleged 'well, you know how it is'.

Age was a more significant factor which I feel affected my interactions within the research setting. Although maturity might be considered an asset in carrying out prison research as it indicates experience, signifying respect and authority, I found the contrary to generate additional advantages. A large majority of the prisoners were older than me with the average age of New Hall's women, at the time of the research, being 33 years old. I was in my mid-twenties at the time of carrying out the fieldwork, although I suspected many of the prisoners perceived me as somewhat younger. My apparent 'youth' was a common discussion point amongst the prisoners. Unsubtly, women frequently made comments with regard to my age, such as: 'you're just a baby', 'what do your mum and dad say about you doing this [research]?' and so forth. They would regularly ask me how my 'school project' was going. Evidently, I did not present an image of power and authority. In my previous employed position, although I joined the prison service as a teenager, I do not recall experiencing the same level of protection and attentiveness from prisoners as I did on this occasion despite being several years older. Clearly, the image I presented in my employed capacity was one much different. Not only were there conscious transformations made in relation to my physical appearance (i.e. abandoning my suit) and my tolerance for misconduct (i.e. allowing delinquency to go unpunished), but perhaps more significantly, there were inadvertent changes in my behaviour and personal character.

For my part, I felt much more confident and at ease in my employed capacity having close supervision and the support of the establishment and its staff, and therefore exhibited much more self-assurance and poise, in contrast to my more recent image of naivety and inexperience during the PhD fieldwork. I did not consider this a negative dynamic. In some respects, being perceived as naïve, worked to my advantage. This image of a 'green' research student (see also Sloan and Wright, this volume) supported my aim to appear unthreatening, which in all probability contributed to the women's ease in talking openly to me, and in front of me.

Developing relationships and power dynamics

The prison staff had very little involvement in the design, arrangement and organisation of the research. It was assumed I would conduct the research complying with all prison procedures and causing little disruption to the regime and the prison staff. In the event, there were occasions when due to not receiving notification on alterations to regime practices, I was often in danger of causing disruption. Ironically, the prisoners would often notify me of correct protocol to safeguard me from causing commotion to the regime with regard to completing the necessary paperwork and inform me of the organised times for 'movement' around the prison. Prisoners are only permitted to move between areas of the establishment (e.g. to attend work) during 'line route' or 'movement' periods which occur at set hours of the day. The opening of 'line route' involves operational support grade staff supervising the pathways between various areas of the prison, ensuring all women reach their arranged destination. Following the 'movement' period, central control office will conduct 'roll count' which involves accounting for every prisoner by contacting all of their arranged destinations for confirmation of their arrival. If staff require a prisoner to move outside the 'movement' period unescorted (e.g. allowing the prisoner to leave work to attend a doctor's appointment), they are to be issued with a 'movement slip'; this is essentially paperwork authorising their movement which involves a phone call from the sending location to the receiving site, signatures, times stamps and so forth. When taking the women from one site to another to allow privacy when conducting interviews, the prisoners would inform me of correct movement times and ensure I completed their movement slips correctly when allowing them to 'move' unsupervised, asserting that 'you will get in shit if you do it wrong'.

Occasionally, I experienced some of the women almost 'mothering' me. Often, but not intentionally, I found myself consumed with anxiety and uneasiness in unfamiliar and challenging positions. For example, during the ethnography I took up a post in a sewing workshop where I positioned myself at a workstation alongside the other women; my intention being to 'blend' into the environment and observe everyday life in the workplace. The women were fully aware of my student researcher status and we would often discuss my research interests whilst at work. I was given a patch of navy blue material (practice cloth for new starters), to allow myself to become familiar with the machinery and refine my technique before I would be assessed for progression into the actual operational line where I would be tasked with sewing elastic waistbands onto male prisoner boxer shorts. Unfortunately, due to my inexperience of using sewing machinery and general lack of skills in needlecraft, I failed to keep up with operations. In truth, I failed to even get started until my station neighbour who observed my embarrassed panic, took pity on me and helped me get underway. My apparent position of vulnerability led to the offering of ongoing support and encouragement throughout my time in the workshop from the women. I recall one occasion where a woman who had been providing me with support during that session had to leave work to attend a visit and she appointed somebody to supervise me, requesting 'Will you keep an eye on Lucy for me while I'm gone?' as if I required a babysitter. Regrettably, I was never promoted from the 'practice cloth', but the women would instead task me with less challenging projects, such as stitching shapes, and would offer congratulations on my slight progression. This mentoring arrangement completely altered the power dynamics in our relationship.

I noticed that 'mothering' was a feature of how older prisoners relate to younger prisoners who were particularly more vulnerable. This 'matronising' seemed more common on the prison wings when the younger girls showed more need for attentiveness, not typically in the sewing room. For example, a number of the older prisoners talked of how they have tried to 'watch over' or comfort the younger prisoners who were self-harming. The older women regularly depicted imprisonment as especially difficult for the younger girls, and would often refer to them as the 'youngsters' or the 'babies'.

Similar to my experience in the workshop, I attended volleyball training practice, feeling compelled after receiving an invitation from a woman I had been working alongside in the workshop. Despite my best efforts, I was not only hopeless, but very much a hindrance, causing disruption to the flow of the game and preventing a victory for whichever team that was burdened with me. In spite of my ineptness, the women were kind and encouraging, assuring me that I would improve with practice. What positively came from this interaction was an occasion to exhibit my sense of fun and humour with the women, allowing them to make jokes of my incompetence, diminishing any image of power I might have previously displayed. This image of a 'dippy', naïve student did not jeopardise my attempts at effectively collecting data, although unintended, I felt it essentially worked to my advantage by allowing me to appear unthreatening and approachable. This became evident when they would commit actions forbidden by the prison in my presence, such as trading items and smoking in no-smoking areas. They were aware of the fact that I was intentionally overlooking and not reacting to any misconduct I observed. In a respect, I was demonstrating a sense of loyalty to the prisoners by not reporting such actions to staff. I was, however, conscious that by immersing myself with the women in such a way, I could be perceived by staff as 'taking sides' with the women.

Neutrality and sympathy

Whilst my aim was not to distance myself from staff, other researchers have reported intentionally doing so in order to develop rapport and credibility with their study group (Cohen and Taylor, 1972). However, this research aimed not only to explore the needs and experiences of incarcerated women at New Hall through discussion with the women but also to explore the prison employees' observations and experiences of working with these women; dissociation from staff would jeopardise this opportunity. Therefore, the initial intention was to follow the advice of King and Liebling (2008: 444): 'retain your neutrality; try not to take sides'.

Although there are general expectations on qualitative researchers to remain objective, maintaining a neutral position is not so straightforwardly accomplished for various reasons. First, some might argue the impossibility of my capacity to remain completely impartial based on my previous knowledge of and experiences within the prison service. Second, some might contend that as a result of my gratitude in receiving support and ongoing access to the establishment exclusively for the purpose of conducting my own research, I might feel compelled to display a sense of loyalty to the organisation. Indeed, it would be difficult to write a hypercritical report on an institution that had previously employed me and had accommodated my requests in doing research, but at the same time, the gatekeepers were fully aware that my approach was not a quest to 'dig up dirt' or expose poor treatment or conditions, but to better understand the experiences of repeatedly imprisoned women serving short-term sentences, constructively highlighting system failures, without being severely critical. The institution was aware that my motivations were to help the prison help the prisoners who were generating increasingly high reoffending figures, and that my methods involved encompassing the views and opinions of not only the women but also those who work with the women. Not at any stage did I feel any pressure nor expectations from the establishment to generate particular findings.

Throughout the fieldwork, I avoided feeding back any findings to the prison until the fieldwork was complete in agreement with King and Liebling (2008: 445) that sharing information with officials before the fieldwork is complete 'is potentially difficult, especially if views of reality differ, if bad news emerges, and is likely to undermine prospects of maintaining a "neutral" position in the eyes of staff and prisoners'. One of the most uncomfortable situations during the fieldwork was receiving complaints from prisoners about the prison, its services and the regime. However, these were not reports of serious incidents or abuse but more of a general frustration at the lack of support within the prison. My initial concerns were that reporting negative feedback of this type to management could have been viewed as me taking sides with the prisoners, although these frustrations were generally shared by prison workers. Staff frequently complained of reduced spending in prisons, limiting their capacity and impacting the quality of the services they delivered. Fortunately, this meant that I was not placed in a compromising position between the prisoners and those who confine them. Unlike Crewe (2009) who talked of the anxieties he faced in having to decline requests from prisoners to bring innocuous items into the prison, the women at New Hall made no demands or requests that would place me in such an intricate position. Despite my seeming naivety, the women made no attempts to exploit my vulnerability in such a way, and as previously revealed, the women made great efforts to safeguard me from generating conflict with prison officials.

Although I expressed great interest in listening and understanding the prisoners' views and opinions about their imprisonment, positive or negative, it was made clear to the women that my function was not to impose changes or resolve issues since I did not hold the power or authority to do so, but to accurately depict their experiences and outlooks in my research write-up. Prisoners did not challenge this explanation of my role and since I was generally seen as powerless, I felt I was essentially being used as an outlet for their complaints and aggravations rather than being expected to resolve their issues. Like

Crewe (2009) I felt I became a 'lightening rod' for complaints and grievances from prisoners after developing a reputation for being a good listener. At the time, there was also the prospect of my returning to New Hall for employment post-PhD, this generated a number of concerns, including that, if re-entering the site as a member of staff, I would have a duty to the prison to enforce rules and impose discipline upon those who violate or challenge regulations. After making assurances to prisoners of my non-alignment and impartiality, I would be conscious of appearing deceptive and was concerned about the potential to generate anxiety in those women who had previously disclosed negative personal feelings against the prison and staff or performed prohibited acts against prison regulation in my presence.

Becker (1967: 239) highlights the issue of researchers being 'caught in a crossfire' in his paper, suitably titled 'Whose Side Are We on?' Becker strongly believes that qualitative research cannot be value free, and therefore 'the question is not whether we should take sides, since we inevitably will, but rather whose side we are on' (1967: 239). In contradiction to Becker's claim that it is impossible to not take sides, Liebling (2001) argues that the prison researcher does not have to take only one side, but that an appreciation and degree of allegiance to both sides is possible. Liebling claimed that building rapport with all contributors by supporting all sides is not only achievable, but vital. In the context of my research, although it might be assumed that the two sides in the power dynamic are to be the prisoners and those that confine them, it was rather 'the prison' as the subordinate, and 'the Government' (those who generate sentencing laws, dictate the prison regime, set the prison targets, restrict the funding and so forth) as what Liebling (2001) describes as the 'superordinates'.

In agreement with Becker, completely impartial research is improbable in this type of environment due to the human nature of research and the level of intimacy with the prisoners I experienced during the intensive fieldwork period. With the focus of my study being on the prisoners and their experiences, it was difficult to not feel sympathy with the women, something which Becker (1967) considered perfectly normal and logical. Many of the staff and workers at the prison also exhibited sympathy for the short-term prisoner population and their frustrations, which is arguably a natural effect of working so closely within such a confined environment (Arnold, 2005: 416). It would seem inconceivable to some that these women, who have been removed from society for transgressing society's norms by committing criminal acts, some violent, would engender feelings of sympathy, but human nature sees us make attachments that may seem illogical.

All things considered, prisoners are human beings and my choice of an ethnographic approach combined with the very personal nature of the discussions caused me to form relationships with them. I was conscious that my involvement with prisoners could be open to criticism in terms of researcher bias, but I consider it both valid and unavoidable that our real selves, personal biographical experiences and personalities become 'entangled' with others in the dynamic. Although a concerted effort was made to retain neutrality, I found it was impossible to disregard sympathy. Becker strongly maintains that all research is inescapably contaminated by these emotions and despite best efforts to minimise individual values and biases, they cannot be eradicated. Being sympathetic and taking one side or another could undoubtedly impact on the data but it does not invalidate it. Ethnographers and qualitative researchers invariably leave an individual mark on the data collection process.

Emotions

Whilst the majority of research relationships are uncontentious, on occasions researchers can find their emotions caught up with the field-research experience, especially when undertaking research of a sensitive or emotional nature (Smith and Wincup, 2000). Whilst the nature of the research undertaken here in practice had a great deal of involvement with participants in an intensive environment discussing emotional and sensitive topics, I am mindful that my emotional response to the field-research is of relevance. Understandably, it is hard to not be affected emotionally to respondents describing difficult or distressing experiences, which is certainly the situation I endeavour to illustrate here. Although it is acknowledged that one might be affected in an emotionally positive way, during this research which focussed on the women's problems and negative experiences that had led to their imprisonment, the emotions demonstrated (and felt) were predominantly ones of distress.

The very act of exploring women's imprisonment proved to be an emotionally exhausting experience. I was moved by the strengths and insights demonstrated by the women in sharing their stories and felt privileged to have been permitted access to their emotions and experiences, but at the same time I found the undertaking of the field-research at times emotionally challenging. The repeated listening for long periods of time to emotionally distressed women's detailed and often graphic reports of traumatic life experiences, such as incidents of brutal domestic violence, rape and sexual abuse throughout their lives – often starting in childhood – self-harm and suicide attempts, homelessness, battles with drug and alcohol addiction and having children removed and the pains of separation, is a psychologically taxing experience for the researcher, but undoubtedly more so for the women sharing their accounts.

Many occasions saw older respondents exhibiting concern for my emotional state and questioning my boundaries for hearing sensitive detail before continuing. Despite my efforts in appearing composed and unaffected by their reports, they would often verify 'are you okay with me telling you about this?' before revealing disturbing or upsetting information. I would positively assure them of my aptitude to cope with hearing their accounts and encourage them to continue. There were times when I watched the women weep, particularly when talking about estrangement from their children, and it did require great effort to contain my reactions. Admittedly, this type of emotive demonstration from some discussants contributed to my inability to disregard feelings of compassion and empathy for the women and the traumatic experiences some have suffered. Although many of the women commented on how they found our discussions satisfying, valuable and 'healing', the reality of the situation is that nothing was practically resolved through these interactions (other than for my own gain in nearing the completion of my doctorate).The women did not just suffer for the period of my research project but continue to suffer and were not able to walk away from these problems at the end of it all as I was; yet despite this, they continually expressed concern for my welfare. I was intensely mindful of the fact that, given certain circumstances, arguably any woman might find herself in a similar situation, and it was difficult not to envisage how different my own life would be if I were to endure some of their life events. In some respects, I saw aspects of myself, my friends and my relatives in the women I interviewed. Arguably, this realisation encouraged me to listen more intently to their reports. Not only can the interviewing experience have an emotional effect on the researcher during the actual encounter, but it was also problematic bringing these discussions to a close and walking away from the prisoners and their problems at the end of the research day without harbouring feelings of guilt. Although I could not disconnect my emotions and reactions from the research process, I would argue that they positively led me to a deeper understanding of the reality for these women.

Conclusion

Through self-reflexivity, I have examined the identities I inhibited through my research study. I have reflected on my experience as an ex-prison employee turned 'visiting' student researcher and on the various nuances of shifting positionality in the prison. This has included a consideration of how my personal characteristics and social identity came into play within the research, shedding light on not only the advantages my previous experience brought, but also the negative dimensions.

Lee (1993) has argued that when researchers emphasise the problematic nature of field research, the depiction is often one of a 'heroic tale' in which the disinclination of those being studied is overcome as a result of the diligence and cleverness of the researcher. This is not a 'heroic tale'; admittedly, there were times when I failed to manage my researcher self appropriately in a way that shaped the research process. I cannot claim that the openness of the women I encountered was a result of my skill and artifice; instead, my unintentional but apparent youth, naivety and vulnerability in the research setting built a two-way supportive relationship that stimulated openness.

By allowing such transparency and openness with regard to my own emotions, character and behaviour within the research setting, I run the risk of feeling uneasy and perhaps slightly foolish. However, this is a risk worth taking, because at the same time it allows the data collected during my research experience to be interpreted in its wider context with an honest consideration to how the research process was moulded by the person I am and the image I presented.

Notes

1. 'The Repeat Imprisonment of Women Serving Short-Term Custodial Sentences at HMP New Hall'. This work was supported by the Economic and Social Research Council ES/I02218X/1.
2. For an account of ethnographic research which focused on race, class and gender, see Phillips and Earle (2010).

Further reading

King, R. D. and Liebling, A. (2006) 'Doing Research in Prisons', in R. King and E. Wincup (eds) *Doing Research on Crime and Justice*, Second edn (Oxford: Oxford University Press).

Martin, C. (2000) 'Doing Research in a Prison Setting', in V. Jupp, D. Davies and P. Francis (eds) *Doing Criminological Research* (London: Sage).

Smith, C. and Wincup, E. (2000) 'Breaking In: Researching Criminal Justice Institutions for Women', in R. D. King and E. Wincup (eds) *Doing Research on Crime and Justice* (Oxford: Oxford University Press).

References

Arnold, H. (2005) 'The Effects of Prison Work', in A. Liebling and S. Maruna (eds) *The Effects of Imprisonment* (Cullompton: Willan Publishing).

Becker, H. (1967) 'Whose Side Are We on?' *Social Problems*, 14, 3, 239–47.

Bosworth, M., Campbell, D., Demby, B., Ferranti, S. M. and Santos, M. (2005) 'Doing Prison Research: Views from Inside', *Qualitative Inquiry*, 11, 2, 249–64.

Campbell, R. (2002) *Emotionally Involved: The Impact of Researching Rape* (New York: Routledge).

Carlen, P. and Worrall, A. (2004) *Analysing Women's Imprisonment* (Cullompton: Willan).

Cohen, S. and Taylor, L. (1972) *Psychological Survival* (Harmondsworth: Penguin).

Crewe, B. (2009) *The Prisoner Society: Power, Adaptation and Social Life in an English Prison* (Oxford: Oxford University Press).

Gelsthorpe, L. (1990) 'Feminist Methodologies in Criminology: A New Approach or Old Wine in New Bottles?', in L. Gelsthorpe and A. Morris (eds) *Feminist Perspectives in Criminology* (Milton Keynes: Open University Press).

Genders, E. and Player, E. (1995) *Grendon: A Therapeutic Prison* (Oxford: Oxford University Press).

HM Inspectorate of Prisons (2013) *Written Evidence from HM Inspectorate of Prisons* [accessed online, 9 September 2014], http://www.publications.parliament.uk/pa/cm201314/cmselect/cmjust/92/92we03.html

King, R. D. (2000) 'Doing Research in Prisons', in R. D. King and E. Wincup (eds) *Doing Research on Crime and Justice* (Oxford: Oxford University Press).

King, R. D. and Liebling, A. (2007) 'Doing Research in Prisons', in R. King and E. Wincup (eds) *Doing Research on Crime and Justice*, Second edn (Oxford: Oxford University Press).

Lee, R. (1993) *Doing Research on Sensitive Topics* (London: Sage).

Liebling, A. (1992) *Suicides in Prison* (London: Routledge).

Liebling, A. (2001) 'Whose Side Are We On? Theory, Practice and Allegiances in Prison Research', *British Journal of Criminology*, 41, 3, 472–84.

Malloch, M. S. (2000) *Women, Drugs and Custody: The Experience of Women Drug Users in Prison* (Winchester: Waterside Press).

Martin, C. (2000) 'Doing Research in a Prison Setting', in V. Jupp, D. Davies and P. Francis (eds) *Doing Criminological Research* (London: Sage).

Mills, J. (2004) *'There's a Lot in Those Keys Isn't There?' The Experience of a Female Researcher Researching Rape in a Male Prison Undertaking the Research as a Key Holder* (National Criminal Justice Reference Service: US Department of Justice).

Ministry of Justice (2010) Compendium of Reoffending Statistics and Analysis, Ministry of Justice Statistics Bulletin, https://www.gov.uk/government/uploads/system/uploads/attachment_data/file/199224/compendium-of-reoffending-statistics-and-analysis.pdf [accessed online, 09/September/2014].

Morris, T. and Morris, P. (1963) *Pentonville: A Sociological Study of an English Prison* (London: Routledge and Kegan Paul).

Phillips, C. and Earle, R. (2010) 'Reading Difference Differently? Identity, Epistemology and Prison Ethnography', *British Journal of Criminology*, 50, 2, 360–78.

Scully, D. (1991) *Understanding Sexual Violence* (London: Harper Collins).

Smith, C. and Wincup, E. (2000) 'Breaking In: Researching Criminal Justice Institutions for Women', in R. D. King and E. Wincup (eds) *Doing Research on Crime and Justice* (Oxford: Oxford University Press).

Sparks, R., Bottoms, A. E. and Hay, W. (1996) *Prisons and the Problem of Order* (Oxford: Oxford University Press).

Warren, C. A. B. (1988) *Gender Issues in Field Research* (Newbury Park, CA: Sage).

20
The Ethnographic Practitioner

Joel Harvey

Introduction

In this chapter, I will introduce the idea of working as an ethnographic practitioner in secure forensic settings. This chapter will be reflective and will draw on my personal experience of being immersed in therapeutic practice in prisons and other secure settings *after* I had first and formerly been an ethnographic prison researcher.

Having briefly introduced ethnographic approaches to research in general, I will reflect on my experience of carrying out an ethnographic study in a young offender institution, Her Majesty's Young Offender Institution (HMYOI) Feltham, in West London. I will then focus on the influences of my prior research experience on my decision to become a practitioner and the way I conducted that role. I will reflect on the 'role reversal' that occurred in the process of moving from 'observer' to 'practitioner', and I will focus on two main ideas that this transition elucidated: first, the idea of 'insider-outsider', and second, the importance of 'keeping context in mind'. I will then examine what ethnography can offer therapists in prisons, or other secure settings, and I will end by reflecting briefly on ways that ethnographic principles could be applied to therapeutic practice.

Ethnography is a well-established research method which involves *understanding* the experiences of a particular group of people, the contexts in which they live and the relationship between their experiences and the context in which they are embedded. In their classic book *Ethnography: Principles in Practice*, Hammersley and Atkinson (1997) state that carrying out an ethnography 'involves the ethnographer participating, overtly or covertly, in people's daily lives for an extended period of time, watching what happens, listening to what is said, asking questions – in fact, collecting whatever data are available to throw light on these issues that are the focus of the research' (p. 1).

So, an ethnography usually involves spending prolonged periods of time with people in their own environments, often living alongside them, in an attempt to appreciate their experiences. The ethnographer often takes on a role in the particular context being examined. For example, if we were interested in the experience and the meaning-making of factory workers, we might decide to work on a production line; if we wanted to understand fisherman on the islands off Scotland, we might take a role on the boat in order to access that world by doing exactly the same job as the people we were studying. This would be termed 'participant observation'. Other ethnographers might not participate but might only be 'observers'. They might locate themselves in a particular environment, for example, a police station, and carry out observation and interviews in that setting, in order to understand the role and culture of police staff. However, they would not take on a specific role within that environment.

Importantly, ethnography can be seen as both a process and an outcome. The process involves carrying out the interviews, being present for a prolonged period of time carrying out observations and taking detailed notes about the process. As an outcome, the research can then be written up as an ethnography. The outcome involves producing what Clifford Geertz calls a 'thick description' of the lives on the group of interest (Geertz, 1973). The outcome is a written account that communicates to the reader the experience of the particular group being studied.

Ethnography has grown up in the field of social anthropology, and many classic studies were conducted outside Western societies. These include Malinowski's (1922) study of the Trobriand Islanders, Evans-Pritchard's (1937) *Witchcraft, Oracles and Magic among the Azande* and Douglas's (1966) *Purity and Danger.* There are a host of more recent ethnographic studies which explore life in Westernised societies. For example, Anderson (2001) carried out an ethnographic study for four years in inner-city Philadelphia and published the book *Code of the Street: Decency, Violence and the Moral Life of the Inner City.*

As detailed in this volume, ethnographies have taken place in prisons. There are the 'classic' US prison ethnography studies of Clemmer's (1940) *The Prison Community* and Sykes' (1958) *The Society of Captives*. Ethnographic studies in the UK have also been published, which have examined the culture of prisoners in a medium-security men's prison (Crewe, 2009), ethnicity and masculinity in two English men's prisons (Phillips, 2012) and the experience of maximum-security men's prisons (Drake, 2012).

Although there is a growing body of contemporary ethnographies of the world of prisoners themselves, there has been less ethnographic observation of the prisoners' engagement in forensic clinical practice. In one study, Waldram (2007) carried out an ethnographic study of a sex offender treatment programme in a Canadian prison. He explored how prisoners 'tell their stories' within the treatment programmes, and he spent 18 months following the programme and their progress. Allowing informants to tell their stories is a key aspect of ethnographic research.

There are complex practical and ethical problems in carrying out an ethnography in its purest form in prisons. For example, if a researcher were interested in using ethnography to understand the prisoner's experience in full, it would be difficult for him or her to go out and commit a crime to become a true 'participant observer' in the process of being imprisoned. However, the prison ethnographer can attempt to get close to people's experience by spending prolonged periods of time in the prison. Whether one is a 'true' participant-observer or more of an 'observer', what is distinctive and essential about ethnographic research is the core intention of learning about the experiences, beliefs and meaning-making of people living in a particular setting. In order to learn about another's social world, Goffman (1961) would argue that it is necessary 'to submit oneself to the company of the members to the daily round of petty contingencies to which they are subject' (Goffman, 1961: 7). Being present with a particular group, absorbing what is seen and heard (or not heard), and then reflecting on these observations and conversations, is at the heart of ethnographic research. Indeed, 'being present' is argued to be an important component of any form of prison research (King and Wincup 2002).

Reflections on being a prison ethnographer

More than 10 years ago, I carried out ethnographic fieldwork of HMYOI Feltham, a young offenders' institution for young people aged 15–20 (Harvey, 2007). I carried out the study on the part of the prison which accommodated young people aged 18–20. I spent 10 months there and had full access to the prison. I held keys and could come and go through the gate and to different wings of the prison the same as staff members. I was particularly interested in the role of social support in prison, from both prisoners and staff. I carried out interviews with staff and prisoners, used questionnaires and carried out social network analyses. The network analyses involved interviewing every young person on a wing, to ascertain whom they considered to be their 'mates' and the extent to which they trusted them.

I was also particularly interested in understanding the psychosocial experience of the first month in custody, which, as we know, can be a high-risk period for suicidal behaviour. To develop this understanding, I interviewed 70 prisoners after they had been in prison for 72 hours and then re-interviewed them at 10 days and then 30 days, to see how they had subsequently adapted to life in the prison. I was interested in examining what helped young men adapt to life inside and what made it difficult for them. From these interviews, I identified three different forms of adaptation (practical, social and psychological) and developed a model of adaptation (Harvey, 2007).

An essential part of this 'embedded' study, or 'ethnography', was being able to spend a substantial amount of time 'hanging out' on the prison wings, the education department, workshops, exercise yards, health care, reception and visits hall. On some days, I would be present before the prisoners were unlocked, shadow prisoners throughout the entire day, and be there until lock-down. I kept a notebook and pen with me at all times and would note down my observations or my discussions with staff and prisoners. This information was then used to help understand the material I gathered from my more structured interviews with prisoners and staff. Indeed, using different methods allowed for data triangulation, 'the checking of inferences drawn from one set of data sources by collecting data from others' (Hammersley and Atkinson, 1997: 230). If I had only come into the prison, carried out the interviews and walked out again, I would not have developed an understanding of the context and I think I would perhaps not have been as attuned to the young person as they were describing their experience of imprisonment to me.

Becoming attached to a prison is a prerequisite to understanding the dynamics of life there and the social relationships that lied therein. Without this constant presence, I would have lost much of the richness of the research and gained only a superficial picture of life at the prison (Harvey, 2007). As Hammersley and Atkinson (1997) stated, 'it is only through watching, listening, asking questions, formulating hypotheses, and making blunders that the ethnographer can acquire some sense of a social structure of the setting and begin to understand the culture of the participants' (p. 100). So, I could observe everyday practice without getting caught up in it; I could listen to conversations between prisoners on the wing whilst they were playing pool; and I could walk with staff and prisoners as they moved from one area to another. If a prisoner was relocated from the wing to the health-care centre, I could then have *time* to go and spend time in health care, as he attempted to adapt in this new environment. I could attend visits halls and witness prisoners' reactions before, during and after visits with people from the outside world. I would spend time in reception and on the first night centre to understand these important points of transition. I would walk with prisoners as they walked from reception to the wing for the first time. So in Feltham, through extended contact I began to understand particular people, interactions or events in their wider social context, and this understanding might not have been achieved on a shorter visit.

Yet at the same time, I did not have a role to fulfil within the prison structure. I was able to 'observe' practice but was not a practitioner. As an outsider looking in I could ask naïve questions, be curious and reflect. My reason for being there was solely to *understand* the experience of imprisonment for young people rather than work with them. In fact, the role I had was to process what was being said, reflect upon it and *understand*. Each conversation I had with staff and young people helped build my understanding of their experience. I was there to understand how experiences were constructed, the use of language, youthful and professional argot, and the forms of symbolism that mediated prison life. I wasn't there to carry out psychological assessments or interventions with young people, or contribute to risk management panels, or develop the service. I wasn't there as a qualified practitioner. There was one exception: I had the same responsibilities of sharing information, if I felt that the young person was at risk of harm to themselves or others. However, my intervention role stopped there and I obviously was not in a position where I would be expected to work with the young men.

Reflections on moving from ethnographer to practitioner

Whilst I was carrying out my study, I decided I wanted to make the transition from research as prison ethnographer to practise as a clinical psychologist. I remember on one particular day I observed a psychiatric nurse assessing a young man who was feeling low in mood and who had suicidal thoughts. He helped the young man think about his difficulties and offered reassurance and support. At this moment I felt that I wanted to move from being an 'observer' of practice to being a 'participant' in practice. Given my background in psychology, the most obvious route to becoming a practitioner was to train as a clinical psychologist. Therefore after completing my ethnographic research at Feltham, I trained and qualified as a clinical psychologist, and then I returned to various secure settings to work as a practitioner. Those settings included a prison, an adolescent forensic unit and a medium secure unit, and I worked with young people and adults.

This shift, from 'observer' to 'practitioner', a 'role-reversal' if you like, enabled me to reflect on a number of different concepts that have relevance to therapy provision in criminal justice settings. The shift from one role to another allowed me to approach similar situations from different perspectives. My previous experience as a prison ethnographer enabled me to contrast those experiences with those of a practitioner in similar contexts. My ethnographic practice allowed me to understand the settings more thoroughly than I would have done, had I only experienced them as a practitioner. Also, those processes of ethnographic observation then informed the way I worked as a practitioner on the inside. Thus two particular themes or constructs became salient to me as a practitioner, which I will consider next: 'insider-outsider' and the importance of 'keeping context in mind'.

Insider-outsider

As an ethnographic researcher, I was very much an 'outsider' to the prison establishment. Although, as an ethnographic researcher, I had full access to different areas of the prison, I was an 'outsider' in that I was not part of the establishment with a defined role within the structure. My identity, as mentioned above, was rather fluid and to some extent fragmented and this had to be managed and negotiated on a daily basis. Although I had keys and could access different areas of the prison, my access to prisoners for interviews had to be constantly negotiated; the prison officers were the 'gatekeepers' who enabled me to carry out these interviews. I had limited legitimacy in the institution and no structural position within the prison.

My first role working in a prison was as a trainee clinical psychologist in a Young Offender Institution (YOI) in the North West of England. I was a National Health Service (NHS) employee and the NHS Trust for which I worked had been commissioned to provide mental health services in the prison, although it had only been commissioned to provide such a service one day per week. Interestingly, the position as a psychologist on an 'in-reach' team – a telling phrase – meant that we came from the 'outside' into the 'inside' prison community: borrowing from social anthropology I was in a liminal position, in a zone between two boundaries. I was at once an 'insider', gaining access to prison records and providing psychological therapy, but at the same time I was neither an 'outsider', employed by the prison service directly nor present in the institution on a daily basis.

However, the key difference between being an ethnographic researcher and being a practitioner was that, as a practitioner, I had a defined role: I was there to provide psychological therapy. In this sense, I was an insider by virtue of having a legitimately defined role. I had key roles and responsibilities. But what struck me during this early training position was that although I had a more clearly defined role within the prison, I, paradoxically, ended up understanding the prison much less than I had when I was more of an 'outsider' as an ethnographic researcher. As on many prison in-reach teams, the psychologist might not be there full-time but might only be in the prison a couple of days a week. During this limited time, young people needed to be seen, appointments had to be organised, and the task was to provide psychological therapy sessions. Furthermore, when I was a trainee psychologist, prisoners were brought to me in the health-care centre, and because I was only there one day a week, I didn't have the time to go on the wings. I was struck by this model of service delivery. What was most striking was that I did not get to know the prison: I did have a tour of the prison, and there were times when I did go on the wings to see some young people or speak with staff. However, they were the exception rather than the rule. This was in sharp contrast to my previous experience of being in prison, when, as a researcher, I had spent prolonged periods of time across different areas of the prison, building relationships with staff and coming to understand the emotional climate of different parts of the prison. But, as a practitioner, although I was an 'insider' by dint of having a role within the structure of the prison, the way in which the role was constructed in fact placed me in a relatively more peripheral position.

These early reflections stayed with me, as I went on to work in a medium secure unit. Post qualification, I took up a full-time post as a psychologist on a low-security ward in East London, fully an 'insider' now, even more so than as part of an in-reach team. Moreover, whereas before I had only worked in the prison for one day a week, I wondered whether I might have a greater understanding of the patient's life as I was now in a full-time post. Indeed, I was keen to make sure I understood the institution and actively tried to spend time on the ward in which I was based, spending more 'informal' time with patients, getting to know staff on an individual basis. I did this outside the one-to-one therapy time and other clinical duties. In some ways, I was attempted to adopt a style I had when carrying out my prison ethnography. I wanted to know the individual climate of the ward, to understand how patients made the transitions between different wards, to think about their social life on the ward, and to ensure I was attuned to the needs of staff. Whilst I managed, to some extent, to spend some time doing this, this occurred when I had time in-between therapy sessions, multidisciplinary meetings and running offending behaviour programmes. These efforts, which take time, were not explicitly part of the core roles of a clinical or forensic psychologist. The job was to deliver psychological therapy, carrying out risk assessments, train staff, offer consultation and so on. For example, the role involved assessing the risk clients posed to themselves and others and to work as part of a team to make decisions about whether not clients could be discharged from secure conditions. It also involved working with clients working therapeutically with clients who were experiencing psychosis.

So, whilst being more of an 'insider', as a full-time member of staff (rather than a service commissioned into the prison), the defined role of psychologist still determined me to occupy a more peripheral position, compared to the role as prison ethnographer. Of course, the role of prison ethnographer enabled me to have more time and freedom, given that my sole task was to *understand* the experience of prisoners, and I obviously didn't have to spend time carrying out therapeutic work. But the role of the psychologist in the prison or secure unit was not as focused on *understanding* the service user's *experience* of the institution in which they reside, as a prison ethnographer might. This task of understanding, or *verstehen,* is central to ethnographic research (Seymour-Smith, 1986). Of course, therapists, psychologists and counsellors in secure units do develop an understanding of the context, but such an understanding is not necessarily a core aspect of the role. Instead, the role might be, to name but a few tasks: to offer Cognitive Behavioural Therapy (CBT) sessions for clients who present with low mood, suicidal thoughts and anxiety; to carry out detailed risk assessments of future violence, such as the HCR-20; or to run a sex offender treatment programme. Of course, these tasks are important and central to the role; but it is paradoxical that a sole focus on these tasks might then detract from an understanding of context.

As an ethnographic researcher, and more of an 'outsider', by the time I left HMYOI Feltham, I knew the prison relatively well, although of course not fully. However, by the time I left the medium-secure unit where I worked, I had some understanding of the low-secure ward where I was based but less understanding of the rest of the establishment. 'Getting to know' the establishment was not a central task. In fact, attempts to 'get to know', 'hang-out' and spend time developing rapport with staff and service users were to some extent an 'additional' part of the role and a peripheral position to occupy. 'Getting to know' the place was not written into my job descriptions nor related directly to key competencies by which I was assessed as an applied psychologist. Our task-focused, performance-orientated institutions reduce the amount of time an individual therapist has to soak up the culture of the places where they work.

Keeping context in mind

But why does this understanding of wider institutional context matter? Is that not just the different concern of the ethnographer who describes a world, compared with a practitioner who has a job to get on with? My experience of being an ethnographic researcher made me focus on understanding context, in particular the way that people relate to their environment. Then, as a practitioner, I came to realise that the understanding which ethnographers have of people in environments is essential for practice. Harvey and Smedley (2010) put forward several reasons why it is important to take context into account. They argue a contextual understanding is necessary in order to help the therapist understand how problems might develop or be exacerbated during confinement, to understand the barriers to therapy provision in a prison (i.e. lock-down, the transient nature of the prison population, the turbulence of individual biographies), to be mindful of critical incidents that might have happened in the prison that might impact upon the client (i.e. suicide of a prisoner, physical assaults), to be able to work systemically along with other members of staff, to acknowledge that prisons are low-trust environments and the impact this might have on the provision of therapy, and to acknowledge the imbalance of power between the client and therapist. Taking a contextual approach also encourages therapists to think about *what* to assess and *how* to assess. It makes us question whether the assessment tools used in the community, to measure depression, for example, are adequate. Do they, for example, capture notions of *prison induced distress* (Liebling, 1992)? Are these measures contextually relevant? Also, if we pay attention to context, interventions might focus more on helping prisoners alleviate the pains of imprisonment, alongside offering offending behaviour programmes. Whilst of course, as we know, therapeutic work is carried out today by individual therapists to help prisoners cope with the experience of imprisonment, perhaps the dominant focus of offending behaviour programmes might sometimes overshadow this. Importantly, taking a contextual approach encourages the therapist to resist an internal pathological model of psychological difficulties.

Taking a contextual approach to clients' needs allows the therapist to depart from a solely pathological model of emotion and behaviour. The responsibility of the wider social system in the development of these difficulties comes into focus and enables practitioners to think about the pains of imprisonment and what can be done to help manage the emotional experience. It would be of interest to think about how ethnographic method might be applied to therapeutic practice. Ethnographers place an understanding of the person in situ at the heart of their analyses, and this is important for practitioners too.

It has been argued here that it would be useful to place understanding of context more at the core of therapeutic work. Rather than seeking to understand only the individual, it is necessary to be aiming to understand their experience of the institution in which they're based. Whilst many practitioners do take into account systemic factors, especially systemic practitioners, and whilst many professionals embrace the notion of a reflective practitioner or scientist-practitioner, what I'd like to end this chapter by thinking about how therapists, counsellors or psychologists, might incorporate some of the methods from ethnography into their practice.

Developing as an ethnographic practitioner

Is it, however, possible to develop ethnographic practitioners? Could therapists in prisons, or other secure settings, borrow the methods of ethnography and develop these into their role? How could they simultaneously be an insider and an outsider when we have a job to do simply on the inside? How can therapists step outside the context in order to understand it? It is the 'outsider' prison ethnographer who has the time and 'permission' (through the aims of the research endeavour) to observe, reflect on and understand the experience of people within a particular context. By contrast, as an 'insider' practitioner, there is less time and permission (as there are different aims for the role) to observe, reflect and take time to understand the context in which clients live. Whilst of course, as I have mentioned above, individual therapists do take context into account in their therapeutic work, there is less facilitation of this, even though these people are more closely embedded into the institution.

How might practitioners think differently if NHS induction programmes stressed the importance of understanding the context in which we work? Of course, these programmes cover health and safety, security and risk, but do they embrace a necessity to soak up the context in which we work? Are there opportunities for shadowing staff and reflecting afterwards and for carrying out detailed observations? What if such staff were able to be ethnographers, if they took detailed notes, and were able to reflect upon them? Reflective practice is an important aspect of ethical practice as a psychologist (BPS, 2009), and it would be of interest to think about the role that ethnographic principles might have in relation to practice.

Moreover, prior to obtaining a position in a particular institution, do different professional training, emphasise the need to acknowledge and understand the context where the forensic practitioners will be working?

How could these ideas apply to multidisciplinary teams? Could it be envisaged that a member of staff is freed from their duties to spend a week in an ethnographic role whose task is to immerse themselves in wider procedures and understand broader contexts of practice? If they kept detailed field notes and analysed them, this data could be valuable for the team. Perhaps such a model could work whereby there's an exchange of professionals across different wards or wings and for therapists to begin to have a dialogue about what they've understood from their role as an ethnographic practitioner.

Then there are those micro-moments, where the practitioner might adopt the role of ethnographer when observing an interaction on the wing. Here, they might understand a particular aspect of prison life or experience on a medium-secure unit ward and spent an hour 'hanging out', observing, having conversations and then perhaps writing this up in reflective notes afterwards, in an attempt to foster more profound understandings of social interactions in the prison. This would not be work directed towards a specific patient, rather it is an approach with a more collective general aim of understanding a particular aspect of the workplace culture. I'm sure this occurs already but is rarely explicitly operationalised.

There might also be opportunities in clinical supervision to think about ethnographic components of work. Perhaps if practitioners were at times to adopt the position of 'participant-observer' and attempt to develop a 'thick description' of a particular aspect of prison life, these reflections and conversations in supervision could open up broader discourses when thinking about our work with clients. For example, could such 'thick descriptions' be written up and taken as a discussion piece in supervision? Peer supervision might of particular value here. Moreover, it would be important for the team as a whole to embrace such knowledge exchange and to be open to reflection.

As with most practical suggestions, there are of course tensions. The obvious tension is time. Therapists work in challenging resource-limited environments and the ideas of a therapist being freed from regular clinical duties to 'hang out' on the wing for a relative prolonged period of time might appear unrealistic.

But, on the other hand, if such work leads to better outcomes in terms of the therapy we provide, then it might be justified. Proving this would be another question and a research study in itself.

Second, because the practitioner is already embedded as an insider in the institution, it is questionable how far he or she can 'step-back' as an 'observer'. But whatever we do, in research, practice or elsewhere, we bring our perspectives to bear on what we encounter and we need to reflect upon that. Therefore, any models of ethnographic practice would have to think about the practitioner's own biases and assumptions. In fact, taking on the role of ethnographic practitioner might help us think about our own assumptions and biases more explicitly. In practice, models such as the 'reflective-practitioner' and, of course, the 'scientist-practitioner' exist (Schön, 1983; Lane and Corrie, 2006). Being an ethnographic practitioner, in a way, is analogous here, but the difference is that ethnography brings a different kind of research method and a specific set of concerns into focus, namely, contextual factors. Whilst the reflective practitioner might reflect *on* action and reflect *in* action (Schön, 1983), the ethnographic practitioner, by contrast, would be reflecting more on what other actors are doing and on the context, rather than reflecting primarily on their own practice. Also, whilst the reflective practitioner reflects in order to act – that is to practise – an ethnographic practitioner primary goal is to *understand*. Of course, this might lead to further action, but that is not the initial goal. Moreover, the method of data gathering as an ethnographer might result in further depth of understanding.

Conclusion

To conclude, therapists working in prisons are trusted with working with vulnerable people and through the writing of reports and the completion of risk assessments they directly contribute to the construction of knowledge and the narrative of their clients. With this comes the responsibility of holding in mind the experience of clients who are held in deprived, controlled and often unpredictable environments. It is important that therapists are given the opportunity to understand these contexts in a deep and meaningful way. To do so, they might benefit from integrating some ideas from ethnography into practice, as well as from finding more opportunities to free themselves to become attuned to the changing socio-political experience of secure confinement. By adopting the stance of ethnographic practitioner, not only might therapists continue to be attuned to the needs of clients, they might also become more active agents of change in reforming secure services to meet the needs of clients. In this sense, the ethnographic practitioner could transform the world they have come to understand.

Further reading

Atkinson, P., Coffey, A., Delamont, S., Lofland, J. and Lofland, L. (eds) *Handbook of Ethnography* (London: Sage).

Drake, D. and Harvey, J. (2014) 'Performing the Role of Ethnographer: Processing and Managing the Emotional Dimension of Prison Research', *International Journal of Social Research Methods,* 7, 5, 489–501.

Harvey, J. (2007) 'An Embedded Multi-Method Approach to Prison Research', in R. King and E. Wincup (eds) *Doing Research on Crime and Justice,* Second edition (Oxford: Oxford University Press).

References

Anderson, E. (2001) *Code of the Street. Decency, Violence and the Moral Life of the Inner City* (London: W. H. Norton and Company).

BPS (2009) *Code of Ethics and Conduct* (Leicester: BPS).

Clemmer, D. (1940) *The Prison Community* (New York: Holt, Rinehart & Winston).

Crewe, B. (2009) *The Prisoner Society: Power, Adaptation and Social Life in an English Prison* (Oxford: Oxford University Press).

Douglas, M. (1966) *Purity and Danger: An Analysis of Concepts of Pollution and Taboo* (London: Routledge).

Drake, D. H. (2012) *Prisons, Punishment and the Pursuit of Security* (Basingstoke: Palgrave Macmillan).

Evans-Pritchard, E. E. (1933/1976) *Witchcraft, Oracles and Magic among the Azande* (New York: Oxford University Press).

Geertz, C. (1973) *The Interpretation of Cultures* (New York: Basic Books).

Goffman, E. (1961) *Asylums Harmondsworth* (Penguin).

Goffman, E. (1963) *Asylums: Essays on the Social Situation of Mental Patients and Other Inmates* (London: Penguin Books).

Hammersley, M. and Atkinson, P. (1997) *Ethnography: Principles and Practice* (London: Routledge).

Harvey, J. (2007) 'An Embedded Multi-Method Approach to Prison Research', in R. King and E. Wincup (eds) *Doing Research on Crime and Justice,* Second edition (Oxford: Oxford University Press).

Harvey, J. (2007) *Young Men in Prison: Surviving and Adapting to Life Inside* (Cullompton: Willan Publishing).

Harvey, J. and Smedley K. (2010) 'Introduction', in J. Harvey and K. Smedley (eds) *Psychological Therapy in Prisons and Other Secure Settings* (Cullompton: Willan).

King, R. and Wincup, E. (eds) (2002) *Doing Research on Crime and Justice* (Oxford: Oxford University Press).

Lane, D. A. and Corrie, C. (eds) (2006) *The Modern Scientist-Practitioner: A Guide to Practice in Psychology* (New York: Routledge).

Liebling, A. (1992) *Suicides in Prison* (London: Routledge).

Malinowski, B. (1922–61) *Argonauts of the Western Pacific: An Account of Native Enterprise and Adventure in the Archipelagos of Melanesian New Guinea* (New York: Routledge).

Phillips, C. (2012) *The Multicultural Prison: Ethnicity, Masculinity, and Social Relations among Prisoners* (Oxford: Oxford University Press).
Schön, D. A. (1983) *The Reflective Practitioner: How Practitioners Think in Action* (New York: Basic Books).
Seymour-Smith, C. (1986) *MacMillan Dictionary of Anthropology* (London: MacMillan Press).
Skyes, G. (1958) *The Society of Captives* (Princeton: Princeton University Press).
Waldram, J. B. (2007) 'Narrative and the Construction of "Truth" in a Prison-Based Treatment Program for Sexual Offenders', *Ethnography* 8, 2, 145–69.

Part IV
For Prison Ethnography
Introduction to Part IV

Jennifer Sloan

The theme running throughout the final part of the Handbook is to consider what it is we need ethnography for. The chapters in Part IV are all implicitly underpinned by the notion that ethnography is a broadly positive tool – an approach to be valued for its depth and insight as well as the humanity it brings to the social sciences. Few would argue that these characteristics are not inherently valuable to research processes, particularly in the exploration of those institutions that operate beyond public view. Ethnography, however, as with any research approach, has limitations. Its external validity, and thus the extent of its generalisability, can be called into question.

Ethnography's strength in gathering deep and detailed insights has the capacity to provide great swathes of information. But this strength might also be viewed as its weakness. The purpose of a single ethnographic study is not to qualify the patterns and aggregations that quantitative data generate, nor is it often the basis upon which policy is formed and shaped. However, the contributions to this part of the Handbook demonstrate how the different ways researchers use an ethnographic lens to examine the inner life of prisons can reveal wider patterns in practices of imprisonment, at both micro-organisational and macro-political levels. When considering ethnographic studies alongside wider trends in the penal realm or by comparing different ethnographic studies, far more is revealed about the human experience and its relationship to political-economic structures than can be captured by statistics alone. As Jewkes so eloquently pointed out in the Foreword to this Handbook, statistics more often serve to 'dazzle' rather than to reveal.

This part of the Handbook is opened by Thomas Ugelvik's compelling chapter which argues for the usefulness of a global prison ethnography that aims to elucidate three levels of knowledge about incarceration – the 'everyday interaction and frustration on the wings', the level of state power and the links between the prison and the global sphere. Noting that prisons are 'increasingly part of a regime of international mobility control', Ugelvik argues for the advancement of ethnographic projects in prisons and invites us 'to broaden our theoretical and analytical horizons and study prison wings as part of the rest of the world'. In doing so, he argues, the results of prison ethnographic practice become much more transferrable in terms of being globally relevant.

It is through the inspection of the practices and perspectives of other jurisdictions that we are able to discover more about our own realm and, in turn, about the impact of the researcher upon the ethnographic process. In Chapter 22, Tomas Max Martin carefully demonstrates this in his considerations of the Ugandan prison system, highlighting the variety of means he used in undertaking his research. The importance of his personal 'differences' is revealed as a means of inspiring trust and negotiating his position as a non-threatening 'other', as well as a means of providing new perspectives on justice. He discusses the complexity of 'negotiating boundaries in an opaque environment' and the importance of the resonance between a researcher's personal anxieties and the 'wider presence of insecurity, vulnerability and ambiguity of knowledge in the field'. The chapter demonstrates the practical importance of reflective prison ethnography in establishing the prison (and prison ethnography) as a global phenomenon to be understood as an international challenge – just as Ugelvik proposes.

Similarly, in Chapter 23, Mahuya Bandyopadhyay shows the importance of her differences and similarities in undertaking prison ethnography in Indian prisons, and the importance of noting their post-colonial context. Her recognition of temporal structures and use of 'thick description' provides yet another perspective to the prison setting which is best found and woven together through skilled ethnographic processes. She discusses relationships and tensions in the field, raising the idea that a 'heightened negative emotional context and experience' can be used as a tool in ethnographic practice. In an extremely detailed chapter that discusses notions of rapport, emotionality, credibility and practices of subversion and transgression, Bandyopadhyay's work (which she describes as a postscript to her earlier book, Bandyopadhyay, 2010) gives further weight to Ugelvik's arguments about extending ethnographic theorising. She too seeks to 'turn the anthropological gaze on prison ethnographers' and looks to an increase in prison research across the globe, but particularly in South Asia.

Bandyopadhyay notes that prison ethnography 'transgresses ontological positioning in making full sense of the self'. The positionality of the researcher and the importance of ethnography from the inside are becoming more important and thus increasingly recognised – as discussed in Part III of the Handbook, 'Of Prison Ethnography'. In arguing 'for ethnography', William Davies, in Chapter 24, utilises his study on short-term prisoners to introduce a different 'insider' angle that bears on the ethnographic process: prison ethnography as a tool for former prisoners. Despite some challenges with access, Davies discusses the importance of being open about his 'position' as an ex-prisoner and his desire to use his identity as a means of establishing a rapport and relationship with current prisoners. Davies demonstrates the way prison ethnography is useful as a means of mobilising (to use Piacentini's terminology from Chapter 4) his own (former) status as a prisoner to add perspective and depth to ethnographic encounters. He points to the importance of deeper insiderness to overcoming otherwise unseen or poorly appreciated 'barriers to knowledge, meaning making and understanding'. In this way, Davies' use of autobiographical elements in his ethnographic approach allowed other perspectives to emerge, enriching prison ethnography and stretching its boundaries beyond those conventionally associated with insider status. Davies' chapter provides an important context for academic voices that have been so rarely heard in prison ethnographic practice, those of prisoners or ex-prisoners themselves (albeit the growth in convict criminology is addressing this). His experiences also remind ethnographers to reflect upon the importance of the self within their work, as well as to recognise that the ethno*grapher* and the ethno*graphy* exist in an impenetrable symbiosis that is missing from other research methods.

In the final chapter of the Handbook, Beyens and Boone take up the challenge posed by Ugelvik to link ethnographic research to wider global processes. Their insightful chapter describes the use of Dutch prisons to house Belgian prisoners in order to address the imbalance of prison numbers between the two jurisdictions. Through this work we begin more to tangibly see the ways in which prison processes are extending beyond or between nation states. Looking at the consequences of such a regime for prisoners and staff alike, Beyens and Boone highlight the similarities and differences of prison experiences provided by the two nations, as well as the differences experienced by the researchers. Their study sheds critical light on the way the practice of reflecting upon the familiar through the lens of the 'foreign' can provide hitherto obscured perspectives.

This final set of chapters and the Handbook as a whole demonstrate that the sum of the richness and vitality of the ethnographic endeavour in prisons is much more than its individual parts. Each chapter provides the shadows and sheds light upon certain areas of imprisonment, showing differences and similarities in ethnographic prison research and its potential to expose the extraordinary range and depth of international prison practice. This concluding part of the Handbook demonstrates the range of international practices, the innovations that are possible and the commitments that are required for prison ethnography to thrive. Through these accounts from Africa, India, England and mainland Europe, the differing realities of prisons, prisoners and ethnographers emerge. In this way, we are able to see how the processes of imprisonment are both unique and yet consistent for all those subjected to it. The authors in this part, and elsewhere throughout the Handbook, offer compelling visions of what prison ethnography is for, the urgency of being 'for prison ethnography' and inspiration for taking it further.

These chapters and the Handbook, as a whole, demonstrate the proliferation and use of imprisonment as a worldwide phenomenon of control and restraint imposed upon prisoners, prison staff and researchers. The overwhelming power and hegemony of prisons as the ultimate symbol and substance of modern punishment are here placed into perspective as institutions that are replete with the intricacies, delicacies and nuances of human life. The detailed, texturised and seldom seen side of prison life and of prison power is the gift and revelation that prison ethnography elaborates for all who care to see.

Reference

Bandyopadhyay, M. (2010) *Everyday Life in a Prison: Confinement, Surveillance, Resistance* (New Delhi: Orient BlackSwan).

21
Global Prison Ethnography

Thomas Ugelvik

Introduction

According to the UN Department of Economic and Social Affairs (UN-DESA), in 2013, 232 million people worldwide, or 3.2 per cent of the world's population, were living in a country other than the one they were born in, compared with 175 million in 2000 and 154 million in 1990.[1] Two facts can be inferred from this simple statistic. On the one hand, most people still live and die in the country where they were born. They are protected, taxed and – when appropriate from the point of view of the powers that be – imprisoned by the same state apparatus that first issued them a birth certificate and counted them as part of the exclusive group called 'state citizens'. On the other hand, the international mobility rate is increasing rapidly. This is, in part, a willed effect of international political changes. From a European perspective, the increased movement of EU (European Union) citizens has been one of the main objectives of the transformation of the Union from primarily an economic cooperation agreement to what is today arguably looking more and more like a federal state. Briefly put, the relationship between the state and the people who for some reason find themselves on the state's territory (including increasing numbers of non-citizens) is changing in this age of globalisation.

Processes of globalisation bring new possibilities: goods, services, ideas and (privileged) human beings are mobile and able to circulate across vast distances and old borders in ways unthinkable only a generation or two ago. But globalisation also results in specific problems, challenges and risks. Wars, conflicts and natural disasters, an unstable and unpredictable global economy and its effects on a global employment market all have effects which transcend national boundaries.

The effects of these changes can be seen on prison wings around the world. The population controlled by the penal arm of the state is no longer largely restricted to citizens of the state (O'Nolan, 2011). Western European countries in particular are now imprisoning an increasing number of non-citizens (Ugelvik, 2014a). In certain parts of Europe, the over-representation of non-EU citizens in prison is many times their share of the general population (Melossi, 2013); the situation has been compared with the over-representation of blacks in US prisons (Wacquant, 1999). The development should be seen as connected to changes in wider society; what has been called the 'hyper-criminalisation of immigrants', and in particular of so-called third-country nationals, has been seen to play an instrumental role in the production of a vulnerable and exploitable workforce (De Giorgi, 2010).

Prison researchers have very often taken the nation-state as their default contextual frame for their analyses. In this chapter, I will argue that international and global developments are making this myopia untenable. According to O'Nolan,

> The increased presence of foreign nationals in European prisons can only be accurately interpreted in the context of globalisation processes, increased mobility, changes in modes and patterns of crime, as well as by reference to structural and individual discriminatory processes.
>
> (2011: 385)

I will not present analyses of empirical material in this chapter. Instead, my aim is to discuss the consequences that changes associated with globalisation could and should have for prison ethnography, as well as to invite others to explore the possibilities of a truly global prison ethnography. Prisons are changing with the societies they are part of. The traditional ethnographic focus on prisons as nation-state institutions has left a regrettable knowledge gap. I will argue that as prison ethnographers, we need to re-conceptualise the boundaries of our discipline to keep up. I will, more precisely, explore the current development where prisons are being used by states to respond to the effects of globalisation and discuss how this might be explored ethnographically.

Why global prison ethnography?

As a research method, ethnography has always been connected to 'the small scale' and the local level of everyday interaction. For ethnography to stay ethnography, this cannot change. As ethnographers, we need to focus on the local, but we should – theoretically, empirically and analytically – acknowledge that the particular view from a specific prison today inevitably is influenced by social forces that transcend national borders. To be able to do this, we need to connect analyses on different levels; we need to employ an effective ethnographic zoom. The local level of everyday interaction will of course still be key, but we should strive to see the local as part of the national and even the global. I would like this chapter to be an invitation to broaden our theoretical and analytical horizons and study prison wings as part of the rest of the world. In the following, I will discuss examples of how this might be done, and the effects it may have.

How can macro-processes – like globalisation – be studied ethnographically? How can the study of everyday life grasp lofty and abstract processes that transcend national boundaries? According to Burawoy (1991b, 2000a, 2000b), we need to investigate how global changes are manifesting themselves on the local level. But we also have to go further; collecting anecdotal evidence of the global in the local is not enough. The challenge for ethnographers is to 'ground' globalisation and show how specific events are connected to more general processes; how the flow of people, goods, and discourses are making an impact on local, national, and global levels simultaneously. We need to approach the micro–macro link from the ground up, but also try to understand the reciprocal influence between levels. On the micro-level, a prison wing is a specific place where specific people are interacting. As ethnographers, we should study this process in all its specificity. But as prison researchers, we know that prisons are more than arenas for interaction. They are places where different people with very different experiences and expectations have to coexist and, if possible, make the best out of a difficult situation. Increasingly, such difficulties include language problems and cultural differences between prisoners from different parts of the world. They are also institutions where a form of state power is exercised. From justice, via incapacitation and deterrence, to rehabilitation and positive personal growth, prisons have specific abstract goals that need to be 'translated' into practice on the wings. Today, the logic of citizenship is increasingly being put to use on the prison wings. European states are introducing policies that separate between citizen prisoners and foreign prisoners. Finally, prisons today are influenced by forces and developments that transcend the nation-state. When the global is impacting on the national, the results can still be found on the local level. The global is, in short, always present in the local. Globalisation, oriented prison ethnographers need, then, to find ways to manage the difficult zoom between (1) the micro-level of everyday interaction, (2) what is in this context the meso-level of nation-state optics and projects and (3) the macro-level of international movements and global flows and forces. Analyses on all three levels will be important and necessary if we want to fill the knowledge gaps that globalisation processes have created.

The micro-level: Everyday interaction and frustration on the wings

Prison populations have grown in most European countries over the last few decades. Simultaneously, the prison populations have changed profile considerably in many jurisdictions. The number of foreign national prisoners in the UK system (England and Wales) trebled between the early 1990s and 2006, increasing from 3,446 (7.8 per cent of the total prison population) in 1993 to 10,289 (13 per cent) in April 2006 (Bhui, 2008). Still, the UK is one of the jurisdictions in Western Europe with the smallest proportion of foreign national inmates; the average proportion of foreign national prisoners in Western European prison systems is currently 26 per cent (Ugelvik, 2014a). In stark contrast, Eastern European countries normally have very small numbers of foreign national prisoners, ranging from Poland and Romania, both with less than 1 per cent of foreigners in their prison populations, to Slovenia, in this context the most 'Western' of the Eastern European countries with 10.7 per cent foreigner prisoners. The Slovenian prison system is thus close to the UK situation when it comes to the incarceration of foreigners. Western European correctional services, then, have to cope with increasing numbers of foreign nationals in their institutions. Eastern European governments, on the other hand, have to deal with growing numbers of their citizens incarcerated in foreign countries and foreign governments putting pressure on them to return these prisoners to serve out the rest of their sentences in their country of origin.

In most jurisdictions, 'foreign prisoners' will obviously constitute a very complex and heterogeneous group, whose only common distinguishing features are incarceration combined with a relationship of non-belonging vis-à-vis a specific nation-state. Some have lived in the country they are imprisoned in for years and are fully integrated members of the national community in every respect except the fact that their passport has the wrong colour. Others have recently arrived, possibly without valid travel documents, and their citizenship and identity may be under question. This complexity is a challenge for prison officers and prison ethnographers alike. In fact, it is often easy to forget that we are all foreigners once we, as tourists, move across a domestic border and venture into foreign territories (Hudson, 2008). The everyday difficulties associated with housing all these foreigners who might have different wants and needs than what one commonly finds amongst domestic prisoners, combined with the ever-growing task of transferring prisoners and deporting newly released former prisoners, will be a formidable challenge for European criminal justice systems in years to come.

This development plays itself out and has effects locally, on specific prison wings where specific people are incarcerated. Staff, for instance, are often frustrated at the lack of knowledge (and time to develop such knowledge) and available resources to work constructively with foreign nationals. Foreign national prisoners are frustrated at the general uncertainty, discrimination, and racism they often experience, as well as the many everyday mundane problems resulting from their status as foreigners. According to Banks (2011), foreign nationals in prison typically experience isolation and language barriers, they often have limited or no family contact, only a limited understanding of the prison and criminal justice system, and many experience problems linked to immigration-status, and anxiety related to the prospect of post-sentence immigration detention and deportation.

As a result, the everyday life on the wings is impacted in many ways. The most common and significant problem reported by foreign national prisoners, in general, is the lack of knowledge of the national language (Kalmthout et al., 2007; Bhui, 2009; Kaufman, 2012). In many cases, both verbal and written communication is severely hampered. This may again lead to feelings of social isolation, uncertainty and helplessness. A lack of understanding of the native language will colour every part of the everyday prison experience. Prisoners are frustrated at not being understood by staff, of having little to read in their own language and no television channels, and at missing out on basic provisions because they had not understood instructions.

Communication problems may result in more than just everyday frustrations, however. The decision to grant prisoners' early release is often based on a risk assessment where the previous criminal and prison records are important parts of the decision-making process. An average prisoner will have a comprehensive computer file full of information for prison officers to consider in decision-making processes. Most foreign national prisoners, however, lack such a history, and often look like walking and talking question marks from the perspective of the prison officers responsible for making, for them, important and life-changing decisions. Prison and court officials often decide to err on the side of caution. Foreign nationals are also very unlikely to be given home detention curfews and release on temporary licence, regardless of the fact that they often have very good prison records and may be regarded as 'model prisoners' (Kalmthout et al., 2007; Bhui, 2009). They are also often unable to attend work or school in prison, because of selection criteria that keep them out, even if they may have 'the same rights' as citizens on paper. Important decisions that will impact prisoners' lives in profound and direct ways, that are normally taken based on sound knowledge and detailed information gathered from different cooperating state agencies, will be based on 'best guesses' in the case of foreign nationals. This may, in turn, lead to feelings of being the victim of discrimination, favouritism and even racism. Staff may also be frustrated by a lack of information, of course, and – at least those staff members who are committed to a rehabilitation and reintegration ethos – by being expected to keep foreign national prisoners under inappropriately strict conditions, in some cases on immigration detention orders past their criminal sentence.

To a certain extent, the challenges foreign prisoners are facing are similar to challenges experienced by prisoners in general. Even though 'foreign nationals in prison' as argued above is obviously a very complex category with much internal variety, foreign nationals also have many common experiences and needs, usually linked with the primary problems of family contact, immigration difficulties and language that makes it meaningful to consider them as a distinct group with distinct needs (Bhui, 2009). Many foreigners are isolated, both literally, but also symbolically and culturally. Their foreigner status formally and informally creates specific challenges unique to them.

The meso-level: The prison and state power

When citizenships is an exclusive status that gives bearers rights that are coveted by many, and at the same time the borders are not hermetically sealed, the predictable result is that unwanted foreigners or irregular migrants will be present on any given state's territory. And when they are present, they will soon, to some extent and whether they want to or not, present themselves to the state as someone the state has to consider, as 'state projects' and objects of state knowledge production.

> From the perspective of social accounting, a Nation is similar to a factory. Whether it is people or things that are produced, the keeping of books is subject to the same rules and obligations: One must record exactly what *enters*, what *exits*, establish the *balance* of this two-way movement and *verify*, according to the *state* of the register and the products in the store (inventory and counting), the accuracy of the account of *movements* (what comes in and what goes out).
>
> (Bertillon, 1878, quoted in Neocleous, 2003)

Traditionally the prison has been intimately connected to the nation-state. Indeed, a 'state' as a unique entity has often been defined through its monopoly on the legitimate use of coercive force (Weber, 2004). On this meso-level of analysis, the main challenge of a global prison ethnography is to explore how the everyday life on prison wings is connected to wider state projects, logics and optics. The penal apparatus is a core organ of the state, expressive of its sovereignty and instrumental in imposing categories, upholding material and symbolic divisions, and moulding relations and behaviours. The prison, then, is an institution where a particular form of state power is put into practice. It is a place where a group of people are authorised by the state to exert legitimate power on the state's behalf over another group of people. In our current globalised world, however, these facts – once straightforward – are becoming increasingly complicated.

On the one hand, the state tries to keep unwanted migration to a minimum and keep unwanted migrants under control and, if possible, out of its territory. Internationally, we can see the emergence of an increasingly complex immobility regime of gated communities, ghettoes, detention centres and a range of related practices such as electronic tagging and quarantining that allows states to categorise and track individuals who are deemed to be dangerous or simply 'out of place', in order to bring about their bureaucratic control through spatial seclusion. Hayward recently described the phenomenon of 'kettling' as 'the (legally ambiguous) corralling of protesters into a demarcated, confined space for an indeterminate period without access to food, water or toilet facilities. In short, it is a mass detention in public space' (2012: 13). The prison may be seen as part of this development. Understood as part of a wider immobility regime, the prison is of course one of the mobility control technologies that has the longest pedigree. The transition from forms of punishment directed at the bodies of the punished to forms of punishment directed at their souls does not mean that the prison is not concerned with bodies (Foucault, 1977). As a state technology of movement control that can be studied on the level of everyday practice, the prison is part of a wider field of technologies of statecraft through the administration of bodies in time and space (Ugelvik, 2014b).

On the other hand, the state tries to gain information about, and control over, the unwanted migrants that nevertheless are present. Foreigners in European prisons increasingly find themselves in special wings or even entire institutions for foreign nationals only. In complex societies with considerable minority populations, however, it is not always easy to separate foreign national prisoners from ethnic minority prisoners. In the UK, determining citizenship, at least initially, depends on self-identification; prison officers simply ask where new arrivals were born. Kaufman (2012) shows that this strategy is not without flaws. She finds that the efforts to find foreigners in practice often depend on racialised assumptions about what constitute 'Britishness' and 'foreignness'. As a result, the experience of imprisonment is altered for members of visibly different minorities who have to be able to prove that they belong, and are entitled to stay, in the country after their release.

To be imprisoned is, to an extent, to be made visible, legible and, not least, countable for the state (Scott, 1998; Ugelvik, 2013). Yet, even states that routinely produce detailed statistical analyses of their prison populations often do not know fairly basic information about their foreign national population. Modern state power is based on the desire to name, order and control people (Scott, 1998; Smith, 2009). The dream of state power is the will to know, order and manage (Neocleous, 2003). As Weber and Bowling have stated, 'In a system designed to ascertain those who may move freely, and to immobilise and eject those who may not, matters of identity are central' (2008: 125). Prisoners are, because they are imprisoned, drawn into the orbit of the state, whether they want to be or not. The mechanisms by which the state administers the population, such as the passport, the driving licence, the identity card, as well as the more underhand means of information-gathering such as phone-tapping, bugging and letter-opening, are all important intelligence-gathering tools (Neocleous, 2003). Importantly, these state optics and techniques are constitutive; when the state divides the world into categories, the world changes. The efforts spent to gain knowledge and make people governable have very real consequences. By objectifying this group in a specific way as 'foreign national prisoners', subjects of a certain form of power are constructed. This process should be studied ethnographically.

When someone is imprisoned, however, they are not only made visible for the state and its agents. They are also made available for intervention. In rehabilitation and welfare-oriented prison systems, a prison is thought of as an arena for successful reintegration work. To various degrees across Europe, the prison is described (at least on paper) as a social technology tailored to the overarching goal of increased security on a societal level through the rehabilitation of individuals. Being a prisoner, then, means being put in a particular relationship with the state, as a temporarily excluded project of state rehabilitation agents. What about the foreign national prisoners? A welfare state will normally run on the notion of citizens' rights to welfare. In most countries, some rights and benefits are reserved for people who possess citizenship status. This means that individuals who lack citizenship status are denied the full enjoyment of social, political and civil rights (Bosniak, 2006). As Joppke has observed, 'Because rights are costly, they cannot be for everybody' (1999: 6). How does this play out on the prison wings?

According to the Council of Europe's European Prison Rules on the other hand (Council of Europe, 2006, Section I: 2), all prisoners, including those of foreign nationality, should retain all rights not necessarily taken away by the fact of imprisonment. It seems to be a recurring risk, however, throughout European jurisdictions, that foreign prisoners may not be able to exercise their rights effectively, including their fundamental human rights (Kalmthout et al., 2007). According to Section 33.3 of the same European Prison Rules, 'all prisoners should have the benefit of arrangements designed to assist them in returning to free society after release'. In practice, again, foreign nationals tend to be excluded. Such activities are often in short supply, and foreign nationals are not given priority (Kaufman, 2012). A reason is that foreign prisoners are expected to leave the country – either voluntarily or forcefully – upon release. Many of the rehabilitation measures are seen as directly connected to the welfare system outside and are therefore not deemed appropriate or relevant for prisoners who will not be part of that society anyway. The default assumption is that foreign prisoners will be deported. Such an assumption might aggravate a problematic tendency to exclude vulnerable groups from welfare benefits in society in general, as observed by Barker (2012) discussing the case of Sweden.

From the perspective of Western European prison officials, foreign nationals are increasingly being seen more like potential deportees than potentially rehabilitated members of society, as risks to be managed and expelled, rather than individuals with individual needs. Will the result be the creation of two separate but parallel systems, one for citizens, and another for non-citizens? The European states seem to be cultivating a form of double vision: more sophisticated systems of control and exclusion for some, and more open borders and a higher degree of mobility for others (Bosworth, 2008). What impact will this development have on the local level of specific prison wings? How will it change the prison as we know it?

In 1985, the German criminologist Jakobs wrote of the need to introduce a separate 'criminal law for enemies' or *feindstrafrecht* (Fekete and Webber, 2010). His work was based on the idea of a fundamental divide between citizens (subject to the rule of law) and non-citizens (not legal subjects and, therefore, non-persons in the eyes of the law). According to Fekete and Webber, Jacob's vision is being implemented, more or less informally, around Europe. Foreigners are being subject to harsher penalties than natives and migration status itself has become subject to criminal law and criminal penalties through a development towards what Stumpf (2006) has called 'crimmigration law', meaning a blurring of the difference between immigration control and crime control. As a result, the administration and even criminalisation of some forms of immigration have become key aspects of the governance of many late-modern democracies (Genova, 2002; Aas, 2007b; Dauvergne, 2008; Dal Lago, 2009; Aas, 2011). The presence of large numbers of unwanted immigrants clearly indicates for many the fact that nation states no longer are able to regulate completely the number of foreigners entering a country (Engbersen, 2009). Border control and immigration administration practices should, in such a context, be understood as the enactment of sovereignty, as a 'sovereignty gesture' (Bosworth, 2012) and thus as important tools in state crafting (Schinkel, 2009), and the prison is increasingly being made a part of it. Following Balibar, one could even argue that the nation-state borders now run through the prison wings of Europe:

> Sometimes noisily and sometimes sneakily, borders have *changed place*. Whereas traditionally, and in conformity with both their juridical definition and 'cartographical' representation as incorporated in national memory, they should be *at the edge of the territory*, marking the point where it ends, it seems that borders and the institutional practices corresponding to them have been transported *into the middle of political space*.
>
> (2004: 109)

In any case, whilst European welfare systems can (more or less) successfully limit the constituency that they serve, the same is not true for European penal systems. This predictably creates particular problems in penal systems that are heavily welfare oriented. The more welfare oriented a criminal justice system is in fact, the more sophisticated information it will depend on, and the more problematic foreign nationals may turn out to be. Prison ethnography should try to stay on top of the development; a global prison ethnography would make it possible to study state power in the age of globalisation.

The macro-level: The prison, international mobility and globalisation

We live in a time that seems obsessed with international movement. Studies within the broad globalisation paradigm seem often to emphasise flow and borderlessness as the norm to the extent that they risk making immobility and borders look as though they no longer exist. Discourses about mobility-as-liberty and mobility-as-progress are frequently accompanied by notions of movement as healthy and even moral. From this perspective, a sedentary life is a life that is not lived to its full potential. *Peregrinor, ergo sum* (I travel, therefore I am).

If we regard the freedom to be mobile as a resource, however, it is clear that the capacities for international mobility are unequally shared. Consider the opening up of the borders in the EU to enable the enactment of the EU mantra of free mobility. The so-called borderless Schengen area is undoubtedly dependant on the closing down of and detailed control over, mobility at the outer borders (Bosworth, 2008; Brown, 2010; Melossi, 2013). The historically speaking relatively recent introduction of passports is another example – we live in an age where nation-states are increasingly working together on the important task of identifying and regulating moving bodies and denying and refusing any illegitimate movement. What is different today is that human mobility needs to be framed in relation to the global political system of nation-states, who set and control the parameters of international movements and seem to prefer relatively immobilised subject populations (Salazar and Smart, 2011).

Globalisation thus paradoxically produces significant new forms of immobility and closure for some categories of persons alongside the increased mobility of others, what Shamir (2005) has called a 'mobility gap'. As a form of human experience, border-crossing mobility could still be said to be the exception rather than the norm. International borders are not singular and unitary, but are designed to encourage some kinds of mobility (business travellers, tourists, migrant workers, students) and discourage other (illegal migrants, refugees). Following Salazar and Smart (2011), one could say that mobility is the key difference and otherness producing machine of our age, involving significant inequalities of speed, risks, rights and status. Consider, for instance, the difference between EU citizens and so-called third-country nationals.

The prison is a case in point. In addition to being connected to a wider range of state institutions and forms of state power, the prison today is increasingly part of a regime of international mobility control. In the process, the very core of the prison as a state technology is changing. There are several results. One is an emerging risk-management system that has a global reach. In the context of the EU, border control cooperation, a common asylum-seeker registration and deportation system and shared responsibility for the return of illegal immigrants to their point of entry are all examples with high priority (Broeders, 2007; Balibar, 2010). The borders around the Schengen area are being fortified because old borders between member states have evaporated. According to the EU Internal Security Strategy (EUISS), the various forms of serious and organised international crimes are the most urgent challenges to EU security. Even petty crime such as burglaries and car thefts are often seen as local manifestations of border-crossing crime, with international criminal networks necessitating a concerted European action. The notion of 'international crime' is, of course, hardly a new invention (Knepper, 2011). More generally, the modern state has always had to cope with non-citizens behaving badly. It is the scale of the phenomenon that is new; from being a relatively marginal issue, the foreigners, asylum seekers and third-country nationals have become important objects of control and administration, not only for the nation-states, but also for the European Union as a whole (Aas, 2007a, 2007b; Weber and Bowling, 2008; Pakes, 2013). Seen from this perspective, the prison is part of a wider field of border control technologies, together with international police databases, agencies working with deportation of unwanted foreigners, immigration detention centres and so on. In short, the prison is becoming a vital part of an international migration control system encompassing practices of border control and immigration removal and deportation. So we are no longer faced with a prison as a technology of selective immobility; prisons are also aiding in the forced movement of people across borders in new ways.

These international and even global changes also manifest themselves locally, on specific prison wings. Many foreign national prisoners have a deportation order added to their prison sentence, either by the court as part of sentencing, or by the immigration authorities in a separate process. In practice, it will often be down to the prison locally to effectuate the deportation together with police and immigration officers. The prison is thus made part of the 'deportation machine' (Fekete, 2005). In short, the question of deportability (Genova, 2002) is taking centre stage when prison officers are making everyday decisions. Some jurisdictions, such as France and the UK (Wacquant, 1999; Banks, 2011; Bosworth, 2011; Kaufman, 2012), imprison people on an immigration order in regular prisons, alongside prisoners serving a penal sanction. When deportation procedures are put on hold, deportable former prisoners are just kept in prison in some cases, sometimes for months or even years on end. Over the last decade, the non-criminal prison population in the UK, for instance, has almost trebled, according to Banks (2011).

Immigration detention in prison often happens following a penal sanction, when the immigration authorities have not been able to effectuate deportation in time for the release date. Some prisoners have no valid travel documents. Some countries have no embassy in the country where their citizens are imprisoned, making the process of return – voluntary or coercive – difficult. Some embassies refuse to issue travel documents unless the imprisoned foreign citizen appears in person. The deportation process is adding difficult new tasks to prison officers' and prison managers' schedules that are already quite full in many places.

National governments are increasingly bound by decisions taken at the supranational level. Much has been written about the decline of the nation-state and its power in the era of globalisation (Bauman, 1998; Creveld, 1999; Beck, 2002). Some have argued that we are moving towards a form of supranational control-without-a-state, where the national governments are replaced, or, at least, where the power of the nation-state and national institutions are watered down (Mathiesen, 2008). The state is allegedly losing much of its importance and its traditional power base is eroding, so that we are living in a post-national world where the state has abdicated and surrendered its power to other agents and organisations on other levels. Others (Neocleous, 2003; Schinkel, 2009; Neumann and Sending, 2010) have claimed that the state is just thriving in new ways that are difficult to analyse from the point of view of traditional state theory. Many prison scholars would argue that traditional forms of state power such as the prison and the related state monopoly on legitimate violence seem to be doing just fine; the increasing prison populations around the world can attest to that. In addition to this, prisons seem to work well both symbolically and practically as a tool of border control (Bosworth, 2008). According to Melossi (2003), the 'deviant immigrant' has played a vital part in the intra-European construction of a shared European identity. It might also be that border-crossing and international crime is being used to 'govern through crime', as Findlay (2008) has argued with reference to Simon (2007). The prison is then, still, placed in the core of state sovereignty as one of the fundamental tools of statecraft.

Conclusion and suggestions for future research

The division of labour between academic disciplines has resulted in criminology being preoccupied with the national and with the specific nation-states. Crime and justice have traditionally been seen as phenomena on the national level. This chapter has argued that the notion that there is a distinction between the domestic and the international, or between 'inside' and 'outside', should be challenged (Loader and Percy, 2012). We are living in an era where the received inside–outside binary has been radically disturbed. This has consequences for prisons as well as for prison ethnographers. Prison ethnography can no longer strictly be interested in the nation-state.

As a technology of state mobility control, we need to understand that the prison is also part of a wider international regime of practices, policies and systems whereby states increasingly exert power through the administration of, and control over, mobility. I have argued for the need for prison ethnographies that see the prison as part of a wider international mobility control regime employed by states to exert and reproduce sovereignty in new ways. We need to reposition the prison conceptually as part of a wider field of interconnected technologies of immobility and forced mobility and understand that the ways into and out of the prison may lead from and to other forms of immobility and forced mobility. In short, we need to take Wacquant up on his challenge to study prisons 'both as a microcosm endowed with a distinctive material and symbolic tropism and as a template or vector of broader social forces, political nexus, and cultural processes that traverse its walls' (2002: 386). However, the boundaries of prison ethnography must be redrawn not only to include society outside the prison but also to encompass the world outside the limited social space, that is, the nation-state.

Much work is yet to be done. I will briefly suggest a few possibilities that seem to have promise for prison ethnographers:

- According to Burawoy (1991a), we are living in a world where space itself has become a more floating and immaterial concept. In many ways, prisons are exceptions to this. Prisons are built according to a very concrete and closed notion of space. For most prisoners, the world is no more open than it was a century or two ago. They are held behind concrete walls and often only have very limited access to a telephone and no Internet access. Even in a context of globalisation, the prison world is in most ways as closed as ever. Prison ethnographers should study how prisoners experience the enforced immobility and the lack of contact with the world and their loved ones that many take for granted today.
- Fraser (2013) recently pointed to a paradox that even though criminologists long have argued for more transnational approaches, criminological knowledge remains clustered in a relatively narrow range of geographical sites. Understandings of crime and criminology in the South also too often are defined through the lens of the North (Aas, 2012). This chapter has admittedly been lopsided in favour of (Western) European perspectives. Prison ethnographers need to examine the world beyond the Global North. This work is already being done by Bandyopadhyay (2006), Darke (2013), Jefferson (2014) and others. We should also develop this and try to study the movement between North and South and the interconnected international regime of power that prisons, as local ethnographic sites, are part of.

- Prisons are increasingly being used for immigration detention and other immigration control purposes. Prison-like immigration detention centres are opening in all European jurisdictions to make the control of deportable foreigners possible and facilitate their deportation. A significant part of the prison population in many jurisdictions have been imprisoned today for having committed immigration offences and not crimes in the classical sense. In Norway, the normal sentence for violating the re-entry ban (an immigration offence) was recently raised from 60 days to 1 year for the first offence, and 18 months for repeated offences. Compared with general sentencing levels for more traditional offences, re-entering the country after being deported is now considered to be a relatively serious crime. This blurring of the borders between immigration control and crime control should be studied ethnographically.
- Finally, we should study what happens when a tool that was custom made to do a specific job is being used for something else. What happens in more welfare-oriented prison systems when institutions are filled with prisoners who lack the right to basic welfare provisions according to national legislation? According to O'Nolan (2011), a range of measures is used by states to discourage 'less eligible' immigrants from coming and staying within their boundaries. A governmentality of immigration is being developed, an incentive structure taking as its fundamental mechanism the difference between citizens and non-citizens. Theodore (2011) has described this as the 'attrition strategy', the notion that measures can be set up to make unauthorised immigrants 'self-deport' and leave the country 'voluntarily'. This logic seems to be colonising the prisons of Europe to a certain degree. Prison ethnographers should study the effects of such a policy and how it plays out on the prison wings.

Acknowledgements

I would like to thank Anette B. Houge, Jennifer Sloan and Kjersti Lohne for insightful comments to earlier versions of this chapter. The writing of this chapter has been funded by the European Research Council (ERC starting grant ERC-2010-StG_2009120).

Note

1. http://www.un.org/apps/news/story.asp?NewsID=45819andCr=migrantsandCr1=#.U42VUHY4UdU (accessed 03 May 2014).

Further reading

Aas (2007b) is a broad introduction to the many issues related to crime and crime control in the era of globalisation. Stumpf (2006) was amongst the first to use the term 'crimmigration' to describe the progressive intertwining of immigration law and penal law. The notion of global prison ethnography is heavily inspired by Burawoy's writings on global ethnography (see e.g. Burawoy, 2000b). Bhui (2009), Bosworth (2012) and Kaufmann (2012) provide important analyses of how the developments described in this chapter play themselves out in specific institutions.

References

Aas, K. F. (2007a) 'Analysing a World in Motion: Global Flows Meet "Criminology of the Other" '. *Theoretical Criminology*, 11, 2, 283–303.

Aas, K. F. (2007b) *Globalisation and Crime* (London Thousand Oaks: Sage).

Aas, K. F. (2011) ' "Crimmigrant" Bodies and Bona Fide Travelers: Surveillance, Citizenship and Global Governance', *Theoretical Criminology,* 15, 3, 331–46.

Aas, K. F. (2012) ' "The Earth Is One but the World Is Not": Criminological Theory and Its Geopolitical Divisions', *Theoretical Criminology,* 16, 1, 5–20.

Balibar, É. (2004) *We, the People of Europe: Reflections on Transnational Citizenship* (Oxford: Princeton University Press).

Balibar, É. (2010) 'At the Borders of Citizenship: A Democracy in Translation?' *European Journal of Social Theory,* 13, 3, 315–22.

Bandyopadhyay, M. (2006) 'Competing Masculinities in a Prison', *Men and Masculinities,* 9, 2, 186–203.

Banks, J. (2011) 'Foreign National Prisoners in the UK: Explanations and Implications', *The Howard Journal of Criminal Justice,* 50, 2, 184–98.

Barker, V. (2012) 'Nordic Exceptionalism Revisited: Explaining the Paradox of a Janus-Faced Penal Regime', *Theoretical Criminology,* 17, 1, 5–25.

Bauman, Z. (1998) *Globalisation: The Human Consequences* (Cambridge: Polity Press).

Beck, U. (2002) 'The Terorrist Threat: World Risk Society Revisited', *Theory, Culture and Society,* 19, 4, 39–55.

Bhui, H. S. (2008) 'Foreign National Prisoners', in Y. Jewkes and J. Bennett (eds) *Dictionary of Prisons and Punishment* (Cullompton: Willan).

Bhui, H. S. (2009) 'Foreign National Prisoners: Issues and Debates', in H. S. Bhui (ed) *Race and Criminal Justice* (London: Sage).

Bosniak, L. (2006) *The Citizen and the Alien: Dilemmas of Contemporary Membership* (Princeton: Princeton University Press).

Bosworth, M. (2008) 'Border Control and the Limits of the Sovereign State', *Social and Legal Studies,* 17, 2, 199–215.

Bosworth, M. (2011) 'Deportation, Detention and Foreign-National Prisoners in England and Wales', *Citizenship Studies,* 15, 5, 583–95.

Bosworth, M. (2012) 'Subjectivity and Identity in Detention: Punishment and Society in a Global Age', *Theoretical Criminology,* 16, 2, 123–40.

Broeders, D. (2007) 'The New Digital Borders of Europe: EU Databases and the Surveillance of Irregular Migrants' *International Sociology* 22, 71–92.

Brown, W. (2010) *Walled States, Waning Sovereignty* (New York: Zone Books).

Burawoy, M. (1991a) *Ethnography Unbound: Power and Resistance in the Modern Metropolis* (Berkeley: University of California Press).

Burawoy, M. (1991b) 'The Extended Case Method', in M. Burawoy, A. Burton, A. A. Ferguson, K. J. Fox, J. Gamson, N. Gartrell, L. Hurst, C. Kurzman, L. Salzinger, J. Schiffman and S. Ui (eds) *Ethnography Unbound: Power and Resistance in the Modern Metropolis* (Berkeley: University of California Press).

Burawoy, M. (2000a) 'Grounding Globalisation', in M. Burawoy, A. Burton, A. A. Ferguson, K. J. Fox, J. Gamson, N. Gartrell, L. Hurst, C. Kurzman, L. Salzinger, J. Schiffman and S. Ui (eds) *Global Ethnography: Forces, Connections, and Imaginations in a Postmodern World* (Berkeley: University of California Press).

Burawoy, M. (2000b) 'Introduction: Reaching for the Global', in M. Burawoy, et al. (eds) *Global Ethnography: Forces, Connections and Imaginations in a Postmodern World* (Berkeley: University of California Press).

Council of Europe (2006) *Recommendation on the European Prison Rules* (Rec (2006) 2) (Strasbourg: Council of Europe, Committee of Ministers).

Creveld, M. V. (1999) *The Rise and Decline of the State* (Cambridge: Cambridge University Press).

Dal Lago, A. (2009) *Non-Persons: The Exclusion of Migrants in a Global Society* (Vimodrone: IPOC).

Darke, S. (2013) 'Inmate Governance in Brazilian Prisons', *Howard Journal of Criminal Justice,* 52, 3, 272–84.

Dauvergne, C. (2008) *Making People Illegal: What Globalisation Means for Migration and Law* (Cambridge: Cambridge University Press).

De Giorgi, A. (2010) 'Immigration Control, Post-Fordism, and Less Eligibility', *Punishment and Society,* 12, 2, 147–67.

Engbersen, G (2009) 'Irregular Migration, Criminality and the State', in W. Schinkel (ed) *Globalisation and the State* (Basingstoke: Palgrave).

Fekete, L. (2005) 'The Deportation Machine: Europe, Asylum and Human Rights', *Race & Class,* 47, 1, 64–91.

Fekete, L. and Webber, F. (2010) 'Foreign Nationals, Enemy Penology and the Criminal Justice System', *Race and Class,* 51, 4, 1–25.

Findlay, M. (2008) *Governing through Globalised Crime: Futures for International Criminal Justice* (Cullompton: Willan).

Foucault, M. (1977) *Discipline and Punish: The Birth of the Prison* (London, New York: Penguin).

Fraser, A. (2013) 'Ethnography at the Periphery: Redrawing the Borders of Criminology's World-Map', *Theoretical Criminology,* 17, 2, 251–60.

Genova, N. P. D. (2002) 'Migrant "Illegality" and Deportability in Everyday Life', *Annual Review of Anthropology,* 31, 419–47.

Hayward, K. J. (2012) 'Five Spaces of Cultural Criminology', *British Journal of Criminology,* 52 3, 441–62.

Hudson, B. (2008) 'Difference, Diversity and Criminology', *Theoretical Criminology,* 12, 3, 275–92.

Jefferson, A. (2014) 'Conceptualizing Confinement: Prisons and Poverty in Sierra Leone', *Criminology and Criminal Justice,* 14, 1, 44–60.

Joppke, C. (1999) *Immigration and the Nation-State* (Oxford: Oxford University Press).

Kalmthout, A. v., Meulen, F. H.-. d and Dünkel, F. (2007) 'Comparative Overview, Conclusions and Recommendations', in A. v. Kalmthout, F. H-v. d. Meulen and F. Dünkel (eds) *Foreigners in European Prisons* (Nijmegen: Wolf Legal Publishers).

Kaufman, E. (2012) 'Finding Foreigners: Race and the Politics of Memory in British Prisons', *Population, Space and Place,* 18, 6, 701–14.

Knepper, P. (2011) *International Crime in the 20th Century: The League of Nations Era, 1919–1939* (Basingstoke: Palgrave Macmillan).

Loader, I. and Percy, S. (2012) 'Bringing the "Outside" in and the "Inside" Out: Crossing the Criminolgy/IR Divide', *Global Crime,* 13, 4, 213–18.

Mathiesen, T. (2008) '*Lex Vigilatoria: Global Control without a State?*', in M. Deflem (ed) *Surveillance and Governance: Crime Control and Beyond* (Colombia: Emerald).

Melossi, D. (2003) '"In a Peaceful Life": Migration and the Crime of Modernity in Europe/Italy', *Punishment & Society,* 5, 4, 371–97.

Melossi, D. (2013) 'The Borders of the European Union and the Processes of Criminalization of Migrants', in S. Body-Gendrot, M. Hough, K. Kerezsi, R. Lévy and S. Snacken (eds) *The Routledge Handbook of European Criminology* (London: Routledge).

Neocleous, M. (2003) *Imagining the State* (Maidenhead: Open University Press).

Neumann, I. B. and Sending, O. J. (2010) *Governing the Global Polity: Practice, Mentality, Rationality* (Ann Arbor: University of Michigan Press).

O'Nolan, C. (2011) 'Penal Populations in a World in Motion: The Case of the Republic of Ireland', *The Howard Journal of Criminal Justice,* 50, 4, 371–91.

Pakes, F. J. (2013) *Globalisation and the Challenge to Criminology* (Abingdon: Routledge).

Salazar, N. B. and Smart, A. (2011) 'Introduction: Anthropological Takes on (Im)Mobility', *Identities: Global Studies in Culture and Power,* 18, 6, i–ix.

Schinkel, W. (2009) 'Dignitas Non Moritur? The State of the State in an Age of Social Hypochondria', in W. Schinkel (ed) *Globalisation and the State: Sociological Perspectives on the State of the State* (Basingstoke: Palgrave Macmillan).

Scott, J. C. (1998) *Seeing Like a State: How Certain Schemes to Improve the Human Condition Have Failed* (New Haven: Yale University Press).

Shamir, R. (2005) 'Without Borders? Notes on Globalisation as a Mobility Regime', *Sociological Theory,* 23, 2, 197–217.

Simon, J. (2007) *Governing through Crime: How the War on Crime Transformed American Democracy and Created a Culture of Fear* (Oxford: Oxford University Press).

Smith, M. J. (2009) *Power and the State* (Basingstoke: Palgrave).

Stumpf, J. (2006) 'The Crimmigration Crisis: Immigrants, Crime, and Sovereign Power', *American University Law Review,* 56, 2, 367–419.

Theodore, N. (2011) 'Policing Borders: Unauthorized Immigration and the Pernicious Politics of Attrition', *Social Justice,* 38, 1–2, 90–106.

Ugelvik, T. (2013) 'Seeing Like a Welfare State: Immigration Control, Statecraft, and a Prison with Double Vision', in M. Bosworth and K. F. Aas (eds) *Borders of Punishment* (Oxford: Oxford University Press).

Ugelvik, T. (2014a) 'The Incarceration of Foreigners in European Prisons', in S. Pickering and J. Ham (eds) *The Routledge Handbook on Crime and International Migration* (London: Routledge).

Ugelvik, T. (2014b) *Power and Resistance in Prison: Doing Time, Doing Freedom* (Basingstoke: Palgrave Macmillan).

Wacquant, L. J. D. (1999) '"Suitable Enemies" Foreigners and Immigrants in the Prisons of Europe', *Punishment and Society,* 1, 2, 215–22.

Wacquant, L. J. D. (2002) 'The Curious Eclipse of Prison Ethnography in the Age of Mass Incarceration', *Ethnography,* 3, 4, 371–97.

Weber, M. (2004) 'Politics as a Vocation', in D. Owen and T. B. Strong (eds) *The Vocation Lectures* (Cambridge: Hackett).

Weber, L. and Bowling, B. (2008) 'Valiant Beggars and Global Vagabonds: Select, Eject, Immobilize', *Theoretical Criminology,* 12, 3, 355–75.

22
Accessing and Witnessing Prison Practice in Uganda

Tomas Max Martin

Introduction

In prison research, gatekeepers are powerful bureaucrats, whose sanctioning makes ethnographic fieldwork within prison walls possible. In the Global South, such sanctioning is more likely than immediately expected as post-colonial prisons are forced open by the proliferation of human rights and as prison managers struggle to ride the tiger of reform towards alliance-building with donors, civil society and international researchers. However, accessing paramilitary state institutions, which testingly reach out to external partners, transcends the initial management of gatekeepers. This chapter briefly introduces the applauded human rights reform process in Uganda and makes a case for the particular kind of knowledge about everyday governance and change that ethnography – especially observations in the field – can offer to gauge prison reform effects. Based on fieldwork experiences from within Ugandan prisons, the chapter explores the register of roles that a researcher may take on to access the people who populate enclosed prison worlds. The management of researcher roles is not simply a question of balancing traction and control of the research process and taking advantage of the researcher's presence in the field. I suggest that Goffman's (1989) notion of the fieldworker as a 'witness' rather points to the fact that these shifting and contradictory roles propel the researcher into observing and participating in the duplicity intrinsic to prison life and to the ways bureaucracies in the Global South engage with development intervention, custodial imperatives and human rights. In conclusion, I argue that this witnessing entails a fusion of methods and ethics. The open and unstructured modus of ethnography may unpack the real local effects of strongly normative concepts like human rights reform, but it also impels and compels the prison researcher to be conscientious about reflexivity and ensuing claims of validity.

Uganda Prison Service: The best of the bad guys

The Ugandan prison population has increased by more than 30 per cent in the last ten years.[1] The justice system lacks resources and fails to deliver justice, gravely exacerbating the overcrowding and the extensive detention under harsh conditions that Ugandan prisoners endure. According to international human rights standards, prisons in Uganda are failed and fragile – with excessive numbers of remand prisoners, overcrowding, poor health services, run-down facilities, hard labour and violence (cf. Tibatemwa-Ekirikubinza, 1995; Oppenheimer, 2005; State, 2006; ICPS, 2008; UHRC, 2009; HRW, 2011), However, the Uganda Prisons Service (UPS) represents a human rights success and it is going through an applauded human rights-based reform process. Headlines such as 'A Taste of Hell in Uganda Prisons' (*The Independent*, 13 April 2010) or 'Prison Staff Accused of Hanging Inmate' (*Daily Monitor*, 9 March 2010) are not uncommon in Ugandan media, but violations of prisoners' rights are also seen to be decreasing according to independent human rights watchdogs. International donors are referring to UPS as 'the best of the bad guys', budgets are increasing, management is tightening and material progress is being felt across the institutional landscape. A new law and new policies of imprisonment explicitly draw upon human rights standards; staff are subject to human rights training; and managers, staff and prisoners alike qualify change in human rights terms, with institutional procedures – from budgeting to complaint handling – being formally framed by human rights.

A significant milestone in this reform process is the 'Open Door Policy' in 2000, which explicitly invited potentially critical external actors into the prison world in order to build new alliances and attract funds. The 'Open Door Policy' has been implemented in the context of significant financial improvements as the UPS budget has gone from approximately USD 7 million in 2002–03 to USD 17 million in 2008–09 (JLOS, 2010). A key element in this policy has been to integrate human rights in line with international standards and best practices, and UPS formally adopted the vision: 'To be a centre of excellence in providing human rights based correctional services in Africa'. This prompted the main watchdog, the Uganda Human Rights Commission (UHRC), to note 'significant' and 'remarkable improvements' in prisoners' rights and to refer to UPS as 'human rights responsive' and 'appreciative' and as making 'commendable steps to curb torture' in its 2009 annual report (UHRC, 2010).

Ugandan prisons seem to 'reform' according to internationally acclaimed standards. Yet, as much as a global discourse like human rights induces massive change, such discourses are concurrently cut to size and adjusted to the given locality by the people who appropriate the ideas and technologies on offer (Tsing, 2005; Li, 2007; Martin, 2014b). Thus, if we want to understand how a phenomenon like human rights reform in Ugandan prisons takes effect in local institutional landscapes, we need to see beyond the ' "ideal appropriation" (the kind dreamed of in project documents)' and explore the ' "real appropriation" (the kind actually undertaken by local people)' (Olivier de Sardan, 2011a: 25). Ethnographic analysis of everyday social practice is an obvious route to take in that respect, and it is consequently also the approach I have applied in my study of the embracing of human rights in Ugandan prisons (Martin, 2013, 2014a, 2014b).

Ethnography: A dip in the witches' brew of prison practice

Foucault argues that 'one must analyse institutions from the standpoint of power relations, rather than vice versa, and the fundamental point of anchorage of the relationships, even if they are embodied and crystallized in an institution, is to be found outside the institution' (Foucault, 1982: 791). It is probably right that the fundamental *point of anchorage* for the power relations that underpin the appropriation of human rights is to be found outside Ugandan prisons. Yet, the fundamental *point of contact* with the real lives of real people is to be found inside Ugandan prisons. This point of contact is the social interface where values, interests, knowledge and power intersect in face-to-face encounters between local social actors (Long, 1992: 214). This interface is the locus of agency, and it is here that the real appropriation of human rights and their effect on the 'real governance' of Ugandan prisons can be studied ethnographically (Olivier de Sardan, 2011b: 25).

It is in this interface, where a global discourse like human rights is 'crystallised' and 'embodied' by local social actors (to paraphrase Foucault above), where everyday governance can be subject to empirical scrutiny. Such scrutiny concerns what Foucault called the ' "real life" in the prisons' – the 'witches' brew' of everyday prison practice – a level of study which his grand genealogical investigation of the disciplinary technologies of power only inferred and acknowledged, but did not take up directly (Foucault, 1991: 81). I have taken this cue on the 'witches' brew' from Li (2007). It is appealing to discover that the author of *Discipline and Punish* (albeit offhandedly) offered such an evocative term for prison ethnography, but a more general point, which Li makes, is that ethnography takes the researcher 'beyond the plan, the map, and the administrative apparatus, into conjunctures where attempts to achieve "the right disposition of things" encounter – and produce – a witches' brew of processes, practices, and struggles that exceed their scope' (Li, 2007: 28). It is not the only route to take, but as pointed out by Li, ethnographic analysis offers a research strategy that can engage and make sense of the complexity of prison practice.

Applying ethnographic methods to prison studies basically implies the use of observation and open-ended interviewing in the field as the primary means of data collection. Fieldwork is a tenet of ethnography, whereby the researcher engages with the people under study, shares their everyday lives as far as possible and converses with them in order to generate data for a detailed description (an ethnography) of the social life of a particular place or institution (Hirsch and Gellner, 2001: 2).[2] Malinowski gave the classic definition of fieldwork as the means to 'get the native's point of view', and with that objective in mind, Malinowski laid out the fieldworker's task 'of drawing up all the rules and regularities of tribal life; all that is permanent and fixed; of giving an anatomy of their culture, of depicting the constitution of their society' (Malinowski, 1922: 11). Malinowski's theoretical focus on regularity has since become overrun by a social scientific interest in change and flux.[3] As Moore puts it: 'Malinowski the theorist has been cast off, but Malinowski the ethnographer lives on' (Moore, 1994: 374) and fieldwork has survived as an 'archetype for normal anthropological practice' (Gupta and Ferguson, 1997: 11).

Observations

Anthropologist Sally Falk Moore makes a candid statement about fieldwork in one of her classic texts on legal pluralism (Moore, 1973). Moore famously compares the implementation of land reform in Tanzania with the pragmatic negotiation of labour relations in the New York garment industry to illustrate the extent to which law effects social change. She bases her analysis of the land reform on her extensive fieldwork in the highlands of Kilimanjaro, but the data material about the New York garment industry that she uses 'comes from having spoken with some people involved in it and reading some books' (Moore, 1973: 723). This is a provocative way to describe the fundamentals of most qualitative research that you can, of course, only get away with if you have that particular author's calibre. However, Moore explicitly posits this particular knowledge of the garment industry against her more profound fieldwork-based knowledge from Tanzania, where she has been and lived and observed everyday practices. Thus, in the simple terms fieldwork-based knowledge adds a powerful ingredient to the (mere) 'speaking' with people and 'reading' about a certain social phenomenon. It adds observation.

Fieldwork in the ethnographic variant used here is more or less interchangeable with participant observation in the sense that observation refers to a composite engagement with people and places of the field through informal talks, observing, spectating, eavesdropping, collective discussing, moving and sitting, hanging out, tagging along and participating in activities where possible. In that sense, observation is visceral and corporal. Goffman defines 'observation' as a technique of:

> subjecting yourself, your own body and your own personality, and your own social situation, to the set of contingencies that play upon a set of individuals... So that you are close to them while they are responding to

> what life does to them... and with your 'tuned-up' body and with the ecological right to be close to them (which you have obtained by one sneaky means or another), you are in a position to note their gestural, visual, bodily response to what's going on around them and you're empathetic enough – because you've been taking the same crap they've been taking – to sense what it is that they're responding to. To me, that's the core of observation.
>
> (Goffman, 1989: 126)

Observation is about learning what happens by being physically and socially close. It is less about picking people's brains. Such observations typically carry most of the data that my analyses of governance and transition in Ugandan prisons are based on and the instances of their generation are diverse. I have made something out of observing small things such as cobwebs on certain doors, how prison officers sat on chairs, how rich and powerful prisoners folded their socks and how heads turned, instantly alert, as an army vehicle was heard in the distance. I have also been in a position to observe staff, prisoners, relatives and court officials move in a veiled and elaborate choreography of corruption as just another sleepy day in court passed by and to sense the rush and *esprit de corps* as the top brass of UPS entered a scene. These catalogues of ad hoc observations also include hours and hours of informal talk in and around all these mundane incidents and spectacular events.

It goes without saying that ethnographic work also entails a refined and crucial practice of interviewing (Hammersley and Atkinson, 2007) – especially the ethnographic skills of letting improvisation and the internal dynamics of a conversation (rather than guided order and replicability) drive an interview in order to pay in-depth attention to the interests and competences of the person interviewed (Olivier de Sardan, 2008: 17). Yet, in my research efforts to trace the tacit road rules of prison governance, the practical norms, which are implicit, informal and play out in everyday prison practices, I have found that it is highly fruitful to prioritise observations as a key method. And fieldwork observations are pregnant with meaning from the very start, when the researcher begins to negotiate access to the field.

Access and roles

Prisons are restrained and restraining sites that set significant boundaries for research – from external and manifest boundaries of walls and procedures to the boundaries of confidentiality and integrity imposed on the self. Accessing prisons is very much a question of negotiating these boundaries, again and again (Waldram, 2009: 4; Bandyopadhyay, 2010: 35). In this process the researcher takes, and is offered, different roles. These roles, more often than not, contest the researcher's integrity by being compromised by different shades of complicity with the pain and suffering that characterise prison life and by different shades of duplicity towards informants, authorities or stated ideals.

Access

Prisons are distinctly securitised bureaucracies and it goes without saying that formalised authorisation is important for access. From the outset, I approached UPS with due consideration to put up a formal, concise presentation of myself, my objectives, my institutional affiliations and credentials and research clearances,[4] and I was all the time conscious of not prompting the UPS management to turn my requests down. This negotiation of access with UPS management was amicable, but it was also a significant point of departure for what Bandyopadhyay refers to as a prison researcher's embarkation 'on a very conscious construction of the "self" in fieldwork' (Bandyopadhyay, 2010: 40). Like Bandyopadhyay, I was also consciously presenting 'a diminutive and restrained self' (2010: 53). I put on a patient and sometimes even docile and naïve air and mimicked modes of interaction around me to signal my willingness to subject to rules, to surveillance, to security and to hierarchical power. I was concurrently striving to hold onto a researcher's identity as independent and empowered by my officially approved quest for knowledge in order not to compromise research integrity or to seem too duplicitous to them (and myself). I did so under the assumption that I had to manage with an inherent suspicion towards research on the part of the prison management. This assumption was, to a great extent, formed by my experiences of gaining access to an Indian prison in the course of my first ethnographic fieldwork in 1999, which took more than two months and included very intense negotiations and compromises on my part (Martin, 2009). In the Ugandan case, my assumptions about access difficulties were wrong. The head of UPS, the Commissioner General of Prisons, matter-of-factly authorised my study. It needs to be remembered that he was in a position to withdraw this permission immediately and that there were many more authorisations yet to be given, but my interest was welcomed, and accessing Ugandan prisons proved to be more 'profane' than expected (Hammersley and Atkinson, 2007: 42). This was a telling indication of the management's confidence in UPS's 'Open Door Policy' and their interest in coming across as a transparent institution. 'We have nothing to hide', senior officers repeatedly told me.

Permission in hand, I entered UPS to meet my liaison officer, a heavy-set uniformed man, who got up from his desk and embraced me. It was an unexpectedly warm welcome. Liebling writes enthusiastically about the prisons that she has studied as being 'open to outsiders', 'positively welcoming', and she concludes that her team of researchers experienced 'far more cooperation than we deserved' (Liebling, 1999: 155). In apparent contrast, Jacobs writes: 'the prison participant observer enters a highly unstable social setting abounding with rumour, suspicion, factionalism, and open conflict. He must daily negotiate the legitimacy, content, and boundaries of this role with a society which is hostile to his presence' (Jacobs, 1977: 216).

Both these quotes correspond with my experiences of qualitative research in prisons. I also received extensive cooperation on all levels and I believe that prison institutions in general tend to invite committed and constructive attention. It is a relatively rare commodity for prison actors to be given an opportunity to explain themselves and an interested researcher is not automatically shut out. That said, I also experienced strong hostility to my presence, which corresponds with Jacobs' quote above. I did not feel personally threatened at any time during fieldwork, but there was an ever-present generalised, institutional hostility towards my inherently questioning presence and my efforts to interrogate the practising of rules and roles of prison life. Prisons are described in the literature as significantly opaque: 'Prisons are pervaded by an interpersonal opacity that thwarts even those who govern, manage and live in them' (Rhodes, 2001: 76). Trying to see through this opacity by crossing boundaries is indeed challenging and spurs hostility and suspicion, but as indicated by Rhodes it also privileges the researcher to participate in a subset of prison life that staff and prisoners share. Anxiety, uncertainty and risk are part of a reflexive understanding of the field. As Rhodes has it (with reference to Waldram (Waldram, 1998)): 'Although the inaccessibility and opacity of the prison make ethnography difficult, they do not necessarily preclude it... restraints imposed on research by prison staff may be similarly folded into the process through which the ethnographer comes to appreciate larger dynamics of restraint governing these institutions' (Rhodes, 2001: 77). Negotiating boundaries in an opaque environment is a methodological condition of prison ethnography, which often also graduates into an analytical insight.

UPS staff were generally very forthcoming and positively surprised by my interest in them. My willingness to report with them on morning parade, sit with them in the sun, walk with them to court and generally hear them out was unusual and most staff quickly warmed up to this rare opportunity to express their grievances. However, they did so in constant consideration of what might be used against them. 'Will I be safe?' one asked directly, when I encouraged him to give an interview, and I am sure most of his colleagues shared this concern. Senior officers routinely made an effort to present me to their staff on parade and assert that they could talk to me: 'Don't fear! He is one of us', they would say. My presence was thereby explicitly sanctioned, but I was also enrolled in the management's sphere of control. The 'us' I was part of was somewhat ambiguous. Staff were free to talk to me, but how freely?

The pervasiveness of this suspicion hit me most vividly in one of the final interviews I did in February 2012. I had known a certain junior officer over a three-year period. He had been directly involved in a number of intense situations that he had commented on with great richness. I had followed him at work and we had talked and I had asked him for an interview, but he had insistently declined. When I came back a year later, he invited me for an evening walk and we ended in the backyard of a restaurant out of sight. I took out my notebook, but he asked me to put it away, since this was 'just talking'. The same evening, I eagerly wrote down this 'talk' on my computer and decided to use the material. As I got back the next time, I told him about my decision and he was not surprised. 'Ah, I knew you had it in your head', he said unconcernedly. 'You swallow this, but don't vomit it out'. I read from a draft paper, where I had quoted him under another name and he just said that I had got it right and continued talking. This time I took notes. However, my mobile phone suddenly beeped because I had received a text message and he gave a start: 'Martin! Are you recording our conversation? Are we already on the internet?!' I hurriedly turned off the phone and we carried on.

It still baffles me that he even considered that I was stealthily broadcasting our conversation online as we sat on broken plastic chairs under a darkening open sky in a remote rural setting talking about the intricacies of corruption and power play between senior and junior officers. It was a telling illustration of the extent to which the field and the kind of practice I was undertaking were pervaded by suspicion, secrecy and insecurity. It was a keen reminder of the responsibility I was under. In my efforts to find out why my informants and their colleagues felt so vulnerable, I had to struggle constantly not to enhance this vulnerability. One small tactic was to avoid displaying any friendship and intimacy with key informants, although relationships deepened, but to be equally carefree with everybody and to maintain this attitude in public. Thus the protective management of vulnerability is not just a matter of appropriate reservations of informed consent, anonymity, etc., but an ever-present and primary factor of the collection of data, of analysing and of writing it all up.

In sum, the prison setting characteristically continues to expose the researcher to a constant fear of losing access (Bandyopadhyay, 2010: 39). The researcher is likely to constantly sense a certain tension that the rules and regulations, which have bent to facilitate access, are always also in a complementary position of flicking back with equal force. In that sense, access is always conditioned, temporal and monitored. Accessing UPS was of course to a great extent routinised as I returned again and again. However, as I negotiated boundary after boundary and gained deeper access into the institutional landscape, I had the concurrent impression that loss of access was always imminent and that the damage would be increasingly irreparable. This 'veiled threat of loss of physical accessibility' (Bandyopadhyay, 2010: 43) also disciplined me and I was always cautious about the politics of requesting access and was never overtly insistent if a request to see a place, follow a procedure or approach a topic was rejected. I just asked again later, or waited.

Roles

As noted by Jefferson, it is not just the keepers of the gate who matter, but also how you approach the gate (Jefferson, 2004: 41). In order to gain and maintain access, a researcher is likely to get mixed up in shifting and conflicting roles. The ethnographic literature is full of typologies of such roles. Jefferson found himself accorded identities ranging from spy and human rights advocate to 'our white man' (Jefferson, 2004: 57). Jacobs sought to vacillate between student, lawyer and sociologist roles with different strings attached to each (Jacobs, 1977: 221–22). I struggled formally to establish myself as a 'researcher', stressing my independence and my interest in learning and understanding as opposed to assessing. This was an uphill task. From what I was subsequently told, most staff and prisoners thought of me as either a Christian missionary, who come in vast numbers to Uganda (and also to the prisons), or an NGO representative, when they first saw me. Those whom I spoke to slowly got a more complex picture, and some then got the impression that I was, in fact, a prison professional. The staff and prisoners I came to know a bit better slowly began to talk to, and about, me as a researcher.

This lack of clarity about my person was, to a great extent, counterweighed by my very indisputable identity as white person (called a *musungu* in local languages). I was persistently referred to as a 'big man', a man of power and wealth, who represented capital in terms of bringing a good digital camera from Europe, paying children's school fees, having the ear of top managers and so on. This capital also caused some caution as I could land staff in problems if I got hurt or witnessed and narrated embarrassing information. I tried to downplay this inequality socially by being sincere and humble, and taking opportunities to present myself as a father, a husband, a working man, who had grown up in the countryside – all in an effort to develop dimensions of my relations with informants that were familiar and close – but this powerfulness was also something that I exploited.

As a white man I was on the one hand able to command some attention, but I was at the same time aloof from prison life and thus not strongly positioned. Whiteness was an indicator of ignorance about local knowledge and of a flighty relationship with Uganda. A Ugandan research colleague, who was mildly surprised by my ability to access UPS, argued that 'an outsider could do a study on prison like no Ugandan', as he put it. UPS, he argued, would be less guarded and believe that I just did my research and left. This relative power and weak positioning enabled me to transverse formal hierarchies and relate to juniors and seniors and prisoners alike. This entailed a need to perform confidentiality very explicitly and to stress that I did not carry information across these hierarchies. I am certain that many informants doubted this at first. A number of staff noted that they had worried that things which I had seen or heard would come to superiors' ears and they subsequently commended that this had not been the case.

Witnessing

According to Goffman, a central role for a fieldworker is that of witness: 'You're artificially forcing yourself to be tuned into something that you then pick up as a witness – not as an interviewer, not as a listener, but as a witness to how they react to what gets done to and around them' (Goffman, 1989: 126). A witness role can be highly challenging in situations of suffering. In one instance I decided to refrain from intervening in a situation of explicit violence in order to witness it. I was later compelled to express my fear and disapproval to my key informant, who had taken part in the beating of a prisoner, but it was more of a personal, emotional outburst. In situ, I decided that my brief was to witness. However, this also obliges me to *bear witness*, to produce and impart knowledge, ideally, with an ensuing potential to ameliorate suffering more broadly or more systematically.

The role of witnessing is also a pertinent reminder to resist the pull towards a detective role. As noted by Malkki, the role of 'the police detective discovering what is "hidden", assembling "evidence" to make a strong "case", relentlessly probing for more information' is not a fruitful fieldwork strategy (Malkki, 1995: 51). The researcher gets caught up in her or his own quest to extract truth. The opacity of prison life, the shared uncertainty, the empirical manifestation of cases and investigations and the presence of crime were highly seductive for this kind of clue searching. I was at several instances almost obsessed with different whodunit projects, which in hindsight was unproductive. Data collected became contrived by investigation and diverted attention from what people had to say. Moreover, the information was too specific to anonymise.

One example was my witnessing of a spectacular escape that resulted in the conviction and imprisonment of a junior prison officer. The escape happened a few metres from where I was sitting and I had followed the involved officers over some time. I subsequently used a lot of energy in talks and interviews to figure out whether the officer was guilty. In the end, the point I learned from the event was that this was not so important. Staff were undecided about or even not very interested in whether he had done it or not. The escape had been 'tricky' and blame was likely to land somewhere. Staff generally found that the officer was convicted due to his comportment in court, his lack of discipline, his history, his bad luck and most importantly that he had said too much. I noticed this layer in the narratives quite late because I had been preoccupied with the issue of guilt and facts.

The investigative drive was also a quest for certainty on a personal level. I was really close to this particular event and as things went from bad to worse, I started to worry that I could become personally involved – maybe even framed as a co-conspirator of some sort. The anxiety was far-fetched, but nevertheless duly felt. I have come to interpret this anxiety as a resonance with a wider presence of insecurity, vulnerability and ambiguity of knowledge in the field. Staff and prisoners managed this insecurity daily, not knowing what might, in fact, hit them the following day. In that sense, the closeness of fieldwork had spilled over into a personal anxiety that had attuned my research to notice something important. Whereas I struggled to control my anxiety by establishing certainty about the escape, my informants rather emphasised issues of relations and security to explain what had happened and why things had gone wrong. My own sense of insecurity gave perspective to one of the most persistently voiced and signatory traits of staff life: *to keep quiet.*

According to Olivier de Sardan, the management of researcher roles, the 'staging', should not be glorified or denied. Roles taken and offered should, rather, be consciously utilised to either minimise or take advantage of the researcher's presence in the field (Olivier de Sardan, 2008: 47). I appreciate this point, but I find that roles of prison ethnography, at least, are in many ways imposed upon the researcher and it makes good sense to learn from them in a conscientious way, rather than merely struggle to instrumentalise them.

Complicity, ethics and reflexivity

The apprentice is a traditional role to play on for a fieldworker, who wants to approach a situation of participation and to shorten distances between the self and others in the field (Bundgaard, 2003). Apprenticeship – even as an openly artificial form of taking up minuscule tasks – is a fruitful way to find a place to settle and work from, when conducting fieldwork in a bureaucracy, where everybody else is explicitly tasked and mandated (Martin, 2006: 33). In a violent space characterised by suffering and vulnerability, this is obviously a highly contentious route. It was impossible for me to enrol as a member of prison staff or a prisoner, but a few moments of quasi-apprenticeship nevertheless emerged. I was invited to join a posse of prison staff who went to recapture an escapee. A few days later, I was asked if I might want to drive them, which I declined as I would not be directly complicit in the possible beating and killing in the course of the recapture. Apart from such blatant and fairly easy choices, apprenticeship also opens up a slippery slope of identification and emotional attachment with actors in the field. Rhodes, for example, notes the ethical problems of Fleisher's work (Fleisher, 1989), who enrolled as correctional officer as part of his fieldwork strategy and ended up siding with his fellow guards' defence of maximum-security imprisonment as a commendable means to create a peaceful prison environment (Rhodes, 2001: 73).

However, complicity can also be much more implicit and ambiguous. Many staff directly pointed out that my research was a living example of UPS's 'Open Door Policy'. My research was, in itself, a consolidation of UPS's image as an increasingly human rights observant, well-governed institution that is eligible for funding and readily able to expand its capacity to confine men and women. Although a prison researcher might not sympathise with violence or provide its transport, s/he can easily end up considering to what extent s/he is being put to the service of grander reproductions of power and knowledge that ultimately enlarges prison pain. As put by the veteran prison scholar and activist Angela Davis, a prison researcher is potentially always facing the complex challenge to work to 'create more humane habitable environments for people in prison without bolstering the permanence of the prison system' (Davis in Jones, 2006: 82).

Yet, inadvertent involvement can also be more benign. One example from my fieldwork includes a situation where I joined prisoners and staff on a long hike to court. Very few staff and prisoners mistook me for a prisoner during fieldwork. There are very few European prisoners in Uganda and I must have looked far too confident at close range. However, on this particular hike, as I walked with the handcuffed prisoners in civilian clothes, a great deal of the people who we passed were dumbfounded. *'Ah! – Do white people also steal?'* staff laughingly told me one had cried in the vernacular language. Another had shaken his head and commented that the hand of the law had become so long that it even caught white people. Later in the day the extent to which my mere presence gave perspective to crime and punishment turned much more concrete. Both staff and prisoners agreed that the court officials had been uncomfortably surprised by my presence as a potential source of embarrassment and external assessment. Consequently, an unusual number of cases were dismissed that day and others were given bail and community service without much ado (to the voiced irritation of the resident prosecutor). The prisoners were jubilant and I was subsequently begged by others to please go to court when their cases were due – even a year later.

When studying wielders of state power, identification with the people studied and defence of their interests is not self-evident (Pels, 1999: 112). Yet, the closeness of fieldwork entails a commitment to take seriously what one is told and to try to be on the same wavelength as the people in the field (Olivier de Sardan, 2008: 20). This quest to understand and to stay close is challenged by the presence of humiliation, exploitation and physical violence, which immediately call for distancing. I did not manage to handle that without some level of duplicity. On one occasion, for instance, I was following a disciplinary case that a key informant of mine had investigated and forwarded to a senior officer.

I had the impression that he expected that the prisoner would be or had been beaten, since it involved a fight and since fighting prisoners often get a corresponding physical punishment. As we were walking towards the office where the adjudication was about to take place, he wanted to know if prisoners were beaten in my country – as if to get a sense of where I stood if things got rough. I said no but I found myself quickly adding that prisoners were often strapped and isolated in Denmark. I was not a stranger to violence against prisoners, I signalled, in order not to scare him off and think twice about letting me tag along. I negotiated a boundary this way, I thought, but I was also complicit in rendering prison pain mundane (for a similar point, see Hammersley and Atkinson, 2007: 211).

Identity doubling, impression management and the wearing of masks are part of any fieldwork, ranging from forced conversion, conscious betrayal to instinctive survival (Pels, 1999: 101). Managing these roles is an inherently ethical task and the intricacies and nuances of doing it right is typically built up during fieldwork, but this management ability can also be worn down. One example was my initial effort to decline politely staff's persistent offers to have my car washed by the prisoners. I did not want to be complicit in the taken-for-granted exploitation of prisoner labour. After some time I gave up and found solace in getting a legitimate opportunity personally to assist the prisoners, who washed my car with some sugar and soap. As I drove out from my last prison visit at the conclusion of the final spell of fieldwork, I found myself mildly irritated that I, for a certain reason, left with an unwashed car.

As noted by Rhodes, prison ethnography is significantly self-conscious (Rhodes, 2001: 72). This self-consciousness is potentially also a consciousness of selves and of others. This leads Liebling to argue that qualitative enquiry into prison life is more susceptible to pain (Liebling, 1999: 165). Prisons are places of explicit human suffering. 'To be sure', Jacobs states, 'prison is neither a pleasant place to live, to work or to carry out fieldwork' (Jacobs, 1977: 228). During my fieldwork in UPS, I listened to the stories of torture survivors. I was dumbstruck when put in front of more than a hundred squatting men in a small dilapidated ward and one said: 'Just give us a comforting word, Mr Tomas.' I was (and still am) embarrassed that I refused to give a prisoner UGX 800 (less than USD 1) for the syphilis medicine that he asked for, because other prisoners started shouting: 'You give one, you give us all.'

In order to deal with such ethical problems, I have followed the code of ethics of the American Anthropological Association (AAA, 1998), but such codes offer little guidance on how actually to respond to situations like the ones above. I have therefore come to agree with Pels that '[w]hile ethical standards aspire to transcendence, they can only be judged contingently, in political context' (Pels, 1999: 103). Ethical research is an ongoing responsibility to respond to those studied (Meskell and Pels, 2005: 3). It is about negotiation, rather than adjudication, about intersubjectivity and concrete practices of responsible interaction. Ethical research is therefore more about methods than about following transcendent codes and guidelines from an authoritative 'constitutional realm' (Meskell and Pels, 2005: 10). Meskell and Pels call for an embedded ethics, which fuses ethics with methods: 'This would include using our methodology to anticipate where, when, and how we are bound to encounter relations of power that help or frustrate our goals, the goals of the people we move among, and the methods that help us or our potential collaborators to achieve those goals' (2005: 22). Fieldworking enables a methodological choice to witness and an ensuing obligation to bear witness in a reflexive and conscientious way.

Flyvbjerg flatly states that '[l]ike other good craftsmen, all the researchers can do is use their experience and intuition to assess whether they believe a given case is interesting... and whether they can provide collectively acceptable reasons' (Flyvbjerg, 2002: 80–1). Such 'collective acceptability' can be directly derived from the feedback from the field in concerted efforts to get reactions from informants and actors in context (Flyvbjerg, 2002: 81). Acceptability, of course, also comes from choice and use of theory but, not the least, from explicating the research instruments. As bluntly put by Kapferer, 'the experiencing, body and reflective consciousness of the anthropologist becomes the crucial scientific instrument' (Kapferer, 2007: 82). Reflexivity offers a positioning of this instrument. A thorough description of the concrete as well as the analytical steps taking in the research process invites the reader not just to accept, but also to question, the data. Sanjek refers to this methodological move as showing 'the ethnographer's path' (Sanjek, 1990). Sanjek importantly stresses that 'subjects of ethnography are more interesting than the authors', but he also argues that writing the researcher into the narrative is not just whimsical self-absorption (Sanjek, 1990: 413); it is an opening up of the text to further collective acceptability. What did you do and why? Who did you talk to and learn from? What did you bring back to document it? This kind of reflexivity is a claim to validity (Sanjek, 1990: 394–5) and a way to explicate what Olivier de Sardan calls ' "the anthropological pact", which confirms in the reader the idea that the anthropologist did not invent the discourse he relates nor dream up the description he proposes' (Olivier de Sardan, 2008: 50).

In keeping with Meskell's and Pels' points above about the fusion between methods and ethics, I suggest that explicating the ethnographer's path is not only a claim for validity but also a claim for a contingent ethics. Restitution is not only a means of verification, but an ethical feedback to the field. And writing up is a constant balancing of bearing witness and not enhancing vulnerabilities or the permanency of prison pain by 'steering between abstract and fetishized representation' (Rhodes, 2001: 77).

Conclusion

In sum, I have argued that an ethnographic approach enables a study of everyday practice and an in-depth analysis of local events that may enhance our understanding of the 'real' appropriation of policy and reform in prison settings. The research design is not filtered through a hypothesis or a normative perspective, but actively seeks an open, or 'unstructured' (Rhodes, 2001: 77), modus in order to base the analysis on an account of the local social actors' view and situations (Olivier de Sardan, 2008: 3). This modus enables the researcher to scoop up some scrambled evidence about everyday life from the 'witches' brew' of prison practice. Of the many roles that the researcher takes on in this process (not least to negotiate access), I suggest that Goffman's description of the role of the witness is most compelling. Returning to Goffman's quote above (Goffman, 1989: 126), the prison ethnographer moves in to exercise an 'ecological right to be close', often including 'sneaky means' of complicity and duplicity that one needs to learn from and handle with deep ethical concern. This is very much a bodily process, whereby the ethnographer, by design or default, responds 'to what's going on' and become 'empathic enough' by 'taking the same crap' as the people around her or him to sense what it is these people are responding to. This form of witnessing is a particularly pertinent way to unpack the real, local effects of such a strongly normative and universally 'self-explanatory' concept as human rights and to discern the local, unwritten, tacit road rules of practical norms that staff and prisoners draw so extensively on to govern penal bureaucracies in practice.

Acknowledgements

I would like to thank the Uganda prison officers, who made time and took interest in talking to me about their work and allowed me to tag along behind them, when they were on duty. I would also like to express my thanks to the editors Jennifer Sloan, Deborah Drake and Rod Earle for their comments and encouragements. Also a special thanks to my family, who faithfully endure my many absences.

Notes

1. World Prison Brief from the International Centre for Prison Studies. Available at: http://www.kcl.ac.uk/schools/law/research/icps (accessed 13 August 2014).
2. The fieldwork from which I draw the main points of this chapter ran over a three-year period from an initial period from April to August 2009, a second in March 2010 and a final period from January to February 2012.
3. Since the publication of Marcus' influential article (1995), 'multi-sitedness' has been the watchword with which to reinvent fieldwork and update this jaded colonial

practice to include post-colonial insights and global complexities by 'freeing of ethnographers from the conceptual boundaries of the delimited site and allowing them to follow movements of people, ideas, and objects, to trace and map complex networks' (Candea, 2009: 169).

4. During the research, I was enrolled as a PhD student at the Graduate School of International Development Studies and affiliated with the Danish Institute for Human Rights, Denmark, and the Makerere Institute for Social Research, Uganda, and my research had been cleared by the Uganda National Council for Science and Technology. Moreover, my close colleague and fellow prison researcher, Andrew Jefferson of the Danish NGO Dignity, had met with the Commissioner General of Prisons and introduced my proposal to the UPS management.

Further reading

Goffman, E. (1989) 'On Fieldwork', *Journal of Contemporary Ethnography*, 18, 2, 123–32.

Martin, T. M., Jefferson, A. M. and Bandyopadhyay, M. 'Sensing Prison Climates: Governance, Survival and Transition', *Focaal*, 68, 3–17.

References

American Anthropological Association (AAA) (1998) Code of Ethics of the American Anthropological Association (AAA), http://www.aaanet.org/issues/policy-advocacy/upload/ethicscode.pdf (accessed 3 June, 2014).

Bandyopadhyay, M. (2010) *Everyday Life in a Prison: Confinement, Surveillance, Resistance* (New Delhi: Orient BlackSwan).

Bundgaard, H. (2003) 'Lærlingen: Den Formative Erfaring', in K. Hastrup (ed) *Ind i Verden. En grundbog i antropologisk metode* (Copenhagen: Reitzel).

Candea, M. (2009) 'Arbitrary Locations: In Defence of the Bounded Field-site', in M.-A. Falzon (ed) *Multi-sited Ethnography: Theory, Praxis and Locality in Contemporary Research* (Farnham: Ashgate).

Fleisher, M. (1989) *Warehousing Violence* (Newbury Park: Sage).

Flyvbjerg, B. (2002) *Making Social Science Matter: Why Social Inquiry Fails and How It Can Succeed Again* (Cambridge: Cambridge University Press).

Foucault, M. (1977) *Discipline and Punish: The Birth of the Prison* (London: Penguin).

Foucault, M. (1982) 'The Subject and Power', *Critical Inquiry*, 8, 777–95.

Foucault, M. (1991) 'Questions of Method', in G. Burchell, C. Gordon and P. Miller (eds) *The Foucault Effect: Studies in Governmentality* (Chicago: University of Chicago Press).

Goffman, E. (1989) 'On Fieldwork', *Journal of Contemporary Ethnography*, 18, 2, 123–32.

Gupta, A. and Ferguson, J. (1997) 'Discipline and Practice: "The Field" as Site, Method, and Location in Anthropology', in A. Gupta and J. Ferguson (eds) *Anthropological Locations: Boundaries and Grounds of a Field Science* (Berkeley: University of California Press).

Hammersley, M. and Atkinson, P. (2007) *Ethnography: Principles in Practice*, Third edition (Abingdon: Routledge).

Hirsch, E. and Gellner, D. N. (2001) 'Introduction: Ethnography of Organizations and Organizations of Ethnography', in D. N. Gellner and E. Hirsch (eds) *Inside Organizations: Anthropologists at Work* (Oxford: Berg).

Human Rights Watch (HRW) (2011) *Even Dead Bodies Must Work: Health, Hard Labor and Abuse in Ugandan Prisons* (New York: Human Rights Watch).

International Centre for Prison Studies (ICPS) (2008) *World Prison Brief: Uganda* (London: International Centre for Prison Studies).

Jacobs, J. B. (1977) *Stateville: The Penitentiary in Mass Society* (Chicago: University of Chicago Press).

Jefferson, A. M. (2004) *Confronted by Practice: Towards a Critical Psychology of Prison Practice in Nigeria*. PhD Dissertation, University of Copenhagen, Copenhagen.

Justice Law and Order Sector (JLOS) (2010) *Justice Law and Order Sector Midterm Evaluation* (Kampala: Republic of Uganda).

Jones, D. (ed) (2006) *Humane Prisons* (Abingdon: Radcliffe Publishing).

Kapferer, B. (2007) 'Anthropology and the Dialectic of the Enlightenment: A Discourse on the Definition and Ideals of a Threatened Discipline', *The Australian Journal of Anthropology,* 18, 72–96.

Li, T. M. (2007) *The Will to Improve: Governmentality, Development, and the Practice of Politics* (Durham: Duke University Press).

Liebling, A. (1999) 'Doing Research in Prison: Breaking the Silence', *Theoretical Criminology,* 3, 147–73.

Long, N. (1992) 'From Paradigm Lost to Paradigm Regained?', in N. Long and A. Long (eds) *Battlefields of Knowledge. The Interlocking of Theory and Practice in Social Research and Development* (London: Routledge).

Malinowski, B. (1922) *Argonauts of the Western Pacific* (London: Routledge and Kegan Paul).

Malkki, L. (1995) *Purity and Exile. Violence, Memory and National Cosmology among Hutu Refugees in Tanzania* (Chicago: University of Chicago Press).

Marcus, G. E. (1995) 'Ethnography in/of the World System: The Emergence of Multi-Sited Ethnography', *Annual Review of Anthropology,* 24, 95–117.

Martin, H. M. (2006) *Professional Formation and Survival: Dealing with Contradiction in Ugandan Nursing,* PhD Dissertation, University of Copenhagen, Copenhagen.

Martin, T. M. (2009) 'Taking the Snake Out of the Basket: Indian Prison Warders' Opposition to Human Rights Reform', in S. Jensen and A. M. Jefferson (eds) *State Violence and Human Rights: State Officials in the South* (Oxford: Routledge-Cavendish).

Martin, T. M. (2013) *Embracing Human Rights: Governance and Transition in Ugandan Prisons,* PhD Dissertation, Roskilde University, Roskilde.

Martin, T. M. (2014a) 'The Importation of Human Rights by Ugandan Prison Staff', *Prison Service Journal,* 212, 45–51.

Martin, T. M. (2014b) 'Reasonable Caning and the Embrace of Human Rights in Ugandan Prisons', *Focaal,* 68, 68–82.

Martin, T. M., Jefferson, A. and Bandyopadhyay, M. (2014) 'Sensing Prison Climates: Governance, Survival and Transition', *Focaal,* 68, 3–17.

Meskell, L. and Pels, P. (2005) 'Introduction: Embedding Ethics', in L. Meskell and P. Pels (eds) *Embedding Ethics* (Oxford: Berg).

Moore, S. F. (1973) 'Law and Social Change: The Semi-Autonomous Social Field as an Appropriate Subject of Study', *Law and Society Review,* 7, 719–46.

Moore, S. F. (1994) 'The Ethnography of the Present and the Analysis of Process', in R. Borofsky (ed) *Assessing Cultural Anthropology* (New York: McGraw-Hill).

Olivier de Sardan, J.-P. (2008) *La riguer du qualitatif. Les contraintes empririques de l'interpretation socio-anthropologique,* unpublished translation into English by Antoinette Tidjani Alou 'Rigorously Qualitative. Epistemology, Fieldwork and Anthropology' (Louvain-La-Neuve: Academia-Bruylant).

Olivier de Sardan, J.-P. (2011a) 'The Eight Modes of Local Governance in West Africa', *IDS Bulletin,* 42, 22–31.

Olivier de Sardan, J.-P. (2011b) 'Local Powers and the Co-delivery of Public Goods in Niger', *IDS Bulletin,* 42, 32–42.

Oppenheimer, B. J. (2005) 'From Arrest to Release: The Inside Story of Uganda's Penal System', *Indiana International and Comparative Law Review,* 16, 117–44.

Pels, P. (1999) 'Professions of Duplexity: A Prehistory of Ethical Codes in Anthropology', *Current Anthropology,* 40, 101–36.

Rhodes, L. A. (2001) 'Toward an Anthropology of Prisons', *Annual Review of Anthropology,* 65–83.

Sanjek, R. (1990) 'On Ethnographic Validity', in R. Sanjek (ed) *Fieldnotes: The Makings of Anthropology* (Ithaca: Cornell University Press).

State, U. D. O. (2006) *Uganda: Country Reports on Human Rights Practices* (Uganda: Bureau of Democracy, Human Rights and Labor).

The Independent (2010) A Taste of Hell in Uganda Prisons, 13 April, The Independent, http://www.independent.co.ug/features/features/2769-a-taste-of-hell-in-uganda-prisons (accessed 3 June, 2014).

Tibatemwa-Ekirikubinza, L. (1995) *More Sinned against than Sinning* (Copenhagen: University of Copenhagen).

Tsing, A. L. (2005) *Friction: An Ethnography of Global Connection* (Princeton: Princeton University Press).

Uganda Human Rights Commission (UHRC) (2009) *Annual Report 2008* (Uganda: UHRC).

Uganda Human Rights Commission (UHRC) (2010) *Annual Report 2009* (Uganda: UHRC).

Waldram, J. B. (1998) 'Anthropology in Prison: Negotiating Consent and Accountability with a "Captured" Population', *Human Organization,* 57, 238–44.

Waldram, J. B. (2009) 'Challenges of Prison Ethnography', *Anthropology News,* 50, 4–5.

Wimba, F. and Adure, J. (2010) 'Prison Staff Accused of Hanging Inmate', *Daily Monitor,* 9 March, 2010, http://www.monitor.co.ug/News/National/-/688334/875496/-/wj7g38/-/index.html (accessed 3 June, 2014).

23

Deviation and Limitations of (Prison) Ethnography: Postscript to Fieldwork in an Indian Prison

Mahuya Bandyopadhyay

Introduction

Incarceration is extremely hard to document ethnographically. Social anthropology with its ethnographic method possibly offers an expedient way of representing spaces of incarceration and expressing marginalised voices within them. These statements express the inherently paradoxical encounter between ethnography and prisons. Rhodes (2001), in a path-breaking review essay on the anthropology of prisons, argued that there is a need for prison ethnographers not just to get inside prisons and describe life within prison walls, but more significantly to 'interrupt the terms of the debate' (2001: 75). Wacquant (2002) articulated otherwise: that in a context of eclipsed prison ethnography, it is more important for ethnographers to enter prisons and fill the void in the literature on prisons, through 'thick descriptions' of a range of different kinds of carceral spaces. In this chapter, such observations about the anthropology of prisons form a backdrop for reflections on their methodological import for prison ethnographers.[1]

As if in response to the problems of accessibility, the emotional scarring, ethical dilemmas and a sense of quiet derision that hangs on with almost every prison researcher, the notion of quasi-ethnography (Inciardi, 1993) has been offered as a way of reconciling the rather difficult terrain of prison research and the disciplinary regulative ideals of the social anthropological method.[2] In fact, this label makes ethnography possible in a space otherwise deemed inaccessible to the ethnographer and her methodological and technical tools and strategies. The prison is an opaque institution; two fundamental ways in which this opacity is maintained is through constant and rigorous surveillance and minimal interface of the institution with the world outside. The ethnographer, in entering the prison, challenges both these aspects of prison life. I, possibly like many other prison ethnographers, found the quasi-ethnography label to be an enabling category that aptly described my research experience in the post-colonial prison.

Quasi-ethnography suggests both a deviation from 'ethnography' as well as limitations in the ethnographic project and method, when applied to prison spaces. Even though these limitations stem from the structural constraints inherent in prison spaces, they have the potential to limit prison research practice and prison ethnographers in many other ways. Prevailing over these limiting tendencies entails countering the structural barriers of access, as well as the well-worn assumptions and established theoretical constructs and empirical categories of prison spaces. That researchers must continually push the methodological boundaries of ethnographic research in order to ask and answer the questions that cannot be tackled through the conventional methods has been stressed often enough (Liebling, 2001; Rhodes, 2001; Bosworth, 2005; Jewkes, 2013). Prison ethnographers entering prisons all over the world have followed this advisory, resulting in a vibrant and emerging field of ethnographic writing on prisons.[3] My concern in this chapter is to explore the lessons that prison ethnography can enable for ethnographic practice and the method, more generally. How can prison ethnographers speak to, and connect with, a larger academic community of anthropologists, rather than addressing prison ethnographers alone?

I focus on the kinds of ethnographic practices that may deem a piece of ethnographic work as quasi-ethnography and show how this can be rather limiting for fieldwork in unconventional, particularly closed off and terribly insular sites of research. Through introspection, I turn a critical lens on my fieldwork practices and draw out methodological strategies that anthropological fieldwork has not focused on. These strategies are discussed with reference to rapport building and emotion work, language and argot, the issue of time in prison and the practices of subversion. The chapter begins by briefly drawing the readers' attention to the dominant tropes of representation of prisons in India in particular and the post-colonial prisons of the Global South in general. Here I address the question: What are the broad 'terms of the debate' with regard to prisons in India? Having begun with the premise and faith that ethnographic research in prisons can disrupt this dominant, near-hegemonic imagery, in the second section of the chapter, I present the challenges in realising such a project, whilst offering possible methodological cues that reorient ethnographic practice. The management of, and negotiations with, such deviations in prison ethnographic practice may be used to draw out larger methodological lessons. Some of these may be typical to the particular prison climate[4] that I was researching and others may apply to the study of prisons, more generally.

Prison in India: Colonial and post-colonial images

The dominant discourse of the prison in India revolves around epithets and themes such as remnants of a colonial prison; the well-ordered prison; the poor, overcrowded post-colonial prison; the dehumanised prison; the repressive prison reminiscent of a police state; and the reformatory prison aligned to the notion of a welfare state. The contradictions in these thematic representations are evident and the prison researcher is likely to encounter a curious amalgam of all or most of these themes in writings on the prison in India. The prison in India has been characterised as a colonial institution, originally created for the maintenance of colonial order. The colonial prison was perceived as a site where essential social categories were reflected, internalised and embedded, thereby providing an orientalist model of society constructed around an essentialism of caste and religion. Studies of colonial prisons (and other institutions) argue that discipline, incarceration and medical intervention in nineteenth-century India were implicated in the British effort to ease governance of the colonial society. However, this is not to say that the model of the British prison system was replicated in India. Rather, the study of the colonial prison suggests that cultural specificities and values resulted in local and unique structuring of institutional spaces, practices and everyday lives. Moralities and value positions embedded in caste, custom, race and religion were used to 'contest the universalising ambitions of modern penology' (Arnold, 2007: 182). Further, the colonial prison was not just a site of oppression but also an institution that was used by the nationalists as a public arena to declare their opposition. Colonial rule was thus responsible, partially at least, for framing the prison paradoxically, both as a site of oppression and as a site of resistance. The paradox of the colonial circumstance had a definite impact on everyday life in the contemporary prison as it grappled with reconciling the apparently contradictory aims of reform and deterrence. The independent state also had the responsibility of expressing a clear break from colonial practices, even whilst accepting the progressive ideals of the modern institutions established through colonial rule. In the contemporary world, the latter objective translates as the compulsion that most states feel to connect with and adhere to larger global practices.

The picture of the well-ordered prison, equally central to the image of the prison in India, entails the following: holding prisoners safely; maintaining strict discipline within prison walls; ensuring the lawful and humane treatment of prisoners whereby the residual rights of prisoners are protected; and sustaining the isolation of the prison from the rest of society, both symbolically and in substantive terms, minimising the communication and expressive contexts between these two realms. This image of the well-ordered prison is also thus fundamentally linked to the performance of all these functions with minimum disruptions and chaos, implying reasonability and the organised, optimum and effective use of resources to meet goals.

In reinventing the modern methods of punishment and dealing with deviance, the post-colonial prison has also earned the classificatory derogatory label of the dehumanised prison. Why is this marked out as a special epithet for post-colonial prisons? Aren't all prisons essentially dehumanised spaces? In India, as in many post-colonial contexts, the prison exhibits dehumanisation through problems such as overcrowding and underfunding, the lack of basic infrastructure, severe human rights violations and the inability to banish completely the older methods of punishment that focus on bodily harm, the arbitrary exercise of power and a denial of what would be considered the 'residual rights' of prisoners. All such classificatory tags of dehumanised prison, well-ordered prison, post-colonial prison are often embedded in the notion of poor prisons. The post-colonial prison also invokes, rather strongly, the image of the prison on a path of reform. The notion of reform is relevant to understand the changes that the prison system is undergoing with a focus on a human rights perspective and an awareness of the colonial underpinnings of coercive institutions. The prison was also being reimagined as a *shongshodhanagar*, meaning 'a place for reform': how prisoners could be set on a path to reform and rehabilitation, and the positive role of the prison in this process were critical concerns. The everyday realities of contemporary prisons reflect these concerns, often in fragmented ways. Despite the overwhelming positioning of the prison as a well-ordered organisation, the daily realities, in coping with its paradoxes, appear ill-disciplined, chaotic and arbitrary.[5]

Negotiating ethnographic practice

Prison ethnographers have articulated changes in ethnographic practice in myriad ways: as negotiating the tensions between the roles of researcher and participant observer (Castellano, 2007); as learning to be critical of rapport as a form of control (Reeves, 2010); as understanding and coping with the 'panoptic culture of suspicion' and practising 'deliberate naïveté as a strategy' (Waldram, 2009: 4); or as using the personal frustration and isolation one experiences and works with to understand the delicate nuances of prisoners' lives (Rhodes, 2009). A dominant thread in personal and method-related reflections on prison ethnographies is the question of constraints and access, how to negotiate it and not jeopardise it. Wacquant engages with two other significant limitations: the 'professional organisation of the academe' and the 'lowly social and therefore, scientific status of the object of investigation' (2002: 388). Both these, to my mind, place the researcher in a complex paradox. The researcher is very aware of studying those with very limited capacity to express and exercise agency whilst at the same time being subjected to similar processes of denial and limited capabilities. However, most prison researchers negotiate and develop unique routes of circumventing the limitations. Rhodes (2009), for instance, describes four factors that mitigated the limitations of her research in a supermax prison. These were the simple passage of time, collaboration, isolation and frustration. Whilst temporal rhythms of the fieldwork process and the strategy of collaborations have been written about, isolation and frustration are rarely perceived as positive forces. Most prison researchers experience isolation and frustration in heightened forms, which feature in discussions about the difficulties of doing prison research and the emotional impasse it often creates for the prison ethnographer. How is it possible to rethink this heightened negative emotive context and experience as an ethnographic tool?

As a prison researcher in India, I found myself occupying a rather marginal position in relation to my discipline and its overriding concerns. Not only were there no Indian prison ethnographies to fall back on, I felt the need to justify an ethnographic stance for issues that were largely considered to be the domain of 'social work'. The sense of marginality and disempowerment, a function of the organisation of disciplinary practice, the subjects of study and their location and label, thus governs prison work. I will show how some of the critical markers of classical ethnographic practice were altered whilst doing fieldwork in a prison in India. Embedded in the ensuing discussion on rapport and emotionality, the temporal rhythms and structuring of fieldwork, the use of language to understand the everyday realities in the field and to represent it and the practice of subversions are ways of rethinking and reimagining the strategies of anthropological fieldwork.

Rapport, emotionality and anthropological credibility

Ethnography privileges rapport building, immersion in the 'field' and in the everyday life of the community being researched. Establishing a good rapport and developing bonds with the community, combined with a 'reflective detachment', has, in the Malinowskian tradition, been considered crucial to any anthropological enterprise. As Liebling points out, 'to do ethnographic research in a prison... what you need most of all is full use of yourself' (Liebling, 2001: 475). I examine the implications of making full use of oneself in prison fieldwork, suggesting two contradictory ideas: first, this is an import from conventional ethnographic styles and prison fieldwork and is far from conventional; and second, prison ethnographers learn to transgress their ontological positioning, in making full use of themselves. I found immersion rather difficult and characterised my relationship with the field as 'controlled detachment'. Emotional distancing from my informants was, primarily, a result of the detachment that was built into the field situation itself. In part, this is characteristic of most field situations. In the prison, however, the detachment arose not merely from the interactional setting, but also from the imposition of rules and regulations that governed both the fieldworker and the informant. The method of participant observation required establishing rapport and closeness. However, I constantly negotiated the twin processes of distancing and closeness. My analysis and writing is a product of this dilemma in fieldwork and the ways in which I sought to resolve it. The strategies used to deal with this predicament, however, had a partly serendipitous pattern, in so far as they evolved as immediate, extemporaneous responses to situations.

My discomfort at not being able to replicate the experience of fieldwork I had read and heard about was instrumental in my constant struggle to build close relations with the prisoners. The very nature of the field demanded a certain kind of interaction with it, one that I refer to as maintaining a 'decent and tactful distance'. The ensuing conflict became an integral part of my field experience. Making a choice between whether to be closer to a particular prisoner or whether to protect my position as a researcher in the institution was an everyday task. Let us consider, for instance, the issue of doing favours for the prison inmates. I tried to avoid doing too many favours for the prisoners. This practice of doing favours, carrying out small requests for one's informants and exchanging gifts are established ways in which rapport in the field is built. In prison, many of these 'favours' were implicated in the larger and significant domain of ethics in fieldwork. When was a rule break justified? Who would be punished if a transgression became visible and known? Was I not putting my own fieldwork and access to the prison, as well as the inmate's positioning within the system, at risk through these 'favours'? In a context of such vexed and overlapping questions of research ethics, organisational rules and personal ethics, I found myself negotiating the business of doing favours rather carefully. Sometimes I carried letters to a 'lover' in another jail, bought cosmetic items for the women, lent money and wrote petitions. The decision to do a favour or not was based on the level of trust and closeness that I had with the concerned prisoner. Since all these favours would be considered 'illegal' by the authorities, I also weighed the gravity of the offence I was going to commit, and then made a decision. Balancing the efforts to build rapport with the prisoners and maintaining a distance from them, which was vital for retaining my access to the site, is a serious dilemma in prison research. The self-consciousness about being close and feeling a bond with the 'subject' of my study and suggestions of my distance from them only led to increasing self-doubt about the validity of my fieldwork process and the data I was collecting.

Tremendous significance has been placed on affect, sympathy and empathy in the doing of ethnographic fieldwork. The prison ethnographer thus bears what I refer to as the 'burden of affect' in more ways than one. Building rapport, feeling close and bonding emotionally with the researched is one aspect of this burden of affect. In ethnographic research, however, the emotional bonding and rapport building are not really considered burdensome; in fact, this is one of the redeeming facets of the otherwise long and arduous process of fieldwork. Jewkes (2012) persuasively argues for the methodological significance of the emotive content of prison fieldwork with the belief that the acknowledgement of emotions experienced by prison fieldworkers and their own subjective experiences in the field enable a deeper and nuanced understanding of the meanings of incarceration.

Forming close, spontaneous attachments with the prisoners implied momentarily forgetting my fieldworker self. Simultaneously, I was often reminded by the prisoners about my status as an outsider, primarily marked off as someone who went home every day. These reminders appeared to be rude and insensitive but they brought the 'fieldworker' self back into focus. The fieldworker self and the emotional, connected empathic self are often fused in the situation of the field. However, this is neither a universal nor a necessary experience. Dealing with emotion work in the field then pertains to not just finding the paths to connecting, sharing and finding ways to express one's own emotionality, but also recognising the possibility of not being able to connect. The inability to connect, sympathise and express empathy may be seen as just that: the inability of an individual researcher, despite the acute awareness of the structural constraints and ethical complexities in forging these emotional ties within the prison. Taking cognisance of and articulating this disconnect between the multiple personalities that the fieldworker often assumes enables us to accept the tricky nature of empathy. In prison fieldwork, empathy is laden with existential dilemmas and related ethical and legal concerns. How is empathy to be defined? How can it be reconciled to the many different emotions of anger, fear, frustration, helplessness, pity, aloofness, excitement and joy that one experiences in the field? This process of reconciliation, often rather painful and private, holds the key to our understanding of empathy in the field. To find the will and the social science language to articulate this complex of emotions and their reconciliation adds to the arduous nature of prison fieldwork. To my mind, the prison teaches us that empathy and a sense of deep disconnect can coexist. This helps us to subvert the understanding that rapport building is, essentially, about building harmonious relations with the subjects of enquiry. Disharmony and undercurrents of violence are hardly conducive factors in forging harmonious relationships. In prison, empathy and connections emerge within such a context of disarray and despite it. The prison, as I am sure also occurs with fieldwork in situations of conflict and coercion, teaches us that it is possible to empathise and connect with the field without forging harmonious relations. Friendly conversations, willingness and the ability to listen without judging, paying close attention to nuances of speech delivery, and sensitivity to sense what is expressed are some of the common elements in the practice of rapport building. In prison fieldwork, the ethnographer learns that one can build rapport without these guiding elements. I take this point further and attempt a slightly provocative turn by asking a question: When can the argument replace the friendly conversation in the field? As a friend and fellow ethnographer pointed out to me, in the field you only engage in an argument when you feel secure; not just about your presence in the field, but more so secure in your understanding of the field, with all its complexities, conflicts and subtleties.[6] As ethnographers, we are trained to be wary of the argument. It disrupts the harmony, so essential in collecting ethnographic data. The argument that the situation of disharmony and conflict can generate data is something we tend to forget. Can our fieldwork be subjected to the same argumentative rigour that we apply to our writing and analysis? Is it possible to think of the argument, as well as being argumentative in the field as essential components of the ethnographic toolkit? The argument possibly enables a shift of focus away from the researched and from the fieldworker, thereby dislodging both from the central position they hold in anthropological research.

Does such argumentative rigour in our dialogues with the field interrupt balanced, harmonious fieldwork? Or is our status as ethnographers, entangled in complex power dynamics in the field, not productive for the argument? Much of ethnography involves studying down; implying that the tilt of power dynamics is in favour of the researcher. However, through fieldwork in a prison in India I came to understand that the sense of power the ethnographer has over the subjects of research is drawn more from her primordial identities; rather than from her position and authority as a social scientist. Intersectionalities of race, class and caste identities (in fieldwork in India and South Asia) complicate the dynamics of power relations in the field. Significantly, these intersectionalities are also articulated primarily in terms of primordial identities rather than their entanglements with professional ones of fieldworker, anthropologist, author, writer and so on. As ethnographers navigate their way around these dynamics, they are often only negotiating with and through these primordial identities and/or people's perceptions of them. Establishing primacy of professional identity is rarely a priority. The prison presents a curious case of studying down. The position of power that the ethnographer/researcher may have is attenuated by the application of rules and regulations and by the severe constraints by the legal and institutional framework that governs the relationships between prison insiders and outsiders.

The domains of rapport and gaining access in prison are thus replete with criminal complicity and danger, both having serious legal overtones. In many relatively free sites,[7] rapport does not necessarily imply criminal complicity. Thus whilst the twinning of ethics and complicity is characteristic of most field sites, in prison, this is marked by legal concerns and the fear of the apparent irreversibility of consequences.

Serendipity can account for the differences in field sites and the variety of personal experiences of fields and fieldworkers, but it acknowledges certain fixed ideas regarding methodological training for ethnographic fieldwork. Marcus (2009), in reflecting on fieldwork training in a context of the ever-shifting and dynamic anthropological field, pointed out that doctoral fieldwork projects in many social anthropology departments are like managed 'de facto experiments', collaboratively negotiated by supervisors and research students. The subjects of these negotiations are the 'limits of the norms and forms of the traditional paradigm' (Marcus, 2009: 8). Conserving the valued norm of the craft of anthropological fieldwork is primary. It lends credibility to the anthropological project. Training of new students is focused on maintaining such credibility, even as the notion of the anthropological field has undergone radical and transformative shifts in the past few decades. I reiterate Marcus' argument that, for the methodological training to not be burdened by the norm of conserving the anthropological craft, we need to rethink fieldwork, focusing not on what is imposed by the 'long-standing regulative ideals' (2009: 8) but on what the negotiations of these tell us about anthropological fieldwork and its training. Ethnographic fieldwork in prisons and other restricted organisational spaces, I think, offer great value in such a project of rethinking, as much of the valued craft is reordered, thought anew, with new ethnographic practices emerging and significantly altering the traditional regulative ideals as well as the 'culture of craft' (Marcus, 2009).

The practices of rapport building and establishing close connections with the subjects of research may be negotiated through the fieldworker's engagement in the field, and the disciplinary ideals. In prison fieldwork, a researcher relates to 'immersion' in a peculiar way, deviating notably from the disciplinary ideal of bonding, rapport and emotional connection with the field. Immersion in ethnographic fieldwork would mean being engulfed by the life in the field and partaking of the everyday life in the field. Contrarily for me, immersion implied an immersion of the 'self'. This meant that I accepted the controls on access, took on a certain acceptable demeanour and slowed down the pace of my research work (none of which I really wanted to do). Following such restrictions I hoped would negate whatever threat there was to the question of physical accessibility to the field. The threat of loss of physical accessibility to the fieldwork site, the careful practice of subversions in explicit collaboration with the prisoners and its implicit acceptance by the staff, and the presentation of a diminutive and restrained self, were elements that configured the prison as a field site for me. Whilst disciplinary ideals have privileged empathy as a way of building rapport, the demands that prison fieldwork makes on the fieldworker's ability to empathise are complex, often riddled with ethical dilemmas. Given the near hegemonic influence of rapport building as a strategy in fieldwork, it becomes rather difficult to articulate a question that prison fieldwork in fact very clearly frames – is it possible to gather data without striving to achieve an emotional connection and without developing empathy for the site and the people one is studying? I wish to argue that the business of rapport building, connecting emotionally and feeling and expressing empathy are fundamentally linked to the nature of the research question. This also implies a decentering of the persons involved in the research: the fieldworker and the researched. Through such a decentering exercise, the whole project of empathy may be reimagined. The craft of social anthropological fieldwork and concomitantly its training may thus be recast to focus on ways that field data may be collected without necessarily being emotionally connected to the people and the field.

Language, argot and thick description

In every field situation, learning the language and figuring out the cultural codes are critical processes in understanding and representation. For me, prison fieldwork was located in the city where I had lived and grown up. I had felt fairly comfortable knowing that I would not have to invest time in learning the language. However, as my engagement with the prison deepened I realised that learning the language assumes a different meaning within the prison. I had to learn and be sensitive to the prison argot, the familiar tropes and genres of presenting lives, the discourse markers in both verbal and non-verbal communication, to reading gaze, gestures, demeanour and the stray comments made by prisoners, officers and staff members. Whilst much can be said about each of these aspects, I will highlight this learning process with two examples.

The first one relates to the narratives of prisoners that I collected. I used the term *jibon kahini* or life story to explain to prisoners what kind of information I was trying to gather from them. *Jibon kahini* was a familiar trope for many and it enabled me to get information about prisoners' lives, without asking too many specific and, often, uncomfortable questions. These narrative interviews were spread over several sessions, and sometimes even locations. For instance, I would often carry on a conversation with a prisoner (someone I had interviewed earlier) as he waited in the van outside the court, waiting to be called in. In most of the narratives of young male prisoners, I found that their stories, especially of the crimes committed and/or witnessed, were told with all the flair, twists and turns of a Bollywood film. I had thus to sensitise myself to the Bollywood film genre, its language and narrative style. Prisoners find it difficult to use direct common language to articulate their lives and there is often a great deal of 'narrative debris', in their expressions, in the form gaps, inconsistencies, self-interruptions and frame breaks (McKendy, 2006). Thus familiarity with the argot is only one aspect of developing language skills in the prison; in addition, the ethnographer must learn to understand the narrative techniques, and make sense of the narrative debris characteristic of many prisoner narratives.

The second instance pertains to a conversation I overheard (akin to so many others) amongst officers, where a prisoner was the subject of the 'talk'. A foreign prisoner who was in the main office regarding a petition he was planning to submit told one of the jailors that he really liked the safari suit (a suit that many *babus* (clerks) wear, especially during the summer) the officer was wearing. Where can I get one like that, the prisoner asked. The jailor said, 'you want one? I can get it stitched for you. You give me your measurements and I will get it done'. Another officer sitting at a distance commented, 'Jailor *babu* has made arrangements for *Pujo*'. The others had a hearty laugh and the jailor, at whose expense the joke was, gave a sheepish grin and said: 'what all you say'. Only a detailed interpretive reading of this encounter will qualify it as significant data. The comment 'Jailor *babu* has made arrangements for *Pujo*' implies that the jailor is going to make some money out of this favour that he so willingly promises the foreign prisoner. *Pujo* here refers to an important Bengali festival, which was around the time this conversation took place. Further it must be noted that only a foreigner could address the jailor in that manner and indirectly make a request. Also, the jailor's friendly response is premised on the knowledge that money would not be an issue here. In all other similar transactions where staff members acquired things of personal use for the prisoners, the price was often heavily discussed and negotiated. Both these cases are instances of learning to listen and learning to decipher the codes inherent in these interactions and verbal communications.

Learning a language involves learning the grammar and the spoken word. A critical device that perhaps prison fieldwork taught me was to transgress the boundaries of one's own language. Swear words were not really a part of my everyday language, known, heard or spoken. Swear and cuss words, contrarily, were an inextricable part of how prisoners expressed themselves, not necessarily with me, the fieldworker, but amongst themselves and also sometimes with the warders. Familiarity with the prison argot is surely one way of accessing the language in which prisoners express themselves, but a more nuanced understanding would possibly entail understanding the diverse contexts and meanings which are often implicated in the use of swear words and cuss words, used to represent feelings, everyday practices and prison life generally. A significant aspect of the training in language thus involves learning the otherwise marginal words, phrases and their usage; those that may not form part of formal or informal everyday language in most contexts. Being aware of the 'marginal' in language is one kind of training that fieldworkers need, understanding that this marginal and oft-labelled 'foul' language has the power to communicate effectively and express emotions and feelings in a way that the mainstream language cannot possibly requires the fieldworker to transgress the boundaries of her own understanding of usage of language and their contexts. Is a swear word only used in anger and frustration or in a playful banter? Are they used to symbolise aggression or helplessness, or both? Prison fieldwork teaches us to unravel the subtlety of usage, contexts and meanings of words that would otherwise be recognised as 'foul language'. Can the fieldworker learn to use, understand, write and translate this 'foul' language to communicate what goes on inside these institutions? Becker, for instance, argued that neutral language was central to Goffman's enterprise and this was probably to avoid conventional language and conventional categories of thought (Becker et al., 2004: 264). I wish to argue here that our disciplines, especially social anthropology, despite its diversity of fields and methods, do not really equip us with the tools to do this effectively. The vast gap between the academic language that we write in and the foul language that we often hear in the field is often dealt with by a kind of sanitising, as fundamentally we are taught to write in a way that we do not offend.

Temporal structures

The idea of considerably lengthy anthropological fieldwork is also challenged in the prison. Given the permission limitations of institutional ethnography, time is a significant determinant of the nature and quality of data and, subsequently, analysis. Entry and exit, otherwise largely determined by the needs of the research proposal and the demands of data collection, is severely constrained in prison. It is dictated by the authorities and by the changing conditions in the prison. So for instance, after a jailbreak I was asked to avoid being around for a week or so. It was stated as a request. Similarly, my schedule was often dependent on the welfare officers, who were officially in charge of me. If the welfare officer was on leave, I would be asked not to come. The lady welfare officer was often on leave and after heeding her orders a couple of times, I resisted.

The issue of time too presents a paradoxical situation – in prison and for the subjects of investigation the passage of time is slow. The bureaucratic processes that a researcher must navigate to secure access to the prison also mirror this slow passage of time. Once access is gained, however, there is an urgency to gather as much data as possible, to observe and record as much as possible, simply for the fragile and unpredictable terms of access. At the same time, gaining trust, emotionally adjusting to the demands of fieldwork and trying to position oneself in the field are again time-consuming processes. The official structuring of the researcher's and the subject's time, the contradiction of subjects having all the time in the world, yet not having enough control over it to give it to the researcher as and when was mutually convenient, the urgency to collect data quickly and the slow process of gaining trust – all these issues frame time in prison fieldwork.

Apart from just coping with the frustration of the slow passage of time, I dealt with the complex issue of time in prison fieldwork by situating myself in a few prisoners' lives through different contexts such as the courtroom, the homes and families of prisoners and their case partners in the same prison, and their friends in other prisons in the city. The regulative ideal with regard to time in anthropological fieldwork involves long durations of stay in the field, covering all the cycles in a year or more. Such structuring of anthropological time defines fieldwork and the process of data collection, attributing superficiality to the social practice of ethnographic exploration, which is otherwise marked by a sense of bonding with the place and people one is studying. In prison fieldwork, the researcher is acutely aware of this kind of superficiality that the disciplinary ideals impose, often adding to the structural barriers imposed by the institution.

In transgressing some of these structural limits, the prison ethnographer also adds a qualitative dimension to the notion of anthropological time: that length and duration may not be equally significant across different field sites. In fact, in prison fieldwork *opportune time* presents to the researcher a more compelling dimension to the notion of anthropological time. Here *opportune time* implies temporal situations that are favourably disposed to the relaxation of the controls that are otherwise imposed on both the prisoners and the fieldworker. Prison ethnographers, like prisoners, can learn to create the contexts for such temporal conditions to prevail. The notion of opportune time is, of course, valid for all kinds of field sites. However, anthropological time presumes that the lengthy duration of fieldwork and the focus on covering all cycles in a year creates such *opportune time*. In prison and other sites where access is limited and lengthy fieldwork may not be permissible, the ethnographer learns to create *opportune time*. This may again involve subversion of prison rules, or negotiating rules of access with the staff members and warders in charge, or remaking the everyday to accommodate one's needs.

Subversion/transgression

In spite of the constant surveillance, I was able to practise subversions of the rules that characterised my fieldwork experience, and the field was progressively configured in different, more accessible ways. For instance, the rule that governed my interaction in the 'female ward' was that I could not move out of the official spaces or decide whom I wanted to speak with. The welfare officer decided whom I could interview. But I could subvert this rule as time passed. These subversions did not really emerge from any received pedagogical knowledge. Rather, through my interactions with the prisoners I became a partner in some of their subversive practices. I became adept at speaking in hushed tones in the crowded office, often changing the topic of conversation when we realised someone was listening to our conversation, or pretending to be distant even when some degree of closeness in relations was established. This was markedly different from the fieldwork and rapport building strategies that I had read about (Emerson et al., 1995; Vered, 2000). The practice of subversions not only formed an integral part of my observations of everyday life in the prison, but it was also through such subversions that this everyday life became accessible to me.

I was asked not to talk about the crime and the court cases with the 'under-trial'[8] prisoners. Even though the welfare officer indicated that prisoners don't want to share such information with an 'outsider', I found, to the contrary, that many prisoners were eager to talk about their crime to present themselves favourably. I was told to sit in the schoolroom of the 'female ward', but here again I subverted the rule and often sat with the prisoners in their wards or in the courtyard. It was an unsaid rule that I should not interview any male prisoner twice. But I frequently managed to speak with some of the prisoners I had grown close to and considered to be 'good informants'. I was not supposed to carry anything for the prisoners, but I catered to the requests of many women prisoners for items of personal use, *paan*,[9] cosmetics or sometimes even old clothes. Fieldwork would not have been possible without such subversions that I practised along with the prisoners. They also indicated to me the subversive practices of the prisoners which constituted their everyday lives. The ideas of subversion and the underlife of a total institution were sociological concepts that I was familiar with. However, the actual process of practising subversions was learnt through trial and error and in following my instincts in interactions with both prisoners and staff.

Whilst the prison was a legally binding space, it was also a system where the use of extra-legal authority at all levels of the hierarchy of prison administration was common. This made it difficult for anyone to know what the rules and regulations actually were. In spite of being bound by rules, there was some degree of laxity in their imposition on me, an outsider. Rules were not categorically laid out for me and I often relied on intuition to do the right thing. I interviewed most of the male prisoners in the chaotic noisy office, a space that seemingly rarely allowed moments of privacy. I realised, however, that this din worked to my advantage, as prisoners were more willing to talk in hushed voices, in the midst of this hustle and bustle, rather than in the welfare officer's room within one of the wards where I had held a few interviews earlier. My interviews in the presence of the welfare officer and those in the chaotic main office revealed to me how the chaotic main office could become a subversive site, that presented rich data, and the possibility for prisoners to share intimate aspects of their lives. I often classified the interviews held in the presence of the welfare officer as 'bad' as I thought they told me very little about the prisoner's life, and represented an official point of view. Only on a closer reading did I realise that it provided 'data' to comment not only on the relationship between officers and prisoners but also my relationship with both these communities. In sharp contrast, the following narrative collected in the chaotic environs of the main office seemed aligned to my understanding of 'good' data, thickly described. The narrative is of a 40-year-old male prisoner, serving time for murder. A somewhat truncated version is presented here:

> 'It all happened in connection with the shop that we owned. It was a sweet shop and I would run it with the help of my father. Then it was not doing so well ... So we rented it out to a *marwari*[10] businessman who took it up and restarted the business.... it started doing very well. Actually it is located in a very good place – on the main road. I was working in a factory. But I did not like that so much.... We decided to take back the shop and continue that business. We asked the *marwari* to leave our place but you know how these people are – he refused to get out of our property. He had spent quite a lot of money on the shop – generally decorating it and things like that so I think his intention was to take possession of it by force. They have *goondas* (hooligans, often hired to threaten or use force) and he thought he would get the place without a fight. But I am a very hot-headed person. I cannot tolerate injustice. So one day I just went down to the shop with some boys from my locality. They were supporting me in driving him out of our property. We asked him to leave very politely first. But then the boys in the shop got aggressive. Seeing their approach, the boys who were with me became angrier. You know how they are ... all young boys ... blood is always boiling ... unemployed, nothing to do ... they have a lot of anger trapped inside them and it just bursts whenever there is a little frustration. One thing led to another and before I knew it we were fighting with the boys in the shop. I had picked up a rod from somewhere and I was going to hit this guy, one of the workers and he just ducked so it was an accident. I obviously had no intention of killing anyone. We had just gone there together as a show of strength and to scare them off our property. So because this guy had ducked, the rod hit his head and he died. But you know after the accident we were the ones who took him to the hospital and then all my friends told me that I should not get involved in this. Our *para* (neighbourhood) was a Congress stronghold[11] and so nothing really happened to me as the boys were on my side and that helped. A case was registered though and our shop was sealed off but there was no warrant in my name and so I knew I was safe.' *I asked how it was possible that he had committed this crime and everybody knew about it and yet he was not arrested. Correcting me, he said,* 'it is not that I am a criminal. I don't come from such a background; in my family everybody is decent. You go to my *para* (neighbourhood) and ask anybody and they will all tell you that I am a decent person and that it was all an unfortunate accident.'

This narration expresses the self-perception of a branded 'criminal' serving a sentence. In my interviews in the presence of the welfare officer, prisoners seemed eager to present a 'good' picture of the prison and its administration and spoke more about prison facilities than about their personal lives. Knowledge of the way in which the prison functioned in the past, drawn from the sharing of experiences of long-term warders, officers and prisoners, served as a marker of judging its present state. The officer's presence formalised the setting to an extent that 'informants' avoided venturing deeply into their personal worlds. My demeanour too contributed to the formal and restrained nature of these interviews. In interactions outside this space, I was chatty and always spoke a lot about my own life, delving into instances from my 'life-story' to explain to the prisoners what kind of information I was seeking. In the welfare officer's room and in his presence, I did not talk about my own life. In sharp contrast to the peaceful environs of the welfare officer's room inside one of the wards, the chaotic main office provided the scope for creating a private interactional space where stories of prisoners' lives unfolded.

I was not to develop close relations with the prisoners, and I could not talk to them privately. Yet, it is clear from this extract that I was attained a level of closeness and trust that enables a person to reveal the 'forbidden' and 'secret' aspects of his life. Finding a more or less secluded corner to conduct our interview, mastering the technique of speaking in hushed tones, inaudible to the other people around us, and the strategy of changing the topic of discussion if anyone happened to be within earshot were our subversive practices. Individual rapport in the prison was often circumstantial and erratic. So rapport and the bond between the fieldworker and informant was more firmly entrenched and embodied in the relationship between researcher and prisoner as partners in the subversive process, rather than in the relationship between researcher and informant.

Initially, the jailor or the welfare officer decided my informants and accordingly a signed and stamped slip was made out to call them to the office. I observed that my informants were chosen with great deliberation by the officers present and their 'writers' (convict prisoners who work as helpers of the officers in the main office are known as 'writers'). The deliberation was generally with a view to presenting before me a *bhalo* (good) prisoner. When I suggested that I would like to interview all types of prisoners, the officers would laugh at my supposed naivety. With time, however, I developed close friendships with some of the 'writers' and would urge them to suggest prisoners I could meet and interview. As the writers took on a more proactive role in deciding who was to be called from the male wards, the scope of my access to different kinds of prisoners widened considerably. In fact, as more and more male prisoners shared their experiences of talking to the 'lady researcher', I think my 'interview session' became a desirable subversive site. 'Writers' then informed me about them getting requests from male prisoners who wanted to be interviewed. In the 'female ward', I discovered that I had relatively unhindered access. Here, the lady welfare officer was in charge of me but her frequent and long absences worked in my favour, making it possible for me to be part of 'everyday life', even if for a few hours on a particular day.

The instances presented above unravel many contexts of subversion: first, the transgression of the formal prison rules by the ethnographer; second, the everyday and regular subversive practices followed by the prisoners, in which the staff and authorities were clearly complicit; third, the outstanding and irregular subversions that prisoners displayed on occasion, such as an escape, an argument with authorities, or a riot; fourth, the specific acts of subversions that prisoners practised along with the ethnographer, some of which were related to a transactional relationship between the two; and finally, the subversion of the rules of engagement that were negotiated between the fieldworker and the authorities at the time of granting permission. The latter were not necessarily drawn from any system of written, codified rules. Such complicity entailed grave dangers for both researcher and prisoners. Yet, the subversive practices of prisoners and ethnographer made an interactional space possible. In prison, this space could not have been created simply from following the conventional methods of listening without judgement, sympathising with subjects, and building emotional connections.

Looking ahead of the postscript

My understanding of and writing about prison lives in India can be attributed, in large measure, to these subversive practices, replete with ethical problems. They narrate meaningful lives of prisoners, despite the dehumanisation. This representation has often been viewed, within the discipline of sociology and social anthropology where I am located through training and academic practice, as a rosy picture, as one that does not address the dehumanisation. This image of the prison militates against the dominant discourses of the postcolonial prison, and, in order to validate such images, it is important for prison ethnographers to be able to articulate and defend their use of concepts and methods from within the larger discipline of social anthropology. This articulation is not to be confined to one's observations and experiences of the prison space alone. Dehumanisation within prison and expressions of agency – this is perceived as an oppositional binary. Ethnographic fieldwork, in my case and possibly in many others, will actually debunk this binary. The prison is a dehumanised space; it is simultaneously a space that holds tremendous potential for resistance, a potentiality that is actualised in the everyday life of prisoners.

The established imagery of the prison as a dehumanised space offers a certain kind of critique of governance and presents an ethnography of state by focusing on an institution where there is minimal civil society interference.

This critique is a familiar one to social and political anthropologists: repressive practices of the state; an institution riddled with corrupt practices for the monetary and material benefits of a few; an institution where the state fails in its welfare orientation, and where it is unable to ensure the basic rights of its citizens. What is not familiar is the other kind of critique that emerges – that of the inability of the state to perform effectively in an institution for punishment. The porosity of the institution, the individual and collective efforts at dealing with dehumanisation and the many scripts of subversion that I present (Bandyopadhyay, 2010) offer a critique in both the senses mentioned above. So when human rights are not ensured, prisoners make continual individual and collective attempts to escape complete dehumanisation. These efforts contaminate the established picture of the dehumanised prison and, to a certain extent, also problematise the straightforward critique of the state's inefficiency as provider of its prison populace.

The primary data for this chapter is drawn from my experience of fieldwork in a prison in India, conducted more than ten years ago, but it is emergent and contemporary in many other senses. It is a critical analysis of my own fieldwork strategies and my ethnographic training to comment on prison fieldwork. I turn the anthropological gaze on prison ethnographers. The lack of scholarship on prisons in India, and even in South Asia, in comparison, for instance, to the UK or even the US, which have a far more vibrant community of criminology and prison scholars, is disquieting, to say the least. This chapter thus implicitly offers a critique to the practice and professionalisation of the discipline of social anthropology and sociology in India, where studies of coercive organisations, though central to our understanding of a rapidly changing Indian society, have not really seen the light of day.

Notes

1. The idea for this chapter emerged from my presentation and participation in a seminar, Resisting the Eclipse, in 2012 with prison ethnographers from across the world. I am grateful to Deborah Drake, Jennifer Sloan, Rod Earle and Abigail Rowe for bringing so many prison ethnographers together to brainstorm about methodological and substantive issues. I am also deeply indebted to members of the Global Prisons Research Network, especially Andrew Jefferson and Tomas Max Martin. Their efforts have energised prison scholarship and have enabled many, like me, who were tired of thinking and writing about the prisons in isolation.
2. For a discussion of the limits of research practice in prisons, see Moczydlowski (1992), Inciardi et al. (1993), Owen (1998) and Reed (2004).
3. The ethnographic accounts of Russian prisons (Piacentini, 2004), the supermax in America (Rhodes, 2004), the connections between the prison and the ghetto (Wacquant, 2002), the social anatomy of a medium-security English prison (Crewe, 2009), narratives of prison work and the role of the prison officer (Liebling et al., 2010), ethnographic accounts of reform and human rights in prisons in

Africa (Jefferson, 2005, 2010; Martin, 2014) and the nature of incarceration in a maximum-security prison in Papua New Guinea (Reed, 2004) are a few good examples of prison writing and representation.

4. For a discussion of the concept of prison climate, see Martin et al. (2014).
5. Brown (2007), in discussing reform in the prison in Southeast Asia, argues that the documentation on prisons and prisoner populations contained detailed information, which would suggest 'comparable command' over the prison, but the everyday realities of the prison were often ill-disciplined, arbitrary and negotiated.
6. This is with reference to a personal conversation on fieldwork with a friend and colleague, Ritambhara Hebbar, whose doctoral research is based on intensive fieldwork in a tribal community in Jharkhand, India. I am grateful to her for many conversations comparing fieldwork in two sites: the tribal community and the prison and the insights into our methods that emerged through these conversations.
7. I loosely distinguished between fieldwork in coercive organisations and fieldwork in free, community settings. The latter I described as relative free settings (Bandyopadhyay, 2010).
8. Remand prisoners are referred to as undertrials and are housed in the same jails as the convicts. In India, there are no separate remand prisons, or even separate wards, for the remand prisoners.
9. *Paan* is betel leaf which was generally chewed by some female prisoners along with areca nut and tobacco.
10. The term *'Marwari'* is used to refer to people from the Rajasthan region of India. Historically successful as traders, they are often considered to be synonymous with the business community, especially in West Bengal.
11. The term 'Congress stronghold' implies that there were influential members of the Congress Party in that neighbourhood, and they could use their influence to ward off an arrest and criminal proceedings, at least in the initial period after the crime was committed.

Further reading

Jewkes, Y. (2013) 'What Can Ethnography Offer in an Age of Mass Incarceration?' *Criminal Justice Matters*, 91, 1, 14–15.

Liebling, A. (2001) 'Whose Side Are We On?: Theory, Practice and Allegiances in Prisons Research', *British Journal of Criminology*, 41, 472–84.

Rhodes, L. (2001) 'Toward an Anthropology of Prisons', *Annual Review of Anthropology*, 30, 65–83.

Rhodes, L. A. (2004) *Total Confinement: Madness and Reason in the Maximum Security Prison* (California: University of California Press).

Wacquant, L. (2002) 'The Curious Eclipse of Prison Ethnography in the Age of Mass Incarceration', *Ethnography*, 3, 4, 371–97.

References

Arnold, D. (2007) India: 'The Contested Prison', in Dikotter, F. and Brown, I. (eds) *Cultures of Confinement: A History of the Prison in Africa, Asia and Latin America* (New York: Cornell University Press), pp. 147–84.

Bandyopadhyay, M. (2010) *Everyday Life in a Prison: Confinement, Surveillance, Resistance* (New Delhi: Orient BlackSwan).

Becker, H. S., Gans, H. J., Newan, K. S. and Vaughan, D. (2004) 'On the Value of Ethnography: Sociology and Public Policy: A Dialogue', *Annals of the American Academy of Political and Social Science*, 595, 264–76.

Bosworth, M. (2005) 'Doing Prison Research: Views from Inside', *Qualitative Inquiry*, 11, 249–64.

Brown, I. (2007) 'South East Asia: Reform and the Colonial Prison', in F. Dikotter and I. Brown (eds) *Cultures of Confinement: A History of the Prison in Africa, Asia and Latin America*, pp. 221–68 (Ithaca: Cornell University Press).

Castellano, U. (2007) 'Becoming a Nonexpert and Other Strategies for Managing Fieldwork Dilemmas in the Criminal Justice System', *Journal of Contemporary Ethnography*, 36, 704–30.

Emerson, R., Fretz, R. and Shaw, L. (1995) *Writing Ethnographic Fieldnotes* (Chicago: University of Chicago Press).

Inciardi, J. A. (1993) 'Some Considerations on the Methods, Dangers and Ethics of Crack House Research', in J. A. Inciardi, D. Lockwood and A. E. Pottieger (eds) *Women and Crack Cocaine* (NewYork: Macmillan).

Jefferson, A. M. (2005) 'Reforming Nigerian Prisons: Rebuilding a "Deviant" State', *British Journal of Criminology*, 45, 487–503.

Jewkes, Y. (2012) 'Autoethnography and Emotion as Intellectual Resources: Doing Prison Research Differently', *Qualitative Inquiry*, 18, 63–75.

Jewkes, Y. (2013) 'What Can Ethnography Offer in an Age of Mass Incarceration?' *Criminal Justice Matters*, 91, 1, 14–15.

Liebling, A. (2001) 'Whose Side Are We On? Theory, Practice and Allegiances in Prisons Research', *British Journal of Criminology*, 41, 472–84.

Liebling, A., Price, D. and Shefer, G. (2011) *The Prison Officer* (Cullompton: Willan Publishing).

McKendy, J. P. (2006) 'I'm Very Careful about That: Narrative and Agency of Men in Prison', *Discourse Society*, 17, 473–502.

Marcus, G. (2009) 'Notes toward an Ethnographic Memoir of Supervising Graduate Research through Anthropology's Decades of Transformation', in J. D. Faubion and G. E. Marcus (eds) *Fieldwork Is Not What It Used to Be: Learning Anthropology's Method in a Time of Transition*, pp. 1–34 (Ithaca: Cornell University Press).

Martin, T. M. (2014) 'Reasonable Caning and the Embrace of Human Rights in Ugandan Prisons', *Focaal*, 68, 68–82.

Martin, T. M., Jefferson, A M. and Bandyopadhyay, M. (2014) 'Sensing Prison Climates: Governance, Survival, and Transition', *Focaal*, 68, 3–17.

Moczydlowski, P. (1992) *The Hidden Life of Polish Prisons* (Bloomington: Indiana University Press).

Owen, B. (1998) *In the Mix: Struggle and Survival in a Women's Prison* (New York: SUNY Press).

Piacentini, L. (2004) *Surviving Russian Prisons: Punishment Economy and Politics in Transition* (Cullompton: Willian Publishing).

Reed, A. (2004) *Papua New Guinea's Last Place: Experiences of Constraint in a Postcolonial Prison* (Oxford: Berghahn Books).

Reeves, C. (2010) 'A Difficult Negotiation: Fieldwork Relations with Gatekeepers', *Qualitative Research*, 10, 3, 315–31.

Rhodes, L. (2001) 'Toward an Anthropology of Prisons', *Annual Review of Anthropology*, 30, 65–83.

Rhodes, L. A. (2004) *Total Confinement: Madness and Reason in the Maximum Security Prison* (California: University of California Press).
Rhodes, L. (2009) 'Ethnography in Sites of Total Confinement', *Anthropology News*, 50, 1, 6.
Vered, A. (eds) (2000) *Constructing the Field: Ethnographic Fieldwork in the Contemporary World* (London: Routledge).
Wacquant, L. (2002) 'The Curious Eclipse of Prison Ethnography in the Age of Mass Incarceration', *Ethnography*, 3, 4, 371–97.
Waldram, J. B. (2009) '"It's Just You and Satan, Hanging Out at a Pre-School": Notions of Evil and the Rehabilitation of Sexual Offenders', *Anthropology and Humanism*, 34, 2, 219–34.

24
Unique Position: Dual Identities as Prison Researcher and Ex-prisoner

William Davies

Introduction

It is understood in the research methods literature that rapport building is an essential component of the interviewer–interviewee relationship, and thus it needs to be carefully built up and maintained throughout the research encounter. In this chapter, I suggest that when researching sensitive topics or working in tense environments, rapport building is contingent on proximity, openness and a non-judgemental approach. I argue that my ideas, meanings and understandings were greatly facilitated by utilising my personal history of being an ex-prisoner, which enabled me to build up a rapport with the individual respondents through reciprocal information sharing of personal experiences. This was achieved through taking the time to have a pre-interview discussion with each respondent, during which research ethics and informed consent were covered. Here I was able to discuss my past and the reasons behind my research; this allowed the respondents to view me as closer to their status rather than being a member of the establishment.

This chapter opens up and engages with a discussion relating to the positive impact 'insiders' (in this case ex-prisoners) can have on researching subjects close to them (e.g. prisons) by creating a depth of understanding that a more surface-level approach would struggle to provide. Thus, the chapter inherently makes a case for the importance of ethnography and perhaps, more specifically, for 'insider ethnography' as a means by which to capture texture and depth that is difficult to achieve through other methods or from other positions or roles held by the researcher in relation to the research cohort.

The research setting and respondents

The research setting for my PhD was a local, category B, adult male prison in the North of England and, throughout this chapter, will be referred to as HMP Research. I was granted access to the prison and given keys (a point to which

I return later) in order to enable a greater degree of freedom of movement. During the two weeks that ended up being my research period, I carried out semi-structured interviews with 20 prisoners, each of whom was serving short-term prison sentences of 12 months or less. Of these 20 respondents, 12 were housed on the general population wings and eight on the vulnerable prisoner unit (VPU); of the latter eight, four identified themselves as having committed an offence of a sexual nature, and the remaining four presented themselves as being on the VPU for protection against bullying and other prisoner-related issues.

Initially, in the fieldwork planning stages, it was envisaged that I would be conducting a number of follow-up interviews with the respondents, building up a trustful relationship with them during the process; during which time I would carefully choose when and how to disclose my past experiences with them. However, due to timescales, my access was to be limited to a two-week period. With this new timescale in mind, the importance of being able to establish relationships with the respondents needed to be renegotiated. Having only a short time within which to conduct my research, I was conscious of the need to avoid the scenario of collecting large amounts of data in a short amount of time with no concern for building relationships or cementing the interviewer–respondent relationship; therefore the danger of becoming a 'rapid collector', as Tedlock (2000: 456) identifies researchers, could not be overlooked.

Types of knowledge

In approaching my research I separated knowledge into the *objective* and *subjective* that I would be examining. The notion of *objective knowledge* which I associated with my research extended to the identification of 'what' was being explored; which in this case was the lived experiences of short sentenced prisoners within HM Prison Service. This meant that the specific *objective knowledge* needed was in relation to what a short-term prison sentence constituted, how many were served and by whom. This was knowledge that could be gathered at a distance and needed no real linkage to qualitative methodology. In contrast, the *subjective knowledge* that the research was tasked with identifying was in relation to how the cohort of short-term-sentenced prisoners experienced their incarceration. It is this *subjective knowledge* that I argue was achieved in a shorter space of time than conventional relationship building methodologies, such as reciprocity, and trust building (Adler and Adler, 1998: xv), due to my closeness to the respondents. Through sharing my identity as an ex-prisoner with the respondents being interviewed, it enabled them to view me as something other than an interviewer; they viewed me as an equal, someone who they thought understood their identity as prisoners. This in turn led to an apparent level of openness regarding the asking and answering of questions within such a short interview time frame of one hour; one hour which must include building a rapport with the respondent, collecting the data through the interview and cementing the interview at the end.

Objective knowledge surrounding prisons can be found from a number of sources: the Ministry of Justice Quarterly Statistical Bulletin, weekly prison population figures published online and sentencing statistics, provided within the Ministry of Justice's Criminal Justice Statistics Quarterly collection, being some of the officially published data, supplemented by the work of the Howard League for Penal Reform and the Prison Reform Trust. However, to begin truly to understand the nuances of prison life, *subjective knowledge* of imprisonment must be understood:

> Since we can only enter into another person's world through communication, we depend upon ethnographic dialogue to create a world of shared intersubjectivity and to reach an understanding of the differences between the two worlds.
>
> (Tedlock, 1991: 70)

Subjective knowledge surrounding imprisonment is readily available from a number of sources: Clemmer (1940); Sykes (1958); Carrabine (2004); Liebling (2004) and Crewe (2007) are just a few of the numerous academic studies surrounding prison life and the sociology of prison from the prisoner's perspective. Further to that Arnold, Liebling and Tait (2007) and Arnold (2008) have written about staff experiences (with Arnold also having gone through prison officer training) whilst Crawley (2004) also researched the experiences of prison officers (without having done officer training). In addition to this, there are numerous media pieces written by ex-prisoners who recount their experiences of having served a prison sentence (see Archer, 2002; and Erwin James' regular British newspaper column, along with the work of Rod Earle, 2012 on the differences between his, 'spending time and doing time', within the prison environment). Further to this, we have copious amounts of fictional media representations of prisons such as: *Prison Break, Shawshank Redemption, Oz, Brubaker, Orange Is the New Black*, not to mention contemporary print media representations of 'holiday camps' filled with master criminals playing games consoles and watching television.

Whilst these can all present accurate and vivid insights into prison life from the perspectives of those who live and work within the institution, the experiences of the researcher (or author) do not always match those of the respondent. The closest we see is the work of Arnold (2005, 2008) who, as has been noted, conducted research on prison officers, after having herself undergone prison officer training. Whilst this afforded Arnold an understanding of what a prison officer might go through during their training and might have given an insight into the thought processes of front line prison staff, it does not provide the lived experiences of a prison officer; what it is like physically to lock a prisoner in a cell, or what it is like to have a prisoner become violent without warning. Can you adequately replicate the exact feeling of being 'gassed' or 'shitted up' by a prisoner[1] within the safety of a training session with colleagues?

Barriers to knowledge

When an interviewer meets with an interviewee, they are generally strangers. When two strangers meet within an interview setting, whereby one party wishes to gain personal information from the other, then certain barriers must first be overcome. A respondent will be less likely to discuss personal information with a person they do not trust, like, or have a connection with. They will be less likely to discuss issues which paint them in a negative light to an interviewer who they deem to be in a position of power over them. The prison environment provides all of these obstacles. Therefore when an outsider is interviewing a prisoner, that prisoner will invariably have barriers up. I found that in my research I was able quickly to reduce the negative impact of such barriers by sharing my identity as an insider with them at an early stage; thus enabling a relationship between interviewer and respondent to be built quicker.

Feminist methodologies discuss the importance of relationship building within the interview process in order to enable more detailed data to be collected. Oakley (1981) suggests that researchers should become involved with the creation of the data through the introduction of their own ideas and experiences on the topic under discussion. This links with the insider researcher and status versus that of an outsider put forward by Merton (1972); I saw myself as very much an insider, although technically I would have been an outsider who possessed insider knowledge, gained from experience rather than education or research. Liebling (1999) discusses how, the further into interviews she progressed, the more the respondent appeared relaxed enough to revisit previous questions and expand on answers with more detail, and that participants would return to a topic, change their first response – go deeper, and become fluent, trusting, more open, and the interview would unwind (1999: 158).

In the interviews, I was able to put myself on a relatively equal status with the respondents (it would never be absolutely equal due to the fact that I was free to leave at any point: they were imprisoned).

Creating prison knowledge and overcoming barriers

Ethnographic research is concerned with portraying those who are being researched in as natural a way as is possible. Thus, we would generally expect to see the researcher taking part in some kind of observation, be it covertly, as in Humphreys' (1975) *Tearoom Trade* and Whyte's (1943) *Street Corner Society*; or overtly in Arnolds' (2008) study of prison officers.

Whilst my research may not be 'to the letter of the law' an ethnographic overview of the lived experiences of short-term prisoners (because I was not immersed in their life as a participant, or narrating their existence as they experienced it), I argue that my research has ethnographic edges to it. At one point I did, in fact, live the existence that my respondents were living; I shared the experiences that they were encountering, just at a different point in time. So, whilst ethnographers can view what it might be like to be serving a prison sentence and be able to disseminate that knowledge to a wider audience, they will always be seen by their respondents as 'outsiders'. As my research methodology was one of 'retrospective participant observation' (Bulmer, 1982: 232), I was able to maintain an 'insider' status.

One of the differences between my research and the ethnographic research of other academics is the length of time spent within the prison. Some researchers spend many months: I spent two weeks. Many researchers get to meet their respondents over a couple of meetings and are able to build relationships and trust that way: I was afforded one hour for each of my interviews. It could possibly be suggested that this lack of time spent with respondents would not have allowed me sufficient time to break down the various 'barriers to knowledge' that exist when conducting prison research. However, I argue that the lack of specific face-to-face research time that I was able to spend within the walls of HMP Research did not impact negatively upon my ability to elicit information from the respondents.

The ability to elicit detailed, personal life stories within a short space of time was largely done by limiting the various barriers to gaining *subjective knowledge* that have been identified here (trust building, openness, equal status). In attempting to eliminate or negate the negative effects of the knowledge barriers before the collection of data (individual interviews) begins, the quality of the data does not suffer due to time restraints.

Building relationships within the research environment

Prison consists of power relationships, and that power only invariably travels downwards. This power relationship creates levels of mistrust between those that are governed by the power (prisoners) and those that wield the power (either the institution or the individual members of staff). Building trust between interviewer and respondent is seen as being crucial in the research process (Oakley, 1981; Finch, 1984), this is never so important than in the relationship between prisoners and non-prisoners where the levels of mistrust might be naturally higher due to the them 'versus' us mentality of the prison system (Carrabine, 2004). Mistrust between two parties at this stage would undoubtedly have a negative effect on knowledge barriers. As mentioned previously, many prison ethnographers have been able to negotiate longer time scales within which to conduct their data collection: Arnold (2005) spent 11 weeks training with her cohort of prison officers before collecting data from the research site; Crawley (2004) spent two years in the field collecting data, allowing for trust to be built up over a period of time. It was here that I was first able to utilise my insider status to aid in the trust building process. At the planning stages of my methodology, it was not envisaged that my insider status as an ex-prisoner would automatically be shared, even less so at such an early part of the interviews, or indeed whether such information sharing would take place within each interview. It was later to transpire that reciprocal sharing would, in fact, be integral to it the depth and quality of data that I was able to collect.

Rapport

The most important methodological skill that a researcher can have in their toolkit is that of being able to build a relationship and develop a rapport with those involved in the study:

> Successful research depends on the investigator's trained abilities to look at people, listen to them, think and feel with them, talk with them rather than at them. It does not depend fundamentally on some impersonal apparatus, such as a camera or tape recorder or questionnaire, that is interposed between the investigator and the investigated.
>
> (Polsky, 1998: 119)

At the start of the interviewing process, I knew that more attention was needed to be given towards building trust quickly due to time restrictions. I decided that the quickest way for me to achieve greater trust was through reciprocal sharing, whereby the interview becomes a 'two way street', with information being shared between interviewee and interviewer as the process progresses. Instead of taking a few minutes to discuss the research and the role that the respondent would be playing in it and then starting the interview, I had decided that I would first introduce myself and my history very briefly before moving into a detailed overview of my research and my motivations behind it. Following this, I would then revisit my personal history in slightly more depth and allow the respondents to ask any questions that they wanted; I put no caveats on this and encouraged them to ask anything they liked, which they subsequently did. It was this initial 15 or so minutes that I found crucial in being able to build a relationship with the respondents quickly, whilst also attempting simultaneously to overcome knowledge barriers that arise from initial mistrust.

At the beginning of the interview process, the respondent's motivation might have been one of a 'research bargain' (Martin, 2002) whereby prisoners are grateful for the time spent out of their cell with someone new to talk to. However, this process only ensures that the researcher has a physical body to pose questions to, the process does not guarantee that the respondent will cooperate with the research fully, openly and honestly. The early plan was to utilise my insider status of ex-prisoner much in the same way that Finch (1984) espoused that her insider status benefitted her research:

> Namely that the ease with which one can get women to talk in the interview situation depends not so much upon one's skills as an interviewer, nor upon one's expertise as a sociologist, but upon one's identity as a woman.
>
> (Finch, 1984: 171)

Whilst I am not disputing that Finch's methodology greatly facilitated the collecting of her data (as it did in the prison setting for Quraishi (2008), who utilised his status as a Muslim when interviewing Muslim prisoners), I do argue that simply having *one* connection is not necessarily enough to build trust within the research setting. Whilst it is the case that I utilised my status as ex-prisoner to my advantage in establishing trust at an early stage of the interview, simply being an ex-prisoner did not supersede my skills as a researcher or criminologist. As I will discuss later, there were pitfalls to sharing an identity with the respondents that, at times, might have restricted the level of information provided during the interviews. That is not to say that Finch's 'identity sharing' did not have an important role to play in my data collection. On the contrary, being able to share an identity with such a hard-to-reach and vulnerable group made the overall process of relationship building an easier, and as I suggest, much quicker process.

Fleisher (1998) would argue that is impossible for researchers to gain in-depth information from respondents, and that 'No one, especially a criminal would divulge innermost secrets to a stranger, even a stranger offering a fee' (1998: 53). Here, I expanded on my status as an ex-prisoner to include more specific details regarding that identity; this included personal information such as the offence that I had committed, the sentence that I had received, the time that I had served, and the timescale relating to when and where I served my sentence. The 'fee' I paid to my respondents was not one of money or goods, but information, personal information. For the large part, my personal history shared similarities with my respondents. I was in my late twenties when I went to prison; I served my sentence in a local, adult, category B prison; I served a short sentence. The main differences were that my offences were different from my respondents, and there was a time difference of some 14 years.

Oakley argues that there is 'no intimacy without reciprocity' (1981: 49). The reciprocity in my interviews started before any information was asked of the respondents. By sharing my personal experiences with the interviewees, I was starting the reciprocity progress early; yet, whilst I hoped that this would encourage similar personal disclosure during interviews, I did not think that it was guaranteed. In sharing life histories during the interviews, I had placed myself within close proximity to the respondents, and it is a mixture of this reciprocal sharing of information and close proximity of life histories that I argue enabled me to produce a quality of data that may have taken other, non-insider, researchers longer to acquire.

The importance of proximity within ethnographic research has been suggested to be significant in the collecting of data. What has been largely neglected in such discussions, however, is the role that proximity plays in the process of analysing and presenting the data once collected. At times in the interview process, I found that my cultural and life history proximity to the respondents was in danger of limiting the depth of discussion I had envisaged. During the first couple of interviews, the respondents would sometimes finish a sentence by adding the phrase, 'you know what I mean?' Invariably, because of our shared proximity I did know what they meant, either from past personal experience, or because they portrayed their answer well enough for me instantly to picture what they were discussing. Initially I saw this as one aspect of the interviews that, for me, stood out as proof of my success of building a relationship with the interviewees: they saw me as someone who understood them. However, it could be argued that this was, in fact, having the opposite effect; that because the respondents saw me as being closer to being 'one of them' rather than a representative of the prison system, they did not go into as much detail as they might have done for an interviewer who they saw as having no insight into their daily lived experiences. As such my response to statements that respondents qualified with 'you know what I mean?' was that of 'yes, I do, but the people reading this won't necessarily know what you mean and I would rather tell them in your words than mine'.

Simply by asking respondents to put their experiences in their words is not sufficient to ensure that their thoughts are portrayed accurately. During the interview process, I became aware of thinking at times that certain 'discussion points' such as entry into prison, support for release and familial relationships would be good for the data I wanted to present. This might be seen by some as the beginnings of 'going native', not to the extent that Ferrell (1998) experienced when he ended up in court after participating in activities that he was simply meant to be studying; but native none the less, if it could be shown that I was 'on the side' of the researched (Becker, 1967). By putting forward the lived experiences of current prisoners in their own words, how could I not be seen as being on their side? After all, I was not presenting the side of the establishment or staff to counteract the prisoner's experiences.

Another self-discussion point that I had whilst collecting my data was: Who was I to say that my experiences were the same as those that I was interviewing? What makes an interviewer close in proximity to the respondents? Is it down to the researcher to decide, or those that are being researched?

Simply building rapport with, and locating oneself within, cultural proximity to the respondent is not enough to break down all barriers to knowledge. Within prison there is a very real power differential, and historically, if you are not a prisoner then you are likely to be viewed by prisoners as being on the side of the establishment. The literature surrounding the sociology of imprisonment has long discussed the definitive line between prisoners and the prison (Sykes, 1958; Johnson and Toch, 1982; Carrabine, 2004; Crewe, 2007, 2009; Liebling, 2007). One often cited barrier to gaining information within interviews is the researcher as a key carrying researcher. This power differential is seen to include the researcher when they are in possession of a set of keys with which they can freely navigate the prison environment. It is argued that a researcher loses impartiality when they take possession of prison keys and place themselves in a symbolic position of power over prisoners (Sim, 2003).

Being a key-carrying researcher had an unplanned plus point, in particular, after I had shared with the respondents regarding my life history, they as a whole thought it was positive that an 'ex-con' was able to have keys to a prison which allowed me unrestricted access. When they were told that I actually had keys to another prison as part of my Independent Monitoring Board duties, they seemed even more impressed. As such, this is an anecdotal example of what I thought as being something that I thought gave the relationship between me and the interviewee another connection. It allowed me to be able to identify the keys as 'the elephant in the room'; to be able to present them not as an identifier of the power that only a member of the establishment can possess, but rather they became a nothing, a simple tool with which I was able to come and go as I pleased. After all, keys are common place within the contemporary prison estate. Many non-prison staff hold keys to the establishment they work in. On a number of occasions, various non-respondent prisoners stopped me and asked if I was from *Shelter* (a housing charity) or a probation officer, a drug worker, or from any other voluntary organisation. Keys are also commonplace on residential wings in some prisons now; it is not uncommon for prisoners to have keys to their own cells. Once the master lock had been unlocked by the prison staff, the individual prisoners can lock their cells behind them whenever they like. If they go to work in the morning, they can come back for lunch and let themselves back into their own cell. Keys no longer hold mystical power within the establishment as the prisoners are increasingly aware of the variety of roles within the prison which require a person to carry them.

Vulnerable prisoner units

So far, I have discussed how relationships between researcher and respondents were formed through reciprocal sharing and locating life histories within close proximity to each other. This was done to facilitate the data that can be gained through ethnographic methods when time is limited. This process relied heavily on the speedy building of trust. Even in cases of insider research, there may not be an exact replication of life history between the interviewer and interviewee. Therefore, it can be suggested that relationships cannot always be formed on personal histories. This was the case during my research when interviewing prisoners who had committed offences of a sexual nature, including offences against people under the age of 18.

When offered the opportunity to interview prisoners housed on the VPU, I wasted no time in accepting. When possible, researchers should be opportunistic when additional sources of data are made available, and never more so than in the case of hard-to-reach demographics such as vulnerable prisoners. In relation to some of the more generic prison research focusing on adult male imprisonment in general, the lived experiences of prisoners housed within VPUs go largely under-researched. Part of the intrinsic beauty of the ethnographic approach to research is that it enables us to gain a greater understanding of hard-to-reach groups, affording researchers a greater level of *Verstehen* (Weber, cited in Ferrell, 1998). However, the inclusion of vulnerable prisoners into my research added additional issues to the methodology, in an already time-restricted data collection stage.

One thing that struck me very early on in the interview process, dawning on me literally moments before the first respondent arrived at the interview room, was how exactly was I going to react to the crimes that some of the respondents had committed. I had at no point in the planning of the research thought I would be interviewing prisoners who were labelled by the establishment as being 'vulnerable'. I was not naïve enough to think that everyone on the VPU was going to be a sex offender, or had committed a crime against children, but I was still conscious that there would be the distinct possibility that some of them would have. I had not put any offence-related stipulations forward with regard to the general population, so felt the same should be appropriate for other prisoners interviewed.

The interviewing of vulnerable prisoners not only identified additional barriers to knowledge but also created opportunities to gain a greater understanding of the experiences of a wider range of sentenced prisoners. First, the main barrier to knowledge could be seen in trust and relationship building, a lack of sharing of personal history (yes I knew what it was like to be a prisoner, but the experiences of a stigmatised sex offender or vulnerable prisoner cannot easily be understood without first-hand experience). Simply by definition, prisoners on the VPU are 'vulnerable' (Hudson, 2005) which can create a greater issue with building trust with other people. Offending behaviour courses attempt to make sex offenders take responsibility for their actions and accept their behaviour as deviant; this might make respondents more shameful of their actions and less likely to talk in depth, choosing instead to present their 'frontstage' personas (Goffman, 1990: 32). A number of respondents were actively taking part in behaviour training such as Sex Offender Treatment Programmes (SOTP) which are designed to encourage prisoners to be more open and upfront about their histories and more at ease talking about their histories and experiences and taking responsibility for their actions (Hudson, 2005). It is, therefore, also possible that having been on these types of training courses the respondents saw the research interviews as an environment where they should be using these newly gained skills. Yet, overall, the experience of being locked behind a door is the same so there was at least a starting point with which to make a connection and allow respondents to feel comfortable enough to reveal any 'backstage' personas they may be concealing (Goffman, 1990).

As has already been discussed, it had already been planned how I imagined that I would set about gaining the trust of the respondents through reciprocal sharing of life histories and pre-interview conversations. I was quietly confident that I would be able to speak with the respondents on their level, in their language, on a one-to-one basis with little or no barriers of superiority or subordination between us, in what Tedlock (1991: 70) would identify as an 'ethnographic dialogue' within which a common understanding can be reached to create a shared understanding of the social world being investigated. I was confident that I would be able to get the respondent to feel comfortable enough with me that they would be happy to discuss personal issues. What I had not given any thought to was whether or not I would feel comfortable with them. Everyone has their own preconceived ideas about people and researchers are no different. We all have our own defined thoughts on what is right and wrong; what is acceptable behaviour and what we would constitute abhorrent. Prior to the fieldwork I had spent time reading and detailing how one of the pains of imprisonment was that you are confined with people who you would otherwise never have contact with (Sykes, 1958; Carrabine, 2004). I had read and discussed issues surrounding taking the time and making the effort to get the respondent onside and to build a relationship with them (Oakley, 1981; Finch, 1984), but there was little discussion in these sources regarding what a researcher should do if they found themselves interviewing someone that they simply did not like, and had no desire ever to like or get to know as a person.

This raises the question of emotions and impartiality within research. A researcher who holds insider status would find it very difficult to remain emotionally impartial. To answer the question posed by Becker (1967) who asked 'whose side are we on?', the insider researcher would often share more in common with the researched. The research that is being discussed here is being put forward as impartial, in that the researcher was on the side of the data. That said it would be wrong to insist that during the research I did not find myself getting emotionally involved with the respondents. Yet, there is a difference between being involved (empathising, showing a genuine interest in them) and getting emotionally invested (attempting to change their situation, or portraying them in a good light).

My research differs from that of others in relation to emotional investment. As mentioned above, it was difficult not to get emotionally involved in the respondents' life histories as a number of them resonated with my own experiences. Where my research did differ however is that the emotional investment needed to gain a mastery of the prison environment was minimal compared with the experiences of fellow researchers. Drake and Harvey (2013) discuss how, within separate pieces of research they both identified the sheer amount of emotional demands that their research made of them simply to get them up to speed with the prison environment. They discuss how mastering the physical spaces within the prison, along with prison language 'argot', and day-to-day rules and regulations, was a journey which, once completed, left them feeling as though they had mastered the environment, but had expended a large amount of emotion getting there.

The only real option available with regard to interviewing vulnerable prisoners was to be as impartial as possible at all times; the researcher's approach to the collection of data should not be shaped by their 'socio-historical location, including the values and interests that these locations infer on them' (Hammersley and Atkinson, 1995: 16). It was important then that all respondents, regardless of which group of participants (general or vulnerable) they were identified with, were treated equally within the research. During the planning of the research, when it was decided who would be included in the cohort, the main parameter set was that they were serving a short-term prison sentence. At no point was it felt that there was the need to add a filter which would take the offence committed into account. It was further decided that there should be absolutely no reason to change this when faced with the option of interviewing vulnerable prisoners. However, asking the respondent about the details of their crime was not going to be a question that I had planned to ask in any of the interviews and would only be discussed if the respondent mentioned it first. In hindsight, this meant that I was creating my own 'don't ask, don't tell' scenario. However, it transpired that the vulnerable prisoner interviews were conducted slightly ad hoc in respect to details regarding their crime. It became clear very early in the first interview that, with vulnerable prisoners, the crime committed was an important avenue of questioning; the responses they received from fellow prisoners were closely related to the crimes that they had been sentenced for. Therefore, the question of the offence committed needed to be addressed as I felt that if the offence affected their treatment, then it would also affect how they experienced prison life.

Another reason which made it difficult to avoid the question of the offence committed was due to the validity of the data. If a research question was going to be answered in detail, then the questions asked when gathering the data had to be equally, if not more, detailed. Whilst I was mindful of not making the interview process uncomfortable or upsetting in any way for the respondents, neither did I want to ask them simple 'flowery' questions. I wanted the questions that I was asking them to cause them to stop and think, to make them look into their selves and their feelings and share them on an open platform. By avoiding certain questions early on, I felt that that might be setting the standard for the rest of the interviews. If the respondent was given a way out of answering the first difficult question, then they could see that as a precedent for the refusal to answer any further sensitive or difficult questions. In terms of prison etiquette, the asking of an inmate what their offence was is simply not done and prisoners should 'do their own time' and not get involved in another prisoner's history (Clemmer, 1940; Sykes, 1958). By that being one of the first questions asked in the interview, it set the stage that no real questions could be out of bounds, and that questions of a personal nature would continue to be asked throughout, all of which I felt comfortable asking, and the respondents, through their readiness to answer, appeared comfortable in answering, due to the relationships built up during the initial first ten minutes of the interview.

Conclusion

In this chapter, I highlight the importance of utilising ethnographic and feminist methodologies within prison research. The prison is a closed environment within which the role of superordinate and subordinate (Becker, 1967) is clear and distinct. In such an environment, reaching a stage whereby those who are imprisoned feel comfortable enough to discuss, at length, their personal experiences, should not be taken for granted. Before data can be obtained within one-to-one interviews, relationships between the interviewer and respondent need to be formed within which mutual trust can be nurtured, enabling knowledge barriers, such as lack of trust, to be overcome.

The power relationships between interviewer and respondent can be broken down quicker than in conventional interviewing if the interviewer is able to locate their experiences within the proximity of those being interviewed. Within my research, I utilised my status as an insider to aid in the building of rapport, within which it was possible to form a reciprocal information-sharing relationship with respondents. This, in turn, enabled in-depth data to be collected within a shorter period of time than might be used by other researchers.

That is not to say that the data collected here was better than that collected by others, only that it was not disadvantaged by spending less time interviewing.

However, it is not always possible for the researcher and respondent to build a rapport over shared experiences, as was the case with the vulnerable prisoners within my research. Rather, it brought about questions relating to emotions and impartiality within research. As researchers, we may not always be able only to research the cohorts that we choose: at times additional avenues of research open up to us, and when that happens we must adapt. Even though I shared no proximal knowledge about the offences committed, I was still able to share with the vulnerable prisoners the experience of being imprisoned; that, along with impartiality, enabled me to continue utilising my chosen method of ethnographic interviewing.

The argument that I put forward here is that the data collected within my research was greatly aided by utilising the common experiences of imprisonment that I shared with the respondents. When faced with time constraints in the interview process, the researcher should utilise any and all legitimate and ethical strategies available to gain data within the prison setting. The researcher, and indeed the research methodologies, must be adaptable; through utilising ethnographic methodologies this adaptability is made possible.

Note

1. Both 'gassed' and 'shitted up' are prison slang for throwing urine, faeces or other bodily fluids over prison staff.

Further reading

Carrabine, E. (2004) *Power, Discourse and Resistance: A Genealogy of the Strangeways Prison Riot* (Aldershot: Ashgate).

Sykes, G. (1958) *Society of Captives* (New Jersey: Princeton University Press).

References

Adler, P. and Adler, P. (1998) 'Foreword: Moving Backward', in J. Ferrell and M. Hamm (eds) *Ethnography at the Edge: Crime, Deviance, and Field Research* (Boston: Northeastern University Press).

Archer, J. (2002) *Hell: A Prison Diary*, Volume 1 (London: Macmillan).

Arnold, H. (2005) 'The Effects of Prison Work', in A. Liebling and S. Maruna (eds) *The Effects of Imprisonment* (Cullompton: Willan Publishing).

Arnold, H. (2008) 'The Experience of Prison Officer Training', in J. Bennett, B. Crewe and A. Wahidin (eds) *Understanding Prison Staff* (Cullompton: Willan Publishing).

Arnold, H., Liebling, A. and Tait, S. (2007) 'Prison Officers and Prison Culture', in Y. Jewkes (ed) *Handbook on Prisons* (Cullompton: Willan Publishing).

Becker, H. (1967) 'Whose Side Are We On?' *Social Problems*, 14, 239–47.

Bulmer, M. (1982) 'The Merits and Demerits of Covert Participant Observation', in M. Bulmer (ed) *Social Research Ethics* (London: Macmillan).

Carrabine, E. (2004) *Power, Discourse and Resistance: A Genealogy of the Strangeways Prison Riot* (Aldershot: Ashgate).

Clemmer, D. (1940) 'The Prison Community', *Social Forces,* 19, 3, 442–43.

Crawley, E. (2004) 'Emotion and Performance: Prison Officers and the Presentation of Self in Prisons', *Punishment and Society,* 6, 4, 411–27.

Crewe, B. (2007) 'Power, Adaptation and Resistance in a Late-Modern Men's Prison', *British Journal of Criminology*, 47, 2, 256–75.

Crewe, B. (2009) *The Prisoner Society: Power, Adaptation, and Social Life in an English Prison* (Oxford: Oxford University Press).

Drake, D. and Harvey, J. (2013) 'Performing the Role of Ethnographer: Processing and Managing the Emotional Dimensions of Prison Research', *International Journal of Social Research Methodology*, 15, 5, 489–501.

Earle, R. (2014) 'Insider and Out: Reflections on a Prison Experience and Research Experience', *Qualitative Inquiry*, 20, 429–38.

Ferrell, J. (1998) 'Criminological Verstehen: Inside the Immediacy of Crime', in J. Ferrell and M. Hamm (eds) *Ethnography at the Edge: Crime, Deviance, and Field Research* (Boston: Northeastern University Press).

Fleisher, M. (1998) 'Ethnographers, Pimps and the Company Store', in J. Ferrell and M. Hamm (eds) *Ethnography at the Edge: Crime, Deviance, and Field Research* (Boston: Northeastern University Press).

Finch, J. (1984) 'It's Great to Have Someone to Talk to: Ethics and Politics of Interviewing Women', in C. Bell and Roberts, H. (eds) *Social Researching: Politics, Problems, Practice* (London: Routledge) reprinted in M. Hammersley (ed) *Social Research Philosophy, Politics and Practice* (London: Sage).

Goffman, E. (1990) *The Presentation of Life in Everyday Life* (Harmondsworth: Penguin).

Hammersley, M. and Atkinson, P. (1995) *Ethnography: Principles in Practice,* Second edition (London: Routledge).

Hudson, K. (2005) *Offending Identities: Sex offenders' Perspectives on Their Treatment and Management* (Cullompton: Willan).

Humphreys, L. (1975) *Tearoom Trade: Impersonal Sex in Public Places* (New Jersey: Aldine Transaction).

Johnson, R. and Toch, H. (eds) (1982) *The Pains of Imprisonment* (California: Sage).

Liebling, A. (1999) 'Doing Research in Prisons: Breaking the Silence?' *Theoretical Criminology*, 3, 2, 147–73.

Liebling, A. (2007) 'Prison Suicide and Its Prevention', in Y. Jewkes (ed) *Handbook on Prisons* (Cullompton: Willan).

Liebling, A. (assisted by Arnold, H.) (2004) *Prisons and Their Moral Performance: A Study of Values, Quality, and Prison Life* (Oxford: Oxford University Press).

Martin, C. (2002) 'Doing Research in a Prison Setting', in V. Jupp, P. Davies and P. Francis (eds) *Doing Criminological Research* (London: Sage).

Merton, R. (1972) 'Insiders and Outsiders: A Chapter in the Sociology of Knowledge', *American Journal of Sociology*, 78, 1, 9–47.

Oakley, A. (1981) 'Interviewing Women: A Contradiction in Terms', in H. Roberts (ed) *Doing Feminist Research* (London: Routledge and Kegan Paul).

Polsky, N. (1998) *Hustlers, Beats and Others* (New York: The Lyons Press).

Quraishi, M. (2008) 'Researching Muslim Prisoners', *International Journal of Social Research Methodology,* 11, 5, 453–67.

Sim, J. (2003) Book review of Y. Jewkes (2002) 'Captive Audience: Media, Masculinity and Power in Prisons', *Theoretical Criminology*, 7, 239–42.
Sykes, G. (1958) *Society of Captives* (Princeton: Princeton University Press).
Tedlock, B. (1991) 'From Participant Observation to the Observation of Participation: The Emergence of Narrative Ethnography', *Journal of Anthropological Research*, 47, 1, Spring, 69–94.
Tedlock, B. (2000) 'Ethnography and Ethnographic Representation', in N. Denzin and Y. Lincoln (eds) *Handbook of Qualitative Research*, Second edition (London: Sage Publications).
Whyte, W. (1943) *Street Corner Society: The Social Structure of an Italian Slum* (Chicago: University of Chicago Press).

25

Mixing Detention Cultures: The Belgian–Dutch Case

Kristel Beyens and Miranda Boone

Introduction

In 2009, the then Minister of Justice of Belgium, Stefaan De Clerck, struggled with a long-standing problem of serious prison overcrowding, whilst the Netherlands was closing down prisons due to a decreasing prison population. As the Penitentiary Institution of Tilburg (PI Tilburg), a prison in the Netherlands which is located near the Belgian border, was also facing closure and thus unemployment of its staff, this situation was taken as an opportunity to find a temporary solution for both governments' penitentiary problems. An agreement between the two countries was set, and from February 2010 onwards Belgian inmates in prisons dispersed all over the country were gradually transferred to the Dutch PI Tilburg and were detained under Belgian penitentiary legislation and the Belgian prison regime. The PI Tilburg is run by Dutch staff under shared Belgian and Dutch governance. This has resulted in a unique encounter and melding of different legal regulations, prison regimes and cultures.

From the start, there was a generally negative image of the PI Tilburg in Belgium in the press. The protests mainly targeted the compulsory, opaque and unannounced transfer of prisoners to a foreign country; the bad food; and the distances from their families. Consequently, the 'League of Human Rights' paid a visit to the PI Tilburg and wrote a negative report about the first period of the Tilburg experiment (League of Human Rights, 2011). Later on, the 'European Committee for the Prevention of Torture and Inhuman or Degrading Treatment or Punishment' (CPT) devoted a special visit to the PI Tilburg and published, in 2012, a moderately positive report (CPT, 2012).

Despite this negative publicity, it turned out that prisoners and staff reported relatively positively about their experiences in Tilburg prison in the annual enquiries that were done amongst prisoners and staff in all Dutch prisons. The Dutch Prison Service wanted to find out if this image was correct and how these outcomes could be explained and asked the Research Centre of the Dutch

Department of Justice (WODC) to launch a call to investigate the detention experiences of staff and prisoners in the PI Tilburg. We were very happy to be selected to carry out a ten-month-funded research project, because it would give us the opportunity to investigate this experiment from the inside. The research was conducted by three Dutch and two Belgian researchers, including the authors of this chapter, who also supervised the project and wrote the final report. We chose a semi-ethnographic research design because we were convinced that this was the only sound approach to make a thorough analysis of the experiences of prisoners and staff and the meanings they give to these experiences.

This research fits the purposes of this Handbook in two ways. First, it is ethnographic in the sense that it has used a combination of observation and in-depth interviews to get an inside view on how prisoners and staff in this specific penitentiary institution go about their everyday lives, routines and practices and how they experience these. The short-term character of our research and the limited time we had for observation were compensated for by the bi-national composition of the research team and their familiarity with the respective prison cultures in their respective countries. The exceptional comparative situation in the PI Tilburg more or less forced us to get a deep understanding of the perspectives and cultural context of both the Belgian prisoners and the Dutch staff. For this chapter, we have selected some findings to illustrate how the mix of Belgian–Dutch regulations, staff and prison cultures influences the detention experiences of prisoners and prison staff. Secondly, conducting the research with a mixed Belgian–Dutch research team can be considered as a special form of 'comparative' research. Therefore, the last part of this chapter is devoted to the experiences of the researchers studying this particular situation. It gave rise to interesting discussions and reflections on our researchers' gazes from 'national' positions, looking at 'foreign' or new penal practices. But before doing so, a short introduction to the particular penitentiary and policy context of this penitentiary cooperation between the two countries is given, in order to understand better the experiences that we have studied.

The penal context of the 'Tilburg experiment'

After two decades of rising prison populations and an almost doubling of the prison capacity from 8,000 to 15,000 since 2005, the Netherlands witnessed a decrease in their numbers of prisoners, due to a variety of reasons that are described elsewhere (see Boone and Moerings, 2007, 2008; Van Swaaningen, 2012; Boone and Van Swaaningen, 2013). In 2008, it became clear that this decline was structural, and the decision to reduce the cell capacity by closing prisons was taken by the Department of Justice. This had serious employment implications for the prison staff. In Belgium, however, since the end of the 1980s the prison population has been constantly rising (Beyens et al., 1993; Maes, 2010; Delterne, 2014), resulting in serious prison overcrowding. After more than two decades, with half-hearted attempts to implement a reductionist policy of front- and back-door measures, in 2008 a 'Master Plan for a prison structure in humane conditions'[1] was established in order to expand the existing prison capacity with seven new prisons. It will take, however, several years to realise these building plans. In 2009, the Belgian prison population was 10,238 prisoners for a prison capacity of 8,404, resulting in an overall overcrowding rate of 21.9 per cent. In some 'houses of arrest', where remand prisoners are detained, the overcrowding rate was even higher than 50 per cent (Prison Service, 2010). The prison overcrowding also led to a lot of discontent amongst prison officers, who regularly went on strike to criticise the difficult working conditions and the consequences of the overcrowding. Due to these strikes for the quality of life of the prisoners, the government kept on desperately seeking a temporary emergency solution.

As mentioned earlier, a promising answer to the problems in both countries was found in the transfer of Belgian prisoners to the PI Tilburg. So, in 2009, the Ministers of Justice of both countries signed an agreement – the so-called Nova Belgica Agreement – to formalise this transfer. Since 2010, Belgium has hired extra prison capacity as well as prison staff for a fixed yearly fee of €43,835,000 (in 2013) or €185 per prisoner per day (Delterne, 2014). The agreement of collaboration regulates the relations between the two penal systems in respect of the legal issues with regard to the prison regime, the selection of prisoners, the financial aspects and the transportation of the prisoners between the Belgian prisons and PI Tilburg. The use of the Tilburg prison takes place predominantly under the rule of the Belgian penitentiary laws with regard to the internal and external legal positions of prisoners. In addition, it is operated under a mixed management of Belgian prison governors, who are responsible for the implementation of the Belgian prison regime, and a Dutch management officer, who is responsible for staff and financial matters.

Tilburg prison is still considered a Dutch penitentiary institution on Dutch territory, but, during the agreement, it has been given a particular use or status as a section of the Belgian prison of Wortel, which is located about 45 kilometres from the PI Tilburg. At the time of our research, about 650 Belgian prisoners were detained in Tilburg. Although the initial agreement ran between 2010 and 2012, it was extended until the end of 2015, because the Belgian prison building plans had been delayed.

From a policy perspective, it is interesting to note that the problem of prison overcrowding has not been resolved at all after the hiring of the PI Tilburg. On the contrary, overcrowding has only become worse. With a prison population of 11,645 and a prison capacity of 9,384 (the capacity of the PI Tilburg included), in 2013 the overall prison overcrowding rate increased to 24 per cent (Prison Service, 2014). This means that between 2009 and 2014 the Belgian prison population rose by 13 per cent. This is an important indication of the fact that creating more detention capacity was not a structural solution for the Belgian problem of overcrowding.

Characteristics of Tilburg prison

To appreciate the detention experiences of the prisoners, it is important to understand the material circumstances of their detention. The PI Tilburg has only been used as a prison since 1994. Previously, it was a military barracks, which was converted firstly to a detention centre for irregular migrants, who were awaiting their deportation, and, just before the arrival of the Belgian prisoners, to a prison for women.

It has seven living units for prisoners. Particular to Tilburg is the fact that there are group cells for eight, six and four persons, and mono and duo cells. Each of the eight-person cells has a small kitchen, a shower and a toilet. The living units with more than two-person cells have a recreation room and a big common kitchen where prisoners can prepare meals together in the evenings. The cooking facilities for prisoners are one of the most distinctive and appreciated aspects of Tilburg prison.

The ethnic mix of the Tilburg prison population (about 650 prisoners) is unusual. More than half of the inmates have an irregular or unclear residence status; about two-thirds of the detainees are of non-Belgian origin.[2] The detainees are transferred from Walloon, Brussels and Flemish prisons, resulting in a broad mix of languages, with a substantial number of prisoners who speak French as their first or second language. The majority of the Dutch prison staff, however, do not speak or understand French. Most of the prisoners are sentenced to from three-years of imprisonment up to life. Compared to Dutch standards, in Belgium much longer sentences are imposed. For example, the Belgian prison population has about tenfold the number of lifers compared to the Netherlands.

At the time of the research, about 500 people were employed in Tilburg prison. In contrast to Belgium, they are categorised as 'penitentiary workers' (*penitentiaire inrichtingswerkers*), who are responsible for the daily supervision of the inmates, and security staff. This division of labour allows the penitentiary workers to focus more on a humane and more rehabilitative approach. In addition, several other services, such as management, prison work, medical services, education and sports activities, are carried out by the Dutch personnel. There are also Belgian employees present in the PI Tilburg, such as prison governors and members of the psychosocial staff, who are mainly responsible for the assessment of prisoners in view of release.

Methods

The fieldwork started in February 2012 with a site visit and a long meeting of the research team with the prison governor, where practical arrangements with regard to timing and access to the different areas in the prison were made. During the whole research period (February–June 2012), the research team was welcomed and informed in a very open way by all levels of staff. Although the research time was very limited, fieldwork started with some days of observations in order to get a flavour of the atmosphere in the different sections, to inform the prisoners and staff about the research and to recruit respondents for the semi-structured interviews with prisoners and staff. We were inspired by Liebling and Arnold's (2004) key dimensions measuring the moral climate in prisons to construct the interview schedule for our semi-structured interviews with prisoners and staff. The analysis focused on the material detention circumstances; regime; personal development and reintegration; contact with the outside world; prisoner–staff and prisoner–prisoner relationships; security and order; and fairness.

Using a quota sample, 36 prisoners with diverse detention histories, detention lengths, nationalities and cultural and linguistic backgrounds were selected in order to cover a broad diversity of experiences. Thirty-eight members of staff, with different background characteristics, were also interviewed. All the interviews were recorded, transcribed verbatim and analysed with the qualitative data analysis software MAXQDA. The researchers' experiences in this particular situation will be discussed in the last part of this chapter.

Differences between the Dutch and the Belgian prison legislation and regimes

Some remarkable differences between the Dutch and the Belgian prison legislation and regimes appeared to be particularly influential on the experiences of both staff and prisoners. Below we will pay attention to the three most important aspects: the conditional early release system; security measures such as urine checks and cell inspections; and access to files. In the next section, we will explain *how* these differences influenced the experiences of the Belgian inmates and the Dutch staff.

The conditional release system

In the Netherlands, the system of automatic early release was replaced in 2008 by a system of conditional release. Prisoners, on whom an unconditional prison sentence is imposed of one year or more, can be released after two-thirds of their sentence. Contraindications are formulated in the law (Section 15d of the Penal Code) and consist of the following: (i) serious misconduct since incapacitation, for example behaviour that led to multiple disciplinary punishments; (ii) attempts to escape; (iii) recidivism risk conditions; and (iv) refusal to comply with conditions. Conditional release is granted, unless a court decides on request of the prosecutor to delay or refuse it. Refusals and delays, however, are increasing but are still very rare. It is important to note that in this system prisoners cannot do anything to speed up their release.

Contrary to the Dutch system, conditional release for prisoners with a prison sentence of three years or longer, which is the population in Tilburg, is not granted automatically in Belgium but is decided by multidisciplinary 'sentence implementation courts'. Legally, this category of prisoners can be paroled after having served one-third of their prison sentences; recidivists can be released after having served two-thirds. However, not only time conditions have to be fulfilled; other conditions need to be met before a prisoner can be released on parole, which requires an individual assessment and decision of the sentence implementation court. Advice of the prison governor, based on the report of the psychosocial service, is required. The counter-indications entail: (i) the absence of prospects for the social reintegration of the prisoner; (ii) the risk of committing new serious offences; (iii) the risk that the prisoner would harass the victim(s); and (iv) the attitude of the inmate towards the victim(s) of the offence that led to his conviction. These counter-indications reflect the importance of the social reintegration of the prisoner after his prison term. Therefore, every prisoner has to provide a reintegration plan to prepare for his conditional release during his detention, illustrating his prospects to reintegrate into society and the efforts he has already made in this regard. In order to provide this plan, the inmates need to take initiatives themselves, assisted by the members of the psychosocial service and the external social workers providing educational- and job-related services in the prison.

Security measures

A number of security measures that are quite common in Dutch penitentiary practice are less easily available under Belgian law and thus also less available for the Dutch prison staff in Tilburg prison.

Contrary to Belgian practice, the regular police only rarely intervene in cases of disturbance in prison. Instead, a team of highly trained security personnel is put into action in cases of serious security incidents. This team is formed ad hoc from staff in the prison and has to arrive at the location within three minutes, dressed in the uniforms of the flying squad and armed with batons and shields. In even more serious cases, assistance of the National Division Special Assistance Forces (*Landelijke Bijzondere Bijstandsverlening*) is ensured, which is also the situation in the PI Tilburg. In Belgium, a team like that did not exist at the time of our research, so the prisoners were not familiar with it.

In Belgium, as in the Netherlands, prisoners' bodies and clothing can be searched. According to the penitentiary regulations in both countries, the living area of the prisoner can also be searched (cell inspection). The Dutch legal system also provides the possibility of urine checks (Art. 30 of the Dutch Penitentiary Act) and searches inside the prisoner's body in cases of a serious threat to the maintenance of order and security in the institution, or the prisoner's health (Art. 31 of the Dutch Penitentiary Act). These last two options are unknown to the Belgian system where urine checks are only possible on a voluntary basis. Also, searching inside the prisoner's body is not possible under Belgian law, and this prohibition also applies in the PI Tilburg.

Access to files

Another difference that influenced the experiences of the Dutch prison staff concerns the access prison officers have to the files of detainees. The Dutch Prison Act provides detailed rules regarding content of, and access to, penitentiary files. The Minister of Security and Justice, the prison governor and the selection officer[3] all have access to the penitentiary file. The law says that access can be given to other prison officers or public servants 'as far as necessary for the treatment of a request done by the prisoner himself, for the sake of a pending procedure, to be able to manage the files or to deal with other decisions regarding the prisoner' (Section 40, subsection 2 of the Penitentiary Order). This is a very broad criterion, which results in prison officers having access to a lot of information concerning the penal past of the prisoner and his behaviour in earlier penitentiary institutions. No rules are, however, formulated concerning the handling of files in the Dutch–Belgian agreement. The Belgian penitentiary law does not give any rules either. The prison governor is responsible for the file, but it is considered to be an unwritten rule that prison staff do not have access to files. Compared to Dutch personnel under Dutch regulations, Belgian members of staff thus have no access to information concerning prisoners' criminal and detention records. This Belgian practice was also applicable to the Tilburg situation, with the result that the Dutch prison workers in the PI Tilburg had much less access to information about the Belgian prisoners than they were used to when working in a Dutch prison, which influenced their daily routines. Under Dutch law, the penitentiary file can also be made available to the authorities for the assessment of applications for leave or conditional release, whilst in Belgium – and thus also in the PI Tilburg – this is not the case.

Experiences of the Belgian prisoners and Dutch prison staff

The previous section illustrated how national differences in regulatory frameworks come together in the PI Tilburg and create a new detention situation for the prisoners and the staff. In this section, we will describe how these differences and other cultural differences intervene in the daily practices and influence the routines and experiences of prisoners and staff. Three situations of 'foreignness' will be discussed, that is, staff–prisoner relationships with special attention to the encounter of 'foreign' staff habits, interactions and communication styles and prisoners' habits and needs; food practices; and release practices.

Staff–prisoner relationships

Several prison studies show that the perceived quality of the prisoner–staff relationship has a strong impact on the detention experiences of prisoners (Liebling and Arnold, 2004; Liebling, 2011). Kruttschnitt and Dirkzwager (2011) show that Dutch prison officers score well in this respect compared to English prison officers. In this research, the more responsive attitude of the Dutch prisoners appeared to be an important explanatory factor for the positive evaluation of the Dutch prison regime compared to the English regime.

In our research, when asked what the prisoners experienced as the most striking difference between the Belgian prisons they were transferred from and the PI Tilburg, almost all our respondents pointed to the different approach of the penitentiary workers during daily interactions. Most prisoners valued their humane approach. Compared to the Belgian prison staff, they perceived the Dutch prison workers to be more accessible, friendly, helpful and less authoritative. This difference is best illustrated by the way prisoners had to address the prison workers and the prison officers in the different countries. Whereas they were used to calling the prison officers *'chef'* (chief) in Belgium, they were expected to call the Tilburg prison workers by their first name, which was also always on their nametags.[4] The fact that the staff called the prisoners by their first names was also quite unusual for the Belgian prisoners and introduced a more informal atmosphere during interactions:

> In Belgium, this is common, I am the chief and you are the prisoner, number so and so, your name is not used there. They only use your last name, never your first. Here [Tilburg prison] they all use your first name. I didn't hear that in years, that really affected me.
>
> (Prisoner 20)

The positive attitude of the staff was noticed through their willingness to have a cup of coffee or to smoke a cigarette with the prisoners, to do sports activities or to mingle and chat with them on the yard whilst having their daily walk. The Dutch prison workers' approach had a calming effect on the prisoners, who were very surprised and sometimes could not believe their eyes when they arrived:

> The first day I came here I was very nervous. One of those people said 'hi' to me and within two minutes I felt calm. Just the way they approached me: 'Welcome here! Cup of coffee?' We thought: 'what is happening here?'

> I never experienced something like that. In Belgium you just sit at the wing, this is your cell, 'Bam' they shut the door. And all the other things you have to find out yourself.
>
> (Prisoner 27)

A Belgian prisoner told us how he was struck by the fact that the prison workers always knocked on the door before entering the prison cell and how they made an effort to close it softly. These behaviours were uncommon for the Belgian prisoners and were highly appreciated because they were used to the more distant and often rather unfriendly behaviour of the Belgian 'chefs'. In general, there was a much higher level of routine interactions between the prison workers and the prisoners during the movements, activities and moments of free time, particularly in the sections with multiple prisoners' cells. It is important to mention that the prison workers considered it as a part of their job to have regular interactions and chats with the prisoners, which is less the case in Belgium. They also have the opportunity to pay much attention to this aspect of their work because of the division between penitentiary workers and security staff, as described earlier in 'The penal context of the "Tilberg experiment" '. In cases of serious inconvenience, they can always call the security team into action, whose prompt and resolute interventions really impressed the Belgian prisoners.

During the daily 'walks', or 'airing'[5], the prison workers made efforts to start conversations with the prisoners. In the Belgian prisons, the prison officers mostly 'hide' in separate areas and leave the prisoners alone during their airing time. Although the walking hour can become very risky for vulnerable prisoners, some prisoners indicated during the interviews that they missed this 'private prisoners' time', which they perceived as an opportunity to be 'amongst them', 'to do business' in all senses and thus to engage in typical prisoners' subcultural activities. Thus, a substantial minority of the prisoners we interviewed described the Dutch staff as too social or interactive and experienced their eagerness to communicate as a form of control. They experienced their behaviour as indiscrete or intrusive and as an undesirable interference with their privacy, which is already limited in prison. In particular, those prisoners who did not speak Dutch were sometimes suspicious and wondered what the prison workers were trying to achieve with their responsive attitudes. At the same time, they felt excluded. Both Dutch- and French-speaking respondents shared the opinion that prisoners who only spoke French or another language in which the staff were not proficient did have a disadvantage in this chatting culture. A non-Dutch prisoner expressed it in the following way:

> It is too difficult to speak with the chefs. I do not speak their language. I have asked to follow a course to learn. There are language courses to learn

> to speak with the chefs. They understand each other. There is nothing to say, the chefs, they are not wicked, but I don't understand them. There are not many chefs who speak... there are some chefs who speak a little bit of French, but yes, the rest, they cannot. I have a lot of difficulties to tell them something, I ring, he asks me in Dutch what I have to say to him. But then I can say nothing.
>
> (Prisoner 33)

Linguistically disadvantaged foreign-national prisoners therefore evaluated their interactions with the staff more negatively than the Dutch-speaking respondents because they often did not understand what the conversations were about and sometimes believed that the prison workers were joking with them and felt ridiculed. This shows that, in circumstances where communication is a core element of the prison culture, non-proficiency of language can reinforce exclusion of prisoners, of whom many were already in a more vulnerable position due to their irregular residence statuses.[6]

In this context, it is important to note that more than half of the prisoners did not have a residence status in Belgium and that only 35 per cent of the prisoners were of Belgian origin. Hence, it goes without saying that a large proportion of the prisoners were not proficient in the Dutch language. Although French is the second or even most spoken language amongst the prisoners in the PI Tilburg, the staff were rarely proficient. Most staff members, however, downplayed the language issue. With hands and feet, assistance of other prisoners, or, as a last resort, the interpreter phone, they believed that they could manage the language barrier adequately. During the interviews and observations, it became clear that the prisoners valued these efforts. It is also notable that the French-speaking prisoners talked more about 'les chefs' (the chiefs). This can be understood as an expression of their more arduous adaptation to the Dutch culture of treating prisoners.

A responsive and active attitude towards prisoners by the prison staff has two sides: it serves not only as a humane but also as a controlling approach, which was noted by some prisoners, who became annoyed by the overall presence of the prison workers. Increasing positive contacts and building constructive relations between staff and prisoners are considered to be crucial for building and strengthening the so-called dynamic security (see also Tournel and Kennes, 2011). In the PI Tilburg, the interactions with prisoners are also used to get information about the moods and possible tensions amongst prisoners. This is also a reason why staff members value their positive contacts with prisoners. In the context of the PI Tilburg, this was even more important, because of the lack of background information on the prisoners that the prison workers could make use of and the fact that they were used to having more information about the backgrounds of the prisoners (see previous section). This difference in rules puzzled them a lot, which was illustrated by the fact that several respondents told us they tried to find background information on certain prisoners on the Internet, particularly in cases where they were serving long sentences or when the prison workers did not really trust them. Another factor that demonstrated the importance of maintaining good relations with the prisoners concerned the lack of availability of some safety measures that are very common in the Dutch prison culture, in particular urine checks and cell inspections (as described in the previous section). The efforts they made to get on friendly terms with the prisoners were thus also intended to obtain valuable inside information and to prevent incidents. In this way, power was omnipresent in the PI Tilburg and was an invisible feature of prison life.

Different food practices

Another issue that always immediately turned up in the interviews, but in a unanimously negative sense, was the poor quality and quantity of the servery food in the PI Tilburg. Food and eating are very important moments for having a break in life, which is also the case for prisoners. The Belgian prisoners found it very difficult to adapt to the Dutch servery food habits, where deep-frozen food packages are delivered by a private company and distributed to the prisoners so that they could heat the so-called boxes in the microwave in their cells. This food was rejected by most of the prisoners as distasteful, boring and insufficient. They clearly preferred the food of the Belgian prisons that was prepared in the central prison kitchen. The Belgian prison governor, however, pointed out that the nutritional value of the Dutch food packages was much more balanced and healthier than the fatty food that was usually served in Belgian prisons. Many of the prisoners told us that they categorically refused to eat the food from the boxes, and many ended up in the garbage cans. Some Belgian prisoners told us how they craved their 'home food'. This was even more the case for non-national prisoners with a Mediterranean background. They told us that the food that was served in the Walloon prisons, which were located in the south of Belgium, was apparently more adapted to their needs and tastes. Lacking the food from home could be interpreted as an additional pain of imprisonment.

A more positive side of the food practices in Tilburg prison was the self-cook areas for prisoners in the different sections. The eight-person cells were equipped with a small kitchen, which gave the prisoners the opportunity to cook and eat together. This was welcomed by a lot of prisoners because it compensated for the bad servery food. However, the ingredients had to be bought by the prisoners in the prison canteen, which reinforced the inequalities between the *haves* and the *have nots*. Therefore, the cooking possibilities were a source of inequality, but sometimes also of sociability and even solidarity amongst the prisoners. They shared recipes and invited each other for meals, and the possibility to cook and eat together was regarded by many prisoners as an advantage of the PI Tilburg. We observed how cooking was a vehicle to express a prisoner's identity[7] and that cooking groups were formed along ethnic or national lines. Prisoners even asked to share multiple prisoner cells to be able to cook together. Like Phillips (2012), we too found that the self-cook approach did sometimes cement racial barriers and also that they coexisted with a convivial multicultural sharing of food.

Different release practices

The striking and fundamental differences in the Dutch and Belgian legal systems of release (briefly outlined earlier in the chapter) resulted in differences in prisoner experiences. The Belgian system leads to particular prisoner behaviours, which were quite surprising to those who were not familiar with this system. In line with the research of Claes (2012) in a Belgian prison, we observed how this conditional system of having to prepare for their release put a lot of pressure on the prisoners. The particular situation of being detained in the PI Tilburg even reinforced this and had a major impact on the way the Belgian prisoners experienced their stay and on the way the Dutch prison staff observed these experiences. Although the foundations for these experiences were laid down in legislation, the real impact of the system became clear during our conversations with the prisoners and the staff. The Dutch staff (and the Dutch researchers alike) were astonished by the fact that prisoners were so involved in their own reintegration process. Prisoners were worried that they could not earn enough in the PI Tilburg[8] to pay compensation to the victim, which they were expected to do by the sentence implementation court in order to get parole. To prepare their reintegration plan, prisoners need to show they will have a job when released. Therefore, they needed permissions for day leaves in order to do job interviews outside. Prisoners complained about the strict granting policy of the Belgian prison administration (Direction Detention Management) and the refusals to leave the prison.[9] This involvement and active attitude of the Belgian prisoners was, for some staff members, experienced as a relief compared to the much more passive attitude of many Dutch prisoners, whose potential efforts to prepare their post detention time, or the absence of them, did not change much up to the moment they would be released.

The staff, however, also observed another side of the coin, a side that became gradually clear to the Dutch researchers as well. The involvement of the Belgian prisoners in their release was fully explained by the discretionary release system that legally includes uncertainty about the moment of release. As was described in the section 'Differences between the Dutch and the Belgian prison legislation and regimes', the sentence implementation court will only grant release when the prisoner can show that he has prospects for housing and employment after his detention or when he can convince the court that he has the right attitude with regard to the victim (e.g. admitting guilt, paying victim compensation).[10] The Belgian release system is a clear example of what Crewe calls soft power in prison (Crewe, 2009, 2011a, 2011b). Prisoners are nowadays probably less subordinated to the brute, 'hard power' of their guards, but instead of that, 'soft power' has entered into prison.

Freedoms and releases are linked to the progress prisoners make in their rehabilitation process, for which they are held responsible themselves. In this way, they are forced to resign themselves to risk assessment, treatment programmes and responsibility strategies. In the PI Tilburg, the prisoners have a responsibility to prepare for their release, but the access to training and employment possibilities is very much restrained. Due to this gradual, discretionary system where several hurdles have to be passed, only a small number of those who are eligible for conditional release are actually released on their eligibility date. The majority serve a (much) longer prison term. This uncertainty is added to the fact that the importance of early release is immense due to the long prison sentences that are imposed compared to the Netherlands. For prison officers (and researchers) used to the Dutch situation where prison sentences of more than four years are relatively scarce, it was striking to see how many prisoners were serving 10 or 15 years of imprisonment and rather confusing to find out that they were already quite busy preparing for their release after having only served a few years of their prison terms. This was, at first sight, a positive side of the 'responsibilisation' of prisoners, but it also had a shadow side.

Preparation of conditional release sometimes caused serious emotional stress to the prisoners. The specific situation in Tilburg made it even more difficult for prisoners to meet the legal conditions. For example, due to the limitations of the agreement between Belgium and the Netherlands, the services that were required to assist the prisoners in the preparation of their reintegration plan were absent in the PI Tilburg[11] during the course of the research, which implied that assistance to look for a job during detention was hindered; for example, no special vocational training could be organised. In addition, the psychosocial service, which is responsible for the assessments and the preparation of the advice for the sentence implementation court, was understaffed for a long time, which also caused delays.

The combination of the legal and practical difficulties prisoners had to cope with to prepare for their conditional release meant that a growing group of inmates experienced early release to be a 'mission impossible':

I: So preparation of your early release is actually a big problem?
P: A very big problem, everybody is going to say that, everybody.
I: And what are the consequences, for example with relation to finding a job?
P: That is impossible here.

(Prisoner 30)

Having to endure the uncertainties and the frustration of not being able to meet the requirements of the sentencing implementation court, or the idea that they had to live for many more years after their release under the pressure of the risk of being recalled to prison if they infringed one of their release conditions, they preferred to waive the possibility of conditional release and to serve the full term of their prison sentences.[12]

A particular comparative research experience

Doing this research invited us to reflect on its unique intercultural and comparative character. We have already mentioned that it was a short-term research project, which only allowed for four months of fieldwork. As a research team, we were very much convinced of the added value of our qualitative research design. However, this approach had to be defended during the whole research process because the commissioner of the research project was not very acquainted with the more holistic and situated approach in studying detention experiences using qualitative methods.

Due to the limited time for observation and immersion, we categorise our study as semi-ethnographic. Being in the prison for almost four months to 'hang around' or to interview and being able to visit the different parts of the prison was crucial for us to understand better the discourses of the prisoners as well as of the staff and to recognise institution-specific peculiarities. It also allowed us to make the staff and the prisoners acquainted with our research and to generate trust. We did not 'take sides' (Becker, 1967) and conducted interviews with both prisoners and staff. This double-sided research choice has never been questioned by the prisoners, or by the staff, nor did we have the impression that this prevented either group being honest and open during the interviews. We think that this was possible due to there being little oppositional culture in the PI Tilburg.[13]

The depth of our findings and insights were, however, much stimulated by the unusual comparative context of our research and the multinational (Belgian–Dutch) composition of the research team. Therefore, our research can be regarded as a special form of comparative research: the researcher is foreign to its research object, but, in this case, only partly. In addition, contrary to most other prisons, the PI Tilburg had to construct its own practices and routines right from the start. When we got 'in', it had only had a history of one year. Its daily routine was created by a mix of Belgian and Dutch rules and policies, working and management styles, prisoners' subcultures, expectations and previous detention experiences from the staff as well as of the prisoners. All these elements together generated a unique organisational culture, which may not be regarded or evaluated as Belgian or Dutch.[14] It was, therefore, challenging to try to understand how the different national rules and practices got intertwined, interacted and created a new detention situation to which prisoners as well as staff had to adapt. This mixed Dutch–Belgian situation was studied by a mixed Belgian–Dutch team, all female and all with a good knowledge of the penitentiary and judicial traditions in their own jurisdictions. As ethnographic research aims to understand the world from the perspectives of insiders and within the research subject's emotional-social context, (Siegel, 2010; Jewkes, 2014), this process seemed to be accelerated by the alienating insider–outsider context and the nearness of colleagues, who could explain observations which were puzzling or not understood in first instance.

Nelken (2010) makes a distinction between being 'virtually there', 'researching there' and 'living there'. The three positions are situated differently on the outsider–insider continuum and differ in the way the researcher is able to collect his or her own data, whether (s)he is dependent on primary or secondary data and whether (s)he is able to make sense of the data in a knowledgeable and culturally embedded way. It is clear that 'living there' is, for Nelken, the most preferable position to understand what is at stake and thus for high-quality comparative research. This involves a long-term, cultural and social embeddedness of the researcher in the society being researched, which enables him or her to understand better the practices (s)he is studying. The position of 'living there' is the most informed one, though this is not to say that it is without its own prejudices and biases (Beyens and McNeill, 2013). In the beginning, we positioned ourselves in the 'living there' category (Beyens and Boone, 2013); however, later on we realised that during the research we constantly shifted insider–outsider positions. Where the Belgian researchers were insiders, the Dutch were outsiders, and vice versa. As a learning effect, it became easier to open up for the position of the other and observe what used to be familiar from an outside perspective (Brants, 2011).

Reflections on the position and characteristics of the researcher

Doing this research revealed the importance of the characteristics and skills of the researchers. The interviews were conducted by the supervisors and the researchers of the research team, and in the beginning, teams of two interviewers were formed, combining young and experienced researchers, or a Belgian–Dutch team. In case of solo interviews, we always chose to interview respondents from our own jurisdictions. Soon we sensed that national sameness facilitated the interviews because, although Flemish and Dutch are, in principle, similar languages, each language has its own pronunciation and expressions, which quickly identify the person as Dutch or Belgian. Particularly, for the prisoners, being able to speak with a fellow countrywoman made them feel a bit like 'coming home'. This effect became even stronger in cases where the prisoner only spoke French, since this language is only scarcely spoken by the Dutch prison officers. When doing the interview with a mixed nationality team, it was almost natural that the researcher of the same nationality took the lead, due to her closeness to the background of the interviewee. However, some interviews had to be conducted in French, due to the insufficient proficiency of Dutch of the prisoner. As only the Belgian researchers had the skills of talking in Dutch and French, in this area the country divisions also became articulated.[15] This conflict with sameness and difference taught us how difficult it had to be for the prisoners to function in a context of non-proficiency of the main language in the prison.

Further, it was interesting to find out that, in terms of explanation during the interviews, the prisoners were more likely to explain fully the procedure, for example, when the younger researcher did the interviews alone. With the supervisor, they assumed quicker that the interviewer already knew or understood how things were going and consequently did not elaborate on that. It could, however, be very interesting for us to learn about their interpretation of and views on the system. This confirms the importance of the innocent researcher position in qualitative research (as also noted by Sloan and Wright in Chapter 7, this volume).

The knowledge of the researchers of the national rules and penitentiary policies was a vital element to understand what was going on in Tilburg. However, we constantly had to explain to each other and adjust the gaze of the 'foreign' researcher, who was sometimes a bit too enthusiastic in her admiration for a new practice she discovered. It became clear very soon how we looked at the Tilburg situation from our own national (sometimes biased) backgrounds, and that this also influenced our observations. The truth is in the eye of the beholder. The most interesting – but sometimes also most thought-provoking – aspect for us, as researchers, was that we also learned to look at aspects of our own systems through the eyes of our non-national colleagues. Their positive or negative amazement was very instructive to look at our own systems with a fresh view. Doing the research was thus not only instructing each other but also learning from each other about our own systems through the wonder of our colleagues. This was particularly so regarding the complicated conditional release system, with its different formal and informal practices and levels which influenced the experiences of staff and prisoners. This was the subject of long and interesting discussions about the parallels and particularly the differences in philosophies between the different jurisdictions and even resulted in a comparative PhD project. The same was true for the humane approach of the prison workers, the division of labour between the prison workers and the security staff and the different food, medication and security practices. Step by step, this led to a layered understanding of the detention experiences. By explaining and situating each other within the cultural backgrounds of the practices we observed, we forced ourselves to dig deeper and explain better. We also bumped into particularities, which were sometimes obvious for the national researcher, but not at all for the non-national researcher. And although we could not go that far into contextualising the Tilburg regime and culture, both also needed to be understood from a broader social context in the different countries.

Listening to the prisoners talking about their detention experiences in the Tilburg context also taught us a lot about how they experienced their previous detention in the Belgian prisons because their evaluations and surprise of how things were at PI Tilburg were, of course, influenced by these previous experiences and also by their (mostly negative) views about the PI Tilburg before they were transferred there.

We can conclude that, to understand the life in the PI Tilburg, the choice for a qualitative design was the most adequate. We can only regret that we could not have more time to be there. Therefore, we hope that we can go back before the experiment ends, to see how staff and prisoners have adapted to this situation.

Notes

1. Masterplan 2008–2012 voor een gevangenisinfrastructuur in humane omstandigheden, Brussel, Ministerie van Justitie, 18 April, 2008.
2. In this chapter, we use the term 'Belgian' prisoners to refer to prisoners who are convicted on Belgian territory and, according to Belgian penal law, who would normally serve their time in a Belgian prison. Thus, the term 'Belgian' does not refer to a Belgian nationality.
3. The officer who is responsible for the selection of prisoners for other penitentiary institutions or leaves.
4. Pratt and Erikkson (2013: 18) also describe the informal mode of address in the Nordic prisons as in contrast with the more formal English approach.
5. In Belgium, the common word for the prisoners' daily hour in fresh air outside is 'walk', whilst the Dutch speak of 'airing the prisoners'.
6. See Kox, De Ridder, Vanhouche, Boone and Beyens (2014) for a more profound analysis of the lived experiences of foreign-national prisoners without legal residence in the PI Tilburg.
7. In-depth qualitative research is currently being conducted by An-Sophie Vanhouche (Vrije Universiteit Brussels) to explore further this aspect of identity formation with regard to food issues.
8. The PI Tilburg had the policy to employ every prisoner for four hours a day (half-time employment), which led to a weekly remuneration of €26. Prisoners who previously had the opportunity to work more hours or to earn piece rate wages in the Belgian prisons complained about the limited amount of money they could earn in the PI Tilburg. It is, however, to be noted that in the Belgian prisons there is high prisoner unemployment, implying that many of them have no opportunity at all to earn some income. (The term 'piece rate wages' refers to the fact that prisoners do some small very routinised tasks, and they are paid per task they fulfil and not per hour; so the faster they work, the more they can earn).
9. For an in-depth analysis of Belgian decision-making policies and practices with regard to granting furloughs and penitentiary leaves in Belgium, see Robert and Mine (2014).
10. See also Scheirs (2013) for a comprehensive qualitative study of the decision-making practices of the sentence implementation courts.

11. The Belgian Federal State has three levels of competences. Federal matters contain, besides defence, finances, foreign policies and the Ministry of Justice. Infrastructural competences are for the regions. Person-bound policies such as education, culture and welfare are the competence of the communities. Prison policies thus combine federal and communitarian matters. As the Nova Belgica agreement was only an agreement between the Ministers of Justice of both countries, the Flemish community was not involved, with the result that help and aid services for the prisoners are absent in the PI Tilburg.
12. See also Maes and Tanghe (2014) for an analysis of this phenomenon of 'maxing out' in the Belgian prison system.
13. For an in-depth discussion about the 'taking sides' debate in prison research, see Liebling (1999, 2001) and Beyens et al. (Forthcoming).
14. It was, however, very difficult to avoid a 'nationalistic' interpretation of the functioning of the PI Tilburg. Particularly from a comparative approach, people are inclined to speak in terms of good or bad, or worse or better (also Brants, 2011).
15. Consequently, this division of labour was also extended to the transcriptions and analysis of the interviews.

Further reading

Nelken, D. (2010) *Comparative Criminal Justice: Making Sense of Difference* (London: Sage).

Beyens, K. and Boone, M., assisted by Liefaard, T., Kox, M., Vanhouche, A.-S. and van der Poel, S. (2013) *'Zeg maar Henk tegen de chef'. Ervaringen met het Belgische detentieregime in de PI Tilburg* (Boom: Lemma Uitgevers).

Beyens, K., Kennes, P., Tournel, H. and Snacken, S. (2015) 'The Craft of Doing Prison Research', *International Journal for Crime, Justice and Social Democracy* (forthcoming).

References

Becker, H. S. (1967) 'Whose Side Are We On?' *Social Problems,* 14, 239–47.

Beyens, K. and Boone, M., assisted by Liefaard, T., Kox, M., Vanhouche, A.-S. and van der Poel, S. (2013) *'Zeg maar Henk tegen de chef'. Ervaringen met het Belgische detentieregime in de PI Tilburg* (Boom: Lemma Uitgevers).

Beyens, K. and Boone, M. (2013) 'Comparatief onderzoek naar de beleving van detentie. Hoe wij "met elkaar hebben leren leven"' in C. Kelk, K. Frans and D. Siegel (eds) *Veelzijdige gedachten. Liber amicorum prof. dr. Chrisje Brants,* pp. 365–74, (Boom: Lemma).

Beyens, K. and McNeill, F. (2013) 'Conclusion: Studying Mass Supervision Comparatively', in F. McNeil and K. Beyens (eds) *Offender Supervision in Europe,* pp. 155–69, (Basingstoke: Palgrave Macmillan).

Beyens, K., Kennes, P., Tournel, H. and Snacken, S. (Forthcoming) 'The Craft of Doing Prison Research', *International Journal for Crime, Justice and Social Democracy.*

Beyens, K., Snacken, S. and Eliaerts, C. (1993) *Barstende muren. Overbevolkte gevangenissen: omvang, oorzaken en mogelijke oplossingen* (Vol. 26) (Antwerpen, Arnhem: Kluwer, Gouda Quint).

Boone, M. and Van Swaaningen, R. (2013) 'Regression to the Mean: Punishment in the Netherlands', in V. Rugiero and M. Ryan (eds) *Punishment in Europe* (New York: Palgrave Macmilllan).

Boone, M. and Moerings, M. (2007) 'Growing Prison Rates', in M. Boone and M. Moerings (eds) *Dutch Prisons* (The Hague: BJU Legal Publishers).

Boone, M. and Moerings, M. (2008) 'Detentiecapaciteit en Detentieomstandigheden in Nederland', *FATIK*, 120, 5–10.

Brants, C. (2011) 'Comparing Criminal Process as Part of Legal Culture', in D. Nelken (ed) *Comparative Criminal Justice and Globalization* (Farnham: Ashgate Publishing).

Claes, B. (2012) *Herstel en detentie. Een etnografisch onderzoek in de gevangenis van Leuven Centraal*, Unpublished PhD thesis, Vrije Universiteit Brussel, Brussel.

CPT (2012) *Report to the Governments of Belgium and the Netherlands on the Visit to Tilburg Prison from 17–10 October 2011* (Strasbourg: Council of Europe).

Crewe, B. (2009) *The Prisoner Society: Power, Adaptation, and Social Life in an English Prison* (Oxford: Oxford University Press).

Crewe, B. (2011a) 'Depth, Weight, Tightness: Revisiting the Pains of Imprisonment', *Punishment and Society*, 13, 5, 509–29.

Crewe, B. (2011b) 'Soft Power in Prison: Implications for Staff-Prisoner Relationships, Liberty and Legitimacy', *European Journal of Criminology*, 8, 6, 455–68.

Delterne, S. (2014) *Construire: une réaction suffisante à l'inflation carcérale? A quels coûts?* Paper presented at the Journée de réflexion. 'Des (nouvelles) prisons: et après?' (Brussel: ULB)

Jewkes, Y. (2014) 'An Introduction to "Doing Prison Research Differently" ', *Qualitative Inquiry*, 20, 4, 381–91.

Kox, M., De Ridder, S., Vanhouche, A.-S., Boone, M. and Beyens, K. (2014) 'Detentiebeleving van strafrechtelijk gedetineerden zonder verblijfsrecht', *Tijdschrift voor Criminologie*, 56, 2, 31–47.

Kruttschnitt, C. and Dirkzwager, A. (2011) 'Are There Still Contrasts in Tolerance? Imprisonment in the Netherlands and England 20 Years Later', *Punishment & Society*, 13, 3, 281–306.

Liebling, A. (1999) 'Doing Research in Prison: Breaking the Silence?' *Theoretical Criminology*, 3, 147–73.

Liebling, A. (2001) 'Whose Side Are We On? Theory, Practice and Allegiances in Prison Research', *British Journal of Criminology*, 41, 472–84.

Liebling, A., assisted by Arnold, H. (2004) *Prisons and Their Moral Performance: A Study of Values, Quality and Prison Life* (Oxford: Oxford University Press).

Liebling, A. (2011) 'Moral Performance, Inhuman and Degrading Treatment and Prison Pain', *Punishment and Society*, 13, 5, 530–50.

League for Human Rights, Observatoire International des Prisons and La Ligue des Droits de L'Homme (2011) *Nota naar aanleiding van bezoek aan Tilburg*, 28 Juni 2011.

Maes, E. (2010) 'Evoluties in punitiviteit: Lessen uit de justitiële statistieken', in I. Aertsen, K. Beyens, T. Daems and E. Maes (eds) *Hoe punitief is België?* (Gent: Maklu).

Maes, E. and Tange, C. (2014) 'Langgestrafte veroordeelden in de SURB-wachtkamer voor voorwaardelijke invrijheidstelling: "En attendant Godot"?', in K. Beyens, T. Daems and E. Maes (eds) *Exit gevangenis? De werking van de strafuitvoeringsrechtbanken en de wet op de externe rechtspositie van veroordeelden tot een vrijheidsstraf* (Antwerpen/Apeldoorn: Maklu).

Nelken, D. (2010) *Comparative Criminal Justice. Making Sense of Difference* (London: Sage).

Phillips, C. (2012) *The Multicultural Prison. Ethnicity, Masculinity, and Social Relations among Prisoners* (Oxford: Oxford University Press).

Pratt, J. and Eriksson, A. (2013) *Contrasts in Punishment. An Explanation of Anglophone Excess and Nordic Exceptionalism* (London: Routledge).

Prison Service (2010) *Yearly Report 2009* (Brussel: FOD Justitie).

Prison Service (2014) *Yearly Report 2013* (Brussel: FOD Justitie).

Robert, L. and Mine, B. (2014) 'Kijken in de zwarte doos. Een onderzoek naar beslissingsprocessen betreffende uitgaansvergunningen en penitentiair verlof', in K. Beyens, T. Daems and E. Maes (eds) *Exit gevangenis? De werking van de strafuitvoeringsrechtbanken en de wet op de externe rechtspositie van veroordeelden tot een vrijheidsstraf* (Antwerpen/Apeldoorn: Maklu).

Scheirs, V. (2013) *De strafuitvoeringsrechtbank aan het werk: een entografisch onderzoek naar haar interacties, beslissingsprocessen en-praktijken,* Doctoral Thesis Criminology, Vrije Universiteit Brussel, Brussel.

Siegel, D. (2010) *Maffia, diamanten en Mozart. Etnografie in criminologisch onderzoek* (Den Haag: Boom Juridische uitgevers).

Swaaningen, R. van (2012) 'Reversing the Punitive Turn', in T. Daems, S. Snacken and D. van Zyl Smit (eds) *European Penology?* (Oxford: Hart).

Tournel, H. and Kennes, P. (2011) 'De dilemma's van dynamische veiligheid voor bewaarders', *Panopticon*, 3, 21–36.

Index

Note: Locators followed by 'n' refer to note numbers.

Printed and bound in Great Britain by
CPI Group (UK) Ltd, Croydon, CR0 4YY